Tourism, Tourists and Society

Tourism, Tourists and Society provides a broad introduction to the inter-relationship between tourism and society, making complex sociological concepts and themes accessible to readers from a non-sociological academic background. It provides a thorough exploration of how society influences or shapes the behaviours, motivations, attitudes and consumption of tourists, as well as the tourism impacts on destination societies.

The fifth edition has been fully revised and updated to reflect recent data, concepts and academic debates:

- New content on: mobilities paradigm and the emotional dimension of tourist experiences.
- New chapter: Tourism and the Digital Revolution, looking at the ways in which the Internet and mobile technology transform both tourist behaviour and the tourist experience.
- New end-of-chapter further reading and discussion topics.

Accessible yet critical in style, this book offers students an invaluable introduction to tourism, tourists and society.

Richard Sharpley is Professor of Tourism and Development at the University of Central Lancashire, Preston, UK. He is co-editor of the journal *Tourism Planning & Development*.

Tourism, Tourists and Society

Fifth edition

Richard Sharpley

Routledge
Taylor & Francis Group

LONDON AND NEW YORK

Fifth edition published 2018
by Routledge
2 Park Square, Milton Park, Abingdon, Oxon, OX14 4RN

and by Routledge
711 Third Avenue, New York, NY 10017

Routledge is an imprint of the Taylor & Francis Group, an informa business

First edition published by Elm 1994
Fourth edition published by Elm 2008

British Library Cataloguing-in-Publication Data
A catalogue record for this book is available from the British Library

Library of Congress Cataloging-in-Publication Data
Names: Sharpley, Richard, 1956– author.
Title: Tourism, tourists and society / Richard Sharpley.
Description: Fifth edition. | New York : Routledge, 2018. | "Fourth edition
    published by Elm 2008." | Includes bibliographical references and index.
Identifiers: LCCN 2017054399 (print) | LCCN 2018001459 (ebook) |
    ISBN 9781315210407 (Master ebook) | ISBN 9781351809559 (Web PDF) |
    ISBN 9781351809542 (ePUB) | ISBN 9781351809535 (Mobipocket) |
    ISBN 9781138629394 (Hardback : alk. paper) | ISBN 9781138629493
    (Paperback : alk. paper) | ISBN 9781315210407 (Ebook)
Subjects: LCSH: Tourism—Social aspects.
Classification: LCC G155.A1 (ebook) | LCC G155.A1 S4777 2018 (print) |
    DDC 306.4/819—dc23
LC record available at https://lccn.loc.gov/2017054399

ISBN: 978-1-138-62939-4 (hbk)
ISBN: 978-1-138-62949-3 (pbk)
ISBN: 978-1-315-21040-7 (ebk)

Typeset in Bembo
by Apex CoVantage, LLC

Contents

Preface to the fifth edition

The first edition of this book was published in 1994. In the intervening two decades or more, tourism has continued its inexorable growth, not only cementing its position as one of the world's largest economic sectors accounting for 9 percent of global GDP and almost one tenth of global employment, but also becoming a truly global social phenomenon. The figures speak for themselves. In 1994, international tourist arrivals amounted to almost 520 million; by 2016, that number had almost doubled to 1,235 million whilst, over the same period, international tourist receipts trebled, reaching US$1,220 billion in 2016. But it is not only the overall growth that is significant. New markets and new destinations have emerged with China in particular becoming the largest source of international tourists, whilst domestic tourism, estimated to be six times greater in terms of numbers of trips, has also continued to grow. Again, China is at the forefront; the Chinese make more than two billion domestic trips annually. Thus, tourism continues to represent an enormous and ever-increasing migration of people across international borders and within their own countries and, as such, it not only deserves but demands an understanding of the social processes involved.

The study of tourism, particularly from a sociological perspective, has also developed significantly since 1994. In its first edition, this book sought to consider both tourists themselves and the societies that generate and receive them. Specifically, it introduced basic sociological theory and its relevance to tourism before going on to explore the relationship between tourism and society from two perspectives: the influence of society on tourism and the influence of tourism on society. Subsequent editions have maintained that structure, though adding additional chapters to reflect advances in knowledge and understanding of the social dimension of tourism. In this fifth edition, all existing chapters have been expanded and updated as necessary, whilst a new chapter focuses on the impact of the digital revolution, particularly advances in information and communication technology, on tourist behaviour and experiences. At the same time, every attempt has been made to maintain the accessible style that was established in the first edition, presenting concepts and ideas in an understandable way but also developing arguments that may encourage the reader to look in different ways both at tourism in general and themselves as tourists in particular.

Richard Sharpley
September 2017

Tourism
A sociological approach

Introduction

Tourism is all things to all people. To the holiday-maker, for example, tourism may be the chance to relax and unwind, to 're-create', representing a temporary period of escape from the responsibilities of work and from the stress of everyday life. Equally, it may be seen as an opportunity to do something new, to learn a new skill, to be 'creative' (Richards & Wilson, 2007; Richards, 2011). Conversely, for any one of the hundreds of thousands of tourism businesses around the world – from large, multinational organisations to small, independent operators – tourism is simply, by definition, business, a source of employment and income. At the same time, governments may promote or positively encourage the development of tourism, considering it to be an essential ingredient of broader social and economic development policies (Jenkins, 1991; Telfer & Sharpley, 2016). Yet, to the local residents in popular destinations, the annual influx of hordes of tourists may be seen more negatively as something to be endured or coped with (Boissevain, 1996) or, as more recently in the case of both Barcelona and Venice, to be resisted (Sharpley & Harrison, 2017).

Equally, the *study* of tourism may be approached from a variety of academic backgrounds or disciplines, each providing a valid basis for explanation and argument. For example, economists treat tourism as a discrete form of economic activity, relating the demand, motivation, growth, scale and form of tourism to economic factors; even the impacts of tourism, or externalities, may be explained or justified in economic terms (Dwyer and Forsyth, 2006; Mihalič, 2015; Stabler, Papatheodorou & Sinclair, 2010; Vanhove, 2011). More generally, whilst much of the early research and academic study of tourism originated as a branch of geography, a multidisciplinary approach has been increasingly adopted since the 1970s. There now exists a broad range of tourism literatures based on academic specialisms, such as anthropology (Burns, 1999; Nash, 1981; 1996; Smith, 1989a), psychology (Filep, 2012; Iso-Ahola, 1982; Pearce & Packer, 2013; Ross, 1994), law (Grant & Mason, 2003), political science (Burns & Novelli, 2007; Elliott, 1997; Hall, 1994; Matthews & Richter, 1991), history, (Shackley, 2006; Towner, 1996; Walton, 2005), cultural studies (Chambers, 1997; Meethan, 2001; Smith, 2006; 2009), marketing (Holloway, 2004; Middleton *et al.*, 2009; Witt & Moutinho, 1989) and, of course, geography (Hall & Page, 2014; Williams & Lew, 2015). At the same time, much of the literature focuses upon particular types of tourism itself, such as heritage tourism (Boniface & Fowler, 1993; Herbert, 1995; Timothy & Boyd, 2003; Yale, 2004), rural tourism (Page & Getz, 1997; Roberts & Hall, 2001; Sharpley & Sharpley, 1997; Sharpley, 2007) and special interest (Getz, 1991; Weiler & Hall, 1992) or niche (Novelli, 2005) tourism, or on geographical or political classifications such as, for example, the UK (Yale, 1992), Europe (Davidson, 1998; Pompl & Lavery, 1993), city tourism (Ashworth & Page, 2011; Grabler *et al.*, 1997; Hall & Page, 2003; Heeley, 2011; Law, 2002) or developing countries (Harrison, 1992a, 2001; Reid, 2003; Telfer & Sharpley, 2016).

Despite this enormous variety of perspectives or academic approaches to tourism, however, there is one particular feature of tourism that cannot, or should not, be ignored. Unquestionably, tourism is one of the largest economic sectors in the world. Indeed, tourism is frequently described as the world's largest industry, though it is widely debated whether or not the myriad of businesses and organisations involved in tourism should be collectively described as a single, identifiable industry. For example, it has been suggested that 'referring to tourism as an industry may be a major contributor to the misunderstanding, resistance and even hostility that often plague proponents of travel and tourism as worthy economic forces in a modern economy' (Davidson, 1994: 20; see also Gilbert, 1990). Irrespective of terminology, however, tourism is, according to the United Nations World Tourism Organization (UNWTOa, 2016), ranked as the world's third largest export category after fuels and chemicals, accounting for 7 percent of total worldwide exports and 30 percent of services exports.

When describing tourism as an export sector, reference is being made specifically, of course, to international tourism; that is, tourism that involves travel to and a stay of at least 24 hours or more in a country in which the tourist does not normally reside or work. In other words, tourism differs from other exports inasmuch as it is consumed in the country where it is 'produced'. As discussed towards the end of this chapter, certain types of day visitors or excursionists, such as cruise passengers, may also be categorised as international tourists, although they are not normally included in international tourism statistics. And it is those statistics that reveal the remarkable growth in the scale and value of international tourism since the mid-twentieth century. As can be seen from Table 1.1, since 1950, the year that comprehensive international tourism data were first published, international tourist arrivals have grown consistently. Indeed, arguably no other economic sector can match the long-term growth rate of international tourism.

By the end of the last century, international tourist arrivals totalled almost 690 million; just over a decade later, and despite major events such as '9/11' in 2001, the SARS (Severe Acute Respiratory Syndrome) outbreak in 2003, the Indian Ocean Tsunami in 2004 and the global economic crisis of 2008, international arrivals have continued to increase, exceeding the one billion mark for the first time in 2012. Similarly, the value of international tourism, measured in receipts, has also grown remarkably, totalling US$1,260 million in 2015. Yet, international tourism accounts for only a relatively small proportion of all tourism activity. It is estimated that domestic tourism (that is, people participating in tourism in their own countries) is five to six times greater than international tourism in terms of numbers of trips and, according to the World Travel and

TABLE 1.1 International tourist arrivals and receipts, 1950–2016

Year	Arrivals (million)	Receipts (US$bn)	Year	Arrivals (million)	Receipts (US$bn)
1950	25.3	2.1	2000	687.0	481.6
1960	69.3	6.9	2001	686.7	469.9
1965	112.9	11.6	2002	707.0	488.2
1970	165.8	17.9	2003	694.6	534.6
1975	222.3	40.7	2004	765.1	634.7
1980	278.1	104.4	2005	806.1	682.7
1985	320.1	119.1	2006	847.0	742.0
1990	439.5	270.2	2007	903.0	856.0
1991	442.5	283.4	2008	917.0	939.0
1992	479.8	326.6	2009	882.0	851.0
1993	495.7	332.6	2010	940.0	927.0
1994	519.8	362.1	2011	995.0	1,042.0
1995	540.6	410.7	2012	1,035.0	1,075.0
1996	575.0	446.0	2013	1,087.0	1,159.0
1997	598.6	450.4	2014	1,130.0	1,252.0
1998	616.7	451.4	2015	1,184.0	1,196.0
1999	639.6	465.5	2016	1,235.0	1,220.0

Source: adapted from UNWTO data

TABLE 1.2 International tourism arrivals and receipts growth rates, 1950–2000

Decade	Arrivals (average annual increase %)	Receipts (average annual increase %)
1950–1960	10.6	12.6
1960–1970	9.1	10.1
1970–1980	5.6	19.4
1980–1990	4.8	9.8
1990–2000	4.2	6.5

Source: adapted from (UNWTO, 2005)

Tourism Council (WTTC), if both direct and indirect expenditure is taken into account then global tourism – including domestic tourism – is a $7 trillion industry, accounting for over 10 percent of world GDP and around 9 percent of global employment.

Inevitably, the rate at which tourism has grown over the decades has declined (see Table 1.2).

More specifically, although annual growth in arrivals and receipts averaged 6.2 percent and 10 percent respectively between 1950 and 2010, between 2010 and 2015 the average annual growth rate in arrivals was 'just' 3.9 percent (UNWTO, 2016b), calling into question the UNWTO's long-held prediction that, by 2020 international tourist arrivals will reach a staggering 1.6 billion, generating receipts of well over US$2 trillion (WTO, 1998a: 3). Nevertheless, there can be no doubting either that tourism, both international and domestic, will continue to grow (albeit with some transformations in the scale and direction of tourist flows reflecting, for example, the emergence of China as the dominant outbound tourism market), or that it will remain a global economic force.

Most importantly, however, the sheer scale and value of tourism should not draw attention away from the simple fact that tourism is about people. It is about millions of individuals who comprise local, regional and national societies, travelling domestically or crossing international borders and experiencing and impacting upon different societies. It is about people who are influenced and motivated by the norms and changes in their own society, who carry with them perceptions, expectations and standards based on their own personal experience and background. Above all, tourism is about people, tourists, interacting with other places and other peoples, undergoing experiences that may influence their own or the host community's attitudes, expectations, opinions and, ultimately, lifestyles.

In short, then, the very basis of tourism is people and society. Thus, the study of tourism in general cannot, or should not, be divorced from an examination in particular of what may be termed the 'sociology of tourism'. A fundamental issue, however, is the extent to which tourism, as an essentially social but nevertheless diverse activity, lends itself to sociological study. Specifically, the question to be asked is: is it possible to develop a sociological theory of tourism, or is it only possible to apply sociological theory to different aspects of tourism. Moreover, other academic disciplines, such as psychology and anthropology, have equal claim as a basis for research into social aspects of tourism; indeed, one of the first major texts concerned with the relationship between tourists and the local destination community (or 'hosts') and the social impacts of tourism is sub-titled *The Anthropology of Tourism* (Smith, 1977, 1989a) whilst, subsequently, both disciplines have provided the foundation for a number of books (for example, Abram *et al.*, 1997; Burns, 1999; Franklin, 2003).

The purpose of this introductory chapter is to define the context for a sociological approach to the study of tourism. The first necessary step, then, is to examine what is meant by a sociological approach or, more precisely, the meaning, purpose and extent of sociology as an academic activity. This may then be related to, and used as a basis for the consideration of, the human and social aspects of tourism throughout the rest of this book.

What is sociology?

It is probably true to assert that although most people have some notion of what sociology is about, relatively few are able to define the term accurately. Unlike many other academic disciplines, such as history, geography and chemistry, both the scope and the purpose of sociology are either vague or, in the extreme, incomprehensible to the lay person (Browne, 1992: 1). As a result, sociology is often regarded with disinterest or, at worst, with mistrust by those who have little knowledge or understanding of the subject. Indeed, as Bilton *et al.* (1996: 1) point out, sociologists themselves may often feel tempted to say that they are historians or economists rather than sociologists in order to avoid the difficulty of having to explain what they really do!

This difficulty in defining sociology arises, in part, from the nature of the subject itself. For example, one explanation or description of sociology might be the study of the structure of human society and behaviour or, as Anthony Giddens explains in his widely used book, sociology may be defined as 'the scientific study of human life, social groups, whole societies and the human world as such (Giddens, 2009: 6). Although essentially accurate, this perhaps over-simplifies what sociology is. That is, it is certainly concerned with specific aspects of society, such as the family, class and gender divisions, work, religion or deviance (behaviour which does not conform to what is considered to be 'normal', crime being the most obvious example). Indeed, many introductory sociology texts are structured according to these social institutions (for example, see Abercrombie *et al.*, 2000; Browne, 2011; Giddens, 2009). This is, however, only half of the story. Of equal, if not greater, importance is the approach or perspective which determines how these particular aspects of society and the behaviour of individuals within society are studied. Sociology is, in effect, a *way* of looking at society. As Browne (1992: 2) suggests, 'sociologists use a sociological imagination . . . they study the familiar routines of daily life . . . in unfamiliar ways' or, as Giddens (2009: 6) puts it, 'the sociological imagination requires us, above all, to "think ourselves away" from the familiar routines of our daily lives in order to look at them anew'.

In other words, the basis of sociology is society. Society is made up of individuals who, with the exception of those who make a conscious decision to avoid contact with other people, perform or participate in a huge variety of actions every day. The great majority of these actions are socially acceptable or normative (that is 'normal', expected behaviour); they are also, however, socially determined. That is, an individual's behaviour is generally constrained, or determined, by their society's rules, rules which may be set down by custom, by religion, or by laws. As a result, all the individual actions within a given society tend to occur in a co-ordinated fashion so that social life remains reasonably ordered and predictable. For example, in many Western societies it has long been considered 'normal' for a young person to take a year off in between school and university to go travelling – to take a so-called 'gap-year' (O'Reilly, 2006). Conversely, an individual who does so in, say, his or her forties, might once have been considered unusual, eccentric or even, perhaps, irresponsible. However, as societies develop, social rules or norms also develop and change. In the UK, for example, almost half of all 'gap-year' tourists are now in fact older, middle-aged people taking a career break or even travelling in early retirement. At the same time, it has become more socially acceptable, or perhaps even expected, to do something 'useful' while on gap-year travels, hence the contemporary popularity of so-called volunteer tourism (Callanan & Thomas, 2005; Wearing & McGehee, 2013), a form of tourism that is discussed in more detail in Chapter 4.

The important point, therefore, is that sociology is concerned not only with the structure of society and the behaviour of its members but also with the rules, or wider social forces, that determine social structure and those patterns of behaviour. It is this latter characteristic that differentiates sociology from other disciplines, such as anthropology, and that causes most confusion amongst non-sociologists.

Whereas many people attempt to explain or describe different forms of human behaviour as natural, instinctive or just plain common sense, all of which place the emphasis firmly on the ability of the individual to make his or her own decisions, sociology to some extent rejects notions of individuality and places human behaviour within the wider context of social forces which are beyond the control of the individual. Also, socially normal or acceptable behaviour is, of course, relative to different societies and reflects a particular society's rules or constraints that must be learned by the individual. Thus, 'one person's "common sense" is somebody else's nonsense' (Bilton et al., 1996: 6). For example, in Western societies it is generally accepted as common sense or normal that it should be men, rather than women, who undertake heavy labouring work; in some other countries, such as India, it is more often that such work is done by women, a role determined by the social forces of religion, male dominance and the caste system (Baker, 1990) whilst increasing numbers of women are working on building sites following the recent construction boom in Cambodia (Fox, 2017).

The basic tenet of sociology, then, is that human society and behaviour is structured, moulded and constrained by wider social forces and influences, and it is this approach that underlies sociological research and analysis. Yet, although sociologists share this common approach, there is a variety of theories about what society actually is, how it may be explained and, hence, how it determines individual behaviour. The following section briefly traces the development of sociology as an academic discipline and the evolution of the different theories of sociology (see Swingewood, 1991 and Applerouth & Edles, 2012 for more detail). The relevance of these theories to the study of tourism is then discussed.

The development of sociology

Modern sociology, as a distinct discipline, has its roots in Europe in the mid-nineteenth century. The 'father' of sociology is generally held to be the Frenchman Auguste Comte (1798–1857). Not only did he coin the term 'sociology' but he was also the first to adopt a rigorous, scientific approach to the study and explanation of society. Prior to this time, many people had concerned themselves with the development and structure of society. Early Greek philosophers, such as Plato and Aristotle, had developed theories about the nature of society but, even by the mid-eighteenth century, the work of social theorists, such as Jean-Jacques Rousseau (1712–1778), remained largely based on a philosophical, rather than a formal, scientific, approach to the study of society. As Bilton et al. (1996: 2) point out, 'philosophers and thinkers frequently constructed grand models and schemes about humans and their societies without looking at how societies actually worked'.

One exception was Robert Owen. Born in Newtown, Wales, in 1771, by the age of 28 he was a successful businessman and co-owner of a cotton mill at New Lanark in Scotland. As a social reformer, his business success allowed him to test his theory that individuals are formed by their environment and that the basis of a happy, harmonious society is education. In other words, Owen believed that people are not born with inherently good or bad traits but that they acquire them from their environment. Thus people, particularly children, can be taught 'any language, sentiments, belief, or any bodily habits and manners, not contrary to human nature' (Owen, 1991: 12). He therefore developed a 'model' village around the cotton mill at New Lanark, the purpose of which was to provide a stable, healthy and happy environment for his employees and their families. He provided medical care funded by what was, in effect, an early and local form of National Insurance and the village shop was run as a co-operative. Moreover, various forms of unacceptable behaviour, such as excessive drinking, were discouraged, and all the children in the village received schooling at his 'Institute for the Formation of Character'. In short, Owen adopted and put into practice a sociological approach to providing for his workforce. His motives were treated with suspicion in many circles yet he made what was, arguably, the first practical attempt to test a sociological theory. Interestingly, New Lanark is, today, a major tourist destination in the Clyde Valley near Glasgow (Beeho & Prentice, 1997), as are other 'model' villages in the UK such as Saltaire near Bradford and Bourneville village, established by the Cadbury family in 1895.

In contrast to Owens' practical work, Comte was the first academic to develop a sociological theory, or a basis for the study and explanation of society. His work evolved against a background of profound change in Europe; the Industrial Revolution and rapid scientific and technological developments were transforming traditional rural society whilst dramatic advances were being made in the scientific knowledge which was rapidly replacing religion as the basis for understanding the world. As a result, Comte attempted to apply scientific method to the study of society, believing it to be the path to a full understanding of society and, thereby, the means for improving it. In other words, Comte asserted that true knowledge is scientific knowledge and, therefore, that social phenomena could be explained, understood and controlled scientifically in

PLATE 1.1 Salt's Mill in Saltaire now houses an art gallery, shopping facilities and restaurants

Source: Photo by Richard Sharpley

PLATE 1.2 Shopping in Salt's Mill, Saltaire
Source: Photo by Richard Sharpley

much the same way as natural phenomena. He called this a *positive* approach and, thus, he established positivism as a distinct school of sociological thought.

Positivism falls under the broader heading of structuralism, a wider sociological perspective that not only dominated much sociological research and thought up to the late 1950s, but which also is one of the two major competing theories about the way in which society is structured and develops. Structuralism refers to any form of sociological analysis that is concerned with society as a whole and how it is structured. Stucturalists adopt a macro-sociological approach, taking as their starting point the assumption that there exists a 'central value system which, either by constraint or consensus, normatively prescribes and sanctions role attitudes and behaviour' (Dann & Cohen, 1991). Thus, an individual's values, beliefs and behaviour are, according to structural theory, predominantly shaped, developed and constrained by the social world in which that individual lives. Conversely, structural theory tends to ignore or to play down the role of the individual, the 'human actor', in the formation and development of society; human individuality is, in effect, subordinated to the constraining influence of society. It is this latter characteristic of structuralism that has attracted most criticism, as it *reifies* society. That is, structuralism views society as being real or as a 'thing' rather than as an abstract concept. (Reification is a term used by sociologists to describe the interpretation of a general concept, such as society, as something solid or real.)

Despite this and other criticisms, the structural perspective dominated much sociological analysis from the birth of modern sociology until the mid-twentieth century. Within structuralism, however, there are two distinct and opposing camps. Both adopt the holistic approach to the study of society but, whilst one group concentrates on what is known as consensus theory, the other advocates conflict theory as the basis for sociological analysis.

Consensus theory

A basic assumption of structural sociology in general is that the values, beliefs and behaviour of all the individuals who comprise a particular society are formulated and, most importantly, constrained by what may be described as the rules of that society. Some of these rules may be prescribed by a society's laws which constrain an individual's behaviour by the threat of punishment or sanctions. However, not all of society's rules and constraints are backed up by laws; indeed, most social behaviour is, arguably, constrained by an individual's own beliefs and values. As a simple example, the British are well known for forming queues while waiting to be served in, say, a post office. Jumping the queue is normally considered to be bad manners, yet in many other countries queuing is unheard of and seen, perhaps, as a quaint British custom.

The important point is that, continuing with this example, queuing is not instinctive; people learn that, at least in Britain, it is normal social behaviour to form queues. More generally, individuals are not born with a concept of right and wrong, of what constitutes good or bad manners. These beliefs and values, which effectively constrain an individual's behaviour, are determined by society. To put it another way, at birth an individual is rather like a new computer; the hardware, with particular capabilities, exists but the software has to be installed to make the computer function effectively. Of course, a child inherits certain characteristics from its parents – hence, the 'nature *versus* nurture' debate – but, like a computer, 'software' (that is, beliefs, rules, values) needs to be installed through a process called *socialisation*.

Socialisation continues throughout an individual's life and in all spheres of life. Society's rules and constraints are learned, or internalised, from a variety of sources. Initially it will be an individual's immediate family which has the most influence but school friends, peer groups, institutions such as schools, colleges and universities, the work environment, religion and even the media will constrain and shape an individual's beliefs and behaviour during his or her lifetime. Moreover, the rules that an individual learns are those rules which are generally accepted by a particular society to be appropriate or acceptable. That is, there is a *consensus* about how members of a society should behave, about what the central values and norms of that society are. It is this, according to consensus theory, that determines people's roles and behaviour and ensures the continuation of an integrated, regulated and stable society.

One of the first sociologists to develop a theory of society based on a structural-consensus approach was Emile Durkheim (1858–1917). Following on from and developing the ideas of Comte, Durkheim viewed modern, as compared with primitive, pre-industrial, society as being held together by what he termed organic solidarity. While society as a whole determines an individual's role and behaviour, organic solidarity develops from a new moral consensus which, Durkheim believed, could be disseminated through education. Indeed, one of his objectives was the creation of social harmony through the state's use of sociological knowledge.

A central assumption of organic solidarity as suggested by Durkheim is that society is differentiated into separate areas and institutions, such as education, religion or the family, each of which deals with a particular aspect of social life. Each part plays a necessary role or function in the harmonious continuation of society, the analogy being that society is like a living organism; each part, or organ, is essential to the well-being of the organism. Yet the character of the organism can only be viewed as a whole, rather than being reduced to its constituent parts. Thus, society should, likewise, be viewed as a whole, with societal institutions examined and explained on the basis of their function in society. This approach to sociology became dominant during the first half of the twentieth century and developed into what was seen at the time as *the* sociological theory, namely, functionalism. The American sociologist Talcott Parsons (1902–1979) was, in particular, at the forefront of the functionalist approach to sociology.

Although functionalism has become less popular since the 1960s, it is nevertheless of direct relevance to a sociological approach to tourism. As discussed in Chapter 5, an analysis of tourist motivation cannot be divorced from the function of tourism as, say, an escape from the 'real' world, whilst, at a more socio-psychological level, functionalism provides a framework for examining the satisfaction of needs, such as adventure or curiosity, provided by tourism. Moreover, the functionalist perspective may also be applied to the classification and analysis of tourism as a social system (see Nash, 1981).

Conflict theory

Whereas Durkheimian sociology views human action and behaviour as resulting from wider social forces and influences developed by consensus, conflict theorists, although still adopting the macro, holistic approach, believe that sociological study should be concerned primarily with the influence of societal conflicts, such as domination and subordination. In other words, consensus theory favours the harmonious evolution of society and its rules, values and norms. In contrast, conflict theory is based on the assumption that these rules, values and norms, which are then internalised through the socialisation process, are founded on the ability of a dominant group in society to impose their values and behaviour onto subordinate groups. Through the imposition of their values, dominant groups are able to sustain a social structure that favours their own position in society. Thus, according to conflict theorists, social change must result not from evolution but revolution.

Charles Darwin (1800–1882) attempted to show that evolution was based on conflict and a clash of interests, but it was Karl Marx (1818–1883) who, although a philosopher and an economist rather than a sociologist, was to have a profound influence on this branch of sociology. In brief, Marx believed that the basis of society and social structure is the economy and, in order to survive, people need to produce economic necessities, such as clothing and food. The production of such economic necessities entails an individual's involvement in the system of production, whereby people enter into relations of production. It is these relations which influence and determine social structure and, hence, roles, values and behaviour, because relations of production become class relations. In particular, the working class, the proletariat, become subordinate to the capitalist class, the bourgeoisie.

Under the burgeoning European capitalist system of the nineteenth century, Marx saw the human condition becoming one of *alienation*. In contrast to traditional agricultural societies and production in which people shared all agricultural tasks, as a result of the new methods of mass production and the division of labour, individuals became involved in relatively meaningless tasks which were only part of the wider production system. Consequently, workers became alienated from their work, from the product of their labour, from their fellow human beings, from nature and, ultimately, from themselves. In effect, their labour became a commodity, bought by capitalists for the cheapest price. Thus, labour has a value. Marx labelled the difference between the value of labour (that is, the wages paid to a worker) and the value of the commodities produced as surplus value. This surplus is extracted from the subordinate class through the process of exploitation.

According to Marx, it is surplus value that is the very foundation of the capitalist system. The surplus created within the production system, the profit, enables capitalists to own and control the system of production, including labour, thereby becoming the dominant class. The economically dominant class is also able to dominate other spheres of life, from politics to religion, in the extreme creating an ideology that hides the true nature of social relationships from the subordinate class. Therefore, social progress can only be achieved, Marx argued, by removing exploitation, alienation and economic domination, which in turn can only be achieved by abolishing, through revolution, the economic system (capitalism) which creates those conditions. The responsibility for such revolution lies with the subordinate, working class.

Conflict theory, especially the work of Marx, has attracted both widespread support and criticism. Within the context of this book, it provides a valid basis for what may be described as a neo-Marxist perspective on tourism. It may be argued, for example, that so-called mass tourism, as a subset of leisure in general, is no more than a capitalistic domination or exploitation of working class leisure time. Since the beginning of the nineteenth century, the development of leisure, both as the social condition of time free from work and specific activities that leisure encompasses, may be seen as having been shaped and controlled by the needs of the dominant, capitalist classes (see, for example, Clarke & Critcher, 1985; Rojek, 1993). As some have long argued (Britton, 1982), tourism and, in particular, mass tourism (in the narrow sense of the mass tourism product – the package holiday; but see Chapter 4), is designed, produced, marketed and sold by the capitalists, the tour operators. The consumers (mass tourists) are, arguably, deceived by the lure of a holiday that promises escape from the capitalist system yet which is, in effect, an extension of it.

Thus, the 'revolution' in tourism could be manifested in a widespread rejection of the mass, package tour in favour of more individually oriented forms of tourism. Indeed, to an extent this has been occurring in recent years, the revolution in information technology through the development of the Internet providing tourists with both the knowledge and means to book and travel independently (see Chapter 2 for more discussion). Conflict theory is, therefore, of relevance to the study of the social determinants of tourism, tourist motivation, the nature and political-economy of the tourism industry and the structuralist theory of tourism as a reflection of societal change.

Inevitably, the major criticism of both consensus and conflict theory is that they both, in different ways, over-emphasise the socialisation process, thereby denying the ability of individuals to influence and change society. In addition to the reification of society, an interpretation which attributes abilities and powers to society, such as thought and reason, only possessed by humans, consensus theory tends to view individuals as passive 'robots' conforming to predictable patterns of behaviour. In the context of tourism, one form of such predictable behaviour that may be explained by consensus theory is the annual mass migration of tourists in search of summer sun, behaviour that has been described by one observer as irrational (Ryan, 1997: 3) and once likened by another to that of lemmings (Emery, 1981)! In contrast, conflict theory is based on the premise that the majority of people within society are subordinate to the rules and values of the dominant class; conformity results, therefore, not from harmony and consensus but from power and dependence. However, both consensus and conflict theory adopt an a-historical approach. That is, they ignore the historical development of society and minimise human involvement in society's structural development, whereas there are many examples of human actions that have changed society's norms and values, such as the fight by the suffragettes in early twentieth century Britain to secure equal voting rights for women (Purvis, 2003). In contrast, the second major school of sociological theory, the micro approach, highlights the role of individuals and groups of individuals in the determination, explanation and understanding of social reality. This micro approach to sociology is known as social action theory.

Social action theory

Social action theory, which essentially adopts a humanist perspective to sociology, is a broad heading under which a number of sociological approaches are found. These include the formal sociology of Georg Simmel (1858–1918), a German who was one of the first to reject the positivist, structural approach to sociology, the work of Max Weber (1864–1920), who introduced the concept of *Verstehen* (meaningful understanding) to sociological analysis and explanation, symbolic interactionism, which developed primarily as an American branch of sociology, and the more recent and radical ethnomethodology and phenomenology (see Scott and Marshall, 2005 for definitions and explanations of sociological terminology).

The basic perspective of social action theory is that society is not distinct from, but is formed by, the individuals who comprise it, and that social reality results from the social action between individuals. Such action, or behaviour, in turn results from the way in which one individual understands or interprets the behaviour of another individual, with one of the simplest forms of interpretation between individuals being the spoken word. Through this ability to interpret and understand, the individual thereby takes on a more active and creative role in the development of society.

Thus, for action theorists the development and continuation of society and culture is still dependent on socialisation, but the rules and values that are internalised are neither static, nor are they determined by society. Rather, individual members of society have the ability to adapt and change their behaviour within a process of negotiation, or meaningful encounters, with other members of that society. In short, the rules and values that influence an individual's behaviour are not determined and fixed by a reified society, as proposed by structural theorists, but are continually being changed and adapted by the actions and decisions of individuals within society.

Simmel argued that the fundamental subject of study should be the individual or, more precisely, the ways in which individuals act socially. Society, therefore, results from an intricate amalgamation of the multitude of interactions and relations between individuals; that is, society is made up of individuals who are connected by social interaction. The type or nature of interaction determines different social institutions or groupings, such as the family, marriage or religion, and it was with the form rather than the content of these social groupings, or sociations, with which Simmel was concerned (hence, 'formal' sociology). Thus, Simmel defined the form of a social relationship between two individuals as a dyad; the content may vary (for example, husband and wife, manager and subordinate, teacher and pupil) but the form of the relationship depends on the continued interaction and participation of the two individuals concerned. However, should a third person join the group (which then becomes a triad), then the form of the relationship changes from two-way interdependence into interaction based on mediation. Formalism, then, presents a way of looking at tourist groups, such as comparing the difference between individual and mass tourism, or the role of a tourist guide as the mediator between tourists and local people (Cohen, 1985; Weiler & Yu, 2007).

Similarly, Weber defined society in terms of sociation, but he also sought to link the meaning attached to social action with a more positivist cause-and-effect approach. In other words, he introduced the concept of motivation into sociology, combining an understanding of the meaning of social action with the result of such action. The Weberian perspective is of direct relevance to the study of tourism in general and tourist motivation in particular, providing an alternative basis of analysis to, for example, the functionalist explanation of tourism (see Chapter 5). Of the more recent social action perspectives, symbolic interactionism is, arguably, of most relevance to tourism analysis and research.

Symbolic interactionism

Symbolic interactionism concentrates on the way in which social rules and identities are established through social interaction emphasising, in particular, the importance of the response of other people to an individual's behaviour. Rather than simply internalising society's rules, individuals are able to analyse and adapt their own behaviour; social identity results from the interpretation of the responses of others to an individual's behaviour. To put it another way, social identity, knowing oneself, can only be achieved by interpreting how others respond to our actions, the response being communicated through symbols, such as language, in a social situation. Behaviour and values are developed, therefore, through social interaction.

The most immediate and general relevance of symbolic interactionism to tourism is its potential contribution to an understanding of the tourist-host relationship. Tourist-host encounters are, more often than not, characterised by inequality and a variety of differences between the participants and their expectations (Sharpley, 2014).

Symbolic interactionism provides the foundation for the analysis of, and potential solutions to, the socio-cultural impacts of tourism that result from such unequal or unbalanced encounters. These issues are discussed in Chapter 11.

Additionally, Dann and Cohen (1991) point to a number of other ways in which symbolic interactionism may be applied to tourism. They suggest, for example, that it provides a basis for researching issues of authenticity/inauthenticity in tourist experiences and, in terms of motivation, that it may lead towards an explanation of the desire to escape from the rules and morals of the home society whilst on holiday. That is, the ludic (play) qualities of tourist behaviour, such as excessive drinking and eating or casual sexual encounters, may be associated with an avoidance of normal social interaction that might discourage such behaviour (see, for example, Lett, 1983).

These and other social action theories, including phenomenology and ethnomethodology, have been criticised for over-emphasising the role and influence of the individual in the development of society. It is certainly true that people possess the ability to act individually and creatively, to reason and to make individual decisions, and to make sense of their physical and social world. However, the great majority of people also live according to the rules, values, morals and constraints of their societies and, consequently, most societies maintain a sense of order and harmony. Thus, neither of the two primary sociological perspectives, the macro, structuralist, theories or the micro, social action, theories, can alone fully or adequately explain all social phenomena. Indeed, a kind of halfway house has been proposed by the British sociologist Anthony Giddens. His concept of structuration develops the notion that social structure is both the medium and the outcome of social action or, as he explains 'societies . . . have "structure" insofar as people behave in regular and fairly predictable ways . . . "action" is only possible because each of us, as individuals, possess an enormous amount of socially structured knowledge' (Giddens, 2009: 89). In short, both structuralism and social action play a role in the development of society, yet neither is afforded primacy.

Inevitably, perhaps, these conflicting perspectives on sociology continue to be a subject of debate amongst sociologists themselves. At the same time, it might be argued that traditional sociological theory, much of which developed during a period of remarkable social and economic change during the nineteenth and twentieth centuries, is insufficient to explain the equally remarkable and rapid changes that are occurring in the twenty-first century, not least as a result of the digital revolution. For example, it has been suggested that, in an increasingly mobile and borderless world, sociology must move beyond society to understand contemporary social, political and economic transformations (Urry, 2012). Irrespective of these debates, however, it is important to point out that these different theories or perspectives are just that; they are different approaches, but united by the same objective of studying and explaining the development, structure and functioning of human societies. Indeed, most general texts on sociology utilise some, if not all, of the sociological theories in the analysis of different aspects of society. There is, therefore, no single, all-encompassing theory of sociology and, by implication, no single sociology of tourism, although this has not prevented some from proposing such overarching theories of tourism, such as Dean MacCannell's work on 'The Tourist' (1976; 1989; 2013) and John Urry's widely cited concept of the 'tourist gaze' (Urry, 1990a; 2002; Urry & Larsen, 2011)

These tourism theories, and others, will be discussed throughout this book. For now, however, this brief review of the development of sociology and sociological thought has served simply to highlight the scope and breadth of sociology as a perspective on society, and it is now important to consider how such a perspective may be applied to the study of tourism as a distinct area of social activity.

Tourism and sociology

Tourism is about people and societies. It is a social activity generated by some societies and impacting physically, economically, socially and culturally on others. Some commentators, adopting a structuralist, neo-Durkheimian perspective, would argue that tourism is a reflection of the condition of modern society as a whole (see Krippendorf, 1986; MacCannell, 1989; 2013, and, more generally, Chapter 3). Interestingly, Dann (2002) suggests that tourism is not just about society; it is, in fact, a 'metaphor' for society. In other words, society can be observed through the particular activity of tourism. This, in turn, supports the argument that 'tourism should be studied not for its own sake, but for what we can learn about the world in which we live' (Sharpley, 2011: 29). In other words, tourism, as a specific social institution, offers a lens though which people and society can be studied.

Some take the more specific, pragmatic (and optimistic) view that tourism can be considered a vehicle for the promotion of international peace and understanding, a force for overcoming international barriers and conflict (D'Amore, 1988), a force for social harmony. For example, the World Tourism Organization (now referred to as the UNWTO to distinguish it from the WTO – World Trade Organization) stated in its inaugural Manilla Declaration that 'tourism stands out as a positive and ever-present factor in promoting mutual knowledge and understanding and as a basis for reaching a greater level of respect and confidence among all the peoples of the world' (WTO 1980: 3). This may indeed be the case, although throughout its modern history, tourism has not been the cause but certainly the focus of violence and terrorist activities, as in the case of the Tunisia beach massacre in June 2015 (Ryan, 1991b; Tarlow, 2006).

Others have adopted a more generally pessimistic perspective on tourism, with mass tourism in particular often accused of being a destructive influence on host societies and cultures (but, see Harrison & Sharpley, 2017a). Indeed, following the initial enthusiasm which the then new phenomenon of mass international tourism received in the 1960s, during the early 1970s a number of commentators questioned the true value of tourism by highlighting the non-economic costs of tourism development (for example, Young, 1973; Turner & Ash, 1975; de Kadt, 1979). Subsequently, this negative attitude towards mass tourism, perhaps epitomised by Croall's assertion that 'a spectre is haunting our planet: the spectre of tourism. . . . In its modern guise of [mass] tourism, it can contribute to the continuing degradation of life on our planet' (Croall, 1995: 1), has underpinned the debate surrounding alternative, sustainable forms of tourism. In fact, despite the attention paid to and (perhaps now declining) support for the concept of sustainable tourism development over the last three decades, evidence continues to paint a somewhat damning picture of the consequences of tourism development on destination environments and societies (Hickman, 2007).

Whichever standpoint is taken, however, tourism is an increasingly widespread social activity; it continues to grow in scope, scale and consequence and is, therefore, a valid and important subject for sociological analysis. Furthermore, as a perspective on the phenomenon, sociology offers the potential for explanation and understanding of many factors and issues within tourism. Two approaches may be adopted. On the one hand, it is possible to study tourism within the encompassing discipline of sociology (that is, treating tourism as another social institution, along with the family, work, education and so on), permitting a broader approach to the subject than is often taken. On the other hand, as much, if not more, is to be gained by taking tourism itself as the starting point. In other words, it is possible to study tourism, exploring its inherent concepts, structures, processes and characteristics, by referring to and applying different and relevant socio-logical theory as necessary. It is the latter perspective that provides a platform for much of the discussion throughout this book.

A number of issues, then, immediately become apparent, but two questions in partic-ular arise. First, which aspects of tourism can be usefully examined from a sociological viewpoint and, second, which sociological theories are most applicable to those aspects? In answering these questions another problem becomes evident, namely, which is the most appropriate 'ology' to use? This refers specifically to the study of the socio-cultural impacts of tourism which is not only one of the four main areas of research identified by Cohen (1984) in his review of the sociology of tourism, but also the prime concern of what has been called the anthropology of tourism. Valene Smith's (1989) seminal text *Hosts and Guests: The Anthropology of Tourism*, subsequently revised and updated (Smith & Brent, 2001), includes a number of case studies that could be legitimately claimed as sociological research. Similarly, Burns' (1999) text, *An Introduction to Tourism and Anthro-pology*, covers many issues that are essentially social or sociological. Conversely, issues of authenticity and the commoditisation of culture, topics frequently examined in the literature by sociologists (see, for example, Cohen, 1988a) are no less a valid subject for anthropologists. Moreover, to further complicate matters, a rather fuzzy line exists between a 'true' sociology of tourism and the increasingly popular cultural-studies per-spective on tourism as well as that adopted by proponents of the so-called 'critical turn' in tourism (Ateljevic et al., 2007), the latter exploring many issues traditionally addressed by sociologists or anthropologists.

Nevertheless, a simple response to the first two questions might be that tourism is concerned primarily with the movement of people and, therefore, all areas of tourism should justifiably be included under the umbrella of sociological analysis. A clearer picture is obtained from a brief review of sociological approaches to tourism in the literature and a summary of the sociological theories outlined above and their relevance to the study of tourism.

Sociology and tourism in the literature

In addition to the socio-cultural impacts of tourism, a field of study to which socio-economic impacts may quite legitimately be attached, Cohen (1984), in an early paper, lists three other principal areas of analysis that have emerged in sociological treatments of tourism in the literature. These are, firstly, tourists themselves and their motivations, attitudes, perceptions and so on; secondly, the tourist-host relationship; and, finally, the structure of the tourism system. In fact, since the publication of his seminal paper *Toward a Sociology of International Tourism* (Cohen, 1972) Cohen himself has been a leading figure in the development of the link between sociology and tourism, and his work is referred to extensively throughout this book.

Some of the earliest contributions to sociological research in tourism originated in Germany. Indeed, much the earliest academic work focusing on tourism, predating the emergence of the contemporary literature, was framed within a sociological perspective and dates back to early twentieth century Europe – though mostly published in languages other than English (Dann & Parrinello, 2009a). However, perhaps the first major sociological work in tourism appeared in 1960 (Knebel, 1960, referred to in Cohen, 1984), around the time that mass tourism as we know it today was emerging as a major social force and, not coincidentally, that tourism first became more widely considered as a justifiable and important subject of academic study. Amongst the emerging research, Nuñez (1963) adopted a strictly empirical, as opposed to theoretical, approach in his study of the development of a tourism destination, as did Forster (1964) who documented changes in the structure of the workforce in Pacific island societies resulting from tourism development. In contrast, Boorstin (1964) lamented what he called the *Lost Art of Travel* in his criticism of mass tourism in general, and of mass tourists in particular, who he perceived as cultural dopes easily satisfied by inauthentic, pseudo experiences.

Boorstin's elitist sentiments were echoed to an extent by Mishan (1969), an economist who argued that the growth of mass tourism resulted from the cost of travel being too cheap. That is, the tourism industry, 'in a competitive scramble to uncover all places of once quiet repose, of wonder, beauty and historic interest to the money-flushed multitudes' (Mishan, 1969: 141), ignored the environmental and social costs of tourism development in calculating their prices. The danger was that the longer-term survival of host destinations and communities was threatened by short-term profit motives. The solution according to Mishan: to ban all international air travel! It is, of course, interesting to note that Mishan's argument is now, to an extent, being accepted and debated. That is, mass international air travel, particularly with budget (no-frills) airlines, such as EasyJet or Ryanair, is considered by many to be too cheap in terms of the costs to the environment – air travel, justifiably or otherwise, is seen to be a major potential contributor to climate change (Chapman, 2007; Hares *et al.*, 2010). As a result, there is now increasing political momentum towards charging an environmental tax on air travel (Pearce & Pearce, 2000).

Despite their elitism, the approach of both Boorstin and Mishan is of relevance to the present concern for the impacts of mass tourism (see Chapter 12). Their critical stance with respect to mass tourism was also continued, albeit with a less generalised and more balanced and considered approach, by a number of authors, especially Young (1973) and Turner and Ash (1975). It was also during the 1970s that a more rigorous and theoretical sociological approach was applied to the study of tourism. For example, Cohen (1972) was the first to challenge the generalised notion of the 'tourist' with his model of tourist typologies (discussed in Chapter 4). He went on to develop a phenomenology of tourism (1979b), arguing that not only is there a variety of tourist types, or roles, but also a variety of experiences by which tourists may be categorised.

Perhaps the most influential work to emerge at this time, however, was that of Mac-Cannell (1973 and 1976). In firmly rejecting Boorstin's arguments, MacCannell proposed a new sociological theory of tourism based upon the notion that tourists actively seek the authentic in times and places away from their normal lives. What they actually experience, though, is a reality which is constructed for their benefit, a staged authenticity (MacCannell, 1973). Similarly, Cohen and Taylor (1976) presented the case that tourism is an escape from the alienated condition of modern Western society and a search for self-identity, a theme explored more explicitly by Dann (1977) in an early discussion of tourist motivation. The concept of authenticity and tourist experience/expectations, introduced to tourism research by MacCannell, has since been developed by other authors (see, for example, Cohen, 1988a; Hughes, 1995; Olsen, 2002; Pearce & Moscardo 1986; Wang, 1999a, b) and is directly related to broader issues, such as the development of ecotourism, the commoditisation of culture, heritage and the commercialisation of history, the marketing of 'authentic experiences', and so on.

The theoretical approaches of the 1970s were balanced by empirical studies which were also undertaken during the same period. These were primarily concerned with the different relationships and perceptions embodied within tourist-host encounters and the socio-cultural impacts of tourism development (see Smith, 1977; de Kadt, 1979), and signified the advancement of anthropology as a separate area of tourism research.

Since the early 1980s there has been nothing less than an explosion in the range and depth of research and literature concerned with tourism in general and the sociology of tourism in particular. Most general tourism texts include sections concerned with the social and cultural impacts of tourism, tourist demand and motivation, types or categories of tourists, definitions of tourism or resort life cycles, all of which are topics that respond to sociological treatment, yet most tend to adopt an empirical, 'face-value' approach. At a more specialised level, a number of books and many papers and articles, too numerous to list here, have considered particular aspects of tourism which could be categorised under the heading of the sociology of tourism. Some of the most influential earlier articles are conveniently published in an edited collection (Apostolopoulos et al., 1996), whilst Wang (1999a) considers the link between tourism and modernity in his influential work.

For the most part, the now-established literature addresses specific topics or questions that may be considered 'sociological' rather than adopting a 'broad-brush' sociological approach to tourism, although Pearce's analysis of the social-psychology of tourism covers a range of issues (Pearce, 1982). The topics are diverse. Many, for example, examine the meaning and motivation for tourism as a social activity, addressing topics such as tourism as a form of escape (see Rojek, 1993), as a reaction to modern society (Krippendorf, 1986; 1987), as a search for meaning, self-identity and authenticity, thereby drawing parallels with religious experience (Graburn, 1989; Timothy & Olsen, 2006; Vukonić, 1996), or even tourism as a return to a childlike stage of existence (Dann, 1989; 1996).

Another well-researched area is that of tourist-host interaction whilst much attention has been focused on the influence of social and cultural change on tourism. For example, a number of authors have considered the influence of postmodern culture on the consumption of tourism (Berger, 2011; Munt, 1994; Pretes, 1995; Sharpley, 1996; Uriely,

1997; Urry, 2002; Urry & Larsen, 2011), whilst the more general relationship between tourism and culture is also attracting increasing attention (Rojek & Urry, 1997; Robinson & Boniface, 1999; McKercher & du Cros, 2002; Smith, 2006, 2009).

In addition to this more specialised research, overall sociological treatments of tourism have also been published. Perhaps the most notable and certainly the most widely cited work is that of Urry, in which he has developed a sociological examination and explanation of tourism based upon the central theme of the tourist 'gaze' (Urry 1990a; 2002; Urry & Larsen, 2011). Similarly, Dann (1996) explores tourism from a 'sociolinguistic' perspective, arguing that tourist behaviour is influenced or controlled through the language of tourism as presented in brochures, advertisements and other media. Other authors, including Voase (1995), Ryan (2002) and Franklin (2003) have also approached tourism from an essentially human or social perspective.

More recently, two trends are apparent in the literature that addresses the socio-cultural aspects of tourism. First, what might be broadly termed the sociology of tourism has been embraced by or, perhaps, redefined as the tourist experience. Since 2000, a growing number of journal articles exploring issues that might be considered sociological have been published, including conceptual overviews (Uriely, 2005; Volo, 2009; McCabe, 2002) and a variety of more specific topics that fall within what Quinlan Cutler and Carmichael (2010) refer to as the dimensions of the tourism experience. For them, understanding the experience, from anticipation through to recollection, must be framed by an exploration of the influential realm, including the social environment, and the personal realm which includes both anticipation/motivation factors as well as outcomes, such as satisfaction and emotion. Second, and related, there has been an increasing focus on the role of the tourist in creating experiences, both in the practical sense of co-creating an experience (Prebensen & Foss, 2011) and conceptually as tourism representing an embodied performance (Bærenholdt *et al.*, 2004). Moreover, research within the tourist experience has explored issues previously considered under the sociology umbrella, such as motivation and consumption, and newer themes that suggest, as previously noted, that contemporary social socio-cultural transformations, including within tourism, demand a new set of concepts and approaches. A number of these newer themes, such as the impact of smartphones on tourist photography (see Chapter 7), are discussed later in this book. Nevertheless, as the following sections summarise, many aspects of contemporary tourism may be considered within the framework of traditional sociological theory.

Tourism and sociological theory – a summary

Although this necessarily brief review of the literature demonstrates the evolution of the sociological and anthropological treatment of tourism, it does not indicate the extent to which sociological theory can be usefully applied to tourism. It is important, therefore, to consider not only the ways in which tourism and sociology have already been linked, but also to identify areas of potential research. This is best done by relating the major sociological perspectives outlined earlier in this chapter to relevant issues within tourism.

Structural-consensus theory

The structural, macro-sociological perspective firmly places tourism within the study of society as a whole whilst, at the same time, directing attention towards the wider tourism system rather than towards the individuals who participate in tourism. As a basis for studying tourism the structural approach may be criticised for reifying what is, in effect, the combined actions and behaviour of tourists and those who are employed in, benefit from, or whose lifestyles are affected by, tourism. Nevertheless, a general macro perspective and the more specific functionalist approach provide a foundation for tourism research in a number of areas.

First, it is important to explain and describe the development of tourism within the context of the development of society as a whole and, in particular, how tourism has become institutionalised. The growth and democratisation of tourism from what was once an activity enjoyed by the privileged few to the mass social phenomenon that it is today is frequently explained by the three facilitators: increases in free time; more disposable income; and advances in technology. Whilst these three factors have undoubtedly played a significant role in the emergence of tourism, it is nevertheless a rather simplistic explanation. Tourism is directly related to the development of leisure which, in turn, is linked to societal change and forces. Thus, for example, factors such as industrialisation, urbanisation, mass production and consumption, environmentalism and broader cultural transformations have not only directly influenced the development of tourism and its transformation from luxury to perceived necessity, but also have brought about significant changes in the style or ways in which tourism is consumed and, by implication, produced.

Second, as Dann and Cohen (1991) point out, a macro perspective can be adopted when considering the evolution of the tourism system itself, either as a linear development from local, small-scale beginnings through to international business, or as a cyclical process such as that proposed by Butler (1980a). A functionalist approach either places tourism in the context of its role in the functioning of society as a whole, such as its function in promoting international understanding, or views tourism itself as a social system. In the latter case, different parts of the tourism system may be categorised by function and linked to, for example, product development and marketing.

The greatest potential for tourism research within the holistic, macro approach is in adopting the basic assumption that tourism is a reflection of society. In particular, the positioning of tourism as a search for the authentic (MacCannell, 1976; Wang, 1999a, b) as a reaction to the contrived, inauthentic condition of modern life in tourism generating societies, or even as a sacred experience (Graburn, 1989; Sharpley, 2009a) compared with the ordinary, demands the consideration of factors such as the authenticity of the tourist experience, the commoditisation of culture and tourist motivation, and thematic issues such as the link between postmodernism, consumer culture and contemporary tourism.

Structural-conflict theory

Conflict theory is a valid basis for research into a variety of tourism issues. Brief mention has already been made of the conflict-based relationship between the tourism industry and its customers, manifested in the domination and control of the mass tourism, package holiday market by the tour operators (although this domination is arguably becoming less marked as tourists construct their own holidays – a process known as 'dynamic packaging' – by purchasing various elements of the holiday through the Internet). This relationship is, arguably, founded on paradox and deceit. The product is sold as an escape from the mundane, the ordinary, the routine; it promises change, excitement and temporary freedom from day-to-day institutionalised life. Yet, despite the apparently huge choice available to the customer, the product is standardised and mass produced. Rooms may have more or fewer facilities, accommodation may be self-catering, bed and breakfast or half board, a hotel is near the beach or a bus ride away, or the overall product might be designed to appeal to the 'independent' traveller, as in the case of the tours sold by specialist adventure travel companies. However, the basic product is still the same: transport, accommodation, food and entertainment (Harrison & Sharpley, 2017b). Also, in cases where a tour operator also owns the travel agent, the airline and possibly the accommodation, the entire process is controlled by one organisation. Customer choice is, generally, constrained by price and, far from escaping from the capitalist system, the tourist is actually contributing to it.

Some might argue, of course, that the Internet and, specifically, the potential for dynamic packaging and the ability to make choices based on an ever-increasing supply of information, not least customer reviews placed on websites such as TripAdvisor has, in a sense, liberated tourists from the control of tour operators, empowering them and providing them with much greater choice and flexibility. To a great extent, this is undoubtedly true. A tourist can now independently book flights, accommodation and car hire, purchase travel insurance and so on through the Internet at places, times and costs to suit themselves. At the same time, however, there are many web-based organisations that offer travel services, such as Lastminute.com, Travelocity and Expedia. It could be argued that these organisations have taken over the dominant role of traditional tour operators, so that power has shifted not to tourists, but simply a step down the chain of distribution.

Within the broader, international tourism system, conflict theory brings issues of dependency and tourism-related neo-colonialism into clearer focus. The international tourism industry is becoming dominated by large multinational corporations (MNCs) based both in Western tourism generating countries and, increasingly, in countries such as India, Hong Kong, China and Japan. These organisations frequently support, finance, manage or own the tourism facilities in destination countries or regions, particularly in the developing world, which lack the necessary financial and human resources to develop tourism. The MNCs gain increasing control over tourism to and in the destination (Bull, 1991: 181–197) which, in turn, becomes increasingly dependent on Western finance, products and tourists (see also Bianchi, 2015).

Britton (1982) found that many previously colonised nations, such as Kenya, are particularly susceptible to overseas domination of their nascent tourism industries, a situation he describes as neo-colonialism whilst, more generally, Nash (1989: 39) comments that it is the 'power over touristic and related developments abroad that makes a metropolitan centre imperialistic and tourism a form of imperialism'. In short, conflict theory provides a theoretical basis for exploring both the political-economy of the tourism system and, more generally, the alleged positive contribution of tourism to social and economic development in destination areas.

The third area in which conflict theory is of relevance to tourism is the study of the tourist-host relationship and the concept of commercialised hospitality (Dann & Cohen, 1991). What is, possibly, a unique experience for a tourist may be business as usual for the host whose 'hospitality', in reality, is motivated by profit. Conflict theory also highlights the unequal, transitory basis of tourist-host encounters and the growing incidence of what may be termed 'inverse-exploitation'. Increasingly, tourists may be invited to take a photograph or to visit a local home, only to be asked afterwards for a 'gift', usually money. Such behaviour may be seen as exploitation of both the tourist and a country's tradition of hospitality whilst, overall, conflict theory directly challenges the notion that the development of tourism can lead to greater knowledge and understanding between different peoples and nations.

Social action theory

The micro-sociological approach directs research and analysis towards the tourist as an individual as opposed to the tourism process and system. Focusing on the interaction between individuals, the most logical application of social action theory is to the explanation of the different expectations, perceptions, relationships and outcomes of tourist-host encounters. The success of such encounters is often undermined by misunderstandings based on differences in race, gender, class. For example, potentially meaningful encounters between southern European males and northern European female tourists or between European visitors and Gambian beachboys (known locally as 'hustlers' or 'bumsters') may be limited by opposing expectations and cultural differences. Indeed, the reputation of Gambian bumsters continues to be seen as contributing to negative images of The Gambia as a tourist destination. The analysis of tourist-host encounters may then be related to the broader field of socio-cultural impacts of tourism and an exploration of the practical ways in which such impacts may be reduced.

Social action theory may also be applied to the study of tourist motivation, one of the primary themes in the sociological treatment of tourism. Examining and explaining tourist motivation or, in simple terms, determining the reason why people travel, is a complex process. Motivation is related to both push and pull factors (Dann, 1981); push factors are those which directly influence motivation and may be socially, psychologically, economically or physically determined, whereas pull factors are the attractions of the destination. Thus, the various social action approaches are of direct relevance to an examination of both push and pull factors. These are discussed in greater detail in Chapter 5.

The sociology or anthropology of tourism?

Within the tourism literature there appears to be a degree of confusion as to what constitutes a sociological or an anthropological approach to the study of tourism. For example, Selwyn (1992: 354) describes Cohen as 'one of the most prolific anthropological writers on tourism' and Dean MacCannell's *The Tourist* as 'one of the most influential books in the anthropology of tourism', whereas both Cohen and MacCannell are more generally considered to be sociologists. This blurring of the boundaries between the two disciplines arises, perhaps, because of the overlap in their subject matter. Anthropology is the study of humankind; 'anthropologists are interested in everything human, whenever and wherever it occurs' (Nash & Smith, 1991). Thus, sociology is, arguably, a discipline that falls within the broader concerns of anthropology. Furthermore, anthropology's claim on tourism cannot be disputed: 'modern tourism accounts for the single largest peaceful movement of people across cultural boundaries in the history of the world. Given that, tourism is unavoidably an anthropological topic' (Lett, 1989: 276). Little is to be gained here from a semantic discussion of the two disciplines but a brief consideration of anthropological concern with tourism will clarify the approach adopted in this book.

The application of anthropology to tourism was relatively late in comparison to other disciplines. This, according to Nuñez (1989), was because tourism was considered by anthropologists not to be a proper or serious subject worthy of their attention. Indeed, it was Nuñez himself who was responsible for one of the first anthropological works on tourism (Nuñez, 1963), but it was the publication of *Hosts and Guests* (Smith, 1977) that firmly established tourism as a valid target for anthropologists. Since that time, a sizeable body of literature has been produced concerned with tourism, literature which can be divided into two broad categories: (a) work which empirically assesses the impact of tourism on host societies and cultures and (b) the meanings of tourism to the tourist. The latter category includes such topics as motivation, tourist roles and the semiology of tourism, whilst the dichotomy between the two is embodied in the work of Graburn (1989), who views tourism as a form of sacred journey, and that of Nash (1989) who describes tourism as a form of imperialism. Crick (1989) adds the political economy of tourism to the list of identifiable categories of the anthropological treatment of tourism.

It is immediately apparent that there is a large area of overlap between sociology and anthropology within the context of tourism research. Indeed, the only major difference is that anthropology is traditionally constrained by its holistic, comparative, cross-cultural approach, a fundamental basis of the discipline being that anthropological theories must be applicable to all peoples in all places. However, returning to the main points made throughout this chapter that tourism is, essentially, about people and societies and that tourism itself, rather than associated disciplines, should be the starting point for any analysis or research, then inter-disciplinary conflict becomes irrelevant. It is the perspective adopted that is important so that what we are concerned with, in effect, is the 'humanology' of tourism.

What is tourism?

Such has been the growth and spread of tourism during the latter half of the twentieth century and into the twenty-first that it is now, as Cohen (1974: 527) suggested more than 40 years ago, 'so widespread and ubiquitous ... that there are scarcely people left in the world who would not recognise a tourist immediately'. Tourism, however, cannot be viewed as 'one monolithic, static sort of phenomenon' (Graburn, 1983); it has already been referred to here as both a social and an economic phenomenon and there is a wide variety of other definitions and descriptions attached to the term tourism in the literature. This reflects in part the multidisciplinary nature of the topic (Gilbert, 1990) and in part the 'abstract nature of the concept of tourism' (Burns and Holden, 1995: 5).

Ryan (1991a: 6) demonstrates how tourism may be defined from a variety of viewpoints. For example, an economist might define tourism in terms of the supply of and demand for tourism products, a tourist board might adopt a technical, statistical definition based on purpose and length of stay, or an environmentalist might describe tourism in terms of the legitimised exploitation of natural resources. Despite these differences, however, it is important to establish a working definition of tourism as a foundation for the discussion in the following chapters. As a starting point, Chambers English Dictionary refers to tourism as 'the activities of tourists and those who cater for them', immediately reflecting the traditional dichotomy between tourism as a form of social activity (the focus of this book) and tourism as the industry which enables and facilitates participation in that activity. Similarly, Burkhart and Medlik (1981: 41–43) usefully identify two main groups or classifications of tourism definitions. First, technical definitions attempt to identify different types of tourist and different tourism activities, normally for statistical or legislative purposes, and which, by implication, view tourism as an economic, as opposed to human, activity. Second, conceptual definitions are concerned with the nature and meaning, or essential characteristics, of tourism as an activity (Telfer & Sharpley, 2016).

Technical definitions of tourism

Many of the earlier attempts to define tourism, undoubtedly influenced by the need of tourism destinations for a set of criteria by which to identify and measure tourism, followed the technical, rather than conceptual, perspective (Gilbert, 1990). The first international definition of tourism, proposed in 1937 by a group of statisticians at the League of Nations, defined a tourist simply as someone who travels for 24 hours or more outside their normal country of residence. This definition included those travelling for business in addition to pleasure, health or other purposes, and it also introduced the 'excursionist' as someone who stayed in a destination for less than 24 hours. However, the definition excluded domestic tourism and overlooked the fundamental meaning of tourism as a social activity.

A similar definition, though resorting to the more general description of 'visitor', was produced by the United Nations Conference on Travel and Tourism in 1963 and later adopted by the International Union of Official Travel Organisations (IUOTO), the precursor of the World Tourism Organization (UNWTO). It states that a visitor is:

> any person visiting a country other than that in which he has his usual place of residence, for any reason other than following an occupation remunerated from within the country visited,

a visitor being either a tourist, who stays overnight, or an excursionist on a day visit. According to Murphy (1985: 5) this definition is the most widely recognised, yet its

TABLE 1.3 Technical definitions of tourists

To be included in tourism statistics		*Not to be included in tourism statistics*
Category	*Purpose*	*Category*
Tourists:	holidays	Border workers
non-residents	business	Transit passengers
national residents	health	Nomads
abroad	study	Refugees
crew members	meetings/missions	Members of armed forces
Excursionists:	VFR	Diplomats
cruise passengers	religion	Temporary immigrants
day visitors	sport	Permanent immigrants
crews	others	

Source: adapted from WTO (1994)

focus remains the measurement of tourist traffic and, again, the role of tourists themselves in the tourism process is overlooked. In an attempt to rectify this omission, the Tourism Society in the UK define tourism as

> the temporary short-term movement of people to destinations outside the places where they normally live and work, and their activities during the stay at these destinations; it includes movement for all purposes as well as day visits or excursions.

The major drawback with this definition is that it implies that anyone who travels, for virtually any purpose, is a tourist. Indeed, the UNWTO considers that travel for a variety of purposes, including business, should be included in statistical data. Table 1.3 summarises technical definitions of a tourist.

The inclusion of business and other forms of non-leisure travel contradicts the generally held perception that tourism is a leisure activity whereas, interestingly, the word travel comes from the French *travail*, or work. However, the great majority of research within the sociology of tourism focuses specifically on leisure tourism, or what can be thought of as holidays/vacations.

Conceptual definitions of tourism

In contrast to technical, measurement-based definitions, attempts have also been made to conceptually define tourism from an essentially anthropological perspective. Nash (1981: 461), for example, considers that 'at the heart of any definition of tourism is the person we conceive to be a tourist'. Approaching tourism from the perspective of motivation and touristic practices, he defines tourism as simply the activity undertaken by 'a person at leisure who also travels' (Nash, 1981: 462), thereby firmly identifying tourism as the antithesis to work activities. Smith develops this theme with a more explicit reference to motivation, a tourist being a 'temporarily leisured person who voluntarily visits a place for the purpose of experiencing a change' (Smith, 1989a: 1). Similarly, Graburn emphasises tourism's functional role inasmuch as it 'involves for the participants a separation from normal 'instrumental' life and the business of making a living, and offers entry into another kind of moral state in which mental, expressive, and cultural needs come to the fore' (Graburn, 1983: 11). Finally, in a broader, metasociological sense, MacCannell (1989: 1) describes the tourist as a model of 'modern-man-in-general' and tourism as a modern pilgrimage, a kind of refuge from modernity (Short, 1991: 34). Such conceptual definitions place the emphasis firmly on the implicit leisure role or meaning of tourism. Unfortunately, however, by creating the work/leisure dichotomy, certain categories of travel activity which are strictly neither leisure nor work, such as religious pilgrimages or long-term budget travel (see Chapter 4), are omitted, thereby creating a narrow set of parameters within which to place the activity of tourism.

Tourism as mobility

Clearly, these more traditional approaches to defining tourism explicitly consider it as a separate, identifiable sphere of social and economic activity. That is, tourism has long been thought of as not only a leisure activity, but also one that is both temporally and spatially separated from normal, day-to-day life. In other words, it is motivated primarily by the desire to escape and to experience the 'Other'. Certainly, many forms of 'mass' tourism, from the 'ritualised pleasure' (Shields, 1991) of the nineteenth century seaside resort through to contemporary packaged sun-sea-sand holidays were, and remain, a separate, identifiable activity differentiated by time, location and behaviour from normal social activities and institutions. However, it has been suggested that, over the last thirty years or so, this differentiation has become less apparent: 'tourism is no longer a differentiated set of social practices with its distinct rules, times and spaces (Urry, 1994). Rather, it has become 'de-differentiated' from other social practices, merging into other social activities, such as shopping or eating out. Thus, it can no longer be considered in isolation from other social practices and transformations, particularly those that involve physical (and perhaps mental) travel or movement from one place to another. Hence, tourism is 'increasingly being interpreted as but one, albeit highly significant dimension of temporary mobility' (Hall, 2005: 21).

In other words, the broad concept of mobilities, or the increasing and widespread movement of people, capital, information and material goods both globally and locally, is not only becoming a defining characteristic of contemporary societies. It is also adopting the mantle of a new social scientific paradigm. That is, social and economic life is increasingly patterned and influenced by networks of mobilities (and immobilities) and, therefore, the study of mobilities is increasingly seen as an appropriate theoretical framework for the study of societies more generally. Evidently, tourism is one manifestation of mobility. The dramatic growth in the scope and scale of tourism reflects, or has contributed to, the increasing mobility of both people and the services (finance, information, communication and so on) that facilitate tourism. As a consequence, the study of tourism is increasingly being located within a mobilities framework (Hall, 2005), and it is now being accepted that a fuller explanation of contemporary tourism requires knowledge and understanding of the meanings and implications of the multiple mobilities of people, capital, culture, information, goods and services more generally. This, in turn, suggests that tourism as a social phenomenon may in fact be indefinable; it is, simply, one dimension of mobility.

Holistic definitions of tourism

Although there is merit in the mobilities argument above, it is probably true to state that not only is tourism generally recognised and understood as an identifiable social practice, but also those participating in it recognise and regard themselves, by and large, as tourists. However, the two categories of definition, technical and conceptual, discussed above represent two extremes of a definition continuum (Buck, 1978) which are constrained by their disciplinary focus. Thus, it has been suggested that 'as the tourist is part of the subject world, we should search for other definitions which balance out the need for both measurement and tourist identity' (Gilbert, 1990: 9). In other words, a holistic definition which embraces both the factual and theoretical perspectives of tourism is required. Jafari (1977) goes some way towards achieving this by epistemologically defining tourism as:

> the study of man away from his usual habitat, of the industry which responds to his needs, and of the impacts that both he and the industry have on the host's socio-cultural, economic and physical environments.

The essential point remains that, such is the variety of disciplinary treatments of tourism and given the vast array of activities, motivations, organisations and so on that comprise tourism, to attempt a single, all-encompassing definition is a difficult, if not impossible task. Tourism is, as stated earlier, primarily a social activity. In other words, if people had neither the ability nor the desire to travel from one place to another, tourism would not exist. Thus, tourism is an activity which involves individuals who travel within their own countries or internationally, and who experience and interact with other people and places. It is, in short, a social phenomenon which involves the movement of people to various destinations and their (temporary) stay there.

At the same time, however, tourism on its present international scale could not occur without the existence of a large and sophisticated 'industry' which enables people to be tourists. That is, without the provision of accommodation, transport, entertainment and other facilities, and without the existence of businesses that organise, package and sell tourist experiences or provide essential support, such as insurance, information or financial services, the majority of people would be unable to participate in tourism. Therefore, as a widespread activity that is embedded in modern society, tourism also embraces the following characteristics:

1   It is normally considered a leisure activity, generally associated with short-term escape from the routine or ordinary. An implicit assumption is that tourism involves freedom from paid or domestic work, although some forms of non-leisure travel (for example, pilgrimage, exploration/adventure travel) or work-related travel (for example, conferences, incentive travel) are also accepted as forms of tourism.

2   It is socially patterned. That is, the ability to participate in tourism and the nature of tourism consumption is influenced by tourists' socio-cultural background, with wealth, gender, age, class, education and other social factors all having an influence on the frequency, duration, destination and style of tourists' trips.

3   It is supported by a diverse, fragmented and multi-sectoral industry. Extensive vertical and horizontal diversification has resulted, however, in the domination of the industry by a relatively small number of multinational corporations, mostly based in the industrialised, tourism generating countries. Thus, the structure and characteristics of this industry and its inherent power relationships are likely to be significant determinants of the nature of tourism-related development.

4   It is largely dependent on the physical, social and cultural attributes of the destination and the promise of excitement, authenticity and the extraordinary. It is also, therefore, an 'ecological' phenomenon inasmuch as tourism not only requires an attractive, different environment, but also interacts with and impacts upon that environment.

5   It is a commercial activity based on encounters between tourists and local people or communities. Tourism acts, therefore, as a catalyst in the development of commercialised hospitality, the potential commoditisation of culture, and as an agent of social change.

6   It is a sector of the broader leisure market and reflects trends and changes in tourism generating societies.

Many of these characteristics and issues are addressed throughout this book. Indeed, they constitute a form of agenda for the following chapters, an agenda which may be summarised by observing that a dialectical, or two-way relationship exists between tourism/tourists and society. On the one hand, tourism is itself influenced or impacted upon *by* society. As history shows (see Chapter 2), mass tourism has evolved as a result of transformations and developments in society; it is, in a sense, a social victory (Krippendorf, 1986). More importantly, however, society has been, and continues to be, a powerful force in shaping the character of tourism. That is, a variety of social factors are instrumental in determining the motivation for and style of tourism, influencing how, when, where and why people participate in tourism. On the other hand, tourism itself impacts on societies. In other words, the development of tourism inevitably results in both positive and negative consequences for destination societies. The rapid growth of mass, international tourism since the 1960s has been mirrored by ever-increasing concern about the consequences of that growth on local people in tourism destinations.

This two-way relationship is reflected in the structure of this book. Chapters 3 to 9 focus upon the ways in which society determines, shapes or otherwise influences tourists' behaviour, motivation, consumption and attitudes. The subsequent chapters then explore the ways in which tourism impacts upon destination societies and cultures, with particular emphasis placed on the role of the tourist-host encounter. First, however, it is important to trace the historical development of tourism as socially determined activity as a background to the rest of the book.

Further reading

Apostolopoulos, Y., Leivadi, S. and Yiannakis, A. (eds) (1996) *The Sociology of Tourism: Theoretical and Empirical Investigations*. London: Routledge.
Though published some two decades ago, this edited collection includes a number of early papers that explore tourism from a sociological perspective.

Browne, K. (2011) *An Introduction to Sociology*, 4th Edition. Cambridge: Polity Press.
Exploring the contribution of sociology to the study of tourism requires an understanding of sociological theory. Many introductory sociology texts cover this, but Chapter 1 in this book is particularly accessible to those new to the discipline.

Dann, G. and Cohen, E. (1991) Sociology and tourism. *Annals of Tourism Research*, 18(1): 155–169.
A succinct paper that considers the relationship between sociology and tourism.

Dann, G. and Parrinello, G. (eds) (2009) *The Sociology of Tourism: European Origins and Developments*. Bingley: Emerald Group Publishing.
The study of tourism is often, though erroneously, thought to have begun in the late 1960s and early 1970s. This important text, however, reveals that not only can the study of tourism be traced back to the early twentieth century studies across Europe, but also provides a detailed critique if the relationship between tourism and sociology in an extended introductory chapter.

Discussion topics

▶ Is tourism fundamentally an economic phenomenon or a social phenomenon?

▶ Can the demand for tourism be explained primarily by functional sociology? That is, does tourism play an essential role in the functioning of contemporary society?

▶ Has tourism become a 'social institution'?

▶ Which, if any, sociological theory provides the most appropriate framework for exploring and understanding contemporary tourism?

CHAPTER

2

The evolution of tourism

Introduction

It is widely accepted that the roots of modern tourism lie in the industrial, economic and social transformations that occurred during the nineteenth and early twentieth centuries. Technological innovation and increasing levels of income and free time provided the means for more widespread participation in travel and tourism, whilst changes in the social condition resulting, in particular, from rapid urbanisation and the new, industrial work practices provided the motivation. Thus, it would be logical to assume that tourism is a phenomenon of modern society, emerging as a kind of inevitable by-product of what may be described as the modernisation of society.

Two points must, however, be emphasised here. Firstly, 'like many other modern industries, tourism can trace its ancestry back to the Old Testament' (Young, 1973: 9), the means of travel having been available, albeit to a privileged minority, for thousands of years. For example, sea-going ships were first designed and built around 3000 BC (Casson, 1974: 21) and chariots were first introduced around 1600 BC. Similarly, people have been able to be tourists, in the sense of travelling for pleasure, education, spiritual fulfilment and interest rather than trade or warfare, for as long as they have been physically able to travel from one place to another. Indeed, some of the earliest evidence of tourism is to be seen in Egypt, where ancient graffiti dating back to 1300 BC have been found scratched onto the great pyramids at Giza (Casson, 1974: 32; Holloway, 1998: 16). Therefore, although modern, mass tourism has been a social phenomenon only since the mid- to late-twentieth century, tourism has existed in one form or another for almost as long as societies have existed. Secondly and, perhaps, more importantly, the enabling factors of time, money and transport technology, combined with both the freedom and desire to travel and the evolution of a dynamic and increasingly sophisticated travel sector, are frequently cited as the reasons for the growth of tourism. Although these factors have certainly given the majority of people, initially in the wealthier, developed countries and, in more recent years, in emerging economies such as China, the ability and opportunity to participate in tourism, they do not adequately explain the nature of the evolution of tourism. That is, since the 1600s, an enormous variety of tastes in, and

styles of, travel and tourism have become popular and have either remained fashionable or become less widespread. Such tastes and styles, however, have not been universal, nor have they occurred at the same time in different societies, even though the enabling factors of tourism have been present.

For example, as discussed later in this chapter, the spa towns in Britain, popular from the seventeenth century onwards (Borsay, 2012) became less fashionable as tourist resorts around the end of the eighteenth century. Nevertheless, in a number of European countries, spa towns and cities, such a Budapest, remain popular to this day whilst spa centres offering specialist products, such as thalassotherapy, are an increasingly popular form of health or wellness tourism (Azman & Chan, 2010; Erfurt-Cooper & Cooper, 2009). Similarly, although technological advances in transport made travel to and through wilder, less hospitable landscapes easier, safer and more comfortable, it does not explain why it became popular to visit or gaze upon such landscapes. Or, why is it that many people nowadays eschew modern transport and accommodation facilities to travel in a more 'traditional' style?

In short, different societies have favoured different types of tourism at different periods, and continue to do so. Therefore, the historical and continuing evolution of tourism cannot be explained simply and universally by describing those factors which enable people to participate in tourism. We should consider not only the 'socio-economic, cultural, political and technological context' (Towner, 1996: 6) of tourist generating areas but also those of destination areas. At the same time, broader cultural and ideological factors must also be taken into account, such as the emergence of 'consumer culture' (see Chapter 6) or the ideology of environmentalism.

This suggests, of course, that there are as many 'histories' of tourism as there are societies which participate in tourism (see Walton, 2005) and that a complete discussion of the evolution of tourism is beyond the scope of this chapter. Nevertheless, it is important to trace briefly the historical development of tourism, identifying the major factors and influences that have underpinned the growth of tourism, as a socially determined activity, from an élite activity enjoyed by a privileged minority into the mass phenomenon that it is today. A number of broader cultural factors that pattern contemporary tourism are then discussed in subsequent chapters. (For a detailed discussion of the history of tourism in terms of both content and methodology, see Shackley, 2006; Towner, 1984; 1988; 1995; 1996; Walton, 2005; 2009.)

Tourism in ancient times

For the earliest civilisations, the major factors which inhibited the development of tourism were the difficulty and danger of travelling any distance and, for most people, a lack of money. With the exception of the Minoan (2000–1500 BC) and the Mycenaean (1600–1200 BC) civilisations, road building was virtually unknown and, even by the end of the fourth century BC in Greece, roads were poor and highwaymen frequently preyed on unsuspecting travellers. The most convenient and safe mode of transport was by ship, although even sea travel was not immune to danger from either the elements or piracy and, as most travel was motivated by either trade or warfare, the opportunity to travel for pleasure was very limited.

Nevertheless, tourism of a sort existed within Ancient Greece, although normally associated with attending religious or sporting festivals or consulting oracles. For example, the oracle at Delphi drew people from far and wide to seek advice on various matters, whilst the Pythian Games, also at Delphi, were a popular event. Many sick people travelled to Epidaurus in the hope of being healed by the gods, similar to modern-day pilgrimages to, for example, Lourdes in France (Eade, 1992), but Olympia, home of the Olympic Games, was probably one of the most popular tourist destinations in Ancient Greece. The first Games were held in 776 BC and thereafter attracted thousands of visitors from both Greece and abroad to witness the sporting contests and other events which gave the Games their deep religious significance. Thus, tourism in Ancient Greece 'was not so much a voyage of adventure as a trip in accordance with tradition and ritual. The man who travelled tightened his links rather than liberated himself from his social background' (Sigaux, 1966: 10). In other words, leisure was regarded by the Ancient Greeks not as a time to relax and unwind but more as a means of self-development through education, sport and music; leisure was seen, by the philosophers of the time, as the basis of civilised society. Visits to oracles or festivals were, therefore, part of Greek life, and travel for pleasure was uncommon. As a result, tourism as a form of escape or relaxation, a common motivation for much present-day tourism, did not become widespread until Roman times although holiday resorts were developed near major cities. The most famous of these was Canopus near Alexandria.

One notable exception was Herodotus, a Greek historian who lived during the fifth century BC and died around 425 BC. An educated man from a wealthy background, he spent much of his life travelling and recording what he experienced and is, therefore, often considered to be the first travel writer. Usually travelling by ship, a fact which accounts for his frequent descriptions of harbours and river towns, Herodotus travelled widely around Egypt, Syria, Persia and Asia Minor, reaching as far as Sicily and Italy in the west and Babylon in the east. In his writings, he describes what he encountered on his travels, sometimes relating his own experience and observations, sometimes relying on information from guides and other people he met. He wrote to both inform and to entertain and his work is a unique record of early tourism.

One of the major hurdles which limited the development of tourism in ancient times was overcome by the Romans. In order to administer their expanding empire and to maintain the Pax Romana, it was necessary for the Roman authorities to build a network of roads which not only allowed for the rapid movement of troops and administrative personnel but also increased the opportunity for ordinary citizens to travel. One of the first major highways to be built was the Via Appia, the Appian Way, the construction of which commenced in 312 BC. It eventually stretched across Italy from Rome to the port of Brindisi on the east coast and was one of literally thousands of major and minor roads which, by the first century AD, crossed the length and breadth of the Roman Empire. It was possible to travel along first-class, paved roads all the way from Hadrian's Wall in the north to the southern corners of the Empire in Ethiopia (Young, 1973: 10), with travellers being able to break their journeys at staging-posts, or hotels, along the route. Indeed, travel and tourism during the Roman period was both relatively safe and convenient, yet long-distance travel for purposes other than trade or military service was still uncommon. Even though general holidays and other festivities occupied about half the Roman year, most festivals and other events took place locally and there was no widespread touristic movement between provinces (Sigaux, 1966: 11). Only the wealthier members of Roman society were able to indulge in foreign tourism. Athens and the Greek cities of what is now Turkey, such as Ephesus, were popular destinations and, as a forerunner of the Grand Tours of the sixteenth to eighteenth centuries, young Romans were sent to Athens or Rhodes to be educated. Many Romans also visited Egypt and were as anxious as previous visitors to scratch their names onto famous structures.

More generally, the Romans introduced the concept of tourism as a form of escape. Those in positions of authority, or who could afford to do so, built themselves villas or country houses beyond the confines of the cities, often in the hills to escape the summer heat. The Alban and Sabine hills around Rome offered cool relief from the heat of the city and, by the first century BC, were dotted with summer homes and villas. Nor was this practice restricted to Rome; villas and second homes were found around most cities throughout the Empire. The development of the road network also allowed easy access to coastal areas during the summer months and a string of resorts developed along the northern shore of the Bay of Naples, over one hundred miles from Rome. The wealthier members of Roman society owned villas both in the hills and in coastal resorts; of the latter, the most famous was Baiae, the first of Rome's summer resorts. Originally favoured as a winter resort because of its hot springs (taking the waters being an important ritual in Roman life), Baiae gradually expanded from a peaceful place to relax and to go fishing and boating into a major resort – a process that was to be repeated almost two thousand years later in places such as Spain. As it developed, the town gained a reputation for moral laxity; loud parties, excessive drinking and nude bathing were commonplace and it soon attracted criticism from more straight-laced members of Roman society. For example, Seneca described the resort as the 'home of vice . . . [where] . . . licence is triumphant' (cited in Speake, 2003: 1186), a complaint which fell largely on deaf ears. Indeed, Baiae survived as long as the Roman Empire itself.

Despite the popularity of the coastal resorts around Naples, the establishment of a number of spa towns in various provinces, such as the French towns of Vichy and Aix-les-Bains, which became popular entertainment centres, and the relative ease of travel with the extensive road network, tourism during Roman times was still limited and sporadic. The distances to be travelled were often great and travel during the winter months was often impossible. Nevertheless, the Romans added an important dimension to travel and tourism. Previously, tourism was motivated by trade, health and attendance at festivals or other religious events; the Romans introduced the summer holiday based, to a great extent, on the socially sanctioned principle of pleasure and self-indulgence. It was a form of tourism that disappeared with the decline of the Roman Empire during the fifth century AD and that would not reappear until the twentieth century. Indeed, the fall of Rome signalled the virtual end of tourism as a leisure activity for almost a thousand years, although specific forms of travel and tourism emerged during the intervening period.

Tourism in the Middle Ages

With the end of Roman rule, many roads fell into disrepair and, as a result, most people's mobility was severely impaired. But this was not the only reason for a decline in tourism.

In addition to being extremely uncomfortable, travelling also became a much more dangerous activity, whilst the decline and widespread poverty of Europe during the Dark Ages meant that few people had the means, purpose or inclination to undertake journeys of any distance. Such tourism as existed at this time was limited to local fairs, festivals and religious holidays (literally, holy days); travelling was usually only undertaken for the purpose of trade or government business.

One form of voluntary tourism which was, however, popular during this period was pilgrimage. 'In its purest form pilgrimage was a voluntary journey to worship at some holy shrine, and the journey itself was expected to be hard and fraught with difficulties, a form of penance' (Jebb, 1986: 3; Turner & Turner, 2011). Pilgrimages had been undertaken for some time. Indeed, Bethlehem was frequented by Christian visitors as early as the third century (Sigaux, 1966: 18) but, from about the tenth century, when overland travel became more practicable and as more facilities for travellers became available, greater numbers of people set out on such journeys. Most travelled on foot (although, by the time of Chaucer's Canterbury Pilgrims, horseback had become the favoured means of transport) and the three main destinations were Jerusalem, Rome, and Santiago de Compostella in north-west Spain. All three attracted large numbers of pilgrims. For example, some 300,000 people visited Rome in 1300. However, shorter journeys within one country, such as English pilgrimages to Canterbury or Winchester, were also popular. Interestingly, the pilgrimage route to Santiago de Compostella (known as the Camino de Santiago) has re-emerged in recent years as an increasingly popular tourist attraction/experience. In 2003, for example, some 75,000 people travelled the route either walking, cycling or on horseback (Devereux & Carnegie, 2006), since when the number of tourists travelling along part or all of the route has increased substantially (Lois González, 2013). More generally, pilgrimage and other forms of religious tourism now represent a significant sector of the international tourism market. For example, according to Olsen and Timothy (2006), more than 240 million people annually participate in pilgrimages, whilst a more recent estimate puts the figure at 200 million (ARC, 2014). More broadly, the World Tourism Organization claims that '300 to 330 million tourists visit the world's key religious sites every year' (UNWTO, 2014). Whatever the actual numbers are, however, it is probably true to state that 'it is impossible to understand the development of . . . tourism without studying religion and understanding the pilgrimage phenomenon' of bygone eras (Collins-Kreiner & Gatrell, 2006).

Thus, during the Middle Ages, tourism, as opposed to obligatory forms of travel, was largely associated with religion. The more adventurous also embarked on long-distance journeys seeking fame and fortune, perhaps the most well known being Marco Polo who travelled to China in the thirteenth century. The accounts of his journeys are one of the very few examples of travel writing remaining from this era and it was not until the sixteenth century that individuals not only began to travel for travel's sake, but also began to record and publish details of their travels and adventures for a public that was becoming increasingly interested in stories of faraway, exotic places. One of the better known of these early adventurers was Thomas Coryate who, in 1608, undertook a trip to Venice. His account of his travels, *Coryate's Crudities*, was to inspire others to follow in his footsteps and is an early example of the way in which travel writing, as one medium of the 'language of tourism' (Dann, 1996), is a cultural influence on tourist behaviour (see also Robinson & Andersen, 2002). His writing was both vivid and humorous. For example, during a rough crossing of the English Channel he describes 'varnishing the exterior parts of the ship with the excremental ebullitions of my tumultuous stomach' (cited in Aune, 2012: 217), an experience that has undoubtedly been frequently repeated over the centuries!

Coryate was typical of many tourists of that time inasmuch as his destination was Italy. Though a nation in decline, it was still the intellectual centre of Europe (Turner & Ash, 1975: 31) and one example of the way in which the socio-cultural characteristics of destination areas are an important factor in the development of tourism. Academics, writers, artists and the aristocracy visited and were inspired by Italian art and culture. The artist Dürer, the philosopher Erasmus and the poet John Milton were among the many people who travelled there, whilst the Palladian style of architecture was introduced to Britain by Inigo Jones, following his own visit to Italy in the early 1600s. It was not only to Italy that tourists, in particular the English, travelled. It was one of a variety of destinations that made up what became known as the Grand Tour, a form of travel which was indicative of the re-emergence of tourism as a leisure activity for the first time since the decline of the Roman Empire.

Tourism 1600 to 1800

The seventeenth and eighteenth centuries are of particular importance in the historical development of tourism. Although they preceded the modernisation and industrialisation of society, the period most commonly associated with the birth of modern tourism, it was then that the pattern of tourism development through to the present time was set. In other words, it was this period which marked both the start of the social democratisation of tourism, a process which has culminated with the emergence of mass participation in tourism, and the beginning of the transformation of the fundamental meaning and purpose of tourism.

Two forms of tourism were prevalent during this period. The Grand Tour is 'one of the most celebrated episodes in the history of tourism' (Towner, 1996: 96). It was the main form of overseas travel from the sixteenth to early nineteenth century and is important as not only the first popular style of international tourism but also, as Towner (1996) observes, its legacy can be seen today in the cultural tours of Europe. Almost concurrently, spa tourism emerged in both Britain and Europe (and, to an extent, in colonial America) as the forerunner of modern resort-based tourism, although the patronage of spa towns in different countries varied enormously. Also important during this period were changes in the style of tourism which not only had an impact on the Grand Tour and spa tourism, but which also transformed the meaning of tourism.

The Grand Tour

'Like all tourist movements, the Grand Tour was the product of a particular social and cultural environment' (Towner, 1985: 299). The religious conviction that had motivated overseas travel during the Middle Ages had, during the 1500s, been replaced by more secular desires and, by the start of the seventeenth century, it was customary for the English aristocracy to send their sons, once they had graduated from university, on a tour of Europe. Moreover, underlying the popularity of undertaking a tour in Europe was the fact that the culture to which the British aristocracy aspired was to be found not in Britain but across the Channel, in France and, as referred to above, in Italy.

Usually accompanied by a tutor, the young aristocrat spent a period of anything up to three or four years abroad, the purpose of this extended trip being to complete a young man's education. In a sense, the cultural centres of Europe became a large finishing school for young Englishmen. They enrolled on courses at the universities in major cities and learnt not only academic subjects and languages but also social refinements, preparing themselves for careers as diplomats or in government. For example, amongst those who travelled in Europe in the early days of the Grand Tour (and by the mid-1700s, it is estimated that some 20,000 English were abroad at any one time) was Henry Wooton who, having gone on an extensive tour starting in 1589, was eventually to become the English Ambassador in Venice. The travels of these early Grand Tourists inevitably took them to Italy as part of what Towner (1985) describes as the Classical Grand Tour. The northern Italian cities of Turin, Verona and Venice were on the usual itinerary and the classical tastes of the tourists were also reflected in their routes along the Rhone valley in France. Switzerland, Austria, Germany and Holland were also included on longer tours.

The important point about the Grand Tour, in terms of the historical development of tourism, is that the characteristics of both the Tour and those who participated in it changed over time. In other words, during the two centuries or so that preceded the Napoleonic Wars, the Grand Tour underwent a fundamental transformation and, by the beginning of the 1800s, the purpose, destinations and length of trip of the tourists bore little relation to earlier tours. A greater number of tourists started to tour Europe, but their trips were shorter both in distance and duration; they came from increasingly older age groups; they tended to belong to the professional middle classes rather than the aristocracy; and their purpose was more for pleasure and sightseeing rather than education. In short, the Grand Tour became popularised and the tourists themselves began to gain a reputation for showing little or no interest in the people, language or culture of the countries through which they passed, an accusation that may be directed towards certain forms of modern, mass tourism.

As the Grand Tour became 'invaded by the bourgeoisie' (Turner and Ash, 1975: 41), the aristocracy abandoned the traditional European tour in favour of more socially exclusive resorts or areas elsewhere in a pattern of behaviour that has been repeated throughout the development of tourism since the late eighteenth century. This transformation occurred for a number of reasons, though primarily reflecting the emergence of a new middle class who could afford overseas travel. There was also a gradual shift away from education-motivated touring towards travel as a symbol of the leisured classes, a catalyst being the increasing popularity of travel literature during the eighteenth century which helped to 'spread the culture of travel to the literate middle classes' (Towner, 1996: 102). The notion of sightseeing also came to dominate travel culture. Whereas the early Grand Tourist travelled abroad for 'discourse' (Adler, 1989), to learn languages, to read and to meet and converse with eminent persons, later travellers relied more on visual observation. Initially, such sightseeing was impartial and objective, 'the "eye" . . . was deliberately disciplined to emotionally detached, objectively accurate vision' (Adler, 1989: 18). Soon, however, an element of subjectivity was injected. Nature, landscape and scenic beauty became the object of the tourists' gaze as the Romantic Movement emerged, influenced greatly by the writing of Rousseau. Mountain scenery, once feared or simply considered to be monstrous and ugly in comparison with gentler, more ordered landscapes, became the object of the tourists' attentions and their routes through Europe were adapted accordingly. Switzerland became popular and, towards the end of the eighteenth century, a number of visitors, including William Wordsworth, undertook walking tours there.

In England, too, the Romantic Movement came to dominate the ways in which people viewed the landscape, although more generally travel within Britain was not particularly popular or widespread until the late eighteenth century. Not only was transport slow and uncomfortable but, with the exception of the spa season, domestic travel simply did not constitute part of the culture of the leisured classes.

The change in landscape tastes in England is, perhaps, epitomised by the transformation of the Lake District from what Defoe (1991: 291) described as 'a country eminent only for being the wildest, most barren and frightful of any that I have passed over in England, or even Wales itself' into an area revered by writers, poets and artists alike. What had changed, of course, was not the landscape itself, but people's attitudes towards landscape and scenery. Certainly, improvements in transport made it easier to visit wilder, more isolated areas, yet the representation of the Lake District in art and literature was a powerful influence in the development of aesthetic tastes for landscape. At the same time, rapid social and economic change, in particular the urbanisation and industrialisation of Britain from the 1750s onwards, resulted in rural areas, such as the Lake District, being romantically held as the antithesis to urban life (O'Neill & Walton, 2004). In other words, tourism during the eighteenth century responded to socio-cultural and economic transformations which have continued to guide and influence the way in which mountainous and rural areas are viewed as tourist destinations (see Urry, 1995: 193–210, and Chapter 3).

Tourism and the spa resorts

At the same time as the Grand Tour was becoming popular amongst the English aristocracy, the spa towns of England and Europe were once again becoming popular for the first time since the decline of the Roman Empire. Often described as the first step towards the development of resort-based tourism, renewed interest in the spas resulted from the belief amongst the medical profession at the time that mineral water could be beneficial to the health. Bath, in particular, became nationally and internationally famous, largely because of a book published by Dr William Turner in 1562, drawing attention to the alleged medicinal properties of its waters. Other spas were soon established in England, including Scarborough, Epsom and Tunbridge Wells, and the fashion soon spread across the English Channel as spas in France, Germany and Italy were re-developed to cater for the needs of an increasing clientele.

PLATE 2.1 The Roman Baths, Bath Spa
Source: Diego Delso (delso.photo, *Licence* CC-BY-SA)

It was not long before the spa towns became social centres as well as health resorts. Indeed, health considerations rapidly took second place as visiting spas became an annual event on the social calendars of the upper classes. By the beginning of the eighteenth century, Bath was at the height of its popularity with Richard 'Beau' Nash, the Master of Ceremonies, organising the social life of the town and welcoming each visitor personally. Gradually, more and more facilities were provided to entertain visitors at the spas and they soon became, in effect, holiday resorts disguised as health centres, with only a minority of visitors being in anything but the best of health. A similar process was also occurring in Europe and some German spas, such as Baden-Baden, became little more than gambling resorts. Inevitably, perhaps, the spas began to attract increasing numbers of visitors from the expanding middle and professional classes and their social exclusivity began to suffer. Improvements in transport further increased their accessibility and, as shopkeepers, innkeepers and a variety of other trades moved in to take advantage of the increasing numbers of visitors, the resorts began to move down market. By the end of the 1700s, the spa towns were rapidly being transformed into residential and commercial centres as tourists turned their attention to the seaside resorts and new developments that were to emerge during the following century (for more detail, see Towner, 1996).

Tourism in the nineteenth century

The nineteenth century is, without a doubt, the most important period in the history of tourism. Even by 1800, after 200 years of the Grand Tour and the rise and decline of the spas, tourism was still an activity enjoyed by a relatively small, privileged proportion of the population. For example, it is estimated that about 40,000 English citizens were either living or travelling in Europe at that time (Sigaux, 1966: 66); yet, by 1840, some 100,000 people were crossing the English Channel each year, a figure which rose to one million by the start of the twentieth century (Young, 1973: 18). The main factor which brought about this rapid growth in tourism was, of course, advances in travel technology, especially the introduction of the railways, but society itself underwent a fundamental transformation that was to influence how and where people spent their leisure time in general, and the development of tourism in particular. In other words, the improvements in transport and communications during the nineteenth century, as well as increases in personal income and free time, enabled a far greater proportion of the population to participate in travel and tourism. Importantly, though, changes in the structure of society and social attitudes towards leisure and tourism also determined where, when and how different social groupings participated in tourism. Indeed, the development of tourism reflected broader social transformations. Thus, although the greatest growth in tourism, particularly international tourism, has been experienced since the mid-twentieth century, the foundations for such growth were laid during the nineteenth century, the emergence of seaside resorts in particular representing the first step towards mass participation in tourism.

The development of the seaside resort

As the spas declined in popularity during the late 1700s, the attention of tourists turned towards coastal resorts. Once again, the initial impetus was provided by the medical profession which extolled the supposed recuperative powers of sea water. In 1753, Dr Richard Russell published a famous paper in which he described the benefits of bathing in, and even drinking, sea water and, to practice what he preached, he moved to Brighthelmstone (now Brighton) on the south coast. By the turn of the century Brighton had become a fashionable destination, its popularity having been given an important boost following a visit by the Prince of Wales in 1783, and the town expanded rapidly. Similarly, a number of northern coastal resorts, such as Blackpool, Southport and Scarborough, also grew in popularity. For example, in 1795, Blackpool was described in the *Blackburn Mail* as being 'the first watering place in the Kingdom, whether we consider the salubrity of the air, the beauty of the scenery, the excellence of the accommodation or the agreeable company of which it is the general resort'.

The initial exclusivity of the seaside resorts was dependent on two factors. Firstly, sea bathing was considered to be a medicinal rather than a pleasurable activity and was, therefore, a structured ritual (see Urry, 2002) which, frequently, took place during winter. Secondly, travelling at the end of the eighteenth century was still slow and relatively expensive. For example, the trip from London to Brighton could take up to two days and the cost of such a journey was beyond the means of most people, even if they had the time. Thus, up until the 1830s, the seaside resorts were still the preserve of the wealthier, leisured classes, although some resorts had become accessible to other social groups, largely as a result of new transport services. In particular, the resorts near the Thames estuary became increasingly popular following the introduction of steamboat services. The first service between London and Gravesend started in 1815 and to Margate in 1820 (Holloway, 1998: 22). By 1830, paddle steamers were carrying Londoners in their thousands down the Thames to the Kent coastal resorts, where the famous piers were originally built for landing passengers rather than entertainment.

In 1829, Stephenson's *Rocket* travelled from Liverpool to Manchester at an average speed of 16 miles per hour (26 kilometres per hour), signalling the advent of rail transport and the technological revolution which brought about the birth of mass tourism. The expansion of the railways was remarkable. In 1836, there were 700 miles (1,126 km) of track in England, in 1843 there were some 2,000 miles (3218 km) and, by 1848, the total length of the railways exceeded 5,000 miles (8,045 km). This expansion was matched by the rapid increase in the number of passengers travelling by rail and, by 1847, the annual number of train passengers had risen to 51 million (Holloway, 1998: 24). For the first time, cheap, safe and relatively fast transport was available to the majority of the population, although the railway companies were slow to recognise the potential opportunities of mass leisure travel, and the seaside resorts expanded rapidly. The growth and success of some individual resorts was almost entirely dependent on the railways. For example, Rhyl in north Wales developed entirely as a result of the construction of the Chester to Holyhead railway line and, furthermore, the social status of resorts also depended to some extent on the rail links, although other factors were also important (Urry, 1990a: 22). Some destinations, such as Torquay and Bournemouth, remained relatively exclusive owing to their distance from major industrial cities and the later arrival of the railways, whereas Blackpool had moved downmarket by the 1850s. A number of authors have explored the history of the seaside resorts in some detail (see Towner, 1996: 167–216; Walton, 1983; Walvin, 1978; or, more generally, Pimlott, 1947). In particular, Shaw and Williams (1997) provide an in-depth analysis of the factors that have led to the changing fortunes of coastal tourism resorts.

It was not only the development of the railways that led to the growth and democratisation of tourism at the seaside resorts. Of equal importance were the social changes that were occurring during the nineteenth century which created the time, the money and, perhaps most importantly, the desire to participate in tourism. At the beginning of the century, Britain remained, by and large, a pre-industrial, rural society. About eighty percent of the population lived in rural areas rather than in towns and cities, and social life, including leisure, was determined by traditional customs and the agricultural calendar. The Industrial Revolution, which led to the developments in transport technology, also brought about a variety of transformations and created the social and cultural conditions under which tourism could thrive.

From a positive point of view, there was a general increase in wealth amongst the industrial population as the average income per head quadrupled over the course of the nineteenth century (Urry, 1990a: 18). Although poverty was widespread in the rapidly expanding industrial cities, some working people were able for the first time to accumulate savings to pay for holidays, holidays with pay not being made available until well into the twentieth century. Free time for leisure and tourism was initially limited. Most people worked a six-day week, with Sundays reserved for rest and worship, until half-day holidays were introduced during the second half of the century, and bank holidays in 1871. Also, during this period the leisure time available to the working classes was often structured and organised by the dominant capitalist class as 'part of the phalanx of nineteenth-century regulative mechanisms formed to create an obedient, able-bodied, law-abiding and docile class of working people' (Rojek, 1993: 32). For example, it is no coincidence that both the Football League and Rugby League in Britain were formed in the northern industrial areas towards the end of the 1800s (Clarke & Critcher, 1985: 62; see also Ryan, 1997).

As life became industrialised and urbanised, work time and leisure time became differentiated and the different social classes emerged, often with their separate, class-defined residential areas within towns and cities. The working classes, in particular, found their lives becoming increasingly structured, organised and dominated by the capitalist system. Long working hours, the Protestant work ethic, social reform campaigns and cramped urban areas which lacked space for leisure and recreation all combined to create the conditions under which people longed to escape from the towns and cities. Employers began to realise the benefits of offering regular, official holidays to workers, and wakes weeks, when factories, mills or even entire towns closed for a week's holiday, became commonplace in the industrial north. Importantly, this meant that communities took holidays together and, for many towns, this was manifested in trips to the seaside, with particular resorts becoming associated with different industrial cities or regions. For example, Morecambe catered for tourists from Yorkshire whilst Blackpool was favoured by Lancashire workers; Great Yarmouth attracted miners from the east coast and midlands; south coast resorts near London were mainly visited by day-trippers and others, such as Southport, managed to retain a more exclusive atmosphere. Southwold, on the Suffolk coast, has retained a firmly middle-class public and has sustained growth into the twenty-first century, building a new pier in 2000–2001. Beach chalets here are sold for £35,000 even though they have no sanitation or running water and have no right of tenure.

Thus, mass tourism to the seaside resorts was a direct result of the Industrial Revolution (although, as some have observed, recreational enjoyment of the sea existed well before the discovery of the seaside by the wealthy) and tourism, generally, came to be seen as a formalised and regular form of escape from the stress and strain of modern, industrial life. The development cycle that had become evident through the popularisation of the Grand Tour and the spas once again meant that, as the nineteenth century progressed, the higher social classes had to look further afield to retain their exclusivity. International train travel was introduced with services, such as the Orient Express, offering luxurious travel across Europe. It is also interesting to note that proposals to build a Channel Tunnel were first mooted during the nineteenth century and, at a Select Committee meeting in 1883, the potential cost of building the tunnel was put at £3 million! The Mediterranean resorts along the French Côte d'Azur were popular amongst the European aristocracy and became the favourite haunt of Royal tourists. For example, Queen Victoria visited Cannes in the 1890s, as did the Russian Czar and, at the end of the century, the Riviera was about five times more expensive in real terms than it was during the 1950s and 1960s (Turner & Ash, 1975: 69). However, another vital characteristic of the development of tourism during the nineteenth century was the institutionalisation of tourism and the beginnings of an identifiable tourism industry.

Thomas Cook

Although travel opportunities became available to increasing numbers of people with the rapid development of the rail network, greater wealth and a more formal approach to the provision of free time for those, other than the leisured classes, to whom work was a necessity, 'there was no tradition of travel amongst the new Victorian middle classes' (Young, 1973: 20). In other words, most people had little idea about how to overcome the potential problems of overseas travel, such as language barriers, exchanging money, knowing where to go and where to stay, and so on. What was needed to bring overseas travel within the reach of these potential tourists was an organisation that would provide all the necessary services and help, and that organisation was set up by Thomas Cook. Cook was not the first person to organise tours for the public; Sir Roland Hill is accredited with 'inventing' excursion trains and by 1840 such trips were not unusual. But it was Thomas Cook who did more than anyone to revolutionise tourism, transforming it from the preserve of the privileged classes into an international industry and creating the package tour as one of the most popular forms of tourism (see Brendon, 1991, for a complete history of Thomas Cook).

Thomas Cook's main business was printing but he was also a firm believer in temperance. It was as he was walking to a meeting in Leicester in 1841 that he first had the idea of organising a special train to take delegates to a temperance meeting in Loughborough and, on 5 July 1841, 570 travellers boarded a Midland Counties Railway Company train for the 11-mile journey from Leicester. Each had paid one shilling for the return journey but, more importantly, that short trip was the first step to Thomas Cook becoming a worldwide force in tourism (see Plate 2.2). The success of the first trip soon led to other trips being organised, motivated more by Cook's altruism than a drive to be commercially successful (a characteristic that was to lead to a serious conflict with his son, John, who was more concerned with building a successful business). Soon, he was running regular excursion trips. From 1848, tours were made in Scotland, with 5,000 tourists each season using Cook's services and, in the same year, he took a group to Belvoir Castle. He first contemplated overseas tours in 1850 but the Great Exhibition of 1851, to which he conveyed a total of 165,000 visitors, delayed his ambitions. Indeed, it was not until 1855 that the first overseas Cook's tour occurred and, owing to resistance from the French railway authorities, the tour ended at Calais.

Throughout the 1850s most of Thomas Cook's business was in Britain. From 1862 onwards, following a successful excursion to Paris, his operations abroad began to expand. The first tour to America was undertaken in 1866 and John Cook joined his father as a partner in the business. Thereafter, the organisation's size and prestige expanded rapidly. In some parts of the world, the company began to wield much power and influence. For example, it had control of all passenger steamers on the Nile from 1880 onwards and a

PLATE 2.2 The first tour organised by Thomas Cook
Source: Thomas Cook Travel. Reproduced with permission

virtual monopoly of all tourism from India. The latter included pilgrim traffic to Mecca and the responsibility for the travel arrangements of Indian princes attending Queen Victoria's Jubilee celebrations. In 1872, the first Cook's Circular Notes were issued. These were similar to letters of credit used by travellers during the previous century but were much more flexible as they could be exchanged at any hotel or bank in the Cook's scheme. In effect, they were the ancestors of the modern traveller's cheque which was first developed in the 1890s by American Express. 1872 was also the year when Thomas Cook's first round-the-world tour was organised.

One hundred and fifty years on, Thomas Cook is still a major force in international tourism and the company has continued the tradition of innovation started by its founder in the 1840s. For example, early in 1994 a revolutionary (for then) new information and booking system using a mobile travel kiosk was launched, reducing the need for customers to visit a travel agency and making information and booking services more widely available, thereby making it even easier to book a holiday. Indeed, the greatest contribution that Thomas Cook made to the development of tourism was just that; through his organisational skills, his eye for detail and his contacts he took the worry out of travelling and brought the opportunity of travel to millions. In other words, Thomas Cook was a major influence in the democratisation of travel and tourism, removing much of the mystique of overseas travel and undoubtedly influencing people's attitudes towards tourism. Not that he was without his critics. On the one hand, he set standards of comfort and convenience that brought tourism to the masses but, on the other hand, he could also be accused of diminishing the authentic travel experience (see Chapter 9) and of creating, in the broader sense, the institutionalised mass tourist.

However, whichever viewpoint is adopted, there is no doubting his contribution to what was, in effect, the socialisation of tourism.

Tourism in the twentieth century

In the early years of the twentieth century, the development of tourism continued along the course that had been set during the previous century. The English seaside resorts became increasingly popular and greater numbers of tourists travelled abroad. The upper classes spent their summers on the French Riviera but, for the majority, tourism was still based around the mass exodus to the seaside. Already there were signs of the internationalisation of tourism as large numbers of Americans crossed the Atlantic and it was estimated that, in the years preceding World War I, up to 150,000 American tourists came to Europe each year. Travelling was becoming increasingly comfortable and easy. No passports were required in Europe and many countries became increasingly reliant on tourism as a source of income.

New types of tourism were also becoming popular; skiing holidays in Switzerland had been introduced by Sir Henry Lunn in the 1880s (Holloway, 1998: 26) and, domestically, the countryside was becoming a popular destination for walkers and cyclists. The first holiday camp, Cunningham's, on the Isle of Man, had already been established at the turn of the century (see Ward & Hardy, 1986) and, generally, tourism expanded rapidly. The pattern of development also continued. Those with time and money went abroad, those with less of both went to the seaside resorts and, as more and more people were able to travel, once exclusive resorts became popularised.

The inter-war years

Following World War I, the growth in tourism continued, although there were a number of important developments which had both a direct and indirect influence on the evolution of tourism. Passports were introduced but, in the Europe of the prosperous 1920s, this had little effect on the numbers of people participating in tourism. Trans-Atlantic travel, in particular, grew spectacularly as Americans visited Europe in their thousands, bringing with them styles and fashions that were to dominate the European social scene for a number of years. Tourism offered wealthier Americans the opportunity to escape from the restrictions of their own society, in particular Prohibition, and many spent their summers travelling in Europe or staying on the French Riviera.

It was on the Riviera during this period that sunbathing first became popular. Until the 1920s, most middle- and upper-class Europeans and Americans avoided exposing their skin to direct sunlight. Pale complexions were considered to be a symbol of higher social status, whereas darker, suntanned features were identified with lower, rural classes or black people. Thus, British women in colonial countries, such as India, maintained their strict dress code in order to avoid darkening their skin and, hence, being identified with local people. However, during the years immediately following World War I, sunbathing became an increasingly popular leisure activity and the suntan became highly fashionable. By the early 1920s, social life on the French Riviera centred on the beach and the suntan became a symbol of wealth and of the leisure classes. A hot summer in 1928 finally made sunbathing more popular in England (see Turner & Ash, 1975: 80) and with it emerged an entire new industry, supplying bathing costumes, suntan lotion and so on. Achieving a suntan soon became a major motivation for tourism. It was a visible sign of wealth and prestige in the major northern European urban centres, differentiating between those who could or could not afford a summer holiday by the Mediterranean, and, even with the onset of mass tourism in the 1950s and 1960s, the symbolic importance of the suntan did not decline. Despite extensive publicity and warnings about the dangers of skin cancer resulting from sunbathing, escaping for two weeks in the sun remains a primary motivation for many tourists, at least those from northern Europe and North America. Elsewhere, however, efforts to raise people's awareness of the dangers of excessive exposure to sunlight, such as the 'slip-slop-slap' campaign in Australia, have been more successful.

During the 1920s and 1930s, travelling became much easier for many people. Initially, the introduction of motorised public transport by road in the form of the charabanc, an early type of coach, improved accessibility and the ride on the charabanc became part of the attraction of a trip to the seaside. But it was the motor car that did more than anything to improve personal mobility. International travel was still beyond the means of most people and the car provided a new-found freedom for the middle classes, who were no longer dependent on public transport services. Motoring became a popular leisure activity, new destinations, such as the countryside, became popular and, by the outbreak of World War II, there were some two million cars on the road in Britain. This number, however, was dwarfed by the scale of American car ownership in the United States; according to Aramberri (2017), as early as 1927 there were more than 23 million cars on the road in the US, leading Aramberri (2017: 16) to suggest that the country is the 'native land of mass tourism'.

Inevitably, increasing car ownership and less reliance on public transport resulted in the beginning of the decline of the railways, a process that has continued throughout the twentieth century and into twenty-first. By 1999 there were over 22 million cars on the roads in Britain; at the end of 2014, the number of licensed cars had risen to 29.6 million (DfT, 2015). Not surprisingly, car travel is the most popular mode of tourism transport, both domestically and abroad. In 2005 cars, vans and taxis in Great Britain made 40 billion trips. Total domestic passenger distance travelled increased by 62 percent between 1980 and 2005, from 491 to 797 billion passenger kilometres. Between 1980 and 1990 the increase was 41 percent and, from 1990 to 2005, 15 percent. The distance travelled by cars (including vans and taxis) increased by 75 percent from 388 billion passenger kilometres in 1980 to 678 billion in 2005. The great majority of tourism within Europe is based on the car and the opening of the Channel Tunnel in 1994 further increased opportunities for the British to travel independently by car on the Continent.

Cycling also became more widespread in the early part of the twentieth century. The Cyclists' Touring Club was founded in 1878 and, coinciding with a trend towards healthy activities, the founding of organisations such as the Youth Hostels Association in 1930 and a growing interest in the outdoors, cycling became a popular form of tourism during the 1930s.

With regard to air travel, World War I had stimulated research into aircraft design and, following improvements in safety, the first scheduled fare-paying passenger flight took place between London and Paris in August 1919 (Young, 1973: 24). However, the service was not a success. Flights were relatively slow, noisy and usually very uncomfortable and the service was soon cancelled. Longer journeys required frequent stopovers for refuelling and aircraft tended to be unreliable. It was also, initially, a very expensive way of travelling compared with rail and sea transport and so it was not until after the World War II (international conflict, once again, having provided the impetus for rapid advances in aircraft technology) that air travel became a viable and realistic mode of transport for large numbers of tourists. Nevertheless, by 1939 there were regular air services between all the major European cities and Pan Am was operating a regular trans-Atlantic service.

Another factor that stimulated the growth of tourism in the inter-war years was the increasing amount of free time that people in the UK were able to enjoy, in particular, socially sanctioned free time. Throughout the latter half of the nineteenth century, various pieces of legislation had improved working conditions and reduced the length of the working week. By the 1920s, most people worked a 48-hour week. A number of enlightened employers also gave their workers paid time off, but there was no legal requirement to do so. Throughout the early twentieth century there was increasing pressure for holidays with pay. By the mid-1920s, up to 17 percent of the workforce were receiving paid holidays, but it was not until 1938 that the Holidays With Pay Act was passed, giving all employees a legal right to enjoy paid holidays. With the onset of World War II, it was to be some years before the legislation fully took effect but, since then, people's holiday entitlement has gradually increased. For example, in 1969, 97 percent of all full-time manual workers in Britain received two weeks paid holiday; by 1988, 99 percent received four weeks.

The introduction of holidays with pay firmly established the popularity of the British seaside resorts, confirming their virtual monopoly on British holidays; even by the late 1960s, three-quarters of all domestic holidays were spent at the seaside. Many resorts, such as Scarborough and Brighton, were at the height of their popularity and Blackpool at the end of the 1930s attracted some seven million visitors between June and September each year. Importantly, it was during this time that the family holiday became socially institutionalised.

The holiday camp

One of the major features of tourism in Britain during the inter-war years was the development of the holiday camp (for a history of the holiday camp, see Ward & Hardy, 1986). Indeed, as a result of publicity and nostalgia embodied in television programmes such as *Hi-de-Hi!*, the holiday camp is probably the most widely recognised symbol of British tourism up until the late 1950s. The person normally accredited with the concept and development of holiday camps is Billy Butlin and, certainly, his vision, flair and entrepreneurial skill were significant factors in the growth and popularity of the camps. However, the idea of holiday camps dates back to the turn of the century. Cunningham's Young

Men's Holiday Camp was established on the Isle of Man in 1897 and, by the time Butlin's first camp opened in 1936, about 60,000 visitors a year stayed at Cunningham's. The Caister Camp on the Norfolk coast was founded by John Fletcher Dodd in 1906 as a summer camp for socialists and, throughout the 1920s and early 1930s, a number of organisations set up camps around the coasts of Britain. Some, such as those run by the Holiday Fellowship, were run as non-profit schemes to provide the opportunity for healthy holidays and fresh air for young people. Others, such as camps organised by the Co-operative Holidays Association and the Workers Travel Association (by 1939, the second largest holiday organisation in Britain), provided holidays for workers and their families. A number of these early camps had rudimentary chalets for accommodation but in many others people slept in tents; indeed, 'by 1939 it was estimated that a million and a half people spent their holidays under canvas and in camps of all kinds' (Ward & Hardy, 1986: 42).

Butlin's first camp opened at Skegness on Easter Sunday 1936 and, compared with earlier holiday camps, it was relatively luxurious. It comprised 600 chalets, dining and recreation facilities, a swimming pool, a theatre, tennis courts, services such as child-minding and organised entertainment and, perhaps most important of all, modern sanitary arrangements, which had been noticeable by their absence at many other camps. Holidays, with full board and free entertainment, were offered at an all-in price, ranging from 35 shillings (£1.75) to £3 per week, depending on the season. The camp was an immediate success.

His second camp opened in Clacton in 1938 and more followed after World War II, with other entrepreneurs such as Fred Pontin and Harry Warner building up their own holiday camps. By 1948, it was estimated that one in 20 holiday-makers stayed at a Butlin's camp each year (Ward & Hardy, 1986: 75) and throughout the 1950s and 1960s, the camps remained popular. The Clacton camp was closed in 1983, along with those at Filey and Barry Island, and in recent years the remaining camps have been extensively modernised to compete with newer inland resorts, such as Center Parcs.

Holiday camps were successful for a number of reasons. They provided all-in holidays aimed at the middle, rather than working classes, they retained the atmosphere of a seaside holiday but with much better facilities than in the traditional hotel or boarding house, there was plenty to do, especially in poor weather, and they were bright, fantasy lands where 'campers' could forget about life outside and immerse themselves in a dream world. Their success also depended on people's willingness to be organised; holiday camps were developed when the great majority of the population first enjoyed paid holidays and, for many people, having free time was a novel experience. They were used to the routine of work and the culture of mass production and consumption and, thus, the regimented life of holiday camps reflected the broader social condition of the time. But, from the 1960s onwards, the popularity of holiday camps diminished. Their image as 'camps' became unfashionable and developments in tourism, in particular the growth in overseas holidays, provided competition with which the camps, in their original form, were unable to compete.

Nevertheless, the significance of the traditional holiday camps in the evolution of contemporary tourism cannot be underestimated. As discussed in more detail elsewhere (Sharpley, 2017), the holiday camps developed in the UK, particularly Butlin's camps, were based on Fordist principles of mass production (see also Chapter 4); that is, they were run on the basis of high volumes and low profit margins, offering customers efficiently produced, predictable, standardised, yet enjoyable holidays. In so doing, Butlin established a business model that has been replicated successfully and widely within the tourism sector. In other words, as Sharpley (2017: 103) explains, 'key to [Butlin's] success was attracting large numbers of customers to a site where all their needs could be met cost-effectively . . . though at the same time, injecting an element of luxury and hedonism' and, importantly, at an all-inclusive price. A similar approach was adopted by Club Med which, originally founded in 1950, is now the world's largest all-inclusive club holiday provider with 70 villages located in 49 different countries, whilst the all-inclusive concept has gone on to become a popular form of tourism production and consumption. Not only has it, for example, underpinned the success of luxury resorts in the Caribbean (Issa & Jayawardena, 2003), but also some tour operators, such as First Choice Holidays in the UK, offer only all-inclusive holidays. At the same time, the original all-inclusive holiday camp idea has been refined and developed in a wide variety of tourism products, such as inland resorts and cruise holidays, to the extent that nowadays, innumerable tourists are (unknowingly) enjoying a contemporary 'camp' holiday.

The development of mass tourism

World War II effectively put an end to the development of tourism for a number of years. However, the 70 years or so since the end of the war have been the most spectacular and, from a sociological point of view, the most significant in the history of tourism. Within the modern, Western world and, in recent years, in many emerging economies, particularly in Asia, international tourism has been transformed from a luxury enjoyed by a privileged minority into a leisure activity enjoyed by a large majority of the population. Equally, as a social activity, tourism has become internalised. That is, it has become an accepted, or even expected, part of life, a necessity rather than a luxury, and a mass activity.

As discussed in Chapter 1, the growth in international tourism has, by any standards, been remarkable. From just 25 million international arrivals recorded worldwide in 1950 (by way of contrast, the UK alone attracted more than 36 million international visitors in 2016 – see Visit Britain, 2017), the number of tourists crossing international borders each year has risen consistently. The one billion mark was exceeded for the first time in 2012 and, by 2016, international arrivals totalled 1,235 million. It has been predicted that there will be 1.6 billion annual international arrivals by 2020 (WTO, 1998a: 3) although, with current annual growth rates of around 3.9 percent (UNWTO, 2016b), it is unlikely that this will be achieved. More likely to be met is the World Tourism Organization's prediction of 1.8 billion international arrivals by 2030 but, although in the past tourism has proved to be highly resilient to external challenges and events, such figures must be treated with some caution. Indeed, as discussed shortly, a number of factors suggest that international tourism faces an uncertain future. Nevertheless, when domestic trips (estimated to be some six times greater than international trips), are taken into account, there can be no doubting that the contemporary occurs on a truly mass scale.

It is important to note, however, that although tourism occurs on a global scale, it is not a globalised phenomenon. In other words, as Shaw and Williams (2002: 30) pointed out some years ago, the continuing growth in international tourism in particular 'should not be taken to imply that global mass tourism has now arrived and that the populations of most countries are caught up in the whirl of international travel'. Certainly, the emergence of new markets, such as China, and the increasing accessibility and popularity of new destinations, have had an impact on scale and direction of international tourist flows, but a closer examination of the international tourism data reveals that three distinctive patterns identified by Shaw and Williams (2002: 30) continue to characterise international tourism:

a) *Polarity*: international tourism is still largely dominated by the wealthier, industrialised world, with the major tourism flows being either between the more developed countries or from developed countries to developing countries. Recent years have, of course, witnessed the emergence of newer destinations which are challenging this dominance in terms of arrivals numbers. The top ten international destinations in 2016, for example, included China (4th), Turkey (6th) and Mexico (9th). Equally, new source markets, particularly China, have emerged, yet the flows and, consequently, economic benefits of international tourism remain relatively polarised, 'with exchanges of money generated by tourism . . . [being] . . . predominantly North-North between a combination of industrialised and newly industrialised countries' (Vellas & Bécherel, 1995: 21).

b) *Regionalisation*: not only is international tourism dominated by developed and wealthier emerging economies countries but it is also highly regionalised. The largest international movements of tourists occur within well-defined regions, in particular within Europe. Other significant regions include north America, with major flows between Canada and the United States and the United States and the Caribbean, and within the Asia Pacific region.

c) *European dominance*: the third major characteristic of international tourism is that it is largely concentrated within Europe and, indeed, has probably been so since the eighteenth century during the Grand Tour era. During the early 1960s, Europe's share of world tourism peaked at over 70 percent but, since then, it has gradually fallen and, by 2000, 57.1 percent of world arrivals occurred within Europe. Its share has since continued to decline whilst other regions, in particular the Middle East and Asia and the Pacific have experienced significant growth (see Table 2.1). Nevertheless, it is Europe that, on a global scale, still benefits most in terms of opportunities to participate in, and earnings from, tourism.

The shifts in the share of international tourism are, perhaps best demonstrated in the World Tourism Organization's claim that the world's advanced economies now account for 55 percent of all international arrivals and the emerging economies 45 percent (UNWTO, 2016b); although, taking the above three characteristics of international tourist flows into account, as well as arrivals figures at the national level, it is apparent that whilst tourism may well have been a social victory (Krippendorf, 1986) in wealthy, Western countries, the same cannot be said for many other parts of

TABLE 2.1 Percentage share of international tourist arrivals by region 1960–2015

	Africa	Americas	Asia & Pacific	Europe	M. East
1960	1.1	24.1	1.4	72.6	0.9
1970	1.5	25.5	3.8	68.2	1.1
1980	2.6	21.6	8.2	65.6	2.1
1990	3.3	20.4	12.7	61.6	2.2
1995	3.6	19.8	15.6	58.6	2.5
2000	4.0	18.6	16.8	57.1	3.5
2005	4.6	16.6	19.2	54.8	4.7
2006	4.9	16.0	19.7	54.6	4.8
2007	4.9	15.8	20.4	53.6	5.3
2008	4.9	16.1	20.1	52.9	6.0
2009	5.2	15.9	20.5	52.3	6.0
2010	5.2	15.9	21.7	50.7	6.4
2011	5.0	15.7	21.9	51.9	5.5
2012	5.1	15.8	22.6	51.6	5.0
2013	5.1	15.4	22.8	51.8	4.7
2104	4.9	16.0	23.2	51.4	4.5
2015	4.5	16.2	23.5	51.2	4.5

Source: adapted from UNWTO data

the world. This has significant implications for the potential contribution of tourism to social development in destination areas (see Chapter 10).

To return to the evolution of tourism in the twentieth century, technological advance, the emergence of a sophisticated tourism industry and the development of the package tour did most to influence the rapid growth of international tourism. Following the end of World War II, many surplus aircraft and, during the 1950s, the introduction of jet airliners, set the scene for the rapid expansion of the air transport industry in general and charter air travel in particular (see Holloway, 1998: 32–35). As the large airlines bought new jets, smaller charter companies bought cheap, second-hand aircraft to fly tourists to their holiday destinations and, working on the principle of economies of scale, the cost of international travel became almost as cheap as rail or road travel. The first person to operate a charter holiday flight was Vladimir Raitz who, in 1950, organised a trial trip to Corsica. He went on to build his business under the name of Horizon Holidays (subsequently becoming part of the Thomsons group, now owned by the German company TUI) and, following his success, a large number of other tour operators were established both in Britain and abroad (see Bray & Raitz, 2001).

Since that time, the package tourism industry has become increasingly sophisticated and diversified. Companies have integrated vertically and horizontally so that some tour operators own their own airline, their own chain of travel agents and, frequently, hotels in resorts. The scale of operations has also increased enormously, with some 20 million passengers annually taking package holidays out of Britain, and the introduction of wide bodied jets and increasingly efficient aircraft has extended the package 'pleasure periphery' (Turner & Ash, 1975). Nevertheless, in more recent years, tour operators have had to respond to a number of challenges, not least the development of so-called travel 'e-tailing' (as opposed to retailing) and the dramatic growth in independent holidays booked over the Internet (see Chapter 7). At the same time, the rapid emergence of the budget airlines has provided a flexible and more varied alternative to cheap charter flights, opening up new destinations and, as a consequence, transforming the styles and flows of travel.

Nevertheless, although some have predicted the demise of the traditional package holiday, the evidence suggests otherwise. Certainly, the number of independent holidays has grown significantly, now accounting for more than half of all international holiday trips out of the UK, yet the number of package holidays has remained stable since 1999, at around 20 million a year. However, whilst holidays to Spain, the Balearic Islands, Greece and other traditional package resorts continue to thrive, newer, more distant destinations now appear in the tour operators' brochures. For example, China, the West Indies, India and Australia can all be visited on package tours, and at prices which would have been considered impossible a few years ago. The package product has also diversified. Cultural or sightseeing tours may be combined with more traditional beach holidays on 'two-centre' holidays, such as a week's sightseeing in Sri Lanka followed by a week on the Maldives, and some of the most remote areas of the world can now be visited on package tours.

Tourism in the twenty-first century: towards the future

Any consideration of the evolution of tourism should, perhaps, conclude with a look forward, exploring what past trends and transformations imply for the future of tourism. That future is both easy and difficult to predict; on the one hand it is easy because it is impossible to know if a prediction is accurate until the future becomes the present but, on the other, it is impossible to know what factors, from technological innovation to political or economic events, might influence the future nature of tourism.

Nevertheless, it is evident from the overview in this chapter that the development of tourism over the last 50 years or so has mirrored a pattern of development that has been evident throughout the historical evolution of tourism. In other words, since the earliest times when tourism emerged as an identifiable and distinct sphere of social activity, those destinations or types of travel which were once the exclusive preserve of the well-to-do or the higher social classes have, almost inevitably, become assimilated under the umbrella of mass tourism. For example, the Grand Tour became popularised as the aristocracy were replaced by a middle class more intent on pleasure than learning, whilst both the spas and the seaside resorts soon lost their exclusivity. Similarly, the Mediterranean resorts which were once frequented by the royalty of Europe gradually became less exclusive, firstly with the influx of American tourists in the 1920s and 1930s and, subsequently, as a popular summer destination for car-borne tourists from other European countries. Nowadays, more distant, exotic destinations also attract package tourists as international tourism has become geographically more democratic, whilst once exclusive forms of travel have also been embraced by mass markets.

This process whereby exclusive destinations become caught in the popular, mass tourism net has been called the 'aristocratic model' of tourism development (Thurot & Thurot, 1983). Some would argue that it is overly simplistic to explain the emergence and democratisation of tourism on the basis of 'transport technology or the mechanistic process of successive class intrusion' (Towner, 1996: 13), yet the process has been highly evident within the evolution of tourism. Moreover, it is a process which is also evident in many other forms of consumption, the desire to emulate being a powerful force in people's buying habits and one which, in the context of tourism, has accelerated in recent years. Indeed, up until the onset of modern, mass tourism, the exclusivity of a resort or a form of tourism was normally 'safe' for at least a generation but, 'nowadays, the European upper middle class . . . has been caught up with by the lower classes within a period of ten years' (Thurot & Thurot, 1983). One example is the way in which cruise holidays have become a mass market product. Once an exclusive form of tourism, the 'luxury' of cruising is now available to the masses at relatively low prices. For example, Royal Caribbean currently operate 25 cruise ships, the largest of which, such as the Oasis Class *Harmony of the Seas,* accommodate up to 6,000 passengers and are, in effect, floating holiday resorts (Sharpley, 2017).

The extent to which this aristocratic model continues to influence the development of tourism in the future remains to be seen. The mass package holiday of the 1960s and 1970s is gradually being replaced by a more individual approach to tourism, with self-catering holidays, fly-drive packages, two-centre holidays, ecotourism, adventure tourism, cultural tourism and special interest holidays all becoming more popular. At the same time, the development of low-cost airlines has had a remarkable impact on international travel both within Europe and elsewhere – indeed, it is now possible to fly right around the world using only budget carriers. Within Europe, airlines such as Ryanair, which carries approximately 120 million passengers on its fleet of 350 aircraft (Ryanair, 2017), have underpinned the growth in short-break travel to city destinations, as well as challenging the charter airlines' 'monopoly' on flights to Mediterranean resorts (Farmaki & Papatheodorou, 2015).

Certainly, it is generally predicted that the overall trend will continue to be towards more individualistic, proactive, experiential forms of tourism, although the demise of the organised package holiday cannot be taken for granted. In the UK, for example, package holidays have enjoyed something of a renaissance; in 2014, almost 16 million people purchased such holidays, representing more than 50 percent of all overseas holidays taken by British holiday-makers (Lusher, 2015). This can be explained by a variety of factors: the all-inclusive concept, combining value and quality, has become increasingly popular; the package holiday itself is no longer associated with standardised sun-sea-sand holidays but has become a much more diverse and flexible product meeting the demands of a wide variety of markets and needs; and package holidays continue to represent value, dependability and security. It is for this reason, perhaps, that it is older tourists who tend to favour them.

And interestingly, it is older tourists, or the 'silver' market, who are generally considered to become an increasingly important sector within the overall market for tourism which itself is likely to continue the growth trajectory referred to earlier in this chapter, at least in the shorter term. Globally, a principal contemporary demographic trend is population ageing; 'the number of people over the age of 60 is projected to reach 1 billion by 2020 and almost 2 billion by 2050, representing 22 percent of the world's population' (Bloom et al., 2010: 583). In the major tourism generating countries in particular, this will be manifested in the proportion of population over retirement age increasing rapidly. In Europe, for example, the proportion of the population aged over 65 is projected to rise from 16 percent in 2010 to 29.3 percent by 2060 (Creighton, 2014), with similar growth projected in the US. Moreover, these over-65s are expected to enjoy both good health and relative wealth, pointing to growing demand for tourism experiences that offer quality, comfort, security and relaxation, in all likelihood spread more evenly throughout the year to avoid higher costs and crowding at peak periods.

Other predicted trends include increasing rejection of the traditional sun-sea-sand holidays in favour of healthier, more active holidays, a greater demand for educational or cultural experiences, and products that are more tailored to individual lifestyles. Moreover, the development of high-speed trains and further growth in low-cost airline operations are likely to transform both the flow and duration of travel, with short breaks and city tourism becoming increasingly popular. Indeed, this trend has been in evidence for a number of years, to the extent that there is concern that some cities, such as Prague, have already reached their tourism capacity (Dumbrovská & Fialová, 2014) or, in the case of Barcelona, exceeded it (Sharpley & Harrison, 2017).

Nevertheless, there are clouds on the horizon. In other words, a number of factors may limit the extent to which tourism continues to increase in scope and scale. Some of these are considered at length elsewhere (see Telfer & Sharpley, 2016) but, for the purposes of this brief overview, four issues can be highlighted:

1   There is evidence that climate change is already impacting on destinations in terms of, for example, extreme weather events or decreased snow cover in ski resorts, whilst increasing concerns over the contribution of tourism to climate change, particularly from aircraft and car emissions, may impact upon people's travel decisions and, indeed, the cost of travel (Hall et al., 2015; UNWTO, 2009). In other words, travel flows may potentially change, with subsequent consequences for those destinations affected – both 'winners' and 'losers'.

2   Reference has already been made to the ageing of populations in tourism source markets. On the one hand, this may indeed represent an opportunity for tourism providers to meet the demands of a growing market sector that enjoys health, wealth and time for leisure activities. On the other hand, some argue that increases in the so-called dependency ratio, a measure of the numbers of economically inactive people (children, retired, unemployed, etc.) relative to those in work, will put unsustainable demands on public finances, resulting in lower pensions, higher taxes, longer working and so on (Gee, 2002). As a consequence, both younger and older generations in many Western countries will, by the mid-twenty-first century, have much lower disposable incomes and, hence, spend less on tourism.

3   Over the last decade or so, increasing academic attention has been paid to the challenges facing tourism as a result of a potential decrease in oil production and supply (Becken, 2011; 2015). Specifically, it has been suggested that falling oil supplies and/ or rising prices will impact on the demand for oil-based forms of travel and, moreover, that this may well occur in the near future once 'peak oil' (the point which the maximum rate of oil production is arrived at) has been reached (Leigh, 2011). Events more recently, however, have demonstrated that predicting the future demand for and supply of oil is more complex and that concerns over oil are, if not misplaced, then perhaps premature. For example, in 2015 global oil prices fell to levels not experienced for more than a decade, whilst shale oil extraction in the US, the adoption of new technologies to exploit existing reserves more fully, as well as shifts in demand to renewable energy sources (for example, electric cars are becoming more popular, whilst it has been suggested that electric-powered short-haul flights might become a reality by 2027; see Lee, 2017) collectively support the argument that oil supplies may last much longer than conventionally assumed. Conversely, many reports, including those from major oil producers, still point to oil effectively running out towards the end of the twenty-first century. Either way, the scale and direction of travel will be influenced by the inevitability of declining oil supplies.

4   It has long been recognised that tourism is susceptible to what can be broadly termed political instability (Neumayer, 2004; Sönmez, 1998). Putting it another way, one of the factors underpinning the remarkable growth in international tourism since the 1950s was the fact that it was perceived to be safe, with package holidays in particular considered to be a relatively risk-free way of participating in tourism. However, not only have specific events, such as the Tunisia beach massacre in 2015 when 38 tourists were killed by terrorists at the resort of Port El Kantaoui near Sousse, demonstrated that this is not the case, but a number of other major atrocities since 2000, such as the bombing of a nightclub in Bali in 2002 that resulted in 202 deaths, suggest that such incidents are becoming more frequent. Certainly, according to a recent report, since 2000 there has been a fivefold increase in the annual number of deaths worldwide resulting from terrorism in general, from 3,361 in 2000 to 17,958 in 2013 (IEP, 2014: 2). The great majority of these were in just five countries, namely, Iraq, Afghanistan, Pakistan Nigeria and Syria – none of which have major tourism sectors – yet there is no doubt that safety and security issues, which are also related to health scares, may increasingly become a factor in holiday choices.

To summarise, then, since the mid-nineteenth century tourism has been transformed from an activity enjoyed by a privileged élite into a mass social phenomenon that has become available to ever-increasing numbers of people. Underpinning this democratisation of tourism have been increases in leisure time and disposable income, technological developments and a dynamic innovative travel industry whilst, at the same time, the desire of people to participate in tourism has been a fundamental influence. Indeed, why and how people experience tourism are issues that this book addresses. What is clear is that, subject to potential barriers, tourism will continue to grow, driven by the same factors referred to above. Tastes and fashions will change, as will the characteristics of tourism itself; in the longer term, for example, international tourism may once again become a luxury with the majority of people holidaying domestically. Nevertheless, it is likely that, as a contemporary social institution, tourism will continue to be considered a right rather than a privilege.

Further reading

Towner, J. (1996) *An Historical Geography of Recreation and Tourism in the Western World 1540–1940*. Chichester: John Wiley & Sons.
  A seminal text that explores in detail the development of tourism between the sixteenth and twentieth centuries.

Walton, J. (2000) *The British Seaside: Holidays and Resorts in the Twentieth Century*. Manchester: Manchester University Press.
  An essential read for those with an interest in the modern history of the British seaside resort.

Zuelow, E (2015) *A History of Modern Tourism*. Basingstoke: Palgrave Macmillan.
  This book provides a comprehensive history of the development of tourism from the Grand Tour through to the emergence of mass tourism.

Journal of Tourism History (see www.tandfonline.com/loi/rjth20)
  First published in 2009, this journal publishes research papers addressing a wide variety of topics related to the history of tourism.

UNWTO Tourism Highlights (see http://mkt.unwto.org/publication/unwto-tourism-highlights)
  Published annually, this report provides contemporary data with respect to trends and flows in international tourism.

Discussion topics

▶   To what extent is the continuing growth in tourism still influenced by the principal drivers of technological advances and increases in wealth and free time?

▶   How significant was the holiday camp concept to the subsequent development of mass tourism?

▶   What challenges and opportunities face the development of tourism into the future?

▶   Has tourism genuinely become 'democratised'?

CHAPTER

3

Tourism, modernity and postmodernity

Introduction

Tourism, in particular what is commonly understood as mass tourism, is frequently described as a phenomenon of modern society. It has been referred to as 'the single largest peaceful movement of people across cultural boundaries in history' (Lett, 1989: 276) and, certainly, there is no doubt that it has expanded in both scale and scope throughout the twentieth century and into the twenty-first. Nowadays few, if any, parts of the world have not become tourist destinations – for example, tourists have been visiting the Antarctic for more than a quarter of a century, with 30,369 arrivals recorded in 2015–2016 (IAATO, 2017) – and the overall number of people participating in tourism continues to grow (see Chapter 2). Moreover, tourism's final frontier – space – will soon become a destination; the American Denis Tito (the world's first 'space tourist') funded his own trip to the International Space Station in 2001, whilst organisations such as Virgin Galactic and SpaceX are developing craft that will carry paying toursists into space (see also Webber, 2013).

In one sense, tourism is a phenomenon of modern society because it is modern society that has provided both the means and the opportunity for people to participate in tourism. As described in the previous chapter, the rapid growth in participation in tourism and the ability to travel ever further to more remote or exotic destinations would simply not have occurred without the development of fast, efficient and economical forms of mass transportation, increasingly high levels of disposable income and the provision of socially sanctioned free time, such as bank holidays and holidays-with-pay. At the same time, tourism is a product of modern society inasmuch as people now not only expect to take a holiday, but also frequently feel the need to do so. In other words, modern society motivates people to participate in tourism. Whether to simply escape from the pressures and stress of modern life or to seek authentic, satisfying and meaningful experiences elsewhere, people increasingly believe that the only way to survive in modern society is to regularly remove themselves from it, albeit on a temporary basis. Tourist motivation is considered in detail in Chapter 5 but the point here is that, in short, tourism is both caused and sustained by modern society.

Yet, whilst there is much truth in this proposition, the relationship between the development of tourism and modern society is not so simple or clear cut as it may at first appear. That is, the link between technological advances in, for example, transport, information technology and financial services, increases in wealth and free time, and the growth of tourism is universally accepted. However, these so-called enabling factors of tourism do not explain a whole host of other characteristics of modern tourism. For example, a variety of activities or forms of behaviour can, arguably, provide the same benefits as tourism, so why is it tourism, as opposed to other forms of leisure activity, that has become so widespread? Similarly, why has international tourism, over the space of just half a century, been transformed from a luxury into a perceived 'necessity'? And why have styles of tourism changed? For example, in 1986, beach hotel holidays accounted for 72 percent of all early (that is, by December of the preceding year) holiday bookings out of the UK and beach self-catering holidays accounted for 17 percent. By 1993, the proportion had changed to 38 percent and 36 percent respectively (McCarthy, 1994). More recently, particularly reflecting transformations in both the supply of and demand for tourism resulting from developments in information and communication technology (ICT), specifically the Internet and mobile technology, independent holidays have become as popular (in terms of holidays taken) as package holidays, whilst both short-break holidays and multiple holiday-taking are now common. By 2003, for example, almost one third of British households took three or more holidays (including both domestic and overseas) each year and, according to ABTA (2015), 16 percent took more than three overseas holidays in 2014. Other forms of tourism, such as heritage tourism, urban tourism (see Law, 2002) and ecotourism (see Fennell, 2007; Weaver, 2001), have also become more popular. Indeed, research in the early 2000s suggested that the number of tourists taking ecotourism holidays was growing three times faster than those choosing 'mainstream' holidays and that ecotourism represented five percent of the global holiday market (Starmer-Smith, 2004). The scale of the contemporary ecotourism market is difficult to estimate – no specific data exist – although claims that 20 percent of all international travel is nature based and that the demand for so-called responsible holidays is growing (CREST, 2016) suggest that participation in ecotourism continues to increase. More generally, some claim that the traditional package holiday is being increasingly rejected in favour of more individualistic forms of tourism, although, as shown in the previous chapter, figures show that the package holiday remains as popular as ever. The overall growth in tourism, however, is accounted for by other forms of tourism.

These trends in demand may be simply put down to changes in fashion, but changes in fashion may, in turn, be related to changes in the nature of modern society itself. In other words, the developments and trends that have occurred, and continue to occur, in tourism cannot be simply explained as resulting from the technological and other advances associated with the modernisation of society. It is surprising, therefore, that relatively little attention has been paid to the ways in which both the significance of tourism as a form of consumption and also styles of tourism may be influenced by cultural changes and developments in the tourist's home society and environment (G. Taylor, 1994). Nevertheless, it is important to do so. Tourism, as a social activity, is central to the modern leisure experience and cannot, or should not, be considered in isolation from the wider cultural framework within which it occurs; as Urry (1990b: 23) confirms, 'explaining the consumption of tourist services cannot be separated off from the social relations in which they are embedded'.

In particular, it is important to consider what is meant by the term 'modern society'. That is, a distinction must be drawn between modern society in a temporal or periodic sense (modern as opposed to old, pre-modern or traditional) and modern society in the cultural sense. When analysing and explaining the development of tourism as a modern phenomenon it is, generally, the former approach that is adopted. As we have already seen, the birth of tourism as we know it today occurred when society was undergoing a process of industrialisation. Rapid technological advances throughout the modern era, commencing with the development of the railways during the nineteenth century, followed by the introduction of the motor car and, latterly, developments in aircraft technology, have resulted in the opportunity to travel being more widely available. At the same time, the mass tourism industry has been able to spread its net ever wider around the world; more and more countries now lie within what has been called the 'pleasure periphery' (Turner & Ash, 1975) of modern, industrialised societies.

In order to understand fully the link between society and the development of tourism, in particular trends and changes in tourism practices rather than tourism as an overall human activity, it is necessary to consider the nature or condition of modern societies. That is, modern, industrial societies are characterised by a combination of economic, political, social and cultural processes that together create a form of social life that sociologists call 'modernism'. These processes are constantly evolving and adapting according to the needs and demands of society so that, whereas modern in the temporal sense is a fixed state, modernity as a social condition is dynamic. It has been suggested that as modern societies become post-industrial, with their economies becoming increasingly dependent on the tertiary service sector, modernity is being replaced by the condition of postmodernity (see Harvey, 1990; also, Docherty, 2014).

Interestingly, some claim that we have now progressed beyond postmodernity into a more complex condition of post-postmodernity (Walby, 1992) whilst terms such as post-millennialism are also sometimes referred to. For the purposes of this chapter, however, a discussion of the manner in which society has transformed from modernity into a cultural condition that may be characterised as postmodernity will suffice. Hence, this chapter introduces the concept of postmodernity and examines the relationship between tourism and contemporary culture, in particular the way in which certain characteristics of postmodern society impact on tourism. Thus, it provides a broad picture or framework within which the more specific discussion of society's influence on the consumption of and motivation for tourism in the following chapters may be located. First, however, it is important to consider the nature of the relationship between tourism and culture, before examining the specific implications of contemporary culture for tourism.

Tourism and cultural change

It has long been recognised that a positive relationship exists between the consumption of tourism and the cultural characteristics of modern societies (Urry, 1988; 1990a; 1994; 2002). In a simple sense, for example, for tourism as a social activity to occur on a widespread scale it must be socially or culturally sanctioned; there are many cases of societies where specific forms of tourism are encouraged or discouraged, or where different social groups are culturally permitted greater or less opportunity to participate in tourism. Indeed, as indicated in the preceding chapter, the evolution of leisure and tourism in most Western societies has, throughout history, been organised and managed as a means of sustaining preferred socio-cultural arrangements (Rojek, 1993).

More specifically, an identifiable relationship has long existed between what may be described as the cultural condition of societies and the style or meaning of tourism, with transformations in the former almost invariably reflected in changes to the latter. For example, reference has already been made to the English Romanticism of the late eighteenth and early nineteenth centuries which not only changed people's attitudes towards rural environments, such as the Lake District undergoing a perceptual transformation from a region considered both unattractive and dangerous into one where 'all is but peace, rusticity and happy poverty, in its neatest, most becoming attire' (Gray, 1884: 226), but also set the tone for the touristic enjoyment of such areas. According to Harrison (1991: 21), for the Romantics

> the only right and proper way to enjoy the countryside was to walk through these landscapes in solitude and contemplative mood and thereby to achieve a new sense of solace, consciousness and spiritual awareness.

Arguably, this cultural shaping of attitudes towards rural areas, what Harrison (1991) describes as the 'countryside aesthetic' remains today a powerful influence on the style of rural tourism, particularly amongst middle-class urban visitors (see also Urry, 1995: 211–229; Wilson, 1992).

Similarly, other tourism practices reflect broader cultural change. The widespread practice of sunbathing, for example, originated from new fashions amongst the social élite on the French Riviera in the 1920s and the resultant desirability of a suntan (previously associated with lower social classes, such as outdoor manual labourers). So too has the changing role and style of the holiday camp mirrored broader cultural transformations, from the early, rudimentary camps such as Cunningham's, established on the Isle of Man in 1897, through the heyday of the collective entertainment of Butlin's (see Ward & Hardy, 1986), to the emergence of the more sophisticated holiday villages of the 1990s, such as Center Parcs, and the development of up-market all-inclusive resorts, such as the Sandals chain in the Caribbean (Sharpley, 2017).

Although there is widespread evidence of a relationship between tourism and culture, it has not always been the case that this relationship has taken the form of tourist practices directly reflecting culture and cultural change. Indeed, it has been suggested that, in addition to the reflective relationship exemplified above, there are three other possible forms of the tourism–culture relationship (Urry, 1994). First, tourism and culture may be in opposition or develop in opposite directions; second, tourism may lead to or indicate future cultural change and, third, 'that tourist practices simply are cultural, that is, they comprise signs, images, texts and discourse' (Urry, 1994: 223). Urry goes on to argue that the relationship has changed over time. During the nineteenth century, tourism and culture were largely in opposition. Thus, contrasting with 'the bourgeois culture with its concerts, museums, galleries, and so on' (Urry, 1994: 234), tourism for the masses was centred on the rapid development of the seaside resorts. These places of ritualised pleasure (Shields, 1991) were the embodiment of mass, low culture, set apart from the high culture of the bourgeoisie which included, in a touristic context, the romantic, 'serious' participation in rural tourism mentioned above.

During the twentieth century, up until the 1970s, the tourism-culture relationship gradually transformed to the extent that tourism practices came to reflect cultural change. That is, the emergence of a culture based upon mass production and mass consumption was reflected in the development of mass forms of tourism. Importantly, however, as a social activity tourism was still separate or differentiated from broader cultural change. In other words, although the Fordist production methods which were attached to tourism (see below), whether in the context of the holiday camp or the mass package holiday business, mirrored the wider production/consumption system, tourism remained, at least for the masses, a separate, identifiable activity differentiated by time, location and behaviour from other activities and institutions.

Since the 1970s, it is argued, this differentiation between tourism and other practices has become less apparent. 'Tourism is no longer a differentiated set of social practices with its distinct rules, times and spaces' (Urry, 1994: 234); rather, it has merged into other social activities such as shopping or watching television. Purchasing ethnic goods, such as South American wood-carvings or Indian clothing, from specialist shops, eating in Greek or Italian restaurants or simply watching one of the multitude of travel pro-grammes on television are all examples of how tourism has diffused into everyday life. Many people are tourists most of the time and, in short, tourism has, simply, become cultural.

There are, then, two broad stages in the relationship between tourism and the cultural condition of society. Throughout most of its development, tourism has been separated off from other social activities and institutions, reflecting the differentiation both within and between other social practices and institutions, such as social class, employment or gender roles. Even tourism itself has been subject to differentiation; different resorts or types of holiday became associated with different social groups, whilst the emergence of mass tourism has been contrasted with the so-called 'lost art' of travel (Boorstin, 1964). Thus, as we shall see shortly, until the latter part of the twentieth century, tourism reflected the modern period. However, as suggested above, tourism has now entered a second stage of development where it is less distinct from other social practices. It has become de-differentiated (Lash, 1990: 11) from other activities, reflecting the wider emergence of economic, political, social and cultural processes that have been collec-tively referred to as postmodernity.

It is this transformation of culture from a condition of modernity to postmodernity that, for two reasons, is of greatest relevance to the study of tourism. First, it is suggested by some that, as a result of the alleged transformation from a condition of modernity to postmodernity in many Western societies, tourism practices have also become postmod-ern. In other words, the de-differentiation of tourism from other social activities, rep-resenting the marriage of 'different, often intellectual, spheres of activity with tourism' (Munt, 1994: 104), has brought about a variety of new, 'postmodern tourisms' (Munt, 1994: 104). These are discussed later in this chapter.

Second, the emergence of consumerism or consumer culture is considered by many to be a defining characteristic of postmodern cultures. That is, 'consumption has been seen as epitomising this move into postmodernity' (Bocock, 1993: 4). Tourism is, in a sense, consumed; tourists are 'consumers, whose primary goal is the consumption of a tourism experience' (McKercher, 1993: 11). Therefore, it is also important here to consider the potential influence of postmodern consumer culture on the specific practice of the consumption of tourism. This issue is addressed in Chapter 6.

Before looking at the relationship between postmodern culture and tourism practices, it is first necessary to consider what is meant by the terms modernity and postmodernity and the evidence that suggests society is moving from the former condition to the latter.

From modernity to postmodernity

It is difficult to grasp the notion that society or, more specifically, the social and cultural character of life in modern society, is undergoing an identifiable process of transformation from one condition to another. Indeed, there is much debate amongst sociologists themselves as to whether modern society has moved beyond modernity and is now identified by a set of characteristics that may be amalgamated and described as the condition of postmodernity. As Urry (1990a: 83) states, 'in some ways it is difficult to address the topic of postmodernism at all. It seems as though the signifier postmodern is free-floating, having few connections with anything real, no minimal shared meaning of any sort.'

Moreover, even if there exists agreement that society has undergone a cultural shift into a condition of postmodernity, there is a continuing debate as to what the term means. This debate, according to Hollinshead (1993), centres on a number of questions, including does postmodernity exist? Is it a cultural style, an historic period or an economic phase? Is it an on-going academic craze? Or is it a self-perpetuating, 'self-validating discourse on the part of a whole host of individuals concerned about their own legitimate place in society?' (Hollinshead, 1993).

To answer these questions is beyond the scope of this chapter. However, what is certain is that many of the economic, political, social and cultural forms that characterise modernity have changed or are in a process of change. The extent to which these changes are inter-related and signify an identifiable and all-embracing development in the nature of contemporary society is arguable but, nevertheless, postmodernity is a term that can be usefully applied to the organisational and cultural condition of modern society in the late twentieth and early twenty-first centuries.

The purpose here, then, is not to analyse the arguments for and against postmodernity (for example, see Harvey, 1990; Jameson, 1984; Lash, 1990; Lyotard, 1984; Sim, 2011; and, more generally, Hall *et al.*, 1992b). But it is important to outline what is meant by postmodernity and to highlight common themes among its various definitions before considering the links between postmodern society and tourism. The problem remains that there is little agreement as to what postmodernity actually is. Generally, postmodernity is seen to represent the end of the structured, organised and rational state of society. It signifies the replacement of 'the dominance of an overarching belief in "scientific" rationality and a unitary theory of progress' (Jary & Jary, 1991: 487) by an emphasis on choice, a plurality of ideas and viewpoints, image and the ephemeral, and the 'eclectic borrowing and mixing of images from other cultures' (Voase, 1995: 67).

In other words, postmodernity represents a departure from modernity or, as Bocock (1993: 78) puts it, 'the term post-modern can be seen as an analytical category which serves to highlight certain features of socio-cultural life, features which contrast with those in the paired analytical category of the modern'. A logical starting point is to consider briefly modernity, or the modern condition, from which postmodernity has evolved.

Modernity

The emergence of modern societies in a temporal, periodic sense can be traced back to the Europe of the sixteenth and seventeenth centuries with successive agricultural, scientific and industrial revolutions. It was during this period that, rather than being dependent on and controlled by nature, societies were increasingly able to dominate their natural world to their own advantage. Thus, the advent of the modern era was dependent on technological advance and scientific knowledge and those increasingly few societies today which have yet to embrace or to come under the influence of modern technology are described as pre-modern, traditional or authentic (see Chapter 9).

It was much later that modernity, 'that distinct and unique form of social life which characterises modern societies' (Hall *et al.,* 1992a: 2), became an identifiable social condition. Its origins lie in what is known as the Enlightenment Project, a period of intellectual thought dating back to the eighteenth century but the major tenets of which are reflected in modernist thought and culture (Pagden, 2013). During an age when 'the scientific domination of nature promised freedom from scarcity, want and the arbitrariness of natural calamity' (Harvey 1990: 12), the Enlightenment thinkers envisaged a similar situation whereby society, through the accumulation and application of rational, scientifically based knowledge, could be released from the constraints of irrational forms of thought, such as religion, superstition, myth, prejudice and ideology. Distancing themselves from history and tradition, they foresaw the triumph of reason and objective, rational knowledge and, through scientific progress and social scientific knowledge, they sought 'mental liberation and social betterment amongst humanity generally' (McLennan 1992: 330). In particular, the Enlightenment thinkers believed that all natural and social phenomena could be scientifically explained and, therefore, that there was only one solution to any problem, a position that was soon to be challenged. But their support for scientific, technological and economic progress in pursuit of an improved human condition continued through to the height of modernity.

The real foundations of modernity were laid during the industrialisation and urbanisation of society during the nineteenth century, based upon the social and political institutions that evolved in the wake of rapid change. Five main processes, in particular, emerged to give modernity its identifying character:

a)   the development of political, secular systems and the concept of the nation-state, supported and sustained by large-scale bureaucratic systems which increasingly sought to organise, regulate and control social life;

b) the growth and expansion of the capitalist economy based upon private owner-ship, leading to mass production and consumption and, internationally, the distinc-tion between the industrialised, developed countries of the West and the rest of the world;

c) the evolution of national and international society into a system determined by class, gender, race, occupation and wealth;

d) the cultural transformation of societies from religious to secular and the emer-gence of popular forms of art, entertainment and music; and

e) the demise of individuality and development of the mass market with the public perceived as a homogeneous group with similar tastes and attitudes.

The major characteristic of modernity which emerged from the nineteenth century onwards, however, was that virtually every aspect of society and social life became dif-ferentiated. Guided by the over-riding objective of human and technical progress, mod-ernism eschewed history and tradition. The past, the present and the future became separated, the present providing the opportunity to work towards an assured, better future. Time itself became a resource and, whereas during the pre-modern, agricultural era leisure and work intermingled within social life, a distinction came to be made between work time and leisure time. As tourism developed as an identifiable, widespread leisure activity it also became a differentiated, separate sphere of social life with its own distinct time. Moreover, it was also differentiated by location; work and home life were in the towns, tourism took place at the seaside. Urbanisation led to the differentiation between the countryside and towns and cities and their associated social systems, so much so that modernism largely came to be associated with the structure and order of urban society. For example, the inner-city tower-block architecture of the post-war period is often considered to be the most visible physical representation of moder-nity. Employment and work practices in capitalist industry resulted in differentiation between classes and occupation, the family became differentiated by gender roles; even nature and society became differentiated. Internationally, distinctions emerged between nation-states, between East and West, between North and South. In short, modernity 'involves "structural differentiation", the separate development of a number of institu-tional and normative spheres, of the economy, the family, the state, science, morality, and an aesthetic realm' (Urry, 1990a: 84).

This differentiation, according to Urry, is both horizontal, representing distinctions between different institutions, roles, activities and so on, and vertical, as in differentia-tions within different spheres of social life. In other words, not only is there a distinc-tion between, say, tourism and other forms of leisure activity but also, in modernist culture, a distinction between 'traditional' or authentic travel and (mass) tourism (see Chapter 9). Similarly, distinctions exist between classical and popular music and within other art forms, and between mass and élite production and consumption. In recent years, however, this horizontal and vertical differentiation has become less distinct; society has embarked on a process of de-differentiation (see Lash, 1990: 11), the fun-damental trait of postmodernity.

Postmodernity

Although much of the literature on postmodernity is concerned specifically with changes in cultural styles in literature, films, architecture and art, during the latter half of the twentieth century a number of changes in society, its institutions and its direction indicated that a much more fundamental and widespread social movement was underway. In other words, the postmodern style of, for example, architecture which incorporates both contemporary and classical or traditional styles is symptomatic of a much deeper-rooted shift in both the structure of society as a whole and its values and culture. Whether this shift has been towards a new, distinctive social and cultural experience is open to debate, yet there is little doubt that many of the ideas, objectives and cultural representations of modernity have been rejected and replaced by a new set of identifying characteristics. Thus, postmodernity is, in effect, 'a very loose term used to describe the new aesthetic, cultural and intellectual forms and practices which [emerged] in the 1980s and 1990s' (Thompson, 1992: 226).

Postmodernity can be considered from a variety of viewpoints. For example, in terms of the development of society, the modernist project of progress and change which rejected history and tradition has been replaced by a new concern for conserving, representing or recreating the past. Whether as a particular style of interior decoration, a style of building or as a tourism product in the form of heritage attractions, the past is being merged into the postmodern present. In other words, the past and the present have become de-differentiated as society appears to be gaining a preference for stability rather than change. Similarly, the distinction between society and nature has become de-differentiated as it has become increasingly recognised, under the aegis of the environmental movement, that, in order to survive, society must co-exist with rather than dominate nature.

Other structural differentiations, both horizontal and vertical, have also been reversed or removed. For example, class distinctions and boundaries are becoming less clear cut and bear more relation to family background and tradition as opposed to wealth or occupation. The emergence of multinational corporations and the interdependence of economies and organisations across international borders (as powerfully demonstrated during the global economic crisis of 2008) has diminished the distinct status of the nation-state whilst the increasingly cosmopolitan character of many societies has led to a de-differentiation of race, religion and culture. For example, it is claimed that in Sydney it is possible to eat out at a culturally different restaurant every night for a year! Paradoxically, the alleged globalisation of society (Hay & Marsh, 2000) has also served to heighten the awareness of how various societies and peoples are culturally different, in some cases leading to a resurgence of nationalism and fundamentalism. Indeed, recent political events in both Europe (the Brexit vote; the increasing popularity of right-wing nationalist parties) and in the US (the election of Donald Trump as President) are, for some, evidence of a process referred to as 'de-globalisation' (Yafei, 2017). The concept of globalisation is considered in more detail later in this chapter but, for now, it should be noted that 'postmodernism is . . . [also] . . . anti-hierarchical' (Urry, 1990a: 85); distinctions between high and low culture are disappearing as classical music becomes popular (in the mid-1990s, for example, the violinist Vanessa Mae popularised classical music whilst a number of so-called 'crossover' groups continue to apply classical styles to more popular music/songs), as art and commerce merge and, through techniques such as audience participation, the contemplation of art becomes entertainment.

Further evidence of de-differentiation is to be found in the way in which reality is represented. That is, a major distinction between the cultures of modernity and postmodernity is that 'modernism conceives of representation as being problematic whereas postmodernism problemises reality' (Lash, 1990: 13). Modernity was concerned with reality and fact based upon logical and scientific explanation; representations of reality, through the arts, advertising and the news media, reflected the importance placed on reality. Under postmodernity, however, it is claimed that there is a diminishing distinction between reality and representations of reality. Such has been the growth in the production of images, representations and simulations, exacerbated by the explosion in electronic imaging, such as television, video, films and, in particular, the increasing dominance of digital communication technology, specifically the Internet and social media, that image is merging into reality. In some instances, such as computer games, representations and simulations replace reality whilst widespread use of social media has blurred the distinction between actual and virtual reality or between fact and fiction. For example, there are increasing concerns over the spread of so-called 'fake news' through social media (Allcott & Gentzkow, 2017). Social life in general and social identity in particular have become dependent on image, as styles and fashions represented in the media are translated into reality by an increasingly image-conscious consumer society. The result is that postmodern society is dominated by image, by pastiche and by reproductions that lack depth and substance. It has become a 'world of sign and spectacle . . . in which there is no real originality. . . . Everything is a copy, or a text upon a text, where what is fake seems more real than real' (Urry, 1990a: 85).

There are a number of identifying characteristics which indicate that, socially and culturally, modern society is evolving from a condition of modernity into a new state that may be described as postmodernity. Not all modern societies are becoming, or have become, postmodern and some may be more or less postmodern than others. For example, America may be described as more postmodern than the majority of, if not all, European countries. Furthermore, different areas or regions within societies may possess cultural attributes which, to a greater or lesser extent, resemble those proposed by postmodernists, whilst not all aspects of culture within society need to be postmodern. Nevertheless, modern societies are increasingly adopting the characteristics of postmodernity, these being:

a) a plurality of viewpoints and ideas, replacing the modernist concept of a uniform, mass society, and a corresponding rejection of all-embracing sociological theories. 'The idea that all groups have a right to speak for themselves, in their own voice, and have that voice accepted as authentic and legitimate is essential to the pluralistic stance of postmodernity' (Harvey, 1990: 48);

b) the fusion or de-differentiation of distinct areas of social and cultural activity and structure and the unification of popular, mass consumer culture with 'high' culture, particularly in the commercial appropriation of culture (Zukin, 1990);

c)   lifestyles which are increasingly dominated by spectacle, image, visual media and what has been called the 'three-minute culture', resulting in ephemerality and a concentration on surface appearance rather than cultural depth;

d)   the merging of the past into the present and a preference for stability, implying a condition of discontinuity and a lack of historical progression (even though, para-doxically, postmodernity is considered to be the next stage in society's development after pre-modern and modern). 'Postmodernity abandons all sense of historical continuity and memory, while simultaneously developing an incredible ability to plunder history and absorb whatever it finds there as some aspect of the present' (Harvey, 1990: 54);

e)   the breaking down of traditional social structures and the emergence of new group-ings and movements, such as conservation groups, political groups, new age travel-lers, women's associations, special interest groups and so on which cross over ethnic, class, occupational and religious boundaries;

f)   identity formation through consumption. 'Under modern conditions, work roles in production processes were defined as being central for identity, which is in contrast with consumption patterns of action being posited as central to post-modern iden-tity construction' (Bocock, 1993: 79).

There are many other elements and characteristics of contemporary society that the-orists claim to be indicative of a move into postmodernity. At the same time, there are others who completely reject the notion of postmodernity, either as a cultural paradigm or as a new social and cultural epoch, writing it off simply as a term used to describe developments in society and culture that depart from the sense of order, rationality, cohesion and uniformity that typified modernity. Whichever viewpoint is adopted, however, a number of fundamental changes are occurring in society which may have a corresponding effect on tourism.

Postmodernity and tourism

Tourism, according to Urry (1990a: 87), is 'prefiguratively postmodern because of its particular combination of the visual, the aesthetic, and the popular'. In other words, certain characteristics of postmodernity have always been identifiable in tourism, in particular the emphasis on spectacle and entertainment. For example, the English sea-side resorts of the late nineteenth and early twentieth centuries, through to the heyday of holiday camps in the 1950s (see Ward & Hardy, 1986), vied for business by offering the best entertainment, the longest pier, the brightest lights or the most exciting funfair. Blackpool, with its tower, ballrooms, piers, promenade, zoo, illuminations, gardens and Pleasure Beach was, perhaps, the most postmodern resort of all, offering a world of image, illusion and fantasy in contrast to the reality of social life in the northern indus-trial towns and cities. Importantly, the social life of the tourists in the seaside resorts, thriving on spectacle and mass entertainment, made little or no distinction between art, culture and society; the holiday experience was characterised by the de-differentiation that has come to identify postmodernity.

It is upon this concept of tourism as the consumption of fantasy, images or representations of reality, rather than reality itself, that much of the relevant literature remains focused. For example, as a result of the illusory, contrived and image-based nature of contemporary society, tourists seek out and, according to Boorstin (1964), are satisfied with 'pseudo-events' and contrived spectacles. They have become an army of semioticians (Culler, 1981: 127), looking for signs or images of cultural practices and attractions rather than seeking to understand their true meaning. The local tourism industry is obliged to satisfy this demand and, as tourist experiences become increasingly removed from reality, tourism develops into a 'closed, self-perpetuating system of illusions' (Cohen, 1988b: 30). In the extreme, these illusions or representations may be simulacra, or copies for which no original exists, and tourists become travellers in 'hyper-reality' (Eco, 1995).

One example of this is the successful promotion of Santa Claus as a tourist attraction in Lapland (Pretes, 1995), whilst the Disney theme parks are frequently cited as the epitome of the postmodern tourism experience (Munt, 1994). More specifically, the Holy Land Experience theme park in Orlando, Florida might be considered a postmodern, hyper-real tourist attraction (see www.holylandexpereince.com).

Similarly, MacCannell (1989) argues that tourists do, in fact, seek authenticity, yet are frustrated by representations of authenticity being staged for their benefit. Thus, reality is constructed and tourists consume images of reality (Harkin, 1995; Hughes, 1995), although it has been suggested that the search for authentic experiences need not necessarily end in frustration or failure. Different tourists have different motivations and expectations and the experience of reality results from a form of negotiation between the tourist and the tourism setting (Pearce & Moscardo, 1986). Much may also depend on the way in which images of reality are presented to tourists through advertising (Silver, 1993).

Many of these issues are addressed in greater detail in subsequent chapters. Of concern here, however, is the way in which postmodern culture has influenced tourism as a particular sphere of social activity. That is, even though tourism has long displayed some of the characteristics of postmodernity, that postmodernity has until more recently been contextualised by tourism. In other words, whilst on holiday the social condition of tourists was essentially postmodern, yet tourism remained a distinct social activity, separate and differentiated from normal, modern, day-to-day social life. Specific periods of time were set aside for tourism, such as public holidays and the annual week or fortnight's holiday, and tourism occurred in distinct places, such as the seaside or the countryside. Thus, tourism, both temporally and spatially, provided a contrast to normal life; indeed, it was, and still is, that contrast which is the major attraction of tourism.

To a great extent, the contrast or differentiation between tourism as a separate and identifiable sphere of social activity has diminished. Tourism has become de-differentiated from, or merged with, other cultural and social activities to the extent that it may be suggested that most people are tourists most of the time. This can be better explained by considering a number of different types of tourism which can be related to the cultural transformation of contemporary society. These 'postmodern tourisms' result primarily from the de-differentiation of tourism place and tourism time, and from the merging of past and present manifested in the nostalgic yearning to experience heritage and authenticity (in the historic or pre-modern sense).

Tourism place

Traditionally, people have travelled away from their place of residence and work in order to participate in tourism, a process still typical of much contemporary tourism. This relocation is not purely in the simple sense of moving from one place to another, from the city to the seaside or from one country to another. It also involves a change of social and cultural environment from, for example, the urban environment (signifying work, constraint, normality) to the holiday environment (signifying fun, escape, relaxation and so on). Throughout the modern era, the popularity of the traditional seaside resorts may have waned in favour of an ever-increasing choice of different and more distant overseas destinations, but the basic formula has remained the same. More recently, however, new tourism destinations and attractions have emerged which indicate that the tourism place, where people participate in tourism, has become increasingly de-differentiated from the normal, day-to-day social place and, implicitly, the need for a change of environment has diminished.

PLATE 3.1 A thermal power plant in Iceland features on sightseeing tours

Source: Photo by Richard Sharpley

A primary example of this 'postmodernisation' of tourist place is the development of urban tourism. If the residents of the English city of Bradford in the late nineteenth century had been able somehow to see into the future, they would have no doubt been amazed to discover that, in the 1990s, about six million people each year choose to visit their city as tourists. In the early 1800s, Bradford was a small rural market town in which wool spinning and cloth manufacture were undertaken as cottage industries but, by the middle of the century, it had become the centre for wool production in the UK. This established the foundation for the city's subsequent industrial and economic development but, from the mid-twentieth century, the textile sector fell into decline. The decision was taken to reinvent Bradford as a tourist destination based on its industrial and cultural heritage. It also became home to what is now the National Science and Media Museum as well as a base for visiting natural and cultural sites in the region (including Saltaire, the 'model village' referred to in Chapter 1) and, in so doing, established a strategy that post-industrial urban centres around the UK and elsewhere have followed (Heeley, 2011; Spirou, 2010). Certainly, almost every major town and city in the UK now promotes itself as a tourist destination, frequently basing their tourism product on heritage which is a major manifestation of postmodern tourism. The important point is that there no longer needs to be a contrast between tourism place and normal work/residence place. People can be tourists in their own town as the social activity of tourism itself becomes entwined with other social and cultural activities. Factories and other workplaces, both historical and modern, have become tourist attractions, whilst the development of new complexes which permit a variety of social activities literally under one roof has further spread the location and diversity of tourist place into the urban area. Shopping malls, in particular, have served to de-differentiate between activities such as shopping, eating, going to the cinema and other forms of entertainment; Urry (1990a: 147) cites the West Edmonton Mall in Canada which, in 1987, attracted over nine million visitors, making it the third most popular tourist attraction in North America after Disneyland and Disney World.

Perhaps one of the best British examples of the shopping centre as a tourist attraction continues to be the Intu Metrocentre in Gateshead in the north-east of England. First opened in 1986, it offered some three miles of shopping malls, a multi-screen cinema, restaurants and an indoor fairground, Metroland, and included a number of themed areas, such as the Mediterranean village where restaurants and cafés were designed in Greek and Italian styles. It has since been refurbished, though retaining a multi-screen cinema and family entertainment centre and opportunities for eating at a variety of contemporary bars and restaurants. The postmodern fusion of image and fantasy replacing reality has been taken to its extreme by the development of inland resorts, such as the Center Parc complexes. Here, simulation has been superimposed on reality in the ultimate manifestation of the de-differentiated, postmodern tourist place, an artificially created 'tropical' environment built in the normal, traditionally non-tourism place. Thus, inland villages represent the quintessential postmodern tourism place.

Another example of a postmodern, hyper-real attraction is the Loro Parque, or Wildlife Park, in Puerto de la Cruz, Tenerife. In addition to the more usual exhibits, the Loro Parque is also home to the world's largest 'Penguinarium': 'Imagine standing in shorts at a temperature of 22C and being transported into an authentic Arctic eco-

PLATE 3.2 The Eden Project in Cornwall, England, built in disused clay pits

Source: Photo by Richard Sharpley

PLATE 3.3 Former dock buildings in Liverpool now house an art gallery

Source: Photo by Richard Sharpley

system . . . these penguins and other Antarctic seabirds will be inhabiting a replica of an Antarctic island at a temperature of -2C' (see: www.canaries-live.com/UK/penguinar ium.html). The point, of course, is that a hyper-real environment has been created in what is, in effect, an enormous fridge – the penguins themselves were hatched from eggs in the Penguinarium and live in an artificial 'Antarctic' environment.

Film tourism, too, is a phenomenon that may be seen as the experience of postmodern tourism places. It has long been recognised that people are drawn to the filming locations of movies and TV shows; that is, they are 'sometimes induced to visit what they have seen on the silver screen' (Riley *et al.*, 1998: 919; see also Connell, 2012 for a comprehensive review of film tourism). The benefits of such tourism to the destination can often be substantial in terms of visitor numbers and visitor spending – the *Lord of the Rings* trilogy, for example, had a major positive impact on tourism to New Zealand following the release of the first film in 2001 (Buchmann *et al.*, 2010; Grihault, 2003) – whilst research constantly demonstrates the advantages of promoting film/TV locations as tourist attractions (Croy, 2010; Kim & Richardson, 2003; Tooke & Baker, 1996). However, the very fact that people are travelling in ever-increasing numbers to visit imaginary places created for visual consumption in cinemas or on television suggests that film tourism is a powerful form of postmodern tourism.

Tourism time

As tourism has increasingly merged with other social and cultural activities, so too has the time spent being a tourist become less distinct from other time, such as work time and shopping time. Indeed, shopping, eating out, going to the theatre and participating in sports or hobbies have, in many instances, become tourist activities. For example, a weekend city-break may include the traditional activities of sightseeing and staying in a hotel, but shopping and visiting the theatre or cinema are also likely. Also, the time made available for tourism has also increased, as has the definition of what tourism time is. Thus, tourism is no longer restricted to the annual holiday; weekend breaks, additional short holidays, day and even half-day trips are now considered to be tourism time.

Nor does an individual have to leave home to be a tourist. As discussed in Chapter 5, the tourism experience does not start and end with the physical departure from and return to the home environment. Anticipation and day-dreaming in the planning process and remembering or reminiscing after the holiday are equally part of the tourism experience but, in the context of postmodern culture, such is the bombardment of images of other cultures, peoples and places presented by the media, whether incidentally or in specialist television programmes and newspaper and magazine articles, that armchair tourism has become a reality. Continuing developments in digital imaging technology, particularly in the field of virtual reality, will ensure that people can become tourists whenever they desire and without ever having to leave their own homes. To an extent, this has already occurred – the advent of Google Earth, for example, has made it possible for people to 'visit' places through their computer screens. Whether such 'virtual' tourism will eventually replace actual travel experiences remains to be seen for, as Guttentag (2010) observes, virtual reality can never replace authentic reality. That is, it is debatable whether tourists themselves would accept virtual reality as a substitute for a 'real', embodied tourism experience and, hence, it must be questioned whether virtual reality 'experiences could ever be considered a form of tourism' (Guttentag, 2010: 648).

The impact of digital technology on tourism is considered at greater length in Chapter 7 but, more generally, it can also be suggested in the context of postmodern tourism time that the plurality and multi-ethnicity of many modern societies, evidenced by the cultural diversity of restaurants, shops and entertainment in many towns and cities, means that, consciously or subconsciously, people are tourists for much of the time.

Time compression and tourism

One of the main characteristics of postmodernity is the merging of different time periods. Postmodernists look to the past as a sign of stability, and symbols of the past are reconstructed or represented in the present. Styles of architecture, interior design and clothing fashions are the most common examples where the past is visually represented in the present, but tourism is also a sphere of social activity where the past, and the future, become compressed into the present. Moreover, postmodernity's fondness for pastiche and image is particularly evident within the context of tourism.

There are two areas where the past, or representations of the past, influence tourism. Firstly, the enormous growth in the heritage industry (see Chapter 9) and the ways in which the past is represented are indicative the attraction of nostalgia as a tourist attraction. 'Postmodernism and the heritage industry are linked, in that they both conspire to create a shallow screen that intervenes between our present lives, and our history' (Hewison, 1987: 135). The past is brought into the present and is put on display through a variety of modern interpretative techniques, such as videos, the re-creation of noises and smells and live re-enactments, which represent the past, not as it was but as we wish to see it. History thus becomes a commodity, a tourist attraction based upon visual spectacle that is devoid of any true analysis of the past, a representation that bears little, if any, resemblance to reality. 'The postmodern past is one where anything is possible, where fantasy is potentially as real as history because history as heritage dulls our ability to appreciate the development of people and places through time' (Walsh, 1992: 113). One example of this is the Jorvik Viking Centre in York. First opened in 1984 and recently re-opened following serious flooding in late 2015, the Centre, developed on the site where the remains of a thousand-year-old Viking settlement were discovered, provides 'a groundbreaking visitor experience where you take a journey through the reconstruction of Viking-Age streets and experience life as it would have been in tenth century York (Jorvik, 2017). Much of that experience is created by technology and imagination; as Hewison (1991: 161) notes, 'significant finds from the archeological dig that produced Jorvik Viking Centre could be displayed on the top of a single table'. However, this does not deter tourists; in 2015, the Centre welcomed its 18 millionth visitor. In short, tourism based upon heritage is fundamentally postmodern (see Timothy & Boyd, 2003; Herbert, 1995; Timothy, 2011 for a more complete analysis of tourism and heritage).

The second way in which a relationship exists between the postmodern compression of the past into the present and tourism is linked to the issue of tourist experiences and the search for authenticity (see Chapter 9 for more detail). If true authenticity is seen to lie in other times and places (that is, in destinations or countries that have yet to adopt the characteristics of modern, Western societies), then tourism that is motivated by the desire to experience cultures that are essentially pre-modern is an attempt to merge the past into the present. Tourists who travel to developing countries superimpose different, past cultures onto their own, modern experience; in effect, they compress the past into their own present. It is, however, an unreal past. Just as heritage presents a rose-tinted version of history, so too do tourists in many destinations experience a sanitised experience of local, historical culture. They experience visual representations, a romanticised version that is confirmed by the images reproduced in the media, that in many cases bears little resemblance to the reality of life in the countries being visited. It is famous sights, colourful festivals, exotic food and the promise of adventure that sells tourism, not images of poverty, starvation, illness and other problems that beset many developing countries. This has important implications for the future development of tourism, particularly with respect to the way in which many destinations are permitted to represent themselves (to become modern), in a world that, some would argue, is transforming into a global village.

Tourism and the global village

It has long been claimed that the world is getting smaller, that the world is becoming a global village and that, internationally, society is undergoing a process of globalisation. As McGrew (1992: 65) noted a quarter of a century ago, 'globalisation has become a widely used term within media, business, financial and intellectual circles, reflecting a fairly widespread perception that modern communications technology has shrunk the globe'. Information technology that allows us to see history in the making and to communicate with people on the other side of the world at the touch of a button, transport technology that has brought distant countries ever closer in terms of travel time and opened up the whole world to international tourism, 24-hour dealings on the world's financial markets and a whole host of other factors have led to the impression that, in a physical sense, the world is, indeed, becoming smaller.

But globalisation is concerned with rather more than the increasing speed and ease of international travel and communication. It is about a world where there is greater interdependence between nation-states; where the activities and influence of political, economic, industrial, religious and environmental organisations transcend national boundaries; where the events in one country can have serious and immediate effects on another country far away; where there has been a significant migration of people; above all, where there is increasing recognition that 'spaceship earth' is one world shared by a huge diversity of peoples with the potential to develop into the first global civilisation (see Perlmutter, 1991). Four characteristics of globalisation are identified by Steger (2003: 9–12):

a) the development of social networks that transcend traditional economic, political, cultural and geographic constraints;

b) the 'expansion and stretching of social relations, activities and interdependencies' (Steger, 2003: 11);

c) an increase in the growth and intensity of such relations and activities; and

d) the creation and intensification of social interconnectedness and interdependence at a subjective level; that is, growing awareness amongst people of being part of an interconnected, global society.

For Steger (2003) then, globalisation is a social phenomenon which he defines as:

> a multidimensional set of social processes that create, multiply, stretch, and intensify worldwide social interdependencies and exchanges while at the same time fostering in people a growing awareness of deepening connections between the local and the distant.
>
> Steger, 2003: 13)

Similarly, Scholte (2002: 13) considers globalisation to be 'the spread of transplanetary – and in recent times more particularly supraterritorial – connection between people'. However, he goes on to suggest a number of qualifications that reflect other commentators' criticisms of the concept of globalisation, not least the fact that it does not signify the collapse of territorial boundaries, boundaries which nation-states are increasingly concerned about protecting. At the same time, globalisation, as in a global society/ space, does not preclude discrete, sub-global societies and spaces, nor does it imply global cultural homogenisation. Nor is globalisation universal; whilst some societies are increasingly connected, others remain excluded, leading to the conclusion it is an inherently political phenomenon – that is, globalisation empowers some but disempowers others. It is for these reasons that some suggest that not only are we entering a phase of de-globalisation, that in response to supranational power and the threat of cultural homogenisation nations and societies are re-asserting their political, economic and cultural independence, but also that such a process is necessary to maintain and strengthen national economies (Postelnicu et al., 2015).

Irrespective of these debates, there is evidence that globalisation is an identifiable process. For example, the demands made upon the United Nations as a peacekeeping force, the expansion and increasing influence of multinational corporations, the global reach of the Internet and social media, the attention paid to international problems, such as drug production and smuggling, pollution and global warming, the interdependency of the world's financial markets, the worldwide impact of political instability, terrorist atrocities or conflicts, such as the contemporary political instability in the Middle East, and the internationalisation of communities based upon religious, ethnic and cultural factors all point to the dissolving of national boundaries. Moreover, tourism itself has undoubtedly contributed to, and is affected by, the process of globalisation. Increasing knowledge and understanding of different nationalities and cultures has broadened people's horizons whilst the internationalisation of many countries' populations has undoubtedly led to a significant increase in tourism.

As to the cause of globalisation, there is less agreement (Hirst & Thompson, 1999). It has been variously attributed to technological advance, the development of a world economy, political factors, or a combination of all three (see McGrew, 1992). Equally, there is disagreement as to the longer-term consequences of globalisation, although it is generally accepted that it will not be a smooth, harmonious process. In particular, the greater uniformity, integration and homogeneity of society that some envisage in the global village of the future is likely to be countered by efforts to retain national or local control and identity, resulting in a reactive de-globalisation process already referred to. More specifically, and as discussed in Chapter 12, tourism can both increase and decrease the gulf between different nation-states. Nevertheless, a number of links can be identified between globalisation and tourism:

a) One of the major characteristics (and causes) of globalisation has been the rapid advance in information technology. Tourists now have access to information and images of virtually every destination in the world, which may be combined with visual images on the television (for example, 'reality' images, such as news pro-grammes, specialist travel programmes and nature programmes, or representational images presented in TV series) and in other media. As a result, tourists demand greater choice and variety and are able to make better informed decisions. At the same time, the tourist industry is more rapidly susceptible to localised problems reported on the world stage. For example, the activities of terrorist groups or threats of muggings and other crimes can lead to rapid cancellations of holiday bookings.

b) The continuing globalisation of the international economy has a number of char-acteristics, in particular the greater interdependency of nation-states and the ability of one country's financial policies to have an impact on the economies of other nation-states. Indeed, such is the extent of international financial dependency, par-ticularly as revealed in the global financial crisis in 2008, that some people ques-tion the concept of the nation-state as a separate, identifiable form of society. Of equal importance has been the collapse of the centrally planned economies and the emergence of the free market in the former Eastern Bloc countries as well as the increasing influence of China in the global economy which has sig-nalled the advent of a truly worldwide capitalist economy and the gradual post-industrialisation of the advanced, Western economies. The latter has been matched by the industrialisation of a number of developing countries, in particular in the Far East, which means that, in a sense, the capitalist system which was once limited to individual nation-states has emerged as a worldwide economic phenomenon. This is part of what has been described as the age of 'disorganised capitalism' (Lash & Urry, 1987). The implication for tourism is that international tourism will continue to increase but with much of the growth accounted for by tourism from newly industrialised nations and also from those countries whose economies have been released from central control. For example, in March 1994, the Cyprus Tourist Organisation signed an agreement with its Russian counterpart as the first step towards the development of charter package tourism to the island. By 1997, some

7 percent of arrivals to the island were from Russia. Of greater significance, China is now the world's largest market for international tourists; in 2015, some 127 million China travelled overseas, spending US$292 billion compared with the next largest market, the US, whose citizens spent US$113 billion on overseas travel (UNWTO, 2016b). Not surprisingly, therefore China is seen by many destinations as a prime tourist market, though the increasing dependence on Chinese tourists has not been without problems (Cohen, 2017).

c) It is generally accepted that globalisation is leading towards greater cultural homogeneity amongst nation-states. For example, it is not unusual to see younger local people in many developing countries adopting the Western dress code of jeans, T-shirts and baseball caps, whilst the spread and popularity of symbols of American culture, such as McDonald's, is testament to the increasing uniformity of the world. This homogeneity, referred to by one commentator as the *McDonaldization of Society* (Ritzer, 2015), is exacerbated to an extent by tourism, although the activities of multinational corporations and worldwide communication have done more to spread Western culture around the globe. Cultural homogenisation may be linked to tourism in contrasting ways. On the one hand, it may lead to an increase in tourism as countries which have become Westernised appear 'safer' to potential tourists whilst, on the other hand, increasing cultural homogeneity may reduce the attraction of some destinations. In the latter case, it will be necessary for resorts and destinations to improve the quality of their tourism product in order to compete against other, similar destinations. Such a situation already exists around the Mediterranean coastal resorts where, for example, in the late 1980s, Turkey capitalised on the poor image of the Spanish resorts. Efforts by the Spanish to improve the quality of their destinations have now succeeded in returning Spain to its position as the most popular European tourist destination.

d) The international tourism industry is becoming increasingly dominated by large, multinational corporations (MNCs). Both vertical and horizontal integration (see Holloway with Taylor, 2006: 178–184) within the industry has resulted in the creation of large organisations with operations in many countries and which own or control, through management agreements and franchises, many, if not all, elements of a tourism 'package'. Thus, it is not unusual to book a holiday, travel to the destination, stay in accommodation and go on organised tours with different companies that are all owned by one parent company. Deregulation of the airlines and a number of other factors will continue to lead to the domination of the industry by a few major 'players', with the result that tourists, smaller businesses and even some entire tourist destinations will be increasingly at the mercy of the large MNCs.

Tourism, post-Fordism and post-industrialism

Modern society and the more general characteristics of modernity are inextricably linked to the industrialisation of society. The nineteenth century modernist project of progress and economic growth, based upon the control and domination of nature and the resulting transformation of natural, raw materials into tangible and saleable commodities, was firmly rooted in the development of industrial processes and systems. These processes, in turn, led to the rapid urbanisation of Western societies and the corresponding evolution of social structures and institutions which came to represent the differentiated condition of modern society.

During the first half of the twentieth century modern industrial methods of mass production dominated Western economies but, more recently, there has been a recognisable shift towards new forms of production and consumption which reflect certain characteristics of postmodern society. This shift is marked by a growth in the tertiary service sector rather than in manufacturing industries, and a reorganisation of economic processes based upon flexible production. However, the new, post-industrial age has signalled, in particular, the end of the organised, rigid socio-economic structures of modernity and the advent of what has been termed post-Fordism.

Following the pioneering work of Henry Ford in developing mass production techniques for the manufacture of motor cars, the term Fordism has been used to describe both the system of mass production and the resultant mass consumption of the modern industrial era. Fordism was based on four main principles which became applicable to the production of most mass-produced goods (see Murray, 1989). Firstly, all products were standardised which meant that, in turn, each part and task involved in production could also be standardised. Following from this, certain standardised tasks could be undertaken by machines. Thirdly, those tasks which could not be relegated to machines were performed by workers who concentrated on one particular task. Finally, the assembly line system introduced greater efficiency by bringing the task to the worker rather than *vice versa*. The main characteristic of mass production was high set-up costs but low unit costs and, overall, its success depended on, amongst other things, economies of scale, long runs of standardised products, a willing workforce and, most importantly, a mass market that would accept mass-produced, standardised products.

A similar, but simpler, process is identifiable in the development of mass tourism and, in particular, the package holiday (Sharpley, 2017). The product, the holiday, is 'manufactured' by tour operators using the standard components of transport, accommodation and attractions. Each component part is further standardised by, for example, providing one-class, charter air travel and a minimum choice of basic meals in hotels. Unit costs (that is, the cost of the holiday) are minimised by high levels of 'production' and are ensured by techniques such as the block booking of hotel rooms and fitting a greater number of seats into aeroplanes used for charter flights than would normally be found on scheduled flights (see Yale, 1995). Equally, as with all forms of mass production, the continued success of the mass, package holiday is dependent on the acceptance of the product by the consumer. In other words, tour operators are only able to sell cheap, mass-produced package holidays to a large number of tourists if the tourists themselves are willing to accept the lack of choice, the impersonal service, basic standards of food and accommodation, and cramped transport. (Indeed, a common criticism of package holiday tourism is that the tourist is frequently treated more like a unit of production than as a customer!) Once an element of choice or a demand for non-standard products enters the system, then the basis of mass production is undermined; the principles of Fordism no longer apply.

Since the late 1960s, Fordist methods of mass production in general have been challenged by both workers and consumers alike and some have suggested that modern societies have entered the era of post-Fordism, an age where the consumer has begun to dictate, rather than accept, what is produced. In other words, the relationship between production and consumption has undergone a fundamental transformation (see Featherstone 1990; 1991). In the Fordist era, the role of production was dominant and, in the context of tourism, the producers of tourism were largely able to control the development and style of the mass consumption of tourism. More recently, however, consumers have adopted the dominant position; production methods have become more flexible as manufacturers, aided by advanced production technology and improved information systems, have had to become responsive to more rapid changes in consumer demand. Consumers themselves have become more quality conscious and demand a greater variety of products and styles, whilst products have a shorter 'life' as fashions change according to the image portrayed in the media. Many changes in demand are related to surface appearance; the basic product remains the same but the demand for colour, style or accessories changes. For example, the success of the clothes manufacturer Benetton is largely based on the company's ability to react quickly to changes in fashion colours, producing the same basic garments but in each year's new colours. Additionally, manufacturers have had to become more aware of different specialised and niche markets; the mass market approach has been replaced by market segmentation and the need for a variety of market research techniques.

Overall, the increasingly dominant role of the consumer and the growing demand for individualistic, niche products is indicative of the emergence of postmodern culture, a significant characteristic of which is, as we have seen, the growth of consumer culture. Chapter 6 considers this topic in more detail but it is interesting to point out here that, within the context of tourism, the transformation from a Fordist to a post-Fordist system of production and consumption is, arguably, less marked than in other areas. It has long been predicted that tourists will become more quality conscious and are demanding more specialised, tailor-made forms of holiday and travel experience (for example, see Lickorish, 1990; Poon, 1993) and, certainly, there is now an ever-increasing variety of tourism products on offer. Newer, more distant destinations are being added to the range of package holidays offered by tour operators and different types of holidays, from adventure trips in the more exotic or remote regions of the world to winter-sun holidays for the older generations, are being supplied by specialist operators. At the same time, new products and attractions have been developed to satisfy the demands of an increasingly tourism- and leisure-oriented public whilst many popular overseas destinations, such as Spain and Cyprus, have recognised the importance of improving standards and quality to maintain market share. Nevertheless, recent experience, at least in Britain, demonstrates that the original Fordist-type basis of the package holiday remains, in absolute terms though not as a proportion of the total number of holidays taken, as popular as ever. In the 1980s, discounting campaigns mounted by major tour operators and travel agents resulted in a rise of some 40 percent in level of bookings, the implication being that price was still the dominant factor in mass market holiday purchasing.

Similarly, it was reported in April 1994 that Britannia, Thomson Holidays' then charter airline, was to increase the number of seats on its long-haul Boeing 767 flights, sacrificing passenger comfort for cheaper holidays (Atkins 1994). Recent evidence suggests little has changed. Although late discounting has been replaced by early-booking discounts, the major selling 'tool' remains price and, despite the opportunities for independent travel booked via the Internet, tour operators are still successfully selling large numbers of package holidays. Similarly, charter airlines continue to maximise the number of seats on their aeroplanes, even on long-haul flights, applying mass-production techniques to make exotic destinations, such as the Cuba, more affordable to the mass, package tourist. Equally, the success of the low-budget airlines, such as Ryanair and EasyJet, is based on the low prices they charge for flights, demonstrating that tourists are willing to forgo quality/service for price. Therefore, mass tour operators in Britain appear to be resisting the trend towards a consumer-oriented industry, although this is, perhaps, evidence of the effects of post-industrialisation.

Rather than looking at changes in the manufacturing and consumption process in particular, the concept of post-industrialisation is concerned with the transformation of modern economies in general, the main proposition being that modern, industrial societies are becoming increasingly dominated by service economies. Within service economies, both the kinds of work that people do and traditional social structures based upon occupation have fundamentally altered. Manual jobs have been replaced by machines and some would argue that the expansion of the service sector has led to jobs which involve creativity, social interaction and the delivery of a service rather than the production of an inanimate object, jobs which are, therefore, more satisfying and worthwhile. Others would argue that, although the nature of work has changed, resulting in a less clear distinction between the traditional working class and an expanding middle class, new social distinctions are appearing. In a postmodern society that is increasingly dominated by information technology and communication, power resides with those who have access to and use of information; in conflict theory, the capitalists (the owners of the production process) have been replaced by the bureaucrats, but the relative position of the workers remains unaltered.

Whichever viewpoint is adopted, the evidence suggests that, in the case of tourism, there is a move towards the provision of specialist, niche market products and an expansion in both the range and quality of holidays on offer yet, despite the generally accepted post-Fordist attitudes towards production and consumption, mass market package tourism remains firmly embedded in the industrial era (Harrison & Sharpley, 2017a).

Tourism and the environment

One of the principal areas in which postmodernity differs from modernity is within the context of the environment or, more precisely, concern for the environment. Continuing the basic tenet of the Enlightenment project, modernity sought human and economic progress through the domination and exploitation of nature; an objective which modern, Western societies appear, by and large, to have achieved. Most Western societies are able to live beyond the constraints of nature; natural resources are exploited to provide fuel, shelter and food, there are cures for most common illnesses, and people are generally able to travel where and when they want without having to wait for favourable weather conditions. In short, most people, at least in the developed world, are able to live in societies that have overcome their subordination to most of nature's constraints, although natural disasters, such as earthquakes, hurricanes and floods, do not respect national or developmental boundaries. The Indian Ocean tsunami of 26 December 2004 was, in particular, a devastating reminder of nature's power and impartiality, bringing death and destruction on an unimaginable scale to coastal regions – and tourist resorts – around the Indian Ocean (Sharpley, 2005a).

In recent years, in particular since the early 1980s, modern society has become increasingly concerned with the conservation, rather than the exploitation, of the environment. Governments, societies and individuals alike have become more aware that, in the long run, the survival of the human race depends not on the domination of nature and the environment but the harmonious, sustainable co-existence with our natural surroundings. Issues such as the destruction of the rain forests, the greenhouse effect and global warming resulting from the burning of fossil fuels, acid rain, and the depletion of the ozone layer have all become of international concern. Similarly, specific cases of resource depletion, such as excessive and indiscriminate whaling, have been publicised by the activities of conservation organisations, whilst green political parties have challenged the policy of economic growth which is the driving force behind capitalist economies. The history, political and social development of environmentalism and the green movement is beyond the scope of this chapter (for example, see Porritt, 1984; Adams, 1990; Yearley, 1991) yet concern for the environment is not only evidence of the reflexive nature of postmodern culture (the interest in preserving the past being another example) but also, arguably, one of the greatest challenges facing the future of the international tourism industry. Indeed, climate change has not only become a dominant international issue, both politically and environmentally, but also one that will impact directly on tourism in terms of both travel behaviour and destination planning and management. Mass air travel, in particular, is seen as a potential major contributor to climate change (hence current proposals to levy environmental taxes on air transport), whilst actual climate change may have a significant impact on the volume, nature and direction of travel flows in the future (Hall & Higham, 2005; Hall et al., 2015).

Concern about the negative impacts of tourism has been expressed for almost as long as tourism itself has existed as an identifiable, modern leisure activity. For example, in 1848 Thomas Cook wrote in his handbook for visitors to Belvoir Castle that 'to the shame of some rude folk from Lincolnshire, there have been just causes of complaint at Belvoir Castle: some large parties have behaved indecorously . . . conduct of this sort is abominable, and cannot be too strongly reprobated' (cited in Ousby, 1990: 89). In Britain the national park movement, culminating in the 1949 National Parks and Access to the Countryside Act, was the first attempt to reconcile the demands of tourists with the need to protect the environment, but it was not until the late 1960s and early 1970s that concern about the effects of tourism became more widespread. A number of authors (Mishan, 1969; Young, 1973; Turner & Ash, 1975; Rosenow & Pulsipher, 1979) expressed alarm at the rapid spread of mass, package tourism, predicting that the economic benefits of tourism could soon be outweighed by the costs associated with tourism's negative impacts: 'the time has now come . . . to take the Goddess of Tourism off her pedestal and to place her in the garden with other statues' (Young, 1973: 168).

Since the 1980s new, alternative forms of tourism have been suggested to counter the impacts of mass tourism; variously termed as responsible tourism (Goodwin, 2011), green tourism (Jones, 1987), appropriate tourism (Richter, 1987), good tourism (Wood & House, 1991) or ecotourism (Fennell, 1999; 2007), they all share the viewpoint that tourism should be sustainable. At the same time, an enormous volume of literature produced by academics, researchers and tourism organisations has been published, all suggesting that tourism should be developed in harmony with the environment, maintaining a balance between the needs of local communities, visitors, the tourism industry and the physical, social and cultural environment. Various organisations, such as Tourism Concern, the Ecumenical Coalition on Third World Tourism or the International Centre for Responsible Tourism strive to increase awareness of the impacts of tourism and to promote forms of tourism (other than mass tourism) that respect the local environment and the needs of local communities. Others stress that the responsibility for sustainable tourism lies with tourists themselves, seeing the way forward as the development of 'good' tourism (Wood & House, 1991).

The impacts of tourism on the environment, the mechanisms and principles of alternative, sustainable tourism development and the arguments surrounding the viability of alternative forms of tourism to mass tourism are widely discussed and described in the literature. Indeed, since the early 1990s, no other single issue has attracted as much attention, the concept of sustainable tourism development spawning innumerable books and articles, providing the focus of many conferences, and even enjoying its own dedicated journal. The purpose here, however, is to consider the extent to which the growth in tourism environmentalism is linked to the reflexive nature of postmodern culture.

Concern for the environment as a general and widespread social transformation is undoubtedly a major characteristic of postmodernity, representing the de-differentiation of society and its natural environment. As Munt (1994: 105) observes, concern for the environment and sustainability are the 'highest order discourse of postmodernisation'. It is also evidence of a significant departure from the Enlightenment/modernist project of progress through the control and exploitation of natural resources. The relationship between environmental concern, tourism development and postmodernity is not, however, quite so clear cut. Three points, in particular, cast doubt on the underlying motivation for the promotion of environmentally friendly, sustainable tourism:

a)   Much of the research into tourism is concerned with ways in which it may be more sustainable. In other words, it suggests methods of optimising the economic benefits of tourism to host countries whilst, at the same time, minimising the impacts of tourism on the environment. Rarely, however, is the question about the sustainability of tourism, in particular international tourism, as an overall social and economic development activity ever raised, although more recent research has addressed this issue (Wall, 1997; Mowforth & Munt, 2009; Sharpley & Telfer, 2015; Telfer and Sharpley, 2016).

> There is no example of tourist use that is completely without impact. If the primary goal is one of protection and preservation of the environment in an untouched form then, in all truth, there cannot be tourism development at all.
>
> (Cater, 1993: 89).

Unlike other forms of economic activity that impact upon and deplete the world's natural resources, the continuing existence of tourism is generally accepted, no doubt because it is an activity that is enjoyed by a large number of people. It is also frequently motivated by the desire to escape from modern society, which includes escaping from the concerns, such as environmentalism, of modern life. Thus, it may be argued that much of the environmental concern surrounding tourism is motivated not by the need to protect the environment *per se*, but to sustain it as the resource upon which tourism depends. In short, the ultimate purpose is to sustain tourism itself (see Jenner & Smith, 1992; Sharpley & Telfer, 2002; 2015).

b)   Tourism is a global activity and, increasingly, new tourism generating countries are emerging. But, the great majority of tourists originate in the developed, industrialised countries which, to a greater or lesser extent, are becoming postmodern and, not surprisingly, most of the multinational corporations involved in tourism are also based in the main tourism generating countries. Conversely, many tourism receiving nations have yet to achieve modern status in an economic and technological sense and are, in effect, culturally pre-modern. Also, many developing countries cannot afford to be environmentally aware; caring for the environment is a luxury to be indulged in once basic needs have been catered for. In other words, they require far greater amounts of foreign exchange than can be earned realistically from the small-scale, sustainable approach advocated by the (Western) promoters of sustainable tourism. Unlike those countries which have established and profitable tourism industries and diverse economies and can afford conservation programmes, developing nations depend on larger-scale tourism development as a vital source of income. Much of the concern for the impact of tourism is an attempt to impose postmodern social values on nations which are unwilling, or in no position, to accept those values.

c)   It is important not to confuse genuine environmental concern with the postmodernist de-differentiation of the past and present. To a great extent, the concept of sustainable tourism proposes the conservation or protection of both the physical and the socio-cultural environment of destination areas. Whilst the protection of the natural environment from excessive or inappropriate tourism development and use falls entirely within the parameters of environmentalism, the desire to preserve social and cultural traditions and practices is linked to the issues of authenticity (see Chapter 9) and time compression. In other words, the preservation of the socio-cultural environment in tourist destinations, as proposed by the tourism industry, is the preservation of *signs* of past cultures (in comparison to postmodern culture). Such environmentalism, therefore, is based upon the need to maintain the appeal of the environment to potential tourists and is, again, an effort to impose postmodern cultural values upon other societies.

Overall, then, the issues of postmodern environmental concern about the impacts of tourism should be considered from a global perspective. Whilst many tourism generating countries reflect the broader, international concern for the environment as a whole, it must be remembered that many countries, particularly in the developing world, are either unwilling or unable, for financial reasons, to embrace the concept of environmentalism and sustainable development. For them, the development of tourism is seen as a valuable tool to aid economic growth and diversification; only when a certain level of economic, technological and social development has been achieved can such countries begin to consider environmental issues.

At the same time, distinctions need to be drawn between the conservation of scarce natural resources, including those upon which tourism depends, and the preservation of societies and cultures which, to tourists from modern societies, symbolise different, past ages. The challenge for the tourism industry is to question its own motives in promoting sustainable or alternative forms of tourism; the challenge for postmodern, environmentally sensitive societies is to allow other societies to develop and modernise.

Tourism and postmodernity: a summary

As a basis for exploring the relationship between tourism and postmodernity, this chapter has suggested that developments and transformations in tourism as a social activity cannot be explained by making reference only to the enabling factors of tourism. Although important, inasmuch as tourists require the time and the means to be able to participate in tourism, of equal if not greater importance is the tourist's home cultural environment which, in a sense, provides the framework within which tourism is consumed. This implies that changes in the cultural condition of the tourist's society are likely to bring about changes in the style and significance of tourism.

There is little doubt that modern, Western societies have experienced a cultural shift from the condition of modernity to a less rigid, structured state that may be described as postmodernity. There is also little doubt that transformations in styles of tourism reflect this shift towards postmodernity, whilst tourism itself has, arguably, become de-differentiated from other spheres of social activity. New tourism 'places' and 'times' have emerged, challenging the traditional position and role of tourism and suggesting there is much truth in the proposition that people are tourists most of the time (Urry, 1995). Equally, new styles of tourism, such as heritage tourism or ecotourism, have become increasingly popular, although the extent to which a causal relationship exists between these and specific characteristics of postmodernity remains debatable. So recognising and accepting the influence of cultural change in tourism generating areas is not only essential for a fuller understanding of tourism consumption patterns. It also provides a broader theoretical basis for assessing tourism typologies, demand and motivation, topics which the chapters following address.

Further reading

Butler, C. (2002) *Postmodernism: A Very Short Introduction.* Oxford: Oxford University Press.
For readers with an interest in exploring the concept of postmodernism in more depth, this book provides a brief but critical introduction to key debates.

Cooper, C. and Wahab, S. (eds) (2005) *Tourism in the Age of Globalisation.* London: Routledge.
Though now dated, this edited collection provides an excellent overview of the relationship between tourism globalisation, with contributions addressing a number or themes including the age of globalisation, the relevance of globalisation to tourism demand and marketing, and implications of globalisation for sustainability.

Pretes, M. (1995) Postmodern tourism: The Santa Claus industry. *Annals of Tourism Research*, 22(1): 1–15.
Focusing on a specific postmodern form of tourism (Santa Claus tourism in Finland), this paper provides an excellent summary of the relationship between postmodern culture and tourism.

Uriely, N. (2005) The tourist experience: Conceptual developments. *Annals of Tourism Research*, 32(1): 199–216.
This paper identifies four conceptual developments in the study of the tourist experience, all of which fall under the umbrella of postmodern theory.

Urry, J. and Larsen, J. (2011) *The Tourist Gaze 3.0.* London: Sage Publications.
Now in its third edition, John Urry's seminal text is firmly located with a postmodern perspective.

Discussion topics

▶ To what extent can tourism be considered to be 'prefiguratively postmodern' (Urry (1990a: 87).

▶ In what ways has tourism become postmodern?

▶ Tourism is often claimed to be evidence of globalisation; equally, however, some suggest that we are now entering an era of de-globalisation. Is tourism contributing to de-globalisation?

▶ Has the production of tourism become post-Fordist, or do the principles of Fordism apply to the production and supply of tourism products and experiences?

4

Tourists
Roles and typologies

Introduction

It is generally accepted that the word 'tourist' first appeared in the English language around the end of the eighteenth century, although there is some debate as to when the word was first actually used (Theobald, 1994). Some, for example, attribute the origin of the term to Stendhal in the early 1800s (Feifer, 1985), whilst others claim that its first known usage was in a 1780 guide book to the Lake District. Certainly, William Wordsworth used the word in his 1799 poem *The Brothers,* whilst in 1800 Samuel Pegge wrote in a book on new English usages that 'a Traveller is now-a-days called a Tour-ist' (cited in Buzard, 1993: 1). This indicates that, originally, 'tourist' and 'traveller' were interchangeable terms describing, in a neutral sense, a person who was touring. More recently, the words 'traveller' and 'tourist' have acquired different connotations. The former, in a touristic sense (as opposed to gypsy, new age traveller and so on), is usually applied to someone who is travelling/touring for an extended period of time, probably backpacking on a limited budget. It connotes a spirit of freedom, adventure and individuality. The word tourist, on the other hand, is frequently used in a rather derogatory sense to describe those who participate in mass-produced, package tourism (McCabe, 2005).

The traveller/tourist dichotomy has, as Buzard (1993: 5) argues, 'more to do with the society and culture that produce the tourist than it does with the encounter any given tourist or "traveller" may have with a foreign society and culture'. In other words, the words 'traveller' and 'tourist' have acquired a socially constructed meaning that goes beyond a basic description of travelling and touring. As a result, it is probably true to say that, at some time or another, most people have tried to distance or disassociate themselves from other tourists, convincing themselves that they are somehow better or enjoying a more meaningful experience. That is, they suffer what Dann (1999) refers to as 'tourist angst', 'that feeling which many tourists are reckoned to display towards fellow vacationers whenever they come into contact with, and seek to distance themselves from, them' (Dann, 1999: 160).

This issue is discussed shortly. But, the important point is that the word tourist is nowadays applied to such a huge number and variety of people undertaking such vastly different types of travel that, as a way of collectively describing the individuals who made an estimated 1,235 million international trips in 2016, as well as the billions who participate in domestic tourism, it is a virtually meaningless term. Putting it another way, even though around three-quarters of all international travel expenditure is leisure or holiday related (WTTC, 2016), to describe all the individuals concerned simply as tourists is to overlook a whole host of different factors, such as length and type of holiday, a person's demographic, social and psychological characteristics or the purpose of the trip, that distinguish them from one another. As Pearce (2005: 2) observes in the first chapter of his book on tourist behaviour, 'tourists are not alike. In fact, they are staggeringly diverse in age, motivation, level of affluence and preferred activities'. For example, strictly speaking a young person embarking on a year's backpacking tour of Asia, a family having a two-week package holiday in Benidorm and an American of Irish descent visiting Ireland to discover his ancestry are all tourists, but there the similarity ends. It is for this reason, perhaps, that an ever-increasing number of labels are attached to different types of tourism/tourists (see Table 4.1). Whilst by no means exhaustive, this list in Table 4.1 reveals the diversity of categories of tourism identified and explored within the tourism literature.

If we are to be able to better understand, explain and predict tourist behaviour, it is therefore necessary to look beneath the all-encompassing label of 'tourist'. We have to ask: who is a tourist, and what are the different types of tourist? We have to consider how tourists may be categorised by their behaviour or the roles they play (Foo *et al.*, 2004; Yiannakis & Gibson, 1992), by their expectations and, adopting a structural approach, the extent to which tourist types and roles are determined by their social environment. This chapter discusses the different attempts which have been made to create typologies of tourists and examines socially determined categories of tourist, such as the 'good' tourist (see Popescu, 2008; Wood & House, 1991), the 'sustainable' (Swarbrooke, 1999) or 'responsible' tourist (Weedon, 2014), the 'new' tourist (Poon, 1993) and the 'post-tourist' (see Feifer, 1985; Urry, 1988; 1990a). It also suggests that a practical, useful typology of tourists should be based upon a broader approach than has been adopted to date.

TABLE 4.1 Tourism types and categories

Tourism type/category	Key publications
Adventure tourism • Soft/hard adventure tourism	Beard, C., Swarbrooke, J., Leckie, S. and Pomfret, G. (2012) *Adventure Tourism*. Abingdon: Routledge. Buckley, R. (2006) *Adventure Tourism*. Wallingford: CABI
Agritourism	McGehee, N. and Kim, K. (2004) Motivation for agri-tourism entrepreneurship. *Journal of Travel Research*, 43(2): 161–170. Phillip, S., Hunter, C. and Blackstock, K. (2010) A typology for defining agritourism. *Tourism Management*, 31(6): 754–758.
All-inclusive tourism • Package tourism	Issa, J. and Jayawardena, C. (2003) The 'all-inclusive' concept in the Caribbean. *International Journal of Contemporary Hospitality Management*, 15(3): 167–171. Pearce, D. (1987) Spatial patterns of package tourism in Europe. *Annals of Tourism Research*, 14(2): 183–201.

Tourism type/category	Key publications
Ashram tourism	Sharpley, R. and Sundaram, P (2005) Tourism: a sacred journey? The case of ashram tourism, India, *International Journal of Tourism Research*, 7(3): 161–171.
Backpack tourism/backpacking	Richards, G. and Wilson, J. (2004) *The Global Nomad: Backpacker Travel in Theory and Practice*. Clevedon: Channel View Publications.
Beach tourism	Cortés-Jiménez, I., Nowak, J. and Sahli, M. (2011) Mass beach tourism and economic growth: lessons from Tunisia. *Tourism Economics*, 17(3): 531–547.
Business tourism	Swarbrooke, J. and Horner, S. (2011) *Business Travel and Tourism*. Abingdon: Routledge.
City/urban tourism	Heeley, J. (2011) *Inside City Tourism*. Bristol: Channel View Publications. Law, C. (2002) *Urban Tourism: The Visitor Economy and the Growth of Large Cities*. London: Continuum.
Creative tourism	Richards, G. (2011) Creativity and tourism: The state of the art. *Annals of Tourism Research*, 38(4): 1225–1253.
Cruise tourism/cruising	Dowling, R. (2006) *Cruise Ship Tourism*. Wallingford: CABI.
Culinary/Food/ Gastronomy tourism	Hall, C.M., Sharples, L., Mitchell, R., Macionis, N. and Cambourne, B. (2004) *Food Tourism Around the World*. Abingdon: Routledge. A-M. Hjalager and G. Richards (2002) *Tourism and Gastronomy*. Abingdon: Routledge.
Cultural tourism • Art tourism • Music tourism	McKercher, B. and du Cros, H. (2015) *Cultural Tourism*: 2nd Edition. Abingdon: Routledge. Smith, M. and Richards, G. (eds) (2012) *Routledge Handbook of Cultural Tourism*. Abingdon: Routledge.
Dark tourism • Disaster tourism • Genocide tourism • Graveyard tourism • Grief tourism • Prison tourism • War/battlefield tourism	Lennon, J. and Foley, M. (2000) *Dark Tourism: The Attraction of Death and Disaster*. London: Continuum. Sharpley, R. and Stone, P.R. (2009) *The Darker Side of Travel*. Bristol: Channel View Publications. Sion, B. (ed.) (2014) *Death Tourism: Disaster Sites as Recreational Landscape*. London and New York: Seagull Books.
Ecotourism • Soft/hard ecotourism	Fennell, D. (2015) *Ecotourism*, 4th Edition. Abingdon: Routledge. Wearing, S. and Neil, J. (2009) *Ecotourism: Impacts, Potentials and Possibilities?* Oxford: Butterworth Heinemann.
Education tourism	See for example British Educational Travel Association (www.betauk.com).
Event tourism	Getz, D. (2005) *Event Management and Events Tourism*, 2nd Edition. New York: Cognizant Communication Corporation.
Farm tourism	Busby, G. and Rendle, S. (2000) The transition from tourism on farms to farm tourism. *Tourism Management*, 21(6): 635–642. Ilbery, B., Bowler, I., Clark, G., Crockett, A. and Shaw, A. (1998) Farm-based tourism as an alternative farm enterprise: A case study from the Northern Pennines, England. *Regional Studies,* 32(4): 355–364.

(Continued)

TABLE 4.1 (Continued)

Tourism type/category	Key publications
Festival tourism	Getz, D. (1991) *Festivals, Special Events and Tourism.* New York: Van Nostrand Reinhold. Picard, D. and Robinson, M. (2006) *Festivals, Tourism and Social Change: Remaking Worlds.* Clevedon: Channel View Publications.
Film tourism • Screen tourism • TV tourism • Movie tourism	Beeton, S. (2005) *Film Induced Tourism.* Clevedon: Channel View Publications. Connell, J. (2012) Film tourism: Evolution, progress and prospects. *Tourism Management,* 33(5): 1007–1029.
Frontier tourism	Krakover, S. and Gradus, Y. (2002) *Tourism in Frontier Areas.* Lanham: Lexington Books. Laing, J. and Crouch, G. (2011) Frontier tourism: Retracing mythic journeys. *Annals of Tourism Research,* 38(4): 1516–1534.
Gap year tourism	O'Reilly, C. (2006) From drifter to gap year tourist: Mainstreaming backpacker travel. *Annals of Tourism Research,* 33(4): 998–1017.
Genealogy tourism	Birtwistle, M. (2005) Genealogy tourism. In M. Novelli (ed.) *Niche Tourism: Contemporary Issues, Trends and Cases.* Oxford: Elsevier, pp. 59–72.
Geotourism	Dowling, R. and Newsome, D. (eds) (2006) *Geotourism.* Oxford: Elsevier.
Green tourism	Gülez, S. (1994) Green tourism: A case study. *Annals of Tourism Research,* 21(2): 413–415.
Health tourism • Spa tourism • Wellness tourism	Erfurt-Cooper, P. and Cooper, M. (2009) *Health and Wellness Tourism: Spas and Hot Springs.* Bristol: Channel View Publications. Smith, M. and Puczkó, L. (2009) *Health and Wellness Tourism.* Oxford: Elsevier-Butterworth Heinemann.
Heritage tourism • Cathedral tourism • Museum tourism	Timothy, D. (2011) *Cultural Heritage and Tourism.* Bristol: Channel View Publications. Timothy, D. and Boyd, S. (2003) *Heritage Tourism.* Harlow: Pearson Education Limited.
Industrial tourism	Otgaar, A., Van den Berg, L., Berger, C. and Feng, R. (2016) *Industrial Tourism: Opportunities for City and Enterprise.* Abingdon: Routledge.
Island tourism	Carlsen, J. and Butler, R. (eds) (2011) *Island Tourism: Sustainable Perspectives.* Wallingford: CABI. Graci, S. and Dodds, R. (2010) *Sustainable Tourism in Island Destinations.* London: Earthscan Publications.
Literary tourism	Hoppen, A., Brown, L. and Fyall, A. (2014) Literary tourism: Opportunities and challenges for the marketing and branding of destinations? *Journal of Destination Marketing and Management,* 3(1): 37–47. Robinson, M. and Andersen, H-C. (eds) (2002) *Literature and Tourism.* London: Thomson.
Marine tourism • Dive tourism	Orams, M. (1999) *Marine Tourism: Development, Impacts and Management.* London: Routledge.

Tourism type/category	Key publications
Mass tourism • Package tourism	Aramberri, J. (2010) *Modern Mass Tourism*. Bingley: Emerald. Harrison, D. and Sharpley, R. (eds) (2017) *Mass Tourism in a Small World*. Wallingford: CABI.
Medical tourism	Connell, J. (2006) Medical tourism: Sea, sun, sand and . . . surgery. *Tourism Management*, 27(6): 1093–1100.
Mountain tourism • Glacier tourism	Richins, H. and Hull, J. (eds) (2016) *Mountain Tourism: Experiences, Communities, Environments and Sustainable Futures*. Wallingford: CABI.
Nature tourism	Chen, J. and Prebensen, N. (eds) (2017) *Nature Tourism*. Abingdon: Routledge. Newsome, D., Moore, S. and Dowling, R. (2013) *Natural Area Tourism: Ecology, Impacts and Management*, 2nd Edition. Bristol: Channel View Publications.
Niche tourism	Novelli, M. (ed.) (2005) *Niche Tourism: Contemporary Issues, Trends and Cases*. Oxford: Elsevier.
Religious tourism • Spiritual tourism • Pilgrimage	Raj, R. and Morpeth, N. (2007) *Religious Tourism and Pilgrimage Festivals Management: An International Perspective*. Wallingford: CABI. Timothy, D. and Olsen, D. (eds) (2006) *Tourism, Religion and Spiritual Journeys*. London: Routledge.
Responsible tourism	Goodwin, H. (2011) *Taking Responsibility for Tourism*. Oxford: Goodfellow Publishers.
Retail/shopping tourism	McIntyre, C. (ed.) (2012) *Tourism and Retail: The Psychogeography of Liminal Consumption*. Abingdon: Routledge.
River tourism	Prideaux, B. and Cooper, M. (eds) (2009) *River Tourism*. Wallingford: CABI.
Royal tourism	Long, P. and Palmer, N (eds) (2008) *Royal Tourism: Excursions Around Monarchy*. Bristol: Channel View Publications.
Rural tourism	Roberts, L. and Hall, D. (2001) *Rural Tourism and Recreation: Principles to Practice*. Wallingford: CABI. Sharpley, R. and Sharpley, J. (1997) *Rural Tourism: An Introduction*. London: International Thomson Business Press.
Sex tourism	Ryan, C. and Hall, C.M. (2001) *Sex Tourism: Marginal People and Liminalities*. London: Routledge.
Slow tourism	Dickinson, J. and Lumsdon, L. (2010) *Slow Travel and Tourism*. London: Earthscan. Fullagar, S., Markwell, K. and Wilson, E. (eds) (2012.) *Slow Tourism: Experiences and Mobilities.* Bristol: Channel View Publications.
Slum tourism	Frenzel, F., Koens, K. and Steinbrink, M. (2012) *Slum Tourism: Poverty, power and Ethics.* Abingdon: Routledge.
Space tourism	Webber, D. (2013) Space tourism: Its history, future and importance. *Acta Astronautica*, 92(2): 138–143.

(Continued)

TABLE 4.1 (Continued)

Tourism type/category	Key publications
Sports tourism • Cycling tourism • Surf tourism • Golf tourism • Winter sports tourism	Hinch, T. and Higham, J. (2011) *Sport Tourism Development*, 2nd Edition. Bristol: Channel View Publications. Ritchie, B.W. and Adair, D. (eds) (2004) *Sport Tourism: Interrelationships, Impacts and Issues*. Clevedon: Channel View Publications.
Suicide tourism	Gauthier, S., Mausbach, J., Reisch, T. and Bartsch, C. (2015) Suicide tourism: a pilot study on the Swiss phenomenon. *Journal of Medical Ethics*, 41(8): 611–617.
Tea/coffee tourism	Jolliffe, L. (ed.) (2007) *Tea and Tourism: Tourists, Traditions and Transformations*. Clevedon: Channel View Publications. Jolliffe, L. (ed.) (2010) *Coffee Culture, Destinations and Tourism*. Bristol: Channel View Publications.
Trekking tourism	Gyimóthy, S. and Mykletun, R.J. (2004) Play in adventure tourism: The case of Arctic trekking. *Annals of Tourism Research*, 31(4): 855–878.
Volunteer tourism	Wearing, S. (2001) *Volunteer Tourism: Experiences that Make a Difference*. Wallingford: CABI. Wearing, S. and McGehee, N. (2013) Volunteer tourism: A review. *Tourism Management*, 38: 120–130.
Wedding tourism	Johnston, L. (2006) 'I do Down-Under': Naturalizing landscapes and love through wedding tourism in New Zealand. *ACME: An International Journal for Critical Geographies*, 5(2): 191–208.
Whale watching/tourism	O'Connor, S., Campbell, R., Cortez, H. and Knowles, T. (2009) *Whale Watching Worldwide: Tourism Numbers, Expenditures and Expanding Economic Benefits*. Yarmouth, M.A.: International Fund for Animal Welfare.
Wildlife tourism • Safari tourism	Newsome, D., Dowling, R. and Moore, S. (2005) *Wildlife Tourism*. Clevedon: Channel View Publications.
Winter–sun tourism	Vaughan, D. and Edwards, J. (1999) Experiential perceptions of two winter sun destinations: The Algarve and Cyprus. *Journal of Vacation Marketing*, 5(4): 356–368.

Tourist or traveller?

When the word tourist was first used it was synonymous with traveller. That is, it was used in a totally neutral sense to describe a person who was touring for, normally, the purpose of pleasure or leisure. During the first half of the nineteenth century, distinctions came to be made between tourist and traveller, or tourism and travel, distinctions which implied as much, if not more, about the character of the individuals concerned as about the actual means of travel. The tourist, as opposed to the traveller, not only became associated with mass forms of travel but also with a particular mentality or approach to the travel experience. In effect, 'high culture, the culture of the traveller, saw itself as the polar opposite of low culture, the culture attributed to the tourist' (Rojek, 1993: 174), a distinction immortalised, perhaps, by Henry James' description of tourists as 'vulgar, vulgar, vulgar' (cited in Pearce & Moscardo, 1986: 121).

Writing in 1869, James was referring specifically to American tourists in Europe. However, not only do his sentiments reflect the continuing dichotomy in the way that people view tourists and travellers, but they are also evidence of a debate that continues unabated to this day (see Dann, 1999; McCabe, 2005; O'Reilly, 2005; Richards & Wilson, 2004). Moreover, it is a debate that underpins many issues within the sociological treatment of tourism, including tourist motivation, the social significance of tourism and the search for authentic tourist experiences. These issues are addressed in subsequent chapters but it is important here to explore the traveller-tourist dichotomy in more detail.

The distinctions between the two terms are, arguably, most evident in the literature on travel (Robinson & Andersen, 2002). Again, it was in nineteenth century writing that the distinction first emerged (see Buzard, 1993) but the trend continues. Nowadays, much travel literature tends to emphasise and, perhaps, glorify in the unusual, the different or the unique way of travelling from one place to another. Indeed, since the publication of Ted Simon's (1980) still-popular book *Jupiter's Travels,* detailing his four-year journey around the world by motorbike, numerous travel books have been written that focus more on the experience of travelling rather than on the places visited (including a more recent account by Ted Simon (2007) himself of his attempt to re-create – unsuccessfully – his travels of the 1970s). Typically, authors' accounts of cycling, walking, running, or sailing particular journeys predominate; if it has been achieved against a background of political turmoil or civil war, under harsh weather conditions or without the approval of the authorities, then so much the better! To put it another way, modern travel literature 'writes out' the tourist (Dann, 1999); rather, it emphasises the feelings and emotions which the authors 'experience and communicate, along with the questions of self-identity they rhetorically pose in their descriptions of far-flung places, sentiments which have the cumulative effect of physically and psychologically distancing themselves and their readers from the more familiar voyage of today: the tourist' (Dann, 1999: 160).

As a result, such writing not only glorifies 'travel' in opposition to the more mundane, unexciting practice of 'tourism', but also undoubtedly encourages many others to seek out similar places and experiences. Likewise, earlier editions of some contemporary series of guide books, in particular the Lonely Planet *Travel Survival Kits,* can be seen as emphasising the individualistic, adventurous approach in contrast to the easy, comfortable, package tour. Not only do they mould the visitor's perceptions of the destination (Bhattacharyya, 1997), but they also verify the self-image of those who wish to distinguish themselves from the tourist. However, it is interesting to note that Lonely Planet guides and other similar series, such as Rough Guides, have now become mainstream, widely used publications, in a sense as much as an 'institution' of tourism as independent travel has become (see below). Nevertheless, the point here is that, as the number of places around the world yet to become tourist destinations continues to diminish, for travellers it is not *where* but *how* that has become important.

As important as travel literature has been in forging distinctions between the tourist and the traveller, however, the underlying cause was, and remains, technological advances in transport. During the latter half of the eighteenth century the development of rail transport not only heralded the advent of modern mass tourism (see Chapter 2) but, more specifically, was also as the prime culprit of the demise of 'real' travel. For example, John Ruskin wrote that the train 'transmutes a man from a traveller into a living parcel' (cited in Buzard, 1993: 33). More than a century later it is ironic that, in an age of supersonic air travel (until Concorde was taken out of service in the early 2000s), international train journeys (preferably hauled by a steam engine) are now promoted as a return to the days of real, authentic travel. In short, it is not the actual form of transport but its degree or stage of technological advance that determines its acceptability and authenticity to travellers. No doubt a trip on a jet plane will one day be sold as an authentic experience of real travel!

Of more importance are the social distinctions inherent in the traveller/tourist argument. All tourists, in general, are looked down upon by other tourists who, arguably, consider themselves to be undeserving of the tourist label. Also, it is a process or reaction that is found across the entire spectrum of touristic activity and one which does not always respect traditional social groupings or distinctions. For example, backpackers, particularly those on longer-term trips, are at pains to call themselves travellers rather than tourists (see O'Reilly, 2005; Riley, 1988); indeed, there is an increasingly extensive literature focusing specifically on the 'backpacker' (for example, Cohen, 2011; Richards & Wilson, 2004; Uriely *et al.*, 2002). Travel is associated with adventure, authentic experience, taste, individuality and self-discovery, whereas tourism is pre-packaged, pre-paid, comfortable and predictable. Travellers make their own choices; tourists have their decisions made for them. Travel is seen to be somehow 'better' than tourism, travellers 'better' than tourists, irrespective of class, wealth, education, age, nationality and other social distinctions (see also Elsrud, 2001; Murphy, 2001).

At the same time, distinctions are made within similar forms of tourism, such as package beach holidays. Some people believe that certain destinations are not suitable or are too 'touristy' and so a fortnight's holiday in, say, the Seychelles or the Maldives may be perceived to be better than two weeks in Majorca; the two products are, in effect, the same, the primary difference being the cost. Even independent travel, or backpacking, is not immune to this process. Different countries are hierarchically listed according to degrees of difficulty, danger or hassle for visitors whilst, as Riley (1988) observes, a 'road culture' exists whereby individuals seek to enhance their status by claiming to have travelled for longer, visiting more places yet 'surviving' on less money, than other travellers.

Comparisons may also be made between different nationalities of tourists (Pearce, 2005: 32–35). For many years the American, 'if it's Tuesday it must be Belgium' style of touring Europe bore the brunt of the anti-tourists' criticism. Attention then shifted towards groups of camera-toting Japanese tourists and the allegedly German habit of getting up early to claim the best places around the swimming pool whilst nowadays, both the Chinese (Cohen, 2017) and Russian (Reisinger *et al.*, 2013) markets have been the focus of criticism. Tourist differentiation is even apparent within the context of a single mode of transport. As the opportunity for travel became more widespread during the 1800s, 'status distinctions came to be drawn less between those who could and those who could not travel but between different classes of traveller' (Urry, 1990b). For example, charter flights are more 'touristy' than scheduled flights – though the increasing pervasiveness of budget, no-frills airlines has lessened this distinction – and in China rail travel on normal speed (as opposed to newer high-speed trains) is segregated into two classes of travel – 'soft seat' (first class) and 'hard seat' (second class).

Simply put, all tourists (and travellers), as Culler (1981: 130) argues, 'can always find someone more touristy than themselves to sneer at'. Disliking and trying to avoid other tourists at the same time as trying to convince oneself that one is not a tourist is, in fact, all part of being a tourist. The basis of the conflict is a kind of social arrogance which can be linked directly to the aristocratic model of tourism development described in Chapter 2. Throughout the nineteenth century, criticism was directed at ordinary people who, taking advantage of the new forms of transport, were able to travel both at home and abroad in ever-increasing numbers, thereby threatening once exclusive destinations. The implication was that not only would the new mass tourists impinge on the enjoyment of the previously privileged minority who had the time and money to travel but also that they were, somehow, unable to appreciate the travel experience.

For example, the poet William Wordsworth fought vigorously against the extension of the railway line to Windermere in the English Lake District in the mid-1800s, fearing it would bring large numbers of people more intent on simple pleasures than admiring the sublime beauty of the region. Thus, as travel became increasingly democratised, the moral and cultural benefits of travel were seen to be becoming correspondingly diluted. As the growth of mass tourism has continued throughout the twentieth century and into the twenty-first, this perceived gulf between the traveller and the tourist has intensified; as more and more people become tourists, the less and less do they wish to be labelled as such.

One of the fiercest critics of mass tourists, highlighting the traveller/tourist dichotomy, is Daniel Boorstin. In lamenting what he terms *The Lost Art of Travel* (Boorstin, 1964), he describes the onset of mass tourism as 'the decline of the traveller and the rise of the tourist'. The difference, he continues, is that:

> The traveller, then, was working at something; the tourist was a pleasure seeker. The traveller was active; he went strenuously in search of people, of adventure, of experience. The tourist is passive; he expects interesting things to happen to him . . . he expects everything to be done to him and for him.
>
> (Boorstin, 1964: 85)

The modern tourist, according to Boorstin, has become a passive onlooker who travels in organised groups, enjoys contrived, pseudo-events, rarely experiences or seeks the real or authentic and, as Cohen (1988b: 30) puts it, 'seeks to enjoy the extravagantly strange from the security of the familiar'. It is important to point out that Boorstin is, in fact, concerned with the overall state of modern society and simply uses mass tourism as an illustration for his arguments. Nevertheless, his opinions reflect the continuing and widely held belief that travellers are different and in some way superior to tourists, a belief that is based upon a number of misconceptions and generalisations.

1   The art of travel imagined and, perhaps, romanticised by the protagonists of the
    traveller/tourist dichotomy has not been lost; it has been overtaken by modern
    technology (see de Botton, 2002). In particular, advances in information technol-
    ogy have rendered the recreation of 'traditional' travel impossible. It matters little
    what mode of transport is used for what distinguishes early from modern travel
    is not the speed, comfort or type of transport but the expectations and knowl-
    edge of what will be encountered either *en route* or at the destination. Television,
    radio, magazines, education, guide books, the experiences of family and friends and,
    in particular, the Internet have irrevocably altered the fundamental experience of
    travel to the extent that the traveller/tourist knows what to expect and what will
    be found. Innumerable websites, such as TripAdvisor, can be found that describe
    visitors' experiences of hotels, resorts, airlines and so on, whilst Google Earth can
    transport the potential visitor to the potential destination and provide almost any
    information that he or she may need. In short, advances in information technology
    have, in a sense, removed the excitement or discovery from travel, making it pre-
    dictable, planned and, perhaps, 'safe' (although it is, of course, still possible to travel
    without having previously accessed relevant websites).

2   Rather than leading to greater harmony and understanding, tourism serves to
    highlight social distinctions and conflict. Different modes and standards of travel,
    different classes of accommodation, different destinations and even the difference
    between those who are able or unable to participate in travel and tourism are, to an
    extent, no more than a reflection of wider social differentiation and stratification.

3   Travel cannot be separated from tourism. Not all travellers are necessarily tour-
    ists but all tourists are, by definition, travellers. There is, therefore, little point in
    attempting to distinguish between the two in a collective sense except, perhaps, as
    a marketing exercise. That is, the perceived difference between travel and tourism
    may be used as means of distinguishing between different types of holiday and for
    appealing to different market segments. For example, a month-long overland trip
    in a truck through South America may be sold as authentic travel but, from the
    tour operator's point of view, it is no less a package holiday than a two-week beach
    holiday (see Chapter 9).

4   The experience of independence associated with travel, as opposed to tourism, for
    the most part does not strictly exist. Bookings are made through travel agents or
    online travel and accommodation sites, itineraries and accommodation are arranged
    with the help of specialist guidebooks, and most travellers follow recognised routes.
    Moreover, tourists increasingly make decisions on the basis of the advice or expe-
    rience of other tourists posted on websites such as TripAdvisor and travel blogs
    (Ayeh *et al.*, 2013; Fotis *et al.*, 2012). It is also ironic that events such as 'Indepen-
    dent Travellers' Fairs' are supported by a sophisticated sector of the travel industry
    and, increasingly, 'gap year' travel is seen by many (though perhaps not by 'gappers'
    themselves), simply as an extended holiday between school and university.

5   By attempting to differentiate between the traveller and the tourist, generalised
    characterisations of each emerge. The word tourist, in particular, has come to be
    associated in a derogatory sense with mass tourism (which is also an overused and

misunderstood term), yet those who continue to denounce mass tourism disregard the enormous variation in the motivation, experience and behaviour of different tourists. Similarly, there is no single type of traveller. For example, as discussed shortly, independent travel (or the generic term 'traveller') is widely associated with the younger, explorer type, yet it is a form of tourism which appeals to many socio-economic groupings and, as noted in Chapter 1, a significant proportion of people taking extended periods of travel or 'gap years' are now middle-aged or retired. Certainly, some of the most influential modern travel writers do not fall into this category!

In short, then, there is no such thing as *the* tourist or *the* traveller. Such distinctions are normally self-imposed labels and, therefore, within the context of the modern tourism system, it may be concluded that a traveller is simply one type of tourist.

Tourists: types, categories and roles

An understanding of tourist categories and roles is essential, along with other factors, to the explanation and prediction of consumer behaviour within tourism. One of the earliest attempts to distinguish between different types of tourism was made by Gray (1970) who coined the terms *sunlust* and *wanderlust* tourism. Sunlust tourism is essentially tourism that is resort based and motivated by the desire for rest, relaxation and the three Ss – Sun, Sea and Sand – whereas wanderlust tourism is based on a desire to travel and to experience different peoples and cultures. Implicit in each term are the characteristics of each form of travel; for example, climate and comfortable and familiar accommodation and cuisine will be more important to the sunlust tourist whereas the wanderlust tourist will be more interested in different cultures and the potential for experience and learning. As the two terms imply, sunlust and wanderlust are essentially categorisations based upon the purpose of the trip. They are a useful, though basic, form of market segmentation, describing rather than explaining or predicting the demand for tourism.

Since then a number of typologies, concentrating on the tourists themselves, have been developed. Some of these concentrate on tourists' behaviour whilst others adopt a more socio-psychological approach.

Cohen's typology of tourists

Erik Cohen was the first to propose a typology of tourists based upon sociological theory. That is, unlike previous attempts to categorise tourists, such as Gray's sunlust-wanderlust concept which focused upon tourists in isolation of any conceptual framework, Cohen developed his typology of tourists 'on the basis of their relationship to both the tourist business establishment and the host country' (Cohen, 1972: 164). In other words, his starting point was to relate tourist behaviour to the tourism destination environment.

His work is also based on the fundamental assumption that all tourists, even those with a thirst for adventure and excitement, are unable to escape totally from the influence of their home environment. In other words, all tourists can be located along a 'familiarity-strangerhood continuum'. According to Cohen, all tourists carry with them their values and behaviour patterns when they travel and, as a result, need something to remind them of home, such as a newspaper, familiar food or a friend. At the same time, the way in which they view, and react to, new places and cultures is also determined, to a greater or lesser extent, by their home environment and culture. In short, tourists travel in an 'environmental bubble' (Cohen, 1972: 166). Importantly, however, not all tourists are equally constrained by this bubble. On the one hand, some tourists, those at the familiarity end of the continuum, are unable to escape at all; they seek out the normal or the familiar and are unwilling to try or risk something new or different. On the other hand, others are able to break free from the bubble; they seek out the novel and unusual, and are found at the strangerhood end of the continuum.

Cohen's starting point is, therefore, similar to Boorstin's view of the mass tourist inasmuch as he suggests that tourist behaviour is structurally determined by the tourist's home social environment. But, unlike Boorstin's single and somewhat derogatory generalisation, he suggests that different tourists are more or less able to adapt to and experience the unfamiliar. Thus, progressing from the familiarity to the strangerhood position, four different types of tourist are identified:

a) The organised mass tourist: The organised mass tourist is probably the type that conforms most closely to the stereotypical image of the tourist. On a package tour, the organised mass tourist travels around in air-conditioned coaches on a pre-arranged, inflexible itinerary, stays in hotels which recreate the home environment, makes virtually no decisions and at all stages of the trip is shielded from any possible contact with the host country's culture. If on a beach holiday, the organised mass tourist remains within the hotel complex, with the exception of an occasional organised tour, and at no time does he or she venture outside the environmental bubble. Domestic tourists on package trips, such as a week in Blackpool, also fall into this category.

b) The individual mass tourist: Individual mass tourists are similar to the organised mass tourists inasmuch as their holiday or trip is arranged and booked through an operator. Less constrained by desired safety of the familiar, they are able to exercise a degree of personal choice and control. For example, a fly/drive holiday, where tourists choose their itinerary but still stay on the beaten track combines familiarity with a certain amount of novelty and is likely to appeal to individual mass tourists. In other words, they rely on the established tourism system, but are able occasionally to escape from their environmental bubble.

c) The explorer: The characteristics of the explorer approximate to the behaviour of the independent tourist. The explorer makes his/her own travel arrangements, tries to avoid the tourist trail as far as possible by getting off the beaten track and attempts to associate with local people and culture by learning the language, eating in local restaurants and so on. In short, the explorer seeks novel experiences and largely rejects the familiar. But, a reasonable level of comfort and security is sought and although the explorer, for the most part, is able to escape the environmental bubble, some of the values and routines of home life are retained. For example, accommodation used by fellow travellers may be preferred and many explorers travel secure in the knowledge that they have their return ticket home.

d) The drifter: At the opposite extreme from the organised mass tourist, the drifter attempts to merge into local communities, living and working with local people. The desire for strangerhood is maximised; the drifter has no fixed itinerary and becomes immersed in local culture and customs. Tourism and tourists are considered to be phoney and so all contact with the tourism system is avoided. Escape from the environmental bubble is almost complete, contact with the familiar is minimal and the sense of novelty is at its highest.

Cohen (1972: 68) categorises the first two types of tourist, the organised and the individual mass tourist, as 'institutionalised' tourists. That is, their tourism experience is planned, controlled and provided by the mass tourism industry. In order to serve their large number of customers as rapidly and efficiently as possible, each part of the tour or holiday is planned, packaged and predictable; novelty for the customer is, in many instances, a mass-produced and inauthentic version of local culture (see Chapter 9). The inherent safety or familiarity of the package holiday is a significant attraction to the institutionalised tourist. Conversely, drifters and explorers are 'noninstitutionalised' (Cohen, 1972: 169) tourists, requiring little contact with the tourism establishment. As Cohen argues, drifters and explorers often act as pathfinders for the mass tourism industry; destinations 'discovered' by or popular amongst explorers and drifters often become commercialised and open up to the mass tourism market. For example, Goa and Kovalam were once well-known haunts of travellers in India; both are now directly served by charter flights from Europe and are popular winter-sun package destinations.

One problem with Cohen's typology is that the institutionalised/noninstitutionalised forms of tourism are not entirely distinct; whilst the traditional package-type institutionalised holiday remains as popular as ever, the concept of noninstitutionalised travel has become ever more tenuous. For example, the increasingly large number of people who travel 'independently' – backpackers, explorers, overland travellers – tend to rely on the tourism industry (albeit, not the mass package sector) as much as any other tourist. They use specialist guide books, such as Lonely Planet or Rough Guide books, which refer them to destinations, accommodation, restaurants, transport routes, budget flight agencies and so on that are frequented by other travellers. They often follow popular trails and, in many countries, a local tourism industry has emerged to serve the particular needs of independent travellers. Moreover, it has been found that solo travellers are rarely solitary travellers; that is, they often seek out company of other travellers (Mehmetoglu, 2003). In the extreme, the independent traveller's needs are provided for by specialist operators running overland trips for anything up to six months' duration – adventure travel, certainly, but as institutionalised as the two-week summer package. In short, although it can be argued that explorers' 'approach to and preferences for travel do differ from traditional mainstream tourism' (Loker-Murphy & Pearce, 1995: 841), independent travel has, in the context of the tourist's relationship with the tourism industry, become as institutionalised as mass tourism.

Similarly, it is unclear where the contemporary 'independent' tourist fits into this typology. As noted in previous chapters, advances in information technology and the rapid growth of budget airlines, both short-haul and, increasingly, long-haul, have enabled significant numbers of tourists to avoid using travel agencies or tour operators to book and experience their holidays. In Cohen's terminology, therefore, they are in a sense 'explorers'. However, many if not all such 'independent' tourists visit and stay in places they are familiar with or simply construct their own 'package' holiday (so-called dynamic packaging), frequently sharing their holiday with people who have booked through a tour operator. In other words, Cohen's rather simplistic mass/independent and institutionalised/noninstitutionalised dichotomy no longer reflects the breadth, variety and sophistication of the travel industry nor, indeed, the maturation of tourism as a social activity.

It is also debatable whether or not the drifter is a feasible categorisation at all. As the world gets smaller and more homogeneous it becomes less likely that any individual can fully escape the home environment; as the 'global village' emerges so too does a global environmental bubble.

Another criticism is that this categorisation is based on observable tourist behaviour but gives no indication of the reason for that behaviour. Thus, an individual might prefer to be an explorer but, constrained perhaps by financial, work or family commitments, a form of organised mass tourism may be chosen in order to optimise the benefits at a given time. Nor does this typology allow for variable tourist behaviour over

PLATE 4.1 Mass, all-inclusive tourism resort, Turkey
Source: Photo by Richard Sharpley

time; the implication is 'once a mass tourist, always a mass tourist', whereas tourists frequently take different types of holiday from one year to the next or even within a year.

To return to the example of the independent traveller/explorer, a number of researchers have addressed the roles, attitudes and behaviour of backpackers (for example, Cohen, 1973; Loker-Murphy & Pearce, 1995; Moshin & Ryan, 2003; Noy, 2004; Riley, 1988; Vogt, 1978; Westerhausen & Macbeth, 2003; and more generally, Hannam & Ateljevic, 2007; Hannam & Diekman, 2011). Almost invariably, backpackers are considered to be youth tourists; young people, often at a particular juncture in their lives, undertaking a trip as a rite of passage. But, as already observed, backpack tourism is popular amongst adults of all ages and to assign particular typologies to particular social groups is to overlook the role of the individual in making choices.

Tourist types, tourist numbers

A similar typology to Cohen's is suggested by Smith (1989a). It is again based upon the behaviour of tourists, but Smith also links types of tourists to their numbers with implications about their impacts on the host environment.

a) Explorers: There is a very limited number of explorers, constrained by the ever-diminishing supply of areas to be explored. They are more akin to anthropologists than tourists and fully accept local lifestyles and culture.

b) Élite tourists: Élite tourists, rarely seen, usually include individuals who have been 'almost everywhere' (Smith, 1989a: 12). They participate in unusual activities and adapt fully to local ways but are, nevertheless, on a pre-arranged and, most likely, expensive tour.

c) Off-beat tourists: Equivalent to Cohen's explorer, off-beat tourists are uncommon but seen. They try to avoid other tourists and adapt well to local norms, staying in local accommodation and using local services.

d) Unusual tourists: Tourists who occasionally break away from an organised tour in order to experience some local culture are relatively few in number. They will adapt to local norms for a time but are happier within their own environmental bubble.

e) Incipient mass tourists: Incipient mass tourists represent a steady flow of visitors to a destination that has a reasonably established, but not dominant, tourism industry. The incipient mass tourist will tend to seek out Western style amenities.

f) Mass tourists: There is a continuous influx of large numbers of mass tourists to a destination or resort and they expect Western amenities.

g) Charter tourists: Charter tourists arrive by the planeload in massive numbers. They demand Western style food and accommodation and, in the extreme, the actual destination may be of little importance to them as long as they enjoy their holiday.

Based as it is on tourist behaviour, similar problems emerge with this typology of tourists as with Cohen's. There is also little distinction sometimes between the different categories of tourists; the difference between a mass tourist and a charter tourist is not always clear. Other proposed typologies of tourists also suffer from the same limitations. Cohen (1974: 534) suggests that different types of tourist are distinguishable by what he terms the 'dimensions of the tourist role'. Factors such as permanency, voluntariness, distance and purpose of trip, and recurrence determine whether or not an individual is a tourist and, if so, what type of tourist. Pearce (1982) reviews a number of attempts to formulate tourist typologies and proposes fifteen different types of tourist based upon five role-related behaviour patterns. For example, a jet-setter is identifiable by a luxury lifestyle, a concern with social status, a search for sensual pleasures, interaction with similar people, and frequenting famous places.

Typologies of tourists which rely upon observations of the behaviour and roles of tourists indicate the enormous diversity of activities that are included under the broad heading of tourism. They frequently reveal more about the researcher and the research methods used than about the tourists themselves (Lowyck *et al.*, 1992: 13). However, one attempt to overcome this focuses on the way in which different groups of tourists experience a particular destination (Wickens, 2002). Based on interviews with tourists in Chalkidiki, Greece, five different types of tourist were identified on the basis of their choice of holiday, the activities they participated in and their attitudes to the local community, as follows:

a) *The Cultural Heritage*: a predominant interest in local culture and heritage, or 'Greek life'.

b) *The Raver*: those who emphasised possibilities for hedonistic or sensual pleasures.

c) *The Shirley Valentine*: those (single women) seeking a romantic experience.

d) *The Heliolatrous*: a desire to simply enjoy one or two weeks of sunshine (sunlusters).

e) *The Lord Byron*: those who return to the same resort as an annual ritual.

Similarly, Ryan and Sterling (2001) identified five types of tourist based on observed behaviour amongst visitors to a national park (day visitors; hedonists; generalists; four-wheel drive enthusiasts; and, information seekers) whilst McMinn and Cater's (1998) study of tourists in Belize identified three types of tourist in relation to their environmental behaviour. Other typologies have also been proposed, such as McKercher and du Cros' (2003) cultural tourism typology which segments cultural tourists into five types (serendipitous cultural tourist, incidental cultural tourist, casual cultural tourist, sightseeing cultural tourist and purposeful cultural tourist) whilst Vong (2016) similarly segments cultural and non-cultural tourists within the specific context of casinos in Macau. Alternatively, Zalatan (2004) has developed an 'ex-ante' typology, identifying five categories of tourist (the social tourist, the conventional tourist, the marketing tourist, the planning tourist and the impulsive tourist), in so doing beginning to bridge the gap between typologies as observed behaviour and as drivers (and hence predictors) of demand (see Chapter 5).

Generally, however, typologies tend to be static, not allowing for variations in an individual tourist's behaviour, and view tourists in isolation from broader sociological factors which may determine and explain variations in tourist roles. Nevertheless, attempts to link tourist categories with the tourism experience go some way towards overcoming these limitations of tourist typologies.

Tourists' experiences

Building upon his earlier work in distinguishing between different types of tourist, Cohen addressed some of the inherent weaknesses of his typology in his 'phenomenology of tourist experiences' (Cohen, 1979b). The primary criticism of his initial attempt is that it is overly simplistic to assume that tourists can be categorised along a continuum ranging from, at one end, tourists as mass consumers accepting the superficial, inauthentic product of tour operators (as proposed by Boorstin, 1964) to, at the other end, tourists as modern pilgrims on a voyage of exploration and self-discovery (MacCannell, 1989). This continuum adopts a structural approach inasmuch as each category reflects, or results from, the influence of the tourism generating society. Recognising that tourism is a multi-dimensional phenomenon, Cohen proposes that a micro approach is equally valid in developing an understanding of different tourist types and roles, concentrating not on observed behaviour but on different desired tourist experiences.

Again, the theoretical foundation of this typology is the familiarity-strangerhood continuum, although Cohen is now concerned with the extent to which the tourist enjoys a sense of belonging or, conversely, feels like a stranger in the home environment. Thus, the starting point is to ascertain where the 'spiritual centre' of the individual tourist is located, for different individuals identify with and accept to a greater or lesser extent their home culture and society. At one extreme, the 'centre' is located entirely within the home society and the individual finds no meaning in any other societies and cultures. Implicitly, all aspects of the tourist's home environment and life is satisfying and fulfilling and, therefore, as a tourist, the individual is not concerned with experiencing and learning about other peoples and cultures. At the other extreme lies the modern (in the sociological sense) individual who, alienated from the meaning and values of home society, locates his or her 'centre' elsewhere. In other words, the individual suffers 'placelessness' and believes that a sense of belonging can only be found by travelling elsewhere, to what sociologists term 'The Other'. Thus, in this case, the tourist seeks reality and meaning, or authentic experiences, through tourism (the notion of authenticity in tourism experiences is considered in detail in Chapter 9). Between and including these two points, Cohen identifies five categories of tourist experience:

a) Recreational: The tourist whose centre is located in the home society seeks recreational experiences and has little or no interest in learning about or experiencing the society and culture in which the recreational experience is taking place.

b) Diversionary: The diversionary tourist is an intermediate category. Although alienated to an extent from his or her own society, the individual does not seek authentic experiences elsewhere. In a sense, the purpose of a holiday or trip is to temporarily forget about home.

c) Experiential: The experiential tourist is the modern, alienated individual who seeks authentic experiences elsewhere. Although seeking to experience alternative cultures and societies, the experiential tourist neither identifies with them nor rejects his or her own society. The trip thus compensates for the inauthenticity of home life to which the tourist inevitably returns.

d) Experimental: The experimental tourist is seeking to relocate his or her 'centre', but lies midway between the 'centre' at home and an identified 'centre' elsewhere. Authenticity of experience is essential, but the experimental tourist does not become totally immersed in any one culture.

e) Existential: The existential tourist is the opposite extreme to the recreational tourist. Alienated from the home society, the 'centre' is firmly located elsewhere. The tourist becomes fully immersed in the local, foreign culture and society, finding meaning and belonging in the new chosen 'centre'.

Actual types of tourist may be identified with any one of these five categories. For example, the mass tourist on a two-week beach holiday or a skiing trip closely resembles the recreational tourist whilst a cultural tourist on a tour of, say, the Far East, may be categorised as an experiential tourist. Whilst adding an extra dimension to the behavioural typologies, however, this typology still does not allow for the different needs or requirements of an individual tourist. Nor is it based on any empirical research. It is a theoretical categorisation within which different tourists may be located but, as with other typologies, it considers tourists *per se* rather than in their broader social context.

Psychocentrics and allocentrics

One of the better known and widely cited attempts to link personality traits to tourist types and roles is Stanley Plog's tourist typology (Plog, 1977). Researching the reasons why people who, even though they could well afford it, did not fly, Plog identified two opposing character types at each end of a continuum. Psychocentrics are those who are inward looking, who concentrate on small problems and tend to be less adventurous. The corollary in tourism is the mass tourist looking for the familiar. The psychocentric tourist, therefore, frequents popular, mass tourist resorts either at home or abroad and feels more comfortable surrounded by other tourists. Allocentrics, conversely, are adventurous and are prepared to take risks, as with Cohen's explorer and drifter. The allocentric tourist, therefore, prefers unusual, exotic destinations and enjoys the freedom of relatively autonomous travel. In between the two extremes lie the categories of near-psychocentric, mid-centric and near-allocentric.

Unlike other tourist typologies, Plog goes on to link different types of tourist with different destinations which they are most likely to visit. He suggests that (American) psychocentrics go to resorts such as Coney Island, near New York, whereas allocentrics are to be found travelling in Africa. Mid-centrics, the most numerous category, take their holidays in places such as Europe or Hawaii, destinations which offer the experience of a new, yet sufficiently similar, culture. Similarly, the destination choices of tourists of other nationalities could also be predicted according to this model.

One problem with attempting to link tourist types with destinations in this way is that it is a static model. On the one hand, destinations change and develop over time; as a resort is discovered and attracts growing numbers of visitors it will evolve from an allocentric to a psychocentric destination. On the other hand, the parameters of each category of tourist may also change or become vague. For example, as long-haul charter flights become more available and more exotic destinations are publicised and packaged, psychocentrics might be found travelling to destinations which, according to Plog's model, would normally attract allocentrics. Moreover, as individual tourists become more experienced or progress up what is referred to the 'travel career ladder' (Pearce, 1992), they may become less risk-averse or more allocentric. Thus, although many authors refer to Plog's typology, there is some debate as to its applicability in practice. Indeed, Smith (1990) tested the model against a number of different countries and found that the results did not support Plog's contention that destination choice could be predicted according to personality types. Hence, travel destination choice may be better considered from the perspective of risk (Law, 2006; Sönmez & Graefe, 1998).

As noted above, a number of other attempts have been made to create typologies of tourists (see Lowyck *et al.*, 1992). Little is to be gained from a consideration of them all but, generally, they may be sub-divided into two distinct groups. Firstly, there are those typologies which concentrate on the tourists themselves, their behaviour and their experience (for example, mass tourists, independent travellers, vacationers, cultural tourists, and so on). The great majority of typologies fall within this category. Secondly, there are typologies which are based upon the lifestyle of tourists, such as Dalen's (1989, cited in Lowyck *et al.*, 1992). Dalen applies a four-segment categorisation of lifestyle to tourism and suggests that, for example, the traditional materialist looks for low prices and safe products and, therefore, purchases the mass, package tourism product.

Neither approach is entirely satisfactory in explaining and predicting tourist behaviour. Typologies that concentrate on the tourist *per se* are, generally, descriptive, static and theoretical whilst lifestyle categorisations are often developed in isolation from the tourism system. Some combination might be desirable but, as Lowyck *et al.* (1992: 26) point out, 'studies in which tourism consumer behaviour is linked to general life style variables are generally lacking'. From a sociological point of view, a typology of tourists should be based upon both a micro analysis of tourists themselves and a macro, structural approach which locates actual tourist behaviour and experience within a broader social context. This issue is discussed shortly but, firstly, it necessary to consider what may be described as socially determined tourist typologies.

Socially determined typologies

When a structural perspective is applied to the analysis of tourist typologies it becomes evident that types or categories of tourist have emerged which have more to do with the values of society as a whole than with the behaviour or lifestyle of individual tourists. In other words, certain types of tourists have been given labels that reflect broader, societal attitudes towards tourism and tourists rather than being based on any empirical research of individual tourists. In particular, the term 'mass tourist' is a general, overused and somewhat derogatory categorisation of tourists that bears as much relation to the widespread and continuing concern for the so-called impacts of mass tourism on host societies and environments (Wall & Mathieson, 2006) as it does to the traditional, Boorstin-type attitude towards the tourists themselves. Mass tourism is not a single, specific activity but a phenomenon that encompasses a huge variety of products, demands, destinations, tourists and so on. Clarification is required of what is meant or understood by mass tourism and, hence, the mass tourist label.

What is mass tourism?

Since the 1960s the criticism surrounding mass tourism has increasingly shifted away from the tourists themselves onto the perceived negative impacts of mass tourism around the world. A number of well-known books published during the 1970s (Young, 1973; Turner & Ash, 1975; de Kadt, 1979; Rosenow & Pulsipher, 1979) all point to mass tourism's potentially destructive impact on societies, cultures and environments whilst, during the 1980s, the adverse publicity surrounding some Mediterranean destinations added to the negative attitudes towards mass tourism (and, by association, mass tourists). Moreover, that criticism continues to the present day (Hickman, 2007) although not only do some commentators defend mass tourism (Aramberri, 2010; 2017; Butcher, 2002) but, more recently, the debates have been located within a more balanced understanding of the phenomenon of mass tourism (Harrison & Sharpley, 2017a).

Generally, therefore, mass tourism is seen to have evolved from what Crick (1989: 307) describes as the 'degenerate offspring' of early travel into what some see as an internationally destructive force:

> The tourism industry is in crisis . . . a crisis of mass tourism; for it is mass tourism that has brought social, cultural, economic and environmental havoc in its wake, and it is mass tourism practices that must be radically changed to bring in the new.
>
> (Poon, 1993: 3)

This criticism is indicative of a widespread condemnation of mass tourism which is founded upon a subjective, socially constructed view of mass tourism. Just as mass tourists have come to be seen collectively as what may be described as the lowest common denominator of tourism, so too has the phenomenon of mass tourism itself achieved a notoriety based on generalisations and misconceptions rather than a balanced consideration of the situation. There are a number of different ways of defining mass tourism which provide a more objective basis for analysis.

Mass tourism

Mass tourism is a social, economic, political and geographic phenomenon, commonly used as a means of describing the movement of large numbers of people, usually on standardised, inclusive tours, for the purpose of holiday taking. This movement of people is the manifestation of the fundamental nature of mass tourism, namely, the mass purchasing and consumption of a product. In turn, the product has evolved through technological advance, economies of scale and the combination of a variety of services into a single package.

It is both a tangible and intangible product; the purchase of transport, accommodation and so on is combined with the anticipated benefits of the holiday but, nevertheless, mass tourism is a distinctive type of tourism product that is 'manufactured', marketed and sold. Moreover, according to Shaw and Williams (2002), the consumption of mass tourism is highly spatially polarised, with large numbers of tourists, frequently segmented by nationality, concentrated in a relatively small number of areas. The tourism products in these destination areas are themselves little differentiated, implying a high degree of substitutability between destinations. As a result, their main point of competition is usually price (Shaw & Williams 2002).

A more detailed and nuanced understanding of mass tourism is provided by Harrison and Sharpley (2017b: 7) who identify 11 characteristics that define the phenomenon:

1 There is a regular and systematic movement, involving many industries, of large numbers of people away from their normal places of residence, primarily for holiday purposes.

2 Tourist numbers at destinations are concentrated and seasonal.

3 The major stakeholders in mass tourism – governments and providers of transport, accommodation and attractions – operate in order to make a profit and may benefit from economies of scale.

4 Travel, accommodation and attractions, designed for large numbers of people, are structured and organised by specialist organisations, often with strong links across national boundaries, and often in packages.

5 Control of key elements of the tourism industry rests outside the destinations, possibly with transnational companies.

6 There is concern about the economic, social, cultural or environmental consequences of tourism, which may include commoditisation and standardisation of production, changing social structures, loss of 'authenticity' and environmental degradation.

7 National and international institutions have emerged to support or oppose tourism and respond to its consequences.

8 Impacts are contingent not only on absolute numbers of tourists, but also on the nature of the destination population, its prior experience of tourism, and cultural and other differences between tourist and destination resident.

9 Interaction between tourist and resident is fleeting and superficial and restricted to commercial contexts involving the provider and recipient of services.

10 Where there are marked economic, cultural or social inequalities between tourist and resident, social interaction might be underpinned by stereotypes and/or power disparities.

11 Distinctions might be made between tourists who focus primarily on 'nature' (admittedly a broad term) and those whose activities occur predominantly within an urban environment and, secondly, between those interested primarily in hedonistic pursuits and others involved in 'higher' or more 'spiritual' activities.

According of these criteria, many forms of tourism including those that might be thought of as 'alternatives' to mass tourism, such as adventure tourism or ecotourism, in fact fall under the umbrella of mass tourism. Nevertheless, continuing the argument, the mass tourist is simply an individual who purchases the mass tourism product, a product supplied by the mass tourism industry. To categorise tourists as mass tourists, or even to sub-categorise them as organised, individual, incipient or charter mass tourists, simply identifies them as individuals who, to a greater or lesser extent, consume a mass tourism product. Assumptions about the character, limitations or needs of the mass tourist thus become irrelevant unless the decision-making process leading up to the purchase of the product is also taken into consideration.

Mass tourism: a social construct

As discussed earlier in this chapter, although the word tourist was originally synonymous with the word traveller, distinctions soon came to be made between the two. By the mid-nineteenth century, with the advent of mass forms of transport, the tourist, as opposed to the traveller, became associated not only with mass travel but also with a particular approach to the travel experience. Thus, the term tourist and, in its twentieth/twenty-first century manifestation, mass tourist, has become a socially constructed label attached to particular types of tourism, forms of tourist behaviour, and primarily tourists who are satisfied with inauthentic, 'pseudo' events experienced from the safety of their environmental bubbles. This derogatory connotation has been compounded in recent years not only by the publicised inappropriate behaviour of a minority of tourists, such as 'lager louts', but also by those who promote 'new' forms of tourism as morally superior to mass tourism (Butcher, 2002), to the extent that the problem of mass tourism is seen by some to be not the number of tourists, nor the type of tourism, but the tourists themselves. The socially defined mass tourist has become, in effect, an individual who is neither able to appreciate the tourism experience nor knows how to behave in an appropriate manner whilst on holiday. In this sense, the term mass tourist is a social construct referring to those who seek out and are satisfied by what is considered by some to be the lowest common denominator of tourism.

Mass tourism: tourism for the masses?

A third way of defining or interpreting mass tourism is that it is tourism that is enjoyed by the masses as opposed to the privileged few. As described in Chapter 2, technological advance, increased levels of leisure time and disposable income, and greater freedom of movement have gradually brought travel, and international travel in particular, within reach of increasing numbers of people around the world, most recently of course within emerging economies such as China. If the increasingly rapid process whereby once exclusive destinations and, indeed, exclusive modes of travel, such as cruising, are becoming assimilated under the umbrella of mass tourism is also taken into consideration, then it becomes evident that, globally, tourism is becoming increasingly democratised. Simply put, all tourists are part of the mass democratisation of tourism and, hence, are mass tourists. The distinction must then be made not between mass tourists and other tourists, but between tourists and non-tourists, demanding a sociological explanation of why individuals choose, or are able or unable, to be tourists.

Although it is logical and justifiable to consider all tourism as mass tourism, particularly when it is considered that most, if not all, niche tourism products depend upon and are, essentially, part of the mass tourism system, it is in the second sense (as a social construct) that the term mass tourism remains most widely used, whether generally or in the more specific context of being the alleged antithesis to more appropriate, sustainable forms of tourism. This is, of course, an extreme and inaccurate view. Being a mass tourist is easy, it is safe and, perhaps most importantly, relatively cheap, a combination that continues to ensure the popularity of mass, package tourism. At the same time, 'people seem to enjoy being mass tourists' (Butler, 1992: 32) and they choose to be so. Categorisations that link mass tourists with recreational experiences, with an inability to escape the environmental bubble and with an implied lack of cultural awareness deny the mass tourist any individuality and any ability to choose and to make informed decisions.

Thus, typologies which include the mass tourist as a separate category say more about the researcher than the researched. Lumping together all mass tourists as a single, socially defined category is adopting what Emery (1981: 52) calls the 'lemming hypothesis. We do not know why [mass tourists] move, but we know that, at certain times of the year, they all start moving – and we have a fair idea of the destination.' The inevitable conclusion is, again, that a practical and realistic tourist typology should be based in the broader, social context.

PLATE 4.2 Skiers, Les Deux Alpes, France. Winter sports is a mass tourism activity

Source: Photo by Richard Sharpley

The good/responsible tourist

A second, socially determined type of tourist that has emerged from the concern for the negative impacts of mass tourism is the so-called 'good' (Popescu, 2008; Wood & House, 1991) or 'responsible' tourist, the implication being that mass tourism is 'bad' tourism. Indeed, since the early 1990s innumerable publications have exhorted tourists to act more responsibly, to become 'good' tourists, though this has been criticised as the 'moralisation' of tourism (Butcher, 2002). The way forward to more appropriate, less damaging forms of tourism, often referred to generically as alternative (to mass) tourism (see Smith and Eadington, 1992), is seen to be the responsibility of not only the tourism industry as a whole but also of the individual tourist. In other words, it has become increasingly argued that the solution to the undoubted problems caused by tourism lies not only in new approaches to the development, planning and management of tourism, but also in the adoption of more appropriate behaviour on the part of tourists themselves. As Ludwig, Hilborn and Walters (1993: 36) succinctly argue, 'resource problems are not really environmental problems: they are human problems'.

In a sociological sense, therefore, the emphasis must shift from the structural, mass tourism perspective towards the individual, social action approach. The individual tourist responds to the reactions of others (in this case environmentalists, pressure groups and the impacts of other tourists on host environments and cultures) and demands new forms of tourism. The new, responsible tourist seeks quality rather than value, is more adventurous, more flexible, more sensitive to the environment and searches for greater authenticity than the traditional, mass tourist (see Poon, 1993). This form of tourism, positively contributing to the preservation of the local environment and wildlife whilst providing more 'meaningful' experiences to tourists, is often referred to specifically as ecotourism – as an example, tiger hunting with guns has now been replaced by tiger watching from the safe vantage point of an elephant's back – but the notion of responsibility should, according to Goodwin (2011), apply to all forms of tourism and tourists.

In particular, the good/responsible tourist is exhorted to adopt a new code of travel although, interestingly, is not asked to question whether tourism in any form is appropriate in certain destinations (some would argue that the only good tourist is a non-tourist!). For example, the good tourist prepares for the trip by learning in advance about the destination, ensures that s/he uses a tour operator which is aware of and supports environmental programmes in the host country, behaves in an appropriate manner and recognises local customs whilst abroad and, wherever possible, tries to benefit the local economy rather than international tourism businesses. More generally, the UNWTO (n.d.) offers practical guidance on how to be a 'responsible tourist and traveller' (see Figure 4.1). This clearly applies to all forms of tourism and could be thought of more simply as advice on how to respect the local destination and its communities. However, codes of practice such as this tend to overlook some fundamental features of tourism, tourist motivation and the consumption of tourism (see Chapters 5 and 6; also McKercher, 1993; Sharpley, 2012).

In a broad sense, tourism is associated with holidays which, in turn, conjure up visions of rest, relaxation, fun, escape from the regular and the mundane, freedom from

'Travel and tourism should be planned and practised as a means of individual and collective fulfilment . . . everyone has a role to play creating responsible travel and tourism'. To contribute to this:

Be open-minded to other cultures and traditions. Respect cultural diversity and observe local cultural traditions.

Respect human rights.

Help to preserve the natural environment; avoid buying products made from endangered species.

Respect cultural resources and heritage.

Buy local products to support the local economy; only bargain in recognition of a fair wage.

'Learn as much as possible about your destination and take time to understand the customs, norms and traditions'.

Be aware of local laws and adhere to them.

FIGURE 4.1 The responsible tourist
Source: Adapted from UNWTO (n.d.)

work and so on. The good or responsible tourist, conversely, is being asked to work at tourism, to adopt a fundamentally different approach and interpretation of the tourism experience. Additionally, the concept of the good tourist frequently attracts criticism that it is no more than an attempt to attach an explorer/drifter image to certain tourism products and to develop a niche market for 'aware' tourists. This has led to accusations that the overall idea of alternative tourism is no more than a marketing ploy, a 'green mantle' (Wheeller, 1991; 1992a; 1992b) behind which the tourism industry is hiding.

More specifically, the concept of the good, responsible or eco-tourist relies heavily on the assumption that increasing environmental awareness, and the alleged emergence of green consumerism in general, will inevitably result in more appropriate styles of tourism consumption in particular. This is not necessarily the case. Certainly, since the late 1960s, environmental concern has become one of the most widespread social and political issues, and surveys indicate, as Macnaughten and Urry (1998) pointed out some years ago, that public concern in both the US and UK over environmental issues continued to increase during the 1990s. However, since the new millennium, it appears to have become relatively less important compared with other issues (Wray-Lake *et al.*, 2010). Nevertheless, environmental concerns in general appear to have been translated into people's buying habits in particular; for example, it was found that, between 1990 and 1994, the numbers of people who in generally considered themselves to be either 'dark green' (that is 'always or as far as possible buy environmentally friendly products') or 'pale green' (that is 'buy if I see them') consumers both increased slightly, together representing 63 percent of those questioned (Mintel, 1994).

A subsequent survey by the same organisation (Mintel, 2007) found that green consumerism was continuing to become more widespread, although consumers are more likely to buy environmentally friendly products to feel good about themselves rather than for altruistic reasons. Similarly, Cowe and Williams (2000) found that one third of consumers were seriously concerned with ethical issues when shopping. Interestingly, a more recent study suggested that people who are exposed to green products, such as viewing them on a website, may subsequently behave more altruistically than those who actually buy the products, the implication being that the act of purchasing may make people feel they have done their good deed and consequently act less altruistically when presented with other ethical dilemmas (Mazar & Zhong, 2010). In the tourism context, this may imply that the act of buying a responsible holiday may absolve tourists from any sense of responsibility while actually on holiday; 'responsible tourism . . . appeases the guilt of the "thinking tourist" while simultaneously providing the holiday experience they or we want' (Wheeller, 1991: 96).

Nevertheless, research has consistently revealed pro-environmental attitudes on the part of tourists. For example, one study found that 64 percent of UK tourists believe that tourism causes some degree of damage to the environment and that, generally, UK consumers would be willing to pay more for an environmentally appropriate tourism product (Diamantis, 1999). Another survey, by the charity Tearfund (2000), came to similar conclusions: specifically, it found that 59 percent of respondents would be happy

PLATE 4.3 A baby orangutan in Kalimantan, Indonesia: a popular attraction for ecotourists

Source: Photo by Richard Sharpley

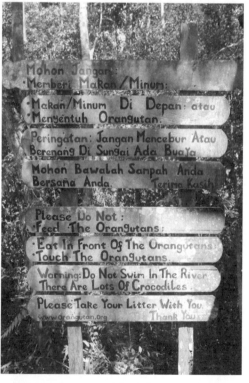

PLATE 4.4 Advice for tourists at orangutan sanctuary, Kalimatna, Indonesia

Source: Photo by Richard Sharpley

to pay more for their holidays if the extra contributed to better local wages, environmental conservation, and so on (see also Goodwin & Francis, 2003). Moreover, it has been claimed that 80 percent of British tourists would be more likely to book holidays with 'responsible' tourism operators (www.responsibletravel.com).

At the same time, the growth in demand for activities or types of holidays collectively referred to as ecotourism would also appear to support the argument that greater numbers of people embrace principles of green consumerism; indeed, ecotourism has long been considered to be the fastest growing sector of international tourism. In the 1990s, for example, Cater (1993), observed that the number of arrivals to certain destinations virtually doubled over a ten year period, whilst others suggest that participation in ecotourism has increased annually by between 20 to 50 percent since the early 1980s (Hvengaard, 1994; see also Steele, 1995). More recently, it has been suggested that ecotourism now accounts for up to 20 percent of all international tourism arrivals (Fennell, 2007) although others make more conservative estimates.

Importantly, however, there is no evidence to suggest that the increase in popularity of ecotourism is directly related to the emergence of green consumerism or wider environmental awareness (see Sharpley, 2006 for a complete debate over the existence of the 'ecotourist'). In fact, a number of researchers refer to consumer ambivalence in the context of environmentalism. For example, despite the apparently large number of green consumers revealed by various surveys, it has been observed that up to one half of those who claim to embrace green values never transfer these beliefs into their consumer behaviour (Witherspoon, 1994). 'Despite the earlier evidence of high levels of environmental concern . . . the proportion of adults who behave in a consistently environmentally friendly consumerist fashion is very low. Fewer than one percent of consumers behave in a consistently environmentally-friendly way' (Witherspoon, 1994: 125). Moreover, studies into the motivation of ecotourists show that the majority seek wilderness scenery, undisturbed nature and the activities that such locations offer as the prime reasons for participating in ecotourism. In other words, it is the pull of particular destinations or holidays (and the anticipated enjoyment of such holidays) that determines participation rather than the influence of environmental values over the consumption of tourism in general. In fact, research into the behaviour of ecotourists in Belize demonstrates that many are motivated by factors other than environmental concern (Duffy, 2002). Thus, care must be taken in assuming that greater numbers of people are becoming or have the potential to be new, good tourists (see Sharpley, 2012).

The volunteer tourist

One form of tourism (or tourist) that has become increasingly prevalent over the last two decades is so-called volunteer tourism. This is not to say that travel for the specific purpose of engaging in voluntary activities is a recent phenomenon. According to Gillette (1999), for example, the first modern international voluntary movement, Service Civil International, was founded in France in the early 1920s whilst both the US Peace Corps and the Voluntary Service (VSO) organisation in the UK had been established by the early 1960s, the latter having placed almost 50,000 volunteers on international development projects over the ensuing years. However, volunteer tourism as a niche tourism market has not only become the focus of academic attention following the publication of Wearing's (2001) text, *Volunteer Tourism: Experiences that Make a Difference*, but it has also become an increasingly popular form of tourism, in particular in the context of gap year tourism, as numerous organisations have been established to meet growing demand.

And it is in this context that volunteer tourism can be considered a socially determined form of tourism and, perhaps, a specific manifestation of good/responsible tourism as discussed in the preceding section. In other words, when prefixed with 'volunteer', tourism is, perceptually at least, transformed from an essentially egocentric or selfish activity (that is, of benefit principally to the tourist) to one which is more altruistic, not only bringing alleged benefits to host communities but also enhancing the volunteer tourists' sense of global citizenship (Butcher & Smith, 2010).

The extent to which these benefits accrue to both the destination and the tourists remain the subject of intense debate, however. Whilst there undoubtedly exist so-called 'deep' volunteer tourists (Callanan & Thomas, 2005: 197), or those with strong altruistic motives, others continue to debate the extent to which volunteer tourists are altruistic 'global citizens' (Lyons *et al.*, 2012). More generally, as an increasingly popular and potentially valuable sector of the international tourism market, volunteer tourism is vulnerable to over-commercialisation with the profit motive sometimes, but not always, undermining the more positive social and environmental credentials of volunteering projects (Tomazos & Cooper, 2012). Certainly, the negative or unintended consequences of volunteer tourism have been long recognised (Guttentag, 2009; Palacios, 2010), including experiences that reinforce rather than challenge cultural stereotyping (Raymond & Hall, 2008; Simpson, 2004) or serve to emphasise inequality (Sin, 2010). Indeed, though a socially 'acceptable' form of tourism, volunteer tourism is seen by many as an oxymoron, calling into question its 'responsible' credentials.

The post-tourist

One feature that unites all the typologies of tourists is that they propose separate and identifiable tourist roles but without making an allowance for tourists adopting either a combination of roles at any one time or a variety of roles over time. For example, an individual may be categorised as a mass tourist, an explorer or a special-interest tourist. Equally, a tourist may be concerned with a safe, recreational experience within the constraints of the environmental bubble or, at the opposite extreme, seeking an 'existential' experience. There is, however, no room in the typologies for an individual to adopt different tourist characteristics or to seek different experiences according to specific needs and constraints whereas, in reality, the distinctions between different categories are likely to be much more blurred. A tourist might be on a pre-paid, packaged tour but, as Rojek (1993: 177) explains, 'there is always room for tourist bypassings and deviations from the tourist script'.

In short, most tourist typologies are static in both time and breadth. Most typologies are also limited by the proposed links between tourist behaviour and the assumed character of tourists. The explorer-wanderlust-allocentric tourist is typecast as being bold, adventurous, independent and empathetic to new cultures and societies, whereas the mass, institutionalised tourist is unadventurous, indecisive, easily pleased by staged, inauthentic events and has little or no interest in expanding his or her cultural horizons beyond the limits of the environmental bubble. Such categorisations, as has already been pointed out, have been developed without taking the broader social context into account but, especially in the case of the mass tourist, they also deny tourists the ability to make choices.

In direct contrast, it may be argued that tourism and tourists have come of age. In other words, the distinction between the traveller and the tourist is, in fact, no more than a manifestation of the first two stages in the evolution of travel and we have now reached the third stage, the era of the 'post-tourist' (Feifer, 1985; Urry, 1988; 1990a: 100). The post-tourist lives in an age of mass communication and rapid advances in information technology; most tourist sights and destinations can be seen, if not actually experienced, on video and television in the comfort of the tourist's own living room. The post-tourist is able, therefore, to make informed decisions and delights in the choice available.

More importantly, the post-tourist recognises and understands the fundamental change that has occurred in the nature of tourism. Armed with a mass of information and images, the post-tourist knows that it is no longer possible to experience authenticity because nothing is new. The pseudo-event or the cheap souvenir is accepted for what it is. Tourism has become a kind of game, 'or rather a whole series of games with multiple texts and no single, authentic tourist experience' (Urry, 1990a: 100) and the post-tourist understands the role he or she plays in that game. The post-tourist chooses sometimes to be a mass tourist, sometimes an independent traveller and sometimes not to be a tourist at all, and accepts the conditions and constraints of each role. For example, the organised, packaged tour is purchased for what it offers – not an authentic cultural experience but the opportunity to collect a set of pre-determined images and sights, saved for all time, perhaps, as photographs. Above all, the post-tourist is aware of being a tourist, of being an outsider, 'not a time traveller when he [sic] goes somewhere historic; not an instant noble savage when he stays on a tropical beach; not an invisible observer when he visits a native compound' (Feifer, 1985: 271).

For the post-tourist, then, the traveller/tourist dichotomy is irrelevant. The traveller has matured and evolved into an individual who experiences and enjoys all kinds of tourism, who takes each at face value and who is in control at all times. In effect, the post-tourist renders tourist typologies meaningless.

Tourist typologies: a broader approach

Throughout this chapter it has been emphasised that a realistic typology of tourists is essential to the explanation, understanding and prediction of tourist behaviour. If this is combined with other factors, such as a consideration of tourist motivation (Chapter 5), a broader foundation for understanding and predicting the demand for tourism is then provided. A number of issues have emerged that point to limitations both in existing tourist typologies and the more general, all-embracing categorisations, such as the 'mass tourist' and the 'good tourist'.

1   Most typologies are static and do not take into account variations in tourist behaviour or experience over time. It is perfectly feasible for an individual to knowingly choose different types of holiday or trip at different times subject to broader constraints or needs. Also, people may mature as tourists as they become more experienced, giving credence to the concept of the post-tourist. They may, in fact, progress through a tourism career (Pearce, 1992; 2005: 50–85), adapting their behaviour in response to changing needs and greater awareness and experience. As Lowyck *et al.* (1992: 28) argue, it must be questioned 'whether it makes sense at all to divide people into different types without taking into account their full life spans'.

2   Most typologies are isolated from the wider social context of the tourist. As a simple example, the most convenient and affordable holiday for a young family might well be of the package variety, yet the parents may have travelled extensively as explorers or independent travellers before being constrained by financial, job or family restraints. Thus, being a mass tourist does not necessarily imply an inability to escape the environmental bubble or, in terms of Cohen's experiential typology, having one's 'spiritual centre' firmly embedded in one's home culture and society.

3   Each typology, in particular those concerned with tourist roles or behaviour, employs a variety of names to describe a lesser or greater number of categories, from Gray's two-category to Pearce's 15-category typology. The important point is that, in the absence of universally accepted parameters and names for tourist categories, researchers create descriptions of different types of tourists according to their own sphere of interest. Thus, some typologies, though looking different, say the same thing.

4   Typologies of tourists tend to be etic, a word used by sociologists to describe a study that is undertaken from the researcher's point of view rather than centring on the object of the research (emic). In other words, the typologies depend more on what the researcher puts into it rather than on unbiased, empirical findings. For example, longer-term independent travellers may be described as adventurous, individual and culturally aware on the one hand, or as lazy, irresponsible 'drop-outs' on the other hand, depending on the experience and opinion of the researcher.

Overall, typologies of tourists tend to be descriptive and, although of interest in terms of highlighting the variety of tourist types and experience, fail to be of direct relevance to a better understanding of the demand for tourism. By concentrating on the tourists *per se* rather than locating tourist categories within the broader social context of the tourists' home environment, many important, if not dominant, factors which determine different types of tourists are excluded from the equation. A tourist typology should not be based upon a one-dimensional, linear progression of observed (or imagined) behaviour or experience, such as the mass tourist to individual drifter continuum, but upon a multi-dimensional matrix which incorporates tourist roles with other factors which influence tourist types. These other factors fall under two broad headings:

Demographic and socio-economic factors

Tourism is not a single product. It encompasses a whole host of different products which are designed, packaged and marketed by the tourism industry to appeal to different potential tourists or, in marketing terms, different market segments (see Middleton *et al.*, 2009). Simply put, the tourism industry recognises that different types of tourism suit different people according to a variety of demographic and socio-economic factors. Logically, each of these factors should be taken into account in the formulation of a tourist typology. There are four principal variables to be considered:

a) Age: An individual's age will determine, to a great extent, the type of tourism that he or she participates in (Pearce, 2005: 28–32). A younger person is more likely to be attracted to independent travel or, perhaps, to the '18–30' style of beach package holiday, whereas older tourists may be less inclined to subject themselves to the relative uncertainty or possible discomfort of independent travel. Equally, an older person may, in a touristic sense, be more experienced and demand more specialised forms of tourism.

b) Life cycle: Life-cycle characteristics play a dominant role in the determination of tourist types. For example, a young, single person has greater freedom to choose different types of holidays (within the constraints of availability of free time, financial resources and psychographic considerations) than, say, a family with young children (Thornton, et al., 1997). At the other end of the scale, 'empty nesters' or people who have retired early have fewer family responsibilities and are able to be more flexible in the timing and duration of trips. They are also likely to have more disposable income.

c) Gender/roles: The gender of tourists may well influence their holiday decisions, irrespective of other factors (Swain & Momsen, 2002). For example, some women may decide to not travel independently or to avoid certain countries for safety reasons. Gender is also of importance within the context of the family because although the rigid roles which normally provide the base of family life become blurred (Clarke & Critcher, 1985: 172), under certain conditions those roles may become amplified.

d) Income/employment: Income and occupation or, more generally, socio-economic grouping, are, perhaps, the most influential factors in determining tourist types. Generally, research has shown tourism to be highly price elastic (for example, see Edwards, 1987; Crouch, 1992); that is, small increases in the cost of a holiday are very likely to result in tourists choosing cheaper destinations. More specifically, those employed in professional or managerial positions benefit from higher levels of income and longer holidays than, say, skilled manual workers and have a much wider choice of what type of holiday to take. The latter group may also be more restricted with respect to the timing of holidays. Thus, it is not surprising that, of the 41 percent of the British population who did not take a holiday in 1992, 45 percent belonged to the D and E (unskilled manual workers, unemployed and pensioners) social group (ETB, 1993). At the same time, the D and E groups (32 percent of the British adult population) accounted for just 13 percent of all holidays taken overseas whilst social groups A and B (professional/managerial; 17 percent of the population) accounted for 30 percent. More recent figures point to a similar trend; research found that, in 2014, 72 percent of the A, B and C1 groups intended to take a holiday, but only 58 percent of the C2, D and E groups intended likewise (BRDC, 2014). The proportion of the population not taking holidays has remained virtually unchanged since the early 1990s; the growth in international travel from the UK has been largely accounted for by people (who can afford it) taking multiple overseas trips each year.

Some of these factors are inter-related and also point to other determinants of tourist behaviour (Pearce, 2005: 40–41). For example, there is an obvious link between age and life-cycle characteristics whilst socio-economic grouping may be related to other variables, such as the level and type of education, which in turn can influence the type of tourism that an individual participates in. Essentially, a clearer and more practical tourist typology may be created by combining the more traditional, role-based approach with the techniques of market segmentation. For example, in the case of independent travellers, the characteristics of a spirit of adventure, an interest in new cultures and so on certainly apply, but they are also more likely to be younger, single and of student status (that is with more time but less disposable income).

Structural social factors

Most tourist typologies adopt a micro perspective. They concentrate on the tourist as an individual and, even when demographic and socio-economic factors are taken into account, the emphasis is placed firmly on the ability of individuals to decide what type of tourist they wish to be. In other words, different types of tourist are taken, in most cases, to be self-determined. The one exception is the 'mass tourist', the implication of most typologies being that people become mass tourists more by default than by design.

It is true that most people are able to choose, within the constraints of time, money, family commitments and so on, what type of tourists they wish to be. An equally valid approach is to consider the extent to which tourist types are structurally determined. The manner in which certain tourist labels, such as the 'mass tourist' and the 'good tourist', are socially constructed has already been considered but a holistic approach reveals that, in some situations, society plays the dominant role in the determination of tourist types.

Non-tourists

Non-tourists, or people who, for whatever reason, do not participate in tourism, are a valid and identifiable category of tourist but not one that is normally included in tourist typologies. They also comprise a category of 'tourist' that remains significantly under-researched, particularly those who make a positive decision not to be tourists, even though they are able to do so. In Britain, the proportion of people who do not take a holiday (a holiday being defined as a stay of four or more nights away from home) remained at around 40 percent of the population for a number of years, despite increasing levels of disposable income and paid holidays – although recent studies suggest that this proportion may have fallen to around 25 percent (BRDC, 2014). Some of these will be people who have made conscious decisions not to be tourists, whilst others may be restricted by factors such as illness or family constraints. For many people, however, their status as non-tourists has been determined by society inasmuch as their labour has been deemed as excess to requirements. In a sense, they suffer, in contemporary parlance, from 'social exclusion', if the ability to take a holiday is seen as a social right.

In other words, for the unemployed the decision to be or not to be a tourist is beyond the control of the individual. The loss of paid employment and an income other than state benefits effectively removes an individual's access to most forms of tourism, especially overseas tourism. The unemployed, non-tourist is, therefore, a manifestation of the conflict theory of society.

Capitalist tourism

As discussed in Chapter 1, a structural-conflict perspective on tourism reveals that the tourism industry is, in effect, a microcosm of capitalist society. The tourism industry, though diverse, fragmented and comprising a large number of private operators, remains dominated by a few powerful, multinational corporations (MNCs). These organisations have concentrated the ownership of different sectors of the tourism system, such as transport, accommodation, entertainment and travel agencies, to the extent that it is possible for one company to own and control all the components of a package holiday. The latter half of the 1990s witnessed a significant degree of vertical and horizontal integration within the British tourism industry, a pattern that has continued on the global stage. As a result, tour operators or intermediaries in particular enjoy a dominant position within the tourism production system, possessing the ability to control tourist flows through marketing and the range of products they produce and promote (see Britton, 1991). This dominance has, to a certain extent, been challenged by the advent of the Internet and the increase in online independent booking of travel services, although this has resulted more in a shift of power within the industry (from tour operators to web-based organisations/intermediaries) than from the producer to the consumer. Therefore, the extent to which tourists as consumers of tourism products are able to influence the kinds of products that are on offer and, hence, the types of tourist they can choose to be, remains largely in the hands of the larger tourism organisations.

In other words, the pluralist approach (power being shared by a multiplicity of groups or organisations), which implies that tourism suppliers follow market trends and consumer demand, 'greatly underestimates the power of business to persuade consumers, through advertising in particular, to make the right choices' (Clarke & Critcher, 1985: 103 and generally for a neo-Marxist perspective on leisure). Tourists can choose to purchase or not to purchase different tourism products, but they have little control over what is on offer. On the other hand, the tourism industry and, in particular, MNCs produce a range of products to appeal to a variety of tourists, products which recognise and, perhaps, reinforce social characteristics and divisions such as age, gender and class. Thus, despite the emergence of post-Fordist production methods in response to more diverse consumer demands, economies of scale have been replaced by economies of scope which allow new products to be introduced, not to satisfy customer needs but to increase diversity, market share and, ultimately, profit. For example, a number of tour operators now offer trips or holidays that are designed to attract the 'good' or eco-tourist, more likely to be a younger, relatively affluent, better educated and well-travelled person looking for authentic yet environmentally friendly holidays. Arguably, such trips play on the environmental conscience of the individual and, whilst developing an image of 'good' tourism, are little more than a niche within the mass tourism market; ironically, the 'good' tourist becomes a mass tourist.

To develop a tourist typology that incorporates a multi-dimensional approach is, perhaps, an impossible task. But, given the limitations of existing typologies, a broader foundation that locates tourists in a social context provides a clearer picture and explanation of tourist categories and roles, contributing to a better understanding of the demand for tourism. It also provides the foundation for a more detailed analysis of tourist behaviour, particularly within the tourism demand process, in the chapters following.

Further reading

Harrison, D. and Sharpley, R. (2017b) Introduction: Mass tourism in a small world. In D. Harrison and R. Sharpley (eds), *Mass Tourism in a Small World*. Wallingford: CABI Publishing, pp. 1–14.

> This chapter explores the concept of mass tourism, suggesting that irrespective of 'typology', all tourists are in fact mass tourists inasmuch as all forms of tourism are simply elements of a mass tourism system.

Horner, S. and Swarbrooke, J. (2016) *Consumer Behaviour in Tourism,* 3rd Edition. Abingdon: Routledge.

> A popular introductory text which includes a chapter on tourist typologies (Chapter 7).

Lowyck, E., Van Langenhove, L. and Bollaert, L. (1992) Typologies of tourist roles. In P. Johnson and B. Thomas (eds), *Choice and Demand in Tourism*. London: Mansell Publishing, pp. 13–32.

> Though now dated, this remains the most comprehensive critique of the concept of tourist typologies.

Song, H. and Li, G. (2008) Tourism demand modelling and forecasting: A review of recent research. *Tourism Management*, 29(2): 203–220.

> Tourist typologies are one potential tool for predicting tourism demand patterns. This paper provides a broader context for understanding the influences on tourism demand.

Discussion topics

▶ Given the remarkable growth in scope and scale of tourism over the last four decades, how relevant are early typologies, such as those proposed by Cohen, to understanding contemporary tourist behaviour?

▶ Do tourist typologies have a practical application to the planning and management of tourism, or are they simply of academic interest?

▶ In the era of the 'post-tourist', are tourist typologies irrelevant?

▶ To what extent is tourist behaviour better explained by tangible demographic and lifestyle factors?

5

Tourism and tourist motivation

Introduction

The study of tourist motivation is concerned with the question, why do people travel? Many attempts have been made to answer this question, ranging from theories based in psychological research to more speculative or apocryphal explanations. For example, the desire to travel is still widely seen as resulting from the 'the travel bug' or 'having itchy feet', a supposed medical condition which John Steinbeck described in *Travels with Charley* as a 'disease [that] is incurable' (cited in Pearce, 1982: 48). The actual meaning of the motivation to travel is also open to wide interpretation. For some, tourist motivation results from deep, psychological needs often unrecognised by tourists themselves, whereas others equate motivation with the purpose of a trip or the choice of holiday.

Whichever viewpoint is adopted, motivation represents the how, why, when and where of tourism. In other words, 'the importance of motivation in tourism is quite obvious. It acts as a trigger that sets off all the events in travel' (Parrinello, 1993: 233). It is not surprising, therefore, that many authors and researchers in tourism have concerned themselves with motivation, recognising it as 'one of the most basic and indispensable subjects in tourism studies' (Wahab, 1975: 44). It is also one of the most complex areas of tourism research. In contrast to early travellers who were motivated by basic needs for survival, present-day tourists are motivated by an enormous variety of factors, many of which are rooted in modern society. As Pearce (2005: 51) notes, 'the motivations or underlying reasons for travel are covert in that they reflect an individual's private needs and wants'. Equally, there have been a number of different approaches, based on a variety of disciplines, to the analysis of tourist motivation. This chapter examines tourism motivation from a sociological perspective considering, in particular, the link between the motivation for tourism and modern society.

Motivation and the demand for tourism

Before looking at the different approaches to tourist motivation, two general points deserve consideration. First, it is important to understand the role of motivation within the overall consumer decision-making process. Although, as already noted, it is motivation that 'kick starts' the entire tourism demand process, it is only the first stage in that process. As Pearce (1992: 113) has observed, 'the term tourism demand should not be equated with tourism motivation. Tourism demand is the outcome of tourists' motivation.' In other words, tourists pass through a number of decision-making stages, or what has been described as a vacation sequence (van Raaij & Francken, 1984), the first of which is the motivational stage. This tourism demand process is discussed shortly but, second, we must emphasise that the demand for tourism, the vacation sequence, cannot be viewed in isolation from the socio-cultural setting within which it occurs. That is, there is little doubt that a number of factors, from financial constraints to values and beliefs, directly influence tourism decision making. Many of those factors themselves are influenced by wider, cultural factors; 'consumption choices simply cannot be understood without considering the cultural context in which they are made' (Solomon, 1994: 536). An understanding of the 'consumer culture' of tourism is also fundamental to the study of the demand for tourism, and is the focus of Chapter 6.

The tourism demand process

At a basic level, tourism is a product that is purchased and consumed. Hence, tourists go through a process of 'acquiring and organising information in the direction of a purchase decision and of using and evaluating products and services' (Moutinho, 1987: 5). In other words, unless a trip or a holiday is an impulse purchase, tourists make a choice on the basis of their personal needs and desires and the extent to which they perceive those needs will be satisfied by a particular trip, holiday or destination. That choice will normally be influenced by factors such as the image (Pike, 2002) or known attributes of the destination, the impact of advertising, the distance and mode of travel to the destination (Nicolau & Mas, 2006), previous experience, the advice of family and friends and so on. Additionally, holiday choice is constrained by factors such as family and work commitments, financial considerations and, of course, the range of products supplied by the tourism industry.

Together, these stages that the tourist goes through represent the tourism demand process. This has been conceptualised by a number of authors. For example, Mathieson and Wall (1982) propose that the tourism demand process involves five sequential phases. These can be expressed diagrammatically (see Figure 5.1).

Stage 1	Stage 2	Stage 3	Stage 4	Stage 5
Felt need or travel desire	Information collection and evaluation	Travel decisions	Travel preparations and travel experience	Travel satisfaction evaluation

FIGURE 5.1 Stages of the tourism demand process
Source: Adapted from Mathieson and Wall (1982: 28)

Within this process, the motivation to participate in tourism is manifested in a 'felt need' to travel, and only when the decision has been made to satisfy that need does the individual move on to the subsequent stages in the process. Similarly, Goodall (1991: 65) suggests that the holiday decision process generally involves the five steps of problem identification (whether or not to take a holiday in the first place), the search for information, the evaluation of alternatives, the purchase decision and, finally, feedback, whereby the evaluation of the holiday experience becomes an additional factor in the next decision-making sequence.

Others have developed more complex models which attempt to define diagrammatically the varying factors that influence the final decision. Schmoll (1977), for example, utilises a four-step sequential process from travel desires, through information search and the evaluation of alternatives, to the purchase decision. That final decision is influenced, according to Schmoll, by forces and pressures that emanate from four separate fields, namely: travel stimuli, in the form of trade or personal information and recommendations; personal and social determinants, which shape motivations and expectations; external variables, such as the image of the destination, past travel experiences and the constraints of time and money; and characteristics of destinations. With the exception of personal/social determinants, each field has an influence on each stage of the decision process.

In a similar vein, Gilbert (1991: 79) identifies four elements of the tourism decision process (see also Cooper *et al.*, 2005: 53):

a) *Energisers of demand.* These are the forces, including motivation, which lead the tourist into deciding to take a holiday in the first place.

b) *Filterers of demand.* Demand is constrained by a variety of demographic and socio-economic factors.

c) *Affectors of demand.* The information about a destination and the tourist's image of it will affect the course of action taken.

d) *Roles.* The role of the tourist as a consumer (for example, as a family member) may determine the final choice of holiday.

Inevitably, these models all over-simplify what in practice is a complex, dynamic and multi-dimensional consumption process. The demand for tourism is, generally, neither a 'one-off' event nor a simple, uni-directional circular process whereby previous travel experiences influence the motivation for, and supplement the information in, the next holiday decision-making process. As Pearce (1992) points out, tourism consumption occurs over a lifetime, during which tourists may progress up or climb a travel career ladder as they become more experienced tourists (see also Pearce, 2005: 50–85; Pearce & Caltabiano, 1983). In the process, their attitudes, values, social relationships or lifestyle factors may all change, representing new influences on decision making. There is also a lack of clarity and distinction between the different stages in the decision process whilst there may, potentially, be a reverse flow of influences. For example, it may be an advertisement or a travel brochure (second stage factors) that creates the need or motivation. Moreover, models of tourism decision making imply a logical and rational process, simplifying a complex process that frequently defies rationality and that has been described as 'discretionary, episodic, future oriented, dynamic, socially influenced and evolving' (Pearce, 1992: 114). Nevertheless, they provide a useful foundation for understanding the demand for tourism, particularly in the way in which they highlight the role of motivation in the process. This is most commonly identified as motivational 'push' as opposed to destinational 'pull', a distinction which serves to separate the motivational stage from subsequent elements of the decision-making process (Klenosky, 2002).

Push versus pull factors

If all the knowledge, information, images and perceptions of a particular holiday or destination are combined, they add up to the overall attraction, or pull, of that holiday choice. Pull factors may be described as 'destination-specific attributes' (Goodall, 1991: 59) within the decision-making process. For example, the destination-specific attributes of a skiing holiday might include accommodation, entertainment facilities, the probability of good snow, the availability of skiing instruction and so on. At the same time, there usually exists a variety of factors that influence, or push, an individual into making a purchase decision. These 'person-specific motivations' (Goodall, 1991: 59) are what push an individual into wanting a particular type of holiday or, indeed, a holiday as opposed to another product, such as a new washing machine. Thus, the skiing holiday might be chosen in preference to, say, a summer beach holiday because an individual has a need or preference for a healthy lifestyle.

The distinction between push and pull factors is of fundamental importance to understanding the role of motivation within the demand for tourism. Generally, it is the push factors, the needs and wants of an individual, that lead to the decision to purchase a holiday in the first place, the nature of those needs determining the type of holiday the individual wants. For example, a person might want to visit friends and relatives but may be motivated by a need for love and affection. Once the decision to take a particular type of holiday has been made, the pull factors of different destinations determine which one is chosen. Thus, 'the key to understanding tourist motivation is to see vacation travel as a satisfier of needs and wants' (Mill & Morrison, 1985: 4).

In short, motivation is the very basis of the demand for tourism. The distinction between push and pull factors may not, in practice, be always clear cut whilst, as suggested earlier, a whole host of other factors, including the socio-economic and psychographic characteristics of the individual and broader, cultural factors, may influence different stages of the process as well as the final choice of tourism product. But, it is effectively motivation that translates an individual's personal needs into goal-oriented behaviour, behaviour from which the tourism decision-making process evolves and progresses. The motivation to satisfy needs, combined with personal preferences, pushes the tourist into considering alternative products; the final choice depends on the pull of alternative holidays or destinations.

In short,

an understanding of tourist motivation is of fundamental importance to the study of tourism demand; an analysis of the motivational stage can reveal the way in which people set goals for their destination-choice and how these goals are reflected in both their choice and travel behaviour.

(Mansfeld, 1992)

There is also great practical value in the explanation and analysis of tourist motivation. Those organisations which are best able to cater for and predict tourist motivation and demand, and hence satisfy the needs of tourists, are likely to be most successful in an increasingly diverse and competitive tourism market.

Perspectives on tourist motivation

The complexity of the concept of tourist motivation is reflected in the widespread and diverse treatment of the subject in the tourism literature. Despite the popularity of the subject, some years ago it was observed that 'no common understanding has yet emerged' (Jafari, 1987: 152). And despite the advances made in many areas of tourism research, it arguably remains the case that consensus has yet to be achieved with regards to the most appropriate approach towards the exploration and analysis of tourist motivation. This can be explained in part by the fact that much of the work concerned with tourist motivation has been theoretical in nature and drawn from a variety of disciplinary foundations. According to Dann, Nash and Pearce (1988), there have also been relatively few empirically based attempts to verify these theories of motivation, a situation mirrored, according to Mansfeld (1992), by a corresponding lack of empirical studies in the wider context of consumer behaviour in general. Much of the research has been based upon content theory, focusing in particular on tourists' needs and, thus, overlooking the processes whereby these needs are transformed into goal-oriented behaviour; as Witt and Wright (1993) argue, needs undoubtedly arouse motivated behaviour, but they do not necessarily predict what that behaviour will be. Over the years, a large number of articles have been published that explore tourist motivation, normally in the context of a particular destination or source market and, in some cases, applying particular motivational concepts. A review of these is beyond the scope of this chapter although a simple online literature search will reveal the diversity of research into the subject.

Generally, then, the literature on tourist motivation encompasses a variety of ideas and approaches. These are summarised by Dann (1981: 205), who defines tourist motivation as 'a meaningful state of mind which adequately disposes an actor or group of actors to travel, and which is subsequently interpretable by others as a valid explanation for such a decision'. What we are concerned with here are the ways in which this 'meaningful state of mind' is determined or, more simply, how it is that people are motivated to be tourists. It must also be stressed that the study of tourist motivation is of most relevance to the category of what may be described as holiday or leisure tourism; that is, tourism that is generally non-essential and for pleasure. The demand for other forms of tourism, in particular business tourism, tends to result from the purpose of the trip rather than from the needs of the tourist.

In his review of the study of tourism motivation, Dann (1981) identifies seven differ-ent perspectives that have been adopted in the literature:

1   *Travel as a response to what is lacking yet desired*
    The motivation for travel lies in the desire to experience something new or differ-ent. People become tourists because their own physical and cultural environment cannot fulfil this need.

2   *Destinational pull in response to motivational push*
    This approach highlights the importance of push factors in tourist motivation. Such factors may be determined by the tourist's home environment or by an individual's own psychological needs.

3   *Motivation as fantasy*
    Tourists may be motivated by the perceived opportunity to indulge in forms of behaviour that would not normally be socially sanctioned or acceptable in their home environment.

4   *Motivation as classified purpose*
    In contrast to push factors, this approach views the purpose of a trip or holiday as the primary motivating factor.

5   *Motivational typologies*
    Typologies of tourists are often used as models of tourist motivation. Within the context of this book, typologies and motivation, though connected, are treated as separate issues (see Chapter 4).

6   *Motivation and tourist experiences*
    This approach suggests that tourist motivation is largely determined by the expected experience in relation to the home environment, in particular by the promise of authenticity.

7   *Motivation as auto-definition and meaning*
    The principles of social action theory, especially symbolic interactionism, can be usefully applied to tourist motivation. The ways in which tourists define and respond to situations is seen as a better way of explaining tourist motivation rather than simply examining their behaviour.

Within these seven perspectives, there are two distinct approaches which may be used as a basis for an examination of tourist motivation. The first is to consider ways in which motivation results from influences external to the tourist (extrinsic motivational factors) and the second is to consider the personal needs of tourists themselves (intrinsic moti-vational factors).

Extrinsic motivation

There are a variety of different forces and pressures which emanate from an individual's social and cultural environment and which may, to a lesser or greater extent, influence that individual's needs and motivations. These pressures may flow from sources such as social norms, the influence of family and friends, the work environment and so on. Therefore, although some may argue that 'motivation is a purely psychological concept, not a sociological one' (Iso-Ahola, 1982: 257), there is little doubt that, in the case of tourism, motivation often results from societal values, norms and pressures which are internalised and become psychological needs. For example, the motivation for many people to take a holiday is to relax, to rest, to have a change and to get away from the routine, mundane constraints of everyday life. These needs can be grouped together under the general heading of escape, or 'avoidance' (Iso-Ahola, 1982: 258) motivations which are, undoubtedly, rooted in society. In short, needs which underpin tourist motivation may be viewed 'in terms of the (tourist) group of which the person deliberately or otherwise is a member' (Dann, 1981: 199), rather than from the individual's psychological condition.

It would be logical to propose that, sociologically, a structural approach to extrinsic tourist motivation should be adopted inasmuch as certain categories of motivation, such as escape, result directly from the pressures and condition of life in a tourist's home society. Indeed, MacCannell's (1989: 3) assertion that, for modern tourists, 'reality and authenticity are thought to be elsewhere: in other historical periods and other cultures, in purer, simpler lifestyles' and that tourism is a search for the authentic that results from the inauthentic, alienated condition of modern industrial society, is firmly based in structural sociology. More specifically, tourist motivation may be viewed from a functionalist perspective; whether motivated by the desire to rest and relax, to 're-create', or to seek authentic experiences, the function of tourism is to redress the balance and harmony of society: 'tourism is social therapy, a safety valve keeping the everyday world in good working order' (Krippendorf, 1986: 525). It is also important to bear in mind that overall tourism demand results from the needs and motivations of individual tourists who, collectively, comprise the market for tourism. Motivation is concerned with the individual tourist and, therefore, a micro, social action perspective is also of value to the study of motivation. (See Dann, 1981, for a discussion of the disciplinary treatment of motivation.)

The tourism-work relationship

Modern tourism and, more generally, leisure originated as a result of the fundamental changes that occurred in the nature and structure of society from the early nineteenth century onwards. People were motivated to participate in leisure activities or to travel by the need to remove themselves physically or mentally from the conditions of life in the cities of the Industrial Revolution. In particular, leisure and tourism became the antithesis to work, a *status quo* that, for many people, continues to this day. Work is, therefore, a primary extrinsic motivational factor for tourism.

Leisure, tourism and work cannot be separated; work provides both the means and the motivation for leisure and tourism and, up to a point, people need to participate in leisure and tourism to continue in work. In this context, work should not only be considered in the narrow sense of paid employment; that is, other commitments, including unpaid/voluntary work and family/home responsibilities, should also be included.

Hence, for the purposes of this chapter, 'work' should be thought of more broadly as obligatory or non-discretionary time activities. Thus, work and leisure are not separate, distinct conditions and, moreover, a relationship exists between the nature or experience of work and the leisure experience (see Parker, 1983). For some people, work may be boring, monotonous, repetitive and something to be endured; leisure and tourism represent freedom and escape from work, and work, therefore, is a means to an end (or, more precisely, simply a source of income). For others, conversely, work may be a way of life. It may be exciting, stimulating and, perhaps, the dominant feature in an individual's life; the role of leisure may thus be subordinated to work. The important point is, however, that different types of work produce different levels of satisfaction. Creative, challenging work arguably produces higher levels of satisfaction whereas more mundane, repetitive forms of work result, generally, in lower satisfaction for the individual. Different work environments produce different individual needs and, hence, different leisure and tourism motivations. In short, 'the experience of work in industrial societies . . . forms the context for the experience of leisure' (Clarke & Critcher, 1985: 17).

Of course, it is not only the work environment which determines an individual's leisure and tourism needs. Nor, under certain circumstances, does the work-tourism relationship apply to particular groups in society, such as the retired or the unemployed, although involuntary non-work may be considered the same as work as a motivational factor in tourism. Moreover, irrespective of employment status, most people are required to engage in some form of obligatory activity during their normal, day-to-day life. Nevertheless, Parker (1983) suggests three basic ways in which the work-leisure (tourism) relationship manifests itself, thereby providing a framework for understanding the links between work and leisure experiences and requirements. Similarly, Zuzanek and Mannell (1983) propose four different hypotheses about the nature of the work-leisure relationship.

1. *Work and tourism in opposition*

Where work and tourism are in opposition, there is a sharp contrast between the experiences of each. The individual is motivated to seek out forms of tourism that offer a distinct change of experience, or even lifestyle, from that found at work. In theory, this relationship should operate in both directions; that is, people in monotonous, production-line type employment are motivated to go on holidays which are stimulating and exciting and which allow them to escape, albeit temporarily, from the reality of everyday life. Conversely, it might be expected that those who are employed in challenging, stressful jobs would seek out quieter, restful or even monotonous types of tourism experience. In practice, however, it has been found that this model is most applicable to those in lower status jobs and for whom tourism compensates (Zuzanek & Mannell, 1983) for deficiencies at work and, by implication, at home. Hence, this model is also referred to as the compensation hypothesis; tourism compensates for deficiencies in the nature of people's work and their obligated lives more generally.

Ryan (1991a: 20), for example, cites the leading role played by the textile workers of Lancashire and Yorkshire in the formation of cycling and rambling clubs in the UK at the end of the nineteenth and in the early twentieth centuries as an historical example of the compensatory nature of leisure experiences. For them, the countryside became a refuge from the conditions of life and work in industrial urban centres. He goes on to describe a situation where the tourist escapes to a fantasy life, the life of the 'idle rich', staying in hotels and enjoying standards of service that could normally only be dreamed of. By saving for the holiday, the tourist is able to indulge in a lifestyle that is in direct contrast to normal life; in compensation for what is missing at work and at home, the holiday represents an inversion of everyday reality. Thus, the tourist is motivated to search out the opposite of the work/home experience. The worker-as-tourist seeks, as Gottlieb (1982) puts it, to be a king or queen for a day, whilst the middle or upper-class tourist seeks to be a 'peasant for a day' in an inversion of their normal work and social environments (Gottlieb, 1982: 173).

The opposition/compensation model of tourist motivation is also applicable to the lifestyle or constraints that are imposed by different types of work, rather than the deficiencies of the work itself. People are constrained by time commitments and codes of dress and behaviour; in contrast, tourism offers the opportunity to escape from these constraining rules and norms, to indulge in 'ludic' behaviour (that is, behaviour that can be described as play). For example, Lett (1983: 54) describes how charter yacht tourists in the Caribbean behave in a manner which is 'an inverted expression of many of the pervasive values and attitudes of middle-class U.S. culture'. Constrained only by time, the tourists ignore the social rules and conventions of their home society and indulge in excessive drinking and sexual activities, behaviour which is 'licensed and excused only because it is temporary and occurs away from home' (Lett, 1983: 53). Similarly, there has long been criticism of the behaviour of some groups of younger British tourists while on holiday. For example, one newspaper report asks: 'What's the problem with British tourists? The mayor of Malia was clear: "They scream, they sing, they fall down, they take their clothes off, they cross-dress, they vomit," he announced back in 2008' (Khaleeli, 2017), behaviour which, though not excusable, can be explained in part by the freedom offered by the holiday context. Lett (1983) emphasises the compensatory character of such behaviour and suggests that it not only refreshes and restores tourists but also prepares them to re-enter their structured, everyday existence.

If tourism presents the opportunity for inversion from one condition (reality) to another (fantasy) and escape from the rules and norms of home society (an escape from responsibility), it is then logical to progress the argument to suggest that tourism, for the tourist, is a form of regression to a childlike existence (Dann, 1996: 101–134). This may be manifested in a number of ways. For example, the freedom from responsibility and decision making, roles taken over by the travel agent or tour operator who, in effect, act *in loco parentis*, may represent a form of liberation which 'becomes no more or less than a return to the realm of childhood' (Dann, 1996: 104). Equally, the choice of destination or attraction offers the opportunity for tourists to immerse themselves in a childlike world. It has been suggested, for example, that the popularity of rural heritage sites, such as Beatrix Potter's Hill Top Farm in the English Lake District, is evidence of tourists' desires to evoke childhood memories, to retrace their steps to childhood places, both real and imagined. Similarly, particular types of holidays or attractions, such as theme parks, permit tourists to participate in childlike behaviour, to play, to enter a world of fantasy, to have fun. In short, the tourist as child is in opposition to, or compensates for, the tourist as adult; tourism is a journey back to a world of freedom, play and a lack of responsibility – of childhood.

2. Tourism as an extension of work

Where tourism and leisure are an extension of work there is, again, a direct link between the work experience and the tourism/leisure experience. Unlike the opposition/ compensation model, however, where the individual is motivated to seek change and escape, the extension model proposes that there is little distinction between patterns of work and patterns of leisure. In other words, tourism and leisure complements rather than contrasts with work. Thus, it is suggested that people who have challenging, stimulating and satisfying jobs, who are in a position of some responsibility, are more likely to choose an independent and stimulating type of tourism. Conversely, those who work in highly regulated, routine and monotonous jobs, who have a passive work role, will adopt a similarly passive attitude towards their tourism and leisure activities. They will choose the mass-produced package holiday which, in effect, mirrors the production-line environment of the workplace. The extreme case would be the individual whose work is central to his or her life and for whom there is little or no distinction between tourism and work, no boundary between work and leisure. For example, a history teacher's holiday might be spent touring historical sites, an activity which could be described as both leisure and work.

The important implication of the theory of tourism motivated as an extension of work is that as work practices change and adapt, so too will the demand for tourism. Many of the main tourism generating countries are being rapidly transformed from industrial to post-industrial economies; primary, manufacturing industries are being superseded by service industries, traditional production lines are becoming increasingly automated. For example, Glasgow in Scotland has lost virtually all its traditional manufacturing industries and is basing its economic regeneration on the development of the tertiary, service sector, including tourism. Some would argue that such a move towards service industry-dominated economies is resulting in more widespread job satisfaction, whilst others would argue that although technology has advanced, the system of production (that is, capitalism) remains unchanged. Whichever viewpoint is adopted, there is little doubt that changes in work practices and environments will impact upon tourism motivation and demand.

3. Neutrality between tourism and work

Both the opposition/compensation and the extension models of the relationship between leisure and work highlight the role of work itself in determining tourist motivation. That is, a causal relationship exists between work and tourism and leisure. In contrast, the third model occupies the mid-point between opposition and extension, suggesting that work has little or no effect on leisure patterns and *vice versa*. In effect, the experience of work and the experience of leisure remain independent; there is no link between the two. As Clarke and Critcher (1985: 19) point out, in this situation it is likely that leisure is seen to be more fulfilling, that work loses its perceived importance and becomes a means to an end. For example, during the 1980s in Britain the work ethic was dominant; by the start of the 1990s, quality of life had become a more widely accepted motivation as people became more concerned with their work-life balance (Guest, 2002). More recently, it is claimed that younger generations, such as the so-called Generation Y and Millennials, give greater precedence to their work-life balance; while seeking to develop successful work careers, of equal importance is the extent and quality of their leisure time, whether spending time with family and friends, engaging in specific hobbies or leisure pursuits, or going on holiday (Smith, 2010). Thus, it is evident that the perceived importance of work as an activity in its own right has diminished, the implication being that the influence of work as an extrinsic factor in tourist motivation is also diminishing in terms of the type of tourism chosen. Nevertheless, the significance of tourism, in particular the annual summer holiday, as an accepted (or even expected) form of leisure activity is such that the role of work as the prime extrinsic motivator of tourism remains virtually unassailable.

Social influences

In addition to work and the work environment as major factors in influencing tourist motivation, a variety of other extrinsic pressures may affect the individual. These pressures are exerted by other people and collectively may be termed social influences (Moutinho, 1987: 5). There are four main sources of social influence in an individual tourist's motivation, each of which requires brief explanation:

1. Family influences

The family can play a significant role in the determination of tourist type (see Chapter 4); irrespective of other factors, the family may be a powerful constraint on the choice of tourism product. Equally, the family can have a significant influence on tourist motivation (Fodness, 1992; Thornton et al., 1997). It is through the family that, initially, most people acquire and internalise their values, beliefs and expectations. Thus, if an individual was brought up in a family which enjoyed regular overseas holidays, it is likely that he or she will be motivated to continue the tradition. Conversely, a negative experience or impression of family holidays may motivate an individual family member into becoming an independent tourist. The VFR (visiting friends and relatives) market is, of course, largely influenced by the family, with the desire to visit relatives, both domestically and overseas, being a powerful tourism motivator.

2. Reference groups

A reference group is any group that an individual turns to as a point of reference for beliefs and attitudes. That is, it is a group against which an individual can judge his or her own beliefs and behaviour. Reference groups may take various forms, such as religious or ethnic groups, work colleagues, or the local neighbourhood, and are either normative (influence general values) or comparative (influence specific attitudes). The level of contact with or adherence to a particular reference group will determine the influence that group has on an individual.

3. Social class

Social class is 'a relatively permanent division of categories in a society, a division that brings about some restrictions of behaviour between individuals in different classes' (Moutinho, 1987: 7). As discussed in Chapter 3, the concept of social class is becoming of less relevance in postmodern societies. That is, the process of de-differentiation is breaking down the traditional distinctions or roles, such as work or gender roles, parameters which distinguished one class from another. As a result, new social groups are emerging which pay little respect to more traditional class boundaries. Nevertheless, members of a particular social class or group tend to have similar values and lifestyles – or as Pierre Bourdieu originally suggested, they possess similar degrees of cultural capital (Bourdieu, 1986) – and it is likely that they will follow standards of behaviour acceptable to that class or group. Therefore, social class/grouping is an important factor in tourist motivation. For example, many destinations are categorised by the social class of the majority of visitors, some being seen as 'up-market', others as 'down-market'.

Different types of tourism may also be class motivated; the working classes have traditionally tended to be attracted by mass tourism or crowds of other tourists, whereas a more solitary approach, what Walter (1982) refers to as romantic tourism, is allegedly of greater appeal to the middle classes. Similarly, newer types of tourism appeal to newer (postmodern) social groupings. For example, ecotourism is ostensibly designed to appeal to that group of tourists whose motivation/behaviour is framed by their shared environmental beliefs and concerns. However, as discussed shortly and following on from the discussion of the 'good' or 'responsible' tourist in the preceding chapter, research has shown that environmental concern is not in fact a major motivational factor amongst ecotourists.

4. Culture

The culture of a society is the combination of its values, morals, behavioural norms, dress, cuisine, artefacts and language. In short, a society's culture is its way of life which is passed on from generation to generation. The culture of a society is dynamic; it may change and adapt over time. Such transformations may be evident in tangible elements, such as tastes in food or music, or in new styles of clothing or architecture; they may also be intangible, as in the alleged emergence of postmodernity (see Chapter 3).

In either case, a society's culture influences the attitudes and behaviour of the individual members of that society. In the context of tourist motivation, the culture of a particular society can be a strong influence on the determination of tourism demand. For example, travel and tourism is more deeply rooted in some cultures than others, or more acceptable in some countries than others. Similarly, different cultures motivate different types of tourism, such as the importance of religious tourism and pilgrimage within Islamic culture, whilst, as discussed in the next chapter, the role or meaning of tourism as one form of consumption may also be directly influenced by cultural factors.

Social influences on tourist motivation are not mutually exclusive. Indeed, it is likely that a combination, if not all, of these four sources of pressure and influence have a bearing on an individual's decision-making process. Some, such as the influence of family, may be more explicit, whilst class or cultural characteristics may be so ingrained as to be unrecognised as positive or negative motivational factors. They may also be combined with motivational forces arising from the work-leisure relationship, so that it may be impossible to highlight any one dominant source of motivation.

Modern society and tourism motivation

Leisure in general and tourism in particular have become institutionalised within modern industrial societies and, to an increasing extent, in many newly industrialised and emerging economies. Certainly, for the majority of the populations of the main tourism generating countries, the summer holiday is an accepted, or even expected, part of life, celebrated as vigorously as other more traditional festivals in the annual calendar. Rapid advances in transport and information technology, economic growth and greater amounts of time available for leisure activities have brought to the masses a degree of freedom and mobility once reserved for the privileged minority. Indeed, it has been argued that 'mobility, vacations and travel are social victories' (Krippendorf, 1986: 523).

Paradoxically, however, those societies which provide the opportunity for travel and tourism also provide the motivation; modern, industrial society has created not only the means of, but also the need for, tourism. For many tourists, the annual holiday represents the chance to rest, to recover from the stresses and strains of everyday life, to get away from it all: 'a hurried mobility has obsessed most of the inhabitants of the industrialised nations. One seizes every opportunity to free oneself from the boredom of everyday life as often as possible' (Krippendorf, 1986: 522). Tourism has become an essential ingredient in a person's life cycle in modern society. In order to survive in modern society, an individual must, periodically, escape from it. Thus, from a structural point of view, tourism is motivated by society and, at the same time, plays an essential function within it. In other words, society itself determines, arguably, the ultimate motivation for tourism.

It is the character of life in modern societies – an amalgamation of the activities, work practices, demands, technological advances, expectations and social values which, together, constitute the modern 'way of life' – that has created the need to escape. This need has been satisfied by increasingly fast, economical and widely available forms of transport. Since the beginning of the industrialisation and urbanisation of societies, people have become increasingly alienated. The division of labour, mass production and automation have alienated people from their work and the product of their labour; greater mobility and communication technology have alienated people from their friends and families; cities have alienated people from nature; people have even become alienated from themselves. Immersed in a world dominated and guided by the economy and economic growth, people have lost their sense of place and belonging; independence and freedom have replaced community, having has replaced giving, materialism has replaced contentment. Manufacturers introduce new products to make every task easier, faster and more painless, yet every technological advance diminishes human contact and reduces the need for social interaction. While the development of social media has increased connectivity between people, not only has there long been concern regarding the impact of Internet use on social well-being in general, but more recently concern has been expressed that social media use enhances a sense of loneliness, specifically amongst younger people in particular (Pittman & Reich, 2016). Overall, as life gets faster, people have less time. The realities of modern life, for many, are a source of stress, constraint, disenchantment and dissatisfaction. People have lost their sense of time and place, they have lost their self-identity. In short, life in modern, industrial society is typified by a sense of 'anomie'.

Anomie is a word used by sociologists to describe 'a situation of perceived normlessness and meaninglessness in the origin [tourist generating] country' (Dann, 1981: 191). According to Dann (1977), anomie is a major extrinsic tourism motivator. Adrift in modern society's headlong rush to achieve economic and material growth, people find themselves wanting to say 'stop the world, I want to get off'. Whether to simply rest for a couple of weeks on a beach, to participate in physical or cultural activities which the hectic pace of life at home does not allow for, or to search for meaning, fulfilment and authenticity in other places and cultures (MacCannell, 1989), people are motivated to escape, temporarily, from their society. Every year, millions of people join together in a kind of migration, 'seemingly of their own free will, but appearing as if they were obeying an order' (Krippendorf, 1986: 522). They willingly subject themselves to traffic jams, delays at airports and all the other problems associated with modern, mass travel in order to refresh themselves, to prepare themselves for work or simply just to convince themselves that, compared to life in other places or countries, things are not too bad after all. Motivated by the realities of everyday life and spurred on by the efforts of the tourism industry, 'people learn to desire vacations . . . for escape purposes and come to think of such vacations as essential for their psychological well-being' (Mannell & Iso-Ahola, 1987: 324).

In short, tourism has become a fact of modern society. Society has created the need and the motivation for tourism, it has created the means by which the great majority of the population may participate in tourism and, in a sense, society sustains tourism as an essential function in the work-leisure cycle. It is for these reasons that some authors (for example, Krippendorf, 1987) maintain that the root of the 'problem' of tourism, as a mass phenomenon that impacts physically and culturally on destination areas, lies not in tourism itself but in the societies that generate tourists. They argue that, unlike early travel, modern tourism is motivated by the need to escape rather than a desire to discover and, therefore, the only way to minimise the impacts of tourism is to remove the need for tourism in the first place. By fundamentally altering the way of life in modern societies, people will no longer feel the need to escape and, by implication, will not participate in tourism. The position of tourism as a socially motivated and maintained activity is such that, unless technological advance in areas like 'virtual reality' can offer a viable and realistic alternative, people will increasingly feel the need to take holidays away from their everyday society.

Intrinsic motivation

The study of motivation has, traditionally, been concerned with the needs and desires of the individual. It is an individual's personal and deep-rooted needs that lead to motivated, goal-oriented behaviour, the goal being to satisfy those needs. The study of motivation has, therefore, been guided by the assumption that 'in order to understand human motivation it is necessary to discover what needs people have and how they can be fulfilled' (Witt & Wright, 1992: 34). Every individual has personal and unique needs, needs which may go unrecognised by, but are still intrinsic to, the individual. In short, the notion of intrinsic need satisfaction has long been considered the primary arousal factor in motivated behaviour and, in the context of tourism, a number of attempts have been made to link intrinsic, psychological needs with identified goal-oriented touristic behaviour.

Maslow's hierarchy of needs

One of the best-known theories of motivation is Maslow's hierarchy of needs (Maslow, 1943). It was originally developed by Maslow in connection with his work in clinical psychology during the 1940s but, since that time, it has been applied widely as a general theory of motivation. It has also been used in specific fields of research, such as motivation in business, and it also forms the basis for much of the work concerned with tourist motivation.

Underlying Maslow's theory of motivation is the concept that all individuals have a number of needs which fall into five broad classifications:

Physiological needs: hunger, thirst, rest, sex, etc.

Safety needs: freedom from threat, fear and anxiety, etc.

Love (social) needs: friendship, affection, receiving love, etc.

Esteem needs: self-esteem, self-confidence, reputation, prestige, etc.

Self-actualisation needs: self-fulfilment, etc.

In addition, Maslow originally proposed that these five classes of needs form a hierarchy (as shown in Figure 5.2 below), each of which must be satisfied before an individual will be motivated by the next class of need in the hierarchy. If none of the needs in the hierarchy have been satisfied, then the basic, physiological needs take precedence and dominate behaviour. Once this need has been satisfied, then it no longer motivates behaviour and the individual will move up to the next level of the hierarchy. This process continues until the final level is reached, the implication being that self-actualisation is the level to which people should aspire (see Cooper *et al.*, 2005).

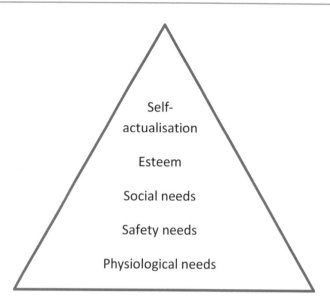

FIGURE 5.2 Maslow's hierarchy of needs
Source: adapted from Maslow (1943)

The appeal of Maslow's theory lies, no doubt, in its simplicity. Maslow himself has recognised the limitations of his model, in particular its relevance and adaptability to the work situation. He has also suggested that the linear progression from one set of needs to the next does not necessarily occur in all cases; not only does he identify seven different 'routes' through the hierarchy but he also states that each set of needs may only be partially satisfied before the next set begins to dominate behaviour. Because of these limitations, Witt and Wright (1992: 36) suggest that Murray's classification of human needs, developed in 1938, provides a better, although more complicated, basis for understanding and explaining tourist motivation. Nevertheless, Maslow's model has been widely adapted by tourism researchers, perhaps because of the way in which a wide range of differing human needs are presented in a simple and understandable framework (Cooper *et al.*, 2005).

For example, Pearce (1988) and Pearce and Caltabiano (1983) have developed a framework for the study of tourist motivation that is initially based on Maslow's hierarchical model. They describe five different levels of motivation, namely, a concern with biological needs, safety and security needs, relationship needs, special interest needs and, finally, self-actualisation needs. They argue that such a framework allows for both biological motives (for example, rest and recuperation) and social motives to be included and that, unlike other theories of tourist motivation, it recognises that motivations may change over time and that tourists may also have more than one motivation. Also, tourist motivation is viewed as a dynamic process; people have a tourism 'career' and move up the tourist ladder at different stages of their life cycle (see Pearce, 1992; 2005). At any stage they may also retire from their tourism career; that is, they may decide not to take holidays.

There is, of course, the danger that the application of Maslow's hierarchy to the specific context of tourist motivation over-simplifies a complex process, providing tidy explanations for observed tourist behaviour without considering a range of other forces and influences on the decision-making process. Certain types of tourism can be related to specific needs; summer-sun package holidays, for example, might satisfy biological needs (rest and relaxation), safety needs (the security of organised, institutionalised travel) and self-esteem needs (being able to display a suntan on returning home), yet intrinsic need satisfaction cannot fully explain tourist motivation. It tells only part of the story. However, it does draw attention to the fact that people have psychological needs that may be satisfied through tourism, needs which may, in fact, go unrecognised by the individual concerned.

Psychological motives for tourism

Dann (1977) suggests that tourism is motivated both socially by the anomic condition of society and psychologically by the need for ego-enhancement. A similar position is adopted by Iso-Ahola (see Mannell & Iso-Ahola, 1987) who sub-divides psychological motivational forces into two simultaneous influences. On the one hand, motivation results from the need to escape from personal or interpersonal environments whilst, on the other hand, there also exists the tendency to seek intrinsic psychological rewards from participation in tourism. The difference between Dann's and Iso-Ahola's position is that the former asserts that escape and the search for reality/meaning is socially determined, whilst the latter argues that tourists seek escape-avoidance from personal, psychological environments. In both cases, however, tourists are motivated by the prospect of 'reward'. In other words, people feel the need to travel not only because of the sense of normlessness and meaninglessness imposed upon them by modern society but also by the need to be recognised, to have their ego or confidence boosted, to personally and psychologically gain from tourism. Thus, whilst on holiday, away from their usual surroundings and friends, people are able to act out an alien personality, similar to the king/queen for a day situation described by Gottlieb (1982). It is more than simply an inversion of the normal and more than indulgence in ludic behaviour. The opportunity for ego-enhancement, for status enhancement, links directly to the potential satisfaction of Maslow's concept of self-esteem needs, achieved through the suntan, showing photographs of places visited, or sending a postcard (or as is more common nowadays, posting an image and text online) as the ultimate status symbol of 'I am here but you are there'. Equally, anomie as a tourist motivator can also be related to Maslow's hierarchy, participation in tourism resulting from the need for love and a sense of belonging.

For example, Dann's (1977) theory of tourist motivation is based upon research amongst tourists visiting Barbados. He found that anomic tourists were married and tended to belong to higher socio-economic groups, whereas ego-enhancement tourists were from a lower socio-economic group and more likely to be female. The demographic characteristics of the latter group related to lower status roles in the tourists' home countries, thus confirming the ego-enhancement motivation of travel. However, a major criticism of Dann's approach, as argued by Pearce (1982), is that in addition to ignoring other possible motivations, it is unclear whether the findings are based upon the tourists' own explanations (i.e. an 'emic' approach) or the researcher's interpretation of the situation (i.e. an 'etic' approach). Such criticism is understandable when it is considered that tourists themselves may have difficulty in recognising or articulating the real, underlying motivations for travel. For example, Crompton (1979) found that respondents to his research had difficulty in explaining the true reasons for destination choice. However, he identified seven psychological push motives for travel: escape from a perceived mundane environment, exploration and evaluation of self, relaxation, prestige, regression, enhancement of kinship relationships, and facilitation of social interaction. These psychological motives represented, according to Crompton (1979: 415), 'a hidden agenda' for tourist motivation.

The same problem in determining the true psychological motivation for tourism has long been recognised. For example, Mill and Morrison (1985: 2) observe that 'tourists themselves may be unaware of the true reasons for their travel behaviour. Individuals are often unaware of the real reasons for doing certain things.' Additionally, people may not always be willing to reveal the real reason for their holiday, such as wanting to impress their neighbours or work colleagues by showing off their suntans. Likewise, Krippendorf (1987: 22) suggests that an individual's motivation to travel will normally repeat 'all the reasons that feature in advertising and which are repeated over and over again in all tourist brochures and catalogues', whilst the true motivations lie hidden in the subconscious. Nevertheless, Krippendorf lists eight different travel motivations that can be identified from the literature: recuperation and regeneration; compensation and social integration; escape; communication; broadening the mind; freedom and self-determination; self-realisation; and happiness.

Motivation by purpose

Owing, perhaps, to the difficulty in ascertaining an individual's underlying motivations for tourism, some authors relate motivation to the purpose of the trip rather than the satisfaction of an identified or hidden psychological need. These may be regarded as intrinsic inasmuch as they relate to the individual tourist's desire for personal reward or achievement of a goal through tourism. For example, McIntosh and Goeldner (1990: 131) list four categories of what they term basic travel motivators:

1. Physical motivators

These relate to the need for rest, participation in sport, relaxing entertainment and other motivations which are connected with health. Common to all physical motivators is the reduction in tension and the refreshment of body and mind through physical activities.

2. Cultural motivators

These are manifested in the desire to see and learn about other countries, their music, food, history, religion, art and so on.

3. Interpersonal motivators

These include visiting friends and relatives, the desire to meet new people and to make new friendships, and escape from the everyday social environment.

4. Status and prestige motivators

These concern ego-enhancement and the desire for recognition, appreciation and attention, and personal improvement. Trips may be related to education or study, the pursuit of hobbies, or business and conference type tourism.

The major problem associated with the motivation by purpose approach is that it describes the outcome or the goal-oriented behaviour that results from a specific need rather than the actual motivation itself. Thus, the desire to learn about other cultures may, in fact, be the outcome of a need to make up for a lack of culture in the home environment, or wanting to make new friends may result from a deeper motivation to avoid loneliness.

Similarly, it would be logical to assume that participation in ecotourism is motivated by the attributes of such tourism (for example, low impact, optimising benefits to local communities and so on); in short, wanting to be a 'good' tourist. However, the true motivation for ecotourism may have little, if anything, to do with environmental concerns. As discussed in the previous chapter, research demonstrates that 'ecotourists' are, for the most part, pulled to eco-destinations by the attraction of the environmental rather than 'pushed' by environmental concerns. For example, Eagles' (1992) study of Canadian ecotourists' motivations identified 15 dominant factors that encourage ecotourists to travel, the majority of which were environmental (see below). Equally, social benefits are identified ('rediscover self', 'be daring and adventurous', 'escape from demands of life') but these reflect the more usual ego-centric character of tourism motivational forces. Similar results were reported by Eagles and Casganette (1995), whilst Wight's (1996) comprehensive study of the preferences and motivations of North American tourism markets concluded that there exist wide ranging preferences and behaviour amongst ecotourists but that, generally, the natural environment and opportunities for active rather than passive participation are important factors in the demand for ecotourism. Again, however, no evidence is provided to suggest that ecotourists are motivated by the 'green' value of wishing to contribute positively to the destinational environment/culture. That is, ecotourists seek to satisfy needs other than behaving in an environmentally appropriate fashion, to the extent that, according to Blamey and Braithwaite (1997) and Palacio and McCool (1997), less than 20 percent of tourists on ecotourism holidays could be described specifically as ecotourists (see also Sharpley, 2006).

Specifically, it was found that, although the motivation for ecotourism vacations is diverse and related to a multitude of variables, ecotourists are, generally, most interested in the physical attractions of destinations and the activities that such destinations offer. Enjoying wilderness scenery and undisturbed nature is the most frequently cited reason for participating in ecotourism, followed by a variety of natural environment, physical or cultural activity motivations (for example, see Figure 5.3)

Motivations	Rank
Wilderness and undisturbed nature	1
Lakes and streams	2
Be physically active	3
Mountains	4
National or provincial parks	5
Experience new lifestyles	6
Rural areas	7
Oceanside	8
Meet people with similar interest	9
Simpler lifestyle	10
Visit historical places	11
Outdoor recreation	12
Be daring and adventurous	13
Cultural activities	14
See maximum in time available	15

FIGURE 5.3 Motivations of significant importance to ecotourists
Source: adapted from Eagles (1992: 6)

Thus, not surprisingly, it is evident that the setting is of greatest importance to the experience of ecotourists. Unfortunately, most of the studies confuse push and pull factors. They relate motivations to the pull, or attraction, of particular settings whilst revealing little about what pushes or motivates ecotourists in the first place. As Wight (1996: 7) argues, 'it may be, however, that the setting is also critical to other, more traditional types of travellers. . . . It is important, therefore, to . . . determine the benefits that eco-tourists seek.' She goes on to identify a number of 'discriminant characteristics' of the benefits sought by ecotourists. These include the avoidance of crowds, the experience of wilderness, learning about nature, the opportunity for physical challenges and, importantly, the potential for bringing benefits to local communities.

Similarly, in an investigation into the psychographic characteristics of nature-based tourists, Silverberg et al. (1996) found that although a conservationist attitude may be a discriminant factor between different clusters of tourists, many of the benefits sought by nature-based tourists are unrelated to environmental concern. For example, the desire to enjoy nature and unspoilt places, to experience wilderness and solitude, relate more to anomie or avoidance needs, whilst it has been argued that ecotourism is both a niche and an expensive product, and is therefore better described as 'ego-tourism' (Wheeler, 1992a). From the available evidence, there is little to suggest that the motivations of ecotourists differ markedly from other tourists and that their true needs bear little relationship to the overt purpose of ecotourism.

Tourism as a sacred journey

Anthropological research into tourism has been divided into two broad areas: assessing the impacts of tourism development on host cultures and societies, and analysing the meaning of tourism to the tourist. Whilst the first area falls under the heading of the social impacts of tourism (see Chapter 12), the second is, essentially, an anthropological study of tourist motivation. A dominant theme within the latter is the notion that tourism represents a modern sacred experience; that tourism embraces, in the broader sense of the word, a spiritual dimension. According to Graburn (1989: 22), 'tourism . . . is functionally and symbolically equivalent to other institutions that humans use to embellish and add meaning to their lives'. If this is so, then it immediately becomes apparent that there is a potential link between the role of tourism as a secular ritual in modern life and more traditional, religious forms of travel, such as pilgrimage. Indeed, as Graburn (1983: 15) asks, 'if tourism has the quality of a leisure ritual that takes place outside of everyday life and involves travel, is it not identical to pilgrimage?'

In recent years, increasing attention has been paid to the relationship between tourism, religion and spirituality. Therefore, this subject is explored in greater detail in Chapter 8.

Tourist motivation and the tourist gaze

Urry (1990a; 1990b; 1992; 2002) describes the activity of tourism as gazing or, more specifically, the tourist 'gaze' (see also Urry & Larsen, 2011): 'What is the minimal characteristic of tourist activity is the fact that we look at, or gaze upon, particular objects' (Urry, 1990b: 26). The actual physical purchases, such as transport, accommodation and food, are incidental to this central feature of tourism; the consumption of these goods and services allows the tourist to gaze upon 'features of landscape and townscape which separate them off from everyday experience' (Urry, 1990a: 3). Tourist motivation results from the need to gaze on sights, places and peoples that are unusual, that are removed from the experience and routine of normal, everyday life; by implication, tourist activity (gazing) is motivated by the need to collect gazes.

The concept of the tourist gaze is widely discussed in the tourism literature. All too often, however, it is also applied over-simplistically. In other words, many refer to the tourist gaze as, literally, the act of tourists gazing or looking at the places and people they are visiting, whereas Urry is more concerned with the forces that determine the nature, direction and significance of the gaze or, more broadly, how they experience places. More specifically, Urry proposes that the tourist gaze is socially constructed; what and how tourists gaze upon is largely influenced by a variety of social and cultural factors which both drive and inform the direction and focus of the gaze. Thus, certain places or sites, such as the countryside, are gazed upon in ways which reflect the cultural significance of those places. Hence, a particular place may be gazed upon differently by tourists from different cultural backgrounds. Moreover, the gaze is dynamic; it responds to wider socio-cultural transformations and will change over time. Generally, however, the tourist gaze is both reflexive and embodied: 'places are chosen to be gazed upon because there is anticipation, especially through daydreaming and fantasy, of intense pleasures, either on a different scale or involving different senses from those customarily encountered' (Urry & Larsen, 2011).

A full discussion of the tourist gaze concept is beyond the scope of this chapter (see, for example, Hollinshead & Kuon, 2013). However, in the context of motivation, there are broadly two different ways in which tourist gazes may be collected, depending on the needs of the individual tourist (Urry, 1990a):

The romantic gaze

The romantic gaze (see also Walter, 1982) is motivated by the desire for solitary enjoyment and experience. It is the equivalent to the search for authenticity and the sacred journey to the 'centre out there'. The romantic tourist seeks reality in other cultures and societies and, broadly, tries to recreate the 'lost art of travel'.

The collective gaze

The collective gaze is communal tourism. It is motivated by the need to gaze at the familiar or to share the non-ordinary with other people. Indeed, it is the shared experience that is of fundamental importance to the collective gaze.

Tourist motivation: conclusions

Throughout this chapter, tourist motivation has been identified with the satisfaction of an individual's needs, needs which push, or motivate, the individual into particular types of behaviour. These needs may result from pressures and forces which are external to the individual, such as the work experience, family obligations or societal norms, from deep-rooted, psychological needs, such as self-esteem or a need for companionship, or from a combination of both. As such, this approach has provided an indication of the enormous range and variety of forces that have the potential to motivate an individual into goal-oriented (specifically, touristic) behaviour. However, as Witt and Wright (1992: 44) argue, 'the study of needs can at best only provide a partial explanation of motivated behaviour'. Other factors must also be taken into consideration if the explanation of tourist motivation is to be of use in predicting tourist behaviour. In particular, it is necessary to look at tourist motivation over time and the way in which an individual's needs may be translated into motivated behaviour.

In theory, tourist decision making follows a logical process which commences with the translation of needs into motivated behaviour. This behaviour takes the form of a consideration of the different products related to the satisfaction of needs and, based upon the available information and the overall image of the destination, the tourist then makes a decision and purchases a holiday. Thus, each stage can be assigned a separate and identifiable position and function within the overall decision-making process. In practice, this process may not be quite so simple and straightforward. The dividing line between different stages is not always distinct and, in particular, the meaning of a holiday to the consumer should also be considered. In other words, tourists experience and purchase more than the actual one- or two-week break. Prior to departure, the process of choosing, of anticipating the holiday (Parrinello, 1993) is all part of the tourism experience and people may be motivated as much by the prospect of having a holiday as by the potential benefits of the holiday itself. Holidays are often purchased many months in advance and the thought of having a holiday, having something to look forward to and to dream about, can be as equally exciting and beneficial (and in many cases more so) than the holiday itself.

Nor does the process finish when the tourist returns home from a holiday. Although the physical state of being on holiday has come to an end, the memories and images of a holiday may remain with an individual for much longer, particularly if photographs have been taken or souvenirs bought. In a sense, the holiday lasts much longer than the actual period spent away and a tourist might also be motivated by the thought of being able to look back on his or her holiday whilst, at the same time, anticipating and planning the next one. So the stages of motivation, choice, holiday purchase and the actual trip become merged into a continual process of anticipation, experience and memory, a process which sustains itself in modern, tourism generating societies which are 'literally saturated with tourist culture' (Parrinello, 1993: 242).

Again, departing from the basic notion of needs resulting in motivated behaviour, tourist motivation is also dependent on the extent to which people expect a particular choice of action to lead to certain outcomes. For example, an individual might want to go on a beach holiday to get a suntan, motivated by the self-esteem need, perhaps, of being able to show off his or her tan. The choice of destination will be motivated not only by the original need to get a tan but also by the extent to which the individual expects to achieve that goal. The individual will thus be motivated to choose a destination that offers the best opportunity for sunbathing and also, perhaps, at a time of year when a suntan is most noticeable (that is, a winter-sun destination). The same principle can also be applied to the influence of socio-economic restrictions on holiday choice. Thus, a person who has a low expectation of being able to afford a particular holiday, will be motivated to choose another type of holiday or, if there is a low expectation of satisfying needs on the alternative holiday, to stay at home.

This approach to motivation is known as expectancy theory (see Witt & Wright, 1992 for more detail). It is a complicated method of analysing motivation, yet it serves to highlight that tourist motivation is, itself, a complex subject. There is a huge variety of push factors that may motivate tourism, and these factors vary between different people. If people's expectations are also taken into account it becomes evident that destination pull factors can play an equally important role in motivation. The implication is, therefore, that to be able to fully understand and predict any one person's motivation for tourism it is necessary to concentrate on that person's preferences, experience, desires and social and economic circumstances.

The situation is further complicated by the fact that tourists may not always be able or wish to reflect upon or express their real motives for travel (Dann, 1981). There is, also, no saying that particular groups of people behave in particular ways, or that particular types of tourism or destinations appeal to particular types of tourist. Essentially, tourist motivation results from a variety of social, economic, demographic and psychological factors peculiar to each individual tourist but, nevertheless, the influence of society and sociological factors, both external and intrinsic to the individual, provide a solid foundation for an understanding of tourist motivation.

Further reading

Most introductory tourism texts include sections or chapters on tourism demand and motivation. For example:

Fletcher, J., Fyall, A., Gilbert, D. and Wanhill, S. (2013) *Tourism: Principles and Practice.* Harlow: Pearson Education (Chapters 2 and 3).

Page, S. and Connell, J. (2014) *Tourism: A Modern Synthesis.* London: Thomson Learning (Chapter 4).

More detailed analyses of tourism motivation are to be found in seminal papers, in particular:

Dann, G. (1981) Tourist motivation: An appraisal. *Annals of Tourism Research*, 8(2): 187–219.

Mansfeld, Y. (1992) From motivation to actual travel. *Annals of Tourism Research,* 19(3): 399–419.

Moutinho, L. (1987) Consumer behaviour in tourism. *European Journal of Marketing*, 21(10): 5–44.

Discussion topics

▶ Why is it important not to confuse motivational 'push' factors with destinational 'pull' factors?

▶ Most people do not know what motivates them to participate in tourism. To what extent do you agree with this statement?

▶ Is tourism primarily motivated by the need to escape?

▶ It is claimed by some that participation in tourism is now a habit. Does this make the study of tourist motivation irrelevant?

6

The consumption of tourism

Introduction

The demand for tourism is a complex, dynamic and multi-dimensional process. It is a process whereby tourists, as consumers of tourism experiences, progress through a number of stages, from the initial identification of the need or desire to travel (the motivational stage) to the final, evaluation and feedback stage. Each stage potentially feeds backwards or forwards into preceding or subsequent stages and, at the same time, a variety of external variables influence of the process. To complicate matters further, for the individual tourist each tourism experience links into subsequent tourism demand processes in a continuous and evolving process. This occurs as long as the tourist continues to participate in tourism and, throughout this 'travel career', it is likely that the tourist's increasing experience and knowledge of tourism will further influence and shape the demand process. It is not surprising, then, that the demand for tourism has been described as 'discretionary, episodic, future oriented, dynamic, socially influenced and evolving' (Pearce, 1992: 114).

Despite this complexity, there are a variety of ways in which the outcome of the tourism demand process may be predicted. As discussed in Chapter 4, early attempts focused upon the construction of tourist typologies which, although suffering a number of shortcomings, provide a basis for understanding how particular types of tourists are likely to behave. That is, they ascribe different styles of tourism consumption to different types of people according to a variety of psychographic variables. As we have seen, however, these typologies do little to explain why people choose to consume tourism in the first place. Therefore, researchers have long been concerned with the analysis of tourist motivation, exploring those social and psychological factors which influence tourists' wants and needs.

An understanding of the tourism demand process and the study of tourist motivation as a primary, integral element of that process is of course important. Nevertheless, of equal if not greater importance is the recognition that the demand for tourism should not be viewed in isolation from the broader cultural context within which it occurs. That is, tourism is just one of a whole host of goods and services that people in modern

societies consume. The relative importance of different goods and services, their meaning or significance, and the manner in which they are consumed is determined as much
by the cultural condition of society as it is by the needs and desires of individual consumers. So an analysis of the demand for tourism is not complete without considering
how the consumption of tourism in particular is influenced and framed by what is
termed 'consumer culture' in general.

Thus, the purpose of this chapter is to explore the link between tourism and the
cultural context of consumption. First, it introduces an important group of variables
which potentially shape or impinge upon the overall consumption of tourism, namely:
the attitudes and values of tourists.

Values and the consumption of tourism

Although motivation is widely considered to be the trigger, or the primary energising
factor in the tourism consumption process, most tourism demand models recognise
the existence of other factors, or 'affectors' of demand (Gilbert, 1991: 79), that may also
influence the behaviour of tourists. A number of these variables may play a direct role
at the motivational stage, determining people's needs and wants and thus being translated through motivation into goal-oriented (tourism consumption) behaviour. Many
of these factors are highlighted in Chapter 5.

The subsequent stages of the demand process, such as the information search, the
comparison of alternatives and final choice, as well as the actual and evaluated experience of the holiday, are also influenced by a variety of factors. These may include past
experiences, the advice of friends and relatives and, in particular, demographic variables.
Indeed, it is 'commonly believed that tourist behaviour [is] affected, if not determined,
by the tourist's age, sex, marital status, education, disposable income, place of origin and
other similar factors' (Pizam & Calantone, 1987: 177). Yet, in much the same way that
tourist typologies are formulated according to the observed behaviour of different types
of tourists, such variables are for the most part descriptive. That is, although they are of
use in segmenting tourist markets and as a basic predictor of how certain groups may
consume tourism, they reveal little about why tourists behave in particular ways.

As a result, some commentators believe that so-called psychographic or lifestyle
variables, including values, attitudes, opinions and interests, are more important factors
in the tourism decision-making process (Luk et al., 1993). Potentially revealing 'more
meaningful information' about tourists' behaviour (Cha et al., 1995: 38), psychographic
analysis has been used by a number of researchers in segmenting tourist markets and
explaining behaviour (for example, Mayo, 1975; Woodside & Pitts, 1976). For the purposes of this chapter it is important to distinguish between concepts such as attitudes,
interests and values. The reason for this is that, although they are frequently and collectively referred to as affectors of demand, and are often used interchangeably, there
are fundamental differences in what constitutes them and how they may influence
behaviour. Moreover, it is values, in particular, that may reflect a society's beliefs or value
systems and thus be structurally determined, and which may influence the demand for
tourism.

According to Rokeach (1973: 18), 'an attitude differs from a value in that an attitude refers to an organisation of several beliefs around a specific object or situation. A value, on the other hand, refers to a single belief of a very specific kind.' In other words, 'values transcend specific objects and situations' (Feather, 1975: 10) and are concerned with desirable or acceptable forms of behaviour or end-states, whereas attitudes are commonly related to specific objects or situations. The implication of this is that values are the dominant force in shaping people's ideas, attitudes and opinions. That is, values precede or guide attitudes and behaviour, serving as standards or criteria for personally and socially preferable conduct or outcomes of behaviour (Kamakura & Mazzon, 1991). Values 'govern a person's lifestyle and provide a direct and useful explanation of the multitude of interests, outlooks on life, consumption practices, and activities that define a lifestyle' (Müller, 1991: 57). Thus, tourists may have different attitudes towards different destinations or types of tourism. Overall, however, the way in which they consume tourism is likely to be influenced by their personal values with respect to, for example, the importance they attach to leisure as opposed to work or to the experiences they seek through tourism.

Concern for the role of values has long been an integral element of the study of consumer behaviour in general; surprisingly, perhaps, relatively less attention has been paid to the role of values on the consumption of tourism in particular. Much of the research into the link between values and consumer behaviour is based upon the pioneering work of Rokeach (1973). He defines a value as an 'enduring belief that a specific mode of conduct or end-state of existence is personally or socially preferable to an opposite or converse mode of conduct or end-state of existence' (Rokeach, 1973: 5). Values represent a set of prescriptive beliefs that guide the choice or evaluation of potential behaviour. It is also evident that, to be socially preferable, some values are structurally formulated; that is, some values represent socially acceptable behaviour and are thus internalised by the individual through the socialisation process (see Chapter 1). Conversely, it is likely that some personal values may result from social interaction.

Not only do individuals carry these beliefs or values which determine their modes of behaviour, they also organise these beliefs into a value system which represents a continuum of the relative importance of the different values they hold. In other words, most people possess multiple values which they prioritise into a system or hierarchy which is 'stable enough to reflect the fact of sameness and continuity of a unique personality socialised within a given culture and society, yet unstable enough to permit rearrangements of value priorities as a result of changes in culture, society, and personal experience' (Rokeach, 1973: 11). Thus, an individual tourist's value system may, in theory, adapt according to social or cultural influences. For example, the contemporary widespread belief that sunbathing may be harmful in the longer term might influence the individual to put 'health' values before 'pleasure' values. Similarly, the alleged increase in environmental awareness throughout society might encourage tourists to place environmental values in a higher position in the value system, although in the context of tourism this does not yet appear to be the case, suggesting that more personal, hedonistic values dominate, in general, the consumption of tourism (Sharpley, 2006).

According to Rokeach, it is also important to distinguish between so-called instrumental values which guide modes of conduct and may be seen, therefore, as means to an end, and terminal values which relate to the desired end-state. Instrumental values, which include concepts such as honesty and responsibility, can be sub-divided into either moral or competence/self-actualisation values, whilst terminal values, such as freedom, self-respect or equality, may similarly have either a social or personal focus. Implicitly, instrumental values are, literally, instrumental in the attainment of terminal, end-state values, although the distinction or causal links between the two are not always clear. For example, honesty might be instrumental in achieving self-respect, whilst environmentally appropriate behaviour might be instrumental in achieving a world of beauty (the latter identified by Rokeach as a terminal value). But both of these instrumental values may become goals in themselves, whilst other single or combinations of modes of behaviour may be instrumental in achieving any one terminal goal. Thus, the terminal value of self-respect may be achieved through a combination of honesty, courage and environmental awareness. Despite this ambiguity, the concept of a value system based upon means and end values provides a useful conceptual framework for understanding how values influence behaviour in a variety of situations, including the consumption of tourism.

In order to try to measure values, Rokeach developed his Rokeach Value Survey (RVS), which consists of 18 instrumental values and 18 terminal values (see Figure 6.1). It is immediately apparent from this list of instrumental and terminal values that there is a close link or relationship between values and motivations as determinants of human behaviour, suggesting that values do indeed play an important role as determinants or predictors of behaviour. For example, the five hierarchical needs identified by Maslow (1943) – physiological, safety, love, esteem and self-actualisation – and which were discussed in the context of tourist motivation in Chapter 5, are generally reflected in many of Rokeach's terminal values.

At the same time, and more specifically, the two primary tourism motivational factors – namely avoidance/escape and self-reward/ego-enhancement (Dann, 1977; Mannell & Iso-Ahola, 1987) – are also implicitly encompassed by terminal values such as pleasure, self-respect and freedom. Equally, many of the other terminal values identified by Rokeach can be transposed onto tourist motivation and behaviour. For example, tourism may satisfy, either directly or through the process of inversion, the 'comfortable life' value, whilst 'happiness', as discussed towards the end of this chapter, is likely to be a dominant influencing value either in many people's tourism decision-making process or in the evaluation of their touristic experiences.

The RVS has been used in a variety of applications (see Kamakura & Mazzon, 1991), including Luk et al.'s (1993) segmentation of tourists' service quality expectations. In its original form it is somewhat complex and, subsequently, it has been simplified and adapted into new value scales for the specific purpose of market research/segmentation and the analysis of consumer behaviour.

One example of this is the List of Values (LOV) scale, a simplified and shortened version of the RVS which is used to identify nine consumer segments based upon the values they endorse.

Similarly, the Values and Lifestyle Scale (VALS) divides American consumers into nine lifestyles or types under four categories based upon their self-images, aspirations, values and beliefs (see Figure 6.2).

Instrumental values	Terminal values
Ambitious *(hard-working, aspiring)*	A comfortable life *(a prosperous life)*
Broadminded *(open-minded)*	An exciting life *(a stimulating, active life)*
Capable *(competent, effective)*	A sense of accomplishment *(lasting contribution)*
Cheerful *(light-hearted, joyful)*	A world at peace *(free of war and conflict)*
Clean *(neat, tidy)*	A world of beauty *(beauty of nature and arts)*
Courageous *(Standing up for your beliefs)*	Equality *(brotherhood, equal opportunity for all)*
Forgiving *(willing to pardon others)*	Family security *(taking care of loved ones)*
Helpful *(working for the welfare of others)*	Freedom *(independence, free choice)*
Honest *(sincere, truthful)*	Happiness *(contentedness)*
Imaginative *(daring, creative)*	Inner harmony *(freedom from inner conflict)*
Independent *(self-reliant, self-sufficient)*	Mature love *(sexual and spiritual intimacy)*
Intellectual *(intelligent, reflective)*	National security *(protection from attack)*
Logical *(consistent, rational)*	Pleasure *(an enjoyable, leisurely life)*
Loving *(affectionate, tender)*	Salvation *(saved, eternal life)*
Obedient *(dutiful, respectful)*	Self-respect *(self-esteem)*
Polite *(courteous, well-mannered)*	Self-recognition *(respect, admiration)*
Responsible *(dependable, reliable)*	True friendship *(close companionship)*
Self-controlled *(restrained, self-disciplined)*	Wisdom *(a mature understanding of life)*

FIGURE 6.1 The values of the Rokeach Value Survey

Source: Adapted from Rokeach (1973: 359–360)

Need-driven groups:	Outer-directed groups:
Survivor lifestyle	Belongers lifestyle
Sustainer lifestyle	Emulator lifestyle
	Achiever lifestyle
Inner-directed groups:	Outer/inner-directed groups:
I-am-me lifestyle	Integrated lifestyle
Experiential lifestyle	
Societally conscious lifestyle	
Self-directed lifestyle	

FIGURE 6.2 VALS categories
Source: Adapted from Shih (1986)

Again, there are evident links between these groups and sub-groups of consumer types and different forms of tourist behaviour, suggesting that the VALS scale represents a useful predictor of tourism demand. For example, the inner-directed socially conscious lifestyle group is made up of 'consumers who are mission- or cause-oriented and have a sense of social responsibility. They favor appeals stressing conservation, simplicity, frugality, and environmental concerns' (Shih, 1986: 4). This suggests that the societally conscious group will seek out appropriate forms of tourism, such as ecotourism. Similarly, the outer-directed sub-group of emulators might be expected to participate in forms of tourism which enhance their status.

Interestingly, although value scales have been found to be reliable predictors of consumer behaviour in general, with the LOV scale being found to be the more accurate (Kahle et al., 1986; Novak & MacEvoy, 1990), there have been relatively few empirical studies into the effect of values on tourist behaviour in particular. In early studies, Boote (1981) discovered that consumer preferences for different chains of family restaurants could be revealed by value-based segmentation methods, whilst Pitts and Woodside (1986) linked ten recreation and leisure choice criteria to a number of instrumental and terminal values in the context of different tourism settings and attractions. They found that 'values were shown to be related to differences in choice criteria and to actual behaviour' (Pitts & Woodside, 1986: 23). Madrigal and Kahle (1994) considered the role of value systems, as opposed to single values, in tourist behaviour and concluded that what they termed value domains 'may be an important set of variables to be considered in predicting what lures tourists to a destination' (Madrigal & Kahle, 1994: 27).

They also suggested that values alone are not a sufficient criterion for predicting behaviour, destination attributes and tourists' demographic characteristics and needs also being important variables. Nevertheless, studies by Pizam and Calantone (1987), Müller (1991), Dalen (1989), Thrane (1997) and, more recently, Mehmetoglu et al. (2010) also support the general argument that 'travel behaviour is significantly associated with a person's general values and vacation-specific values, therefore lending support to the ... theory that values can act as predictors of travel behaviour' (Pizam & Calantone, 1987: 180).

The role of values in determining tourist behaviour must, however, still be considered within the overall context of the decision-making process. That is, although values may be a powerful and influential force in consumer behaviour, there are many other factors which, as we have already seen, may shape tourist preferences and behaviour. More specifically, there is little evidence to suggest that the values that people hold have an effect on all forms of consumption. To put it another way, different types of consumption may be influenced by different values and, therefore, the consumption of tourism may not follow the pattern of other activities. This supports the argument that individuals possess a variety of values, each of which may be more or less influential in different situations. As Madrigal and Kahle (1994) observe, a number of different values may be relevant to particular situations or decisions. These different values are hierarchically ordered in a value system and 'an individual relies on his/her value system to maintain self-esteem or consistency in those situations where one or more conflicting values are activated' (Madrigal & Kahle, 1994: 23). Within the tourism consumption process, the likelihood of value conflict is high, particularly between personal terminal values (for example, pleasure, freedom, happiness) and social values that serve as guidelines for socially acceptable behaviour. In many cases, tourism may provide the opportunity for people to behave in ways that are directly in conflict with their normal values; that is, tourism allows people to escape not only from their home social environment but also from the constraints of their normal social life, constraints which may include many of the socially constructed values that they hold. As a result, it is important to now consider what may be described as the meaning of tourism as a form of consumption in modern or culturally postmodern societies.

Tourism and consumer culture

As discussed in Chapter 5, it is motivation that triggers the tourism consumption process. In other words, if there is to be a demand for tourism, there must also exist needs and wants, or energisers of demand, which through the motivational process become translated into goal-oriented behaviour. Moreover, the manner in which individuals attempt to satisfy these needs and wants through the consumption of tourism – or the character of their goal-oriented behaviour – is to a great extent shaped or modified by a variety of deterministic influences, including demographic factors, roles and values.

Given this primary and fundamental role of motivation and the potentially significant influence of those factors which affect, shape or filter the demand for tourism, it is not surprising that researchers have long been concerned with analysing and attempting to develop an understanding of tourist motivation and the overall tourism demand process. The purpose of such research has been primarily to enable the prediction of tourist behaviour, with evident practical applications in terms of product design, market segmentation and so on.

However, one inherent weakness of much of the work concerned with the demand for or consumption of tourism is that it has adopted an overly tourism-centric perspective. That is, most commentators have traditionally approached the consumption of tourism in isolation from other forms of consumption and from the broader social and cultural influences that pattern or shape consumer behaviour as a whole; in particular, little or no reference is made to the influence of consumer culture on the consumption of tourism. Thus, the existence of tourism as a specific form of consumer behaviour is not questioned. In other words, it is tacitly accepted that ever-increasing numbers of people participate in tourism, but attention is focused primarily on how the demand for tourism is determined by motivational and other factors. As a result, less importance has until recently been attached to the explanation of the significance and meaning of tourism as a form of consumption in general, and the ways in which the consumption or styles of tourism may be influenced by cultural transformations and developments in the tourist's home environment in particular.

To put it another way, the analysis of tourism demand and motivation in the literature is, for the most part, based on the premise that tourism is a satisfier of needs and wants (Mill & Morrison, 1985: 4). The inward, tourism-centric focus of much of the relevant research has meant that, whilst attention has been directed at identifying those needs and wants and how they may be satisfied, in a utilitarian sense, by tourism, less emphasis has been placed on addressing broader, culturally related issues. For example, why is tourism, as opposed to other modes of behaviour, chosen as a form of consumption? Why has international tourism, over the space of some 40 years, been transformed from a luxury into a perceived 'necessity'? Why do styles of tourism consumption change? Many of the needs relevant to tourist motivation, such as the physiological needs of rest and relaxation, or the ego-enhancement needs referred to in the preceding chapter, may be satisfied by a variety of different activities, yet tourism remains an increasingly popular activity, with ever greater demands for specialised, niche products. This suggests that the widely held belief, 'I need a holiday', is as much a cultural construct as it is a rational, need-satisfying course of action. It also suggests, of course, that the consumption of tourism encompasses a meaning and purpose beyond basic, utilitarian need satisfaction.

In short, tourism as a form of consumption central to the modern leisure experience cannot, or should not, be considered in isolation from the wider cultural framework within which it occurs. This is particularly so in those tourism generating societies which have experienced a cultural shift towards the condition of postmodernity because, as proposed in Chapter 3, consumption patterns have become one of the defining characteristics of postmodernity. Whereas, in the modern era, an individual's position or identity was commensurate with his or her work, social class and so on, the de-differentiating process that defines postmodernity has required alternative methods of creating or achieving self-identity. This role has been filled by consumption; indeed, 'consumption has been seen as epitomising this move into postmodernity' (Bocock, 1993: 4) and postmodern culture is very much identified with consumer culture. So it is important to explore how the consumption of tourism is influenced by this broader, postmodern consumer culture within which it occurs.

The evolution of consumer culture

Consumer culture may be defined as the character, significance and role of the consumption of commodities, services and experiences within modern societies. Its existence as a cultural phenomenon implies that consumption, as a social activity, has become culturally significant, particularly in contrast to the role of its opposing phenomenon, production, which was dominant during the modern era. Indeed, as Pretes observes, a fundamental feature of postmodern culture is that 'consumption, rather than production, becomes dominant' (Pretes, 1995: 2). This has not, however, always been the case.

It has long been recognised that a relationship exists between production and consumption of goods and services, a relationship which, as Miller (1987: 134) observes, was traditionally characterised by viewing consumption activities 'as the result of, or as a process secondary to, the development of manufacturing and other forms of production'. Certainly, within the context of tourism, recent years have witnessed a change in the nature of the production-consumption relationship as demonstrated by, for example, increases in the number of specialist tour operators, the promotion of niche markets, the development of more individual, flexible forms of tourism and, in particular, the increasing significance of the Internet in both the supply of and demand for tourism. This change may, in turn, be linked to shifts in consumer culture and the increasingly dominant role of consumers, meaning that, conversely, the role of the producer has been weakened. Thus, consumer culture has evolved and is directly related to the changing production-consumption relationship. Three stages in the evolution of consumer culture have been suggested by Featherstone (1990; 1991).

1   The production of consumption. From the production of consumption perspective, reflecting the traditional view of the production-consumption relationship, consumer culture is related to and emerges from the mass production of goods and services for purchase and consumption, with the producers being able to dictate styles, fashion and taste. As a result of this culture of mass production and consumption, and the inherent need for all commodities to appeal to the widest possible market, high and low culture become merged with the cultural value of commodities tending towards the lowest common denominator. Thus, from this perspective on consumption, the dominant role of the producer leads, perhaps inevitably, to a diluted and homogeneous cultural value of mass goods and services which, in a differentiated, modernist society, serves to reflect 'given social hierarchies' (Miller, 1987: 135). Described elsewhere as a process of 'McDonaldization' (Ritzer, 2015), this approach is of most relevance in the context of tourism to the analysis of earlier forms of mass, package tourism; through developing efficient and predictable means of transporting large numbers of tourists, the producers of package tourism were, to a great extent, able to control the development and style of the mass consumption of tourism, and (cultural) product quality was sacrificed to price. Thus, in short, this perspective proposes that goods (and services) are produced and then consumed as and when individuals have wants or needs that require satisfaction. In this sense, then, consumption can be viewed on the basis of the utility or 'use-value' of commodities (Warde, 1992: 17). It is also, in a cultural sense, production-led. Through Fordist production methods and as an essential prerequisite for such forms of production, producers are able to dictate what, when and how consumers consume (see McCracken, 1986). As discussed in Chapter 2 and elsewhere (Sharpley, 2017), the success of Billy Butlin's holiday camps in the UK was based on his application of Fordist production methods which still arguably, underpin some contemporary forms of tourism, such as the all-inclusive concept.

2   The mode of consumption. In contrast, the second approach or stage focuses upon the mode of consumption, highlighting the culture of consumption rather than simply viewing consumption as the inevitable result of production. It is based upon the notion that, within postmodern, post-industrial societies (or, societies where tertiary, service industries increasingly dominate the economy) traditional social groupings have been replaced by a new and expanding middle or 'service' class (see Urry, 1988; Featherstone, 1990; Voase, 1995). No longer enjoying a sense of self-identity through traditional roles, these new 'service classes' have turned to what and how they consume as markers of identity. Producers have had to respond, leading to a corresponding reversal of power in the production-consumption relationship. This 'use' of consumption is considered in more detail shortly.

3   The consumption of dreams. Of particular relevance to the postmodern consumption of tourism, the third perspective on consumer culture concentrates on 'the emotional pleasures of consumption, the dreams and desires which become celebrated in consumer cultural imagery' (Featherstone, 1990). In this case, consumption neither flows logically from production, nor does it play a role in the determination of social status; the production-consumption relationship becomes irrelevant. Rather, consumption is viewed as the fulfilment of dreams, as a search for pleasurable experiences, as a means of escaping from the rigidity and structure of day-to-day culture and society. Reference is frequently made to the traditional role of fairs and carnivals in the pre-industrial era – they were both local markets and places to indulge in pleasure, to experience unusual or exotic images. It is not surprising, then, that tourism is seen by some as a continuation of the carnivalesque tradition into postmodern consumer culture; the spectacle of mass tourism at the seaside resorts in the late nineteenth and early twentieth centuries and, more recently, the popularity of, for example, theme parks are both seen as evidence of this trend (Urry, 1990a). More generally, of course, the desire to escape from the ordinary and mundane, to consume the dreams and fantasy of travel, is also considered to be a major tourism motivating factor (Dann, 1981).

If these three perspectives on consumer culture are applied to tourism, it is evident that, in recent years, the nature of the consumption of tourism has developed from a producer-led to a consumer-led form of consumption. Earlier forms of tourism leading, in particular, to the development of mass, package tourism were symptomatic of the dominant role of tour operators in shaping holiday tastes and styles based upon the modernist, 'Fordist' approach to mass production. More recently, however, the tourism industry has been obliged to become increasingly responsive to the changing demands of the consumer. What this signifies, in the more general context of consumption, is that the culture of consumption has come to occupy the dominant position in the production-consumption relationship. This has come about, in part, from a variety of factors and transformations within the wider social and economic system in post-industrial societies that have enabled the practice of consumption to assume a leading role in people's lives. Such factors include the large, widely available and ever-increasing range of consumer goods and services, the popularity of 'leisure shopping', the emergence of consumer groups and consumer legislation, pervasive advertising, widely available credit facilities and 'the impossibility of avoiding making choices in relation to consumer goods' (Lury, 1996: 36).

However, it is not only the practice but also the significance of consumption that is of vital importance in the emergence of a dominant consumer culture. We recognise that commodities, whether goods or services, have a meaning beyond their economic exchange or use value. As Lury (1996: 11) explains,

> the utility of goods is always framed by a cultural context, that even the use of the most mundane objects in daily life has cultural meaning . . . material goods are not only used to do things, but they also have a meaning, and act as meaningful markers of social relationships.

In fact, it has been argued that consumption results only from the inherent meaning or significance of goods, their use-value being irrelevant (Baudrillard, 1988), although this is disputed by others (Warde, 1992: 26). Nevertheless, social lives are, in short, patterned, or indeed created, by the acquisition and use (that is, consumption) of things. A well-used example is that of the motor car. In simple utilitarian terms, the car is no more than a convenient, independent, motorised means of travelling from one point to another quickly and in comfort. But, for most people, the choice involved in purchasing a car goes well beyond the practical advantages of car transport; the car is, arguably, one of the most powerful status symbols of the contemporary era.

The combined practice and significance of consumption can, thus, be conceptualised as the 'active ideology that the meaning of life is to be found in buying things and pre-packed experiences' (Bocock, 1993: 50). In other words, consumption in late twentieth century/early twenty-first century capitalist economies 'must not be understood as the consumption of use-values, a material utility, but primarily as the consumption of signs' (Featherstone, 1991: 85). Also, within postmodern culture in particular, this symbolic process inherent in consumption is considered by many to be its role in creating a sense of identity and status or, as Bourdieu (1986) proposes, in establishing distinctions between different social groups. As Miller (1987: 135) argues:

> In a period of strong social stratification, objects tend to reflect given social hierarchies. . . . When, however, this [stratification] breaks down, goods can change from being relatively static symbols to being more directly constitutive of social status. . . . In other words, demand for goods may flourish in the context of ambiguity in social hierarchy.

Such 'ambiguity in social hierarchy' connotes the de-differentiation of social groups in postmodern societies (see Chapter 3); groups which were previously identified and demarcated by work roles now seek identity and status through consumption.

Although much of the consumer behaviour literature is concerned primarily with the role of consumption in identity-construction or group-distinction, it is not the only symbolic or social role of consumption. In other words, the 'act of consuming is a varied and effortful accomplishment undetermined by the characteristics of the object. A given consumption object (for example, a food, a sports activity, a television programme, or an art object) is typically consumed in a variety of ways by different groups of consumers' (Holt, 1995: 1). In other words, although some individual's consumption practices may be identity or status driven – what Holt describes as 'consuming-as-classification' – the same consumption objects, including tourism, may be consumed by others in different ways. Different objects of consumption, whether goods (for example, a car or an item of clothing) or services (for example, a meal in a restaurant) mean different things to different people. Varying significance may be attached to the same object and it is consumed in different ways. Holt (1995) identifies a total of four categories of consumption:

a) consumption as experience;

b) consumption as play;

c) consumption as integration; and

d) consumption as classification.

These four categories provide a useful basis and framework for looking at the different ways in which tourism in particular may be consumed. Before doing so, it is important to emphasise that the main point to emerge from this discussion is that not only have tourists, as in all forms of postmodern consumption, assumed the leading role in the tourism production-consumption relationship, but also the style of tourism they desire and their behaviour as consumers (tourists) will be influenced by the significance attached to the consumption of tourism. In other words, the tourism industry is no longer in the position of being able to dictate the supply of tourism. Tourists are demanding an ever-increasing variety of tourism experiences, experiences which, moreover, have a significance beyond their utility value. That is, tourism provides more than escape, more than two weeks on a beach, more than the chance to explore new places and cultures. Tourism plays a much broader role in people's lives, a role which influences how they consume tourism.

To return to Holt's fourfold categorisation of consumption practices, he suggests that there are two ways of conceptualising consumption – the purpose of consumption and the structure of consumption. In terms of purpose, consumers' actions may be ends in themselves (autotelic) or means to an end (instrumental). Structurally, consumption may be focused directly upon the object of consumption or, conversely, the objects of consumption may serve as a focal point for interpersonal actions. These two dimensions form a grid within which a typology of consumption may be located (see Figure 6.3),

	Autotelic actions	Instrumental actions
Object actions	Consumption as experience	Consumption as integration
Interpersonal actions	Consumption as play	Consumption as classification

FIGURE 6.3 A typology of consumption

Source: Adapted from Holt (1995)

the purpose being to provide a framework for analysing the different ways in which consumers interact with particular consumption objects.

As suggested above, tourism is no different from other consumption objects in that, depending on the significance that people attach to it, they will consume it in different ways. Therefore, this typology can be applied to tourism to reveal the different meaning or significance that culturally frames the consumption of tourism.

Consuming tourism as experience

The consumption-as-experience perspective focuses upon the subjective or emotional reactions of consumers to particular consumption objects.

It is concerned with the ways in which people experience, or make sense of, different objects, or as Holbrook and Hirschman (1982: 132) put it, 'this experiential perspective is phenomenological in spirit and regards consumption as a primarily subjective state of consciousness'. Moreover, 'how consumers experience consumption objects is structured by the interpretative framework(s) that they apply to engage the object' (Holt, 1995: 3). More simply stated, many consumption objects (goods and services) are located or are provided within a social world which provides the framework for their definition, meaning or understanding.

Tourism is no exception to this process. As a form of consumption, it is firmly embedded in tourists' social world and the ways in which people experience, or consume, tourism will depend very much on their interpretation of the role or meaning of tourism within that social world. For example, tourism may be interpreted as a form of sacred consumption (Graburn, 1989). It occurs outside normal (profane) times and places – it 'is a festive, liminal time when behaviour is different from ordinary work time' (Belk et al., 1989: 12) and is consumed as a sacred or spiritual experience. Tourists' behaviour will, therefore, be framed by this sacralisation of tourism and may be manifested in different ways. Thus, some may seek the spiritual refreshment of solitary, romantic tourist places, regarding

> as quintessentially sacred those places . . . that are exceptionally natural, uncrowded, and unspoiled by other tourists. Such places are sacred not only because they are perceived as authentic and unspoiled; there is also some naturism or reverence for nature reflected.
>
> (Belk et al., 1989: 17; also, Walter, 1982)

Conversely, for others the sacred nature of tourism may be reflected in their collective or communal experience of tourist sites and destinations. In other words, the annual holiday becomes a kind of ritualistic gathering where tourists participate in particular types of behaviour; for example, the mass migration of young people to places such as Ibiza, where they indulge in various forms of excessive behaviour, may be described as a cultural ritual no different from, say, the annual family gathering at Christmas.

Importantly, the consumption of tourism is also framed by the experiential aspect of modern consumption as a whole, namely, that 'the consumption experience [is] a phenomenon directed towards the pursuit of fantasies, feelings, and fun' (Holbrook & Hirschman, 1982: 132). In other words, consumption is directed towards the hedonistic pursuit of pleasure, pleasure which, according to Campbell, results not from physical satisfaction but from romantic day-dreaming:

> The essential activity of consumption is thus not the actual selection, purchase or use of products, but the imaginative pleasure-seeking to which the product image lends itself, 'real' consumption being largely a resultant of the 'mentalistic' hedonism.
>
> (Campbell, 1987: 89)

Tourism in particular lends itself to this concept of consumption as the pursuit of illusory pleasure, especially as day-dreaming suggests desires for the novel, different or 'other' (see also Featherstone's (1991: 21) discussion of consuming dreams, images and pleasure). Indeed, novelty seeking has been a fruitful area of research in the context of tourism consumer behaviour (Dimanche & Havitz, 1994; Jang & Feng, 2007; Lee & Crompton, 1992). The implication of this is that, for the most part, the experiential consumption of tourism represents, most frequently, the consumption of dreams, an escape to the non-ordinary, sacred, novel 'other'. It is the experiential participation in the ritual of tourism, a ritual that, however defined by the individual tourist, is the antithesis to the normal or ordinary existence. Thus, if tourists are seeking authenticity (see Chapter 9), that authenticity must also represent 'The Other'.

Consuming tourism as integration

According to Holt, consumption-as-integration is an instrumental action through which consumers are able to 'integrate self and object, thereby allowing themselves access to the object's symbolic properties' (Holt, 1995: 2). The object becomes a constituent element of their identity, either by merging external objects into their self-concept, or by adapting their self-concept to align it with the socially or institutionally defined identity of the object.

In the case of the consumption of tourism, integration is automatic as tourists play an integral role in the production of tourism experiences – as with all services, production and consumption are inseparable and instantaneous, and tourists cannot be separated from the 'product' (see Middleton, 1988: 26). But much depends upon the direction of that integration. A tourist who wishes to be identified with a particular destination's culture or society or with a particular form of tourism may adapt his/her self-concept to 'fit' the identity of the destination or tourism-type. Thus, for example, individuals who see themselves as 'good', environmentally aware tourists will adapt their behaviour by consuming particular types of tourism or by assimilating into the local area; the self is integrated into the object. Conversely, to return to the example of the island of Ibiza, young tourists may behave in a certain way because they wish to integrate themselves into the local tourism cultural scene; they fit themselves to the image of the destination.

On the other hand, certain types of tourism or tourist experience may be integrated into the individual's self-concept in a process of self-extension (see Arnould & Price, 1993, for an analysis of white-water rafting as an example of one such form of tourism); here, the object is integrated into the self.

Consuming tourism as play

The consumption-as-play perspective suggests that people utilise objects as a resource or focus for interaction with other consumers, rather than referring specifically to the experiential characteristics of the consumption object. Thus, in the context of tourism, consuming-as-play does not refer, for example, to the ludic or 'tourist-as-child' (Dann, 1996) character of certain experiences, but to the fact that tourism is used as a vehicle for socialising with fellow consumers of tourism or sharing particular experiences.

This draws attention to the fact that tourism is, frequently, a social experience, an element of which is 'to be able to consume particular commodities in the company of others. Part of what people buy is in effect a particular social composition of other consumers' (Urry, 1990b: 25). In this sense, tourism provides the focus for people to socialise or to fulfil a more performative, reciprocal (Holt, 1995: 9) role in entertaining each other. Equally, tourism may also be a means of sharing unusual or extraordinary experiences; the communal interaction with the consumption object allows tourists to commune or experience *communitas* (again, see Arnould & Price, 1993). In either case, however, the focus is on the communal, social nature of the consumption experience rather than the object of consumption. Up to a point, it becomes less important where tourism is being consumed and, indeed, what the nature of the tourism experience is. More important is the fact that the consumption of tourism is a shared experience, where tourists consume tourism to be themselves, to escape from themselves or to share the unusual with others. In the last of these, the true consumption experience may be the shared 'looking forward to looking back'; that is, the shared experience of something different or even dangerous that will be re-lived in later conversations.

Consuming tourism as classification

Most commonly, consumption is considered a means of classification. Particularly within de-differentiated, postmodern societies, consumers utilise consumption objects to create self-identity and to 'classify themselves in relation to relevant others' (Holt, 1995: 10). It has been argued, for example, that traditional social groupings are being replaced by a new and expanding middle or 'service' class (Featherstone, 1990; Voase, 1995). Within this new social class, there are two identifiable groups, namely, those who possess both economic and cultural capital in significant quantities (the new bourgeoisie), and those who possess cultural capital but less economic capital – the new 'petit bourgeoisie' (Bourdieu, 1986). The latter, larger group are seen as the new taste-makers; having less financial resources, their consumption practices are guided by the identity value of goods and services. 'Style, status, group identification, etc., are aspects of identity-value' (Warde, 1992: 18) and they seek social differentiation and status through different styles, rather than values, of consumption. Different goods and services have different social and cultural values and serve as markers of taste and style. For the new middle classes as a whole, consumption has become one of the primary means of demarcating social status and relationships in a postmodern era where traditional social markers no longer exist.

In the context of tourism, the consumption-as-classification perspective points to the role of tourism consumption in identity and status formation. Tourism has long been a marker of social status and the history of tourism is little more than the story of how tourists have sought social status through emulating the touristic practices of the higher or wealthier classes. Yet, while 'travel has remained an expression of taste since the eighteenth century, it has never been so widely used as at present' (Munt, 1994: 109). In response, the travel industry is developing more specialised, niche products, such as eco (or 'ego') tourism, or styles of tourism which, though relatively affordable, have the aura of status or luxury. An example of the latter has been the introduction of cruise holidays

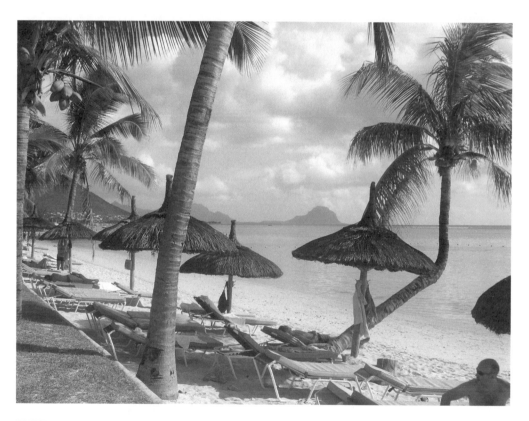

PLATE 6.1 Holidays in Mauritius: a status symbol?
Source: Photo by Richard Sharpley

by some of the larger British tour operators, bringing the 'exclusivity' of cruising within the economic reach of the mass tourist.

Together, these different forms or approaches to consumption in general suggest that a variety of different meanings can be attached to the consumption of tourism in particular. This, in turn, suggests that an understanding of tourist typologies and motivation is not in itself sufficient to have a complete appreciation of the demand process. In other words, there is no doubt that, for many tourists, the prime objective remains the ego-centric desire to escape, rest, relax and have fun. Equally, the way in which they fulfil that desire will be dictated, up to a point, by their individual psychographic characteristics and by particular constraining factors. But there is also no doubt that tourism, as a form of consumption, is culturally framed; the societies which generate tourists can have a major influence on the significance of tourism as a form of consumption in those societies, and are likely to do so as long as consumer culture remains dominant.

Consuming tourism: consuming happiness?

As noted in the introduction to this chapter, tourism is one of innumerable 'things' (Appadurai, 1988) that people in modern societies consume. Indeed, modern societies are essentially consumer societies (Schor & Holt, 2000); as countries develop and become wealthier, not only do their economies become ever more dependent on the demand for or consumption of an increasingly diverse array of goods and services, but their citizens' lives and identities, their subjective well-being (or more broadly, their 'happiness'), are increasingly defined or determined by their consumption practices. And, as de Botton (2002: 9) observes, 'if our lives are dominated by a search for happiness, then perhaps few activities reveal as much about the dynamics of this quest than our travels'. In short, participation in tourism, as a specific and increasingly pervasive form of consumption, may be considered to be the pursuit of happiness.

Yet, the question must be asked: is to consume tourism to consume happiness? Putting it another way, at the end of a paper exploring the relationship between tourism and consumerism, Hall (2011: 301) asks: 'why have so many people increasingly come to believe that consuming such mobility will somehow make them happier and improve their life?' In other words, despite the significant academic attention paid to the issue of tourism motivation, or why people engage in tourism, there remains limited understanding why, or even if, tourism has come to be considered as a potential source of happiness and well-being.

This is not to say that the issue has been completely overlooked. For example, Nawijn (2010; 2011a, b; also Nawijn et al., 2010) has explored the relationship between tourism and happiness from a variety of perspectives, from the differing degrees of happiness during a holiday to the extent to which a holiday provides a longer-term feeling of happiness. Others, too, have considered how tourism may be a source of happiness, both generally (Corvo, 2011: Filep and Deery, 2010) and in the context of specific experiences, such as nature tourism (Bimonte & Faralla, 2012). The outcomes of these studies are, however, inconclusive, suggesting that there is perhaps some validity in the claim made some two centuries ago by Thomas Jefferson, the third President of the United States, that 'travelling makes a man wiser, but less happy' (cited in Sharpley & Stone, 2012: 1).

When Jefferson made this claim, tourism as it is manifested today did not of course exist. Nor could he have predicted that not only would the 'travel' he referred to evolve into the mass social and economic phenomenon that is contemporary tourism, but also that tourism would become a barometer of individual and national wealth. It is no coincidence that the major tourism markets have traditionally been the wealthier developed nations; nor is it surprising that nowadays tourism is growing most rapidly in those countries and regions enjoying the highest rates of economic growth, most notably in China. In other words, as wealth-induced consumption in general increases, so too does the demand for tourism in particular. And if increases in wealth and general consumption can (in principle) increase people's sense of well-being and happiness – an issue that economists and others have long been concerned with (Graham, 2009) – it might be logical to assume that increased consumption of tourism in particular similarly contributes to higher levels of happiness. Certainly, studies have shown that, in general, higher levels of income result in higher reported levels of happiness and well-being, and that within particular countries, individuals who are wealthier are more likely to say they are happy than those on lower incomes. At the same time, however, pioneering research by Easterlin (1975) revealed that, at the national level, increases in overall levels of income measured as per capita GDP were not associated with overall higher levels of happiness – a finding that became known as the Easterlin paradox.

Clearly, an individual's sense of happiness or well-being depends not only on consumption levels or having sufficient wealth to consume (Graham, 2009) but also on a whole host of other non-economic factors. That is, greater wealth and the consequential ability to consume more may not only not lead to greater happiness, but may actually reduce it (DeLeire & Kalil, 2009). Moreover, specific forms of consumption may induce higher or lower levels of happiness; for example, recent work has revealed that consuming experiences brings about longer-lasting happiness than the consumption of material things (Gilovich & Kumar, 2015). Thus, it could be assumed that tourism, as a specific form of experiential consumption motivated by both the desire to escape and the need for self-reward or 'ego-enhancement' (see Chapter 5), results in increased levels of happiness or, at least, higher levels of happiness than other forms of consumption.

Immediately, however, the complex question arises: what is happiness? As Filep and Deery (2010) usefully summarise, the term 'happiness' may be interpreted in a variety of ways although, for the purposes of this chapter, it is simpler to distinguish between the immediate sense of happiness, or hedonic pleasure, and a more fundamental, longer-lasting sense of well-being or contentment, or what is sometimes referred to as 'eudemonia'. Conversely, as Grayling (2008) suggests, happiness is 'too vague and baggy a notion to be truly helpful ... Instead of talking about happiness, one should talk about satisfaction, achievement, interest, engagement, enjoyment, growth and the constant opening of new possibilities.' He goes on to suggest that happiness might only be recognised retrospectively by someone who has been engaged in doing something worthwhile, a point that Hall (2011) also makes when suggesting that forms of tourism based on 'voluntary simplicity', such as volunteer tourism, may result in longer-lasting happiness compared to the immediate but fleeting pleasure gained from self-indulgent, hedonistic holidays. It is also suggested that happiness is not a condition that we can create or achieve entirely through our individual actions or behaviour. That is, research has demonstrated that only 40 percent of variations in happiness are determined by intentional activities, including tourism; 10 percent are determined by life circumstances (relationship, income and so on) and 50 percent by an individual's genetic predisposition (Filep & Deery, 2010; Liu, 2013). In other words, what or how we consume has only limited influence on our perceived levels of happiness.

Whatever the case, it is evident that there is no simple connection between happiness, wealth and tourism. Although experiential/leisure consumption may enhance feelings of happiness (DeLeire & Kalil, 2009; Gilovich & Kumar, 2015), most studies suggest that, beyond a certain level, an increase in wealth and material well-being does not lead to greater levels of happiness. Hence, increasing the consumption of tourism, or having more holidays, may not lead to increased happiness; indeed, according to Nawijn (2011a), although people who take a holiday tend to be slightly happier than those who do not, taking more frequent holidays does not increase happiness. This perhaps suggests that being able to participate in tourism, to be able to satisfy what has perhaps become a socially constructed need (see Chapter 5) – or perhaps even a habit (Henning, 2012) – is a source of happiness; taking additional holidays is, however, not. Moreover, the happiness achieved through tourism tends to be transitory and hedonistic, providing a more fleeting sense of subjective well-being rather than longer-term benefits, whilst levels of happiness vary during a holiday (Nawijn, 2010; 2011a, b). That sense of fleeting happiness may also be enhanced by excessive spending on tourism, on seeking to become a king or queen for a day (Gottlieb, 1982), followed by the reality of returning to day-to-day life.

Of course, happiness is a personal, subjective condition unique to the individual and determined by an enormous variety of cultural, social, psychological and economic factors. Equally, the way in which tourism is experienced is unique to the individual. Hence, there is no simple or single answer to the question: is to consume tourism to consume happiness? For some, such as those with the 'travel bug', who have a love of travel and relish new experiences, the answer may be 'yes'; for others, the answer is undoubtedly 'no'. Fundamentally, however, it must be questioned whether consuming tourism, an activity that is primarily motivated by the desire to escape, to experience something different, can ultimately increase people's happiness. Although the temporary pleasure of hedonic happiness may be felt while on holiday, the very fact of being away, being somewhere and doing something different, not only highlights the distinction between normal and non-normal life, but also suggests that happiness is to be found in either anticipating or recollecting being elsewhere, not in the here and now. Hence, it may be concluded that the route to happiness may not lie in the consumption of tourism (or buying dreams) but in focusing on improving the experience of reality, of normal day-to-day life.

Further reading

Cohen, S.A., Prayag, G. and Moital, M. (2014. Consumer behaviour in tourism: Concepts, influences and opportunities. *Current Issues in Tourism*, 17(10): 872–909.
A relatively recent paper that usefully reviews the research into the consumption of tourism from a variety of perspectives.

Horner, S. and Swarbrooke, J. (2016) *Consumer Behaviour in Tourism*, 3rd Edition. Abingdon: Routledge.
Though not addressing consumer culture in particular, this popular book provides a useful introductory overview of the behaviour of tourists as consumers of tourist experiences more generally.

Lee, M. (ed.) (2000) *The Consumer Society Reader*. Chichester: Wiley.
Tourism is an increasingly popular form of contemporary consumption that occurs within a world increasingly dominated by consumption. This book is a a comprehensive collection of key contributions to understanding the phenomenon of consumption and the consumer society.

Lury, C. (2011) *Consumer Culture,* 2nd Edition. Cambridge: Polity Press.
This second edition of a popular introductory text, which discusses the nature and role of consumption in modern societies, is both readable and accessible to readers new to the subject.

Pearce, P., Filep, S. and Ross, G. (2010) *Tourists, Tourism and the Good Life*. Abingdon: Routledge.
Tourism may be thought of as a search for happiness. Adopting a psychological perspective, this book explores the way in which the consumption of tourism may lead to a sense of happiness or, more generally, well-being.

Discussion topics

▶   Has the consumption of tourism always been a status symbol?

▶   Do different forms of tourism consumption reflect social distinctions more generally?

▶   To what extent is the consumption of tourism likely to reflect people's values?

▶   Does tourism make us happy?

7

Tourism and the digital revolution

Introduction

As noted in Chapter 2, although tourism as a social phenomenon boasts a long history (Casson, 1974), the origins of contemporary mass-scale tourism lie in the industrial, economic and social transformations that occurred during the nineteenth and early twentieth centuries. In other words, people have, in effect, been tourists for as long as they have had the means to travel, although relatively few were actually able to do so. However, not only was the emergence of tourism as a recognised, discrete social 'institution' more recent (the term 'tourism' was first used around the beginning of the nineteenth century), but also the ability of people to travel cheaply, safely and in relatively large numbers occurred only as a result of a combination of factors that, after the Agricultural Revolution (around 1550–1850), reflected the second major influence on the development of modern society, namely, the Industrial Revolution.

More specifically, rapid industrialisation from the mid-1700s underpinned the fundamental restructuring and ordering of society in general, whilst advances in transport technology (the railways) and increases in both free time and wealth provided the means – and widespread urbanisation and transformations in work practices provided the motivation – for increased participation in tourism in particular. In short, the 'trilogy' of technology, leisure time and wealth are widely accepted as the key factors in the emergence of growth of modern tourism. Moreover, as discussed in Chapter 2, they have continued to do so. For example, throughout the twentieth century, advances in aircraft technology brought both short- and long-haul air travel to wider markets whilst, certainly in the world's developed countries, greater prosperity and increases in leisure time stimulated the rapid growth in international tourism (a pattern more recently followed in some emerging economies, such as China).

Nevertheless, in some respects the tourist experience long remained unchanged. Certainly, by the mid- to late 1980s, mass international tourism was firmly established but a tourist going, say, on a summer-sun holiday to the Mediterranean would most likely choose their package holiday from a printed brochure and book and pay for it in a travel agency, though some tour operators offered 'direct' bookings by telephone. They would take their spending money in either currency or, more commonly, travellers' cheques, and it is likely they would carry a guide book with them; at the same time, they would rely on local guides and tourist information centres to help them navigate the destination or go on local tours. Postcards of the destination would be chosen, written and mailed home to friends and family; photographs would be taken on traditional film cameras, followed by the ritual of collecting the 'holiday snaps' from the local photo store. And if urgent contact with home was necessary, expensive international telephone calls could be arranged through the hotel or local exchange. In other words, tourists could travel to a greater choice of destinations at greater speed but at lower cost but, during much of the twentieth century, certain aspects of being a tourist remained very much the same.

Over the last 20 years, however (certainly since the first edition of this book was published in 1994) both the supply and consumption of tourism have been transformed by a phenomenon that has had a fundamental impact on society at the global scale, namely, the rapid and remarkable development of information and communication technology (ICT). Commencing with the introduction of the personal computer, followed by the development of the Internet and subsequent networking facilities including the World Wide Web and email and, more recently, the growth in mobile technologies, most notably the smartphone, advances in ICT collectively represent a third revolution: the digital revolution. This revolution has, perhaps, been most keenly experienced by older generations – the so-called baby-boomers (those born in the population boom following World War II up to 1960) and the generations that precede them. Conversely, those born since the new millennium, sometimes referred to as Generation Z, are 'digital natives' (Selwyn, 2009); they have never known a world without broadband, the Internet, tablet computers, smartphones and the myriad of networks, services and 'apps' that are available to them.

Irrespective of their age, however, the experience of all tourists has been irrevocably influenced by (and, by and large, benefited from) the digital revolution, even for those who eschew many opportunities afforded by ICT developments. For example, although low-cost airlines were able to be established as a result of regulatory changes, or liberalisation policies, in the air transport sector (Dobruszkes, 2006), the success of their business model was dependent on marketing and communicating directly online with the consumer (Horner and Swarbrooke, 2016: 384). And arguably, the competition they created led to lower prices across the airline sector a whole, whilst tourists also benefited from new destinations and new opportunities, such as affordable short-haul weekend breaks within Europe. The ability to access local currency through ATMs whilst abroad is also a function of ICT, as are the satnavs which many drivers depend on during their holidays, whilst one practice that is almost synonymous with being a tourist, namely, photography (Markwell, 1997), has been completely transformed since the introduction of the digital camera in the early 1990s. In fact, there are innumerable examples of how ICT has transformed the tourism sector, as it has contemporary life more generally.

Given the significance of the digital revolution to tourism, it is not surprising that, over the last two decades, increasing academic attention has been paid to the relationship between tourism and ICT, with many books (for example, Benckendorff *et al.*, 2014; Buhalis, 2003; Egger & Buhalis, 2008), articles and a dedicated journal (*Journal of Information Technology and Tourism*) contributing to a burgeoning literature on the subject. At the same time, numerous academic and industry conferences provide a forum for the presentation of latest developments and research in tourism and ICT, most notably the annual International Federation for IT and Tourism Conference (better known as ENTER) which, at the time of writing, has achieved its twentieth anniversary (see www.ifitt.org/experience-enter/). Inevitably, perhaps, much of literature focuses on the application of ICT to the travel and tourism sector; that is, on how ICT can contribute to more effective operations in the hospitality, transport and other related sectors as well as to facilitating destination marketing and management generally (Pearce, 2011). Nevertheless, researchers have also been increasingly concerned with what might be described as the functional benefits that the digital revolution has brought to tourists themselves, such as the ease with which tourism products and services can be booked online (Jacobsen & Munar, 2012), although only more recently has attention begun to be paid to the sociological or psychological consequences of the digital revolution on the tourist experience (for example, Tribe & Mkono, 2017).

Collectively, such is the scope of the literature that, in the context of this book, a complete overview of the impact of the digital revolution on tourism would be an impossible task. Therefore, the purpose of this chapter is twofold; first, it highlights the ways in which ICT, particularly mobile technologies over the last decade or so, have transformed the nature of the contemporary tourist experience; and, second, it explores the manner in which digital technology has influenced both the practice and meaning of an activity that has long been associated with tourism, namely, tourist photography. In order to 'set the scene', however, the next section provides a brief background to the digital revolution.

The digital revolution

Nowadays, the use of ICT is so commonplace in almost all aspects of contemporary social and commercial life that, for people of a certain generation, it is difficult to imagine how they managed before the digital age without personal computers, mobile phones, digital cameras and other 'gadgets' that are now considered essential. Yet, it is not the technology itself that is so remarkable but the speed with which the digital revolution has occurred. For example, although digital mobile phones were widely available from around 1990, and the first 'smartphone', the Simon Personal Communicator, was launched by IBM in the mid-1990s (Tweedie, 2015), the ubiquitous Apple iPhone was first launched only in 2007. In that year, just 122 million smartphones of all makes were sold to end-users; in 2016, 1.5 billion smartphones were sold worldwide, more than double the number sold in 2012 (Statista, 2017). It is now estimated that:

- almost two-thirds of the world's population now has a mobile phone (with 2.2 billion smartphone users);
- more than half of the world's web traffic now comes from mobile phones (Kemp, 2017).

It is also estimated that, in 2017, there were almost 3.8 billion Internet users and around two billion personal computers (PCs) in use. Annual sales of PCs (desktops, laptops and tablet computers) are in decline, however, as people increasingly depend on smartphones for their connectivity needs. Similarly, with regards to digital photography, although the first experimental digital camera was created by an engineer at Eastman Kodak in 1975 (ironically, setting the company on the path to eventual bankruptcy in 2012), it was not until the early 1990s that digital cameras became widely available. And, as with PCs, sales of compact digital cameras, though not the more complex 'DSLR' cameras, have declined as smartphone photography has become more popular.

The foundations of the digital revolution lie, as Benckendorff *et al.* (2014: 9–12) usefully summarise, in the development of computers from the 1950s onwards and, significantly, the invention of the microprocessor in 1970. Since then, technological advances have underpinned the development of smaller, faster, more powerful (and, importantly, affordable) computers with increasingly remarkable memory capacities, digital cameras with an increasingly wide range of capabilities and producing ever-higher quality images and, of course, the smartphone with its ever-expanding range of functions.

Of equal, if not greater, importance, however, has been the development of net-working and the Internet. In other words, whilst the production of ever smaller, more powerful computers and the evolution of user-friendly operating systems, such as Microsoft's Windows system, brought the benefits of computer technology to the individual, it was the development of networking systems that, in effect, allowed computers to talk with each other that proved to be the real catalyst of the digital revolution. The Internet – essentially a network of local networks – was created in 1982. By the 1990s, it had achieved global reach, providing the connectivity necessary for the subsequent development of the World Wide Web (WWW) which became globally available in 1993, as well as email services, an early version of which was Pegasus Mail, launched in 1990. Initially, the WWW offered limited interaction (Web 1.0); that is, people were able to access and view websites but could not interact with or contribute to them, their content being controlled by so-called webmasters. The emergence of Web 2.0, however, allowed for two-way communication between websites and users and the growth in what is referred to as 'user-generated content'. Hence, Web 2.0 was fundamental, for example, to the development of online book-ing/shopping facilities as well as sites that have become seen as an essential source of information for tourists, such as TripAdvisor. Similarly, the success of low-cost carriers such as Ryanair has been built on the customer booking, selecting seats and checking in online, thereby taking a variety of costs out of airline operations. Equally, Web 2.0 supported the growth in online communities, members of which share information, files, photographs and so on; Twitter, Facebook and YouTube are well-known examples of such communities. And, of course, it is in the ability of the user, through their smartphone, to communicate and interact with service and information providers and with other users through social networking sites, that the real impact of the digital revolution lies, both generally and in the specific context of tourism.

The digital tourist

Given the remarkable growth in ownership and use of digital technologies, particularly of smartphones – predictions of smartphone use by 2020 vary wildly from a realistic 3.6 billion (Duran, 2017) to an over-optimistic 6.1 billion (Lunden, 2015) – it might be assumed that adoption of all the facilities and opportunities offered by such technology will be almost universally adopted, with significant implications for both the supply and consumption of tourism. However, this is not necessarily the case. In other words, ownership of a smartphone or computer does not imply the adoption of all its capabilities. For example, in the UK, online booking of holidays has become increasingly popular; according to ABTA (2017), 76 percent of holidays in 2016 were booked online (primarily using a desktop or laptop computer) whilst only 19 percent were booked in-store at a travel agency, yet the same report reveals that 51 percent of overseas holidays were bought as packages. In other words, tourists are increasingly confident in buying a holiday online, but less so in individually purchasing the different components of a holiday online.

Although it is over-simplistic to assume that the continuing popularity of the holiday package reflects limited adoption of online purchasing opportunities (in all likelihood, package holidays remain attractive as a result of their convenience, security and lower costs), it is, however, erroneous to assume that, in the future, we shall all be so-called 'smart' tourists (Gretzel *et al.*, 2015). In other words, although new technologies continually emerge, including ICT, different people adopt them to a lesser or greater extent and with varying levels of enthusiasm. Thus, in considering the impact of the digital revolution on the tourist experience, it is important to recognise that different behaviours may reflect varying levels of ICT adoption and acceptance.

It has long been argued that different people accept or adapt to innovation at different rates and in different ways. For example, in his widely cited 'diffusion of innovations' model, Rogers (1995) identifies five different categories of innovation adopters, namely:

1 Innovators (2.5 percent of people): risk takers keen to adopt new technologies;

2 Early adopters (13.5 percent): embrace change but not obsessively;

3 Early majority (34 percent): happy to adopt, but avoid risk by researching the innovation;

4 Late majority (34 percent): followers who adopt innovation only after majority acceptance, often out of necessity;

5 Laggards (16 percent): sceptical of change, the last to adopt to innovation.

Of course, this model is of relevance not only to consumers or, in the context of this chapter, tourists (most of whom would be able to identify themselves with one of the above categories) but also to producers or suppliers. In other words, a willingness to adopt new technologies or innovations – in effect, to take risks – is a fundamental characteristic of entrepreneurship (Bessant & Tidd, 2015), particularly when innovations prove disruptive to established business models (Charitou & Markides, 2002). Again, the early success of low-cost airlines is a powerful example of an innovation-based disruptive business strategy, with established airlines having to respond rapidly to a new competitive environment.

It should also be noted that the manner in which different people adopt new technologies must be considered within the broader context of innovation. In other words, it is suggested that over the last two centuries there have been waves of innovation (Perez, 2003), from steam power, through electricity and the internal combustion engine to the digital revolution. Moreover, those waves have occurred more rapidly or, more simply stated, the pace of technological innovation is speeding up. As a consequence, in a world in which technological innovation becomes the norm, people tend to adapt to new technologies more quickly. For example, Benckendorff *et al.* (2014: 31) suggest that 'the adoption of smartphones and mobile apps has been much more rapid than earlier adoptions of technologies, such as the Internet, television, electricity and steam-powered transport', although factors such as cost, availability and ease of use must also be taken into account, as should the wider culture of consumption (see Chapter 6).

Nevertheless, there is no doubt that different tourists accept (or, indeed, reject) innovations in ICT in different ways. Hence, in order to understand the influence of the digital revolution on the tourist experience, it is necessary to highlight the reasons why some tourists are slower to respond to the opportunities offered by new technologies than others, particularly as there may be implications for particular market segments. For example, in the UK the so-called 'grey market' (those aged 50 and above) is becoming an increasingly important sector of the tourism market, now accounting for almost 60 percent of all travel and tourism expenditure amongst UK tourists, yet research consistently demonstrates that 'silver surfers' are slower to adopt ICT than younger generations and, when they do so, use it less intensively (Choudrie *et al.*, 2014). Hence, tour operators and other businesses targeting this important market need to tailor their operations accordingly. For instance, a number of UK tour operators use low-cost airlines, such as Ryanair, which requires individual passengers to check in and print off boarding passes online, a task which some older customers may not wish or be able to do. Indeed, as now discussed, age is one of a number of factors that influence the adoption of ICT in tourism.

Factors influencing ICT adoption in tourism

Perhaps not surprisingly, numerous studies have been undertaken into the factors or variables that determine the extent to which tourists adopt ICT in the tourism demand process or, more specifically, in seeking information and making travel purchases. A detailed discussion of these factors is beyond the scope of this chapter although, in their review of the relevant literature, Amaro and Duarte (2013) identify three groups of what they refer to as antecedents of online tourism shopping. These are summarised in Figure 7.1.

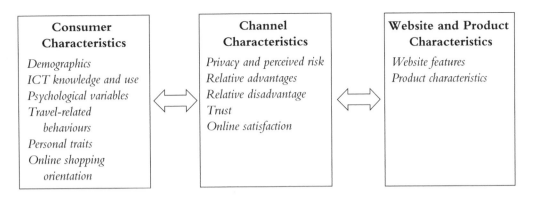

FIGURE 7.1 Factors influencing tourists' ICT adoption
Source: Adapted from Amaro and Duarte (2013: 761)

For the present purposes, two broad groups of variables can be considered:

1   Demographics. Demographic factors include age, gender, education and income levels, all of which may to a lesser or greater extent determine an individual's willingness or desire to embrace new technologies. As noted above, recent research supports the intuitive argument that older people in general are slower to adopt and use new technologies, particularly smartphones, whilst other studies into the use of ICT has found that members of so-called Generation X (those born between 1965 and 1985) are quicker to use mobile technology than the baby boomer generation that preceded them, although the latter recognise its importance and learn how to use it (Yang & Jolly, 2008). Research by Beldona (2005) into the online travel information search behaviour across age cohorts revealed similar results but was less conclusive, baby boomers being found to be more active online than might be expected, although others have found that online purchasing of travel services is directly influenced by generation (for example, Bonn *et al.*, 2000). The point should be made, however, that many studies were undertaken in the relatively early stages of the digital revolution, since when computer/smartphone ownership has increased dramatically and use of the Internet has become more widespread – that is, the 'late majority' are now, in all likelihood, confident and regular users of online travel information and booking services, with a strong orientation towards online shopping. Indeed, Amaro and Duarte's (2013) review of more recent research reveals contradictory results with no clear pattern of demographic influences emerging, although evidence suggests that females use mobile technology and social networks more intensively than males to facilitate travel purchase decisions (Okazaki & Hirose, 2009).

2   Attitudes towards ICT adoption. Broadly speaking, some people are happy to adopt new technology, delighting both in using the equipment itself and the perceived benefits it brings. Others, conversely, may be technophobes; they may have an

innate fear of using new technology and, hence, reject it. Indeed, technophobia related to developments in ICT is a recognised phenomenon, a number of studies exploring what is referred to as 'computer anxiety' and potential means of helping people to overcome it (Brosnan, 1998; Igbaria & Chakrabarti, 1990; Marcoulides, 1989). Interestingly, however, few if any attempts have been made to investigate the implications of technophobia within the specific context of tourism, a surprising omission given the enthusiasm with which the travel and tourism sector has embraced ICT and the extent to which access to many products and services, from booking seats on low-cost airlines or renting an apartment through Airbnb to checking reviews of hotels or restaurants on TripAdvisor, is dependent on computer or smartphone use.

In all likelihood, technophobia or computer anxiety is becoming less prevalent as ICT becomes increasingly integrated into contemporary social life. This is not to say, however, that all the facilities and opportunities offered to tourists by ICT will be fully utilised. In other words, although they may be comfortable using a computer or a smartphone, some people may have negative attitudes towards certain capabilities or functions, their 'technophobia' being manifested in a fear or unwillingness of using it for particular tasks. In particular, the following barriers may exist to the use of ICT in tourism (see also Buhalis, 2003: 127):

1   Security issues. As 'cybercrime' and online fraud become more common, or as the awareness of the potential of such problems increase, some people may be unwilling to enter personal details in general or purchase goods and services online in particular. In short, online purchasing may be seen as risky and, hence, use of ICT may be limited only to information searches.

2   Lack of trust. Such is the volume of information online and the ease with which websites can be set up that people may doubt the origins or accuracy of information obtained online, particularly in comparison with tangible printed information and official sources (for example, tourist information centres).

3   Desire to talk to a real person. Related to the point above, not only may people feel more comfortable discussing/booking tourism services with a real person, either face-to-face in a travel agency or over the telephone, but having a name or contact may make them feel more secure, particularly if committing a relatively large sum of money to a holiday.

4   Perceived difficulty of use/fear of making a mistake. Whilst online information searches may be relatively straightforward, booking or purchasing travel and tourism services may be perceived to be a complex process in which it is easy to make mistakes.

5   Practical issues. In some circumstances, employing ICT for accessing and, in particular, purchasing tourism services may be impractical. For instance, some people may not possess a credit or debit card or prefer to pay cash. In addition, such is the

volume of information available that making informed decisions may be considered to be excessively time consuming.

Despite these barriers, there is no doubt that people are increasingly using ICT for planning and purchasing their tourism experiences; as Pearce (2011: 32) observes, 'the widespread and frequent use of the internet for sourcing information for all types of travel relevant activities is confirmed in many . . . studies'. Indeed, ICT is becoming integral to the tourism demand process and, in many ways, is both transforming and enhancing the tourist experience.

ICT and the tourist experience

Earlier in this chapter, the behaviour of an imaginary tourist on a summer-sun holiday in a pre-digital revolution time was described. If we were to 'fast-forward' to the present, that tourist will have selected, booked and paid for their holiday online; they may also have checked in for their flight online (perhaps downloading their boarding pass onto their smartphone), pre-booked and paid for airport parking online, and perhaps even pre-booked their in-flight meal on line. During the flight, they might

Stage 1: Felt need or travel desire	View photographs/travel marketing on social media sites; need generated from activity on social media.
Stage 2: Information collection and evaluation	Online search for holiday packages/specific components dependent on travel needs; access review sites; consult via social media.
Stage 3: Travel decisions	The holiday/trip purchased online, either as a package or in components (transport, accommodation, transfer/car hire, insurance, special events, restaurants, etc). For some countries, electronic visas purchased online.
Stage 4: Travel preparations and travel experience	Excursion planning via online destination sites/review sites; online checking in; search/evaluate services (clubs, restaurants, sports activities); photography/photo sharing online; online contact with friends and family via social media; communication as necessary with travel organisers.
Stage 5: Travel satisfaction evaluation/memories	Sharing of photographs/experiences via social media; completion of online customer satisfaction questionnaires; writing of travel/holiday blogs; share experiences on travel review sites; upload photographs to image sites (e.g. flickr.com).

FIGURE 7.2 ICT usage in the tourism demand process

watch movies previously downloaded onto their tablet computer/smartphone. On holiday, they will use debit or credit cards to access local currency from ATMs, they will use their smartphone to find restaurants to eat in or places to visit, to take and share photographs, to keep in contact with friends and family at home via email or social media and to navigate around the destination. And on return home, they may select their favourite photographs which they then upload to an online photo-album production service and, perhaps, describe and rate their experiences on review sites. In short, in the space of just 25 years, that tourist's experience has been completely transformed, not least in terms of their relationship with the producers and suppliers of tourism services.

This transformation reflects the extent to which ICT can be used or is influential at each stage in the tourism demand process. Figure 7.2 is an adaptation of the tourism demand process introduced in Chapter 5 (Figure 5.1), indicating the potential contribution of ICT to each stage of the tourism experience.

Generally, the use of ICT in tourism (as more generally) is considered to facilitate and/speed up activities such as the choice and purchase of goods and services, as well as providing immediate access to and meeting a wide variety of information needs whilst offering the tourist greater choice and autonomy in the tourism demand process. At the same time, the travel and tourism sector increasingly seeks to enhance specific tourist experiences through the development of innovative ICT applications.

A number of commentators explore the ways in which the use of ICT may impact on the tourist experience, adopting different perspectives (Benckendorff *et al.*, 2014; Buhalis, 2003; Neuhofer, 2014; Pearce, 2011; Wang & Fesenmaier, 2013; Wang *et al.*, 2012) For example, Benckendorff *et al.* (2014: 261–269) list ten roles for technology (both ICT and other technologies) in creating tourist experiences:

- *an enabler:* technology facilitates and stimulates the demand for tourism; that is, it enables easier access to tourism experiences, further democratising participation in tourism;

- *a creator:* contributes to the creation of new infrastructure that provides novel tourism experiences;

- *an attractor:* technology itself becomes a tourist attraction, from 'hi-tech' theme parks to IMAX cinemas;

- *an enhancer:* technology can enhance the tourist experience, with apps that provide services from visitor orientation to language translation;

- *a protector:* technology helps protect tourists (for example, weather warnings) and the resources that tourism depends upon;

- *an educator:* a principal contribution of technology to the experience is through providing additional dimensions to informing or educating tourists. Examples include audio guides, downloadable podcasts, holographic projections ('talking heads') and augmented reality apps that can be accessed on visitors' smartphones;

- *a substitute:* technology can recreate virtual places or events, the 'real' versions of which are not easily accessible;

- *a facilitator:* essentially, technology assists the tourism sector to provide more efficient, quality services, hence improving the overall tourist experience;

- *a reminder:* smartphones in particular have enabled the capturing and sharing (via social media) of images;

- *a destroyer:* technology-dependent attractions and experiences may suffer from technological failure, thereby diminishing the tourist experience.

Alternatively, Wang *et al.* (2012), focusing specifically on smartphones, explore how the tourist experience can be enhanced by the use of smartphones to rapidly meet a variety of different information needs, those needs being categorised as functional, innovative, hedonic, social and aesthetic. Specifically, their research reveals that the use of smartphones enables tourists to solve problems quickly, to share experiences and to store memories.

For the purposes of this chapter, however, the most useful framework for understanding how ICT in particular can influence the tourist experience is provided by Wang and Fesenmaier (2013) who, in their study of smartphone use amongst American tourists, identified a number of purposes for which smartphones were used and, significantly, how this use not only changed the tourists' behaviour but also their experience; that is, how their feelings and sensations during the trip were influenced by the use of their smartphones. Overall, the study found that the use of smartphones had three broad impacts, namely, 'changing travel planning, constructing and destructing one's sense of tourism, and reconfiguring the relationship amongst tourists, places and others' (Wang & Fesenmaier, 2013: 58). Exploring these in more detail reveals how use of smartphones can enhance the tourist experience but also points to possible negative consequences.

From their research, Wang and Fesenmaier (2013) identified four categories of smartphone use, all mostly related to the connectivity provided through access to the Internet (hence the argument that overdependence on ICT during travel can be a disbenefit or have a negative impact on the tourist experience if such connectivity is sporadic or unobtainable). Two of the four identified uses, namely, 'facilitation' and 'information search' can be thought of as functional uses related to planning and purchasing tourism services. The perceived connectivity and convenience of smartphones was found to influence tourist behaviour in different ways, including:

- More time spent searching for information and planning: the flexibility and ease of accessing the Internet through smartphones means that specific times (e.g. on a computer or visiting a travel agency) no longer need to be set aside for planning/purchasing a holiday. Consequently, travel decisions may be based on 'richer' knowledge, with the result that tourists are more confident in their purchase (for example, good value or the best hotel) and, hence, have a more satisfying experience.

- Alternatively, the flexibility and ease afforded by smartphones reduces the amount of pre-planning; instant access to information may dissolve the information search > planning/purchase > holiday experience stages into one as experiences are sought out and selected throughout the holiday. Consequently, the tourist experience is more flexible, enhanced by the sense of freedom of not being constrained by a completely pre-planned holiday and by being able to 'make it up as we go along'.

- More travel: for some, the ease and flexibility of searching for information and purchasing travel services by phone, along with the enormous variety of information available, enables them to participate in tourism more frequently, although this of course remains constrained by personal financial and temporal resources.

The two other uses of smartphones identified in Wang and Fesenmaier's (2013) study were more directly related to the tourist experience. Inevitably, given the multiple functions of smartphones, they were commonly and frequently used as self-entertainment devices: for listening to music, reading books, playing games, watching movies, accessing the news or more generally just surfing the Internet. Also as a form of entertainment, smartphones were used to send emails, or to converse with others on social media sites although, as discussed shortly, this also falls under the 'communication' use of smartphones. Unsurprisingly, perhaps, smartphones were primarily used in the context of entertainment for the taking and sharing of photographs. This is considered in more detail in the final section of this chapter but, in terms of experience, the 'entertainment' use of smartphones and ICT more generally is a significant contributor to the hedonic aspect of the tourist experience; smartphones are a source of entertainment and fun, contributing to a more relaxing, less stressful experience.

The last use of smartphones identified in the study was 'communication'. In a practical sense, smartphones are, by definition, communication devices; through the connection to mobile phone networks and the Internet, they allow the user to communicate with others in multiple ways. For tourists, however, 'communication' is more than simply a function or an affordance of smartphones. It is, rather, a highly meaningful element of the contemporary ICT-facilitated tourist experience, and it enhances (or transforms) that experience in a number of ways.

First, irrespective of the extent to which they use their smartphones, tourists feel more connected. That is, it is as much the knowledge that they can easily communicate with so-called 'absent others' as it is their actual communication, whether by email, text, social media platform or talking, that enhances tourists' sense of being connected to the 'outside' world beyond the liminal zone (see Chapter 8) that is the destination. And this sense of connectedness adds a positive dimension to the tourist experience through, for example being able to share novel experiences with family and friends or, indeed, hearing about what others 'back home' are doing. Tourists are also more comfortable and relaxed knowing that they can easily be contacted if necessary, although a recognised negative consequence of such connectivity is that they be tempted, for example, to regularly check on work-related emails and others matters. In short, the connectedness afforded by ICT/smartphones diminishes the emotional, if not physical distance between home and the destination, an outcome that may on the one hand be beneficial but, on the other hand, may mean the tourist is never fully 'on holiday'. Consequently, a number of organisations offer holidays in destinations or accommodation facilities where there is no connectivity to the Internet or to phone networks (see, for example, digitaldetoxholidays.com).

Second, tourists feel more informed, more knowledgeable and, hence, more empowered. Being able to familiarise themselves with the destination, to seek out the amenities and facilities that suit them best (and to avoid those that, according to the online reviews of other tourists, should be avoided), tourists feel more in control of their holiday experience. In other words, they feel less dependent on the (profit-motivated) travel organiser, though perhaps more dependent on, but also more trusting of, the online 'word-of-mouth' recommendations of other tourists. Indeed, research has shown generally 'that CGC [consumer-generated content] is perceived as more trustworthy when compared to content from official destination websites, travel agents, and mass media' (Filieri *et al.*, 2015: 175). In addition, the availability of mobile 'augmented reality' applications contributes to their knowledge and enjoyment of sites and attractions where such application are available (Kounavis *et al.*, 2012) although, as considered shortly, tourists may immerse themselves into the technology rather than the attraction itself, with implications for the depth or authenticity of their experiences.

Third, ICT and, in particular, smartphones, allows tourists to be more entertained and, hence, more relaxed; that is, smartphones contribute to the hedonic tourist experience. As discussed above, commonly this entertainment takes the form of taking and sharing photographs on social media sites although smartphones facilitate a variety of other forms of entertainment which, collectively, enhance the overall tourist experience either engaging in 'playful' activities or, more simply, avoiding boredom.

Finally, and importantly, the tourist experience is enhanced by the sense of security implicit in the communication opportunities provide by smartphones. Such security may emanate simply from remaining in touch with those at home whilst, from a more practical perspective, being able to quickly find a hotel room or a taxi (for example, using the Uber app) reduces the challenges or the sense of uncertainty when, for instance, a tourist arrives late at night in an unfamiliar city. However, the sense of security provided by smartphone ownership and use is not unique to tourism. According to Archer (2013), for example, there is an increasing incidence of what he refers to as 'nomophobia' (no-mo(bile) phone phobia) within contemporary society. He suggests that we are becoming increasingly dependent on and addicted to using our smartphones to the extent that 40 percent of people live in fear of being without their phones, whilst other researchers have developed a so-called smartphone addiction scale that identifies the factors that influence and are evidence of such addiction (Kwon *et al.*, 2013).

In all likelihood, most people would recognise their own dependence on smartphones and admit to their unease if they misplace it; moreover, the extent to which smartphones intrude in everyday social life is more than evident to the casual observer. Yet, at the time, there is a growing reaction against the pervasive presence and use of smartphones, as for example revealed in one report which suggests that most British people would support a ban on mobile phones in restaurants (O'Callaghan, 2016). Nevertheless, the use of and dependence on ICT in general and smartphones in particular is pervasive in most spheres of contemporary life, including tourism, raising the question of the extent to which the traditional significance or meaning of being a tourist is being challenged.

The digital revolution: deconstructing the tourist experience?

The contribution of ICT to both the supply of and demand for tourism is considered by most commentators to be a 'good thing'. In other words, much of literature concerned with the digital revolution in tourism advocates the use and development of ICT for streamlining business operations, for more effective communication between businesses and their customers, and for improving the tourist experience, enhancing tourist satisfaction and, hence, gaining more business. And there is no doubt that, in many respects, the digital revolution has had a positive impact on tourism and the tourist experience. That is, today's tourist is (or can be, if the affordances of ICT and smartphones are fully embraced) empowered, informed, entertained and secure, delighting in the opportunities, independence and spontaneity offered by ICT. But is today's tourist still, in fact, a tourist?

According to Tribe and Mkono (2017), the digital revolution is resulting in what they refer to as a condition of 'e-lienation'. In other words, following on from the argument first developed by Karl Marx that the emergence of modern, industrial societies based on capitalism resulted in a sense of alienation for members of those societies (see Chapter 1), the digital revolution has similarly led to a new form of alienation within societies. That is, through their use of ICT and smartphones, people both generally and within specific social groupings (family units, peer groups and so on) are becoming, as human beings, alienated from one another through living and communicating in a virtual, digital world; they are becoming 'e-lienated'.

The extent to which this is occurring is debatable; the 'digital native' referred to in the introduction to this chapter, being able to 'talk' and maintain social relations with innumerable friends and acquaintances, may well feel more connected or less socially alienated than previous generations. Their social relations simply take a different form. Nevertheless, as discussed elsewhere in this book, tourism as a specific social activity has long been driven by a quest for the 'Other' (Urry, 2002). That is, a fundamental motive to participate in tourism is to get away from normal, day-to-day life, to escape (Dann, 1977; 1981; see also Chapter 5), perhaps simply to recreate (as in recreation) on a summer-sun holiday (Cohen, 1979b), or perhaps to seek meaning and authenticity in other places and times, compensating for what is missing in modern, alienated societies (MacCannell, 1989; 2013). At the same, the contemporary tourist is considered to be becoming increasingly 'responsible' (Goodwin, 2011), engaging with and learning about the destination and its communities, seeking or 'co-creating' (Prahalad & Ramaswamy, 2004) positive, meaningful experiences. The digital revolution, however, is arguably undermining these fundamental characteristics of tourism, challenging what it is to be, in a socio-psychological sense, a tourist.

Certainly, at the practical level, the digital revolution has transformed (and improved) the consumption of tourism inasmuch as it is now much easier to travel – not only has the tourism demand process been simplified, but a fundamental shift has occurred in the power relations between producer and consumer. In short, the digital revolution has significantly facilitated what might be referred to as corporeal mobility, to physically travel to and stay in other places. Yet, the significance of being a tourist has been diminished, as the following (deliberately provocative) points demonstrate:

- The digital or 'smart' tourist is never truly away, never truly immersed in the 'Other'. Although they may be physically in the destination, the tourist's use of and dependence on ICT means that they remain socially and psychologically rooted 'at home'. Recounting experiences as they happen, sharing stories and photographs on social media, tourists now experience their holidays or travels through the minds and imagination of those they share their stories with on social media. Moreover, those who maintain contact with their work whilst away (even, for example, just checking emails) cannot be considered to have 'escaped'; the digital tourist, perhaps, continues their normal day-to-day life, just in a different place.

- Traditionally, the lure of tourism lay in the opportunities for adventure, for discovery, for serendipitous experiences. Indeed, as considered in more detail in Chapter 9, the less staged or planned or the more unexpected an experience is, the more authentic and memorable it is likely to be. The contemporary digital tourist, however, can be fully informed; every part of the holiday or trip can be pre-planned and pre-booked online (or booked spontaneously during the holiday), decisions being made on the basis of a thorough information search including tourist review sites. In other words, the digital tourist travels fully prepared; they have, perhaps, experienced their holiday before even leaving home and, consequently tourism is losing the element of fun and adventure.

- The use of smartphones, and the ever-increasing number of 'apps' on offer, precludes immersed, authentic experiences; the digital tourist experiences the destination, the attraction or the place not by visually and emotionally engaging with it, but through technology. For example, the navigation facilities on smartphones mean that tourists are able to find their way around unfamiliar places easily and quickly, but do they 'see' where they are going? Augmented reality apps, designed to enhance tourists' knowledge or understanding of, say a heritage attraction, may be both entertaining and informative, but perhaps discourage tourists from 'feeling' the place they are in, from sensing its history. And as discussed in the next section, the popularity of taking and sharing 'selfies' shifts the focus of the tourist's attention from the place where they are on to themselves; the experience becomes sharing images of the self being anywhere, rather than being in and experiencing somewhere.

There are numerous other ways in which the digital revolution is transforming the tourist experience. For example, tourists may potentially become 'e-lienated' from other tourists as they individually immerse themselves in their smartphones to communicate on social media, play games, read books or simply surf the Internet, reflecting what many see as a wider challenge in social behaviour. At the same time, there are undoubtedly many tourists who control their use of ICT; they use it for its functional benefits but seek out and engage with the 'real world' of the destination. Generally, however, tourism is being transformed by ICT in form and function to the extent that it may, in the future, lose its distinctive social role and significance, becoming, as Hall (2005) suggested some years ago, simply one manifestation of contemporary mobility.

Tourist photography and the digital revolution

As observed earlier in this chapter, one of the most evident impacts of the digital revolution in tourism has been in the realm of tourist photography. Not only has the practice of tourist photography itself been transformed with the advent of digital cameras and, subsequently, the incorporation of cameras into smartphones, but also the significance of photography within the broader tourism experience has also been transformed. Hence, the purpose of this final section of the chapter is to explore briefly this most fundamental and ubiquitous of tourist practices.

Tourism, according to Urry (2002), is motivated by the opportunity to 'gaze' on people, places and attractions that are 'out of the ordinary' (Urry, 2002: 1). What tourists choose to gaze upon may be determined by images they have seen in newspapers, promotional materials, guide books or, in this digital age, on the Internet but, for Urry, the 'tourist gaze' is an essential element of the tourist experience. And of course, the visual consumption of tourist places is not limited to simply gazing on (and remembering) sites and attractions. Tourists and travellers have, for example, always attempted to record their experiences, often through painting (J. Taylor, 1994). However, since its invention in the early nineteenth century, photography has become virtually synonymous with tourism. Indeed, as Li *et al.* (2017: 1) explain,

> although people have for centuries engaged in various forms of tourism . . . Louis Daguerre's invention of photography in 1839 virtually coincided with Thomas Cook's first organised tour in 1841, an event that for many represented the beginning of modern mass tourism.
>
> (Garlick, 2002)

Since then, the histories of tourism and photography have been intertwined (Teymur, 1993: 6) and, as Belk and Yeh (2011: 345) observe, 'the emergence of mass tourism and popular photography owe a great deal to one another'. Consequently, tourism and photography go hand in hand. 'To be a tourist . . . is to be, almost by necessity, a photographer' (Markwell, 1997: 131) or, as Haldrup and Larsen (2003: 24) alternatively observe, 'taking photographs is an emblematic tourist practice; it is almost unthinkable to travel for pleasure without bringing the light-weight camera along and returning home without snapshot memories'. In short, the camera (and now, the smartphone with camera) is, for most tourists, as essential as the passport in international travel and, until the more recent emergence of digital photography, having films processed and printed was a ritualised post-holiday activity.

There can be no doubting, then, the centrality of photography to the consumption of tourism and the tourism experience. Moreover, although the taking of photographs can be thought of in simple terms as something that tourists do to remind them of places visited or of particular experiences – in a sense, the creation of personal souvenirs – the relationship between photography and tourism has always been complex and, in the digital era, is arguably becoming more so. Indeed, a number of points demand consideration.

First, images of places are, or can be, a powerful influence on where people travel and how they view places. In other words, photographs frequently define those places that tourists should visit (Markwell, 1997) – they act as 'markers' of an attraction (see also Chapter 9). Consequently, tourists travel to particular sites or attractions to consume not the site itself, but the previously seen image of that site or attraction.

Additionally, they consume the site by taking their own photograph, reproducing the pictures they have already seen (Jenkins, 2003). Thus, through photography, tourists do not consume actual places/experiences, but images of those places or experiences and, through that process, they verify their anticipated experience. In so doing, they complete, as Albers and James (1988: 136) put it, 'a hermeneutic circle, which begins with the photographic appearances that advertise and anticipate a trip . . . and ends up with travelers certifying and sealing the very same images in their own photographic productions'. In fact, research has shown that even tourists who engage culturally with the destination take photographs that reveal 'ideologies of Western power and dominance' (Caton & Santos, 2008: 7), although other studies suggest more ambivalent evidence of a photographic hermeneutic circle (Garrod, 2008). Nevertheless, it may not always be possible, for technical or other reasons, to complete that hermeneutic circle. Certain places may be 'unphotographable' (Garlick, 2002) in the sense that the image created by another photograph cannot be recreated, resulting in a dissatisfying experience for the tourist.

Second, debate has long surrounded the ethics of tourist photography, it being questioned whether it is 'right' or 'wrong' to take photographs as part of the tourism experience, particularly when those photographs are of local people at the destination (Garlick, 2002). Whilst tourists wish to gaze upon and photograph 'The Other' – the exotic, the unusual – the taking of such photographs may be seen as being at least intrusive, if not exploitative. To take a picture of a local person, whether the subject is aware of it or not, may be thought of as taking something from that person. As Sontag (1977: 14) observes, 'to photograph people is to violate them, by seeing them as they never see themselves, by having knowledge of them they can never have; it turns people into objects that can be symbolically possessed'. Thus, through photography, tourists appropriate the subject, they take symbolic possession of it.

Third, however, and in contrast to the above point, the tourist photograph has long played a role as material (and now digital) evidence of a visit. In other words, not only do tourists take photographs of particular places to verify the experience to themselves (Jenkins, 2003), but it has long been common practice to place themselves in the picture as proof that 'I was here' (Bell & Lyall, 2005). That proof might be required as a status symbol when showing photographs to other people; equally, it might be a means of self-verification of being there, placing the self within a previously viewed image. Either way, the place or experience is consumed not 'in actuality' but through the recorded image of being there.

Moreover, the placing of the self in tourist photographs is of particular significance in the context of this chapter. That is, the transformation in the practice and meaning of tourist photography as an outcome of the digital revolution is, perhaps, best epitomised in the popularity of the 'selfie' (Holiday et al., 2016) in particular, which is evidence of a shift in the role of photography in the tourist experience more generally (Larsen & Sandbye, 2014; Lo et al., 2011). At a practical level, digital photography has not only displaced the traditional post-holiday ritual of having the camera film processed and printed, but has also enabled the instantaneous consumption of photographs (Bell & Lyall, 2005). Digital photographs can be instantly viewed and, importantly, instantly discarded if they do not satisfy the tourist-photographer. By implication, the tourist consumption of places or people through digital photography also becomes instantaneous and fleeting – that is, 'I am here' rather than 'I was here'. The tourist experience takes on a postmodern ephemerality; if that experience is dissatisfying, it can be discarded and forgotten (as can the subject of the photograph) by simply pressing the 'delete' button on the camera.

At the same time, however, as Stylianou-Lambert (2012) explains, the role of the tourist-photographer passively capturing or, more precisely, recreating representational images of places and people to verify their experience has evolved into one where tourist photography has become a proactive, embodied activity, as indeed has the consumption of tourism more generally (Bærenholdt *et al.*, 2004; Edensor, 2000; Larsen, 2005). For tourists, photography is increasingly becoming a performance that 'lights up the tourist experience' (Scarles, 2009: 465). Tourist photography is now 'less concerned with spectatorship and "consuming places" than with *producing* place myths, social roles, and social relationships' (Larsen, 2005: 417, emphasis in original). Moreover, this transformation to a great extent reflects the digital revolution in photography. That is, the adoption of smartphones as means of taking, instantaneously viewing, sharing and deleting images has fundamentally transformed the practice and meaning of photography (Van House, 2011). It has been simplified and transformed into a more controlled, performative, reflexive, de-materialised and social activity that has arguably become an increasingly fundamental element of the tourist experience (Haldrup & Larsen, 2010). Particularly by placing themselves in the image (the 'selfie'), tourists become part of the experience that is then visually shared on social media; the photograph is less about the place or site and more about the photographer, whilst its significance lies in the subsequent sharing of that photograph.

This is not, of course, to say that tourists only take 'selfies'. Much tourist photography remains concerned with capturing pre-determined images that complete the hermeneutic circle referred to previously. Again, however, these de-materialised, digital images can be instantly viewed, altered, shared or deleted; tourist photography in the digital revolution has become less about creating future memories and more about creating and sharing images as an element of the actual tourist experience.

Overall, then, it is evident from this chapter that the digital revolution, manifested in the rapid development of ICT over the last two decades, has had a significant and, in all likelihood, irreversible impact on the tourist experience. Indeed, over the next two to three decades, as the present digital native generation has children and grandchildren who will live in an increasingly technological (and perhaps virtual) world, the tourism experience will continue to be more influenced and transformed by technological development, both in transport and ICT. On the one hand, tourism as we know it today might in fact no longer exist, at least as a mass social activity, having been replaced by virtual tourism experiences. On the other hand, however, people's innate desire to travel, to discover the world they live in and to have 'real' authentic experiences, might underpin a more measured use of ICT, taking advantage of its functions that facilitate day-to-day life (including tourism), but not allowing it to control their lives. Indeed, we might witness a growing demand for 'real' tourism experiences that are 'digital free'. Either way, however, the digital world is here to stay.

Further reading

Benckendorff, P., Sheldon, P. and Fesenmaier, D. (2014) *Tourism Information Technology*, 2nd Edition. Wallingford: CABI.

> The focus of most books addressing developments in ITC and tourism adopt a supply perspective; that is, how tourism businesses and organisation can use technology to become more effective. This book, however, includes a number of chapters that also focus on tourists and their adoption and use of ITC.

Pearce, P. (2011) *Tourist Behaviour and the Contemporary World*. Bristol: Channel View Publications.

> This book provides a detailed analysis of contemporary tourist behaviour; of particular relevance is Chapter 2 (The Digital Tourist, pp. 25–56) which explores tourists' responses to the digital revolution.

Journal of Information Technology and Tourism (see www.springer.com/business+%26+management/business+information+systems/journal/40558).

> First published in 1998, this journal is an essential source of reading of past and present research into the contribution of ITC to tourism and its influence on tourist behaviour and experiences.

Discussion topics

▶ In what ways has development in ITC fundamentally transformed both the supply and consumption of tourist experiences?

▶ There is no doubt that ITC has made it easier to be a tourist. However, is it improving, or simply changing, how people experience tourism?

▶ To what extent do you agree with the argument that the connectivity afforded by ITC, particularly smartphones, means that people are no longer 'tourists' (in the broader sense of being 'away') but are just continuing their 'home' life in other locations?

▶ Will technology-free holidays become more popular?

8

Tourism
Spiritual and emotional responses

Introduction

As noted in Chapter 5, a dominant theme within the sociological and anthropological study of tourism is the notion that tourism represents, for the tourist, a modern sacred experience. In other words, although tourism is, from a practical point of view, about travelling to and experiencing different places, peoples and cultures, it has long been suggested that the activity of tourism embraces a deeper significance, or has a deeper meaning, for the tourist. That is, tourism possesses, in the broader sense of the word, a spiritual dimension. As Graburn (1989: 22) observes, 'tourism . . . is functionally and symbolically equivalent to other institutions that humans use to embellish and add meaning to their lives'.

Not surprisingly, perhaps, within this context attention has been primarily focused upon the extent to which modern tourism practices can be compared with, or are distinct from, traditional pilgrimage in terms of both social form and meaning. Mac-Cannell (1973; 1976), for example, was the first to suggest that the modern tourist is a secular pilgrim, that tourism is a 'secular substitute for organized religion' (Allcock, 1988: 37), providing tourists with the opportunity to seek meaning or authenticity through the rituals of sightseeing. Similarly, Graburn (1983: 15) compares the practice of tourism with that of tradition pilgrimage; he asks: 'if tourism has the quality of a leisure ritual that takes place outside of everyday life and involves travel, is it not identical to pilgrimage?' Other commentators have also explored the link between tourism and pilgrimage, considering the tourist as a pilgrim, and although more recent research into the area of tourism, religion and spirituality explores a number of different issues, ranging from the behaviour of 'religious' and 'non-religious' visitors at sacred sites to the practical management of religious sites and attractions, the most popular theme remains the pilgrim-tourist debate and the links between tourism and pilgrimage within (post)modern societies more generally. For example, in Timothy and Olsen's (2006) edited text *Tourism, Religion and Spiritual Journeys*, the majority of chapters focus on pilgrimage and tourism from either a conceptual or religion-specific perspective whilst more recent texts continue to explore the intersection between tourism and pilgrimage (Badone, 2010; Raj & Griffin, 2015).

However, the spiritual dimension of tourism embraces issues beyond the concept of tourism as a modern, secular pilgrimage. For example, actual pilgrimage to religious centres (or what may be described more generally as religious tourism) is becoming an increasingly significant sector of the international tourist market. Not only have many traditional pilgrimage centres, such as Mecca, Rome, Jerusalem, Lourdes, Santiago de Compostela, Guadeloupe and Varanasi (Benares) remained or re-established themselves as popular contemporary tourism-pilgrimage destinations – it is estimated, for example, that some 240 million people go on pilgrimages annually (Olsen & Timothy, 2006) – but also, as tourism has evolved into a major global social and economic phenomenon, the number of people traveling wholly or partly for religious or spiritual purposes in particular (including attendance at religious festivals/events and visiting religious sites/attractions) has increased both proportionally and in absolute terms. To an extent, this can be explained by both the increased accessibility of sacred places and sites to international tourist markets and also, in recognition of their economic potential, by the greater propensity of governments and other agencies to market such places to tourists (Mintel, 2012; Vukonić, 2002). India, for example, has actively promoted the Mahabodhi Temple in Bodhgaya and other Buddhist sites as attractions to potential spiritual tourists (Contours, 2004). In a similar vein, the annual pilgrimage to Mecca (the Hajj) is not only considered to be the world's largest religious gathering (Ahmed, 1992) but generates annual revenues of approximately US$16 billion. Consequently, the Saudi Arabian government has, since 1980, invested more than $35 billion both to improve facilities for pilgrims and to maximise economic returns from the Hajj (Vijayanand, 2012) and is currently making significant further investments in facilities and infrastructure (Qurashi, 2017)

Conversely, a broadening and, perhaps, secularisation of notions of religion and spirituality has resulted in a wider interpretation of what constitutes sacred tourism places and experiences (Olsen & Timothy, 2006) and, hence, increased participation in such forms of travel. So-called 'New Age' tourism, for example, embraces both travel or pilgrimage to particular 'sacred' (often pagan) sites, such as Glastonbury in the UK, and also the consumption of specific experiences, such as 'holistic holidays' (Smith, 2003) or so-called wellness tourism (Smith & Puczkó, 2009).

At the same time, increasing attention has been paid to what may be described as the 'darker side' of tourism (Sharpley, 2005b). Although travel to 'dark tourism' sites (Lennon & Foley, 2000) has existed as long as people have been able to travel – the gladiatorial games of the Roman era, pilgrimages or attendance at medieval public executions were, for example, early forms of dark, or death-related, tourism whilst, as Boorstin (1964) alleges, the first guided tour in England was a train trip to witness the hanging of two murderers – it is only more recently that academic attention has focused on the alleged phenomenon of dark tourism. Numerous attempts have been made to define dark tourism and to address a variety of issues such as the development and management of dark sites (see Light, 2017; Sharpley & Stone, 2009), yet it is also important to note that visits to dark tourism sites or attractions, whether war graves, sites of famous battles, disaster sites or places where famous people have died (by natural causes or otherwise) may have some deeper, spiritual meaning for the tourist. In particular, whereas more usual approaches to the spirituality of tourism are concerned with the ways in which people may gain greater meaning or understanding of their lives, dark tourism may provide greater understanding of death or mortality.

Yet, discussing the spiritual dimension of tourism, whether generally or in the specific context of dark tourism, presupposes a need for spiritual experiences on the part of the tourist, a need (recognised or otherwise) that may be satisfied by engaging in tourism. However, not all tourists may seek or desire spiritual or transcendental experiences; they may, indeed reject the notion of spirituality, believing that an emotional sense of well-being or connection is achievable at the tangible or material rather than the spiritual level (Elkins *et al.*, 1988). In other words, as is increasingly recognised in the literature, there also exists an emotional dimension to the tourist experience.

This chapter, therefore, is concerned with the broader spiritual and emotional dimensions of tourism, focusing both on tourism in general as a contemporary spiritual and/or emotional experience that may enhance people's lives and also on the 'darker' spiritual dimension of tourism. Of course, actual 'religious tourism' – or tourism whose participants are motivated either in part or exclusively for religious reasons (Rinschede, 1992) – is widely considered to be one of the oldest forms of travel. In fact, institutionalised religious tourism in the form of pilgrimage was, during the

PLATE 8.1 Lincoln Cathedral, UK. A popular religious tourism destination

Source: Photo by Richard Sharpley

medieval period, a widespread social movement that was evident in the world's main religious traditions of Hinduism, Buddhism, Christianity and Islam and, as noted above, remains a popular form of travel, an identifiable and significant sector of global tourism (McKelvie, 2005; Mintel, 2012). Moreover, as Collins-Kreiner and Gatrell (2006: 33) suggest, 'it is impossible to understand the development of . . . tourism without studying religion and understanding the pilgrimage phenomenon'. However, in the context of this book, it is more relevant to focus upon the experiential aspects of religious or spiritual tourism. Therefore, drawing on recent work in the area, this chapter explores the role of tourism as a modern-secular religious or spiritual experience, including a dark-tourism perspective, before going on to consider tourism more generally from the perspective of emotions. First, however, it is useful to examine briefly the transforming role of religion in contemporary society to provide a broad conceptual framework for the rest of the chapter.

From religion to spirituality

It is not possible to explore critically the spiritual dimension of tourism without some understanding of the role or position of religion/spirituality in modern societies. Nevertheless, although a number of studies consider religious tourism within the context of particular religions or religious/sacred sites, rarely is the debate about tourism as a modern sacred experience more generally located in the wider framework of religion in society. That is, religion is often, but erroneously, viewed as a 'given' within the tourism-religion relationship.

Two points must immediately be emphasised. First, 'religion' itself is difficult, if not impossible, to define. Not only are there, of course, many competing sociological and theological perspectives on religion but also, given the numerous religions that may be identified globally, the concept of religion cannot, as Vukonić (2000: 497) observes, 'be described in a simple definition'. Nevertheless, it is generally accepted that religion is, within the context of specific societies, an institutionalised or organised system of beliefs and practices that some or all members of that society follow. Thus, for example, the sociologist Emile Durkheim, referred to in Chapter 1, defined religion as 'a unified system of beliefs and practices relative to sacred things, that is to say, things set apart and forbidden – beliefs and practices which unite into one single moral community called a Church, all those who adhere to them' (Durkheim, 2008: 47). Moreover 'almost all people who follow some form of religion believe that a divine power created the world and influences their lives' (Vukonić, 2000: 497).

Thus, in many if not all societies, religion is an integral part of the social system (Vukonić, 1996: 26), a fundamental element of culture that is manifested in people's attitudes, beliefs and behaviour (Lupfer et al., 1992). Such behaviour, in turn, emanates from two principal sources (Poira et al., 2003). On the one hand, certain religions impose particular obligations and restrictions upon believers, such as with clothing or eating and drinking, or demand adherence to particular rituals; on the other hand, religions also contribute more generally to a society's attitudes and values amongst both believers and non-believers. Together, these suggest that any society's values, attitudes and behaviour (including touristic activity) will vary and, in part, be determined by the nature, extent and strength of religious following within that society. In some countries or societies, the contribution or influence of religion remains dominant, whereas in other (modern and, by definition, secular) societies, religion plays a more limited cultural role.

This leads directly to the second point (and one that underpins the argument that tourism is a modern, secular pilgrimage), namely, that modern societies are generally characterised by increasing secularisation or, to put it another way, by a decline in the perceived relevance or significance of religious institutions and practices. In other words, over the last 150 years or so, modern societies have witnessed a 'shift in the sacred landscape' (Heelas & Woodhead, 2005: 2), evidenced in particular by the decreasing participation in organised religion or, specifically, a decline in attendance at church (Lambert, 2004; Stark *et al.*, 2005), an institution that offers stability, cohesion and spiritual guidance to its followers (Wuthnow, 1998). The diminishing role and significance of religion in modern societies is usually explained by industrialisation, globalisation, consumerism and scientific rationality, although it is suggested that a postmodern search for individual freedom and expression has also reduced dependence on or respect for religious traditions (Tomasi, 2002). Conversely and somewhat paradoxically, however, immigration and cultural pluralism in many modern societies has resulted in the resurgence in participation in organised religion, whilst some commentators suggest that a genuine religious revival is in evidence around the world.

Importantly, the alleged secularisation of modern societies has not resulted in a religious vacuum. That is, religion, in the traditional sense of the word, is not in decline but, rather, is taking on a different form – modern societies remain religious (Tomasi, 2002) but religion has become increasingly de-institutionalised. To put it another way, a more traditional social adherence to religious beliefs and practices has been replaced in modern societies by a more private, individualised 'religiosity without belonging, especially among young people' (Lambert, 2004: 29). Thus, the practice of religion has evolved beyond adherence to religious dogma and unquestioning acceptance of religious institutions and rituals; religious freedom has, in a sense, become freedom from religion. This is, perhaps, most effectively revealed in the distinctions that have emerged between the terms 'religiousness' and 'spirituality'.

a)   Religiousness: Prior to the rise of secularisation, the concept of religiousness embraced both traditional institutional/individual beliefs and activities and the more general notion of spirituality. However, according to Zinnbauer *et al.* (1997), disillusionment with religious institutions and religious leadership has given rise to distinctive meanings of religiousness and spirituality. Thus, religion, or religiousness, has come to be viewed from two perspectives: the substantive approach explores the beliefs and practices of people with respect to a higher power, central to which is the notion of the sacred, whilst the functional approach focuses upon the role that religion plays in people's lives with respect to issues such as death, suffering, and so on. From both perspectives, however, religiousness is now considered narrowly as 'religious institutions and prescribed theology and rituals' (Zinnbauer *et al.*, 1997: 551). Moreover, the term has also come to attract negative connotations, being perceived by many as a barrier to personal experiences of the sacred or spiritual. A number of studies have demonstrated that increasing numbers of people prefer to define themselves as spiritual rather than religious (Zinnbauer *et al.*, 1997).

b)   Spirituality: According to Brown (1998: 1), spirituality

> has become a kind of buzz-word of the age . . . an all purpose word, but one that describes what is felt to be missing rather than specifying what is hoped to be found . . . The spiritual search has become a dominant feature of late twentieth-century life; a symptom of collective uncertainty.

However, from a theological perspective, spirituality is viewed more positively. Rather than a desired antidote to the perceived anomic condition of (post)modern life, spirituality is a 'personal and subjective', as opposed to an impersonal and institutionalised, perspective on religion (Zinnbauer *et al.*, 1997: 563).

This is not to say that that the quest for spiritual meaning and fulfilment is a recent phenomenon, for spirituality is fundamental to traditional religious belief in a higher being external to the self; hence, religion and religious practice has always been an expression of spirituality whilst, more generally, spirituality has always been an element of human existence (Vukonić, 1996). It is a label applied to an enormous variety of beliefs and practices 'concerned with things of the spirit as opposed to the material' (Stark *et al.*, 2005: 7). Spirituality assumes the existence of the supernatural, though not necessarily a god or gods, and therefore represents a wider connotation of the sacred. As a broad concept, spirituality embraces a number of beliefs and practices that do not conform with traditional religions – people may have what they believe to be spiritual experiences even though they may not hold religious beliefs – yet, interestingly, research has also demonstrated that, for many people, the concepts of spirituality and religiousness retain a degree of congruence (Zinnbauer *et al.*, 1997). In other words, it has been found that many of those who consider themselves to be religious also consider themselves to be spiritual, whilst spirituality remains defined in traditionally religious perceptions of the sacred (i.e. belief in God) and of ritual (e.g. prayer, attendance at church). What may be changing is the way that such spirituality is manifested in practice. Shackley (2002), for example, notes that, although church congregations in the UK are declining, tourist visits to churches and cathedrals are on the increase. This, she suggests, may be a consequence of a pressurised modern world that drives some people to seek a 'quick-fix spiritual experience by being a temporary tourist entering a place of worship for a transient, but none the less significant, encounter with the numinous' (Shackley, 2002: 350).

Nevertheless, there is little doubt that the search for the 'spiritual' has, for many, become distinct from the search for the 'religious'. In other words, religion and spirituality are not synonymous and for many in modern societies, religion is no longer of relevance as they search for spiritual fulfilment. Indeed, research has demonstrated, at least in the UK where, for example, church attendance fell by half between 1980 and 2015 with just 5 percent of the population regularly attending (Faith Survey, 2017), that:

spiritual beliefs are not the preserve of the religious . . . a majority of non-religious people hold spiritual beliefs. This is particularly evident when it comes to non-traditional forms of religious beliefs, where it seems to make very little difference whether someone considers themselves religious or not.

(Theos, 2013: 25)

Moreover, the concept of the spiritual, released from the constraints of the prescribed beliefs and rituals of traditional religions, embraces a significantly broader range of practices and beliefs. For example, Heelas and Woodhead (2005) expand on their concept of a shift in the sacred landscape mentioned above by suggesting that the more traditional spiritual 'life as' (that is, life lived as an expected, obligated role conforming to a transcendent authority) has been relegated in favour of a 'subjective life' lived in accordance with an individual's inner needs, desires and capabilities. In other words, there is evidence in many spheres of social life, such as education, health care and employment, that there has been a cultural shift towards a 'person-centred' or 'subjectivity-centred' direction (Heelas & Woodhead, 2005: 5) whilst, for individuals more generally, a life lived according to pre-determined expectations or 'in conformity to external authority' is being rejected in favour of a self-determined, inner-directed life, 'not to become what others want one to be, but to "become who I truly am"'(Heelas & Woodhead, 2005: 3). Moreover, the significance, meanings, relations and connectivities relevant to subjective-life spirituality are also to be found in the real world; hence, spirituality may be thought of simply as a connection between the self and 'this world', implying that a spiritual relationship exists or is sought between people, 'this world' and specific places. Indeed, from a humanistic perspective, spiritual or emotional well-being can be found in harmonious relationships with 'this world' within, according to Fisher, Francis and Johnson (2000), four distinct domains:

- The personal domain, with a focus on the self (meaning, purpose and values in life), creating self-awareness, identity and esteem.

- The communal domain, focusing on interpersonal relationships between the self and others based on morality and culture.

- The environmental domain, with a concern for caring and nurturing the natural environment drawing on a sense of awe, wonder and connectedness with the environment.

- The transcendental domain, focusing on a relationship between the self and 'something or some-One beyond the human level'.

(Fisher et al., 2000: 135)

Consequently, and as noted above, not only have new forms of spiritual tourism, such as 'New Age' or 'wellness' tourism, emerged, but also the variety of places considered 'sacred' (and, hence, the journeys, or pilgrimages, to such places) has increased enormously. Thus, as discussed later in this chapter, contemporary spiritual tourism may also include visits to so-called dark tourism sites (Lennon & Foley 2000; Sharpley & Stone, 2009). At the same time, of course, tourism to places more generally (cities, the countryside, wilderness areas, the seaside) may, as MacCannell (1973; 1976) and others originally proposed, be considered contemporary spiritual experiences (see Jepson & Sharpley, 2015).

This latter point, with specific reference to visiting a traditional tourism destination – the seaside – is considered shortly. The important point is, however, that the concept of religion is both dynamic and difficult to define. Moreover, although many consider that, in modern, secular societies, religion has been replaced by, or has evolved into, a broader-based, secular spirituality, the distinction between traditional religiousness and contemporary interpretations of spirituality may be less clear than is immediately apparent. Consequently, as the following section shows, the distinctions between the pilgrim, the religious/spiritual tourist and the secular tourist are also fuzzier than suggested by earlier writings on the tourism-religion relationship.

The tourist as pilgrim

As mentioned at the beginning of this chapter, many commentators have focused specifically on the notion that modern tourism is a form of pilgrimage. It is accepted, of course, that traditional pilgrimage is motivated by a religious or spiritual quest, whereas generally the same cannot be said for contemporary tourism. However, it is not the original motivation, but the meaning to the individual tourist that is important. In other words, a religious pilgrimage is normally considered to be something serious, legitimate, authentic and of spiritual significance to the participant, whereas tourism, by comparison, is frivolous and superficial (Pfaffenberger, 1983). Yet, if the labels attached to each are stripped away, it becomes apparent that the experience of seeing, for example, the Taj Mahal, may be of equal significance to a tourist as is a visit to, say, Lourdes, for a pilgrim. 'The difference between tourism and pilgrimage lies not so much in any radical phenomenological difference between them . . . but rather in the culturally-supplied language of symbols in which travellers are obliged to express their peregrinations' (Pfaffenberger, 1983: 72).

The argument that tourism is a form of sacred journey is based upon the relationship between work and play (tourism) and, in particular, the location of each. Compulsory activities, such as making a living, take place in the ordinary, home environment, whereas tourism is voluntary and takes place in the non-ordinary environment, away from home. It is, perhaps, for this reason that staying at home during time off from work is not considered to be a true holiday; to stay at home is to do nothing whilst to go away is to do something (Graburn 1989: 23). It also lends credence to the adage that a change (in this case, of location) is as good as a rest. Thus, despite the advent of the 'staycation' (sometimes erroneously considered to be synonymous with domestic tourism) it is considered proper that people work at home and go away for their holidays.

If work takes place in the ordinary environment then, logically, it represents the ordinary experience. It also represents the passing of ordinary time. Normally, the passage of time is marked by regular festivals or events which, traditionally, have a religious or sacred significance. Thus, festivals such as Christmas or Easter represent a temporary shift from ordinary, secular, profane time into sacred time. During these periods of sacred time, the individual is also transferred from the ordinary, profane existence (usually dominated by compulsory activities) into another, non-ordinary state of existence. In modern, secular societies the annual summer holiday is one such event which has come to be equated with the religious festivals in more traditional societies. The week or fortnight away marks a shift from the profane experience of everyday life to the non-ordinary, sacred experience of the holiday. Thus, by comparing the function of religious festivals in traditional societies to that of holidays in modern society, tourism becomes, logically, a sacred journey.

A number of authors have linked the concept of tourism as a kind of sacred journey with Turner's work on pilgrims (see Turner, 1973; Turner & Turner, 2011). This, in turn, represents an extension to the concept that the passage of time alternated between profane (ordinary) and sacred (non-ordinary) time. It also builds upon the notion introduced in Chapter 4 that tourist behaviour is dependent, up to a point, upon the location of an individual's 'spiritual centre' and that tourism is a form of personal transition (Nash, 1996: 39–57). Turner develops the idea that, by taking part in religious rituals or undertaking a pilgrimage, people become divorced from everyday social and economic structures and constraints. Typically, this involves a three-stage process. Initially, people go through the separation stage, where they become separated from their ordinary home environment and society. In terms of tourism, this is the equivalent of travelling to, and arriving at, the destination. They then move into the second stage, into a condition which Turner describes as liminality. That is, people (or tourists) cross the threshold or boundary (from the Latin *limen*) of their normal, ordered and structured society and enter into a state of anti-structure (that is, a situation where the structure and order of everyday life have disappeared). Normal obligations, such as work, no longer exist and new types of relationships, unaffected by the usual social constraints of status and role, are established between individuals and groups. So tourists, while on holiday, are temporarily freed from the demands of their jobs, household chores, social commitments and, generally, the behavioural norms and values of their society. Unrestricted by social barriers, they are able to form groups or relationships with people with whom they would not, perhaps, normally mix and together enjoy the sense of freedom and escape offered by the holiday. Turner describes this sense of togetherness, of sharing, in his context, a religious, spiritual experience, as a state of *communitas*. Passariello (1983) and Lett (1983) use this concept as a basis for explaining the behaviour of, respectively, weekend domestic tourists at a Mexican coastal resort and North American charter yacht tourists in the Caribbean.

The third and final stage is reintegration; people return to their ordinary home environment and social structure. In traditional societies, it is likely that the return from a sacred ritual or pilgrimage, such as a Muslim having completed his pilgrimage, or Hajj, to Mecca, is signified by reintegration into the social group at a higher status. For a tourist, the experience of liminality is more likely to be of a compensatory nature. That is, he or she returns refreshed, renewed and ready to accept the responsibilities and constraints of everyday life. Reintegration is at the same social status or level as separation but the tourist has been spiritually uplifted by the liminal (or liminoid, the word used by Turner and Turner, 2011 to distinguish between secular and liminal, religious experiences) benefits of the holiday. The tourist is motivated in the first place by the psychological need for spiritual regeneration, a need that may be satisfied by a temporary shift away from the ordinary, profane existence into sacred time. The tourist is able to look at life from the outside, from the freedom of the holiday, from the 'Centre Out There' (Turner, 1973).

Smith (1992) proposed that the relationship between tourism and pilgrimage may be conceptualised as a continuum based upon the degree of intensity of religious motivation in what she refers to as the 'quest in guest'. At one extreme lies sacred pilgrimage, a journey driven by faith, religion and spiritual fulfilment; at the other extreme lies the secular tourist who may seek to satisfy some personal or spiritual need through tourism. Between these two points may be found innumerable religious/secular combinations of religious tourism defined by an individual's religious or cultural/knowledge needs. Thus, Smith (1992) suggests that although tourists and pilgrims share the same fundamental requirements for travel (time, financial resources and social sanction), a distinction between tourism and pilgrimage may be identified within the meaning or personal belief attached to each activity. However, whilst this continuum provides a useful means of classifying forms of pilgrimage or religious tourism, it is unable to embrace the diverse and complex interpretations of religion, spirituality and pilgrimage in contemporary society. In other words, there is a need to progress beyond both relatively simplistic structural-functional comparisons of tourism-

PLATE 8.2 War cemetery, France: both a 'dark' site and a site of pilgrimage
Source: Photo by Richard Sharpley

pilgrimage and polarised definitions of the spiritual pilgrim and secular tourist (and identifiable combinations of the two), taking account of the nature of religion/spirituality within modern societies and how this may influence tourist experiences. Therefore, drawing on work in this field, three specific issues are now considered, namely: the spirituality of the journey; the spirituality of religious sites; and the spirituality of tourist places.

The spirituality of the journey

Within the tourism–pilgrimage debate, relatively little attention has been paid to the ways in which the journey itself (irrespective of motive or destination), the act of travelling away and home again, may represent for the participant a spiritual experience. Graburn (2001: 44) relates rites of passage to the journey where 'kinds of tourism may be purposely self-imposed physical and mental tests', such as arduous trips (e.g. cycling across a continent) or backpacking on a minimal budget, yet this tends to be specific to particular journeys at specific periods in people's lives. In other words, it remains unclear to what extent tourist journeys in general are spiritually meaningful or significant.

Addressing this issue, Laing and Crouch (2006) explore the spiritual dimension of what they refer to as frontier tourism, or journeys to the Earth's more remote places involving physical danger and hardship. Relating such journeys to pilgrimage in terms of the nature of the journey, as opposed to its stages, they identify five particular characteristics of pilgrimage that may equally enhance the spiritual significance of frontier travel:

1   Sacrifice, danger and hardship. Journeys to remote, inhospitable places, such as deserts or the polar regions, frequently require frontier travellers to face up to dangerous situations, to endure hardships and make personal sacrifices in terms of personal comfort, safety and well-being. Enduring (and surviving) such dangers and hardships may contribute to a deeper understanding of the self and the learning of personal spiritual truths.

2   Transformation. In addition to the endurance of hardship and danger, frontier travel may provide a transforming experience. That is, it enables people to discover a new or real self through a desocialising process; the standards, conventions and concerns of their home society are shed, enabling the 'real', inner self to emerge. In other words, frontier travel becomes a 'means of spiritual purification' (Laing & Crouch, 2006), a cleansing process resulting in enhanced self-knowledge.

3   Enrichment. Related to the endurance of hardship, the overcoming and danger and the potentially transforming power of the experience, frontier travel may also provide individuals with spiritual enrichment. Such enrichment may emanate from the successful completion of the journey or adventure, or from particular 'moment in time' experiences when everything 'falls into place', representing inner spiritual peace or knowledge. In either case, the experience is enriching inasmuch as it

becomes an abiding memory, a never to be forgotten experience that frames the individual's future life and, perhaps, a form of addiction as similar experiences are continuously sought out.

4   *Communitas*. Not surprisingly, perhaps, Laing and Crouch identify *communitas* as a defining spiritual characteristic of frontier travel. Whilst personal transformation and enrichment may be the outcome of solo journeys, it is the common sharing of the journey, its dangers, hardships, successes and enriching moments amongst the members of the group or team that may provide the most significant or spiritual reward. Such *communitas* develops from the shared experience, from mutual respect and dependence and, perhaps, from the unwritten lore or code of ethics that surrounds particular activities, such as mountaineering.

5   Return. All journeys inevitably involve a return to the traveller's home society from whence the journey commenced. Such return or reintegration may be difficult – the spiritually enriching character of frontier travel may render 'normal' life unattractive. Conversely, the frontier traveller may seek to add meaning to others' lives by sharing his or her experiences, whether through educating them about other places or by motivating them to face up to challenges, to grow spiritually or to seek out similar experiences. In this sense, the frontier traveller becomes a secular 'preacher', conveying the message of the spiritual experiences of travel to frontier places.

Whilst Laing and Crouch's research focuses specifically on those who have participated in, or written about, frontier travel, the outcomes may nevertheless be applied to all forms of tourism. In other words, for frontier travellers, the 'frontier' represents the border between the safe, predictable, ordered and, perhaps, tamed world, and the dangerous, unpredictable, unexplored, untamed and challenging places on or beyond that border. In a sense, however, all people, all tourists, perceive that there are frontiers to their safe, predictable world and existence. Such frontiers may be social, represented by networks of family or friends or by the security of routine and ritual; the routines of work, obligatory activities and leisure often provide the boundaries or meaning of 'normal' life. Conversely, such frontiers may be geographical; the familiarity of place (or the unfamiliarity of other places) may also represent a boundary to people's lives. They may also be defined by an individual's travel experience. Thus, all people have frontiers beyond which, through tourism, they may travel. Consequently, it may be argued that all tourists may potentially experience the spiritual characteristics of frontier travel (or pilgrimage) identified by Laing and Crouch. An obvious example is the backpacker or independent traveller (see Chapter 4). Backpacking, whether or not a rite of passage, may indeed provide meaningful spiritual experiences, whether through hardship, transformation, enrichment or *communitas*. Similarly, secular tourists following traditional pilgrimage routes, such as that to Santiago de Compostella in northern Spain, may experience some or all of the spiritual elements of pilgrimage. However, for a tourist inexperienced in international travel, the first holiday overseas, or a holiday in a more distant, exotic location, may provide similar spiritual experiences. In short, exploring the spirituality of the journey from this perspective provides credence to the argument that contemporary tourism is a modern spiritual experience.

The spirituality of religious sites

The boundaries between tourism and pilgrimage are, arguably, least distinct within the context of religious sites, such as churches, cathedrals, temples and other religiously significant places and structures including, for example, the Wailing Wall in Israel or the Swayambhunath Buddhist Stupa near Kathmandu, Nepal. On the one hand, religious sites act as foci for religious practice, ritual or observance; they attract people who are primarily motivated by the desire for religious experiences of one form or another, from peaceful spiritual contemplation, through an 'encounter with the numinous' (Shackley, 2002: 350), to salvation and healing (Eade, 1992).

On the other hand, they also fulfil a number of other functions. They may be architecturally significant structures in their own right, they may house important works of art, they may play host to a variety of events, such as concerts or exhibitions, or they may simply be iconic tourist sites, visited simply because they are, as Urry (1990a: 12) puts it, 'famous for being famous . . . entail[ing] a kind of pilgrimage to a sacred centre which is often a capital or major city'. It is unlikely, for example, that a tourist in Paris would feel that his or her stay in the city is complete without a visit to either Notre Dame on the Ile de la Cité or the Basilica of the Sacré Coeur on Montmartre; similarly, a tourist stay in Istanbul would almost certainly include a visit to the Sultan Ahmet Camii, or Blue Mosque. In short, there are at least four possible motives for visiting religious sites:

- spiritual/religious purposes, including individual contemplation/prayer or participation in formal services or ceremonies;

- heritage or cultural purposes, such as an interest in architecture or religious culture;

- special interests, for example, musical concerts, brass rubbing, or photography;

- planned or impulse visits 'because it is there'; that is visiting religious sites as iconic tourist markers.

Implicitly, therefore, the management of religious sites is potentially problematic given the diversity of motives amongst visitors, the fact that, frequently, religious visitors are outnumbered by those with other motives (Shackley, 2002), and the need to meet and balance the needs of all visitors whilst recognising that tourism may represent a vital source of income to maintain the fabric of the site. Indeed, with regards to the latter point, the commercialisation or commodification of sacred/religious sites, from charging entrance fees to cathedrals or promoting 'church trails' (Kiely, 2013) to developing a purportedly religious site or experience for commercial gain (the Holy Land Experience in Orlando, USA, being a unique example: see www.holylandexpereince.com), has significant implications for the nature or authenticity of the visitor experience. That is, religious sites may vary from authentic, non-commodified sites to artificially created, commodified and, hence, inauthentic sites (see Figure 8.1).

This in turns suggests that greater knowledge and understanding of the behaviour, expectations and experiences of visitors (both religious and 'non-religious') to religious sites, particularly with respect to the extent to which they seek out or benefit from spiritual experiences, serendipitously or otherwise, may go some way to informing the

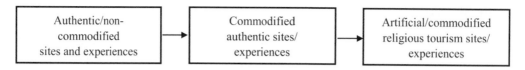

FIGURE 8.1 From authentic to artificial religious sites and experiences

management and promotion of such sites. In other words, whilst it may be safe to assume that certain groups of visitors are religiously motivated, it may be less safe to assume that other, secular visitors do not have some form of spiritual motivation or experience.

A number of studies address this issue, albeit to a relatively limited extent. In an early piece of research, for example, Jackson and Hudman (1995) explored the motivations of visitors to five English cathedrals, finding that less than 4 percent cited religion as the basis for their visit. Overall, the primary reason for visiting cathedrals was an interest in the history or architecture of the building although significantly, those in the older age group (60 or over) cited religion as their main reason for visiting. Conversely, over half of all respondents indicated that their visit 'prompted some type of religious feeling' (Jackson and Hudman, 1995: 43), although the study did not enquire into respondents' self-perceptions of religiousness or spirituality. More broadly, Voase (2007) found that visitors to Lincoln Cathedral in the UK sought, but did not necessarily achieve, a sense of connectivity and human continuity, with the requirement to pay an entrance fee being considered a challenge to any spiritual response to the visit, whilst a more recent study undertaken at Canterbury Cathedral, also in the UK, revealed a desire for more interpretation of both religious and secular attributes of the building (Hughes *et al.*, 2013). This latter research reveals, perhaps, that some major religious buildings function primarily as tourist attractions.

Adopting a different perspective, Collins-Kreiner and Gatrell (2006) compare the differing behaviours of secular and religious tourists to the Bahá'í Gardens in Haifa, Israel, concluding that secular tourists and religious tourists differ greatly in terms of their experience of the site (although this is, to a great extent, determined by the differing structures of tours provided to secular or religious tourists, the former group being permitted only to observe from tourist space, the latter enjoying a more performative role in pilgrim space). More usefully, perhaps, Poira *et al.*'s (2003) study of two groups of tourists at the Wailing Wall in Jerusalem investigates the relationship between tourists' religious affiliation, the strength of their religious beliefs and their subsequent visitation patterns. They identify a strong correlation between religious affiliation of tourists (i.e. their religious heritage) and both their visitation patterns and personal involvement with the site; conversely, strength of religious belief is a less dominant factor. Thus, non-religious Jews feel more involved with the site (the Wailing Wall is considered the holiest religious site for Jewish people) than religious Christians, who do not attach the same religious significance to the site.

Whilst these latter studies perhaps reinforce the perceived distinction between religious and secular tourists in terms of motivations and experiences, research by Williams *et al.* (2006) not only adds a new dimension to the understanding of tourists' relationship with, or response to, spiritual places, but also, importantly, begins to challenge the assumption that religious and non-religious tourists inevitably experience such places in different ways. Based on a survey of visitors to a Welsh cathedral, Williams *et al.* (2006) assess visitors' experience of visiting the cathedral under four broad headings, namely: overall impressions; spiritual and religious; aesthetic and historic; and, commercialisation. Significantly, however, they also segment respondents according to their degree of 'religiosity' (measured, perhaps somewhat simplistically, by frequency of church attendance) in order to identify the extent to which expectations and experiences vary amongst different groups of visitors.

Some results of their research are unsurprising. For example, for 'frequent church-goers' (the most religious group), the overall impression of their visit tends to be most positive; similarly, a majority of this group also claim to 'sense God's presence' during their visit to the cathedral and, overall, feel satisfied and refreshed by their visit. Conversely, only a small proportion of those who never attend church (the least religious group) sense God's presence and are less positive in terms of their overall impressions. Interestingly, however, amongst this latter group there is evidence of a spiritual dimension to the cathedral visit. For example, over one third of non-churchgoers, secular visitors who 'stand outside the Christian tradition', find the cathedral to be spiritually alive, half feel a sense of peace from their visit and a significant majority find the cathedral awe-inspiring and uplifting. In other words, as Williams *et al.* (2006) suggest, 'many aspects of the visit were able to stir the soul' of these secular tourists.

PLATE 8.3 Prambanan Hindu Temple, Yogyakarta, Java. Spiritual site or tourist attraction?
Source: Photo by Richard Sharpley

This particular outcome of this study might support Shackley's (2002) assertion, noted earlier, that the pressures of modern society lead to people seeking a 'quick fix' spiritual experience; in a sense, just as physical hunger may be satisfied by fast food, so too may spiritual hunger be satisfied by fast religion. Conversely, the research may suggest that secular visitors are susceptible to spiritual experiences whilst visiting religious sites, that a lack of apparent religiosity does not preclude some sense or experience of the spiritual. As Williams *et al.* (2006) observe, this suggests that there exists the opportunity for religious sites, such as cathedrals, to 'build bridges between contemporary spiritualities, implicit religious quests, and explicit religious traditions', thereby enabling them to extend the ministry to this group. It also suggests that the distinction between 'pilgrims' and 'tourists' at religious sites may not be as great as previous research suggests (see also Sharpley & Sundaram, 2005). Nevertheless, there is quite evidently a need for wider, more in-depth research in this area focusing upon different sites and different religious contexts.

The spirituality of tourist places

It has long been recognised that certain tourism places (or spaces) may provide tourists with spiritual experiences. For example, it has been observed that, in general, the link between sublimity and religion has long been explicit: 'it is no coincidence that the Western attraction to sublime landscapes developed at precisely the moment when traditional beliefs in God began to wane' (de Botton, 2002: 171). Thus, gazing upon sublime views or landscapes may provide some form of spiritual refreshment or meaning.

More specifically, particular categories of tourism places or destinations have been associated in one way or another with spirituality or spiritual refreshment. MacCannell (1976), of course, in asserting that tourism is a modern form of pilgrimage, implies that reality, meaning and authenticity can be found in other times and places which remain traditional or untainted by modernity. In other words, tourism places in the 'Other' may be the setting for spiritually meaningful tourism experiences. Similarly, the countryside (or, more specifically, the social construct of rurality that may be associated with rural places) has long been seen as possessing a symbolic significance in modern societies. Contrasting with the physical and socio-cultural characteristics of urban areas, the countryside has come to be seen as a rural utopia, a green and pleasant land, offering tourists the opportunity to immerse themselves in a nostalgic past. In other words, as MacCannell (1976) more generally suggests, the countryside is a 'refuge from modernity' (Short, 1991: 34), a place that may provide visitors with spiritually refreshing experiences.

The extent to which this is indeed the case is unclear. On the one hand, it has long been suggested that being in the outdoors, in the natural environment, may be beneficial to mental well-being and may contribute to self-renewal (Burls, 2007; Darker *et al.*, 2007; Kaplan, 1995; Korpela & Hartig, 1996), whilst specific natural places, such as wilderness or forests, can offer spiritual experiences (Fredrickson & Anderson, 1999; Heintzman, 2007). On the other hand, the results of Sharpley and Jepson's (2011) study of tourists' experiences in the English Lake District were more ambiguous.

That is, although certain experiences, such as climbing or gazing at beautiful scenery, elicited in some tourists a sense of spirituality, not only was a quest for the spiritual not considered a motive for visiting the Lake District but also, for many, it was the cultural significance of the area (or more precisely, a sense of place) that generated emotional feelings.

Indeed, although it may be safe to assume that other types of tourist place may also potentially provide visitors with spiritual experiences. such 'spirituality' lies in their history, heritage or links with a more 'authentic' past. In other words, the spirituality of such places lies in the historic meaning or reality they provide in an anomic, (post)modern world – they provide a focal point, a kind of historical spiritual rock in the uncertain and dissatisfying contemporary world of modernity (Hewison, 1987).

In contrast, Bull (2006) explores the extent to which the continuing popularity of a traditional tourist space – the seaside – may be linked either wholly or in part to its spiritual 'pull'; that is, he considers the aspects of coastal-based tourism that might be more spiritual than temporal. There are, according to Bull (2006), three different uses of the sea/coast by tourists:

- activities occurring on, in or under the water (e.g. paddling, swimming, watersports);
- activities that make use of the coastal margin, such as walking or seabird watching; and
- activities that do not depend on the coastal resources but nevertheless occur at the seaside (e.g. socialising, visiting amusement arcades, parks, cafés, and so on).

In the first two cases, it is important to explore why such activities may have a deeper spiritual meaning for visitors; in the third case, the question is: what pulls tourists to the seaside to participate in activities that could take place anywhere?

In addressing these issues, Bull (2006) identifies eight influences that pull tourists to the seaside, each of them possessing 'in some measure a degree of natural spirituality'. At the same time, there are significant symbolic characteristics of the sea that transcend many religions and belief systems and that, collectively, elicit a set of human spiritual responses. These eight influences may be summarised as follows:

1   *Spiritual and physical well-being.* The sea has long been considered beneficial to both physical health (sea water as a natural healer) and spiritual well-being.

2   *Correspondence of the sea's rhythms to life's rhythms.* An unconscious sense of the connectivity between the sea's rhythms (the tides, the waves breaking on the shore) with life's rhythms (heartbeat, breathing, human biorhythms) provides spiritual peace and relaxation.

3   *Freedom of the limitless.* The sea's edge provides the spectacle of infinity, limitlessness, the wonder of the Earth's dimensions; it provides the sense of escape, freedom and unconstrained movement in an environment uncontrolled by humankind.

4   *The beach as liminality.* The coastal margin is a safe liminal space between the danger and unpredictability of the sea and the ordered serenity and stability of the land, from which people may contemplate the 'latent anger and chaos of the ocean, its punishment of sins'.

5 *Adventure and daring.* As with other adventure places, the sea provides opportunities for, and the spiritual refreshment from, participating in adventurous or daring activities and pastimes.

6 *Regression to childhood.* As a liminal space, the beach/sea allows people to return to a childlike existence of fun and play, of innocence and spiritual freedom from adult codes, norms and cynicism.

7 *Return to the womb/pre-terrestriality.* Swimming in the sea may be equated with a return to the womb, a pre-natal comfort, or even perhaps a spiritual link with pre-terrestrial existence.

8 *Surrender to a greater spiritual power.* The sea may draw people back spiritually to their creator and the contemplation of their final resting place. To 'toy' with this greater power (surfing, diving, and so on) is to confront the final journey.

As Bull (2006) accepts, it would be difficult to claim that there is a spiritual dimension to every seaside visit (just as it would be difficult to claim that there is a spiritual dimension every tourist journey or experience). Nevertheless, the seaside does appeal to people's spiritual consciousness and unconsciousness in a number of ways, and provides a setting where a variety of spiritual experiences may be possible. In fact, more recent research reveals that visiting the seaside offers tourists the opportunity 'to think more deeply than normal, to meditate, to be more self-aware and to experience spirituality' (Jarratt & Sharpley, 2017: 15). The question remains, however, whether other tourist places, either in the natural or built environment, can provide similar spiritual opportunities.

The three contexts discussed above, along with the review of the tourism-pilgrimage debate, demonstrate that the distinction between pilgrims, religious/religious heritage tourists and secular/non-religious tourists is less clear than might be initially imagined. That is, the dynamic, multi-layered nature of religion and spirituality in modern societies may be reflected in a multitude of spiritual tourist experiences that have yet to be revealed or understood. Certainly, as the following section now discusses, the concept of dark tourism may also be considered, from a sociological perspective, as a form of spiritual tourist experience.

Dark tourism

The term dark tourism was first coined in 1996 (Foley & Lennon, 1996a, b) but it has been since the subsequent publication of the book, *Dark Tourism: The Attraction of Death and Disaster* (Lennon & Foley, 2000) that increasing academic and media attention has been paid to the subject. This is not, perhaps, surprising, given the fact that tourism (connoting fun, escapism, relaxation, happiness and hedonism) and death/mortality/disaster are not normally spoken about in the same breath, Nevertheless, the idea of dark tourism, or tourism to places or sites associated with death, disaster and suffering, has over the last 20 years spawned an ever-increasing number of academic and media articles (see Light, 2017 for a comprehensive review).

It is not, however, a recent phenomenon. Tourists have long been drawn, purposefully or otherwise, towards sites, attractions or events that are associated with death, violence or disaster, such as the gladiatorial games of ancient Rome. In the modern era, an early example of dark tourism occurred in 1934 when (in somewhat suspicious circumstances) disaster struck the SS Morro Castle, a luxury liner that cruised between New Jersey and Cuba (Thomas & Morgan-Watts, 1988). On the night of 9 September, when the ship was close to the New Jersey coastline, the captain of the ship, Robert Wilmott, allegedly died of a heart attack in his bath-tub and command passed to the first officer. At 2.45am, fire broke out in the ship's lounge and quickly spread, yet the SOS was not sent out until 3.25am. By that time, the ship was ablaze and eventually, 137 passengers and crew perished. Importantly, attempts to salvage the ship were unsuccessful and the smouldering wreck (with numerous victims still aboard) drifted to the shore of New Jersey at Asbury Park. It immediately became a tourist attraction – trips were laid on for people to travel to the site, souvenir stalls were set up and, according to press reports at the time, a carnival atmosphere was enjoyed by the 250,000 people who went to witness the event.

What this disaster demonstrated was that, when such events occur, not only are people drawn to gaze upon them but also there is an 'industry' that is willing and able to provide and enhance such experiences (Kelman & Dodds, 2009). In other words, sites of death or disaster can become a tourist attraction, promoted and visited like any other destination. Thus, more recent examples include 'Ground Zero', where more than double the number of people visited the site the year after '9/11' than when the Twin Towers were standing, trips to New Orleans in 2006 to witness the damage caused by Hurricane Katrina in late 2005 (Gould & Lewis, 2007), and organised tours around Christchurch, New Zealand after the 2011 earthquake (Coats & Ferguson, 2013). Equally, an enormous variety of other types of attraction not related specifically to disasters may be classified as dark tourism destinations. For example, Smith (1998: 205) suggests the sites associated with war probably constitute 'the largest single category of tourist attractions in the world' (see also Butler & Suntikul, 2013; Henderson, 2000; Ryan, 2007), supporting specialised tour operators such as Holts Tours and Midas Tours in the UK.

Yet war-tourism attractions, though themselves diverse, are a subset of the totality of tourist sites associated with death and human suffering (Dann, 1998; Light, 2017; Sharpley & Stone, 2009). Reference is frequently made, for example, to the Sixth Floor in Dallas, Texas from where President Kennedy was allegedly shot (Foley & Lennon 1996a; see also https://www.jfk.org), visits to graveyards (Seaton, 2002), prison tourism (Barton & Brown, 2015; Strange & Kempa, 2003) or slavery-heritage tourism (Buzinde & Santos, 2009; Dann & Seaton, 2001). But there is a wide variety of other tourism sites or attractions that are associated with death, although this may not always be the dominant motivating factor for tourists – it is likely, for example, that the draw of the Taj Mahal is its beauty as a building that epitomises India rather than its function as a tomb.

Importantly, despite both the history and breadth of dark tourism, academic study of the phenomenon is relatively recent. Within the literature, attempts have been made to define or label death-related tourist activity, such as 'thanatourism' (Seaton, 1996), 'morbid tourism' (Blom, 2000), 'black spot tourism' (Rojek, 1993), 'death tourism'

(Sion, 2014) or, more broadly, the 'darker side of travel' (Sharpley & Stone, 2009); to analyse and categorise specific manifestations of dark tourism, from sites of genocide (Auschwitz in Poland, the 'Killing Fields' of Cambodia, the genocide memorials of Rwanda) to 'hyper-real' experiences; and to explore the management and promotion of dark sites. Attention has also been focused, though to a lesser extent, on the reasons or purposes underpinning tourists' desire to seek out such sites or experiences, the proposed 'drivers' of dark tourism varying from a simple morbid curiosity, through *schadenfreude* (Seaton & Lennon, 2004), to a collective sense of identity or survival 'in the face of violent disruptions of collective life routines' (Rojek, 1997: 61), although one commentator suggests that visiting specifically genocide sites satisfies tourists' 'voyeuristic needs' (Schaller, 2007: 515; see also Sharpley & Friedrich, 2017). Conversely, Tarlow (2005) links the attraction of dark sites with either 'reflexive' or 'restorative' nostalgia, though he too resorts to suggesting a wide variety of potential motives for dark tourism consumption.

Moreover, although much has now been written on the subject of dark tourism, as Light (2017) reveals, many questions remain unanswered. For example, is dark tourism generally a tourist-demand or attraction-supply related phenomenon? More specifically, has there been a measurable growth in 'tourist interest in recent death, disaster and atrocity . . . in the late twentieth and early twenty-first centuries' (Lennon & Foley 2000: 3) or are there simply more sites/attractions on offer to ever-increasing numbers of tourists? Does the popularity of 'dark sites' result from only an interest or fascination with death or are there more powerful motivators? Are there degrees or 'shades' of darkness that can be related to either the nature of the attraction or the intensity of interest in death or the macabre on the part of tourists (Stone, 2006; Strange & Kempa, 2003)? And does the popularity of 'dark' sites result from a basic interest or fascination with death, or are there more powerful motivating factors?

Evidently, in order to address many of these questions it is necessary to possess some understanding of tourist behaviour with respect to 'dark' sites and attractions. In other words, the analysis of dark tourism cannot be complete without a consideration of *why* tourists may be drawn towards sites or experiences associated with death and suffering. As noted above, a variety of motives are proposed in the literature, perhaps the most comprehensive list being provided by Dann (1998) who identifies eight possible factors. These include the 'fear of phantoms' (i.e. overcoming childlike fears); the search for novelty; nostalgia; the desire to celebrate crime or deviance; a more basic bloodlust; and, at a more practical level, 'dicing with death' – that is, undertaking journeys, or 'holidays in hell' (O'Rourke, 1988), that challenge tourists or heighten their sense of mortality. However, as Dann (1998) himself notes, these categorisations are largely descriptive and may be related more to specific attractions, destinations or activities rather than the motivations of individual tourists.

Understanding the consumption of dark tourism

The term 'dark tourism' was, as noted above, first coined by Foley and Lennon (1996a, b) in a special issue of the *International Journal of Heritage Studies* and, subsequently, as the title of a book that arguably remains the most widely cited study of the phenomenon (Lennon & Foley, 2000). Their work was not, however, the first to focus upon the relationship between tourism attractions and an interest in death, whether violent, untimely or otherwise. In particular, Rojek (1993) considers the concept of 'Black Spots', or 'the commercial developments of grave sites and sites in which celebrities or large numbers of people have met with sudden and violent death' (1993: 136), as tourist attractions.

Interestingly, Rojek introduces his analysis by making reference to the hordes of sightseers flocking to the sites of disasters, such as the shores of Zeebrugge in 1987 (the capsizing of the ferry *Herald of Free Enterprise*) and Lockerbie in Scotland (the crash site of Pan Am 103) in 1988, before going on to discuss three different examples of Black Spots – the annual pilgrimage to the place where James Dean died in a car crash in 1955, the annual candlelight vigil in memory of Elvis Presley at Graceland in Tennessee and the anniversary of JFK's assassination in Dallas, Texas. These he refers to as postmodern spectacles, repeated reconstructions that are dependent on modern audio-visual media for their continued popularity. Other attractions, such as national and metropolitan cemeteries, are categorised as 'nostalgic' sites and it is only later that he goes on to distinguish disaster sites as being 'analytically distinct from Black Spots as sensation sites' (Rojek, 1997: 63). A similar distinction is made by Blom (2000: 30) who defines 'morbid tourism' as, on the one hand, tourism that 'focuses on sudden death and which quickly attracts large numbers of people' and, on the other hand, 'an attraction-focused artificial morbidity-related tourism'. Thus, the concept of dark tourism is at once rendered more complex by a number of variables, including:

- the immediacy and spontaneity of 'sensation' tourism to dark sites of contemporary death and disaster compared with premeditated visits to organised sites or events related to near and/or distant historical occurrences;

- the distinction between purposefully constructed attractions or experiences that interpret or recreate events or acts associated with death, and 'accidental' sites (that is, those sites, such as churches, graveyards or memorials that have become tourist attractions 'by accident');

- the extent which an 'interest' in death (to witness the death of others, to dice with death in dangerous places, to learn about the death of famous people, etc.) is the dominant reason for visiting dark attractions; and

- why and how dark sites/experiences are produced or supplied – for example, for political purposes, for education, for entertainment or for economic gain.

These issues are addressed again shortly but, to return to the work of Foley and Lennon (1996a: 198), their use of the term relates primarily to 'the presentation and consumption (by visitors) of real and commodified death and disaster sites'. This rather broad definition is later refined by their assertion that dark tourism is 'an intimation of post-modernity' (Lennon & Foley, 2000: 11). That is, first, interest in and the interpretation of events associated with death is to a great extent dependent on the ability of global communication technology to instantly report them and, subsequently, repeat them ad infinitum (hence time-space compression). Second, it is claimed that most dark tourism sites challenge the inherent order, rationality and progress of modernity (as does the concept of postmodernity) and, third, at most sites, the boundaries between the message (educational, political) and their commercialisation as tourist products has become increasingly blurred. As a result of these rather strict, self-imposed parameters, attractions based on events that neither took place 'within the memories of those still alive to validate them' (Lennon & Foley 2000: 12) nor induce a sense of anxiety about modernity do not qualify as dark tourism. Thus, for these authors, dark tourism is a chronologically modern (i.e. twentieth century onwards), primarily Western phenomenon based upon (for reasons they do not justify) non-purposeful visits due to 'serendipity, the itinerary of tour companies or the merely curious who happen to be in the vicinity' (2000: 23). As Reader (2003) suggests, this lack of attention to motivation in general and an evident reluctance to accept that tourists may positively desire 'dark' experiences overlooks an essential dimension of the study of dark tourism.

In contrast to Lennon and Foley's somewhat restricted focus, Seaton (1996) argues that dark tourism has a long history, emerging from what he refers to as a 'thanatoptic tradition' (i.e. the contemplation of death) that dates back to the Middle Ages but that intensified during the Romantic period of the late eighteenth and early nineteenth centuries. He cites a number of attractions, including graves, prisons, public executions and, in particular, the battlefield of Waterloo to which tourists flocked from 1816 onwards and Pompeii, 'the greatest thanatoptic travel destination of the Romantic period' (Seaton, 1996: 239). He goes on to argue that dark tourism is the 'travel dimension of thantopsis' (hence thanatourism), defined as 'travel to a location wholly, or partially, motivated by the desire for actual or symbolic encounters with death, particularly, but not exclusively, violent death' (Seaton, 1996: 240). Importantly and, again, challenging Lennon and Foley's position, Seaton also proposes that:

• dark tourism or thanatourism is essentially a behavioural phenomenon, defined by the tourist's motives as opposed to the particular characteristics of the attraction or destination, and

• thanatourism is not an absolute form; there exists a 'continuum of intensity' dependent upon the motive(s) for visiting a site and the extent to which the interest in death is general or person-specific. Thus, visits to disaster sites such as Ground Zero are a 'purer' form of thanatourism (as long as the visitor was not related to a victim) than, say, visiting the grave of a dead relative.

Based on this behavioural perspective, Seaton suggests five categories of dark travel activities:

1   Travel to witness public enactments of death – though public executions now occur in relatively few countries, Rojek's (1997) sensation tourism at disaster sites may fall under this heading.

2   Travel to see the sites of individual or mass deaths after they have occurred. This embraces an enormous variety of sites, from battlefields (e.g. Gallipoli), death camps

(e.g. Auschwitz) and sites of genocide (e.g. Cambodia's 'killing fields') to places where celebrities died (such as the site of James Dean's death in a car crash referred to above), the sites of publicised murders (e.g. the California house where Nicole Simpson, the estranged wife of O.J. Simpson, was found stabbed to death in 1994), or the homes of infamous murderers.

3   Travel to memorials or internment sites, including graveyards, cenotaphs, crypts and war memorials. The reasons for such visits are diverse, from an interest in brass-rubbing or epitaph collection to pilgrimages to the resting place of the famous, the Père Lachaise cemetery in Paris being an oft-quoted example.

4   Travel to see evidence or symbolic representations of death at unconnected sites, such as museums containing weapons of death (e.g. the Royal Armouries in Leeds, UK) or attractions that reconstruct specific events or activities. As Dann (1998) observes, these 'morbid museums' may focus on selected themes and, thus, be 'less concerned with historical accuracy'.

5   Travel for re-enactments or simulation of death. As Seaton (1996) suggests, this originally took the form of plays or festivals with a religious theme though, over the last century, 'secular derivations', such as the re-enactment of famous battles by groups or societies, have become increasingly popular.

Seaton also notes that, although 'thanatourism' has a long history, it has become increasingly popular over the last two centuries – certainly, Dann's (1998) comprehensive review of the 'dark side of tourism', in which he presents a multitude of examples under five principal headings (perilous places, houses of horror, fields of fatality, tours of torment and themed thanatos) and 11 sub-headings, reveals the diversity of contemporary sites, attractions and experiences that can be referred to as dark tourism. He also suggests that the role of the media has been central to this growth in tourism to sites and attractions associated with death, principally through increasing the geographical specificity of murder and violent death and, more recently, through global communication technology that transmits events almost as they happen into people's homes around the world.

Given the difficulty in attaching an all-embracing label to the enormous diversity of sites, attractions and experiences that may be collectively referred to as 'dark tourism', attempts have also been made to clarify or distinguish between different forms or intensities of dark tourism. For example, Miles (2002) proposes that a distinction can be made between 'dark' and 'darker' tourism based upon the location of the site or attraction. Arguing that there is a difference between sites associated with death, disaster and suffering, and sites of death, disaster and suffering, then 'journey/excursion/pilgrimage to the latter constitutes a further degree of empathetic travel: 'darker tourism' (Miles, 2002: 1175). Thus, a visit to the death camp site at Auschwitz-Birkenau is, according to Miles, 'darker' than one to the US Holocaust Memorial in Washington DC. Moreover, extending his analysis into the temporal dimension (and lending credence to Lennon and Foley's 'chronological distance' argument), he suggests that 'darkest tourism' emerges where the spatial advantage of a site of death is amplified by either the recentness of events (i.e. within recent living memory of visitors) or where past events are transported in live memory through technology. Importantly, underpinning

Miles' argument is the assumption that a dark tourism experience requires empathy/emotion on the part of the visitor – such empathy is heightened by the spatial-temporal character of the site.

In a similar vein, Sharpley (2005b) suggests that, based upon differing intensities of purpose with respect to both the supply of and consumption of dark tourism, different 'shades' of dark tourism may be identified. That is, dependent on both the degree of interest or fascination in death on the part of the tourist and on the extent to which an attraction is developed in order to exploit that interest or fascination, different sites/experiences may be either 'paler' or 'darker'. Thus, darkest or black tourism occurs where a fascination with death is provided for by the purposeful supply of experiences intended to satisfy this fascination, one example being the $65 per person 'Flight 93 Tour' to the Pennsylvania crash site of United Airlines 93 – one of the 9/11 hijacked aircraft – established and run by a local farmer (Bly, 2003). The concept of different shades of dark tourism is also explored by Stone (2006), albeit from a different conceptual basis. That is, he proposes a 'spectrum' of dark tourism, embracing seven categories of dark tourism 'suppliers' related to spatial, temporal, political and ideological factors.

Again, however, the fundamental motivational issue remains unanswered. In other words, despite the variety of perspectives and terminology with respect to dark tourism

PLATE 8.4 The A-bomb dome, Hiroshima, Japan
Source: Photo by Richard Sharpley

within the tourism literature, some commonality on a broad definition is in evidence. That is, dark tourism is typically referred to as visits, intentional or otherwise, to sites/ attractions associated with death and suffering. However, the question of why tourists seek out such dark sites remains largely unaddressed, although Raine (2013) proposes a 'dark tourist spectrum'. Generally, visits to dark sites are seen to be driven by differing intensities of interest or fascination in death, in the extreme hinting at tasteless, ghoulish motivations. More specific reasons vary from morbid fascination or 'rubber-necking' through empathy with the victims to the need for a sense of survival/continuation, untested factors which, arguably demand verification within a psychology context. In particular, in the context of this chapter, however, relatively little attention has been paid to the extent to which the consumption of dark tourism has a spiritual dimension, although Stone and Sharpley's (2008) widely cited paper provides a potential means of understanding or confronting death in modern society.

PLATE 8.5 The 'Killing Fields', Choeung Ek, Cambodia

Source: Photo by Richard Sharpley

Death, society and dark tourism

A paradox exists in modern societies. On the one hand, death is increasingly present, whether in graphic representations in the cinema – the 1998 movie *Saving Private Ryan* gained notoriety for its graphic representation of violent deaths on the beaches of Normandy – on television or in the news. Indeed, modern technology allows viewers, from the comfort of their homes, to witness wars, natural disasters, terrorist atrocities and other events resulting in death and suffering almost instantaneously. Indeed, death and dying is pervasive within popular culture and media output (Durkin, 2003; Walter *et al.*, 1995).

On the other hand, death is also absent in modern societies. That is, death, as the inevitable outcome of human existence, has become increasingly sequestered, or hidden away from contemporary social life. In other words, the communal experience of death, along with social rituals that follow the death of a member of a community, have become increasingly less common, to the extent that dying and, indeed, the contemplation of mortality, have become privatised. Death, dying and mortality are, in a sense, increasingly denied within the public realm and, as a result, modern society has become less well equipped to deal, at a spiritual as opposed to practical level, with death and mortality.

The establishment and evolution of sociology has been concerned almost exclusively with the problems of life, rather than with the subject of death (Mellor & Shilling, 1993). However, almost four decades ago, Berger's (1967) seminal text suggested that death is an essential feature of the human condition, requiring individuals to develop mechanisms to cope with their ultimate demise. He went on to suggest that to neglect death is to ignore one of the few universal parameters in which both the collective and individual self is constructed. Since then, a significant branch of sociology has emerged that focuses on the social context and meanings of death and dying. A full consideration of these is beyond the scope of this chapter (see, for example, Howarth, 2006) but a number of issues are fundamental to understanding the ways in which death has become sequestered, and the implications of this, in modern society.

Of particular significance, in traditional societies death was (and still is) treated as a social or public event. That is, the death of an individual member of a society was viewed as a potential threat to that society. Therefore, an individual's death triggered a set of collective processes or rituals they were designed to counter any threat posed by that death. At the same time of course, and as outlined earlier in this chapter in the discussion of the shift from religion to spirituality, religion and religious practices also held a more dominant position in traditional societies. These religious or superstitious beliefs and rituals were institutionalised and provided people with mechanisms for coping with the death of others or, indeed, confronting their own mortality. Nowadays, of course, in many cultures that still have a dominant religious element, these coping mechanisms still exist.

As societies have modernised, however, religion and religious institutions have become less dominant; scientific knowledge and rationality have replaced religious dogma. Thus, a critical feature of modern society may be seen in the extensive desacralisation of social life which has failed to replace religious certainties with scientific certainties (Giddens, 1991). Instead, whilst the negation of religion and an increased belief in science may have provided people the possibility of exerting a perceived sense of control over their lives (though, crucially, it has not conquered death), it fails to provide values to guide lives, leaving individuals vulnerable to feelings of isolation, especially when ruminating the prospect of death and an end to life projects. In short, members of modern society, by and large, no longer possess the spiritual tools for coping with death, whether their own or that of others.

In addition, a variety of other processes have occurred in modern societies that have further diminished the ability of individuals (or society as a whole) to confront death and mortality. Firstly, the process of dying and disposal has been medicalised and institutionalised; the dying are sent to hospices, undertakers take care of funerals. Thus, the medical profession and the hospice movement have helped relocate death away from the community and into a closed private world of doctors, nurses and specialists (Byock, 2002) and, as a result, processes and activities that often occurred at home have been, in a sense, appropriated by the death 'industry'. At the same time, rapid advances in medical knowledge have strengthened people's belief in longer (if not eternal!) life whilst, culturally, the postmodern, individualised existence focuses on the self, the body and youth. Collectively, these processes have served not to resolve the problem of death by neutralising its implicit threat but, ironically, to leave many people uncertain and socially unsupported when it comes to dealing with mortality. Consequently, members of modern societies suffer what has been referred to as 'ontological insecurity' – that is, a lack of sense of order, meaning and continuity in social life, which in turn leads to a feeling of dread and the consequential bracketing out of social life questions about the social frameworks that embrace contemporary existence.

It is within this context that, under certain circumstances, dark tourism might be seen as a spiritual experience, a means of neutralising the perceived threat of death in modern society. More specifically, dark tourism may provide the means for confronting the inevitably of one's own death and that of others. Dark tourism, with its camouflaged and repackaged 'other' death, allows individuals to (un)comfortably indulge their curiosity and fascination with thanatological concerns in a socially acceptable environment, thus providing them with the opportunity to construct their own contemplations of mortality. With a degree of infrastructure and normality that surrounds the supply of dark tourism, albeit on varying scales (Stone, 2006), the increasingly socially acceptable gaze upon death and its reconceptualisation either for entertainment, education or memorial purposes offers both the individual and collective self a pragmatic confrontational mechanism to begin the process of neutralising the impact of mortality. Consequently, this can help minimise the intrinsic threat that the inevitability of death brings (Stone & Sharpley, 2008). In short, visiting certain dark tourism sites may provide tourists with a mechanism for thinking about death within a safe or, in some circumstance, even light-hearted environment. That is, dark tourism may go some way to providing tourists with a spiritual ontological security.

Of course, given the enormous diversity both of dark tourism places and of the needs, experience and expectations of visitors, the potential effectiveness of dark tourism consumption as a mechanism for confronting, understanding and accepting death will vary almost infinitely. It may be argued, for example, that war cemeteries, sites of mass disasters, memorials to individual or multiple deaths/acts of personal sacrifice and so on may be more powerful and positive means of confronting death than more 'playful' attractions, such as 'houses of horror'. Certainly, a visit to Gallipoli, where the mass graves of the fallen (including that of a young British soldier who died before reaching his 17th birthday) lie above the beaches and cliffs, is an inevitably emotive and meaningful experience, verifying, perhaps, the cultural and popularised representations (both visual – the Mel Gibson movie *Gallipoli* – and musical) of that tragic event. Similarly, the memorial to victims of the 2004 tsunami at Baan Nam Khem in Thailand or the memorial to the victims of the 2002 Sari Nightclub bombing in Bali provide a focus for contemplation, mourning, hope and survival. Conversely, contemporary visitors to places such as Auschwitz, perhaps the epitome of a dark tourism destination, may come simply 'out of curiosity or because it is the thing to do' (Tarlow, 2005: 48) rather than for more meaningful purposes. This latter point, of course, may result in any potential meaning(s) to visitors of mortality, and indeed morality within contemporary society, as consequential and thus additional to any preconceived meanings (or motivations) that may have rested on 'simple morbid curiosity'. At the same time, it would be wrong to suggest that tourists are motivated to visit dark sites in the expectation of neutralising their concerns about death, or that any such spiritual 'refreshment' occurs as a result of visiting a dark site. Nevertheless, relating the demand for dark tourism to the sociological understanding of death provides a useful framework for exploring the spiritual dimensions of the phenomenon of dark tourism.

Tourism: the emotional dimension

Thus far, this chapter has been considering what is broadly referred to as the spiritual dimension of tourism, or the extent to which participation in tourism may provide a sense of spiritual satisfaction or well-being. Over the last decade or so, however, increasing attention has been paid more generally to emotions in the tourist experience (Prayag *et al.*, 2013). In other words, whilst there has long been support for the idea that contemporary tourism is potentially significant as a (secular) spiritual experience, or that spiritual/transcendental experiences might be a specific outcome of participation in tourism, it is only relatively more recently that the importance of understanding tourists' more general emotional responses to tourism has been acknowledged, not least as a basis for better planning and managing tourism (del Bosque & San Martin, 2008). For example, following on from the discussion of dark tourism in the preceding section, it has been suggested that tourists' experiences of dark sites – or the significance of dark tourism more generally – might best be revealed through an exploration of their emotions both prior to and following their visit (Ashworth & Rami, 2015) and, hence, such an exploration might inform the management of dark sites. Interestingly, Ashworth and Rami (2015) also suggest that, from a consumption perspective, an attraction or destination can only be defined as 'dark' if it stimulates 'dark' emotions amongst visitors: 'a dark tourism experience or dark tourism site is one that evokes emotions experienced as unpleasant by an individual, which raises the question: why deliberately experience the unpleasant unless there is a compensating satisfaction?' (Ashworth & Rami, 2015: 320).

It is beyond the scope of this chapter begin to answer that question. Equally, some would contest any distinction that is made between spirituality and emotions, arguing that certain positive emotions contribute to or collectively constitute what spirituality is understood to be. Certainly, in studies exploring the extent to which rural tourists enjoy spiritual experiences, respondents referred to strong emotions, such as 'awe', to describe such experiences (Jepson & Sharpley, 2015). Again, the 'spirituality vs. emotions' debate falls beyond the purpose of this chapter, though it is usefully summarised elsewhere (Vaillant, 2008). Nevertheless, the relationship between spirituality and emotions suggests that, in the context of tourism, the latter cannot be overlooked. Two issues, then, demand attention: first, what are emotions? And second, what is the relevance of emotions to understanding the tourist experience? It is with these questions that this final section of the chapter is concerned.

What are emotions?

At first sight, it would appear to be a relatively simple task to define emotions. After all, as human beings we constantly experience emotions, such as happiness, joy, anger, fear, sadness, guilt, boredom, and so on. More specifically, we feel emotions; we feel happy, we feel angry, we feel sad, we feel bored. Hence, emotions are, in a simplistic sense, feelings. Yet, such a description fails to reveal the true essence of emotions. Why do we experience particular emotions? How do we respond to them? How do emotions differ from mood or from more general dispositions such as optimism or pessimism? Indeed, when emotions are considered in the wider context of human and social existence their complexity as a concept become evident and, as a consequence, it is not surprising that, according to Robert Plutchik, well known for his theories of emotions (for example, Plutchik, 1991), 'there is much disagreement between contemporary theoreticians concerning the best way to conceptualize emotion and interpret its role in life' (Plutchik, 2001: 344).

Despite a lack of consensus over the definition of emotions, there is no doubt that emotions are fundamental to social existence, defining interpersonal interactions and social activities (Barbalet, 2004). Kalat (2011: 437), for example, suggests that 'all of our emotions, within limits, provide richness to our experiences' whilst it is recognised that people tend to remember emotionally arousing information better than neutral information (Levine & Pizzaro, 2004). Emotions are, then, essentially short-term but strong feelings (people typically experience many different emotions during the day and some at the same time, resulting perhaps in having 'mixed feelings' about something). However, the significance of emotions lies not in the actual feelings, but their position in a cause and effect process. In other words, emotions are derived from an individual's circumstances or relationships with others; that is, emotions are a response to external factors or what Plutchik (2001: 347) terms a 'stimulus event'. Moreover, that emotion results in some form of action, for example, responding to fear by avoiding the source of that fear. In short, emotions to a great extent, direct human behaviour (Zautra, 2003).

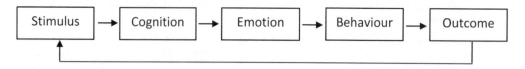

FIGURE 8.2 From stimulus to outcome: the role of emotions

Source: Adapted from Plutchik (2001: 347)

For Plutchik, however, the relationship between cause and response is more complex. Whilst the initial stimulus acts as a trigger, the meaning of that stimulus must be understood, a meaning from which an emotion is derived. That emotion, in turn, leads to some form of response or behaviour, the result of which is an outcome. For example, the initial stimulus might be a threat; this is understood as danger, eliciting the emotion of fear. The resulting behaviour is avoidance or escape, leading to the outcome of safety. Hence, emotions play a pivotal role in people's lives and are, through feedback mechanisms, essentially a factor in the human evolutionary process, as conceptualised in Figure 8.2.

Although there is largely consensus over the role and significance of emotions, there is, however, less agreement over what (or how many) types of emotions people experience. Nevertheless, Hupka *et al.* (1999) suggest that such emotions are universal and, as Ashworth and Rami (2015) note, psychologists have long been concerned with attempting to list or classify emotions. Plutchik (1980) for example, in his well-known 'wheel of emotions', identifies eight primary emotions – namely, joy, trust, fear, surprise, sadness, anticipation, anger and disgust – each of which can be experienced in different levels of intensity. Thus, the primary emotion of fear can be felt less (apprehension) or more (terror) intensively. Significantly, these eight primary emotions are divided into two broad categories: positive (joy, trust, anticipation and surprise) and negative (anger, fear, disgust and sadness), a dichotomy that is widely employed to categorise emotions. In a study of visitor emotions at a dark site, Nawijn and Fricke (2015) similarly categorised emotions into positive and negative, but listed five under each heading: the positive emotions were relief, pleasure, fascination, joy and positive surprise, whereas the negative emotions were anger, sadness, scare, shock and negative surprise.

Numerous other categorisations of emotions exist which, in themselves are of value. Of greater interest, however, is the consequences or implications of the behaviour that follows the experience of these emotions, particularly in the tourism context.

Emotions and the tourism experience

Participating in tourism, or in specific tourism experiences such as visiting a particular attraction or attending an event, can be considered to a stimulus that, through the cognition process, results in emotional feelings on the part of the tourist. Indeed, simplistically speaking, it could be argued that people participate in tourism or go on holiday in anticipation (itself an emotion identified by Plutchik) of positive emotions, such as happiness (see Chapter 6). However, the study of emotions in tourism is concerned more specifically with the issue of satisfaction or, to be more precise, in understanding the emotional or affective components of satisfaction as a basis for both the more effective management of the tourism experience and encouraging positive future behaviour (repeat visits).

This is not to say that tourist satisfaction, as a recognised indicator of successful tourism service performance (Hui *et al.*, 2007), has not been explored in the literature. Indeed, numerous studies have focused on the measurement of tourist satisfaction, such as Akama and Kieti's (2003) study of safari tourists in Kenya and Kozak and Rimmington's (2000) research amongst off-season tourists on Mallorca (see also Dmitrović *et al.*, 2009; Kozak, 2003; Ryan, 2005; Tribe & Snaith, 1998). However, many of these studies tend to focus on cognitive factors, such as memory, reasoning or learning (Koenig-Lewis & Palmer, 2014), whilst emotional or affective factors have been overlooked (Martin *et al.*, 2008). Indeed, satisfaction studies in tourism, in particular in service consumption, more generally have traditionally adopted the cognitive approach based on so-called disconfirmation models, satisfaction being defined as either an evaluation against expectations being met or exceeded (Engel *et al.*, 1993).

Nevertheless, it has become widely acknowledged that, in service contexts in general, emotions (both positive and negative) can be highly influential on both satisfaction and intended behaviour (Oliver, 1997; White & Yu, 2005), whilst research in tourism in particular increasingly explored the relationship between emotions and both satisfaction and future intentions. For example, del Bosque and San Martin (2008) found that both expectations and emotions play a significant role in satisfaction formation; not only do prior expectations influence emotions during the tourism experience (that is, there is an inter-relationship between cognitive and affective components), but also 'emotions play an important role in tourism [satisfaction] since individuals' enjoyment is based on their own experiences' (del Bosque and San Martin (2008: 566). Similarly, Hosany and Gilbert's (2010) study identified positive emotions in satisfying hedonic holiday satisfaction, whilst in the specific context of museums, del Chiappa *et al.* (2014) found that those visitors with more positive emotions reported being more satisfied with their experience than those with less positive emotions, hence concluding that emotions are more significant than cognitive aspects in shaping visitors' satisfaction.

With regards to future intent, Bigne and Andreu's (2004) empirical study of tourists' emotions revealed that those who experienced greater pleasure and arousal demonstrated an increased level of satisfaction and more favourable behavioural intentions, such as loyalty and willingness to pay more. Conversely, although research into emotions and service satisfaction in general has revealed that negative emotions are a predictor of negative behaviour, such as complaints to the service provider or critical reviews (for example, Tronvoll, 2011), Nawijn and Fricke (2015), in their study of visitors to a dark site (a concentration camp memorial), found that strong negative emotions such as sadness and shock actually resulted in positive intent to visit other dark sites.

The research into the role of emotions in tourism suggests that not only is it a fascinating and fruitful of study, but also that understanding tourists' emotional response to their visits is important in practice. That is, tourism providers have much to gain through knowledge of tourists' emotions, potentially enriching the tourist experience and enhancing satisfaction and loyalty. At the same time, however, the contradictory nature of the outcomes of the research suggest there is still much to learn about the emotional dimension of the tourist experience.

Further reading

Religious tourism and spirituality

Raj, R. and Griffen, K (eds) (2015) *Religious Tourism and Pilgrimage Management,* 2nd Edition. Wallingford: CABI.
A comprehensive text that discusses religious tourism and pilgrimage from a variety of conceptual perspectives as well as providing contemporary international case studies.

Timothy, D. and Olsen, D. (eds) (2006) *Tourism, Religion and Spiritual Journeys.* Abingdon: Routledge.
One of the earlier collections to explore in detail the relationship between tourism, religion and spirituality, this remains a key text that explores both conceptual and practical issues concerned with religious tourism as well as presenting studies of tourism within specific religious traditions.

Dark tourism

Lennon, J. and Foley M. (2000) *Dark Tourism: The Attraction of Death and Disaster.* London: Continuum.
The book that originally sparked academic interest in dark tourism. Drawing on a variety of case studies, it introduces and explores the phenomenon, as well as debating issues such as the ethics of presenting death and suffering for touristic consumption.

Sharpley, R. and Stone, P. (2009) *The Darker Side of Travel: The Theory and Practice of Dark Tourism.* Bristol: Channel View Publications.
Perhaps the definitive text book on dark tourism, this book builds on the foundation of earlier studies, both extending the conceptual analysis of the phenomenon and considering the significance and management of specific manifestations of dark tourism.

Stone, P. *et al.* (2018) *The Palgrave Handbook of Dark Tourism Studies.* Basingstoke: Palgrave Macmillan.
A comprehensive and contemporary collection of essays, this book explores a wide variety of issues and themes relevant to knowledge and understanding of the concept of dark tourism.

Emotions and tourist experiences

Robinson, M. and Picard, D. (eds) 2016. *Emotion in Motion: Tourism, Affect and Transformation*. Abingdon: Routledge.
A contemporary collection that considers the relevance of emotion to tourism as both an 'inner journey' and from the perspective of affective responses to particular places and attractions.

Discussion topics

▶   As religious tourism becomes increasingly exploited for its potential economic contribution to destination areas, is the experience of religious tourists likely to become increasingly inauthentic?

▶   If, indeed, modern secular society is defined by a search for spirituality, can tourism fulfil that need?

▶   Is 'dark tourism' simply a convenient label for places and attractions associated with death and suffering, or is it a distinctive form of tourist experience?

▶   Does the 'dark tourist' exist?

▶   In what ways can the study of tourist emotions contribute to more effective destination or event management?

9

Tourism and authenticity

Introduction

The links between authenticity and tourism have been explored by commentators and tourism researchers almost for as long as modern tourism itself has existed. During the nineteenth century, attention was initially focused on the way in which emerging forms of mass transport, in particular the railways, diluted the perceived authenticity of the travel experience. At the same time, the early pioneers of package tourism, such as Thomas Cook, also attracted criticism. For example, Charles Lever, writing in *Blackwoods Magazine* in 1865 about Cook's tourists in Italy, described cities as being 'deluged with droves of these creatures, for they never separate, and you see them forty in number pouring along a street with their director, now in front, now at the rear, circling them like a sheepdog' (cited in Cormack, 1998: 34). Implicit in this statement is the perceived inauthenticity of the tourists' experience, a theme which Boorstin continues and develops in his essay 'From traveller to tourist: The lost art of travel' (1964).

In contrast to Boorstin's thesis that tourists are satisfied with inauthentic, pseudo-events, MacCannell (1989; 2013) adopts a more positive perspective. He argues that living in modern, alienated societies, tourists are motivated by the need to experience authenticity: 'modern man has been condemned to look elsewhere, everywhere, for his authenticity, to see if he can catch a glimpse of it reflected in the simplicity, poverty, chastity or purity of others' (MacCannell, 1989: 41). Thus, for MacCannell, the entire phenomenon of tourism hinges on a quest for authenticity and reflects the deficiencies of modern life; the tourist is a model for 'modern-man-in-general' (1989: 1).

The widely quoted Boorstin/MacCannell debate on the meaning and importance of authenticity has largely dominated the sociological treatment of tourism since the late 1960s. As a result, it has tended to overshadow other equally relevant issues concerned with the connection between authenticity and the tourist experience. For example, the concept of authenticity is frequently used as a marketing tool; holidays are advertised as offering the chance to experience the 'real' Africa, the 'hidden' Asia or, more generally, 'genuine' travel. In many cases, however, the authenticity on offer bears more relation to tourists' expectations (or what tour organisers believe tourists want to see) than to what actually exists.

This then leads on to the question: what is an authentic tourist experience? Visitors to India on a typical Delhi–Jaipur–Agra (Taj Mahal) tour may well believe that they have experienced the 'real' India but, whilst there is no doubting the authenticity of individual sights, collectively they represent one particular image or perception of India: the India of the Moghuls, of royal palaces, of the Raj. That is, they are a sign of 'Indian-ness', a physical manifestation of an image that is, arguably, far removed from the reality of modern India. Thus, the authenticity of the destination is, in a sense, a myth (see Selwyn, 1996).

Another problem to be considered is the extent to which any tourist site or experience may be considered authentic once it becomes packaged and sold as part of the overall tourist product. In other words, once a destination, an event or even a cultural artefact becomes caught up in the tourism system it becomes a commodity. Commodities have a value, normally measured by price, and once culture has become commoditised it can lose its meaning and significance for local people and, potentially, its authenticity to tourists (see Goulding, 2000; Greenwood, 1989; Shepherd, 2002).

Thus, the relevance of authenticity to tourism and the tourist experience is much broader than might at first be imagined. This chapter examines the relationship between authenticity and tourism and considers, in particular, the way in which tourists look to heritage and the past in their search for the authentic.

Authenticity

What is authenticity?

Before looking at the various ways in which authenticity is linked to the tourist experience, it is important to consider what is actually meant by authenticity. It is a word that is frequently used in the academic literature to describe the tourism experience, tourism attractions and events or the motivation for tourism. Equally, it often appears in tourist brochures, advertisements and other travel industry publications, perhaps one of the most over-used words in the 'language of tourism' (Dann, 1996). Despite the widespread use of the word, scant attention is paid to explaining or defining authenticity in relation to tourism. This may in fact be because it is so widely used and because its meaning or interpretation varies according to its use: as Trilling (1974: 11) states, 'the word "authenticity" comes so readily to the tongue these days and in so many connections that it may very well resist . . . efforts of definition'. He goes on to assert, however, that its original usage was in the context of the museum to describe objects which are 'what they appear to be or are claimed to be' (Trilling, 1974: 93), a usage which continues to be the most widely accepted and understood.

Within the context of tourism, the concept of authenticity has become rather more ambiguous. On one hand, the word 'authentic' is frequently used to describe products, works of art, cuisine, dress, language, festivals, rituals, architecture and so on – in short, everything which comprises a country's culture. Generally, something is considered to be authentic if it is made, produced or enacted by local people according to custom or tradition. Thus, in one sense, authenticity connotes traditional culture and origin, a sense of the genuine, the real or the unique. On the other hand, within tourism, it is also used to describe (and sell) different types of travel, certain journeys or even entire holidays. Importantly, it is generally used to distinguish between specialist or niche-market tourism products and mass tourism products, the implication being that mass tourism is, somehow, inauthentic. For example, tour operators which organise adventure travel holidays typically refer to the implicit authenticity of the travel experiences they offer. Thus, Wildfrontiers, a UK-based specialist tour operator, offers 'extraordinary authentic experiences; relax in the best room in a Rajasthan palace hotel, dance around a fire with a pagan tribe in the Hindu Kush, travel with local expert guides to get really under the country's skin' (Wildfrontiers, 2017).

Immediately, then, a difference appears between the two uses of the concept of authenticity within tourism. One is based upon the tangible origin of something; a cultural object or event is either real, genuine and authentic, or it is false, or a fake; the second is based upon a less tangible comparison. For a holiday, a journey or a particular tourism experience to be authentic, it must be perceived to be so in comparison to another experience that is inauthentic. For MacCannell (1989), the inauthentic is modern society, and tourism, therefore, becomes a search for the authentic. It is easy, then, to see how certain forms of travel and tourism come to be described as authentic because, in a sense, mass, package tourism is an extension of modern society and, hence, inauthentic.

Cohen (1988a), in his discussion of authenticity and commoditisation in tourism, furthers the debate by explaining how a word that is normally used to describe something that is real or genuine has also become a socially constructed concept (that is, a description of the condition of modern society). Following Trilling's origination of the word 'authentic' in the museum, curators and ethnographers have tended to view the authenticity of primitive and ethnic art in strict terms; to be authentic, things must have been created by traditional craftsmen using traditional materials. In particular, authentic items must have been made for the use of local people rather than for trade or selling on to strangers; 'the absence of commoditisation . . . [is] . . . a crucial consideration in judgements of authenticity' (Cohen, 1988a).

Most importantly, authenticity is a quality that is perceived to be firmly rooted in pre-modern life, a quality 'of cultural products produced prior to the penetration of modern Western influences' (Cohen, 1988a). In other words, things can only be authentic if they have been created without the aid of modern materials, tools or machinery. Thus, anything, including society, that has been adapted, influenced, altered or, as an anthropologist might describe, contaminated by the modern, Western world, has lost its authenticity.

It is here that authenticity develops into a way of describing the state or condition of societies. If the origin of strictly authentic products lies in pre-modern societies then, by implication, modern Western society, with all its characteristics of alienation, materialism, mass production and consumption and so on, is inauthentic. Conversely, traditional countries or societies (by implication, those in the less developed parts of the world) are more authentic. For the tourist, authenticity or authentic experiences are to be found in pre-modern societies or societies that have yet to become Westernised and developed. This raises issues, as Cohen (2002) notes, about the relationship between tourists' desire or need for authentic experiences, the sustainability of attractions or destinations that might be considered 'authentic', and potential problems of equity. That is, the most appropriate means of sustaining the authenticity or integrity of a particular attraction or place may be to restrict access, yet this course of action might compete with the needs of local communities to profit from tourism.

For example, since the mid-1990s, tourism to Cambodia has grown remarkably. In 1993, just 118,000 tourists visited the country, a figure that had grown to almost half a million by 2000; in 2016, more than 5 million international arrivals were recorded, contributing US$3,212 million in receipts (CMoT, 2017). More than half are drawn to the country's best-known attraction, the Angkor Wat temple complex (featured in the movie *Tomb Raider*), the popularity of which has led to the development of some 450 hotels and guesthouses in the nearby town of Siem Reap. However, although tourism generates significant revenues, the development and volume of tourism is having significant negative impacts on Angkor Wat, threatening both the temple complex itself and the longer-term economic prosperity of local communities (Winter, 2008). At the same time, the transformation of Siem Reap into a tourist cen- tre has diminished its cultural integrity (Sharpley & McGrath, 2017) whilst, despite the apparent economic contribution of tourism, not only has it served to exacerbate inequality within the town (Brickell, 2008), but the region remains one of the poorest in the country (Mao *et al.*, 2013).

To return to the discussion of the meaning of authenticity, the question that then arises is: what are the characteristics of authentic, pre-modern or traditional societies that tourists seek? Is it, for example, simply symbols or signs of authenticity, such as the existence of traditional, non-mechanised farming methods, or do tourists wish to fully immerse themselves in traditional society, to experience a way of life that no longer exists in modern, developed societies?

A full consideration of the characteristics of traditional (authentic) *versus* modern (inauthentic) societies is beyond the scope of this chapter, and much depends upon the perspective adopted. But, given the socio-cultural characteristics of traditional societies (see Figure 9.1 below), it appears unlikely that a meaningful experience of traditional life could be included in the tourism experience. Nevertheless, as discussed later in this chapter, the desire to experience more traditional (and perceptually more authentic) cultures does go some way to explaining, for example, the attraction of the British countryside as a symbol of the pre-industrial, pre-modern era (see Sharpley & Sharpley, 1996) and, more generally, the current fascination with heritage and the past. In a touristic sense, if traditional, pre-industrial society is perceived to be authen- tic, then there is much truth in the suggestion that 'the past is a foreign country' (Lowenthal, 1990).

To summarise, then, authenticity within the context of tourism has two meanings:

1   It is a description of the tangible quality of something (for example, an artefact, a meal, a festival, a building) which is associated with production methods or cultural foundations that are perceived to be pre-modern or traditional.

2   It is a socially constructed, intangible perception of destination societies and cultures, of forms of travel, or of overall tourism experiences that appear to be pre-modern or traditional.

Traditional	Modern

Traditionalism:
  – orientation to the past/tradition
  – inability to adapt to new circumstances
Kinship system:
  – economic, social, legal position
    determined by kin relationships
  – ascription as opposed to
    achievement
Influence of emotion, superstition,
fatalism
	Traditional values less dominant:
	  – ability to change/adapt
	  – challenge to obstacles of tradition
	Open social system:
	  – geographical/social mobility
	  – economic, political, social freedom
	  – achievement as opposed to
	    ascription
	Forward-looking society, demonstrating:
	  – innovation, entrepreneurial spirit
	  – objective, rational approach

FIGURE 9.1 Characteristics of 'traditional' and 'modern' societies

Source: Adapted from Webster (1990)

The Boorstin-MacCannell debate

Though now somewhat dated, the so-called Boorstin-MacCannell debate remains of central relevance to the concept of authenticity in tourism. Indeed, most contemporary commentators continue to refer to the work of both, though particularly MacCannell's theories (for example, Chhabra *et al.*, 2003; Rickly, 2013; Taylor, 2001). It is, therefore, important to review the key points of the debate here.

Both Boorstin and MacCannell take the inauthenticity of modern society as the starting point for their arguments. Indeed, both follow the structural line that the behaviour of modern tourists reflects and results from this inauthenticity, but their conclusions lie at opposite ends of what may be described as the authenticity-inauthenticity continuum. For Boorstin (1964), modern (American) society is contrived, illusory and unreal. People thrive on pseudo-events and this is reflected in the way that the modern, mass tourist is satisfied with contrived, meaningless events which can be viewed, preferably, from the comfort and surrounding of the familiar world. As Boorstin argues, the tourist

> has come to believe that he can have a lifetime of adventure in two weeks and all the thrills of risking his life without any real risk at all. He expects that the exotic and the familiar can be made to order . . . expecting all this, he demands that it be supplied to him. Having paid for it, he likes to think he has got his money's worth. He has demanded that the whole world be made a stage for pseudo-events.
>
> (Boorstin 1964: 80)

The events are supplied by the tourism industry, images of new destinations are contrived by the media and every effort is made to make the tourist feel at home; one of the aims of Conrad Hilton was to create 'a little America' in each of the countries where he opened one of his hotels. As a result, the tourist is increasingly removed from the reality and authenticity of the destination society and 'tourism turns into a closed, self-perpetuating system of illusions' (Cohen, 1988b: 30). In a similar vein, and also as an example of the postmodern hyper-reality (see Chapter 3), the Venetian Resort Hotel Casino in Las Vegas is a contemporary, and rather extreme, example of a 'pseudo' destination.

MacCannell (1989; 2013) adopts the opposite perspective. Rather than simply reflecting or representing the embodiment of the inauthenticity of modern life, the tourist recognises it and becomes a kind of secular pilgrim (MacCannell, 1973) on a quest for authenticity. The very motive for tourism becomes a search for the authentic: 'sightseeing is a kind of collective striving for a transcendence of the modern totality, a way of attempting to overcome discontinuity of modernity' (MacCannell, 1989: 13). The modern tourist looks for meaning in the reality of the life of other people in other places yet, at the same time, accepts the inauthentic condition of modernity. As if to perpetuate the differentiation between the modern and the pre-modern, modern society collects and preserves the pre-modern in museums and heritage centres, in arts, music, fashion and decor, in order to provide havens of reality and authenticity in the turmoil of modern life. For the tourist, the challenge lies in the extent to which he or she is allowed, by the destination tourism industry, to experience the real lives of others. Inevitably, events are staged for tourists but any resulting inauthenticity of experience results not from the demands of tourists for pseudo-events, as Boorstin argues, but rather as 'a structural consequence of the development of tourism' (Cohen, 1988b: 34).

Authenticity and the individual tourist

The arguments of Boorstin and MacCannell represent two extremes and, in reality, it is highly unlikely that tourists who conform to their descriptions exist in any great number, if at all. MacCannell's characterisation of the tourist is more in keeping with a description of an anthropologist and, as McKercher (1993: 11) points out, 'it is a mistake to assume that most tourists are anything more than consumers, whose primary goal is the consumption of a tourism experience'. More simply stated, tourism is most frequently motivated by the desire to escape from, not by the need to become involved in other societies, as suggested by MacCannell. Equally, it is widely accepted that tourists are becoming more discerning and more quality conscious and the tourism industry is having to provide an ever-increasing variety of destinations and products to satisfy demand. Boorstin's tourist, therefore, bears more relation to a caricature of a mass tourist than to anyone who actually exists although, at the same time, it is probable that some tourists come close to his description.

Undoubtedly there are the purists who seek to escape entirely into authentic cultures and societies and others for whom the notion of authenticity does not even come into consideration in their holiday decision-making process. It would be safe to suggest, however, that the great majority of tourists fall between these two extremes in terms of their search for authenticity. At the same time, the alienation that results from the condition of modern society is not necessarily recognised or experienced to a similar degree by all members of society (see Chapter 4 and Cohen, 1979b). For example, many people might be entirely satisfied with their lives, identifying with and accepting the characteristics of modern life, such as a routine job or materialism as a symbol of success. Their centre is firmly rooted in modernity and their sense of alienation is minimal. Other people may reflect on the meaning of their lives and may experience or be more aware of a sense of alienation from modern society. Such differences may result from occupational and educational factors. For example, Cohen (1988a: 376) proposes that intellectuals are, generally, more aware of their alienation than 'the rank-and-file middle-classes, and especially the lower middle class, who still strive to attain the material gains which those beyond them already enjoy'.

The important point is that, if there is indeed a link between alienation and the search for authenticity, then different tourists will be more or less disposed to seek authentic experiences elsewhere. Furthermore, the greater an individual's need to experience authenticity, the stricter will be the criteria by which that individual judges something to be authentic (Cohen, 1988a). Thus, the greater a tourist's alienation from society, the greater will be the emphasis on finding and experiencing authenticity and the stricter will be the rules by which authenticity is judged. In other words, a recreational tourist may well perceive a particular attraction or event to be authentic whereas experiential tourists might see through the staged, contrived nature of the same attraction or event, perceiving it to be totally inauthentic. For example, two different tourists staying at a hotel at a beach resort in Spain may witness a show that includes some flamenco music and dancing. One of these tourists may be a non-alienated, recreational tourist with little desire to seek authenticity, the other a person seeking the 'real' Spain. The first, even recognising the staged nature of the show, may accept it as authentic whilst the second would almost certainly write it off as contrived, false and inauthentic. For the post-tourist, of course, the debate becomes irrelevant; all tourism is a game, all tourist experiences are part of that game and, in recognising this and the tourist's role in the game, the concept of authenticity is not considered (see Chapter 4).

To any individual tourist, then, authenticity is not a given, measurable quality that can be applied to a particular event or product, nor does it provide a simple scale against which a tourist experience may be judged (see Lau, 2010 for a review of authenticity). Rather, the perceived authenticity (or lack of authenticity) of a cultural product or of an overall tourist experience depends upon the relationship between the tourist as an individual and the product/experience with which he or she is concerned. Thus, Wang (1999b) identifies three manifestations of authenticity within tourism: (i) objective authenticity (when an artefact or event is recognised as being authentic); (ii) constructed authenticity, or the authenticity that is imposed onto an artefact or event by tourists or the tourism industry; and (iii) existential authenticity, or a 'state-of-being' related to the activities of the tourist (Wang, 1999b: 352). The latter interpretation is of most relevance here; that is, authenticity is not a fixed, static concept, but negotiable (Cohen, 1988a). In other words, authenticity must be considered from the point of view of individual tourists, their expectations, their experience and their home socio-cultural environment.

In recent years, a number of researchers have explored this issue within empirical contexts. For example, Mehmetoglu and Olsen's (2003) work looks at the different ways in which the tourist experience is considered authentic by visitors to the Lofoten Islands in Norway. They identify three different manifestations of authenticity (social relations, nature and personal achievement) linked to the particular characteristics, needs and experience of the individual tourists. Variations in the experience of authenticity were also highlighted by McIntosh and Prentice (1999) in their study of British visitors to cultural heritage attractions in the UK. In another study, Chhabra *et al.* (2003) assessed the degree of authenticity perceived by visitors to 'Scottish Highland Games' held in North Carolina, revealing (perhaps surprisingly) a significant degree of authenticity experienced by visitors to the event.

It is also argued that perceptions of authenticity are dependent on the relationships that tourists have with people in tourist settings (Pearce & Moscardo, 1986). For example, a tourist in an inauthentic environment, such as a Western-style hotel, may still have an authentic experience by interacting with a local person who works in the hotel. Thus, 'it is the relationship between the tourist and the host which determines authenticity' (Pearce & Moscardo, 1986: 129). The important point is, however, that simple distinctions between the 'authentic' and the 'inauthentic' cannot be attached to particular places or experiences when the role of the individual tourist is taken into account (Olsen, 2002).

Authenticity over time

Just as authenticity is a negotiable process based on the relationship between the individual tourist and the cultural product or event, so too is it possible to suggest that authenticity can develop over time. That is, it is feasible for a product or event that is originally inauthentic to become assimilated into local culture and to become authentic. No culture or society can be static; all cultures are dynamic, new cultural products emerge and, therefore, emergent authenticity (Cohen, 1988a) is a valid and realistic process within the context of tourism. Thus, for example, festivals or events originally staged for the benefit of tourists may, over time, come to be accepted as a local, authentic custom (Xie, 2003). Similarly, crafts or products intended for tourist consumption may also achieve such a status. Tourism may also lead to the revival of old or forgotten rituals or crafts; the passage of time should not be viewed as a sign of diminished authenticity. For example, the traditional craft of greenstone carving in the southern Indian town of Mahabalipuram has been revitalised by the demand for souvenirs. The products, though intended for sale to tourists, are no less authentic than those produced by similar techniques hundreds of years ago:

> Frequently arts, crafts and local culture have been revitalised as a direct result of tourism. A transformation of traditional forms often accompanies this development but does not necessarily lead to degeneration. To be authentic, arts and crafts must be rooted both in historical tradition and in present-day life; true authenticity cannot be achieved by conservation alone, since that leads to stultification.
>
> (de Kadt, 1979: 16)

Overall, then, authenticity is not simply the antithesis to modern life, something that motivates tourists. Nor is it just a label that may be attached to cultural products, events or tourist experiences as a means of comparing them with the inauthentic, the modern or the spurious. It is something that is unique to each individual tourist, possessing a meaning and importance that can only be assessed alongside an understanding of a tourist's experience, motivation, relationship to his or her home environment and reaction to the tourism environment. In other words, authenticity should be judged through the tourist's own eyes, 'what he considers to be the essential marks of authenticity, and which sites, objects, and events on his trip do, in his opinion, possess these marks' (Cohen, 1988b: 37).

Staged authenticity

Of central importance to the consideration of the authenticity of tourist experiences is the notion of 'staged authenticity' (MacCannell, 1973; 1989; 2013). MacCannell (1973: 597) suggests that although the tourist is motivated by the desire for authentic experience and 'may believe that he is moving in that direction', he is, nevertheless, frustrated in his ambition by the way in which experiences have been set up, or staged. In other words, although he may believe he is witnessing authenticity the tourist is, in fact, experiencing only what local people or the tourism industry are allowing him to see.

MacCannell's concept of staged authenticity is based upon the work of Goffman (1959) who divides the structure of social establishments into what he terms as front and back regions. The front region is where the social interaction takes place, where hosts meet guests or where servers attend to customers. The back region is 'the place where members of the home team retire between performances to relax and to prepare' (MacCannell, 1989: 92). Performers (for example, hosts or waiters) appear in both regions, whereas the audience (guests, diners in a restaurant) are only allowed into the front region. Under this simple dichotomy the performance, the show, takes place in the front region but reality exists in the back region. For example, in a restaurant, diners are served and eat their food in the front region, the dining room, but the food is prepared, the plates are washed and so on in the back region, the kitchen. Thus, the front region is removed from reality; the diners do not see their meals being cooked. Conversely, where customers are able to see their food being prepared, the dining out experience might be perceived to be more authentic.

In adapting Goffman's work to tourist settings, MacCannell suggests that the simple front-back dichotomy can be expanded into a continuum which starts at the front and ends at the back and it is from this that the notion of staged authenticity emerges. He proposes that there are six different stages on the continuum which, theoretically, may be identified (see MacCannell, 1989: 101):

Stage One: this is Goffman's front region, the setting which tourists attempt to penetrate or get behind.

Stage Two: although still a front region, this stage has been given the superficial appearance of the back region by, for example, having wine racks on display in a restaurant.

Stage Three: this stage is still firmly embedded in the front region but it is totally organised to resemble a back region.

Stage Four: moving into the back region, tourists are permitted to see this stage. For example, tourists may be taken into the workshops to see the production process of local goods.

Stage Five: this is a back region to which tourists are occasionally permitted entry, such as the flight deck on an aeroplane.

Stage Six: this is Goffman's back region, the ultimate goal of the tourist but one which is rarely, if ever, reached.

When these six stages are applied to the setting for tourist experiences, it becomes evident that a tourist's quest for authenticity can progress along the continuum, but it is unlikely that the tourist will ever reach the sixth and final stage. Each stage offers the tourist apparently increasing opportunities for authentic experiences yet, from stages two through to five, what the tourist encounters is staged authenticity. The tourist is allowed glimpses of the back region, contrived events and attractions that are passed off as authentic, but the final stage of participating in the lives and culture of the host community is rarely experienced.

The tourist, in his quest for authenticity, is doomed to failure. As more and more countries, regions, societies and cultures are caught up in the tourism net, the opportunity for authentic experience diminishes: 'tourists make brave sorties . . . hoping, perhaps, for an authentic experience, but their paths can be traced in advance. . . . Adventuresome tourists progress from stage to stage, always in the public eye, and greeted everywhere by their obliging hosts' (MacCannell, 1989: 106).

One of the main criticisms of MacCannell's model is that it ignores the ability of tourists to understand and interpret the staged authenticity with which they are presented, although it does provide a useful framework for assessing the degree of authenticity inherent in tourist attractions and events. In order to achieve a more realistic model of staged authenticity, the structural approach adopted by MacCannell should be combined with a micro, social action perspective which takes into account the way in which tourists perceive and respond to the situation facing them. Cohen (1979a) combines two types of setting (staged and real) with tourists' impressions of the setting (again, staged and real) utilising a two-dimensional approach to identify four different relationships between a tourist and the tourist setting:

1   The setting is authentic and the tourist recognises it as such.
2   The setting is staged but the tourist, believing it to be real, fails to recognise its contrived nature.
3   The setting is real, but the tourist believes it to be staged and is, therefore, suspicious of its authenticity.
4   The setting is staged and the tourist recognises it as such.

Adding the impressions of tourists to the equation removes much of the finality of MacCannell's concept of staged authenticity. Whereas MacCannell's tourist is never likely to be satisfied and will continue to search for authenticity, tourists in Cohen's settings 1 and 4 above recognise and accept their situation and will be less frustrated. This still represents a rather simplistic approach to the authenticity of tourist experiences and reference should again be made to the arguments presented by Pearce and Moscardo (1986) and more recent research, referred to earlier, with respect to the social role of the tourist as a determinant of the perceived authenticity of tourist experiences. Pearce and Moscardo (1986), in particular, identify nine different tourist experiences in which a tourist's relationship with people, with the setting (backstage or frontstage), or a combination of both can add to the authenticity of tourist experiences.

For example, meeting frontstage people in a frontstage setting, such as the performers in a tourist show, can be as equally authentic as meeting backstage people in a frontstage setting. In other words, authenticity is not dependent on the position along the back-front region continuum and nor is a tourist's recognition of a situation sufficient to determine the degree of authenticity experienced; a variety of other experiences may contribute to the authenticity of a holiday and, in many cases, the backstage/frontstage distinction is irrelevant or not appropriate (Pearce & Moscardo 1986).

PLATE 9.1 Staged authenticity: dance show, Bali, Indonesia

Source: Photo by Richard Sharpley

In short, authenticity may or may not be staged; what tourists experience may be 'real' or it may be planned, a regularly repeated performance. What is important is the total tourist experience and what it means to the individual tourist. Different tourists have different motivations, expectations, knowledge and travel experience and the 'whole issue of whether or not tourists are satisfied with their holiday experience demands a full consideration of the nature of the tourist environment, the tourists' perceptions of that environment and the tourists' need or preference for authenticity' (Pearce & Moscardo, 1986: 129; also Olsen, 2002).

The semiology of tourism

It is apparent that, within the context of tourism, authenticity is not a fixed, given quality or condition of a cultural product but something which is negotiable. In other words, the degree to which a sight or attraction is perceived to be authentic depends upon the relationship between an individual tourist and that sight or attraction. This relationship, in turn, depends to a great extent upon the attitudes, experience and so on of the tourist but, at the same time, the significance attached to a particular attraction or sight goes a long way to determining its authenticity. Something, such as an article of clothing, a souvenir or a festival, might be seen as authentic simply because it is unusual or different rather than because of its inherent quality or cultural meaning; its authenticity results from its difference or, to put it the other way around, its difference is a sign of its authenticity.

Arguably, 'as soon as there is a society, every usage is converted into a sign of itself' (Barthes, 1967, cited in Culler, 1981: 127); that is, everything has a sign as well an original purpose or meaning. For example, the basic purpose of a Rolls-Royce motor car is transport, to carry its occupants from one place to another. To most people, however, a Rolls-Royce is more than just a car – it is a sign of wealth, high status and success. Similarly, a Rottweiler is a dog, but it is also a sign of power and, perhaps, of danger; a passport is a legal, internationally recognised proof of nationality but it is also a sign of travel. The study of these signs, of the relationship between the *signifier* (a Rolls-Royce) and the *signified* (wealth, status), is known as semiology (or semiotics) and it is an approach which can be usefully applied to the consideration of the authenticity of tourist experiences.

Semiology is not a new 'science'. Indeed, two schools of thought regarding the role of signs in social life emerged during the nineteenth century. The Swiss linguist Ferdinand de Saussure (1857–1913) established, within a linguistic context, the two-way relationship between the signifier and the signified, the 'sign' being the 'whole that results from the association of the signifier with the signified' (Chandler, 2002: 19). During the same period, the American Charles Sanders Peirce (1839–1914) was developing a three-part model describing the relationship between the sign (or representamen), the object to which the sign refers, and the interpretant (the sense made of the sign). Combining these two approaches, different forms or types of signs may be identified. An exploration of these is beyond the scope of this chapter although, from a marketing perspective, the application of semiotic techniques may be useful, for example, in interpreting or assessing the effectiveness of tourism advertising. That is, semiology can reveal the 'hidden' signs in advertisements and other promotional material that may be subconsciously read by viewers of such 'texts'. A useful introduction to semiology (semiotics) can be found in Chandler (2002).

In the specific context of tourism and authenticity, Boorstin (1964: 106) complains that 'the French chanteuse singing English with a French accent seems more charmingly French than one who simply sings in French. The American tourist in Japan looks less for what is Japanese than for what is Japanesey.' However, as Culler argues, most tourists are more concerned with finding and experiencing the image or sign of cultural practices and attractions rather than understanding their basic meaning or function: 'all over the world the unsung armies of semiotics, the tourists, are fanning out in search of the signs of Frenchness, typical Italian behaviour, exemplary Oriental scenes, typical American thruways, traditional English pubs' (Culler, 1981: 127). It matters little that pubs are just convenient places for meeting and socialising or that high-rise buildings are a logical way of housing a lot of people in a small area of land; for the tourist, the pub is a sign of Englishness, the skyscraper a sign of New York. As Culler (1981: 127) again argues, 'gondolas are the natural way to get around in a city full of canals . . . [but] . . . tourists persist in regarding these objects and practices as cultural signs'. What tourists want to see and to accept as authentic is something out of the ordinary, something beyond the threshold of their normal day-to-day existence that they can remember and relate to others when they return home. Thus, authenticity becomes a sign and tourism, rather than a search for authenticity, becomes a search for signs.

The relationship between a tourist and a sight is not, however, a simple, two-way process. The tourist has to know that what is being looked at or experienced is an authentic sign, an attraction, that it is something worth visiting. For example, what is it that singles out the Empire State Building as a sign of New Yorkness, when there are many other skyscrapers in the city? The answer, according to MacCannell (1989), lies in a three-way relationship. 'The first contact a sightseer has with a sight is not the sight itself but with some representation thereof' (MacCannell, 1989: 110). This representation may be in the form of a picture, a souvenir, a model or even just a name on a map and is what MacCannell calls a marker. A marker informs the tourist that a sight is worth seeing, that it is an attraction: 'the "real thing" must be marked as real, as sight-worthy; if it is not marked or differentiated, it is not a notable sight' (Culler, 1981: 133). Thus the tourist, in a triadic structure, links the marker with the sight in the process of sightseeing. The Empire State Building appears in all the brochures on New York; it is a symbol, a sign of the city. Therefore, to have an authentic experience of New York the tourist must visit the Empire State Building, along with other recognised symbols of New York, such as Central Park, Times Square and the Statue of Liberty. Preferably, the tourist also buys souvenirs and postcards as a reminder of the experience of New York.

It is the existence of pre-markers (for example, a picture in a brochure or a description in a guide book) and post-markers (souvenirs, photographs, postcards) that confirms a sight or experience as a sign of authenticity. Indeed, 'the postcard, along with the photograph, is the most widely disseminated icon of tourist experience' (Edwards, 1993: 4). In other words, for a tourist experience or product to be authentic it needs to be certified as such. The paradox is that many experiences which conform more closely to the traditional meaning of authenticity go by untried or unnoticed if not marked. To continue the example of New York, using the subway is certainly a more authentic means of travelling around the city than joining a guided tour on an air-conditioned coach yet arguably, because of the perceived danger, many tourists are quite happy to forgo the experience of travelling on the subway. There is a limit to the New Yorkness they wish to experience, a limit which, as the following section considers, may frequently be dictated by the tourism industry.

The marketing of authenticity

> It seems that tourists and indigenous peoples are incommensurably different within the touristic process, and indigenous peoples can only continue to be attractive to tourists so long as they remain undeveloped and, hence, in some way primitive.
>
> (Silver, 1993: 310)

Authenticity is not only perceived by tourism researchers and others to be a prime motivator of tourism; it is recognised by the tourism industry as such. Also, it is widely accepted that the tourism industry plays an important role in shaping tourists' motivation and behaviour because, for many people, the travel brochure (physical or virtual) is the main source of information in planning holidays. Tourists frequently lack the knowledge, experience or access to information necessary to make travel purchase decisions and depend upon tour operators' marketing material, primarily brochures, for that information (Pritchard & Morgan, 1995). In more recent years, of course, the Internet has become a dominant vehicle for the presentation of brochures and other promotional material; however, the principal arguments outlined below remain relevant to all forms of marketing material, whether 'hard copy' or electronic, and in the following discussion the term 'brochure' refers to both traditional and electronic formats (see also Chapter 7). Moreover, the traditional brochure still remains, even in the age of the Internet, a principal source of information for tourists.

It is not only to tourists that brochures are important. The brochure is 'probably the most important single item in the planning of tourism marketing' (Holloway & Plant, 1992: 148). It is the medium through which tour operators sell their product, informing potential customers about the facilities, amenities and activities available, and how much they cost. However, as widely considered in the literature, brochures fulfil a broader function than the conveyance of factual information (Uzell, 1984; Gilbert & Houghton 1991; Pritchard & Morgan, 1995). They also have the power to shape tourists' attitudes and expectations through what information is included or excluded and the way it is presented. In other words, brochures are also influential in determining how tourists perceive a destination: 'there seems little reason to doubt that for many people tourist brochures . . . play a major role in forming their images' (Dilley, 1986), images which result from the information and pictures that tour operators choose to include and, importantly, not to include in their brochures.

Tour operators are motivated by profit and market destinations to appeal to the greatest number of people who are likely to be attracted to their product. Thus, in most cases, there is a logical link between the destination and the potential market. Mediterranean countries are marketed to northern European customers primarily as sun, sea and sand destinations whereas to North Americans they are marketed as cultural and historical destinations, the reasoning being that most Americans go to resorts closer to home, such as the Caribbean, for beach holidays (see Buck, 1977; Britton, 1979; and Dilley, 1986 for earlier research into travel brochures). Beach holiday brochures primarily contain pictures and information about the beach, the hotel, the swimming pool and the nightlife, whereas cultural tourism will be marketed by pictures of historical architecture, traditional industries, information about special interest tours and so on. This is confirmed by research into the way in which British tour operators (both mainstream and specialist) have traditionally marketed Cyprus – primarily a summer-sun destination – in their brochures. Despite the desire of the Cypriot tourism authorities to broaden the appeal of the island, Cyprus is typically represented in the brochures as a familiar, safe, welcoming destination with good beaches, plenty of sunshine and good nightlife. Reference is made to the cultural and historic attractions, particularly by the smaller, specialist operators, but even these strongly feature the sun and beach attributes of the island. Thus, for the most part, tour operators present the island as a sun-sea-sand destination, with the emphasis on fun, relaxation and a hint of romance (Sharpley, 2001).

If this principle is applied to the marketing of authenticity, then it is logical to propose that tour operators represent destination countries in a way which potential tourists perceive them to be rather than how they actually are. These perceptions are not always created by the tourism industry; in an age of mass information and communication, images of many countries in both the developing and the developed world appear regularly in magazines, in films and documentaries, on the Internet and on social media and, of course, in tourist advertisements. However, the tourism industry, through its brochures and other marketing platforms, may reinforce popularly held images of destinations, in particular of those destinations which offer tourists the opportunity to experience 'true' authenticity in the form of pre-industrial, primitive lifestyles. In other words, 'the tourism industry only markets those images that it anticipates will be verified during travel, for tourists' authenticity is not necessarily determined by gaining a genuine appreciation for another culture, but rather by verifying a marketed representation of it' (Silver, 1993: 303).

Inevitably, perhaps, as authenticity is seen to exist in other times and other places (MacCannell, 1989), many destinations marketed on the basis of authenticity are in the developing world. Compared with rapid industrialisation and technological advance (and resultant alienation and inauthenticity) in the Western world, the countries of the developing world are seen as offering authentic, timeless experiences. Brochures describe destinations that have 'many unusual and fascinating examples of human cultural activity, past and present; . . . [where] . . . the pageant of human life is older, more varied, or just different from that at home' (Dilley, 1986: 60). They use clichés such as 'discover the undiscovered' or 'enjoy the unspoilt paradise' to emphasise that, although tourism has arrived, the modern world has yet to penetrate the destination. The images in the brochures tend to be selectively biased towards what a potential visitor expects to see in a country, an image of authenticity based upon pictures, films and historical associations. For example, travel brochures offering tours of India invariably include pictures of the Taj Mahal, the forts of Rajasthan, the houseboats on Dal Lake in Kashmir and of pilgrims bathing in the water of the River Ganges at Varanasi, attempting to recreate, perhaps, the days of the Raj. Furthermore, pictures of local people tend to conform to standard images, such as women wearing colourful saris and adorned with dramatic jewellery. Similarly, Britton (1979: 323) found that 'local residents are generally absent from illustrations; when they are shown, they likely appear as stereotyped stage props, such as a smiling Jamaican nimbly balancing a tray of cocktails on his head'.

What the brochures do not usually show are details and pictures of a destination's level of industrialisation, its problems of poverty, over-population and pollution, the signs that it is becoming Westernised. In other words, tourist brochures, not surprisingly, do not include images that are likely to deter visitors. Tourists, even those on a quest for authenticity, are trying to escape, albeit temporarily, from the pressures and problems of the modern world and the marketing of a destination and the tourism system within it tends to shield visitors from the realities of the country. In effect, the tourism industry markets and operates a sanitised authenticity; visitors to India may be aware of the poverty, but they do not wish to be reminded of it as they see the tourist sights.

As the countries of the developing world become more industrialised and more Westernised, the authenticity marketed by the tourism industry is increasingly divorced from the reality of the country; the authenticity marketed and sold becomes a myth, and will become more so as local people and local tourism industries recognise that their appeal and, more importantly, their value to tourists lies in their traditional culture rather than their emerging modernity.

Herein lies the paradox of tourism development in many countries. As discussed in Chapter 10 (and see Cohen, 2002), the major rationale for promoting tourism is its potential contribution to social and economic development in destination areas. But the appeal of many destinations, their authenticity, becomes challenged by the objective of that tourism-related development – modernisation. Thus, in the extreme, authenticity as demanded by tourists may be confined to themed centres, such as the Polynesian Cultural Centre in Hawaii, where 'a satisfactory fiction emerges wherein a guest can imagine for a brief time that the idyllic life of Polynesia . . . described by Robert Louis Stevenson . . . is a "reality"' (Stanton, 1989: 247).

Authenticity and the commoditisation of culture

A common thread throughout this chapter is that authenticity, within the context of tourism, is a product, a commodity. It is not a quality or a condition of something but, for many, an essential ingredient of the tourist experience. Tourists are motivated by a search for authenticity, whether as an actual experience or as a sign of something different from their ordinary, everyday existence, and the tourism industry markets authenticity as it would market any other tourism product. As tourism as a whole is a product that is produced, bought and sold then, logically, authenticity and the cultural products that represent it also have a value. It is important to consider the extent to which this centrality of authenticity to the tourism experience has led to what Cohen (1988a) describes as the commoditisation of culture. It should be noted that the term commoditisation is often used interchangeably with commodification. Some claim that these terms are distinctive in that commodification refers to any good or service being accorded an exchange value (that is, it becomes a commodity) whereas commoditisation describes the process by which a brand or type of product loses its uniqueness, identity or, perhaps, authenticity. Hence, for the purposes of this chapter the term commoditisation is used and the question that must be asked is: does the commoditisation of culture dilute, or even destroy, its meaning and authenticity?

One of the most widely held assumptions about the development of tourism is that, generally, it leads to cultural change within the destination society. Wall and Mathieson (2006: 262) identify three major forms of culture which attract tourists and are, hence, susceptible to change:

a) inanimate forms of culture, such as historical buildings and monuments or traditional arts and crafts;

b) forms of culture which are reflected in the normal, day-to-day life and activities of people in destination societies;

c) animated forms of culture, involving the participation of people, such as religious events, carnivals, and traditional festivals.

All forms of culture are dynamic and liable to change over time, with or without the influence of tourism. Worldwide advances in information and communication technology, the pervasive influence of the Internet and social media, satellite television and the international spread of symbols of modern Western culture, such as the oft-cited example of the McDonald's fast-food chain, have a far greater influence on cultural change than tourism. But, following the onset of tourism the normal life of a host society, its values, lifestyles and customs, may adapt over time through processes known as acculturation and cultural drift. In other words, 'when two cultures come into contact of any duration, each becomes somewhat like the other through a process of borrowing' (Nuñez, 1989: 266). Generally, tourists are less likely to borrow from their hosts than vice versa (although there are undoubtedly exceptions) and tourism is perceived, therefore, to be a powerful agent of change, particularly in those societies with fragile or less dominant cultures. These issues are considered in greater depth in Chapter 12.

In contrast to a gradual cultural change contributed to by the influence of tourism, certain forms of culture, in particular arts and crafts (that is, material forms of culture) and festivals or ritual events, can be changed or adapted specifically for tourists. They are either produced or performed for the specific purpose of being sold to tourists (Cohen, 1988a) or, in other words, they become commoditised. Such a process is inevitable as tourists, constrained by the short duration of their holidays, demand instant culture and authentic souvenirs to take home with them. Also, from the host society's point of view, if the most is to be made of culture as a commercial product, it must be 'available and presentable; packaged for consumption into easily digestible and, preferably, photogenic chunks' (Simpson, 1993: 166). Thus, it is a process that is also often perceived as leading to the production of inauthentic, fake art and a loss of meaning to the producers: as Greenwood (1989: 173) explains: 'local culture . . . is altered and often destroyed by the treatment of it as a tourist attraction. It is made meaningless to the people who once believed in it'. This need not, however, always be the case.

Arts and crafts

In many destinations, both the purpose and the style of cultural products have been adapted to appeal to the tourist market. What were once religious or ceremonial artefacts are now mass produced and sold to tourists in a process of cultural commoditisation that can be identified in many countries around the world. Many works presenting case studies of such commoditisation are listed by Wall and Mathieson (2006: 272). Typically, traditional art forms, designs and production techniques tend to disappear as simpler and less sophisticated replacements associated with the techniques of mass production are provided for tourist consumption. One such example is the 'raksa' devil dance masks of Sri Lanka (see Simpson, 1993). Originally used in a number of different contexts, such as folk dramas, festivals and rituals of exorcism and healing, the masks represent the images of a variety of deities and demons. They have a fundamental meaning and significance to the performance of such rituals and, at the same time, the production of the masks is also a recognised and socially important activity within the local community. However, the rapid growth of tourism to Sri Lanka during the late 1970s and early 1980s resulted in the masks being recognised as an appealing and commercially attractive representation of Sinhalese culture for the tourist market. As they became mass produced, not only did they lose their cultural meaning and authenticity as masks of different sizes, decoration and colours were produced to suit the taste of tourists, but also the status of the manufacturers in Sinhalese society deteriorated.

At best, the reproduction of cultural artefacts for tourism retains the quality and style, if not the meaning or authenticity, of the originals; at worst, they 'consist of stylised works which bear only the most tenuous relationship to anything in the traditional culture' (Mathieson & Wall, 1982: 168). In short, they typify what has been called 'airport art', manifested by a general deterioration in quality resulting, in particular, from the breaking of the connection between art forms and their original purpose. For example, Buddhist 'tankas', or paintings, which adorn Buddhist temples in Tibet and Nepal are now mass produced and widely available for sale to tourists in Kathmandu. They can also be found in specialist shops and markets in the Western world along with a huge variety of other cultural artefacts from areas such as Asia and South America. This export business has further severed the products from their cultural roots, although it can be argued that the internationalisation of culture also leads to a more widespread knowledge and appreciation of such art forms.

Despite the emphasis placed on the perceived negative impacts of the commoditisation of arts and crafts, tourism can also make a positive contribution to the continuation or re-emergence of traditional art forms. For example, Graburn (1976: 42) describes how tourists' demands for carvings made by the Canadian Inuit has led to a huge increase in production. Rather than resulting in a dilution of authenticity, the carvings are of a much higher standard than most souvenir crafts and are based upon aspects of the traditional Inuit lifestyle. Through their production of tourist souvenirs, the Inuit are not only able to earn a living but also to preserve their cultural identity. In the case of the Indians of the south-western United States, a variety of art forms have been combined into a new, authentic artistic culture: 'massive in-migration and mass tourism have not been disruptive. Rather, the contact with Anglo society offered extended markets that served to heighten artistic productivity and to revive old traditions' (Deitch, 1989: 235). Similarly, Ryan and Crotts (1997) report how the Maori in New Zealand have preserved and revitalised Maori values and beliefs through the touristic reproduction of art forms.

In short, tourism can undoubtedly lead to the mass production of fake cultural objects that bear little resemblance, either in form or in meaning, to their original purpose and are, therefore, inauthentic. Equally, re-emergent or new arts and crafts also result from the demands of tourists for cultural souvenirs. Thus, just as all forms of culture are in a state of constant change and development, these new products are no less authentic to either the producers or the consumers than those from previous cultural periods (see also Ariel de Vidas, 1995).

Festivals, events and rituals

Owing to the constraints that characterise tourism, cultural events which are based upon religious or traditional heritage, such as festivals, re-enactments of historical or mythical events and religious ceremonies, and which are intended as an attraction for tourists, will normally occur outside normal time and space. That is, the reason or tradition underlying the event becomes secondary to the event itself as the timing and content is adapted to suit the needs of tourists. For example, when researching Sinhalese devil dances, Simpson (1993: 168) found that 'the necessity for short, concise and essentially visual modes of presentation is at odds with the styles of performance the Berava adopt in their own ritual performances'. In this situation, it is highly likely that the meaning and significance of the event to the performers and local audiences is lost, even though to tourists it may appear authentic.

Examples of commoditised cultural performances occur all around the world, from staged dance performances given by African villagers to 'Hula' girls greeting tourists arriving at Honolulu airport in Hawaii. One of the first, and most widely quoted, studies into the tourism-related commoditisation of a cultural event was that by Greenwood (1989). He describes the way in which the Alarde, a public ritual in the Basque town of Fuenterrabia which commemorates the town's victory over the French in 1638, became a major tourist attraction as a result of its taking place during the height of the tourist season. The local authorities decreed in 1969 that, in order to allow large numbers of visitors to witness the Alarde, it should be performed twice on the same day. Within two years 'what was a vital and exciting ritual had become an obligation to be avoided . . . [and] . . . the municipal government was considering payments to people for their participation in the Alarde' (Greenwood, 1989: 178). It had become a commercial tourist attraction, devoid of all meaning to the participants. It is interesting to note, however, that, more recently, Greenwood accepts that the Alarde is once more a public event, but more significant now as a contemporary political statement than as a recreation of an historical event.

As with arts and crafts, there are also many situations where the commoditisation of cultural performances does not necessarily lead to a loss of meaning and authenticity. On the contrary, the opportunities and the financial rewards presented by the demands of tourists for authentic experiences can lead to the preservation and development of traditional, cultural events. Also, as Cohen (1988a) points out, the meaning of such events can change, but remain authentic, for the producers. For example, a festival might lose its religious significance through commercialisation but gain an equally important significance to the participants as a representation of local culture. McKean (1989) describes the case of Bali where ritual performances serve two distinct purposes within Balinese society. On one hand, festivals and rituals are performed for tourist consumption, providing a popular attraction at the same time as representing an important source of income. On the other hand, in a process of cultural involution, the commercial tourist version allows the Balinese to retain their traditional cultural skills and practices and to perform to local audiences, thereby preserving authentic cultural events within an increasingly modern social and economic context. Indeed, 'younger Balinese find their identity as Balinese to be sharply framed by the mirror that tourism holds up to them, and has led many of them to celebrate their own traditions with continued vitality' (McKean, 1989: 132; see also Picard, 1995). A similar process was identified by Xie (2003) with respect to the aboriginal bamboo-beating dance on Hainan Island, China. Here, dances performed for tourists' consumption have become an important element of aboriginal cultural identity.

In some cases, cultural events and festivals, whilst being major tourist attractions, retain their importance and authenticity within the host society. In other words, although attracting large numbers of tourists and, indirectly, generating tourist spending, their original function and purpose are not adapted or compromised by the demands of tourism but remain firmly rooted in the destination's cultural heritage. For example, the Changing of the Guards at Buckingham Palace in London draws large crowds but its role as a tourist attraction is incidental to its primary function. Similarly, the annual carnival in Rio de Janeiro, historically a celebration of freedom from slavery, is a festival performed by the people for the people. Again, the carnival is a major tourist attraction but it is neither motivated by, nor held for, tourists. It provides an authentic tourist experience but the importance and meaning of the carnival has been retained.

More generally, the commoditisation or commercialism of cultural performances cannot, and should not, lead to accusations of inauthenticity. People all around the world pay to see or experience performed cultural arts and events, from street buskers to major national theatre and dance companies and orchestras. Indeed, many art forms require financial support to survive and it is often tourism that provides that support. For example, it is often stated that many London theatres would go out of business if it were not for tourism. Yet it would be unheard of for a production of a Shakespeare play or a performance of Mozart's music to be described as inauthentic! Three points deserve emphasis when considering the link between the commoditisation of culture and the authenticity of tourist experiences.

a) Different tourists, depending on their experience and expectations, have different perceptions of authenticity, but most adopt a broader, less purist stance than would, say, an anthropologist. Thus, many forms of cultural productions, whether performed or material artefacts, are accepted as authentic by tourists even if they have been adapted to the requirements of tourism.

b) Very often, the tourism-induced commoditisation of culture leads to the preservation and recreation of traditional, authentic cultural art forms, whilst those which are strongly rooted in local culture retain their integrity and meaning despite tourism. Furthermore, culture is not static but continually evolves and takes different forms. Disneyland is as authentic as a traditional Buddhist festival and perceptions of authenticity or inauthenticity should not be clouded by what may be described as cultural arrogance.

c) Generally, the decision to commoditise (or protect) culture lies with the producers, not the consumers. In the extreme, as has long been the case of the Himalayan kingdom of Bhutan, the number of tourists and where they may go in the country is strictly controlled to protect the authenticity and integrity of religious festivals and ceremonies, although recent evidence suggests the Bhutanese authorities are relaxing controls in order to enhance the country's earnings from tourism (Tourism Council of Bhutan, 2015). As Cohen (1988a) argues, in order to avoid the blanket condemnation of the assumed negative impacts of cultural commoditisation, research should be emic (that is, from the point of view of the host society) and should assess over time the perceptions of both locals and tourists (see also Chapter 10 on host perceptions of tourism).

Authenticity, the past and nostalgia

If the past is a foreign country, nostalgia has made it the foreign country with the healthiest tourist trade of all.

(Lowenthal, 1990: 4)

One of the major themes throughout this chapter is that the notion of authenticity, within the context of tourism, is inextricably linked to the past, to an earlier, pre-modern era. In other words, authenticity and reality are to be found in other times and places which offer a sense of tradition and authenticity that has been lost in modern society (MacCannell, 1989). Similarly, the tourism industry implies, with its promises of 'unspoilt paradise', 'undiscovered peoples and places' and 'authentic culture', that tourists can, somehow, become time travellers; by boarding an aeroplane they can be transported back in time to places which offer the chance to experience life as it used to be. Thus, tourists are motivated by the inauthenticity of modern life, by the alienated, anomic condition of industrialised society, to seek meaning and reality elsewhere. In effect, the past has become a tourist destination.

The past has also become big business, for this concentration on the past is not limited only to tourism. Indeed, tourism is symptomatic within the modern world of a much broader and deeper-rooted concern for, and interest in, history and heritage. 'Today a great deal of time and energy is dedicated to looking backwards, toward capturing a past which, in many ways, is considered superior to the chaotic present and the dreaded future' (Dann, 1994: 55). In many aspects of life, from home decor to clothing fashions, from architecture to advertising, images, designs and styles of the past are used and recreated to signify an era that is, somehow, better than the present. For example, the use of festoon blinds, William Morris style wallpaper, brass lamps and Victorian pine furniture are popular ways of recreating a more traditional, familiar and friendly style of home furnishing in contrast to the perceived stark, characterless quality of many modern homes.

At the same time, saving, conserving and presenting the past is becoming a more widespread concern and activity. Landscape conservation was originally motivated by the desire to protect the natural environment from encroaching urbanisation and

PLATE 9.2 Nostalgia: 1940s weekend in Pateley Bridge, North Yorkshire, UK
Source: Photo by Richard Sharpley

industrialisation; nowadays, symbols and relics of that industrialisation are themselves conserved and protected. Moreover, the past that is protected, recreated or simply looked back upon with nostalgia is becoming increasingly close to the present. For example, it is not uncommon for relatively modern, twentieth century buildings, such as Southwark bus station in London, to be added to the ever-growing collection of so-called listed buildings (that is, legally protected from demolition or significant alteration) in Britain. Indeed, it is in Britain that interest in the past is arguably most prevalent. Almost every town and city boasts a museum or heritage centre and 'it seems that a new museum opens every week or so' (Urry, 1990a: 104), whilst nostalgic events, such as 1940s weekends, are becoming increasing popular (see Plates 9.2 and 9.3). Notably, the National Trust is, with more than four million members, the largest conservation organisation in Europe. Its properties, which include 775 miles of coastline, 248,000 hectares of land and over 500 historic buildings, attract more than 11 million

PLATE 9.3 Nostalgia:1940s weekend in Pateley Bridge, North Yorkshire, UK
Source: Photo by Richard Sharpley

visits each year (see www.nationaltrust.org.uk), although some of the Trust's policies, particularly related to its portfolio of stately homes, has attracted criticism.
(Weideger, 1994).

This ever-increasing interest in the past, feeding what Hewison (1987) refers to as
the heritage industry, is widely believed to be caused by nostalgia, a condition which
'now attracts or afflicts most levels of society' (Lowenthal, 1990: 11). Nostalgia was
once looked upon as a physical illness and even during World War II it appeared on the
US Surgeon General's list of standard illnesses suffered by American army personnel.
Nowadays, nostalgia is generally considered not only to be a yearning to experience or
remember a past that was somehow better than the present, but also the driver of many
forms of tourism (Jarratt & Gammon, 2016). At the same time, however, it is argued
that nostalgia does not simply reflect an interest in or yearning for the past; rather, it is 'a
positively toned evocation of a lived past in the context of some negative feeling toward
the present or impending circumstances' (Davis, 1979: 18, quoted in Dann, 1994: 65).
In other words, nostalgia results from dissatisfaction with the present and concern for
the future, a situation that Hewison (1987) links to 'Britain in a climate of decline [thus],
in the face of apparent decline and disintegration, it is not surprising that the past seems
a better place' (Hewison, 1987: 43).

Reflecting the enormous increase in both the number and the diversity of heritage attractions, there has been a corresponding and growing debate surrounding the
development, marketing and role of heritage. A full consideration of the relevant issues
is beyond the scope of this chapter (see, for example, Timothy & Boyd, 2003; Herbert,
1995; Timothy, 2011), although a number of important questions are linked to the
notion of authenticity. Primarily, many would argue that heritage sites or attractions
do not present 'real' history. That is, they represent the past in a way that is attractive
to (paying) visitors; they portray a sanitised past, a golden age with the 'bad bits' taken
out. In other words, the more traditional role of history (education) has been replaced
by 'infotainment'. This argument is further strengthened when the heritage site itself
becomes the attraction. That is, many heritage centres represent the past through a
variety of modern interpretative methods, from static displays, videos and 'talking heads'
to the recreation of 'authentic' sounds and smells and journeys back in time in 'time
capsules'. In many cases, there is little if any evidence of historical remains, the heritage
attraction being created on the sites of past events or even mythical, literary associations.
In short, it is the display, the interpretation that becomes the attraction, not the history
it represents.

It is also important, within the context of authenticity, to consider whose heritage is being represented. For example, according to Tunbridge and Ashworth (1996),
much heritage is 'dissonant'; that is, the heritage presented bears more relation to the
heritage of visitors and, hence, what they expect to see or experience, rather than
the 'true' history of the site. Equally, the purpose of presenting heritage might be to
achieve political objectives, to convey impressions or messages that go beyond the
original significance of the site or event. A full discussion of these debates is beyond
the scope of this chapter but, in the present context, it is useful to consider how the
tourism industry, recognising and attempting to satisfy the tourist's nostalgic yearn-
ings, has appropriated heritage. Dann (1994) suggests four ways in which nostalgia is

linked to tourism and in which the tourism industry attempts to evoke, for the tourist, a sense of authenticity rooted in the past:

1   Hotels. In an era when hotels are becoming increasingly similar and standardised, when one hotel lobby or room looks much the same as any other irrespective of the city or country in which it is located, a sense of authenticity, distinction and the luxury of a golden age can be achieved by recreating an image of the past. For example, Indian hotels which utilise buildings which were once, and in some cases still are, the palaces of maharajahs, transport guests back to the days of colonial India. Similarly, the famous Raffles Hotel in Singapore was refurbished during the 1990s to recreate the atmosphere of the early 1900s. Most cities can boast an hotel noted for its individuality and authentic atmosphere, but such authenticity is only available to those who can afford it.

2   Museums. MacCannell writes: 'the best indication of the final victory of modernity over other socio-cultural arrangements is not the disappearance of the non-modern world, but its artificial preservation and reconstruction in modern society' (1989: 8). One of the major physical manifestations of the power of nostalgia within the context of tourism is the proliferation of museums and, in particular, heritage centres which attempt to present not only artefacts from the past but also life as it was in days gone by.

    Modern methods of interpretation, such as audio-visual displays, re-enactments using actors, 'living museums' (for example, Beamish Open Air Museum in County Durham, UK or Williamsburg, Virginia) and the use of 'timecars' to carry visitors back in time through a heritage display (as at the Jorvik Viking Centre in York or The Oxford Story in Oxford), are frequently used to recreate the past. However, a major problem, as mentioned above, is that nostalgia acts as a kind of rose-tinted filter, creating a past that is safe, secure and devoid of unsavoury facts of past times, such as poverty, illness, dangerous working conditions, child labour and so on. In other words, 'myths of the past are created – the past is seen in the way in which we would like to see it, and not the way it was' (Wheeler, 1992). Thus, tourists find a reality based not in the past, but on a modern representation of the past (see Hewison, 1987; Wright, 1985; Lumley, 1988; Walsh, 1992).

3   Infamous sites. Dark tourism and the fascination or otherwise in places and attractions associated with death, disaster or destruction was considered in detail in Chapter 8. In the context of this chapter, though, the popularity of infamous sites, such as the Auschwitz in Poland, the Bloody Tower in London and the Bridge over the River Kwai in Thailand, may be explained by morbid curiosity, as may the seven-mile traffic jams of sightseers on the main road to Lockerbie the day after the explosion of Pan Am Flight 103 in December 1988 (see Rojek, 1993: 137 and for a discussion of tourism to 'black spots'). However, Dann (1994: 61) relates the desire to visit such places to the ability of nostalgia to discard unpleasant experiences. The reality of the attractions then lies in the evidence they present of past threats to society, to ordered life, to continuity and to identity. In other words, people visit infamous sites to confirm their own survival.

4   Industrial centres. Much of the growth in the number of heritage centres and museums has been based upon the representation of the industrial past. New Lanark in the Scottish Clyde Valley, the Wigan Pier Heritage Centre, and the Rhondda Heritage Park in South Wales are just three examples of the over 460 museums in Britain which display industrial material. Certainly, much of the popularity of such centres is based upon a nostalgia for industrial machinery and processes, such as the steam engine, which are no longer used. However, by drawing attention to the work of others, in other times and under conditions that are unacceptable today, they also represent a yardstick against which the reality and authenticity of modern and post-industrial society may be measured. Importantly, modern industrial heritage centres may also fulfil a political objective; the opening of the visitor centre at the Sellafield nuclear power station on the north-west coast of England (the world's first large-scale nuclear power plant which first generated electricity in the early 1950s, now being de-commissioned) was as much a public relations exercise as an attempt to inform or educate. At its most popular, the visitor centre attracted more than 1,000 visitors a day but declining numbers resulted in its eventual closure (see Temperton, 2016)

Perhaps the best example of the link between tourism and the experience of authenticity as represented by the past is the popularity of the British countryside as a tourist destination (see Roberts & Hall, 2001; Sharpley & Sharpley, 1997). If tourism is, indeed, a search for the authentic motivated by the inauthenticity and meaninglessness of modern society, then the countryside is the ultimate representation of the pre-industrial life. The countryside originally emerged as an identifiable, distinct tourist destination during the rapid industrialisation and urbanisation of British society during the nineteenth century. Romanticised by the poets and artists of the late eighteenth and early nineteenth centuries, it became the symbol of a life lost to the demands of industry and the capitalists. In the twentieth century, the countryside has come to be seen as the antithesis to modernism; visually and socially it has escaped the regulation and regimentation of modern urban life, representing freedom, nature and reality. However, the tourists' rural landscape is idealised by nostalgia. Modern machinery, housing, motorways, electric power cables and, more recently, wind farms, have no place in authentic countryside and the efforts of conservation organisations are firmly directed towards the maintenance of a kind of Wordsworthian image of the countryside within the framework of late twentieth century society. The countryside 'has become so imbued with literary and painterly associations that we do not really see the landscape that lies before us. We substitute a countryside of the mind, shaped by our cultural perspectives and reflecting our psychological needs' (Hewison, 1993).

The same criticism may be directed towards the perceived authenticity of tourist attractions and destinations as a whole. By continuing to look to the past for authenticity, reality and meaning, the tourist experience will be increasingly caught in a time warp and the culture that is packaged and presented to tourists will bear less and less resemblance to the reality of the destination. The challenge for the future, for both tourists and the tourism industry, is to view the culture and authenticity of destinations and host societies in their own right, rather than in comparison to the tourists' own culture and society. In other words, authenticity is rooted as much in the present as it is in the past and, as more and more countries develop and modernise, their emerging culture and modernity must be accepted as authentic. To do otherwise, to perceive authenticity as being in other times and places (that is, the past), would result in tourism becoming based on myth and fantasy, the representations of authenticity in the host societies becoming as meaningless and inauthentic as the societies from which tourists, temporarily, escape.

Further reading

Knudsen, B. and Waade, A.M. (eds) (2009) *Reinvesting Authenticity: Tourism, Place and Emotions*. Bristol: Channel View Publications.
Rethinking the notion of authenticity in tourist experiences, this book examines contemporary performances of authenticity in travel and tourism practice.

Ryan, C. and Aitken, M. (eds) (2005) *Indigenous Tourism: The Commodification and Management of Culture*. Oxford: Elsevier.
Focusing particularly on indigenous communities and minority groups, this comprehensive collection explores the ways in which tourism may lead to the commodification of societies and culture.

Smith, V. (ed.) (1989) *Hosts and Guests: The Anthropology of Tourism*, 2nd Edition. Philadelphia: University of Pennsylvania Press.
This remains the 'classic' text that explores how tourism may act as an agent of commodification of host cultures.

Wang, N. (1999) Rethinking authenticity in tourism experience. *Annals of Tourism Research*, 26(2): 349–370.
This seminal paper is a 'must-read' when studying authenticity in tourism, introducing as it does the wisely cited concept of existential authenticity.

Discussion topics

▶ To what extent do you agree with the argument that most tourists neither seek nor expect to have authentic experiences?

▶ If tourism is the business of selling (and consuming) experiences, is it inevitable that all tourism products and services are commodified and, hence, technically inauthentic?

▶ One tourist's authentic experience is another tourist's inauthentic experience. Discuss.

▶ For the 'post-tourist', is the concept of authenticity meaningless?

10

Tourism and development

Introduction

A two-way relationship exists between tourism and society. On the one hand, tourism and tourists are influenced by society; that is, society creates both the ability and the desire amongst its members to participate in tourism whilst also influencing how people behave as tourists. On the other hand, tourism and tourists impact upon society. As an export industry, international tourism is unique in that the customer (the tourist) travels to where the product is 'produced'; tourism is consumed, as it were, on site. Domestic tourism, too, involves the movement of large numbers of people from one place to another and, in both cases, a wide range of activities, facilities, attractions and amenities are provided to satisfy their needs. Inevitably, then, tourism impacts upon the environments and societies within which it occurs. Of these two types of tourism-society relationship, this book has so far been concerned with the former – the influence of society on tourism. In this and subsequent chapters, attention now turns to the ways in which, conversely, tourism impacts upon those societies which are tourist destinations.

It has long been recognised that the development and growth of tourism, in particular mass tourism, can result in a variety of negative consequences for destination environments and societies. During the 1960s, what Jafari (1989) refers to as the 'advocacy' stage or period of tourism development, tourism was for the most part viewed favourably as a means of creating income and employment, particularly in disadvantaged or less developed countries or regions. By the 1970s, however, as mass tourism grew dramatically in both scale and scope, increasing concern was voiced over the potential impacts of tourism (Jafari's 'cautionary' stage). A number of authors at that time drew attention to these impacts (for example, Young, 1973; Turner & Ash, 1975; de Kadt, 1979), their approach epitomised perhaps by Mishan, an economist, who wrote:

> Travel on this scale with the annual need to accommodate tens of millions, rapidly and inevitably disrupts the character of the affected regions, their populations and ways of living. As swarms of holiday-makers arrive . . . hospitality vanishes, and

> indigenous populations drift into a quasi-parasitic way of life catering with con-
> temptuous servility to the unsophisticated multitude.
>
> (Mishan, 1969: 142)

Primarily, attention was and, by and large, remains directed towards two areas of concern: the nature of the relationship between tourists as 'guests' and the destination societies that play host to them, and the impacts of tourism on the physical environment. A number of early texts explored both of these areas, whilst one of the first texts to address specifically the socio-cultural aspects of tourism development was *Hosts and Guests: The Anthropology of Tourism* (Smith, 1977). Since then, an ever-increasing number of books and articles have considered the cause and nature of the impacts of tourism on the physical and socio-cultural environments in destination areas (see Mason, 2008; Wall & Mathieson, 2006), providing the foundation for an equally large and diverse literature on the potential solutions to these 'problems' of tourism which fall broadly under the umbrella of so-called sustainable tourism development (Sharpley, 2009b).

In the context of this book, it is the tourist-host relationship and socio-cultural impacts of tourism that are of greatest relevance. These separate yet inter-related issues are discussed in Chapters 11 and 12. Of equal importance, however, but less widely considered in the literature, is the potential role of tourism in the overall development of destination areas. That is, the justification for promoting tourism is generally that it makes a positive contribution towards economic and social 'development'. The objectives and processes inherent in achieving such development are, however, less frequently touched upon in the tourism literature, notable exceptions being Britton (1982), Clancy (1999), Erisman (1983), Opperman (1993), Opperman and Chon (1997), Pearce (1989), Reid (2003) and Wahab and Pigram (1997), whilst the most comprehensive texts on the relationship between tourism and development are those by Sharpley and Telfer (2015) and Telfer and Sharpley (2016). In other words, the general and widely held assumption is that tourism plays a positive role in the development of destination areas and societies and that, as a consequence, the primary challenge then becomes minimising the negative consequences of tourism in order to optimise that developmental role. Less often asked are the questions: what is development? What processes lead to development? And can tourism play an effective role in development?

The purpose of this chapter is to address these questions, assessing in particular the potential for social development through tourism. In so doing, it provides a broader foundation for understanding and explaining the characteristics of the tourist-host relationship and for exploring the inevitability of the socio-cultural consequences of tourism.

Tourism: a tool for development?

Given the rapid and continuing growth in both domestic and international tourism, it is not surprising that in many countries it is regarded 'as an important and integral aspect of their development policies' (Jenkins, 1991: 61) – although in many countries, particularly those with a limited or immature economic sector and a lack of viable alternatives, tourism is often an option of 'last resort' (Lea, 1988). This potential role of tourism in promoting or encouraging development springs primarily from the economic benefits that result from the development of tourism itself. Not only does international tourism generate significant sums in terms of tourist spending – in 2015, for example, international tourist receipts amounted to some US$1,260 billion – contributing significantly to the income and foreign exchange earnings of destination areas (up-to-date tourism statistics are available from both the UN World Tourism Organization (www. unwto.org) and the World Travel and Tourism Council (www.wttc.org)), but it also supports a large and diverse industry. As a result, tourism is estimated to account for around 9 percent of both global GDP and global employment, figures which are, by any standards, impressive. International tourism also accounts for around 7 percent of total global exports (goods and services) and 30 percent of services exports. It is, therefore, one of the world's most significant export sectors.

It is in the lesser developed, peripheral countries in particular that tourism is considered an important and effective means of achieving development; indeed, in many of the so-called least developed countries (see below), tourism is amongst the top three sources of foreign exchange and has underpinned the graduation of three countries (Maldives, Cape Verde and Samoa) out of least developed status (International Trade Forum, 2011). However, defining what is meant by less or least developed countries is a difficult task (see, for example, Opperman & Chon, 1997: 4–5; Sharpley, 2015). In particular, there is an enormous diversity of countries that comprise the 'developing world'. Geographical, political, historical, economic and socio-cultural characteristics and structures all influence a country's level or rate of development (Todaro & Smith, 2014), as well as its tourism development potential. However, developing countries are typically classified according to national and/or per capita income, non-economic development indicators, such as life expectancy, literacy or environmental factors, or a combination of the two. The World Bank, for example, classifies all countries according to per capita gross national income (see Table 10.1), accepting that level of income does not necessarily reflect development status. Consequently, less than half of the 80 countries classified as high income are generally considered to be amongst the group of developed nations.

The term least developed country (LLDC) is also increasingly used to distinguish the world's poorest nations from the total of approximately 180 developing countries.

TABLE 10.1 Per capita GNI country classifications

	Low income economies	Lower-middle income economies	Upper-middle income economies	High income economies
Per capita GNI	$1,045 or less	$1,046-$4,125	$4,126-$12,745	$12,746 and above
Number of countries in group	31	51	53	80

Source: Compiled from World Bank (2017)

To be added to the list of LLDCs (which, in the review of 2016, comprised a total of 48 states: see Table 10.2) a country must have a per capita income below $1,035, as well as satisfying complex 'economic vulnerability' and 'human resource weakness' criteria. Many of these countries are referred to by de Rivero (2001) as NNEs, or 'non-viable national economies', suggesting that they cannot be regarded as 'developing' countries in any sense of the word. Interestingly, a number of LLDCs have either established or nascent tourism sectors which, though small by international standards, are significant in terms of the local economy. For example, in the West African country of The Gambia the tourism sector is small in terms of arrivals (approximately

TABLE 10.2 List of least developed countries (2016)

Afghanistan	Madagascar
Angola	Malawi
Bangladesh	Mali
Benin	Mauritania
Bhutan	Mozambique
Burkina Faso	Myanmar
Burundi	Nepal
Cambodia	Niger
Central African Republic	Rwanda
Chad	San Tome and Principe
Comoros	Senegal
Democratic Republic of The Congo	Sierra Leone
Djibouti	Solomon Islands
Equatorial Guinea★	Somalia
Eritrea	South Sudan
Ethiopia	Sudan
Gambia	Timor-Leste
Guinea	Togo
Guinea-Bissau	Tuvalu
Haiti	Uganda
Kiribati	United Republic of Tanzania
Lao People's Democratic Republic	Vanuatu
Lesotho	Yemen
Liberia	Zambia

Source: UN (2016)

*At the time of writing, Equatorial Guinea was to graduate from least developed country status in June 2017

130,000 annual international arrivals), yet it contributes some 60 percent of total exports. In such a case, however, tourism may be considered an economic survival as opposed to development strategy. Conversely, as noted above, tourism has supported some countries in their graduation from LLDC status. The Maldives, for example, which attracted almost 1.3 million visitors in 2016 with tourism contributing about 75 percent of its GDP, graduated from LLDC status in 2011. More recently, Samoa graduated in 2014.

The characteristics of underdevelopment

Developing countries, to a lesser or greater extent, share a number of features that characterise the condition of underdevelopment.

a) Economic dependence on a large, traditional agricultural sector and the export of primary products

Most developing country economies are dependent on agricultural production and exports for employment, income and foreign exchange earnings. Conversely, the industrial/manufacturing sector may be small and technologically deficient. Typically, over 60 percent of the workforce is employed in agriculture in developing countries compared with less than 5 percent in developed countries. At the same time, low productivity and international price support mechanisms limit their ability to compete in global markets for primary products.

b) Low standards of living

A variety of factors contribute collectively to low standards of living. Reference has already been made to low income levels (average per capita income) although it is important to point out that average income gives no indication of income inequality both between and within countries. It was observed some years ago that few developing countries 'enjoy the luxury of having less than 20 percent of their population below the poverty line' (de Rivero 2001: 64). Since then, and reflecting the first of the Millennium Development Goals (1990–2015) to reduce by half the proportion of people living on less than $1 a day and of the subsequent Sustainable Development Goals to completely eradicate poverty by 2030, some significant progress has been made in reducing levels of poverty. Overall, it is claimed that 'the poverty rate in the developing world has plummeted from 47 percent to 14 percent in the period between 1990 and 2015 – a 70 percent drop' (MDG Monitor, 2017) whilst, most notably, the number of people in China living in poverty declined by some 470 million between 1990 and 2005. Care must be taken with such figures, however. For example, China accounted for more than 75 percent of the global decrease in poverty between 1990 and 2005; if China was excluded from the figures, then global poverty would have been reduced by just 5 percent between 1980 and 2010 (OECD, 2013). Moreover, it was noted in 2004 that

46 developing countries were, in terms of average income, poorer than they were in 1990 (UNDP, 2004), whilst in India, 20 percent of the population currently remain classified as living in extreme poverty. This equates to 270 million people, around one third of the world total. Sub-Saharan Africa continues to suffer the highest regional levels poverty; in the three decades from 1980, the proportion of the population living in poverty only fell from 52.7 percent to 46.8 percent while, reflecting population growth, the actual number of poor people in the region almost doubled, from 210 million in 1981 to 415 million in 2011 (Asitik, 2016: 4). It should also be noted that around half the world's population continues to live on less than US$2.50 a day, an income that, by any standards, represents poverty.

In addition to low incomes, other indicators of living standards include health, child mortality, education/literacy levels, access to clean water, and so on, all of which are reflected in the current Sustainable Development Goals (Table 10.3).

TABLE 10.3 The Sustainable Development Goals, 2015–2030

1.	End poverty in all its forms everywhere
2.	End hunger, achieve food security and improved nutrition and promote sustainable agriculture
3.	Ensure healthy lives and promote well-being for all at all ages
4.	Ensure inclusive and equitable quality education and promote lifelong learning opportunities for all
5.	Achieve gender equality and empower all women and girls
6.	Ensure availability and sustainable management of water and sanitation for all
7.	Ensure access to affordable, reliable, sustainable and modern energy for all
8.	Promote sustained, inclusive and sustainable economic growth, full and productive employment and decent work for all
9.	Build resilient infrastructure, promote inclusive and sustainable industrialization and foster innovation
10.	Reduce inequality within and among countries
11.	Make cities and human settlements inclusive, safe, resilient and sustainable
12.	Ensure sustainable consumption and production patterns
13.	Take urgent action to combat climate change and its impacts
14.	Conserve and sustainably use the oceans, seas and marine resources for sustainable development
15.	Protect, restore and promote sustainable use of terrestrial ecosystems, sustainably manage forests, combat desertification, and halt and reverse land degradation and halt biodiversity loss
16.	Promote peaceful and inclusive societies for sustainable development, provide access to justice for all and build effective, accountable and inclusive institutions at all levels
17.	Strengthen the means of implementation and revitalize the global partnership for sustainable development

Source: Adapted from UN (2017)

c) High population growth and high unemployment/underemployment

Over 80 percent of the world's population live in developing countries, a proportion that will continue to grow given higher birth rates on average (around 2 percent annually) than in developed countries (about 0.5 percent). In the period between 1995 and 2025, the population of many developing countries will double. Consequently, the incidence of under-employment and unemployment in developing countries, typically averaging between 8 and 15 percent of the total workforce though often double this figure amongst the 15–24 age group, will increase significantly.

d) Economic fragility

The economies of many developing countries are weak, characterised by low financial reserves, severe balance of payment deficits and high levels of international debt. Limited natural resources and industrial production necessitates high levels of imports to meet basic needs, yet exports typically cover around only two-thirds of developing countries' import bills. The resultant levels of international debt and interest payments have resulted in many developing countries becoming ensnared in the debt trap, hence the frequent calls for their debt to be written off by Western creditors.

e) Limited or unstable socio-political structures

Whilst underdevelopment is frequently claimed to result from inequalities in the global distribution of economic and political power (with international tourism widely seen as a manifestation of such inequality), the political and social structures within developing countries may also determine the extent to which development occurs. Certainly since the latter part of the twentieth century, an increasing number of countries in the developing world have adopted democratic political systems (Potter, 2000), though not necessarily with a corresponding increase in development. However, the distribution of power in developing countries often tends to favour a small, powerful élite whose position is frequently strengthened and legitimised by the democratisation process. At the same time, it has been increasingly recognised that the nature of governance or the effectiveness of state intervention is a significant factor in the development process in developing countries. In other word, a lack of progress and development has come to be equated not with power imbalances with the global political-economy, but with the concept of the 'failing state' (Di John, 2010; Ghani & Lockhart, 2008). That is, it is the inability or unwillingness (or both) of national governments to fulfil their responsibilities (essentially, to provide security for and promote the social and economic well-being of their citizens) that lies at the root of continuing underdevelopment in general and a failure to achieve development through tourism in particular (Din, 1982; Southgate, 2006; Ussi & Sharpley, 2014).

Inevitably, these characteristics of underdevelopment are not equally evident in all developing countries, whilst other indicators, such as gender-related issues (Momsen, 2004), the ability to exercise human rights (Nkyi & Hashimoto, 2015), or safety and security must also be included as measures of development. Moreover, many developed nations also have 'less developed' regions and face a number of developmental challenges, whether environmental, social (crime, inequality, education, health) or economic (poverty, unemployment). Nevertheless, within the developing world tourism is increasingly viewed as a means of addressing underdevelopment which, by implication, suggests that tourism may also impact positively on some or all of these specific challenges. As Roche (1992: 566) comments:

> whether for good or ill, the development of tourism has long been seen as both a vehicle and a symbol at least of westernisation, but also, more importantly, of progress and modernisation. This has particularly been the case in Third World countries.

In this context, the emphasis is placed on the potential economic benefits accruing from the development of tourism mentioned above, in particular its contributions to foreign exchange earnings and the creation of income and employment, and on the benefits of utilising tourism, as opposed to other economic activities or industries, as a vehicle for development. There are a number of reasons why tourism may be seen as an attractive development option:

a) International tourism has demonstrated consistent growth since the 1960s. Long-haul travel, in particular, has becoming increasingly popular yet appears to be less price and income sensitive than more traditional, short-haul tourism, whilst the emergence of new markets, in particular China and other Asian counties, has driven the continuing growth of international tourism in recent years. Over the last half century or so, international tourist arrivals have averaged 6.2 percent annual growth although, inevitably, the rate of growth has been steadily declining; between 1950–1960 and 1990–2000, for example average growth rates declined from 10.6 percent to 4.8 percent (see Table 10.4). Since then, and despite a variety of factors that have impacted negatively on arrivals, not least the global economic crisis of 2008, international tourism has proved to be highly resilient, achieving 3.4 percent average

TABLE 10.4 International tourism arrivals and receipts growth rates, 1950–2000

Decade	Arrivals (average annual increase %)	Receipts (average annual increase %)
1950–1960	10.6	12.6
1960–1970	9.1	10.1
1970–1980	5.6	19.4
1980–1990	4.8	9.8
1990–2000	4.2	6.5

Source: adapted from WTO (2005)

annual growth between 2005 and 2010 and, more recently, 3.9 percent average annual growth between 2010 and 2015 (UNWTO, 2016b).

b) Tourism to less developed countries has, in theory, the effect of redistributing income from richer to poorer countries. However, it has long been recognised that the net retention of tourist expenditures varies considerably from one destination to another, dependent on the extent to which 'leakages' occur – that is, on how much is spent on imported rather than on locally produced goods to meet the needs of tourists.

c) In many instances, individual countries or trading blocks, such as the European Union, impose restrictions of one form or another to protect their internal markets. In principle, international tourism faces no such trade barriers. That is, generating countries rarely place limitations on the right of their citizens to travel overseas, on where they visit and how much they spend (although travel advisories are one form of limitation on travel). Thus, destination countries have free and equal access to the international tourism market. However, the extent to which destinations can take advantage of this 'barrier-free' market is, of course, determined by international competition in general and by the structure and control of the international tourism system in particular, as well as by more practical issues such as transport links and the scale of the local tourism sector. Indeed, as the following section demonstrates, developing countries continue to enjoy a relatively limited share of global tourist arrivals and receipts.

d) Worldwide, the growth in demand for international tourism both to and between less developed countries is likely to continue.

e) Compared with other industries, tourism is often considered to have relatively low 'start-up' costs. Indeed, many attractions, such as natural scenery, beaches, mountains and climate, are, in effect, 'free'. However, as standards, expectations and competition grow, successful tourism development is becoming increasingly dependent on high levels of infra- and super-structural investment.

It is not, of course, only in developing countries that tourism's development potential has been recognised; tourism is also an important economic sector in most industrialised countries. In Europe, for example, there has long been evidence of national government support of the tourism sector, in some cases dating back to the 1920s and 1930s (Shaw & Williams, 1994: 67) and, in some countries, 'tourism – along with some other select activities such as financial services and telecommunications – has become a major component of economic strategies' (Williams & Shaw, 1991: 1), particularly in the context of the development of peripheral regions and the socio-economic regeneration of rural areas (Hoggart et al., 1995; Cavaco, 1995). Similarly, it was recognised in the early 1990s that huge potential existed for tourism development in the 'new' (i.e. former Eastern) Europe, although 'the question of the nature, speed and quality of international tourism development . . . [was] . . . likely to be one of the more critical components of the region's precarious post-communist pathway' (Hall, 1993: 356). For many of the countries, that potential has been realised, facilitated in no small measure by the remarkable success of low-cost airlines such as Ryanair and EasyJet.

In short, it is widely held that tourism can play a significant and positive role in national, regional and local development. This developmental role of tourism is frequently referred to in generalised terms, perhaps best summarised by the WTO's assertion in the Manila Declaration on World Tourism (WTO, 1980: 1) that:

> World tourism can contribute to the establishment of a new international economic order that will help to eliminate the widening economic gap between developed and developing countries and ensure the steady acceleration of economic and social development and progress, in particular in developing countries.

However, no reference is made to the meaning, process and objectives of that 'development'.

At the same time, much empirical research has been undertaken into the economic, social and cultural impacts, both positive and negative, of tourism development. Rarely, however, are such studies located within the broader context of development as a whole. As Pearce (1989: 15) argues, research into the impacts of tourism development has, for the most part, been 'divorced from the processes which have created them' and little reference is made to the 'changing framework within which all development strategies, including tourism, have been formulated over the last fifty years' (Harrison, 1992a: 10).

As a result, many important issues and questions about the role, meaning and process of tourism-induced development have until more recently been left unanswered, particularly about the extent to which tourism does in fact encourage or lead to development. The first task, then, is to consider what is meant by 'development'.

Development

What is development?

Development is a term that is widely used yet, despite numerous attempts to do so, appears to defy definition. Part of the problem is that it is an ambiguous term that is used to describe both a process through which a society moves (or, implicitly, progresses, although progress itself is not synonymous with development) from one condition to another, and also the goal of that process; the development process in a society may result in it achieving the state or condition of development.

Yet development does not refer to a single process or set of events, nor does it imply a single, static condition. Thus, development may be seen as a term 'bereft of precise meaning . . . [and] . . . little more than the lazy thinker's catch-all term, used to mean anything from broad, undefined change to quite specific events' (Welch, 1984: 4). As Wall (1997: 34) summarises, development can be referred to 'as a philosophy, as a process, as a plan and as a product'.

Traditionally, development has been defined in terms of Western-style modernisation achieved through economic growth. As the national economy grows, the national productive capacity increases and, as long as output expands at a rate faster than the population growth rate, then development is said to be occurring. This perceived role of economic growth acting as a catalyst for development meant that, initially, economic growth and development were one and the same. Indeed, through-out the 1950s and 1960s, the path from underdevelopment to development was seen to lie along a series of economic steps or stages through which all nations, both developing and developed, must proceed (Rostow, 1960). Within this context, devel-opment and underdevelopment came to be defined according to economic measure-ments, such as gross national product or per capita GNP, or according to economic structural criteria. However, this narrow economics-based definition, giving primacy to production and output, overlooked the 'human element' of development. The emphasis on economic development and the inherent assumption that economic benefits would trickle down or diffuse to the wider population meant that problems of health, education, income distribution, unemployment and so on had become sec-ondary to the drive for growth.

However, by the late 1960s it became clear that, in many countries, economic growth was not only failing to solve social and political problems but was actually causing or exacerbating them. As a result, the aims of development became more broadly redefined. Initially, development came to be seen as a process of modernisation with the emphasis on 'how to inculcate wealth-oriented behaviour and values in individuals' (Mabogunje, 1980: 38). Characterised by investment in education, housing and health facilities (with corresponding 'social indicator' measurements), modernisation was nevertheless still firmly rooted in the economic growth perspective. To be modern was to desire and consume goods and services normally produced in developed countries and, therefore, development was dependent on increased production and consumption.

By the 1970s, the pendulum was beginning to swing away from development as an economic phenomenon towards the broader concept of development as the reduc-tion of widespread poverty, unemployment and inequality. Indeed, many policy makers rejected economic growth as the objective of development; people, rather than things, became the focus of attention. Seers (1969: 33), in particular, challenged the traditional economic development arguments when he asserted:

> The questions to ask about a country's development are therefore: What has been happening to poverty? What has been happening to unemployment? What has been happening to inequality? If all three of these have declined from high levels, then beyond doubt this has been a period of development for the country concerned.

To these three conditions he later added a fourth: self-reliance. The oil crisis of the early 1970s had revealed the cost of dependence of many countries and, for Seers, development now implied the need to reduce or eliminate dependence on another country wealthier or more powerful (Seers, 1977). Thus, not only had the concept of development expanded beyond economic growth and industrial expansion to include broader social objectives collectively described by Mabogunje (1980: 39) as 'distributive justice', but the notion of self-determination was also being introduced. No longer was development considered to be a process lying in the control of, or to be guided by, the advanced, Western nations; 'development can be properly assessed only in terms of the total human needs, values, and standards of the good life and the good society perceived by the very societies undergoing change' (Goulet, 1968: 387).

In short, in the space of some 40 years the concept of development evolved from a process narrowly defined (by the Western, industrialised nations) as economic development to a complex, multi-dimensional process requiring the transformation of social and political structures as well as more traditional developmental goals. It has evolved into the process whereby a whole society or social system advances from a condition of life that is deemed to be unsatisfactory (by the members of that society) to a condition that, according to that society's values, better provides for the overall well-being of its members. It is the process for obtaining 'the good life' (Goulet, 1968), central to which, according to Goulet, are three basic values representing the condition of life sought by all individuals and all societies:

a) The sustenance of life: all people have basic requirements, such as food, shelter and health, without which a state of underdevelopment exists.

b) Esteem: all individuals seek self-esteem, a sense of identity, self-respect or dignity. The nature of esteem varies from one society to the next and may be manifested in increased wealth and material well-being or, conversely, in the strengthening of spiritual or cultural values.

c) Freedom: in the context of development, freedom represents increased choice for the individual members of society and freedom from servitude to ignorance, nature, other societies, beliefs and institutions. Significantly, for Sen (1999), freedom in it broadest sense lies at the heart of development.

More specifically, Sen equates 'freedom' with capability; as McGillivray (2008: 34) explains, 'capability is treated as the freedom to promote or achieve combinations of valuable functionings'. Thus, development may essentially be seen as the development of human capabilities, a perspective reflected in the United Nations Development Programme's *Human Development Report 1995* (UNDP, 1995). This defines development as 'the ability to lead a long, healthy life, the ability to be knowledgeable and the ability to have access to the resources needed for a decent standard of living (UNDP, 1995: 18).

Overall, then, development can be thought of as a 'far-reaching, continuous and positively evaluated change in the totality of human experience' (Harrison, 1988: xiii) within which at least five dimensions are identifiable (see Goulet, 1992: 469–470):

a) an *economic* component: the creation of wealth and the equitable access to resources and material goods;

b) a *social* component: health, education, employment and housing opportunities;

c) a *political* dimension: human rights, political freedom and the ability on the part of societies to select and operate political systems that best suit their needs or structure;

d) a *cultural* dimension: the protection or affirmation of cultural identity and self-esteem;

e) the *full-life paradigm*: the meaning systems, symbols and beliefs of a society.

To these should be added, perhaps, the *ecological* dimension, reflecting the emergence of environmental concern and the concept of ecological sustainability as a guiding principle of all development processes. Collectively, these dimensions are broadly reflected in the UN's Sustainable Development Goals (see Table 10.3) whilst nowadays, the most widely accepted measure of development is the annual UNDP Human Development Index (HDI) which ranks countries according to a variety of economic and social indicators (see also Dasgupta & Weale, 1992).

Overall, then, the concept of development has evolved over time from a process or condition defined according to strict economic criteria to a continual, global process of human development. It is a complex, multi-dimensional concept which not only embraces economic growth and 'traditional' social indicators, such as healthcare, education and housing, but which also seeks to confirm the political and cultural integrity and freedom of all individuals in society. It is, in effect, the continuous and positive change in the economic, social, political and cultural dimensions of the human condition, guided by the principle of freedom of choice and limited by the capacity of the environment to sustain such change.

This is, perhaps, best summarised in the UNDP's most recent definition of human development. Though recognising that there remains no consensus over the term, the 2010 Report (UNDP, 2010: 22) defines human development as

> the expansion of people's freedoms to live long, healthy and creative lives; to advance other goals they have reason to value; and to engage actively in shaping development equitably and sustainably on a shared planet.

The question then to be addressed is, how does this process come about (and, implicitly, how can tourism, in particular, contribute to it)? This is best answered by referring to what are known as the theories or paradigms of development.

Theories of development

Development theories are, essentially, broad philosophies which guide development plans and strategies. Modern development thinking evolved out of the global climate of political and economic change following the end of World War II. The economic reconstruction of Europe supported by the Marshall Aid programme, the emergence of the two 'super-powers' and resulting international tensions and, culminating in the Cold War, the rapid and widespread retreat of colonialism and the desire for development in the underdeveloped countries themselves were all instrumental factors in the emergence of development economics. Thus, reflecting the initial concepts of development discussed in the previous section, early development policy was influenced by the success of European reconstruction based on economic growth, aid and intervention and it was taken for granted that the Western, capitalist process of development was a necessary path to be followed by the underdeveloped countries in their transition towards becoming developed.

Since then, four main schools of development thought, or development theories, have evolved, each of which, by and large, has emerged as a result of increasing knowledge and understanding of the developmental process and a consequential rejection of preceding theories.

Modernisation theory

The basis of modernisation theory is that modernisation is an endogenous, or internal process which realises the potential for development in all societies. Different societies may be identified as being at different points on the traditional–modern continuum, or having reached different stages in the process of transforming from a traditional to a modern society. The position of different societies in this process is determined by measures such as GNP, per capita income, various social indicators and acceptance of modern values (for example, the desire to progress, to acquire, and so on), but the important point is that all societies are considered to be following this evolutionary path to modernisation. Harrison (1992a: 9) describes this as a process of 'Westernisation, whereby the internal structures of "developing" societies become more like those of the West, allegedly by emulating Western development patterns'. This is manifested in increasing urbanisation and industrialisation, the emergence of modern values and institutions and greater rationalisation and differentiation of social structures and roles. Implicitly, therefore, modernisation depends upon a transformation in the values and norms in traditional societies, values and norms which may, at the same time, represent barriers to development. Once those barriers have been removed or minimised, then modernisation, based upon economic growth, occurs (see also Harrison, 1988: 30.)

The evolutionary stages model of modernisation was translated into economic theory by Rostow (1960: 4) who claimed that:

> It is possible to identify all societies, in their economic dimensions, as lying within one of five categories: the traditional society, the preconditions for take-off, the take-off, the drive to maturity, and the age of high mass-consumption.

He argued that developing countries are at either of the first two stages but the decisive stage, the 'great watershed in the life of modern societies' (Rostow, 1960: 7) is the take-off stage where one or more significant manufacturing sectors emerge and induce growth in associated sectors and industries. For developing countries, the benefits of such economic growth 'trickle down' or diffuse through the spread of 'growth impulses', such as capital, technology or value systems, from the more developed to the less developed areas, eventually leading to an adjustment in regional disparities. The ways in which this necessary economic growth, leading to development, can be sustained has been the subject of debate amongst economic growth theorists. Some, for example, propose the 'big push' theory, whereby a wide range of industries in a country are helped and supported; others, conversely, suggest that economic growth and, hence, development occurs through backward linkages resulting from the establishment of particular sectors or industries (Telfer, 2015).

Modernisation theory has been criticised on a number of grounds, in particular its use of 'traditional' and 'modern' as vague, ambiguous, ideal type classifications of societies, the implied mutual exclusivity of the two conditions and the inevitability of the replacement of tradition with modernity. It has also been criticised for its Western ethnocentricity and its fundamental doctrine of economic growth but, above all, for its failure to consider development in terms of global inter-relations and the way in which the term diffusion 'serves as a code word for capitalist expansion in its economic, political, cultural guises' (Fitzgerald, 1983: 14).

Nevertheless, it is evident that there are strong links between modernisation and tourism; the justification for tourism-related development is based upon the economic growth potential of tourism. That is, tourism (as a sector or actual resort) is seen as a growth pole from which economic benefits diffuse through the economy; tourism is promoted on the basis of its contribution to income and employment generation and the creation of backward linkages throughout the economy, concepts which are firmly rooted in modernisation theory. Implicitly, development occurs as a result of tourism-related economic growth. In practice this theory has guided a number of tourism development projects, such as Cancun in Mexico (see Torres, 2002; Wall, 1997), yet, more often than not, the expected benefits have not accrued to destination areas. This can be partly explained by the second development theory: dependency theory.

Dependency theory

Dependency theory, often more broadly termed underdevelopment theory (UDT), arose in the 1960s as a critique of the modernisation paradigm; its roots, however, lie in the structuralist economic policies adopted in Latin America during the preceding decade. Following the Great Depression, the export-oriented Latin American nations were suffering severe economic problems, the fundamental cause of which was identified as the continent's disadvantaged position in the world capitalist system. As a result, the UN's Economic Commission for Latin America (ECLA) advocated a strategy of import substitution supported by state planning and intervention. The policy of import substitution based upon state support soon proved to be unsuitable as a development strategy, inasmuch as it did little to improve the situation. But it provided the foundation for the emergence of dependency theory, a school of thought based on Marxist theory (see Chapter 1).

Dependency has been defined by Dos Santos (1970: 231) as

> a conditioning situation in which the economies of one group of countries are conditioned by the development and expansion of others. A relationship of interdependence between two or more economies . . . becomes a dependent relationship when some countries can expand only as a reflection of the expansion of the dominant countries.

In other words, it is argued that the diffusion of Western capital, technology and value systems achieves essentially the opposite of what modernisation theory proposes. This is because, within global economic and political structures, the wealthier, Western nations utilise their dominant position to exploit weaker, peripheral nations (mirroring earlier colonial ties). As a result, the ownership of enterprises in less developed countries frequently lies with Western companies, expatriate workers occupy managerial positions and profits are returned to the parent company, thereby restricting the countries' developmental opportunities. In short, the external economic and political structure of less developed countries means that they are unable to 'break out of a state of economic dependency and advance to an economic position beside the major capitalist industrial powers' (Palma, 1995: 162). In effect, capitalist developments in the core, metropolitan centres perpetuate underdevelopment in the periphery.

Some of the earliest thinking about dependency theory reflected the basis of Marxist structural-conflict theory. For example, Baran (1973) argued that, in much the same way that the capitalists are able to exploit the workers, as discussed in Chapter 1, the actual economic surplus produced by less developed countries (LDCs) is either expropriated by foreign enterprises, misused by the state or squandered by the traditional élites. The possibilities for development are thus limited and for developing countries to grow economically, the solution lies in withdrawal from the world capitalist system and development guided by a socialist political system (Baran, 1963).

This position is expanded upon by Frank (1969) who bases his arguments on the assumption of a single, capitalist world system that has existed since the fifteenth century. Within this single capitalist system, underdevelopment results not from the particular socio-economic characteristics of LDCs (that is, the barriers to development suggested by modernisation theorists) but from the historical relations between metropolitan centres and underdeveloped satellites, relations that exist both within and between countries.

Thus, development and underdevelopment are part of the same economic process, the former being dependent on the latter and made possible through the economic exploitation of satellites by metropolitan centres. Within a country, 'the hinterland supplies the city and is exploited by it; in turn, the city ... is dependent on the metropolitan countries of the West' (Harrison, 1988: 82). Therefore, the existence of the world capitalist system prevents the development of LDCs, resulting in underdevelopment.

A number of other contributions have been made to dependency theory, the different approaches to which have been summarised by Todaro (1994). He suggests that there are three distinctive models within dependency theory:

1   Neo-colonial dependence model: underdevelopment which results from the historic evolution of an unequal relationship between the core and the periphery.

2   False paradigm model: underdevelopment which results from the imposition of inappropriate, Western-based development policies in the periphery.

3   Dualistic development model: development that reinforces the dualistic, rich/poor nature of societies within and between underdeveloped and developed countries.

One of the major criticisms of dependency theory is that it does not hold true for all LDCs. In other words, some countries, such as the so-called 'tiger economies' of south-east Asia and, of course, China, have been able to break out of the dependency/underdevelopment situation and, since World War II, many LDCs have experienced higher growth rates than developed countries. Moreover, other than proposing withdrawal from global economic and political systems, it does not provide any tangible methods of achieving development. But important parallels can be drawn between dependency theory and tourism, parallels which, as discussed later in the chapter, raise significant doubts about the true effectiveness of tourism as a means of encouraging development.

In one particular sense, tourism reflects the dualistic development model as tourism, certainly to LDCs, tends to amplify or reinforce economic and socio-cultural differences between tourists and their hosts. This, in turn, is related to the way in which dependency theory more generally informs much of the research into the negative impacts of tourism on destination areas and communities. That is, it is widely recognised that international tourism 'has evolved in a way which closely matches historical patterns of colonialism and economic dependency' (Lea, 1988: 10). Certainly in the initial phases of the development of international tourism from the 1960s, the ownership or control of the main sectors of the industry lay, for the most part, in the hands of Western transnational corporations (McQueen, 1983). Where developing countries were unable to afford the creation of attractions, facilities, tourism infrastructure and so on, the investment came from the West. Thus, tourism destinations became dependent on metropolitan centres for capital, technology and expertise and, as a result, tourism came to be viewed as a form of neo-colonialism or imperialism (Nash, 1989). At the same time, the fact that, up until the late 1990s, some 80 percent of international tourists came from just 12 (wealthy) countries demonstrated the dependency of many destinations on the West for tourists themselves. Furthermore, this pattern of development is reinforced within many less developed countries by common structural distortions in their social and economic organisation, particularly when they have been exposed to colonial or imperialist domination (Britton, 1982). In more recent years, this dependency on the West for both finance and tourists has diminished with the emergence of countries such as China as both global economic powers and major new international tourism markets. Moreover, in most countries the tourism sector comprises primarily smaller, locally owned businesses. Nevertheless, multinational corporations remain dominant. In the accommodation sector, for example, the French Accor group owns or manages more than half a million hotel rooms worldwide whilst for Marriott International, the figure is over 1.1 million rooms (Statistica, 2016).

The implications of this dependency for the tourist-host relationship in particular is explored in more detail in Chapter 11. For now, it is important to point out that the nature of tourism development in many countries can be explained by dependency theory. A number of authors have examined the so-called centre-periphery dependency model within the context of tourism in a general sense (for example, Britton, 1982, 1987; Høivik & Heiberg, 1980; Wall & Mathieson, 2006), whilst others relate it to specific types of destination, such as small islands (Bastin, 1984; Wilkinson, 1989). Macnaught (1982: 377), for example, considers the critical issue in tourism development in Pacific island communities to be not 'the type of development but the extent to which the political and social autonomy of the destination area is undermined'. In either case, the conclusion is usually that the potential contribution of tourism to broader social and economic development is restricted or diminished by the political and economic framework of the tourism system.

The 'neo-classical counter revolution'

During the 1970s, as dissatisfaction with dependency theory grew, a variety of new approaches emerged which served to redirect attention away from the more traditional economic growth models of development. In particular, issues such as environmental degradation and basic human needs came to the fore, whilst concepts such as 'space-ship earth' brought about a more global perspective on development. It was not until the 1980s and the Reagan-Thatcher era, however, that a new identifiable develop-ment theory emerged. Following neo-classical economic theory, which suggests that international trade can be a positive force in export-led economic development, the neo-liberal theorists of the New Right claimed that the path to economic, social and political development lay in the modern free-market capitalist system. The problems facing developing countries were seen as resulting not from market imperfections but from excessive state intervention (as proposed by dependency theorists) in the form of, for example, foreign exchange controls, pricing controls and unrealistic levels of state ownership and investment.

Influenced by the pro-market position, the neo-classical counter revolution was manifested in development policies that built upon the fundamental reliance on the free market and that favoured market liberalisation, the privatisation of state enterprises and overall reduction of state intervention. In particular, it guided the policy of the World Bank and the International Monetary Fund (IMF) and their Structural Adjustment Lending programmes, which rendered loan facilities conditional on specific policy and economic structure changes in loan-receiving countries (Mosley & Toye, 1988). Thus, Structural Adjustment Lending focused on the need for micro and macroeconomic adjustments, specific policy instruments including:

- credit ceilings and control of the money supply;
- exchange rate adjustment and liberalisation;
- deregulation of prices of goods and services to remove pricing distortions;
- fiscal policy, especially reductions in public expenditure;
- trade and payment liberalisation, including the removal of import quotas;
- institutional reforms, with particular emphasis on privatisation and reducing state influence.

Implicitly, these pre-conditions imposed by lending programmes based upon structural adjustment were a reaffirmation of the role of capitalism and the marketplace in devel-opment. As a result, the neo-liberal policies of the 'counter revolution' have attracted criticism similar to that levelled at the modernisation paradigm with respect to the dominance of Western countries and social and environmental issues. Furthermore, it is generally agreed that structural adjustment programmes have not been successful (Harrigan & Mosley, 1991); indeed, the conditions attached have tended to depress incomes and investment, whilst in many countries social and economic conditions have declined. Pastor (1987), for example, found that funding programmes in Latin America resulted in higher inflation and a real reduction in wages. Consequently, the World Bank and the IMF introduced Poverty Reduction Strategy Papers (PRSPs) as a requirement for their lending to the poorer developing countries. Essentially, PRSPs offered the government and civil society in these countries the opportunity to partici-pate in and, hence, take ownership of, their development strategy, thereby countering criticism that inappropriate, Western-centric economic structural reform was being imposed through the Word Bank/IMF's lending programmes. However, it has been found that, ironically, the very countries most needing financial support have been unable to encourage participation owing to their lack of development and resources (Lazarus, 2008) and, hence, PRSPs have also come to be seen as an unsuccessful approach to funding development schemes.

Tourism development in many countries has benefited from international structural funding. For example, Inskeep and Kallenberger (1992) describe a number of resort developments, including Pomun Lake in Korea and Antalya in Turkey, that benefited from World Bank support. Diamond (1977) similarly evaluates investment in tourism in Turkey during the 1960s and early 1970s, whilst Lee (1987) outlines the way in which European financial aid for tourism development has been provided to the Africa, Caribbean and Pacific (ACP) region through the Lomé Convention. Similarly, many rural tourism projects in Europe have benefited from EU structural funding through the so-called LEADER programme (for example, McAreavey & McDonagh, 2011)

Little attention has been paid in the literature to the effects of Structural Adjustment Lending programmes on tourism development in particular, a surprising omission given the economic value of tourism as a sector of international trade. Curry (1992) explored the effects of economic adjustment programmes on the hotel sector in Jamaica, identifying, in some instances, a negative impact on hotel profitability. More generally, Dieke (1995) assessed the implications of lending programmes on tourism in African economies, concluding that they served to highlight the 'strategic importance of the private sector in tourism development' (Dieke, 1995: 87)

In many cases, this has actually strengthened existing dependency on the metropolitan dominated tourism system, such as in The Gambia where, at the same time, 'per capita income actually fell between 1985 and 1994 . . . whilst lower levels of public spending, the removal of subsidies and other policy measures . . . have led to deteriorating socio-economic conditions for the majority of Gambians' (Sharpley & Sharpley, 1996: 29).

The alternative development theory

The fourth, and, chronologically, the most recent development theory to emerge, is that of alternative development. Most recently manifested in the widespread acceptance and adoption of sustainable development, a concept which 'has achieved virtual global endorsement as the new [tourism] industry paradigm since the late 1980s' (Godfrey, 1996: 60), alternative development is a broad-based approach which has been born out of frustration with the failure of preceding and fundamentally Western-biased, economic growth-based development policies. In contrast to these, alternative development implies a break with the linear model of economic growth (Redclift, 1987), adopting a resource-based, 'bottom-up' approach focused primarily on human and environmental concerns.

Alternative development embraces a number of principles which define its perspective and objectives. They are also clearly reflected on the principles of sustainable development in general and of sustainable tourism development in particular (see UNEP/WTO, 2005). Primarily, the theory of alternative development recognises that development is a complex, multi-layered process that is related to environmental, cultural, social, as well as more traditional economic factors. Also, it has as its starting point the belief that development should be endogenous. That is, it is a process that starts within, and is guided by the needs of, each society; it is not something that should be implemented, imposed or controlled by other societies. Thus, alternative development is centred upon the satisfaction of basic needs, it encourages self-reliance and it should be in harmony with the environment.

The idea of basic needs emerged at the 1976 International Labour Office (ILO) conference on world employment and was later adopted by institutions such as the World Bank. The ILO stressed the benefits of employment creation over economic growth, employment being a necessary prerequisite to the satisfaction not only of fundamental human physiological needs (the provision of shelter, warmth, food, and so on) but also social, cultural and political needs (Streeten, 1977). Aimed at the world's poorest people, the basic needs approach suggests that development depends ultimately on the fulfilment of people's potential to contribute to and benefit from their own community. The notion of a grassroots, community focus to development, building on Schumacher's (1974: 140) argument that 'development does not start with goods; it starts with people and their education, organisation and discipline' is implicit in the alternative development approach, as is the requirement for self-reliance.

The concept of self-reliance is the antithesis to dependency theory. It argues that human development is not possible in the context of development programmes based on core-dominated economic growth, a situation that results in cultural dependency (Erisman, 1983). Communities, therefore, should be allowed to assert their right to make their own decisions according to local needs. Galtung (1986: 101) suggests that, as a fundamental basis for achieving self-reliance, a society should

> produce what you need using your own resources, internalising the challenges this involves, growing with the challenges, neither giving the most challenging tasks . . . to somebody else on whom you become dependent, nor exporting negative externalities to somebody else to whom you do damage and who may become dependent on you.

Importantly, this suggests that self-reliance does not imply isolation; rather, it should be the goal of local, regional and national communities in an interdependent world. Moreover, it also relates to another principle of fundamental importance to alternative development, namely, that the environmental constraints to development should be recognised and taken into account. This was a consideration not apparent in preceding development theories, but one that reflected increasing concern, certainly within the developed world, about the environmental problems of resource depletion, pollution and population growth. In other words, alternative development was the first development theory to embrace the notion that there is an intrinsic relationship between development and the physical and human environment; 'many forms of development erode the environmental resources upon which they must be based, and environmental degradation can undermine economic development' (WCED, 1987: 3).

In short, alternative development places the emphasis on development that satisfies local communities' needs, that is controlled by that community and which is in harmony with the environment, principles which also underpin the notion of alternative tourism. Just as, during the 1970s, increasing public awareness of environmental issues in general led to the emergence of a global environmental movement, so too was increasing attention paid to the negative consequences of mass tourism development in particular. The 1970s was the decade 'in which the potential conflicts of tourism and the natural environment were realised' (Dowling, 1992: 37) and, in response to the growing recognition of the socio-cultural impacts of tourism, the early tourism literature reflected the emergence of alternative development thinking. For example, Emery (1981) considered 'alternative futures' in tourism, whilst Dernoi (1981) proposed alternative tourism as 'a new style in North-South relations'. The concept of environmental harmony and self-reliance, fundamental requirements of alternative development, also became the focus of research into alternative tourism, the latter manifested in what became known as the community approach to tourism development (Murphy, 1985).

TABLE 10.5 Characteristics of mass vs. alternative tourism

Conventional mass tourism	Alternative forms of tourism
General features	
Rapid Development	Slow development
Maximises	Optimises
Socially/environmentally inconsiderate	Socially/environmentally considerate
Uncontrolled	Controlled
Short-term	Long-term
Sectoral	Holistic
Remote control	Local Control
Development strategies	
Development without planning	First plan, then develop
Project-led schemes	Concept-led schemes
Tourism development everywhere	Development in suitable places
Concentration on 'honeypots'	Pressures and benefits diffused
New building	Re-use of existing building
Development by outsiders	Local developers
Employees imported	Local employment utilised
Urban architecture	Vernacular architecture
Tourist Behaviour	
Large groups	Singles, families, friends
Fixed programme	Spontaneous decisions
Little time	Much time
'Sights'	'Experiences'
Imported lifestyle	Local lifestyle
Comfortable/passive	Demanding/active
Loud	Quiet
Shopping	Bring presents

Source: Telfer and Sharpley (2016: 57)

The primary justification of alternative tourism is that it is just that: an alternative to, specifically, mass tourism. Thus, the proponents of alternative tourism advocate tourism that is, for example, small scale, under local control, that is developed in harmony with the local physical and socio-cultural environment and that optimises the benefits to local communities (Table 10.5). In short, it is a form of tourism that benefits, rather than exploits, destination societies.

The concentration on small-scale, local projects has led to accusations that alternative tourism is a micro solution to a macro problem; it offers an alternative to mass tourism, but does not provide solutions to the alleged problems of mass tourism. As a result, the concept of alternative tourism has been widely criticised (for example, see Butler, 1980b; Smith & Eadington, 1992). Nevertheless, it provided the catalyst for the emergence of the concept of sustainable tourism development, arguably the most debated issue in tourism during the 1990s and certainly the most widely adopted set of principles and guidelines for the development of tourism. Therefore, it is important to consider how effective or viable sustainable tourism is as an approach to achieving development, a question that can only be answered by first looking at the concept of sustainable development itself.

Sustainable development

Sustainable development represents a development philosophy and set of principles that, from the early 1990s, not only set the agenda for global development policies in general but also provided a framework for the planning and management of a multitude of economic activities and sectors, including tourism. Some argue that, since the late 1990s, it has been superseded by the notion of human development and a focus on specific challenges, such as poverty alleviation, health and education, as manifested in the targets within the Millennium Development Goals and the Sustainable Development Goals discussed earlier (Knutsson, 2009). Nevertheless, sustainable development remains popular in policy circles at the international, national and local levels and in the context of tourism in particular, yet the validity of both the overall concept and the specific proposals for its achievement contained within a variety of documents remain the subject of intense debate. This controversy surrounding the notion of sustainable development has arisen, in part, from a lack of agreement over the actual meaning of the term; indeed, innumerable definitions have been suggested. However, the most popular and enduring remains the Brundtland Commission's definition of sustainable development as 'development that meets the needs of the present without compromising the ability of future generations to meet their own needs' (WCED, 1987: 48).

Though politically attractive and applicable to many forms of development, this definition does not explain what sustainable development is or how it can be achieved. This task is, perhaps, best approached by thinking of sustainable development as the fusion of two processes, namely 'development' plus 'sustainability' (see Lélé, 1991). The development element has already been discussed in this chapter and, therefore, sustainable development may be thought of as alternative development that is 'sustainable'. What, then, is meant by sustainability?

In a strict sense, if something is sustainable, it can continue or be continued indefinitely. Within the context of this chapter, sustainability refers more specifically to the Earth's capacity to support human existence, also indefinitely. In other words, the Earth comprises a closed, finite ecosystem within which the human economic system of production and consumption, or human activity supporting and leading to development, represents a sub-system. The global ecosystem is, therefore, akin to a 'single spaceship, without unlimited reservoirs of anything, either for extraction or for pollution, and in which, therefore, man must find his place in a cyclical ecological system' (Boulding, 1992: 31). In short, the global ecosystem is the 'source of all material inputs feeding the economic subsystem, and is the sink for all wastes' (Goodland, 1992: 16). These source and sink functions of the planet have a finite capacity to, respectively, supply the needs of production/consumption and absorb the wastes resulting from the production/consumption process. This means that, for any form of economic activity, including tourism, to continue indefinitely, attention must be paid to three factors:

1 The rate at which the stock of natural (non-renewable) resources is exploited or reduced by human economic activity must be balanced with the development of substitute, renewable resources.

2 The rate at which waste resulting from human economic activity is deposited back into the ecosystem must be within the capacity of the environment to assimilate or absorb that waste.

3 Global population levels and, perhaps more importantly, per capita levels of consumption. It is generally accepted that the level of consumption currently enjoyed by individuals in Western societies would be unsustainable if translated into per capita consumption on a global scale.

Sustainable development, then, is development that not only recognises but works within the constraints of the environmental limits of human activities; it is an approach that accepts that development of any kind cannot be separated from concern for and the protection of the environment in general and the resources upon which human existence depends in particular.

A number of attempts have been made to convert this philosophy into a global development strategy. One of the first was the Brundtland Commission's report *Our Common Future* (WCED, 1987) which based its proposals on two fundamental concepts. Firstly, development should be directed towards meeting the needs of all, thereby extending to them the opportunity to fulfil their aspirations for a better life. Subscribing to the principles of alternative development, the report states that 'the satisfaction of human needs and aspirations is so obviously an objective of productive activity that it may appear redundant to assert its central role in the concept of sustainable development' (WCED, 1987: 54). Secondly, development should occur within environmental limits which, importantly, are 'imposed by the present state of technology and social organisation' (WCED, 1987: 8) rather than by the environment itself. The means of achieving development remains, according to the report, economic growth. As a result, the report has been criticised as a return to classical growth theory disguised in the respectable garb of environmentalism. Conversely, *Caring for the Earth – A Strategy for Sustainable Living* (IUCN, 1991) places the emphasis firmly on the necessary change in attitudes and practices amongst people in all societies. In other words, sustainable development is dependent upon sustainable lifestyles, recognising that 'resource problems are not really environmental problems: they are human problems' (Ludwig *et al.*, 1993: 36).

A complete discussion of these and other reports are beyond the scope of this chapter (see Reid, 1995; Sharpley, 2009b). At the same time, the concept of sustainable development continues to dominate global development debates, providing the focus for a number of major international events, from the 1992 'Earth Summit' in Rio de Janeiro and the World Summit on Sustainable Development ('Rio +10') in Johannesburg in 2002 to the 2012 UN Conference on Sustainable Development ('Rio +20'), again in Rio de Janeiro, whilst more recently, environmental issues have been encapsulated within the concern over global warming and climate change and the progress made at the 2016 Paris conference (see UNFCCC, 2017). Nevertheless, based upon the focus and proposals of the main policy documents, it is possible to identify and summarise the basic principles and objectives of sustainable development. Essentially, the concept of sustainable development embraces three fundamental principles:

1   An holistic approach: sustainable development demands an approach that embraces both developmental and environmental issues within a global social, economic, political and ecological context.

2   Futurity: the focus of sustainable development is upon the long-term capacity for continuance of the global ecosystem, including the human sub-system.

3   Equity: sustainable development is development that is fair and equitable and which provides opportunities for access to and use of resources for all members of all societies, both in the present and future.

These principles underpin the objectives of sustainable development, and essentially embrace the objectives of alternative development (self-reliance, the satisfaction of basic needs and community-based development leading to an overall improvement in the quality of life for all), whilst ensuring that the activities and processes supporting such development are, as discussed above, within the Earth's environmental source and sink capacities. Importantly, in order to achieve these objectives, certain requirements must also be fulfilled:

1   Global sustainable development can only be achieved if national and international political and economic systems are dedicated to equitable development and resource use.

2   Technological systems must be harnessed in order to search continuously for new solutions to environmental problems.

3   All societies need to adopt a new, sustainable lifestyle.

The extent to which these are possible and, indeed, the extent to which sustainable development represents a viable method of achieving long-term, global development remains the subject of intense debate. Nevertheless, many countries, societies and economic sectors are committed to working towards the stated objectives of sustainable development, building upon the 'Agenda 21' framework originally set out at the Rio de Janeiro Earth Summit in 1992. Tourism is no exception. For example, the document *Agenda 21 for the Travel & Tourism Industry: Towards Environmentally Sustainable Development* (WTO/WTTC, 1996) established an initial agenda for the future global development of tourism, whilst innumerable policy documents and industry initiatives focus on tourism and sustainable development (see Telfer & Sharpley, 2016: 71–80). Equally, a large section of the tourism literature, including a dedicated journal (*Journal of Sustainable Tourism*) is dedicated to the topic. Nevertheless, as with sustainable development in general, doubts remain about the viability of the concept of sustainable tourism development in particular.

Sustainable tourism development

The concept of sustainable tourism development is as ambiguous and contradictory as the broader theory of sustainable development (for a detailed critique, see Sharpley, 2009b). For tourism academics and practitioners, it has become a catch-all phrase; 'to some . . . [it is] all about new products or market segments, to others, it is a process of development, while still to others it represents a guiding principle to which all tourism should aspire' (Godfrey, 1996: 61). It is also variously defined, although the WTO/WTTC document referred to above is one example of how the Brundtland Commission's definition is appropriated for specific sectors: sustainable tourism development is 'development [which] meets the needs of present tourists and host regions while protecting and enhancing opportunity for the future' (WTO/WTTC, 1996: 30). To complicate matters further, a variety of other terms, such as ecotourism (Fennell, 2007), rural tourism, low impact tourism (Lillywhite & Lillywhite, 1991), alternative tourism, soft tourism (Kariel, 1989), responsible tourism (Goodwin, 2011; Harrison & Husbands, 1996), green tourism (Beioley, 1995) and nature tourism (Newsome *et al.*, 2013; Whelan 1991) have been widely perceived to be synonymous with sustainable tourism.

Despite the variety of definitions and terminology, there are, generally, two broad interpretations of sustainable tourism development. On the one hand, it is possible to talk in terms of 'the development of sustainable tourism', a perspective which focuses on the tourism product with the overall objective being to sustain tourism itself. Referred to by Hunter (1995) as a tourism-centric approach, this is the most usual interpretation. On the other hand, a broader 'sustainable tourism development' approach may be adopted, which views tourism as a means of achieving overall sustainable development. The former term does not mean the same as the latter but, within the tourism literature, the two are frequently utilised interchangeably. It is, arguably, the latter that should be the focus of sustainable tourism; if sustainable tourism is based upon the principles and objectives of sustainable development, then 'tourism must be a recognised sustainable economic development option, considered equally with other economic activities when jurisdictions are making development decisions' (Cronin, 1990: 14). In other words, if tourism is to contribute to (sustainable) development, which is the primary purpose of promoting tourism in the first place, then it is the potential role of tourism in broader development policies, rather than sustaining tourism itself, that should be the focus of sustainable tourism development. This means that, rather than competing for scarce resources, the emphasis is placed on considering tourism in the context of the most appropriate and efficient shared use of resources, on a global basis, within overall developmental goals. In some cases, this may result in tourism being rejected as a development option.

The principles and practice of sustainable tourism are widely discussed in the literature. Since the late 1980s there has been a plethora of policy documents, planning guidelines, statements of 'good practice', case studies, codes of conduct for tourists and other publications concerned with the issue of sustainable tourism development. These have been produced at all levels and by an enormous variety of tourism organisations in the public, private and voluntary sectors. The general principles of sustainable tourism as embedded in these documents are summarised in Table 10.6.

At first sight, these overall principles of sustainable tourism development appear to conform to the broader principles of sustainable development. The sustainable use of natural resources and the development of tourism within physical and socio-cultural

TABLE 10.6 Sustainable tourism development: a summary of principles

- The conservation and sustainable use of natural, social and cultural resources is crucial. Therefore, tourism should be planned and managed within environmental limits and with due regard for the long-term appropriate use of natural and human resources.

- Tourism planning, development and operation should be integrated into national and local sustainable development strategies. In particular, consideration should be given to different types of tourism development and the ways in which they link with existing land and resource uses and socio-cultural factors.

- Tourism should support a wide range of local economic activities, taking environmental costs and benefits into account, but it should not be permitted to become an activity which dominates the economic base of an area.

- Local communities should be encouraged and expected to participate in the planning, development and control of tourism with the support of government and the industry. Particular attention should be paid to involving indigenous people, women and minority groups to ensure the equitable distribution of the benefits of tourism.

- All organisations and individuals should respect the culture, the economy, the way of life, the environment and political structures in the destination area.

- All stakeholders within tourism should be educated about the need to develop more sustainable forms of tourism. This includes staff training and raising awareness, through education and marketing tourism responsibly, of sustainability issues amongst host communities and tourists themselves.

- Research should be undertaken throughout all stages of tourism development and operation to monitor impacts, to solve problems and to allow local people and others to respond to changes and to take advantage of opportunities.

- All agencies, organizations, businesses and individuals should co-operate and work together to avoid potential conflict and to optimise the benefits to all involved in the development and management of tourism.

Source: Telfer & Sharpley (2016: 63)

PLATE 10.1 Sustainable tourism: Ecolodges, Las Terrazas, Cuba
Source: Photo by Richard Sharpley

capacities is of fundamental importance, consideration is given to the equitable access to the benefits of tourism, and the concept of futurity is implicit within the principles. At the same time, the principle of community involvement appears to satisfy the specific requirements of self-reliance and endogenous development that are critical elements of the theory of sustainable development.

However, there are a number of ways in which tourism challenges the concept of sustainable development and which, following the central theme of this chapter, cast doubt on the overall contribution of tourism to development in destination areas. First, in a general sense, it does not appear that tourism can be developed in accordance with the fundamental principles of sustainable development outlined earlier.

A holistic approach

Despite the requirement that any form of development can only be sustainable if it is considered within a global socio-economic and ecological context, most sustainable tourism strategies in practice tend to focus almost exclusively on localised, relatively small-scale development projects, rarely transcending local or regional boundaries, or on particular industry sectors. This is, perhaps, not surprising given the diverse and fragmented nature of the tourism industry, and it is certainly not to say that localised destination or sectoral strategies are not necessary. However, it is also vital to place such strategies within the wider, global picture. Most, if not all, sustainable tourism development strategies fail to do so. As a result, issues of both the scope of tourism in terms of resource exploitation and its scale as a global activity are overlooked. In effect, the entire world is tourism's resource base, yet a destination or sectoral focus means that broader questions of resource use are ignored. For example, ecotourism development in Costa Rica or Belize may locally conform to sustainable principles (Weaver, 1994), but the system of international air travel that carries tourists to those destinations may not. At the same time, a holistic approach would demand that attention is paid to all tourism. Just as many environmental problems have become global, rather than national, issues, so too is tourism a global phenomenon. Thus, developing sustainable forms of tourism in some areas simply sweeps the problems of tourism under the carpet of other destinations and, as Klemm (1992) suggests, 'the real challenge for the future is to provide sustainable tourism for the mass market' (see also Weaver, 2017).

Futurity

There is little doubt that futurity is a primary concern of sustainable tourism development, yet it is the future viability of tourism itself rather than the contribution of tourism to long-term sustainable development that predominates sustainable tourism strategies. There is, therefore, little evidence within sustainable tourism development principles of concern for the potential contribution of tourism to long-term development goals.

Equity

Although most sustainable tourism development strategies emphasise the importance of community-based or collaborative, tourism planning, the objective being a more equitable share of the benefits accruing from tourism development, in reality both the flows and the structure of international tourism suggest that equitable development through tourism is unachievable. Despite the emergence of newer popular destinations and new tourism generating countries, the major international tourism flows and corresponding economic benefits remain highly polarised and regionalised. Europe and North America are, in particular, the main beneficiaries of tourism development, yet even within the developing world tourism has been monopolised by a few countries to the exclusion of the rest (Brohman, 1996). Moreover, in many developing countries which are popular tourism destinations, tourism is frequently distributed unevenly, diminishing the opportunities for equitable development through tourism even on a national scale. Tourism is frequently concentrated within enclave resorts or tourist ghettos, contributing to socio-economic inequities through a developmental process which, ironically, is often promoted by the central governments of the countries in which the resorts are located (Pearce, 1989: 95).

This situation is exacerbated by the structure of international tourism. Not only are tourist flows dominated by Western, industrialised nations, but also the 'three most lucrative components of . . . [international] . . . tourism (i.e. marketing and the procurement of customers, international transportation, and food and lodging) are normally handled by vertically integrated [Western owned] global networks' (Brohman, 1996). Although the increasing influence of the Internet and social media has served to challenge the traditional structures within the tourism sector (see Chapter 7), there nevertheless tends to be a lack of local community control over resource use and, in particular, a significant proportion of tourism earnings is lost through overseas leakages. Studies have shown that such leakages, in the form of profit repatriation and payments for imports of goods and services, may often be substantial, especially in smaller, tourism-dominated economies. For example, the import content of tourism in the Pacific Islands has generally been found to vary between 50 percent and 90 percent (Craig-Smith, 1996: 43).

In short, the patterns and structures of international tourism, particularly between the metropolitan centres and peripheral developing nations, reinforce rather than diminish global socio-economic inequities. Thus, unsurprisingly, although localised, small-scale (alternative/sustainable) developments attempt to reverse this trend, much international tourism still reflects the problems of dependency.

This last issue, the inequity of tourism-related development, highlights an overall question about the potential contribution of tourism to development in destination areas. In other words, the nature of tourism, in terms of both the ownership and control of the production system and the direction and scale of tourist flows, militates against the potential developmental benefits of tourism. Not only does the ownership or control of tourism services and facilities frequently lie in the hands of Western organisations (although, of course, this is not always the case), but also those organisations, particularly tour operators, are able to control tourist flows and, through their marketing and advertising strategies, the expectations and behaviour of tourists. Thus, the financial benefits of tourism are rarely fully realised in destination areas, whilst opportunities for development arising out of tourism remain subject to the activities of the organisations which control the tourism production system.

The activities of tourists themselves are also an important factor in optimising the contribution of tourism to development. Sustainable development is dependent upon the adoption of sustainable lifestyles; similarly, sustainable tourism development is dependent upon sustainable (that is, appropriate or, as discussed in Chapter 4, 'good') tourist behaviour. However, as McKercher (1993) observes, tourists are consumers, not anthropologists, and they consume tourism for fun, entertainment and escape. In other words, for tourists themselves to make a positive contribution to development by, for example, travelling independently (that is, avoiding the Western-owned tourist production system), staying in locally owned accommodation, attempting to learn about and integrate into local communities and so on, requires them to work at tourism. But, as we have seen in the preceding chapters, this overlooks many of the realities of the consumption of tourism; the notion of the so-called 'good' tourist has not been manifested widely in practice and, although evidence, particularly with respect to tourism and climate change (see Høyer, 2000), suggests that tourists are now becoming more aware of the environmental impacts of travel, tourism remains a largely eco-centric, 'selfish' activity. The implications of this for the nature of the tourist-host relationship are considered in Chapter 11.

Generally, then, not only have many questioned the extent to which tourism can be mapped onto the broad principles and objectives of sustainable development (Berno & Bricker, 2001; Sharpley, 2000; 2009b), but also it is accepted that there are few, if any, examples of 'true' sustainable tourism development in practice. Moreover, there is recent evidence to suggest that idealistic support for the concept is on the wane, whilst the manner in which tourism has evolved over the last 25 years — that is, since sustainable tourism development was first proposed in 1990 — suggests there is little appetite for more sustainable, responsible behaviour amongst industry players or, indeed, amongst tourists themselves. In other words, despite the political rhetoric, the continuing publication of policy documents focusing on sustainable tourism development and numerous national and local initiatives, not only do many destinations still promote tourism growth policies (perhaps inspired by the explicit celebration of tourism's continuing growth by bodies such as the UN World Tourism Organization and the World Travel and Tourism Council), but also tourism has continued to evolve in an unsustainable manner. Specifically, the years since 1990 have witnessed:

- continuing growth in international tourism, surpassing the one billion mark in 2012 and reaching 1,235 million in 2016;
- continuing emergence of new destinations, with more than one third of all nations receiving at least one million tourists annually, indicating the increasing spread of tourism on a mass scale;
- the emergence of new markets, particularly in Asia, driving the growth in tourism;
- economic liberalisation, democratic freedoms, cheaper transport costs and the logic of the market that have supported the increases in supply of and demand for tourism;
- increasing dependence on tourism as an agent of economic development round the world;
- limited evidence of adoption of 'responsible' tourist behaviour.

Collectively, these trends point to the continuation of what has been described as the 'industrial model' of tourism development (Pollock, 2012), a model based on maximising economic gain but which challenges the very notion of tourism as a vehicle of development.

Tourism and development: a summary

The justification for developing and promoting tourism, particularly in the lesser developed parts of the world, is that it represents an effective means of encouraging wider social and economic development in destination areas. This potential role of tourism is primarily based upon its economic contribution in terms of foreign exchange earnings, the generation of income and employment, the development of backward linkages throughout the local economy and so on, and there is little doubt that, in many countries, tourism has become a significant and, frequently, the largest economic sector. This tourism-related developmental process remains firmly rooted in modernisation theory, a development paradigm which, as we have seen, has long been superseded by other theories. Development, as a process and a goal, embraces a much wider set of objectives than simply economic growth; it seeks equitable, fair and endogenous development based on self-reliance and the satisfaction of basic needs within sound ecological principles. That is, it seeks the social development goal of the 'good life' and individual well-being.

It is evident that tourism, as a potential contributor to this development process, has a number of characteristics that militate against achieving its objectives (see McKercher, 1993). The tourism production system largely reflects the tenets of dependency theory and, although increasing attempts are being made by local and national governments and, indeed, by certain sectors of the tourism industry, to implement sustainable tourism development policies, significant doubts remain about the viability of this approach. The difficulties associated with achieving sustainable tourism development raise questions about the overall viability of sustainable development itself. Thus, although tourism undoubtedly makes a significant contribution to economic growth in many countries (and future policies should, arguably, be directed towards increasing this contribution), the nature of tourism is such that there is an inevitability about the social and cultural consequences of tourism, consequences which challenge tourism's contribution to social development. It is with these consequences that the following chapters are concerned.

Further reading

Holden, A. (2013) *Tourism, Poverty and Development*. Abingdon: Routledge.
> Poverty reduction is fundamental to development and is a key goal on the global development agenda. This book provides a detailed introduction to the relationship between tourism and poverty within the context of developing countries.

Mowforth, M. and Munt, I. (2016) *Tourism and Sustainability: Development, Globalisation and New Tourism in the Third World, 4th Edition*. Abingdon: Routledge.
> This book provides a comprehensive and detailed critique of contemporary approaches to tourism development within the framework of development, globalisation, power relations and sustainability.

Sharpley, R. and Telfer, D. (2015) *Tourism and Development: Concepts and Issues,* 2nd Edition. Bristol: Channel View Publications.
> The first section of this book provides a detailed introduction to tourism, development and development theories. It then goes on to explore key issues related to

tourism and development, as well as an analysis of barriers and challenges to the achievement of development through tourism.

Telfer, D. and Sharpley, R. (2016) *Tourism and Development in the Developing World,* 2nd Edition. Abingdon: Routledge.
This text explores the role of tourism in development from a variety of perspectives including globalisation, planning, community responses and the consumption of tourism

Discussion topics

▶ What are the key characteristics of tourism that make it attractive as a development option?

▶ As primarily an engine of economic growth, how realistic is it to claim that tourism can stimulate 'development' as currently defined?

▶ Are alternative forms of tourism more sustainable than mass tourism?

▶ Why is there little evidence of sustainable tourism development in practice?

11

The tourist-host relationship

Introduction

It is virtually impossible to be a tourist in isolation. Unless travelling across uninhabited areas or regions it is inevitable that, sooner or later, tourists come into contact with other people. These may be either fellow tourists or members of local communities in tourism destinations although typically, it will be a combination of both types of contact, the extent or intensity of each being dependent on a variety of factors. For example, mass, institutionalised tourists on a two-week sun, sea and sand holiday are likely to have more interpersonal contact with fellow tourists than with local people, whilst an independent traveller or explorer may actively seek out contact with members of local communities. For the explorer, meeting local people and learning about their way of life may be a primary tourism motivator whereas, for the mass tourist, such contact may only be incidental to the holiday.

Whatever the type or extent of interpersonal contact that tourists experience, they will, almost certainly, come into contact with local people. Even if not actively seeking to meet locals (or, as is sometimes the case, making a positive effort to avoid contact), tourists in resort areas stay in hotels, eat in restaurants, drink in bars and buy souvenirs in shops and interact with members of the local community. In other words, even within a simple buying-selling context, tourists have a form of relationship with local people; indeed, more generally, tourism as a social activity has long been thought of as 'the quintessence of relationships which result from travel and sojourn by outsiders' (Hunziker & Krapf, 1942: 21, cited in Dann & Parrinello, 2009b: 15).

Broadly, this relationship between tourists and local people is frequently referred to as the host-guest relationship (Smith, 1989a), although the notion that members of local communities in destination areas are willing 'hosts' to tourist 'guests' has increasingly come under scrutiny. For many tourists this relationship may be fleeting and, indeed, go unrecognised as such; for others, meaningful, two-way and authentic (see Chapter 9) contact with local people may be the basis of the entire tourist experience. In either situation, however, a variety of social processes are at work which not only determine the nature of the relationship itself but also go a long way towards indicating the potential positive or negative impacts of tourism development on destination communities. That is, it has long been argued that fundamental to the successful development of tourism is a harmonious relationship between tourists, the people and places they encounter, and the organisations and businesses that provide tourism services (Zhang et al., 2006). Putting it another way, a positive local community attitude towards tourism and tourists, or what Snaith and Haley (1999: 597) refer to as a 'happy host', is considered essential to tourism development as the success and sustainability of the sector depends upon the goodwill of local residents (Jurowski & Gursoy, 2004; Pérez & Nadal, 2005). If this is not the case then, as experienced in Barcelona is 2015 and Venice in 2016, the local population may protest against tourism and tourists (Sharpley & Harrison, 2017). Hence, the main practical reason for developing an understanding of the processes involved in encounters between tourists and local people is to be able to plan and manage the development of tourism in a manner which minimises potential negative consequences (and optimises the benefits) for host communities (Andriotis & Vaughan, 2003).

The purpose of this chapter is to examine the varying nature of the relationship between tourists and local people in destination areas. In particular, it considers whether tourism can lead to balanced and equal two-way relationships between tourists and locals, thereby acting, as some would desire, as a vehicle towards greater international harmony and understanding (WTO, 1980), or whether it simply amplifies their social, cultural and economic differences, reinforcing existing attitudes and prejudices. It also reviews briefly the extensive literature on how local destinations communities perceive tourism and the factors that influence their perceptions (see also Deery et al., 2012; Nunkoo et al., 2013; Sharpley, 2014). In so doing, this chapter serves as a foundation to the discussion of the social and cultural impacts of tourism in Chapter 12.

Characteristics of tourist-host encounters

The relationships between tourists and local people are almost infinitely variable (see Pearce, 1994). Tourists are motivated by an enormous variety of factors, they carry with them different attitudes and expectations, they may be more or less experienced as tourists, they are on different types of holiday or trip, and they come from a variety of socio-economic backgrounds. Equally, the economic, social and technological conditions within a tourism destination country or region, the size, type and maturity of its tourism industry, and local cultural and religious factors will all have much bearing on the way in which local communities regard tourists. In short, such is the variety of factors which may influence the relationships that develop between tourists and local communities that it would be logical to conclude that there are as many different types of tourist-host encounters as there are tourists and that, consequently, the analysis of such encounters is a difficult, if not impossible, task.

Despite this variety, it is possible to make some general observations about the nature of tourist-host encounters. For example, it would be logical to assume that the greater the economic, cultural and social differences between a tourist and a member of the destination community, the less balanced, or more unequal, will be the relationship between them. The relative wealth of Western visitors to developing countries is a particularly visible basis for an unequal relationship (and conforms to the dualistic development model of dependency introduced in the preceding chapter); in many instances, just the cost of the flight to some developing countries may be the equivalent of twice or more the average annual local income. Less obvious differences, such as conflicting attitudes towards punctuality, may also result in less tolerant contact. Conversely, the relationship, for example, between an American tourist and a Canadian host is likely to benefit from a much greater degree of initial commonality in culture, language and outlook although, even then, their interaction might be influenced by their individual sense of nationalism or national identity. Indeed, a study by Griffiths and Sharpley (2012) revealed that the relationships between English tourists and Welsh hosts vary according to different intensities of nationalistic feelings amongst both parties.

Another general observation is that in most tourist-host encounters the tourist is on holiday whereas the host, more often than not, is employed in the tourist industry and is, therefore, at work; in a sense, the encounter takes places within a tourism culture that is distinctive from both the tourist's and the host's 'normal' existence (Reisinger & Turner, 2003). Again, however, cultural, social and economic distances are likely to amplify potential differences. Thus, links exist between the structure and nature of international tourism development as a whole and the types of tourist-host encounters that result in different destinations around the world. This issue is explored later in this chapter but, as a starting point, it is important to consider a number of characteristics which, to a lesser or greater extent, are applicable to all types of contact between tourists and local people.

One of the earliest attempts to analyse the nature of the contacts between tourists and local people in destination areas identified five particular characteristics common to most situations (see Sutton, 1967). These refer in particular to international tourism, although certain characteristics may also be applicable to tourist-host encounters in the context of domestic tourism. It was argued that, as a rule, contact is transitory, that both parties seek instant satisfaction (for example, the tourist purchasing a souvenir, the shopkeeper making a sale), and that the relationship is asymmetrical or unbalanced (the tourist benefits from greater wealth, the shopkeeper from better knowledge about the value of his goods). Also, it was suggested that the encounter was a new or unusual experience for the tourist and, finally, that a cultural gulf usually existed between the parties involved in the encounter. A similar perspective was adopted by a UNESCO report (1976) which highlights four characteristic features of tourist-host relationships, particularly within the context of mass tourism:

1   Most encounters between tourists and members of the local community are transitory. In other words, most tourists stay in a resort for only one or two weeks and although the encounter may be considered unusual, exciting and different from the tourist's point of view, for the host it may be simply 'business as usual'. As a result, the relationship is likely to be shallow, superficial and based upon different expectations. However, where visits are of a longer duration or, as is often the case, tourists return to the same resort year after year, more meaningful relationships may occur.

2   Most encounters are constrained by temporal and spatial restrictions. Tourism is usually restricted to certain seasons of the year and, within those seasons, tourists are restricted by the length of their visit. Thus, they may try to see as much and do as much as is possible within the time available, a situation which local people may take advantage of by becoming exploitative, charging higher prices and so on. Tourist-host relationships may also be restricted by the location and spread of tourist-related services. Hotels, restaurants, bars, night-clubs and other facilities and attractions in resort areas are frequently concentrated in particular areas, sometimes in tourist zones or 'ghettos' located well away from towns and villages, making it difficult for less interested or motivated tourists to see the 'real' host country. Moreover, tourists are frequently discouraged from venturing out on their own and are sold tours, ensuring that the majority of tourists' spending is within the tourist area and minimising the opportunity for tourist-host encounters based upon anything but commercial interest. In the extreme, such as at all-inclusive enclave resorts (Freitag, 1994; Anderson, 2011) tourists may have no need to leave the confines of their resort and are unlikely to experience any encounter other than with resort staff.

3   Tourism is an economic activity. The majority of people who work in the tourism industry do so to earn money and most interaction between tourists and local people usually takes the form of an economic transaction. As a result, many tourist-host encounters lack spontaneity; shows, tours and even visits to shops are frequently pre-planned to both fit in with tourists' tight schedules and to provide them with the maximum opportunity for spending money. Relationships which were once motivated by traditional hospitality may also become commercialised. For example, in the south-eastern Turkish village of Harran, famous for its beehive-style houses and religious history, it is not unusual for tourists to be invited in to local people's homes for tea and then for payment to be demanded before departure. Similarly, some years ago it was reported that certain types of tourists (particularly rude or arrogant visitors) in Venice are charged at least double the locals' price in bars and restaurants. There are 'two or even three price lists: one for tourists, one for locals, and a third for "sympathetic" tourists who make more effort than the usual grunted demand' (Moore, 2007). Conversely, when the Cyprus Tourism Organisation (CTO) proposed the development of agro-tourism in some mountain villages as part of its tourism diversification programme, local villagers were astounded by the suggestion that they should charge visitors for their hospitality.

4   Tourist-host encounters, on the whole, tend to be unbalanced. That is, local people may feel inferior when faced with ostentatious displays of wealth, and may resent being in a subservient position to people who are on holiday.

A further characteristic applicable to many tourist-host encounters is an apparent lack of knowledge, understanding or sensitivity on the part of tourists to local culture and custom in tourism destination areas. Whilst of greater relevance to the potential impacts of tourism in general, such shortcomings, often combined with preconceptions and stereotypical images of the host community and culture, further limit the opportunity for balanced or meaningful tourist-host encounters. Additionally, this characteristic is related to the broader issues of tourist motivation, the nature and structure of international tourism and, in particular, the manner in which destinations are marketed to potential tourists. For example, some years ago one tour operator's brochure described The Gambia as

> perfect for sun lovers with palm studded beaches, friendly people and year round sunshine. With all its exotic charm, remember this is Africa: life here is slower, standards can vary and public services aren't as reliable as in other resort areas.
>
> (Thomsons, 1994)

No mention was made of the economic, religious or social structures of the country and first-time visitors to Africa would, almost undoubtedly, have carried with them some preconceived images of 'Africa' based upon media images and the connection between The Gambia and Alex Hailey's *Roots* rather than actual knowledge or experience. The website of the main independent tour operator now offering holidays in The Gambia currently states that: 'A Gambia holiday has its own sense of magic; a quiet alchemy of light and beauty, incarnated in the golden sands of its beaches, the endless skies and stunning sunsets, and in the smiles of its welcoming people' (Gambia Experience, 2017). Again, potential visitors are given little information to prepare them for the realities of the country.

This last point raises the question of whether it is the responsibility of the tourism industry to fully inform potential visitors or whether the onus should fall upon tourists themselves to find out as much as possible about their chosen destination (that is, to be 'good' tourists). For example, when the popular Caribbean destination of the Dominican Republic was devastated by Hurricane Georges in 1998, a number of tourists expressed dissatisfaction that they had not been told that they were travelling in the hurricane season, a response that continues to occur, as when Jamaica was hit by a hurricane in the 2007 hurricane season. Wherever that responsibility lies, it is certain that many tourists arrive at their destination totally unprepared for interaction or social contact with local people and, as a result, tourist-host encounters will be constrained and hampered by their lack of knowledge and understanding.

It is, of course, both easy and somewhat dangerous to generalise the varied and complex social processes and interaction involved in encounters between tourists and local people. Some or all of the above characteristics are likely to be identifiable in most tourist-host encounters and are equally applicable to both international and domestic tourism. For example, there is no reason why contact between a tourist and a local villager in the British countryside will not be as superficial, unbalanced, transitory and influenced by general preconceptions as such contacts in a developing country. At the same time, however, it is important to point out that encounters between tourists and local people occur in a variety of situations and may benefit from positive and informed perceptions and motivations on both sides. That is, it should be emphasised that the early studies referred to above were primarily concerned with tourist-host encounters which occur in the first of three principal settings described by de Kadt (1979: 50), namely, 'where the tourist is purchasing some good or service from the host.' Similarly,

Krippendorf (1987) identifies three types or intensities of business-based encounters: continuous contact between tourists and people working in tourism businesses; irregular contact in non-tourism businesses; and regular contact with people who only partially depend on tourism for their income.

But of course, not all encounters are motivated by or result in commercial exchange. Thus, de Kadt (1979: 50) proposes two additional settings for encounters: where tourists and hosts 'find themselves side by side' and where they purposefully meet to exchange 'information or ideas'. Interestingly, however, largely overlooked in these models is arguably the most common form of encounter: where there is no contact or communication at all, where tourists and hosts are simply sharing space. It is, therefore, possible to conceptualise a continuum of tourist-host encounters based on the nature of contact and subsequent host perceptions (see Figure 11.1). At one end of the continuum, tourists and hosts purposefully come into contact within a commercial exchange setting: the tourist is buying/consuming a product or service which the host is selling/providing. In this context, it is probably incorrect to refer to the two parties as 'guests' and 'hosts', 'customer' and 'service provider' being more appropriate terminology (Aramberri, 2001). At the other end of the continuum, and significantly, encounters are not purposeful; tourists and local people involuntarily share the same space. And where local people are involuntarily sharing that space with large or what they might perceive to be excessive numbers of tourists, then they are more likely to have negative attitudes towards tourism and tourists. For example, anti-tourism protests in Venice have been in response to the city (population 55,000) absorbing more than 60,000 tourists every day (Squires, 2016); tourism is seen as very much impinging on the lives of local residents (Settis, 2016).

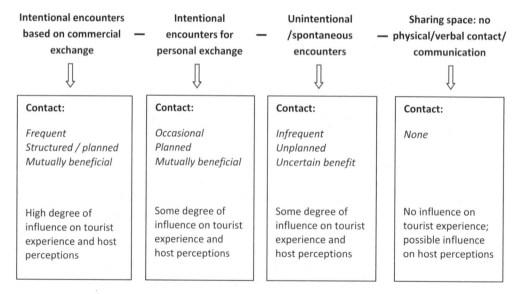

FIGURE 11.1 A continuum of tourist-host encounters
Source: Sharpley (2014: 39)

Evidently, the model in Figure 11.1 is unable to reflect the diversity and complexity of tourist-host encounters and the broader contexts in which they occur; indeed, each and every encounter between a tourist and a member of the destination community is unique, a 'one-off' experience that will, for both the tourist and the host, inevitably differ to a lesser or greater extent from previous and subsequent encounters.

Nevertheless, it demonstrates the enormous variety of settings and forms of tourist-host encounters and, in particular, the importance of recognising the significance of these to understanding how and why local people in destination areas perceive and respond to tourism and tourists in different ways.

Host perceptions of tourism

It is widely accepted that tourists are groups or populations with very different characteristics and attitudes, with clearly identifiable preferences, tastes and perceptions (Brougham & Butler, 1981). These differences can lead to a variety of tourism impacts in destination areas and to different attitudes towards encounters with local people. It is not surprising, therefore, that a considerable amount of research has been (and continues to be) undertaken into the desires, motivation and behaviour of tourists in relation to their impact on destination societies.

It is equally unsurprising that research has long been undertaken into how destination communities, broadly referred to as 'hosts', perceive tourism or, more precisely, what their attitudes towards tourism and tourists are. Indeed, since the mid-1970s when Doxey (1975) proposed his oft-cited 'Irridex' model (see below), 'research on resident attitudes of tourism ... [has become] ... one of the most systematic and well-studied areas of tourism' (McGehee & Anderek, 2004: 132). Underpinning the early research was both the growing concern with regards to the negative consequences of tourism development on destination environments and societies and also recognition, as noted above, that 'the perceptions and attitudes of residents toward the impacts of tourism are likely to be an important planning and policy consideration for the successful development, marketing, and operation of existing and future tourism programs and projects' (Ap, 1992: 665). As a consequence, attention initially focused on the extent to which local residents perceived or experienced the impacts of tourism. Referred to by McGehee and Anderek (2004: 132) as the 'tourism impact' phase of host perception research, studies typically sought to identify the experience of impacts amongst host communities and the factors that determined the nature of that experience, such as place of residence or working in the tourism sector.

For example, Pizam (1978) looked at the attitudes of the residents of Cape Cod, Massachusetts, towards tourism, theorising that their perceptions would be a function of their economic dependency on tourism. He found, perhaps not surprisingly, that a positive correlation existed between residents' work and their attitudes towards tourism: 'it was found that the more dependent a person was on tourism, as a means of livelihood, the more positive was his overall attitude towards tourism' (Pizam, 1978: 12). In another study of resident perceptions, Belisle and Hoy (1980) discovered that local people's perceptions of tourism became less favourable the further their distance from the tourist zone, again indicating that those who are more directly involved in the tourism industry are more likely to have positive feelings towards tourism development. Similarly, Brougham and Butler's (1981) study of resident attitudes on the Sleat Peninsula, Isle of Skye, found that significant differences in perceptions of tourism were identifiable in relation to location of residence, but that other factors, such as age and language, also resulted in varying opinions of the benefits or disbenefits of tourism. Similarly, Akis et al. (1996) found that in Cyprus a positive correlation exists between levels of income and attitudes towards tourism although, certainly in the case of the resort of Agia Napa, resentment is felt towards young tourists who attract complaints amongst local people of being noisy and frequently drunk.

A number of other 'impact' studies are frequently referred to (for example, Haralambopoulos & Pizam, 1996; Liu & Var, 1986; Milman & Pizam, 1988; Perdue et al., 1987; Rothman, 1978; Sheldon & Var, 1984; Um and Crompton, 1987), the great majority of which tend to be largely descriptive. That is, the studies present the results of various research projects but do not fully explain why local people in tourist destination areas have either positive or negative perceptions of tourism. Consequently, and perhaps in response to Ap's (1990: 615) observation that

> unless researchers launch out of the elementary descriptive stage of the current state of research and into an explanatory stage, where research is developed within some theoretical framework, they may find themselves none the wiser in another ten years' time

the research adopted a 'tourism perceptions' approach (McGehee and Anderek, 2004: 132). In other words, recognising that it is more useful for planning and management purposes to understand how and why tourism is perceived by local residents and, in particular, the factors that might determine those perceptions, researchers shifted their attention from exploring the impacts of tourism as experienced by local residents to developing knowledge and understanding of those perceptions. Two perspectives have been adopted within this approach, namely: identifying variables that may determine or predict residents' perceptions, and segmenting local communities according to their level of support for tourism.

Variables influencing host perceptions

As considered elsewhere (Harrill, 2004; Sharpley, 2014), much of the research commonly focuses on the identification, measurement and comparison of the variables that may determine how tourism is perceived (though not necessarily responded to) by local residents. These variables may be explored under two broad headings as identified by Faulkner and Tideswell (1997), namely, 'extrinsic' variables, or those which relate to the destination, and 'intrinsic' variables which relate to the individual host. Typically, extrinsic variables refer to factors related to the stage and nature of tourism development and other characteristics of tourism. For example, studies have long explored how host perceptions vary according to the maturity of the tourism sector (Allen et al., 1988;

Sheldon & Abenjona, 2001;Vargas-Sánchez *et al.*, 2009), whilst factors such as the number and type of tourists (Johnson *et al.*, 1994; Sheldon & Var, 1984), their nationality (Pizam & Sussman, 1995) and their density relative to the destination (Bestard & Nadal, 2007), as well as broader issues such as seasonality (Belisle & Hoy, 1980), have all been addressed.

Conversely, research into intrinsic variables focuses on person-specific factors. Such studies have long addressed fundamental issues such as economic dependency on tourism in terms of both income and employment (King *et al.*, 1993; Wang & Pfister, 2008), revealing not surprisingly that economic engagement in the tourism sector tends to result in more positive attitudes towards tourism, whilst studies have also explored the influence of where residents live, the hypothesis being that the nearer people live to the tourism zone, especially if they are not economically dependent on tourism, the more negative will be their perceptions of tourism. However, this has not always been found to be the case (Raymond & Brown, 2007). At the same time, demographic variables, such as age, gender and level of education, have been considered as possible variables in host perceptions (Haralambopoulos & Pizam, 1996; Mason & Cheyne, 2000), suggesting for example that older people may hold less positive attitudes than younger generations. But again, no correlation has been found between such variables and differences in perceptions of tourism.

More recent research has focused on more personal variables related to the individual host, such as the potential influence of their values on their perceptions of tourism (Choi & Murray, 2010; Woosnam, 2012), as well as their sense of social identity and status (Palmer *et al.*, 2013). Similarly, residents' sense of community attachment based on factors such as length of time lived in the destination area or having extended family living nearby have also been considered as potential variables (Nepal, 2008; Ross, 1992). Yet, despite the overall number and scope of these 'variables' studies, what is of particular note is the fact that few if any consistent relationships have been identified between particular variables and host perceptions of tourism.

Segmentation studies

One of the criticisms of much of the research into host perceptions of tourism is that local residents in destination areas are frequently considered to be a homogeneous group (Andriotis & Vaughan, 2003). In other words, it is assumed that, in any given destination, local residents will have similar attitudes towards tourism and, by implication, will respond in similar ways to its perceived impacts. Quite evidently, however, this is a false assumption. Just as tourists differ in their motivations, values, expectations and experiences, so too do local residents differ in terms of their demographics, lifestyle choices and so on and their attitudes to tourism will vary accordingly. For example, one person may move to a particular place to take advantage of the opportunities for employment in tourism; another, however, might choose to live in the same place for family reasons and, for them, tourism might be an irrelevance.

Consequently, a number of studies have sought to identify how residents' perceptions vary according to different clusters. For example, Davis *et al.* (1988) segmented

Florida residents by their attitudes towards the State's tourism development efforts, revealing five clusters ('Lovers'; 'Love 'Em for a Reason'; 'In–Betweeners'; 'Cautious Romantics'; and 'Haters'), the latter two pointing to a significant anti-tourism segment of the population. In contrast, Fredline and Faulkner (2000) explored residents' reactions to a major event, the Gold Coast Indy race in Australia, identifying clusters according to degree of perceived benefit from the event, whilst Pérez and Nadal's (2005) study clustered residents of the Balearic Islands according to their support for new tourism developments. However, although these studies reveal distinctions in attitudes towards tourism between different groups of local residents – that is, they describe different segments – they do not adequately explain why these distinctions exist, a criticism that is directed towards the host perception research more generally. In other words, most 'perception studies tend to reduce the reality of the . . . [host] . . . gaze to what is visible; yet we know what is visible is not the whole truth' (Moufakkir and Reisinger, 2013: xiii). As a result, there have been calls for a broader approach to exploring residents' perceptions of tourism which takes into account the dominant social, cultural and economic factors in the lives of residents or, in other words, an approach that is based upon an understanding of the social reality of the host community (Deery *et al.*, 2012; Sharpley, 2014).

Nevertheless, and of particular relevance to this chapter, attempts have been made to explain conceptually the nature of the relationship between tourists and hosts at the level of individual interactions, most commonly through the application of social exchange theory.

Understanding tourist-host interaction: social exchange theory

Following his criticism of host perception research noted above, Ap (1992) subsequently proposed that the theory of social exchange, a sociological concept firmly rooted in social action theory, could provide a useful framework for the analysis of the tourist-host relationship. Since then, social exchange theory has been applied in many studies, albeit rather simplistically (and erroneously) to justify the intuitive argument that those residents who perceive the costs of tourism to be greater than benefits will hold more negative perceptions.

Social exchange theory, which is generally concerned with explaining the exchange of resources (physical or symbolic) between people or groups of people, is similar to Nash's (1989: 44) suggestion that 'the relationship between tourists and their hosts includes certain understandings that must be agreed and acted upon' or, in other words, is a sort of transaction. When applied to tourism, social exchange implies that both tourists and hosts undergo a process of negotiation or exchange, the ultimate aim of which is to maximise the benefit to each from the encounter. For the tourist, the benefit may be the purchase of a product or service or, more generally, a desired experience; for local people, the benefit may be economic gain.

The exchange process itself follows a sequence of events, commencing with the identification of need satisfaction (Ap, 1992). That is, unless a need or a motivation exists, there is no reason for either party to initiate an exchange. Thus, unless a community has a need to develop tourism or sees tourism as a means of economic and social improvement, it is unlikely to be willing to become involved in or to welcome the development of tourism. The one exception may be where a community has a tradition of hospitality with no expectation of payment or reward, although such a tradition is likely to become rapidly commercialised with the advent of regular tourism. Once needs have been recognised, both the tourist and the host enter into an exchange situation that must be rational and that results in satisfactory benefits. In other words, both parties act in a rational manner that will result in the desired benefits, although those benefits will be optimised rather than maximised. For example, as argued in Chapter 10, tourism development is normally undertaken for the potential economic and social developmental benefits that it will bring to a community, such as improved standards of living, better transport services and so on. The greater the perceived benefits, the more positive will be local people's attitudes towards tourists. But certain costs are involved, such as having to put up with crowds or higher costs in the shops during the tourist season. Once those costs begin to outweigh benefits, then attitudes towards tourism and tourists will become increasingly negative (as, again, witnessed in recent years in Barcelona, Venice and other major tourism centres).

Importantly, the social exchange, or tourist-host encounter, must be reciprocal. 'Reciprocity suggests that the resources exchanged should be roughly equivalent' (Ap, 1992: 675) and, therefore, neither party should feel they are being exploited. Once either the host or the tourist recognises a lack of reciprocity; for example, when a tourist feels that he or she is being 'ripped off' by the prices being charged for a souvenir or when hosts believe that they are being taken advantage of, such as when tourists intrude on their privacy by taking photographs, then the exchange becomes unbalanced. In this situation, the host is more likely to adopt a more negative attitude towards encounters than tourists because what is 'business as usual' for local people is a one-off experience for tourists. If the conditions of rationality, the optimising of benefits and reciprocity are fulfilled, then the exchange will be perceived as fair and equitable; if the host and the tourist both feel that they have achieved a fair and satisfactory outcome, then each will have a positive perception of the encounter. For example, in an early study, Belisle and Hoy (1980) found that the residents of Santa Marta, a resort on the coast of Colombia, South America, had a generally positive attitude towards tourism and tourists. Despite higher seasonal food prices and a greater incidence of robberies, drug smuggling and prostitution, tourism was seen as having led to improved local transport infrastructure and higher employment, benefits which, on balance, outweighed the costs. Similarly, the study of resident perceptions towards tourism development in Cyprus revealed an overall positive attitude amongst local people (Akis *et al.*, 1996).

Paradoxically, the need satisfaction that initiates the social exchange situation in the context of tourism can also frequently lead to unbalanced tourist-host encounters. Tourism is normally supported and promoted by host communities for the expected benefits of employment opportunities, higher income and social improvement but, as tourism in any resort develops, and as the local community becomes relatively more dependent on tourism as a source of income, then a subtle shift occurs in what may be described as the balance of power in tourist-host relationships. Either the social impacts begin to outweigh the benefits to the local community (see Chapter 12) or local people find themselves in the situation of needing tourists more than tourists need them. In both cases, local people's attitudes and perceptions of tourists will begin to alter and become increasingly negative as individually or as a society they become increasingly dependent on tourists.

In more recent years, a number of researchers have explored host or local community attitudes towards tourists and tourism development in more detail, contributing to a more in-depth understanding of the issue whilst building upon the previous research. For example, Gursoy and Rutherford (2004) developed and tested a new theoretical model based upon social exchange theory. Segregating residents' attitudes under five separate cost-benefit factors (economic benefits; social benefits; social costs; cultural benefits; cultural costs), they identified nine variables that determine the extent of local people's support for tourism development, including: the level of community concern; eco-centric values, utilisation of the tourism resource base, the state of the local economy and community attachment, as well as social, economic and cultural benefits.

Collectively, the literature demonstrates that hosts' perceptions of tourists and tourism development are numerous, variable and influenced by a number of different factors, although certain common themes have emerged from the research. For example, more positive attitudes are in evidence amongst those who work within the tourism sector. It is also important to note, of course, that tourism development is dynamic and the context for tourist-host encounters can also change, influencing the nature of those encounters. Hence, it is important to consider the tourist-host relationship itself as a dynamic process and one which may change in response to other factors.

The tourist resort life cycle

Most of the studies into host perceptions of tourism and tourists tend to be undertaken at a particular point in time. That is, research is carried out at a certain stage in the development of tourist destinations, at a particular point in what may be described as the life cycle of a resort, although one notable exception is Pi-Sunyer's (1989) longitudinal analysis of resident perceptions of tourists in a Catalan resort. Whilst such studies undoubtedly provide a valuable insight into the factors and variables which determine the nature of tourist-host encounters, it is also important to consider how host perceptions change over time, in particular how the nature of the relationship is influenced by the developmental stage of the destination. In a widely quoted study linked to product life-cycle theory in marketing, Butler (1980a) suggests that tourist destinations evolve through a six- or seven-stage process:

1   The exploration stage. The first stage in the development of a tourist destination is characterised by relatively small visitor numbers. It is the stage when a resort or destination is 'discovered' by independent travellers or other explorer-type tourists and, as such, they will be accepted by local residents more as guests than as paying customers. Thus, commercial development of tourism is minimal, contact with

local residents is balanced and frequent, and little or no marketing or promotion of the resort is occurring.

2   The involvement stage. As the number of visitors begins to increase, local people begin to provide facilities and accommodation. The potential for tourism development is recognised and, although still low key, some marketing is undertaken which further increases the number of visitors. As a result, the approach to tourism becomes more commercial although the relationship between tourists and local people remains harmonious.

3   The development stage. As tourist destinations progress into the third, development, stage they become transformed from relatively unknown, quiet destinations (what a travel writer would describe as 'undiscovered') into fully fledged resorts. Initially a wide range of locally owned businesses are set up to provide for the needs of tourists, but control of tourism rapidly passes to external organisations such as large hotel groups and international tour operators. The explorer or niche-market visitors have been replaced by mass, institutionalised tourists and the tourist-host relationship suffers as it becomes based on commercial transactions. Indeed, local residents become increasingly marginalised as tourism becomes dominated by external interests.

4   The consolidation stage. The consolidation stage is marked by a slowdown in the rate of increase of visitors. Rather than new businesses opening up, the existing hotels, restaurants and other facilities are more concerned with controlling costs. The destination has lost its exclusivity and 'unique selling points' and it has joined the ranks of many other similar destinations. During the season the resident population is vastly outnumbered by tourists, most of whom stay in an identifiable and distinct tourist zone within the resort. Thus, only local people involved in the tourism industry have any direct contact with tourists, usually on a transitory, business related basis.

5   The stagnation stage. Eventually the destination reaches a stage where its capacity has been reached or even, at times, exceeded. No new tourists are attracted to the resort which has become dependent on repeat business. The decline in growth has resulted in a lack of investment and so less attention is paid to the upkeep of buildings and infrastructure. Environmental, social and economic problems begin to emerge and the destination, in terms of both visitors and prices, moves downmarket.

6   The decline stage. Finally, the destination enters the stage of decline. Visitor numbers begin to fall as newer, more attractive resorts are developed (or, as in the case of British seaside resorts during the 1980s, overseas holidays become increasingly affordable and popular). The larger tourist businesses begin to pull out of the destination and new uses have to found for tourist accommodation and other facilities. Hotels may be converted into retirement flats or nursing homes and tourism activity falls to a low, but perhaps regular, level with minimal contact between visitors and members of the local community.

7   The rejuvenation stage. Rather than allowing the destination to completely decline, the signs are recognised and new uses, new markets and new sources of investment are sought. Attractions are updated and efforts are made to re-market the

destination with a new, modern image. For example, the resort may begin to market itself as a business and conference centre, the season may be extended with new products, such as summer walking holidays being promoted at winter skiing destinations, or accommodation and facilities are improved and updated to keep in line with developments in other resorts.

A number of attempts have been made to link Butler's model to the 'life cycle' of actual tourist destinations, yet there are conflicting opinions as to its applicability and it has been criticised and defended in equal measure (Getz, 1992; Haywood, 1986). In the early 1990s, for example, Ioannides (1992) compared the growth and development of tourism in Cyprus with Butler's exploration, involvement and development stages, concluding that the high level of local involvement combined with increasing dependence on overseas tour operators and a mass, charter market indicates that the development stage had been reached.

Subsequent research indicated that Cyprus has, in fact, moved into a period of consolidation and potential stagnation (Sharpley, 2001). Similarly, the tourism history of British seaside resorts is another example of how destinations can progress through Butler's hypothetical process; some, such as Brighton and Torquay, have undergone rejuvenation, whereas others are clearly in a state of decline (see Agarwal, 1997). Conversely, Getz (1992), in a study of tourism development at the Niagara Falls, concludes that Butler's stages of consolidation, stagnation, decline and rejuvenation are not separate and identifiable but a perpetual process. That is, tourism planners and managers respond continually to shifts in demand and other problems which tourism destinations face and, rather than sinking into inevitable decline, destinations enter a stage of maturity: 'for old destinations like Niagara Falls, and for most urban tourism areas, "maturity" will likely be a permanent condition' (Getz, 1992: 768). Other work related to the concept of the resort life cycle includes research by Agarwal (2002) and Weaver (1990), whilst Butler himself has edited two complete volumes on the subject (Butler, 2006a, b).

The important point to consider is how the developmental process of tourist destinations relates to the tourist-host relationship and, in particular, the perceptions of local people of tourism and tourists. Some links are identifiable through the degree and type of contact that local people have with tourists as Butler's model develops but, in another widely cited study, Doxey (1975) proposes a four-stage 'Irridex' process whereby the attitudes of local people change as tourism develops.

At the exploration stage, when there are relatively few visitors and contact between tourists and local people is likely to be frequent and balanced, the attitude of the host population is one of euphoria. Visitors are welcome, both as a form of new contact with 'the outside world' and as a new source of income which, in many cases, is an important supplement to household earnings. However, as the level of tourism begins to grow, fewer members of the local population come into contact with tourists. Nor are tourists a rare sight; they begin to be taken for granted and the tourist-host encounter is motivated less by mutual personal interest than by commercial gain on the part of locals. Thus, the attitude of the majority of residents, in particular those who have limited or no contact with tourists, is one of apathy.

The third stage in Doxey's model is one of annoyance. Large numbers of tourists mean that the day-to-day life of residents becomes disrupted; there are queues in shops, traffic jams, local shops turn to the more profitable business of selling souvenirs and, generally, local residents are marginalised in their own town. The perceived benefits of tourism to the host community are beginning to be outweighed by the disruption that tourism is causing, a situation that leads, finally, to antagonism towards tourists. Local people have become dependent on tourism; they are no longer in control of the situation, the standard of living in the resort is declining as the quality of tourism facilities and the type of tourist becomes down market. The tourists and their money, once so openly welcomed, are now blamed for the changes that have taken place in the destination. In short, Doxey suggests that the growth and development of tourism can be mirrored by an increasingly negative attitude towards tourists amongst local people.

Similarly, Ap and Crompton (1993) identify four different strategies that local residents adopt in response to the level of tourism development. That is, they describe the actions taken by local people that result from their attitudes towards tourists. At the euphoric stage, local people embrace tourism; they make positive efforts to meet and develop long-term relationships with visitors, many of whom may return on a regular basis. As the number of tourists grows and encounters become more formal, local apathy is marked by tolerance towards tourists. Despite some of the problems that tourism brings, the general feeling is that the local economy benefits from the income from tourists, and local residents, therefore, tolerate the occasional disruption to their lives caused by tourists. However, as local residents become irritated by the presence of tourists they adjust their behaviour: activities, such as shopping, may be rescheduled to avoid crowds or they will go to places which they know will be quieter. Such a strategy is not always possible, in particular when tourism has reached the stage of consolidation, when tourism dominates their lives and local people have become antagonistic towards tourists. In this situation, if they are able to do so, residents may withdraw; they either move away temporarily, perhaps during the main season, or they may permanently move away from the area. For example, following the rapid development of Agia Napa, a mass tourism resort in Cyprus, the entire original village relocated a few kilometres away to avoid the problems and social impacts of tourism. A study by Brown and Giles (1994) identified similar responses to tourism on the part of local people, but to a more limited extent; they found that, typically, members of local communities in destination areas simply reorganise their daily lives to avoid tourists and tourism areas.

Both Butler's (1980a) resort life-cycle models and Doxey's (1975) 'Irridex' have been criticised for their linearity and assumptions of responses to tourism. Nevertheless, the implication of these studies is that not only will local people's attitudes and perceptions vary according to the level and type of tourism development, but that they will also adapt their behaviour accordingly. Much depends on the extent to which an individual is involved in the local tourism industry; it is likely that a person who earns a living from tourism will remain at the apathy/tolerance stage until business begins to decline, whereas residents who are not directly involved and who, therefore, suffer from the negative impacts without enjoying any apparent benefit, may quickly become antagonistic towards tourists. In either case, the end result is a tourist-host relationship that is unequal and unbalanced, a situation which may be related to the nature of tourism and tourism development itself.

Tourist host encounters and dependency

Much of the literature on the tourist-host relationship adopts what may be described as a micro perspective. That is, it considers the nature of the relationship from the point of view of individuals or localised groups of tourists and locals. In order to fully understand the ways in which the tourist-host relationship develops, we must consider the broader forces and influences that come into play, in particular the relationship between tourist generating countries or regions and tourist destinations. For example, it would be logical to assume that the local community in a destination that is fully in control of its tourism development would be more favourably disposed towards tourists than, say, local people who feel that, in some way or another, tourism has been imposed upon them or that they have become dependent on tourism and, by implication, tourists. For the latter community, tourism may be considered to be a form of imperialism or neo-colonialism and, from a sociological point of view, the resultant tourist-host relationship may be one based upon conflict.

The relationship between tourism and dependency in general has already been explored in Chapter 10. However, the concept of neo-colonialism is of particular relevance to the present discussion and warrants further consideration. Imperialism or colonialism is essentially the expansion of a particular country's economic, political or military interests abroad and, in a sense, international tourism may be viewed as a new, modern form of colonialism. The basis of this argument is that, as we have seen, the great majority of tourists have traditionally originated in the modern, developed countries of the Western world; more recently, other major markets have emerged, particularly China, though the argument remains valid. At the same time, the tourism industry that facilitates the movement of tourists and the development of tourist facilities is itself based largely in the major tourism generating countries. Thus, being the suppliers of large numbers of tourists and, frequently, owning or managing facilities and attractions in destination areas as well as providing the necessary financial investment, the metropolitan centres of Europe, North America and, increasingly Asia are able to exercise some degree of power and control over the development of tourism. This is particularly marked in developing countries but even Mediterranean destinations, such as Spain and Greece, have, in a sense, become colonised by their northern European neighbours. In the case of ex-colonies in the developing world which have gained their political independence from Western powers, this new dependence on the West for both the financial support to develop tourism and tourists themselves is, therefore, seen to be a return to the old days of colonialism, or neo-colonialism.

For example, The Gambia is a small, West African state which gained its independence from Britain in 1965. At that time the country was virtually unknown as a tourist destination; indeed, only 300 tourist arrivals were recorded for the 1965–1966 winter season (Dieke, 1993). Subsequently, and mainly as a result of its popularity as a winter sun destination, The Gambia achieved steady growth in the number of tourist arrivals and, by the mid-1990s, almost 90,000 tourists were visiting the country each year. Tourism was also contributing some 10 percent to the country's gross domestic product (GDP), earning about £16.5 million annually and, at that time, The Gambia's Ministry of Information and Tourism hoped to increase tourism's contribution to GDP to 25 percent. However, whilst such figures indicated a reasonably healthy growth in tourism, they hid a number of important facts which demonstrated a less than healthy dependence on overseas finance and organisations.

This dependence was revealed in late 1994 when, following a military coup late that year, tourism to the country collapsed, with significant knock-on social and economic consequences for local communities. Underlying the collapse of tourism was the fact that around 60 percent of visitors to The Gambia came from Britain, with about 40 percent of all visitors at that time travelling with the tour operator Thomsons (the principal tour operator to The Gambia is now The Gambia Experience). Following the coup, Thomsons, along with other British tour operators, responded to Foreign Office advice and temporarily stopped flying tourists to The Gambia on safety grounds (but see Sharpley et al., 1996). As a consequence, the local tourism industry ground to a halt. Since then, tourism to The Gambia has gradually recovered, though the dependence on the UK for tourist arrivals remains the same (Sharpley, 2009c, d).

Wall and Mathieson (2006) identify three conditions, some or all of which may be linked to the concept of neo-colonialism and all of which are evident in the example of tourism development in The Gambia, which indicate a country's dependence on an overseas-controlled tourism industry. First, many developing countries have become dependent on tourism as a source of foreign exchange. Thus, although the original policy of developing and promoting tourism may have been to develop and diversify the local economy, thereby enabling a greater degree of self-sufficiency, many countries have been unable to do so. For example, Cyprus turned to tourism to stimulate economic growth and diversification following both independence from Britain in 1960 and the Turkish occupation of northern Cyprus in 1974. Tourism became the dominant industry on the island, by the end of the 1990s accounting for over 40 percent of all exports and around 20 percent of GDP, with the result that the Cypriot economy was largely dependent on tourism and, as with The Gambia, disproportionately dependent on tourism from Britain (see Sharpley, 2001). Second, a large proportion of the earnings from tourism flow directly back to the tourism generating countries, both as profits from investments and as payments for imports to satisfy the needs of tourists. In some countries, such 'leakages' can be as high as 70 percent of the earnings from tourism. Third, tourism, as a form of neo-colonialism, is evidenced by foreign nationals holding management and other senior positions within the tourism industry, which is also another way in which the profits from tourism leak out of the country.

Often described as the economic costs of tourism development, these characteristics of neo-colonialism are by no means universal. Many destinations in both the developing and developed world have built up valuable and thriving tourism businesses based on policies which ensure local ownership and the retention of profits. For example, in Thailand foreign ownership of any business is limited to 49 percent whilst in India no foreign national is permitted to work in the tourism industry. It is, therefore, over-generalistic to claim, as does Nash (1989: 39), that it is the influence of tourism generating countries 'over touristic and related developments abroad that makes a metropolitan centre imperialistic and tourism a form of imperialism'. Also, many countries have undertaken tourism development programmes voluntarily and willingly and, by retaining their political, if not economic, independence, are able to dictate their own future. Bhutan, which has traditionally limited the number of tourists arriving each year and has controlled their activities so as not to disrupt and commercialise local culture, is an extreme but good example of how the promise of rapid economic growth has been rejected in favour of retaining independence and cultural and political integrity, although the longer-term sustainability of tourism in Bhutan is now in some doubt (Brunet et al., 2001; Telfer & Sharpley, 2016: 54–55). But, in the context of tourist-host relationships, the development of tourism almost inevitably leads to some degree of economic dependence on the part of host communities and, therefore, the concept of tourism as a form of neo-colonialism provides a useful, broad basis for considering the longer-term direction and evolution of interaction between tourists and local communities in all destination areas.

For example, the sense of economic dependence felt by destination communities may serve to undermine the potential for meaningful, balanced tourist-host relationships, especially if an historic, colonial link exists. Thus, local people in India may well perceive that the attitude of British visitors has changed little since the days of the Raj and may feel resentful towards them, whilst in The Gambia, a country once at the centre of the slave trade, local people who work in the poorly paid, foreign-dominated tourism industry may also feel that little has changed. Similarly, local communities may have generalised attitudes towards visitors which are, again, amplified by their actual or perceived economic dependence upon them. For example, Pi-Sunyer (1989: 195) describes how the development of mass tourism in a Catalan resort led to stereotypical descriptions being applied to different nationalities of visitors. In the eyes of local people, Germans, French and Italian visitors lost their individuality and became identified by particular negative attributes, a process resulting from 'the pressures and sheer magnitude of mass tourism ... and ... the sense of loss of control that such an influx implied' (Pi-Sunyer, 1989: 195)

Nor is economic dependence and the resulting attitude towards tourists limited to international tourism. Local communities in a rural area in England, such as a national park, may be as equally dependent on domestic tourism from towns and cities as is a developing country on international tourists from a modern, Western country. The purchase of large numbers of local houses or apartments by tourists as second, holiday homes, leading to local people being unable to afford to buy their own homes, then becomes little more than a localised form of colonialism. In a similar vein, increasing attention is now being paid to the issue of 'resident tourists', second-home owners and migrant workers who serve the needs of new tourist populations in international destination areas. For example, it has been observed that conflicts exist between British migrants/second-home owners and local communities in southern Spain (O'Reilly, 2003), with British 'in-comers' unwilling or unable to assimilate into the local society; indeed, British migrants in Spain now stand to represent the expatriate community in local elections. More generally, it has been found that complex relationships exist between local people and different types of tourist-migrants (Williams & Hall, 2000). However, the important point is that, generally, the economic dependence which comes hand in hand with virtually all levels of tourism development beyond the exploratory stage implies a lack of absolute control on the part of host communities and, hence, some degree of inequality in the resulting relationship between local people and tourists is inevitable.

Tourist-host relationships: harmony or conflict?

As pointed out earlier, encounters between tourists and local people in destination areas are frequently described as host-guest relationships, a term which implies a sense of willingness, equality and harmony. In other words, it implies that tourists are invited as welcome (but paying) guests and that local people are happy and willing hosts. Thus, host-guest relationships within a destination society may be viewed as a form of structural consensus, as long as tourism is seen to be mutually beneficial and that the transactions or social exchanges between visitors and local people is fair, balanced and equitable. However, the analysis of the nature of contacts between tourists and members of local communities leads to a contradictory conclusion. That is, such encounters, when considered within the dynamic context of tourism development and the life cycle of tourist destinations, become identifiable with the gradual erosion of equality and balance in the relationship and the growing domination of the needs of tourism and tourists. In particular, the nature and economic rationale of tourism development indicates that, for the most part, encounters between tourists and local people bear more relation to conflict theory than harmonious interaction, the exception being contacts in non-tourist areas or where visitors make a conscious effort to meet local, 'backstage' people.

The main point to emerge is that meaningful and balanced encounters between tourists and local people can only occur in situations of mutual dependence and where the local community has retained control over the development of tourism. As residents become more dependent on tourists as a source of income and as control falls into the hands of national or international organisations, the balance of power within the tourist-host relationship falls firmly in favour of the tourist. 'Whenever tourism activity is concentrated in time and space, builds rapidly, dominates a local economy, disrupts community life, endangers the environment, and ignores community input, the seeds of discontent are sown' (Haywood, 1988: 105). If harmony is to be maintained and, by implication, the benefits to both tourists and local people optimised on a continual basis, the solution would appear to lie in maintaining the involvement and control of the community as a whole in the development of tourism, or in what was originally referred to by Murphy as a community approach to tourism development (see Murphy 1983; 1985; 1988; also Hall & Richards, 2003).

The community approach to tourism development in its original form was, in effect, the precursor of what has become sustainable tourism development. Fundamental to the approach is the recognition that a thriving and healthy tourism industry depends upon an equally healthy and thriving local community. It is the local community that benefits from tourism but, at the same time, it is the local community that bears the costs of tourism and has to pick up the pieces once the tourists have gone. In other words, tourism is a resource industry, and local communities are as much a resource, or part of the tourism product, as are tourist facilities and attractions.

The basic requirement for the community approach to tourism development is that all members of communities in tourist destination areas, rather than just those directly involved in the tourism industry, should be involved in the management and planning of tourism. The purpose of this approach is to ensure that the objectives of tourism development coincide with the community's wider social and economic goals and that the tourism industry 'gives back to the community while extracting a living from it . . . [and] . . . that both the industry and its community base can benefit mutually from a long-term partnership' (Murphy, 1983: 181).

The concept of community involvement has, over the years, been incorporated in a number of tourism planning and development projects, such as the former partnership or Tourism Development Action Programme (TDAP) approach in the UK in the 1990s. Primarily intended to develop partnerships between the public and private sectors as a more effective means of planning and financing tourism developments, TDAPs also had the purpose of achieving more widespread support and involvement amongst local communities. The extent to which this has been achieved is debatable. Involvement tended to be limited to those who had a direct, usually financial interest, whilst decisions were frequently based upon personal as opposed to community-wide concerns. Nevertheless, it is widely recognised that harmonious tourist-host relationships are dependent, at least in part, on the involvement of local people in tourism planning at a community level. Pearce (1994: 117) also includes the education of both local people and communities, community ownership of tourist facilities, the facilitation of local residents' way of life and the undertaking of constant monitoring and research as equally essential ingredients of community-based tourism development (Timothy, 2002).

In reality, such involvement is unlikely (Jamal & Dredge, 2015; Taylor, 1995; Tosun, 2000). Tourism is an economic activity which involves tourists who are willing to spend money in return for certain goods and services, and organisations and businesses which will provide those goods and services at a profit. Under such circumstances, balanced and harmonious tourist-host relationships are only likely to occur when the tourism product is small scale, locally owned and controlled, and not the major source of income and employment for the local community. As soon as the hosts become dependent, either on tourists themselves or on outside organisations, they become, in effect, a commodity. The profits of tour operators and other organisations represent a form of exploitation and the tourists, along with the tourism industry, are the exploiters. The tourist-host relationship becomes based upon conflict and, as considered in Chapter 12, the local community may begin to suffer from the social and cultural impacts of tourism.

Further reading

Moufakkir, O and Reisinger, Y. (eds) (2013) *The Host Gaze in Global Tourism.* Wallingford: CABI.

In comparison to most research which considers the 'gaze' in tourism from the perspective of the tourist, this book explores how host communities gaze on tourists. As such, it offers a novel contribution to the wider literature on tourist-host relationship in general and host perceptions of tourists in particular.

Sharpley, R. (2014) Host perceptions of tourism: A review of the research. *Tourism Management,* 42(1): 37–49.

Reviewing the major contribution to the host perceptions of tourism literature, this paper discusses the main themes and trends in the research, highlighting limitations and suggestioning alternative approaches to exploring host-guest relations.

Wall, G. and Mathieson, A. (2006) *Tourism: Change, Impacts and Opportunities.* Harlow: Pearson Education.

This book continues to be one of the key texts that explores in depth the economic and socio-cultural consequences of tourism, including an in-depth consideration of tourist-host relationships.

Discussion topics

▶ To what extent are encounters between tourists and local people inevitably asymmetrical, or unbalanced?

▶ Given that tourist-host encounters are, for the most part, based on some form of commercial exchange, is it more appropriate to describe tourists as 'customers' and hosts as 'service providers'?

▶ What are the limitations of one-off, quantitative studies of host perceptions of tourism and why would in-depth qualitative studies provide a more revealing and accurate understanding of how destination communities perceive and respond to tourism and tourists?

12

Tourism
Socio-cultural consequences

Introduction

The growth and development of tourism during the latter half of the twentieth century and first part of the twenty-first century has been remarkable. Between 1950 and 2000 the annual number of international tourist arrivals rose from 25 million to 687 million, since when the number has increased inexorably. As detailed in Chapter 1, the one billion mark was surpassed for the first time in 2012 and, by 2016, 1.235 billion international arrivals were recorded worldwide. Over the same period, foreign exchange receipts from tourism also increased remarkably, from US$2.1 billion to US$1.26 billion in 2015. However, the rate of growth in international tourism since 1950 has not been constant. That is, a number events of global significance, such as the OPEC oil crisis in the 1970s, the Chernobyl disaster in 1986, the Gulf conflict in 1991, '9/11' in 2001 and, most recently, the global economic crisis of 2008 had repercussions throughout the tourism industry causing a temporary slowdown in the growth of arrivals. For example, international tourist arrivals fell by 35 million in 2009 compared with the previous year.

Nevertheless, tourism continues to demonstrate remarkable resilience to such global events, with declines in arrivals (both global and regional) almost always proving to be temporary. Throughout the 1990s, international tourism grew at an annual average of 4.2 percent whilst, since 2000 and despite other major events impacting on global tourism, including the Bali bombings in 2002, the SARS outbreak in 2003, the Indian Ocean tsunami in December 2004 and, more recently, the increasing threat of terrorist attacks on tourists, figures have continued to rise. Indeed, between 2010 and 2015, international arrivals grew at an annual average of 3.9 percent, cementing international tourism's position as both a major social phenomenon and as one of the world's largest economic sectors. Moreover, if domestic tourism (that is, people engaging in tourism in their own countries) is taken into account, then the overall scale and value of global tourism becomes evident. It is estimated, for example, that the number of domestic tourist trips is some six times greater than that of international trips (in other words, around 85 percent of all tourism activity worldwide is accounted for by domestic trips), whilst the economic contribution of domestic tourism is also highly significant. For example, the UK is a major international destination, attracting almost 36 million international visitors in 2015 who generated over £22 billion in revenues. Yet, domestic tourism, including day trips, generated more than £74 billion whilst total tourism earnings in the UK, including those generated by outbound tourism, totalled more than £127 billion (Tourism Alliance, 2017). At the global scale, the World Travel and Tourism Council estimates that the tourism sector generates more than US$7.6 trillion annually (WTTC, 2017: 1).

In short, there is no doubting the economic value of tourism. As discussed in Chapter 10, in addition to being a significant generator of foreign exchange, tourism can act as a catalyst for economic regeneration and diversification whilst, as a relatively labour-intensive industry, it is an important source of employment in both developed and developing countries; around 10 percent of the world's workforce is employed in tourism. Thus, as tourism continues to grow both in scale and scope, it is not surprising that many countries have leapt onto the tourism bandwagon, developing and exploiting their natural resources in an attempt to gain their share of the multi-billion dollar tourism market.

From a social and cultural perspective, this rapid expansion of tourism is important in two respects. First, within individual destination areas or countries, the development of tourism as a vehicle for economic modernisation and diversification almost invariably leads to changes and developments in the structure of society. Indeed, for destinations the fundamental purpose of developing tourism is to promote economic and social development and, therefore, some of these changes may be welcome. For example, general, society-wide improvements in income, education, health care, employment opportunities and local infrastructure and services are all elements of social development. Conversely, other changes may be less welcome. Traditional social or family values may be challenged, new economically powerful groups may emerge, or cultural practices may be adapted in order to suit the needs of tourists. In other words, destination societies may both benefit from and suffer the less desirable consequences of tourism as an economic development strategy. The dilemma facing many destinations, therefore, is how to achieve a balance between these benefits and costs of tourism development (Telfer & Sharpley, 2016).

Second, 'tourism is unique as an export industry in that consumers themselves travel to collect the goods' (Crick, 1989: 334). The tourism product is 'exported' to tourists who travel to the destination, carrying with them the values, beliefs and behavioural modes of their own, home society as a form of cultural baggage. Thus, as the volume of international tourism has increased, so too has the contact between different societies and cultures. To some observers, this interaction between tourists and local communities threatens to dilute or even, potentially, destroy traditional cultures and societies: 'tourists seem to be the incarnation of the materialism, philistinism and cultural homogenisation that is sweeping all before it in a converging world' (Macnaught, 1982: 365). To others, it represents an opportunity for sharing, for peace, understanding and greater knowledge amongst different societies and nations (Moufakkir & Kelly, 2010).

Whether considering the effects on a destination society brought about by the consequences of tourism development, the influence of ever-increasing numbers of tourists coming into contact with alien cultures, or a combination of both, it is inevitable that tourism, as a fundamentally social activity, will have an impact on those societies and cultures involved in tourism.

The rapid growth in tourism since the 1960s has been mirrored by increasing concern about the impacts of tourism on host destinations and, over the years, a large body of literature has emerged that is concerned with both an analysis of the physical, social, political or cultural impacts of tourism development and with potential solutions to the perceived problems (see, for example, Britton, 1982; Budowski, 1976; Butler, 1991; Croall, 1995; de Kadt, 1979; ETB, 1991; Hickman, 2007; Holden, 1984; Murphy, 1985; Smith & Eadington, 1992; Wahab & Pigram, 1997; Wall & Mathieson, 2006).

Much of the academic literature, reports in the media and what Wall and Mathieson (2006: 221) describe as 'colourful stories', adopt a negative stance, highlighting those aspects of tourism which are seen to be destructive or disadvantageous to tourist destinations (see Travis, 1982). Much of the concern for the consequences of tourism development has long appeared to be framed by a pessimistic, if not apocalyptic view, one which considers mass tourism in particular to be inevitably destructive – a theme continued in Hickman's (2007) book *The Final Call: In Search of the True Cost of our Holidays*. Also, the analysis and criticism of the social and cultural impacts of tourism is frequently based on a number of assumptions which, potentially, distort the overall picture. For example, it is often assumed that the social and cultural impact of tourism is a one-way process, that the flood of (usually Western, though now also increasingly from other countries, particularly China) tourists visiting countries in the developing world almost invariably results in the Westernisation of traditional cultures. At the same time, however, in recent years there has been increasing evidence of the capacity of destination to absorb tourism being reached or exceeded, with local residents in cities such as Barcelona and Venice responding with calls to limit or reduce tourism (Sharpley & Harrison, 2017). In other words, the pessimistic prophesies of some commentators are, perhaps, being proved correct (see, for example, Connolly, 2017).

The purpose of this chapter, then, is to examine both the positive and negative social and cultural impacts of tourism and to consider the extent to which the qualitative assessment of socio-cultural impacts can be measured against broader social and cultural change and the tangible, quantitative impacts of tourism development.

Tourism, society and culture

Murphy (1985: 117) describes tourism as a 'socio-cultural event for the traveller and the host'. It is a social process which, in the context of both domestic and international tourism, brings together people from different regions and different countries in a form of social interaction (see Chapter 11). The resulting tourist-host relationship may frequently impact in a variety of ways upon both the local community and on visitors. Tourism is also, from the point of view of destination areas, a means of improving and modernising the economic and social condition of the host community (that is, encouraging development) and, therefore, tourism may be described as an agent of socio-cultural change.

It is difficult to distinguish between changes or impacts that are specifically social and those which are cultural. The condition and structure of a society and its cultural characteristics are interlinked and changes in one almost inevitably lead to changes in the other. For the purposes of this chapter, however, the social impacts of tourism may be considered to be those which have a more immediate effect on both tourists and host communities and their quality of life, whereas cultural impacts are those which lead to a longer-term, gradual change in a society's values, beliefs and cultural practices. In other words, social impacts are those concerned with issues such as health, moral behaviour, the structure of the family, gender roles, crime and religion, whilst cultural impacts may determine behavioural and attitudinal changes, such as dress, food and social relationships, as well as changes in the production of cultural practices and artefacts. Before describing the specific social and cultural impacts of tourism, it is important to consider, firstly, the factors which determine the degree of socio-cultural impact and, secondly, the extent to which it is tourism and tourists, as opposed to other factors, that lead to social and cultural change.

Factors influencing socio-cultural change

Although it is possible to make general observations about the potential socio-cultural impacts of tourism, the degree to which these impacts influence or are experienced by host communities and tourists depends on a number of factors. Generally, it is logical to suggest that the greater the gulf between the tourism generating country and the destination in terms of culture and economic development, the more significant are the social and cultural impacts likely to be (WTO, 1981). Other, more specific factors may also be identified:

Types/numbers of tourists

Both the volume and the type of tourist are significant factors in determining the potential socio-cultural impacts of tourism. As a general rule, explorer-type independent travellers who are relatively few in number and are more willing to seek out, experience and understand local culture are likely to have less impact than large numbers of mass tourists who demand facilities and amenities to which they are accustomed in their home society. Smith (1989a: 12) links tourist types to potential impacts on host societies, following a continuum from low numbers/low impact to high volume charter tourists/high impact, whilst there are also connections between tourist types and behavioural characteristics and the way in which tourists interact with local communities (see Chapter 4). In some circumstances, an independent traveller may have more impact on an isolated community that has not been exposed to tourism than a large number of tourists in an established destination. Conversely, mass tourism in a self-contained club resort may have relatively little impact on the socio-cultural character of the country in which it is located although, as is often the case, such resorts may cause resentment amongst local people who feel that they are unable to benefit economically from tourists (Freitag, 1994).

However, all-inclusive resorts may in fact provide substantial socio-economic benefits. For example, in addition to meeting substantial demand for all-inclusive holidays (i.e. tourists who seek safe, luxurious holidays in an exotic location), the resorts on the island of Jamaica collectively generate the largest contribution to GDP on the island whilst, in terms of employment, they create relatively more jobs than conventional hotels. For example, research has shown that 5-star all-inclusives create between 1.5 and 2 jobs per room compared with 1 job per room in a conventional hotel. At Sandals Resorts in particular, staff are relatively well paid and benefit from free meals and transport; it is claimed that they can save up to one third of their monthly salary. All line staff receive at least 120 hours of training each year and, in 2003, Sandals Montego Bay initiated a skills training centre for local school leavers. Additionally, Sandals established a Farmers Programme in 1996, under which local farmers were encouraged to supply produce to the resorts. By 2004, 80 farmers were supplying hotels across the island and total annual sales had risen to US$0.3 million. Local craft producers are also able to sell their products to tourists within the resorts whilst, finally, it is important to note that, with the exception of those in Cuba, all Sandals resorts are owned by the original Jamaican company, limiting the problem of profit-repatriation associated with other international hotel chains (Issa & Jayawardena, 2003; see also Naidoo & Sharpley, 2016, for a discussion of enclave tourism in Mauritius).

PLATE 12.1 Angkor Wat, Cambodia: Cultural heritage threatened by tourist numbers

Source: Photo by Richard Sharpley

Importance of the tourism industry

The primary purpose of tourism development is, as we have seen, socio-economic growth and development. In those destinations where tourism is part of, or leads to, a mixed economy, the socio-cultural impacts of tourism are likely to be weaker or less widespread than in a country where tourism is the major industry. Where local communities become entirely dependent on tourism, the socio-cultural impacts of tourism are likely to be most keenly felt. Furthermore, diverse economies are more likely to be able to support and supply the local tourism industry, reducing the need for imports and spreading the socially beneficial impacts of employment and income generation.

Size and development of the tourism industry

In a similar vein to the degree of dependence on tourism, both the size of the tourism industry and its stage of development are important factors. A relatively large number of tourists in small communities will have greater impacts on local residents, whereas larger communities are likely to remain relatively unaffected by tourists. It is for this reason that a number of tourist destinations, such as the Seychelles, are adopting the policy of promoting themselves as up-market destinations, hoping to attract a smaller number of higher spending tourists. The purpose of this is to reduce the potential negative impacts of tourism whilst maintaining the economic benefits to the destination. It must also be remembered that the stage of tourism development in a destination will determine the degree of socio-cultural impact; established resorts will experience less continuing change than a newer destination.

The pace of tourism development

Many tourist destinations have experienced the rapid and relatively uncontrolled development of tourism. In such cases, the socio-cultural impacts of tourism are likely to be greater than in countries or destinations which undertake a slow and controlled tourism development programme. In principle, therefore, local communities should be allowed to gradually adapt to the needs and benefits of tourism and tourists rather than having to undergo a process of rapid upheaval and change.

All tourism destinations are different and the influence of these factors in determining the degree to which the socio-cultural impacts of tourism are experienced is also variable. Nor are such impacts restricted to developing countries or international tourism in general, although much of the literature concentrates on these areas. For example, the local communities in many rural, coastal and urban tourism destinations in Britain are affected to some degree by domestic tourists. Overall, however, the level of impact in a tourism destination will result from the 'interaction between the nature of the change agent and the inherent strength and ability of the host culture to withstand, and absorb, the change generators whilst retaining its own integrity' (Ryan, 1991a: 148).

The implication is that the study of the socio-cultural impacts of tourism must be approached with some caution. It is inevitable that some change will occur as a result of tourism but such is the variety of factors influencing socio-cultural change that each case must be considered individually. For example, it would be logical to expect that the changes resulting from the development and growth of tourism in the Greek Cyclades islands would be relatively uniform but a study by Tsartas (1992) indicates otherwise. The islands of Ios and Serifos are similar in size, population and original socio-economic conditions but it was found that, owing to different types of tourism development (mass-charter tourism on Ios, moderate and controlled tourism on Serifos), different socio-cultural impacts were experienced on each island. The speed with which tourism had been developed, the length of time over which development had occurred and a variety of economic and political factors also played a role in determining the perceived socio-cultural impacts on each island.

Tourism as an agent of socio-cultural change

When visible and identifiable social and cultural changes occur in regions or countries which have adopted a policy of tourism development, it is frequently tourism, as opposed to other factors, that is seen to be the cause of such change. Also, the socio-cultural consequences of tourism are generally perceived to be negative, in particular in the context of tourism development in less developed countries which, rightly or wrongly, may be considered more susceptible to Western influences. Yet, whilst there is little doubt that tourism can bring about changes which may both benefit host communities and be viewed as a 'cost', it is important to point out that, in most cases, tourism contributes to social and cultural change rather than being the cause of such change.

All societies and cultures are changing and, as a global, homogeneous culture emerges (see Chapter 3), no society is immune from outside influence. For example, there are very few communities which do not have access to a television and, hence, images of other countries and cultures. The activities of multinational corporations, internationalising Western culture (for example, McDonald's in Moscow, Kentucky Fried Chicken in Beijing), are catalysts of social change, whilst many countries are undergoing a process of industrialisation, urbanisation and rapid population growth which, potentially, have a far greater impact than tourism on social and cultural structures and values. As Smith (1989a: 9) points out, 'culture change, in the form of modernisation, has made impressive inroads into the backward areas and the poverty pockets of the globe, and the process is both ongoing and accelerating'. She goes on to conclude, in her study of Inuit tourism in Alaska (Smith, 1989b: 75), that it is the effort of the government to improve housing, education, medical care and infrastructure, rather than the growth of tourism, which has been the key element in bringing about modernisation and cultural change.

Frequently, little effort is made to distinguish the effects of tourism from other cultural changes occurring globally and it would seem that, owing to the highly visible nature of tourism and tourists, the development of tourism has become a scapegoat for socio-cultural change (Crick, 1989). It is important, therefore, to recognise the dynamic character of all societies and cultures and to consider the potential socio-cultural impacts of tourism against this background. It is also important to set the parameters within which the impacts of tourism are assessed. In other words, impact studies often display what Wood (1980: 562) describes as a 'western ethnocentrism and romanticism', a bias which, linked with the concept of postmodernity (see Chapter 3), assumes that it is better to preserve cultures which are traditional or pre-modern rather than allowing them to develop or modernise. Thus, tourism developments which, from the Western point of view, 'threaten' the social and cultural characteristics of many destinations are perceived as negative impacts although it is quite possible that local communities support such changes. Within the study of the socio-cultural impacts of tourism, it is necessary 'to go beyond evaluations based on Western romantic ideals of cultural preservation to analyse the precise components of cultural change' (Wood, 1980: 565) and to assess the extent to which tourism is one of these components.

The social impacts of tourism

Although the social and cultural effects of tourism are linked and distinctions may be difficult to identify (Lea, 1988: 62), for convenience they are divided here under separate headings. The social impacts of tourism, those which have a more immediate and visible effect on destination communities and, to an extent, on tourists themselves, may also be sub-divided into impacts resulting from the development of a tourism industry and the impacts of tourist-host interaction.

Social consequences of tourism development

Tourism is normally planned and developed as a source of income and foreign exchange, thereby providing the resources for social and economic development within destination communities. The actual economic costs and benefits of tourism development, such as the generation of income and the multiplier effect, are widely discussed in the literature (for example, see Dwyer *et al.*, 2010; Tisdell, 2013); here we are concerned with the social consequences of these costs and benefits. Generally, 'tourism creates new opportunities in the formal and informal sectors of the economy, new criteria of social status, and contributes to changes in such basic social institutions as the family' (Harrison, 1992b: 22). A number of more specific positive and negative effects are identifiable:

Improvements in the quality of life

In many instances the development of tourism results, directly and indirectly, in improvements in the quality of life of local communities in destination areas. In less developed areas, basic infrastructural improvements required by tourism, such as roads and transport links, communication and information links, the supply of power, clean water, sewage disposal systems and so on may all be of benefit to local communities, whilst facilities and amenities provided for tourists in both new and established resorts also represent general social improvements. For example, the income from tourism frequently supports a wider range of shops, restaurants, theatres and other facilities which are of equal benefit to local communities.

The development of tourism can also lead to an improvement of the physical environment, supporting the conservation and renovation of traditional buildings or environmental improvement programmes. More generally, tourism should, at least in theory, lead to greater investment in education, health and other social services to benefit the community as a whole, although this is not always the case.

Frequently, however, the growth of tourism is not matched by social improvements for local communities. It is generally accepted that jobs in tourism, other than management positions, tend to be low paid, low status and, frequently, seasonal. This is certainly the case in many beach resorts; for example, locals employed as waiters, bar tenders and other similar jobs in hotels in The Gambia earn barely enough to cover their travelling expenses and the work is seasonal.

It is also interesting to consider the employment situation in many post-industrial cities, such as Glasgow, where tourism is being promoted as one of the primary ways of transforming the city from a manufacturing to a service-based economy. Many of Glasgow's unemployed people used to work in shipbuilding or heavy engineering and it is difficult to consider jobs in tourism as suitable alternative employment (see Damer, 1990). Tourism can also result in inflated land and house prices, extensive second-home ownership (Hall & Müller, 2004), inflation and loss of services as, for example, local shops convert to more profitable souvenir outlets.

Changes in the role of women

In many traditional societies, the role of women, particularly younger women, has been strictly governed and defined by social, religious and economic constraints. Indeed, the apparent male domination of many societies is plainly evident to tourists visiting many countries in the developing world. Nevertheless, the employment opportunities offered by tourism have gone a long way to reducing women's economic dependency on the family, representing a new freedom which, although putting strains on the traditional family structure and challenging broader social values, has improved the social condition for many women (see, more generally, Kinnaird & Hall, 1994; Sinclair, 1997). For example, Reynoso y Valle and de Regt (1979: 130) found that the development of tourism opened up a range of job opportunities for women outside the home, challenging the traditional position and machismo of the Mexican male. In other cases, the improved status of women need not necessarily lead to family or social stress. In Cyprus, where the rapid growth of tourism since independence in 1960 created a large number of new jobs (by the early 2000s, tourism accounted for some 25 percent of all employment in Cyprus, although this proportion has declined in more recent years), 'the improved financial status of females did not create conflicts between parents and children and husbands or wives, nor did it challenge the authority of the parents or husbands' (Andronikou, 1979: 249). It has to be added that, under the Cypriot constitution, women enjoy equal rights and many senior positions are currently held by women.

Tourism has also opened up opportunities for women in what may be described as the informal employment sector. In most tourist destinations, particularly in the developing world, the growth of tourism is accompanied by an increase in the number of people who work in unofficial jobs, such as fruit sellers, beach hawkers, garment manufacturers and, perhaps the most emotive subject of all, as prostitutes in the flourishing 'sex tourism' destinations, such as Thailand and the Philippines (Bauer & McKercher, 2003; Clift & Cater, 2000; Ryan & Hall, 2001). This issue is considered in greater detail later in this chapter but there is no doubt that tourism, in both the formal and informal employment sectors, is largely dependent on women. The extent to which this has improved the social status of women varies from society to society; for example, in Bali, 'women are central to the culture, and are indispensable to tourism. Without them the industry would collapse' (Osborne, 1993: 11) whereas, in many other countries around the world, the status of women in the industry is still subordinate to that of their male colleagues.

Changes in community structure

The development of tourism can result in a number of changes in the structure and cohesion of local communities in destination areas with, again, developing countries being most susceptible. The lure or attraction of working in the tourism industry, offering not only employment but the opportunity to meet foreign visitors, draws many younger people to tourist development areas. This has resulted in increased rural-urban migration, a phenomenon which, although not directly caused but nevertheless exacerbated by tourism, leaves many rural areas with a disproportionately aged population and a lack of younger people to continue working in traditional agricultural businesses. Within resort areas it tends to be the younger generations who desire the upward social mobility offered by involvement in tourism and studies have shown that tourism tends to accentuate class differences, polarising local populations and creating a new younger, more prosperous group, perhaps with a broader, less traditional approach than the older generations.

The social impacts of tourist-host interaction

It is inevitable that the physical presence of tourists and their behaviour in tourist resorts and destinations will have some form of impact on local communities. Some of these impacts may be immediate, such as inappropriate behaviour, displays of conspicuous consumption or simply the inconvenience and nuisance caused by large numbers of holiday-makers who may have little or no intention of meeting with or getting to know members of the local population (see Chapter 11). Other effects may be more gradual, such as the local community adopting the behaviour, attitudes or moral codes of visitors through a process of acculturation. Most of the literature on the social impacts of tourism concentrates on the impacts of tourists on host populations but, socially and culturally, tourism is a two-way process. That is, although the physical flows of tourism are largely typified by the annual mass migration from northern Europe to the Mediterranean or, more generally, from the modern, developed nations to lesser developed or developing countries, it does not necessarily imply that the social effects of tourism also flow in one direction.

Relatively few attempts have been made to explore how local cultures and people may impact on visitors; within the tourism literature there is a noticeable lack of research into tourist-host encounters from the point of view of tourists. In one sense, crimes against tourists, such as pick-pocketing or mugging, fall into the category of impacts on tourists, although this is normally considered a result of tourism development in the destination. Tourists are also sometimes the target of politically motivated activities. Since the advent of modern, mass travel, particularly to more remote destinations, there have been a number of well-publicised incidents where tourists have been attacked, kidnapped or murdered by terrorists or other groups for political ends. Notable examples of this include the massacre at Luxor in Egypt in 1998, the kidnap and subsequent death of tourists in The Yemen, also in 1998, and the murder of eight tourists in Uganda in March 1999 and the Bali bombings in 2002 whilst, more recently, the attack on visitors to the Bardo Museum in Tunis (22 deaths) and the massacre of tourists on the beach in at Port El Kantaoui (38 deaths), both in Tunisia in 2015, had a major impact on the country's tourism sector. The link between tourism and politics is explored in the literature (Elliott, 1997; Hall, 1994; Matthews & Richter, 1991), as is the more specific relationship between tourism and terrorism (Pizam & Mansfeld, 1996; Richter & Waugh, 1986; Ryan, 1991b; Sönmez, 1998).

It is also not uncommon for tourists to contract minor, usually stomach, ailments whilst abroad and, as greater numbers of tourists travel to more distant, exotic locations, the incidence of more serious illnesses is on the increase. For example, between 2001 and 2006, there were a total of 10,889 cases of malaria in the UK, with 58 people dying from the disease (Smith, 2007). Interestingly, it has also been reported that a number of 'old' diseases, such as diphtheria, which have been virtually eradicated in Western societies, are now spreading as a result of tourism to previously inaccessible areas (see Clift & Grabowski, 1997). Similarly, evidence indicates that tourism has caused an increase in cases of typhoid in the UK – in 2006, there were 248 cases, 122 of which were contracted overseas (Smith, 2007). The SARS outbreak in 2003 was also a dramatic example of how international tourism can lead to the rapid and global spread of disease. Both crime and health problems are common reverse impacts of tourism although, more typically, they are considered to be two of the risks of participating in tourism. Nevertheless, it is possible to identify a number of other ways in which local communities impact on visitors in a socio-cultural sense.

It is highly likely that fashions and tastes have become internationalised partly, if not solely, as a result of tourism. The multi-ethnic character of many populations and the influence of the media also play a significant role, but there is little doubt that overseas travel goes some way to reducing what may be described as cultural xenophobia in tourism generating countries.

For example, international cuisine, clothing styles and music are now more widely accepted in Britain than some years ago. Local host communities may also impact on tourists in terms of adapting, for better or for worse, the attitudes and perceptions of visitors towards host societies and cultures. For example, in a study of young, British tourists visiting Greece and Morocco, Pearce (1982: 89) found that the tourists saw the Greeks as more religious and less affluent than expected and Moroccans were poorer and more greedy and mercenary than expected. In both cases, the study revealed that tourists returned home with a more positive attitude towards their own country, a finding which implies that an exploration of possible changes in tourists' perceptions of their own society and culture as a result of overseas travel remains a fruitful research topic.

It is important to note that the impact of local people on tourists is dependent on the nature of the encounter. In a study of Greek tourists visiting Turkey, Anastasopoulos (1992) concluded that the negative attitude of the Greeks towards their hosts derived largely from the organised, packaged nature of the tour and the role of the tour guides. This study, along with those by Milman *et al.* (1990) and Pizam *et al.* (1991) also found that there is little empirical evidence to support the view that tourism can lead to greater understanding and harmony and that, in certain circumstances, host communities have a negative impact on visitor perceptions.

A further aspect of socio-cultural impacts on tourists is the way in which tourists adapt their behaviour as a result of encounters with local people. It would be logical to propose that the more contact a tourist has with local people, the less institutionalised the setting and the stronger the local culture, the more likely is the tourist to become acclimatised or 'acculturated'. For example, it is accepted that longer-term independent travellers undergo a period of culture shock when first travelling but that they gradually adapt to their new environment, often to the extent that they find it difficult to re-adjust to their own home culture and society when they return (Furnham, 1984). In some cases, cultural characteristics of the destination society, such as the religion, might be adopted on a permanent basis by the tourist. Again, research is required to explore the two-way nature of the socio-cultural effects of tourism but, generally, it is still local communities which 'suffer' social impacts of tourism to a greater extent. These impacts are manifested in a variety of ways:

The demonstration effect

One of the most visible and common social impacts of tourism, in particular in the context of tourism to less developed or poorer countries, is the introduction of alien values and ways of life into relatively traditional or isolated societies. As a result, local communities begin to adapt and change their own values and modes of behaviour, often in an attempt to emulate those of tourists, in a process known as the demonstration effect.

Up to a point, such a process is inevitable. Whilst on holiday, tourists demonstrate levels of affluence that are usually beyond the reach of local people, affluence which may be apparent simply because tourists can afford to travel in the first place. Frequently, they also display their relative wealth by their styles of dress, the camera or other technological equipment they carry with them or by indulging in conspicuous consumption. Such displays of wealth may often lead to resentment amongst local communities, particularly if they believe that they will be unable to achieve a similar level of affluence themselves. This resentment might be increased by the symbols of tourist development, such as expensive hotels or tourist zones, beaches or clubs which are 'off limits' to local people, and by the behaviour of tourists who do not respect local morals and customs. For example, the development of tourism on the island of Phuket in Thailand caused considerable local resentment, especially with respect to the 'privatisation' of public beaches, and led to the formation of the Phuket Environmental Protection Group to fight for the preservation of the remaining undeveloped beaches (Rattachumpoth, 1992). It is also likely that local people, in particular the younger generations, will begin to question and challenge local custom and tradition and will begin to strive for the material and financial affluence so openly displayed by tourists.

At a basic level, this demonstration effect may be manifested by local people adopting Western styles of dress and indulging in types of behaviour that lead to increasing polarisation between the older and younger generations. With the advance and spread of information and communication technology and the influence of mass, international media, such a process is, perhaps, inevitable and is merely accelerated by tourism. However, regular displays of wealth may entice people to work in the tourism or other service industries or, of greater consequence to host societies, migrating to the tourism generating countries. One way of achieving this is by befriending tourists in the hope of achieving an invitation to visit, offers of financial support or, in the extreme, permanent relationships. For example, in the early days of its tourism development, The Gambia was particularly popular amongst single, middle-aged Scandinavian women. In some cases, relationships between female tourists and local men became more permanent, occasionally resulting in marriage, and a number of couples returned to Scandinavia. Similarly, in other countries, such as Thailand and the Philippines, it is recognised that younger females often view Western male tourists as potential tickets to a better life and become involved in relationships as a means of migrating abroad.

Thus, the demonstration effect can lead to a number of social impacts in destination communities. On a positive note it may result in economic and social development within the community by encouraging people to work for things they lack but, more commonly, it can amplify the financial and moral gap between generations. It can encourage behaviour that undermines or challenges traditional values whilst advancing the spread of Western, cultural homogenisation, and it may disrupt the social structure of local communities as younger people move to urban centres, tourism development areas or abroad to tourism generating countries. More generally, it can also lead to local communities developing inaccurate, stereotypical attitudes towards tourists based upon their observations of behaviour which itself is usually untypical, freed as tourists are from the social constraints and rules of everyday life.

Crime

The association between travel and tourism and crime is not a new phenomenon; throughout the centuries travellers had to endure not only slow and uncomfortable travelling conditions but also the regular attention of people anxious to divest them of their belongings. Crime has also been an accepted feature of tourism in some countries for many years, such as in Italy where people on motorbikes snatch handbags from unsuspecting pedestrians (Country Reports, n.d.; Johnston, 2005). However, there has been increasing publicity about tourism-linked crime, such as that following the murder of a number of tourists in Florida in 1993 and 1994 and, in more recent times, the sexual assault of female tourists in India, whilst tourists in Cancun, Mexico are considered to be highly susceptible to criminal activity (Agren, 2017).

Although there is little evidence to directly link an increase in crime with the development of tourism, there is no doubt that where there are tourists in any significant numbers there will also be people attempting to benefit illegally from the presence of those tourists (Pizam, 1999; see Pizam & Mansfeld, 1996 for a broad treatment of tourism and crime issues). One early study found a positive connection between tourism and the level of crime in Florida, noting that the incidence of crime rose during the main tourist season (McPheters & Stronge, 1974), whilst Wall and Mathieson (2006: 244–248), in a review of existing literature, concluded that there is a positive correlation between crime and tourism. It would be logical to suggest that this link exists because, to local members of the criminal fraternity, tourists represent easy pickings. Not only are they in unfamiliar surroundings, but they will also often be carrying large amounts of money, credit cards, expensive cameras, mobile phones, laptop computers, and so on. Also, in some countries, British and other passports are a valuable commodity on the black market. Thus, the potential gain for thieves may be high and, as Wall and Mathieson (2006) point out, the risk of detection is often low.

In addition to criminal activities which are directed against individual tourists, other illegal activities may also thrive as a result of tourism. For example, in those countries where the official exchange rate overvalues the local currency, it is not unusual for black markets in currency exchange to exist, offering tourists far higher rates than available legally. Other illegal activities may include gambling, trading in counterfeit goods and so on. For local societies in destination areas, the impacts of tourism-related crime are increased expenditure on law enforcement during the tourist season, financial loss as a result of fraud and black market dealings and, potentially, a fall in the number of tourist arrivals should a resort gain an unfavourable reputation for criminal activities, such as theft or mugging.

It should be noted that it is not always tourists who are the victims of crime (Ryan 1991a: 159); often, it may be tourists themselves who commit crimes or become involved in illegal activities. This might be simply violent or drunken behaviour, resulting in a fine or a short term in prison, but tourists also engage in more serious crimes, such as drug smuggling, which in some countries can result in long jail sentences and in others, a potential death sentence.

Language

In most tourist-host encounters, language is the primary means of communication. More generally, language is also a significant cultural characteristic of any society and tourism can have both immediate and longer-term impacts on host communities. This is most likely to occur in larger, more established tourist destinations which attract mass tourists. In this situation local people are, in effect, obliged to learn and use the language of the dominant nationality of visitors in order to be able to deal and communicate with visitors on either a commercial or personal basis. Thus, most local people in Spanish tourist resorts who regularly come into contact with tourists speak English and in the Turkish resort of Alanya, German is widely spoken.

It is not only through commercial necessity that foreign languages may be adopted or, in the case of some more isolated areas, that local dialects or languages begin to die out. The demonstration effect may result in local people wanting to learn the language of tourists and, either intentionally or unintentionally, adopting their mannerisms. Similarly, visitors may learn foreign languages or adopt local accents. For example, longer-stay British visitors in the United States frequently develop an American 'twang' in their speech. In more remote areas where the traditional, indigenous language is not widely spoken or only popular amongst the older generations, tourism may represent a threat to the very existence of that language. Thus, Brougham and Butler (1981) found that many local people on the Isle of Skye in Scotland felt that tourism was a major factor in the diminishing use of Gaelic, mainly as a result of increasing second-home ownership and the influx of seasonal workers from the mainland. Conversely, the impact of tourism on language may represent a benefit to local people, resulting in more job opportunities for those who learn a second language or become multi-lingual.

Religion

Traditionally, religion was a major motivating factor of travel and tourism (see Chapters 2 and 8) and even nowadays a significant proportion of domestic and international tourism is for religious or spiritual purposes. According to the UNWTO (2014), for example, well over 300 million tourist visits are made to the world's main religious sites each year whilst the annual number of pilgrimage trips worldwide is conservatively estimated to total 155 million (ARC, 2011). Since the advent of modern mass tourism, the relationship between tourism and religion has undergone a fundamental transformation, as the majority of tourist visits to religious shrines, holy cities, temples, cathedrals, churches and other symbols or centres of religion are no longer for purely spiritual purposes. In other words, religion has become a commodity, a tourism product, and religious festivals or buildings have become spectacles to be gazed upon and collected along with other sights and attractions. As a result, in many destinations there has been increasing conflict between local communities, devout visitors and tourists. For example, simply the physical presence of large and often noisy groups of tourists who, frequently, take photographs of religious festivals or people worshipping with little consideration for the participants is a common and widespread problem. Visits to monasteries, religious retreats and centres of learning may also disrupt the lives of the inhabitants; even in Bhutan, where the number of tourists has until recently been strictly controlled, the authorities were compelled to prohibit tourists from visiting certain Buddhist monasteries as they were disturbing the monks.

Another situation where conflict may arise is where the traditional importance or meaning of religious rites or practices are not recognised, understood or respected by tourists. For example, in India, tourists frequently attempt to take photographs of the 'burning ghats', places alongside the River Ganges in Varanasi where deceased Hindus are cremated, thereby causing great offence to local people. In extreme cases, disrespect for local religious custom may have severe consequences, such as tourists being physically attacked for taking photographs in temples or churches where it is forbidden.

Whilst it is easy to blame tourists for impacting upon local religious custom and practice, they themselves are often exploited by religious institutions, usually as a source of revenue. In some churches or cathedrals, collection boxes are often strategically placed near entrances and it is not uncommon to find book shops, souvenir stalls or even tea shops and restaurants located in religious buildings. In other cases, religious buildings have adopted a clearly definable dual purpose, separating their traditional function as a place of worship from their attraction to tourists and, hence, their earning potential. For example, entrance to a side chapel at St. Paul's Cathedral in London is free for worshippers, whereas entrance charges are levied on tourists visiting other parts of the building, including the crypt and the Whispering Gallery. Similarly, charges have been introduced for tourists wishing to visit Westminster Abbey. It may be argued that tourists are being taken advantage of and that the fundamental meaning and purpose of the building is being abused, but tourism represents a significant source of income for essential repair and maintenance work. In this sense, the relationship between tourism and religion is positive inasmuch as tourism is contributing towards the preservation of a building which is of religious, architectural and national importance (see Bates, 1994 for a consideration of the problems facing Westminster Abbey as both place of worship and a major tourist attraction in London).

Prostitution

One of the most emotive and publicised social impacts of tourism on destination countries, especially in the developing world, is the alleged effect it has on moral behaviour in general, and prostitution in particular. Cities such as Bangkok in Thailand and Manila in the Philippines have gained reputations for being the sex capitals of the world, an image that has undoubtedly been reinforced by media attention and the availability of 'sex tours' that are openly advertised in some tourist generating countries. There is also no doubt that it is this image that draws many male Western tourists to these destinations.

Prostitution as a tourist 'attraction' is not limited to south-east Asian countries. Amsterdam's red-light district has long been a tourist sight, London's Soho is famous for its sex shows and, as Ryan (1991a: 163) points out, the legalised brothels of Nevada are widely advertised in tourist centres such as Las Vegas. Indeed, virtually every major town and city around the world, whether or not a tourist destination, has a red-light area. It is difficult to assess the extent to which tourism has led directly to an increase in prostitution and, frequently, the role of tourism in this context is overstated. On the one hand, the development of tourism creates the conditions under which prostitution may thrive; tourists have temporarily left the restrictions of their own society and may be willing to indulge in activities which they would not normally consider at home (see Chapter 5). Also, they are assured of anonymity, they may be willing to spend freely and, more generally, sex (the fourth 'S' after Sun, Sea and Sand) has been both an implicit and explicit part of tourism advertising for many years. For example, the Seychelles were once promoted as islands of love (see Turner & Ash, 1975) and at one stage suffered from one of the highest rates of venereal disease in the world.

On the other hand, prostitution as a social impact of tourism must be considered in a broader context. For example, Thailand has a reputation as a 'sex tourism' destination (see Seabrook, 1996; Wall & Mathieson, 2006: 243) The clubs and bars of the Patpong area of Bangkok are frequented by tourists and in popular beach resorts, such as Phuket and Koh Samui, it is easy for Western visitors to find a Thai 'girlfriend' who will remain with them for the duration of their stay. Although the clubs of Bangkok undoubtedly depend on tourism for their business, and prostitution in beach resorts has certainly increased because of tourism, it has been estimated that, overall, there are up to one million Thai women who are involved in prostitution (Harrison, 1992b: 25). Of these, it has been alleged that only about 7 percent depend on overseas visitors, indicating that tourism has become the scapegoat for a wider social problem. The real cause of prostitution in Thailand possibly lies in the country's role as a rest and recreation centre for American soldiers during the Vietnam war, cultural norms and practices and, as is the case for most women who turn to prostitution, poverty. In countries without social welfare and with a social and cultural tradition which rejects unmarried mothers, prostitution may offer the only hope of survival. In this sense, and putting the wider moral issues to one side, tourism-related prostitution may actually be viewed as a benefit to those concerned.

The conclusion must be that, generally, tourism does not actually cause prostitution but contributes to it, although there are extreme cases, such as young boys in Sri Lanka being forced into male prostitution, where the link is more direct. At the same time, as many studies demonstrate (Bauer & McKercher, 2003; Opperman, 1998; Ryan & Hall, 2001; Shaw & Williams, 2000), the link between tourism and the commercial sex industry, and its impacts risk, are complex; that is, broad generalisations about the cause/effect of sex tourism cannot be made. Nevertheless, it is important to emphasise that the social impact may be devastating, particularly with the spread of AIDS and other sexually transmitted diseases. Equally, as Wall and Mathieson (2006: 244) observe, greater understanding of a number of related issues is required, including:

- the sociological issues of denying human rights through forced prostitution, child exploitation and the commercialisation of women;
- the conflict between religious laws and the existence of red-light districts;
- the impacts of prostitution on traditional family structures.

Overall, it may be hoped that the publicity surrounding sex tourism and prostitution, especially in developing countries, will highlight the wider social problems in those countries and lead to greater controls but, at the same time, sex tourism represents the darker side of tourism-induced exploitation of people and their culture.

The cultural impacts of tourism

Many of the impacts of tourism on host destinations and societies are relatively immediate, affecting family and social structures, gender roles, moral behaviour and so on. Over time, the culture of host societies may also change and adapt either directly or indirectly as a result of tourism. Much of the literature concentrates on the way in which cultural forms, such as arts and crafts or animate expressions of culture (such as carnivals, festivals, religious events and historical re-enactments) change as a result of tourism-related commoditisation (see Chapter 9). For example, traditional art forms and techniques may be trivialised and become mass produced for the tourist market, whilst tourism may be responsible for the transformation of cultural events into commercialised, staged spectacles which are devoid of all cultural meaning to the participants. Equally, tourism can provide both the impetus and the financial support for the preservation or revitalisation of traditional cultural practices. One of the principles of sustainable tourism development is that tourism should contribute to the conservation of local culture by, for example, designing and constructing buildings in the vernacular style using traditional materials and methods.

Artefacts, music, festivals and other practices are only symbols and expressions of culture, or cultural products. That is, the true culture of a society refers to its values and norms, its actual identity. It indicates the meanings people attach to different social institutions, such as education, religion, work and leisure, and, in effect, a society's culture is its way of life. All cultures and societies, unless totally isolated from the outside world, are constantly changing and developing, both as a result of changes within society and from outside influences. Internal economic, social and environmental developments within a society may be reflected in broader, cultural change, whilst international communication and information systems, advances in transport technology and a whole host of other factors have contributed to a sharing and dissemination of national cultures around the world. This has been manifested, in particular, in the spread of Western culture, or what has been referred to as the 'coca-colonisation' of the world.

One such factor which has contributed to cultural change is international tourism, especially tourism to countries which, culturally, are significantly different from the tourism generating country. It is difficult to separate the influence of tourism from other factors which induce cultural change and, as a high-profile industry, it is frequently blamed for changes that are almost inevitable with or without the development of tourism. But it is generally accepted that tourism accelerates cultural change through the process of acculturation.

Tourism and acculturation

The theory of acculturation is that, when two different cultures come into contact, over time they will become more like each other through a process of borrowing (Nuñez, 1989). That is, each society, to a greater or lesser extent, will adopt the values and attitudes of the other. By implication, if one culture is stronger or more dominant than the other, then it is more likely that the borrowing process will be one way. The extent to which this will occur is also dependent on a variety of other factors, such as relative social and economic characteristics, the nature of the meeting, and the numbers of people involved. Thus, tourism, as an economic activity based upon interaction between different societies and cultures, inevitably results in some form of acculturation.

In many instances, tourism induced acculturation may be slight and impossible to differentiate from broader cultural change. Thus, tourism between Europe and North America has little cultural impact when compared with the influence of television, the Internet and the steady drift of American culture across the Atlantic. In other situations, tourism may be the dominant factor in cultural change, particularly in relatively isolated, developing countries. For example, since the early 1960s, when it became a popular destination for travellers on the Europe to India overland trail, Nepal has become a mainstream tourist destination on the subcontinent (although the area in Kathmandu where the 1960s 'hippies' found lodgings is still known as 'Freak Street'). From just 6,000 arrivals in 1962, in 2016 around 750,000 tourists visited the country; of these, only 66,500 (8.9 percent) go on treks in the mountains (Government of Nepal, 2016). Although the largest markets for tourism to Nepal are, unsurprisingly, India and China, much of the visible Westernisation of Kathmandu has resulted directly from tourism (see Liechty, 2005).

The degree of acculturation experienced by a destination society depends on a variety of factors. Different types of tourists have different expectations, demands and motivations and, generally, acculturation is directly linked with the nature of tourist-host encounters (see Chapter 11). When such encounters are minimal or non-existent, such as when local populations are shielded from tourist resorts, then acculturation will also be limited. For example, most of the tourism development at Monastir on the Tunisian coast is in the *Zone Touristique*; there is little contact between tourists and nearby villages with the result that, in comparison with the tourist towns of Monastir and Sousse, there is little evidence of Western culture. Moreover, where tourism is predominantly organised and institutionalised, the level, type and duration of contact between tourists and local people and, hence, the potential for acculturation, is often in the hands of culture brokers. These may be tour operators, tour guides, translators or local representatives of holiday companies, all of whom act as mediators between tourists and local people. As Wall and Mathieson (2006: 269) explain, by controlling tourist-host encounters they may also play a positive role in minimising the social and cultural impacts of tourism.

Tourism and cultural dependency

In the extreme, the cultural impact of tourism may result in the situation where the destination society becomes culturally dependent on the tourism generating country (see Erisman, 1983), the difference between this and acculturation being the degree of control exercised by the local community. In other words, the implication of acculturation is that the cultural transformation of a society may be conscious or subconscious but it is, nevertheless, voluntary. Conversely, cultural dependency is an involuntary condition, where the culture of a host society is 'so conditioned by and so reflects the expansion of an external culture that there is a dominant/subordinate relationship between the cultural centre . . . and the cultural periphery' (Erisman, 1983: 342). It results from economic and political dependency, a situation that has emerged in some developing countries which have come to be increasingly reliant on tourism, and represents foreign control over the cultural development of society. In a sense, cultural dependency signifies the final stage in the process of tourism-related neo-colonialism, the final abdication of the control of a tourism destination's economic, social and cultural future into the hands of a foreign country. Though not widespread, some destinations in the West Indies have, according to Erisman (1983), become culturally dependent on the United States.

Managing the socio-cultural impacts of tourism

As tourism has developed in more and more countries around the world (in fact, few if any countries are not now tourism destinations) and as tourism has become more widely depended upon as a driver of economic growth and development, increasing attention has been paid to the impacts of tourism on the society and culture of host populations. Academics, researchers, pressure groups and the tourism industry itself have long been concerned about the negative effects of tourism and, since the 1980s, new, alternative forms of tourism have been suggested to minimise these impacts. Initially, these new forms of tourism were proposed specifically as alternatives to mass tourism which, during the 1990s, became widely condemned as destructive force; indeed, it was claimed that, to be sustainable, tourism should follow strategies other than mass tourism development (Pigram, 1990). Since the early 1990s, of course, and as discussed in Chapter 10, sustainable tourism development has become the buzz word of tourism; that is, development that respects the environment, optimises benefits to tourists and to local communities and which minimises harmful effects on the tourism environment (Sharpley & Telfer, 2015; Telfer & Sharpley, 2016). Even when appropriate policies exist, however, these may be ignored (Plate 12.2).

In principle is difficult to argue against the logic and objectives of sustainable tourism development although, as suggested in Chapter 10 and elsewhere (Sharpley 2009b), it is unlikely to provide in practice any long-term solutions to the problems of mass tourism development. Indeed, there is much controversy about the effectiveness and practical worth of sustainable, alternative tourism in a world in which tourism continues its inexorable growth on a mass scale, whilst in recent years the residents of a number of popular destinations, notably Barcelona and Venice, have demonstrated against further growth in tourism. Similarly, in 2017 it was reported that the mayor of the Croatian city of Dubrovnik was seeking to cap daily visitor numbers at 4,000 to protect the heritage site (Morris, 2017). In other words, resistance to tourism's continuing growth is being increasingly demonstrated by the residents and authorities in destinations themselves.

Nevertheless, an increasing number of tourism organisations have embraced the concept of responsible or sustainable tourism in an effort to mitigate tourism's negative impacts. These vary from individual organisations or tour operators offering holidays

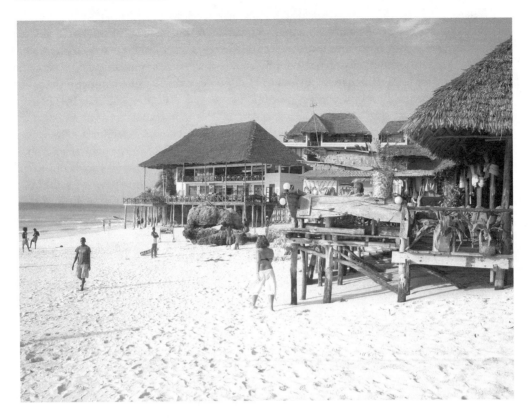

PLATE 12.2 Nungwi Beach, Zanzibar: Excessive development
Source: Photo by Richard Sharpley

that are designed to involve tourists in local community or environmental projects to local, community-run projects (Mann, 2000). There are also a number of schemes that involve groups of businesses in working towards sustainable tourism development, an early example being the ECOMOST project, established by the International Federation of Tour Operators, which sought to increase the sustainability of tourism in the Balearics (IFTO, 1994). Contemporary initiatives include:

a) The International Tourism Partnership (ITP): This developed from the successful International Hotels Environment initiative originally launched in 1992. For some 20 years it was a programme within the Prince of Wales' International Business Leaders Forum but is now hosted by Business in the Community, a British-based business community outreach charity promoting responsible business. ITP is made up of 18 corporate members that represent 23,000 properties and 1.5 million employees around the world, and seeks to promote and develop sustainable practices within the global hospitality sector.

b) Tour Operators' Initiative (TOI): Founded in 2000, the TOI was a voluntary, non-profit initiative open to all tour operators. In 2014 it merged with the Global

Sustainable Tourism Council (GSTC), an international organisation that has the aim of establishing and maintaining standards for sustainable tourism. With a diverse membership across the tourism sector, it establishes 'minimum requirements that any tourism business or destination should aspire to reach in order to protect and sustain the world's natural and cultural resources, while ensuring tourism meets its potential as a tool for conservation and poverty alleviation' (GSTC, 2015).

Other initiatives include the Global Partnership for Sustainable Tourism, a UN-backed initiative launched in 2011 that seeks to promote sustainable tourism practices around the world, and the Travel Foundation, a UK-based charity that works with outbound tour operators to manage tourism more sustainably in the destination (www.thetravel foundation.org.uk), a UK-based charity that works with outbound tour operators to manage tourism more sustainably in the destination. There also exists a number of businesses that market 'responsible' holidays; for example, Responsibletravel.com is an online travel agent that provides holidays 'for people who've had enough of mass tourism' (www.responsibletravel.com).

Generally, however, tourism development has been responsible for a variety of negative impacts around the world, some of which threaten entire ecosystems yet measuring them as a basis for their effective management is problematic. In other words, whilst it is relatively easy to measure or define physical or environmental impacts, applying concepts such as physical or ecological carrying capacity as the limits to development (see Coccossis & Mexa, 2004; O'Reilly, 1986), the same cannot be said for socio-cultural impacts. In other words, what are the yardsticks by which social and cultural change are measured, and what are the limits beyond which such change should be halted?

In one respect, any form of tourism which impacts upon the life of local communities beyond an agreeable or acceptable limit (from the point of view of the residents) can be said to have exceeded the destination's social carrying capacity. That is, the scale and type of tourism should, in theory, be restricted to that which optimises economic and social benefits to the local community without causing undue problems. When considering social and cultural change, however, impacts are too often judged according to the values of modern Western societies rather than against the actual needs of the communities in destination areas. Too often, a Western cultural arrogance dictates what is right or wrong for other societies and cultures, societies which should be allowed to benefit from tourism, to modernise, to enjoy the standards of health, education, transport and housing that are taken for granted in the developed world. Similarly, with respect to domestic tourism in the UK, for example, it is frequently the residents of towns and cities who try to impose their values on the residents of rural areas with little understanding for the needs of rural communities.

Tourism is a contradictory phenomenon (Crick, 1989). It depends upon an attractive environment, yet threatens to destroy it; it trivialises and commoditises cultural production, but can also preserve culture (see Grahn, 1991); it brings economic benefits to communities, yet it undermines traditional family and social structure; it provides opportunities for younger people, yet it polarises generations; it can lead to international understanding, yet it reinforces prejudices and international differences. By its very nature, tourism is a source of conflict and the imposition of the values of tourists, in defining the social and cultural limits for tourism development, does little to reduce that conflict. Tourism does have socio-cultural consequences which may be viewed as either positive or negative but the responsibility for assessing those impacts, for setting the limits of change, lies not with tourists or the tourism industry, but with host communities themselves. And as noted above, host communities are beginning to take on that responsibility.

Further reading

Hall, C.M. and Lew, A. (2009) *Understanding and Managing Tourism Impacts: An Integrated Approach*. Abingdon: Routledge.

This book, providing a detailed analysis of the consequences of tourism, includes a chapter on tourism's socio-cultural impacts followed by a chapter proposing an integrated approach to the effective management of such impacts.

Hickman, L. (2007) *The Final Call: In Search of the True Cost of our Holidays*. London: Eden Project Books.

Written by a journalist, this book offers an alternative, highly readable and challenging perspective on the social and cultural costs of tourism development.

Wall, G. and Mathieson, A. (2006) *Tourism: Change, Impacts and Opportunities*. Harlow: Pearson Education.

This book is an updated and revised version of Mathieson and Wall's seminal 1982 text *Tourism: Economic, Physical and Social Impacts*. Combining the original detailed analysis of tourism's impacts with additional sections addressing contemporary issues and challenges, the section on socio-cultural impacts remains the most comprehensive exploration of the subject.

Discussion topics

▶   In what circumstances can mass tourism development have fewer socio-cultural impacts on destination communities than alternative, smaller-scale forms of tourism?

▶   Should destination communities, as recipients of its economic benefits, be willing to accept or absorb the socio-cultural costs of tourism development?

▶   Is tourism simply a scapegoat for socio-cultural transformations that occur as a result of other factors, such as globalisation?

▶   Does the solution to tourism's socio-cultural impacts lie in the adoption of more responsible behaviour on the part of tourists?

13

Postscript
Tourism and society – towards the future

Predicting the future of any sphere of social or economic activity is fraught with difficulties. At best, a reasonable picture can be built up from the analysis of past trends, historical evidence, relevant current information and educated guesswork; at worst, it can amount to little more than crystal-ball gazing. Attempting to forecast future trends in tourism is no exception, although there has been no lack of attempts to do so (for example, Gössling *et al.*, 2009; Martin & Mason, 1987; Yoeman, 2011; 2012). Certainly, statistics which detail the historical growth in tourism arrivals, tourism flows and other information can be combined with relevant factors, such as demographic trends and changes in the supply of tourism, to provide a reasonably accurate idea of the shorter-term future. Nevertheless, accurate predictions require accurate information and it is generally accepted that, on a worldwide basis, tourism statistics tend to be of variable quality.

At the same time, tourism is a notoriously fickle business. It can be affected by exchange rate fluctuations, economic recessions in tourism generating countries, adverse political conditions in destination regions, wars, changes in taste or fashion, natural disasters and a host of other factors. Nevertheless, as highlighted in Chapter 10, international tourism has grown steadily since the 1960s; initially, such growth was quite spectacular although in more recent decades the annual growth rate in arrivals has been steadier. Thus, as can be seen from Table 13.1 (and from Table 1.1 in Chapter 1), over the longer term, tourism has proved to be relatively immune to short-term political and economic upheavals. In fact, only the events of 11 September 2001 ('9/11') and the impacts of the global economic crisis in 2008/09 resulted in worldwide negative growth in international arrivals and, on both occasions, growth resumed the following year. Nevertheless, other events and tragedies, such as the bombing in Bali in late 2002, the Indian Ocean tsunami in 2004 and, more recently, terrorist activity in North Africa and the Middle East, have had a more localised effect on tourist flows but, overall, tourism continues to demonstrate healthy growth worldwide.

Specifically, since 1980, the number of international tourism arrivals has grown at around 4 percent annually, a rate of growth which is forecast to continue well into the twenty-first century. Indeed, between 2005 and 2010 an annual growth rate of

TABLE 13.1 International tourist arrivals and receipts, 1950–2016

Year	Arrivals (million)	Receipts (US$bn)	Year	Arrivals (million)	Receipts (US$bn)
1950	25.3	2.1	2000	687.0	481.6
1960	69.3	6.9	2001	686.7	469.9
1965	112.9	11.6	2002	707.0	488.2
1970	165.8	17.9	2003	694.6	534.6
1975	222.3	40.7	2004	765.1	634.7
1980	278.1	104.4	2005	806.1	682.7
1985	320.1	119.1	2006	847.0	742.0
1990	439.5	270.2	2007	903.0	856.0
1991	442.5	283.4	2008	917.0	939.0
1992	479.8	326.6	2009	882.0	851.0
1993	495.7	332.6	2010	940.0	927.0
1994	519.8	362.1	2011	995.0	1,042.0
1995	540.6	410.7	2012	1,035.0	1,075.0
1996	575.0	446.0	2013	1,087.0	1,159.0
1997	598.6	450.4	2014	1,130.0	1,252.0
1998	616.7	451.4	2015	1,184.0	1,196.0
1999	639.6	465.5	2016	1,235.0	1,220.0

Source: adapted from UNWTO data

3.4 percent was achieved whilst more recently, the growth rate between 2010 and 2015 was 3.9 percent (UNWTO, 2016b). Moreover, that growth is forecast to continue. The World Tourism Organization has long predicted that, by 2020, annual international tourist arrivals will reach 1.6 billion – though current trends suggest this is over-optimistic – and 1.8 billion by 2030. These figures should, however, be treated with some scepticism as it assumes not only ever-increasing demand for international tourism (requiring a global increase in wealth and other factors), but also the ability of the travel and tourism industry (and the environment) to sustain such growth.

Generally, the World Tourism Organization has identified two sets of variables which will influence the way in which tourism develops into the future. These are market forces, or factors which include changes in the demand for and supply of tourism products and services, and exogenous variables, factors which although not directly connected with tourism can still have impact upon it. The latter group includes political, economic, legislative, technological and social trends. From a sociological perspective, there are factors identifiable in both sets of variables which will combine to influence the future direction and growth of tourism in both a domestic and an international context, and certain observations can be made.

Certainly, the demand for tourism in the major generating countries will be influenced by a variety of factors. Demographic and social trends, such as ageing populations, increasing numbers of single or childless households, couples having children later in life, the early retired and populations which enjoy greater levels of both free time and disposable income, will result in both the absolute numbers of tourists increasing and an increase in the number of holidays taken by individuals. Moreover, different types of tourism will be required. The increasingly important 'silver' or 'grey'; market (over 50 years of age, perhaps retired), for example, may have particular demands and need. Importantly, the present middle-aged and younger generations are those who have grown up with tourism. They are used to tourism, they do not see it as a luxury but as an essential feature of modern social life, and many are experienced tourists. Conversely, it might be argued that transformations in economic structures in general, and levels of disposable income in particular, combined with demographic changes, may in fact restrict the growth in demand for tourism. For example, in the UK there are ever-increasing levels of household debt whilst the cost of housing has also impacted severely on household disposable income. Along with changes in the tax system (to fund an increasingly ageing population) and less generous pensions in the future, these factors may mean that tourism may become less affordable, particularly if environmental taxes are added to the cost of travel.

There may also emerge a two-tier demand structure for tourism, namely, those who are content with the traditional, institutionalised type of package holiday, and those who demand a greater variety of destination and type of holiday. The latter may also become identified as the new type of environmentally aware tourists, 'good' tourists who demand sustainable tourism products although, as discussed in earlier chapters, this is more likely to result from the cultural (postmodern) values in tourism generating countries than from a genuine concern for the environment.

New tourism generating countries are also appearing on the world tourism map, both as a result of the industrialisation of some developing countries and the spread of democracy. The countries of Eastern Europe and the former Soviet Union, for example, are regarded as a valuable potential source of tourists; indeed, Russia has emerged as a significant tourist market and is becoming an increasingly 'valuable' source market in terms of tourist spending. It is China, however, that is currently having the greatest impact on international tourist flows. Having experienced annual average economic growth of around 10 percent since the early 1980s and with some 225 million households described (in wealth terms) as middle class (Economist, 2016: 2), China is now the world's largest source of international tourists who account for 20 percent of global tourist spending. Moreover, whilst 75 percent of UK residents and 46 percent of US residents currently hold passports, just 1.5 percent of 1.3 billion Chinese residents do so. Simply stated, the Chinese now have the time, money and freedom to travel *en masse*, and will continue to do so for the foreseeable future in ever-increasing numbers. Consequently, it is equally unsurprising that many destinations are targeting Chinese tourists although this is proving to bring both benefits and challenges to destinations popular with Chinese tourists (Cohen, 2017).

Along with China, other emergent economic powers in the Far East, such as Korea (now seventh in the word in terms of international tourist spending), Taiwan and

Thailand have joined Japan as major tourism generators, although much of the international travel generated is inter-regional. In other words, these new tourism generators are becoming tourist destinations in their own right and, consequently, the Asia and Pacific region has over the last two to three decades accounted for the largest growth in international arrivals. For example, between 1980 and 1990 the region achieved growth of about 10 percent per annum compared with less than 4 percent annual growth in Europe. And that growth has continued; in 2016, tourist arrivals in the Asia and Pacific region grew by 8.6 percent over the previous year and it is now the world's second most visited region, enjoying a 25 percent share of worldwide tourist arrivals. In contrast, in 2016 Europe's share of total international arrivals fell for the first time below 50 percent, indicating a fundamental transformation in global tourist flows. It should also be noted that, in addition to being the world's largest generator of international tourism, China is the fourth most popular destination, attracting more than 59 million international visitors in 2016. The great majority of these, however, originate from Hong Kong, Taiwan and Macao (all recent data from UNWTO, 2107).

The growth in tourism will be facilitated by increasing efficiency within the tourism industry, in particular within the context of air transport where technological advances in both aircraft and information/management systems will ensure that, subject to energy costs, prices will remain at a low level. As a result, international tourism is likely to be characterised by ever-increasing long-haul as well as intra-regional travel. The remarkable growth in the low-cost budget airline sector will, in particular, contribute to this trend, subject to political interventions in response to concerns over climate change. Over the last decade, many parts of Europe have been opened up to tourism by airlines such as EasyJet and Ryanair, and the budget airline phenomenon has now spread globally. Moreover, although low-cost airlines typically operate on short- to medium-haul routes, some budget airlines, such as Norwegian, have recently commenced flights to long-haul destinations, such as from London to Los Angeles.

There is optimism that tourism, as an economic activity, will maintain and strengthen its reputed position as the world's largest industry. However, that optimism must be tempered by the recognition that tourism, perhaps more importantly, is a social activity. Some societies generate tourism, others receive and depend on tourism and, therefore, the international travel and tourism industry depends on both the continuing desire of individuals to travel and the willingness of host societies to receive and absorb tourists in ever greater numbers. In other words, developments and changes in the structures and values of societies may influence future developments in tourism both positively and negatively. For example, globalisation is a double-edged sword; first, it may lead to greater homogenisation, integration and universalisation amongst the world's nations which, as discussed in Chapter 3, may result in either an increase or a decrease in tourism. Second, it may lead to a resurgence in nationalism and, perhaps, an eventual reaction against the inherently imperialistic nature of international tourism. Similarly, much of the tourism to destinations outside the developed, Western world depends upon and is motivated by the 'otherness', or the distinct social and cultural characteristics of those destinations. Maintaining those characteristics in order to remain attractive to tourists, those destinations may, in the extreme, become little more than 'living museums' satisfying the thirst of tourists for 'authentic' experiences. And third, as discussed elsewhere in this book, there is increasing evidence of destinations attempting to limit further growth in tourism. In 2016, for example, residents in cities such as Venice and Barcelona demonstrated against the incessant growth of tourism and the consequential decline in their quality of life whilst in 2017, the authorities in Dubrovnik proposed a significant reduction in tourist numbers (specifically, cruise tourists) to protect the city's fragile heritage. In short, international tourism may, in the longer term, achieve the opposite of its primary purpose of economic, technological and social modernisation and development in destination countries, whilst destinations themselves may increasingly resist further growth in tourism, despite its economic development potential.

At the same time, tourism will remain a fickle industry, susceptible to a variety of internal and external influences. As more distant, exotic destinations become popular, for example, the use of tourism and tourists for political ends may become more widespread. It is an unfortunate fact but, perhaps, no coincidence that a feature of international tourism in the late 1990s was an increasing incidence of terrorist attacks on tourists. During the early years of the twenty-first century this has, sadly, continued to be in evidence, most notably with the bombing of the Sari nightclub in Bali in October 2002, the Sharm-el-Sheikh bombings of May 2004 in Egypt and, in 2015, the massacre of international tourists on a beach in Tunisia.

Societal change in tourism generating countries may also influence the future development of tourism. For example, less than 100 years ago it was unfashionable to have a suntan. If fashions were to change once again, or concern about the cancer risks of sunbathing were to increase further, the impact on the traditional sun, sea and sand summer package business could be catastrophic. Changes in work practices and more flexible approaches to education, such as a change in the traditional three term and long summer holiday system of schooling, would be of benefit to tourists, the industry and destinations alike as the constraints of seasonality are removed. In a more general sense, the quality of life in modern, Western countries may improve to the extent that, as Krippendorf (1987) hopes, people will no longer feel the need to escape. Moreover, fashions may also change. In the UK in 2007, for example, it was reported that domestic caravanning was experiencing a surge in popularity. And of course, climate change may have a significant impact on future flows of tourism.

Equally, the development of technology, such as virtual reality (see Chapter 7), or the spread and acceptance of attractions such as the inland resort concept, such as Center Parcs, may prove to be a more enjoyable and relaxing experience than the 'actual reality' of tourism which is becoming increasingly characterised by crowds, delays, pollution, traffic jams, mass production and so on. Whatever the future holds for tourism, however, it is essential that knowledge about the interdependence between tourism and the societies that motivate, generate and receive tourists is increased and used to guide its future development to the benefit of all.

Further reading

A small number of texts consider the future of tourism. These include:

Yoeman, I. (2011) *Tomorrow's Tourist: Scenarios and Trends*. Abingdon: Routledge.

Yoeman, I. (2012) *2050: Tomorrow's Tourism*. Bristol: Channel View Publications.
Both of these texts provide thought-provoking future scenarios for tourism.

Journal of Tourism Futures (see: www.emeraldinsight.com/journal/jtf).
A relatively recent journal, launched in 2015, which publishes contemporary and challenging papers addressing the future of tourism.

Discussion topics

▶   Does tourism have a future?

▶   In the future, will tourism once again become the privilege of the élite?

▶   What does the history of tourism tell us about its future?

References

Abercrombie, N., Warde, A., Deem, R., Penna, S., Soothill, K., Urry, J. and Walby, S. (2000) *Contemporary British Society*. Cambridge: Polity Press.

Abram, S., Waldren, J. and Macleod, D. (ed.) (1997) *Tourists and Tourism: Identifying with People and Places*. Oxford: Berg.

ABTA (2015) Caution remains in 2014 but Brits expect to spend more on holidays in 2015. Association of British Travel Agents. Available at: https://abta.com/about-us/press/caution-remains-in-2014-but-brits-expect-to-spend-more-on-holidays-in-2015 (accessed 27 March 2017).

ABTA (2017) *Holiday Habits Report 2016*. Association of British Travel Agents. Available at: https://abta.com/assets/uploads/general/2016_Holiday_Habits_Report.pdf (accessed 6 October 2017).

Adams, W. (1990) *Green Development: Environment and Sustainability in the Third World*. London: Routledge.

Adler, J. (1989) Origins of sightseeing. *Annals of Tourism Research,* 16(1): 7–29.

Agarwal, S. (1997) The resort cycle and seaside tourism: An assessment of its applicability and viability. *Tourism Management*, 18(2): 65–73.

Agarwal, S. (2002) Restructuring seaside tourism: The resort lifecycle. *Annals of Tourism Research*, 29(1): 25–55.

Agren, D. (2017) Cancun crime wave threatens tourist mecca. *USA Today*. Available at: www.cnbc.com/2017/08/02/cancun-crime-wave-threatens-tourist-mecca.html (accessed 7 September 2017).

Ahmed, Z. (1992) Islamic pilgrimage Hajj to Kabba in Mecca, Saudi Arabia: An important international activity. *Journal of Tourism Studies*, 3(1): 35–43.

Akama, J. and Kieti, D. (2003) Measuring tourist satisfaction with Kenya's wildlife safari: A case study of Tsavo West National Park. *Tourism Management*, 24(1): 73–81.

Akis, S., Peristianis, N. and Warner, J. (1996) Resident attitudes to tourism development: The case of Cyprus. *Tourism Management,* 17(7): 481–494.

Albers, P. and James, W. (1988) Travel photography: A methodological approach. *Annals of Tourism Research*, 15(2): 134–158.

Allcock, B. (1988) Tourism as a sacred journey. *Loisir et Société*, 11(1): 33–48.

Allcott, H. and Gentzkow, M. (2017) Social media and fake news in the 2016 election. Available at: https://web.stanford.edu/~gentzkow/research/fakenews.pdf (accessed 31 March 2017).

Allen, L., Long, P., Perdue, R. and Kieselbach, S. (1988) The impacts of tourism development on residents' perceptions of community life. *Journal of Travel Research,* 27(1): 16–21.

Amaro, S. and Duarte, P. (2013) Online travel purchasing: A literature review. *Journal of Travel & Tourism Marketing*, 30(8): 755–785.

Anastasopoulos, P. (1992) Tourism and attitude change: Greek tourists visiting Turkey. *Annals of Tourism Research*, 19(4): 629–642.

Anderson, W. (2011) Enclave tourism and its socio-economic impact in emerging destinations. *Anatolia*, 22(3): 361–377.

Andriotis, K. and Vaughan, R. (2003) Urban residents' attitudes toward tourism development: The case of Crete. *Journal of Travel Research*, 42(2): 172–185.

Andronikou, A. (1979) Tourism in Cyprus. In E. de Kadt (ed.) *Tourism: Passport to Development?* New York: Oxford University Press, pp. 237–264.

Ap, J. (1990) Residents' perceptions research on the social impacts of tourism. *Annals of Tourism Research*, 17(4): 610–616.

Ap, J. (1992) Residents' perceptions on tourism impacts. *Annals of Tourism Research*, 19(4): 665–690.

Ap, J. and Crompton, J. (1993) Residents' strategies for responding to tourism impacts. *Journal of Travel Research*, 32(1): 47–50.

Apostolopoulos, Y., Leivadi, S. and Yiannakis, A. (eds) (1996) *The Sociology of Tourism: Theoretical and Empirical Investigations*. London: Routledge.

Appadurai, A. (1988) *The Social Life of Things: Commodities in Cultural Perspective*. Cambridge: Cambridge University Press.

Applerouth, S. and Edles, L. (2012) *Classical and Contemporary Sociological Theory*, 2nd Edition. Thousand Oaks, CA: Sage Publications.

Aramberri, J. (2001) The host should get lost: Paradigms in tourism theory. *Annals of Tourism Research,* 28(3): 738–761.

Aramberri, J. (2010) *Modern Mass Tourism*. Bingley: Emerald.

Aramberri, J. (2017) Mass tourism does not need defending. In D. Harrison and R. Sharpley (eds) *Mass Tourism in a Small World*. Wallingford: CABI, pp. 15–27.

ARC (2011) *Pilgrimage Statistics: Annual Figures*. Alliance of Religions and Conservation. Available at: www.arcworld.org/downloads/ARC%20pilgrimage%20statistics%20155m%2011-12-19.pdf (accessed 20 May 2016).

ARC (2014) *Pilgrim Numbers*. Alliance of Religions and Conservation. Available at: www.arcworld.org/projects.asp?projectID=500 (accessed 18 March 2017).

Archer, D. (2013) Smartphone addiction. *Psychology Today*. Available at: www.psychologytoday.com/blog/reading-between-the-headlines/201307/smartphone-addiction (accessed 13 October 2017).

Ariel de Vidas, A. (1995) Textiles, memory and the souvenir industry in the Andes. In M. Lanfant, J. Allcock and E. Bruner (eds) *International Tourism: Identity and Change*. London: Sage Publications, pp. 67–83.

Arnould, E. and Price, L. (1993) River magic: Extraordinary experience and extended service encounter. *Journal of Consumer Research*, 20 (June): 24–45.

Ashworth, G. and Page, S. (2011) Urban tourism research: Recent progress and current paradoxes. *Tourism Management,* 32(1): 1–15.

Ashworth, G. and Rami, I. (2015) Have we illuminated the dark? Shifting perspectives on dark tourism. *Tourism Recreation Research*, 40(3): 316–325.

Asitik, J. (2016) *Entrepreneurship: A Means to Poverty Alleviation in Northern Rural Ghana*. PhD Thesis, University of Central Lancashire. Available at: http://clok.uclan.ac.uk/15482/ (accessed 7 June 2017).

Ateljevic, I., Pritchard, A. and Morgan, N. (eds) (2007) *The Critical Turn in Tourism Studies: Innovative Research Methods*. Oxford: Elsevier.

Atkins, D. (1994) Britannia waives the legroom, *Daily Telegraph*, 16 April.

Aune, M. (2012) Thomas Coryate. In G. Sullivan and A. Stewart (eds) *The Encyclopedia of Renaissance English Literature*, Oxford: Blackwell, pp. 216–220.

Ayeh, J.K., Au, N. and Law, R. (2013) 'Do we believe in TripAdvisor?' Examining credibility perceptions and online travelers' attitude toward using user-generated content. *Journal of Travel Research*, 52(4): 437–452.

Azman, I. and Chan, K. (2010) Health and spa tourism business: Tourists' profiles and motivational factors. In L. Puczko (ed.) *Health, Wellness and Tourism: Healthy Tourists, Healthy Business*, Proceedings of the TTRA Europe 2010 Annual Conference, 1–3 September, Budapest, pp. 9–24.

Badone, E. (ed.) (2010) *Intersecting Journeys: The Anthropology of Pilgrimage and Tourism*. Champaine, IL: University of Illinois Press.

Bærenholdt, O.J., Haldrup, M., Larsen, J. and Urry, J. (2004) *Performing Tourist Places*. Aldershot: Ashgate.

Baker, S. (1990) *Caste: At Home in Hindu India*. London: Jonathan Cape.

Baran, P. (1963) On the political economy of backwardness. In A. Agarwala and S. Singh (eds) *The Economics of Underdevelopment*. Oxford: Oxford University Press, pp. 75–92.

Baran, P. (1973) *The Political Economy of Growth*. Harmondsworth, Penguin.

Barbalet, J. (2004) Consciousness, emotions and science. In J. Turner (ed.) *Theory and Research on Human Emotions*. Bradford: Emerald, pp. 245–272.

Barthes, R. (1967) *Elements of Sociology*. New York: Hill and Wang.

Barton, A. and Brown, A. (2015) Show me the prison! The development of prison tourism in the UK. *Crime, Media, Culture*, 11(3): 237–258.

Bastin, R. (1984) Small island tourism: Development or dependency? *Development Policy Review*, 2(1): 79–90.

Bates, P. (1994) Pilgrims or tourists? *In Focus*, Tourism Concern 11: 14–15.

Baudrillard, J. (1988) *Selected Writings*. Cambridge: Polity Press.

Bauer, T. and McKercher, B. (2003) *Sex and Tourism: Journeys of Romance, Love and Lust*. New York: Haworth Hospitality Press.

Becken, S. (2011) A critical review of tourism and oil. *Annals of Tourism Research*, 38(2): 359–379.

Becken, S. (2015) *Tourism and Oil: Preparing for the Challenge*. Bristol: Channel View Publications.

Beeho, A. and Prentice, R. (1997) Conceptualising the experience of heritage tourists: A case study of New Lanark World Heritage village. *Tourism Management*, 18(2): 75–87.

Beioley, S. (1995) Green tourism – Soft or sustainable? *ETB Insights, Vol 6*, London: English Tourist Board: B79–89.

Beldona, S. (2005) Cohort analysis of online travel information search behavior: 1995–2000. *Journal of Travel Research*, 44(2): 135–142.

Belisle, F. and Hoy, D. (1980) The perceived impact of tourism by residents: A case study in Santa Marta, Colombia. *Annals of Tourism Research*, 7(1): 83–101.

Belk, R. and Yeh, J. (2011) Tourist photographs: Signs of self. *International Journal of Culture, Tourism and Hospitality Research*, 5(4): 345–353.

Belk, R., Wallendorf, M. and Sherry, J. (1989) The sacred and the profane in consumer behaviour: Theodicy on the Odyssey. *Journal of Consumer Research*, 16 (June): 1–38.

Bell, C. and Lyall, J. (2005) 'I was here': Pixilated evidence. In D. Crouch, R. Jackson and F. Thompson (eds) *The Media and the Tourist Imagination: Converging Cultures*. Abingdon: Routledge, pp. 135–142.

Benckendorff, P., Sheldon, P. and Fesenmaier, D. (2014) *Tourism Information Technology*, 2nd Edition. Wallingford: CABI.

Berger, A. (2011) Tourism as a postmodern semiotic activity, *Semiotica*, 183: 105–119.

Berger, P. (1967) *The Sacred Canopy, Elements of a Sociological Theory of Religion*. New York: Doubleday.

Berno, T. and Bricker, K. (2001) Sustainable tourism development: The long road from theory to practice. *International Journal of Economic Development*, 3(3): 1–18.

Bessant, J. and Tidd, J. (2015) *Innovation and Entrepreneurship*, 3rd Edition. Chichester: Wiley.

Bestard, B. and Nadal, R. (2007) Attitudes toward tourism and tourism congestion. *Région et Développment*, 25, 193–207.

Bhattacharyya, D. (1997) Mediating India: An analysis of a guidebook. *Annals of Tourism Research*, 24(2): 371–389.

Bianchi, R. (2015) Towards a new political economy of global tourism revisited. In R. Sharpley and D. Telfer (eds) *Tourism and Development: Concepts and Issues,* 2nd Edition. Bristol: Channel View Publications, pp. 287–331.

Bigne, J. and Andreu, L. (2004) Emotions in segmentation: An empirical study. *Annals of Tourism Research*, 31(3): 682–696.

Bilton, T., Bonnett, K., Jones, P., Stanworth, M., Sheard, K. and Webster, A. (1996) *Introductory Sociology*, 3rd Edition. Basingstoke: Macmillan.

Bimonte, S. and Faralla, V. (2012) Tourist types and happiness: A comparative study in Maremma, Italy. *Annals of Tourism Research*, 39(4): 1929–1950.

Blamey, R. and Braithwaite, V. (1997) A social values segmentation of the potential ecotourism market. *Journal of Sustainable Tourism*, 5(1): 29–44.

Blom, T. (2000) Morbid tourism: A postmodern niche with an example from Althorpe. *Norwegian Journal of Geography*, 54(1): 29–36.

Bloom, D., Canning, D. and Fink, G. (2010) Implications of population ageing for economic growth. *Oxford Review of Economic Policy*, 26(4): 583–612.

Bly, L. (2003) Disaster strikes, tourists follow. *USA Today*. Available at: www.usatoday.com/travel/vacations/destinations/ . . . /2002–08–30-disaster-tourism.html (accessed 22 November 2003).

Bocock, R. (1993) *Consumption*. London: Routledge.

Boissevain, J. (1996) *Coping with Tourists: European Reactions to Mass Tourism*. Oxford: Berghahn Books.

Boniface, P. and Fowler, P. (1993) *Heritage and Tourism in the Global Village*. London: Routledge.

Bonn, M., Furr, H. and Hausman, A. (2000) Employing Internet technology to investigate and purchase travel services: A comparison of X'ers, boomers, and mature market segments. *Tourism Analysis*, 5(2–3): 137–143.

Boorstin, D. (1964) *The Image: A Guide to Pseudo-Events in America*. New York: Harper & Row.

Boote, A. (1981) Market segmentation by personal values and salient product attributes. *Journal of Advertising Research*, 21: 29–35.

Borsay, P. (2012) Town or country? British spas and the urban–rural interface. *Journal of Tourism History*, 4(2): 155–169.

Boulding, K. (1992) The economics of the coming of Spaceship Earth. In A. Markyanda and J. Richardson (eds) *The Earthscan Reader in Environmental Economics*. London: Earthscan, pp. 27–35.

Bourdieu, P. (1986) *Distinction: A Social Critique of the Judgement of Taste*. London: Routledge.

Bray, R. and Raitz, V. (2001) *Flight to the Sun: The Story of the Holiday Revolution*. London: Continuum.

BRDC (2014) Holiday Trends 2014. BRDC Continental. Available at: http://mediafiles.thedms.co.uk/Publication/ee-nor/cms/pdf/BDRC%20Continental%20Holiday%20Trends%202014%20Report.pdf (accessed 19 April 2017).

Brendon, P. (1991) *Thomas Cook: 150 Years of Popular Tourism*. London: Secker & Warburg.

Brickell, K. (2008) Tourism-generated employment and intra-household inequality in Cambodia. In J. Cochrane (ed.) *Asian Tourism: Growth and Change*. Oxford: Elsevier, pp. 299–310.

Britton, R. (1979) The image of the Third World in tourism marketing. *Annals of Tourism Research*, 6(3): 318–329.

Britton, S. (1982) The political economy of tourism in the Third World. *Annals of Tourism Research*, 9(3): 331–358.

Britton, S. (1987) Tourism in small developing countries: Development issues and research needs. In S. Britton and W. Clarke (eds) *Ambiguous Alternative: Tourism in Small Developing Countries*. Suva: University of the South Pacific, pp. 167–186.

Britton, S. (1991) Tourism, capital and place: Towards a critical geography of tourism. *Environment and Planning D: Society and Space*, 9(4): 451–478.

Brohman, J. (1996) New directions in tourism for Third World development. *Annals of Tourism Research*, 23(1): 48–70.

Brosnan, M. (1998) The impact of computer anxiety and self-efficacy upon performance. *Journal of Computer Assisted Learning*, 14(3): 223–234.

Brougham, J. and Butler, R. (1981) A segmentation analysis of resident attitudes to the social impact of tourism. *Annals of Tourism Research*, 8(4): 569–590.

Brown, G. and Giles, R. (1994) Coping with tourism: An examination of resident responses to the social impacts of tourism. In A. Seaton (ed.) *Tourism: The State of the Art*. Chichester: John Wiley & Sons, pp. 775–784.

Brown, M. (1998) *The Spiritual Tourist*. London: Bloomsbury.

Browne, K. (1992) *An Introduction to Sociology*. Cambridge: Polity Press.

Browne, K. (2011) *An Introduction to Sociology,* 4th Edition. Cambridge: Polity Press.

Brunet, S., Bauer, J., De Lacy, T. and Tshering, K. (2001) Tourism development in Bhutan: Tensions between tradition and modernity. *Journal of Sustainable Tourism*, 9(3): 243–263.

Buchmann, A., Moore, K. and Fisher, D. (2010) Experiencing film tourism: Authenticity and fellowship. *Annals of Tourism Research*, 37(1): 229–248.

Buck, R. (1977) The ubiquitous tourist brochure: Explorations of its intended and unintended use. *Annals of Tourism Research*, 4(4): 195–207.

Buck, R. (1978) Towards a synthesis in tourism theory. *Annals of Tourism Research*, 5(1): 110–111.

Budowski, G. (1976) Tourism and conservation: Conflict, co-existence or symbiosis? *Environmental Conservation*, 3(1): 27–31.

Buhalis, D. (2003) *eTourism: Information Technology for Strategic Tourism Management*. Harlow: Pearson Education.

Bull, A. (1991) *The Economics of Travel and Tourism*. London: Pitman.

Bull, A. (2006) Is a trip to the seaside a spiritual journey? Paper presented at the *Tourism: The Spiritual Dimension* Conference, University of Lincoln, UK (unpublished).

Burkhart, A. and Medlik, S. (1981) *Tourism: Past, Present and Future*, 2nd Edition. Oxford: Butterworth Heinemann.

Burls, A. (2007) People and green spaces: Promoting public health and mental well-being through ecotherapy. *Journal of Public Mental Health*, 6(3): 24–39.

Burns, P. (1999) *An Introduction to Tourism and Anthropology*. London: Routledge.

Burns, P. and Holden, A. (1995) *Tourism: A New Perspective*. Hemel Hempstead: Prentice Hall International.

Burns, P. and Novelli, M. (eds) (2007) *Tourism and Politics: Global Frameworks and Local Realities.* Oxford: Elsevier.

Butcher, J. (2002) *The Moralisation of Tourism: Sun, Sand . . . and Saving the World?* London: Routledge.

Butcher, J. and Smith, P. (2010) 'Making a difference': Volunteer tourism and development. *Tourism Recreation Research*, 35(1): 27–36.

Butler, R. (1980a) The concept of a tourism area cycle of evolution. *Canadian Geographer*, 24: 5–12.

Butler, R. (1980b) Alternative tourism: Pious hope or Trojan horse? *Journal of Travel Research*, 28(3): 40–45.

Butler, R. (1991) Tourism, environment, and sustainable development. *Environmental Conservation*, 18(3): 201–209.

Butler, R. (1992) Alternative tourism: The thin end of the wedge. In V. Smith and W. Eadington (eds) *Tourism Alternatives: Potentials and Problems in the Development of Tourism*. Philadelphia: University of Pennsylvania Press: 31–46.

Butler, R. (2006a) *The Tourism Area Life Cycle, Vol 1: Applications and Modifications*. Clevedon: Channel View Publications.

Butler, R. (2006b) *The Tourism Area Life Cycle, Vol 2: Conceptual and Theoretical Issues*. Clevedon: Channel View Publications.

Butler, R. and Suntikul, W. (ed,) (2013) *Tourism and War*. Abingdon: Routledge.

Buzard, J. (1993) *The Beaten Track*. Oxford: Oxford University Press.

Buzinde, C. and Santos, C. (2009) Interpreting slavery tourism. *Annals of Tourism Research*, 36(3): 439–458.

Byock, I. (2002) The meaning and value of death. *Journal of Palliative Medicine* 5: 279–288.

Callanan, M. and Thomas, S. (2005) Volunteer tourism: Deconstructing volunteer activities within a dynamic environment. In M. Novelli (ed.) *Niche Tourism: Contemporary Issues, Trends and Cases*, Oxford: Butterworth-Heinemann, pp. 183–200.

Campbell, C. (1987) *The Romantic Ethic and the Spirit of Modern Consumerism*. Oxford: Blackwell.

Casson, L. (1974) *Travels in the Ancient World*. London: George Allen and Unwin.

Cater, E. (1993) Ecotourism in the Third World: Problems for sustainable tourism development. *Tourism Management*, 14(2): 85–90.

Caton, K. and Santos, C. (2008) Closing the hermeneutic circle? Photographic encounters with the other. *Annals of Tourism Research*, 35(1): 7–26.

Cavaco, C. (1995) Rural tourism: The creation of new tourist spaces. In A. Montanari and A. Williams (eds) *European Tourism: Regions, Spaces and Restructuring*. Chichester: John Wiley & Sons, pp. 129–149.

Cha, S., McCleary, K. and Uysal, M. (1995) Travel motivations of Japanese overseas tourists: A factor-cluster segmentation approach. *Journal of Travel Research* 34(1): 33–39.

Chambers, E. (1997) *Tourism and Culture: An Applied Perspective*. Albany: State University of New York Press.

Chandler, D. (2002) *Semiotics: The Basics*. London: Routledge.

Chapman, L. (2007) Transport and climate change: A review. *Journal of Transport Geography*, 15(5): 354–367.

Charitou, C. and Markides, C. (2002) Responses to disruptive strategic innovation. *MIT Sloan Management Review*, 44(2): 55–64.

Chhabra, D., Healy, R. and Sills, E. (2003) Staged authenticity and heritage tourism. *Annals of Tourism Research*, 30(3): 702–719.

Choi, C. and Murray, I. (2010) Resident attitudes towards sustainable community tourism. *Journal of Sustainable Tourism*, 18(4): 575–594.

Choudrie, J., Pheeraphuttharangkoon, S., Zamani, E. and Giaglis, G. (2014) Investigating the adoption and use of smartphones in the UK: a silver-surfers perspective. *Hertfordshire Business School Working Paper*. Available at: http://uhra.herts.ac.uk/bitstream/handle/2299/13507/S154.pdf?sequence=2 (accessed 7 October 2017).

Clancy, M. (1999) Tourism and development: evidence from Mexico. *Annals of Tourism Research*, 26(1): 1–20.

Clarke, J. and Critcher, C. (1985) *The Devil Makes Work: Leisure in Capitalist Britain*. Basingstoke: Macmillan.

Clift, S. and Cater, S. (2000) *Tourism and Sex: Culture, Commerce and Coercion*. London: Pinter.

Clift, S. and Grabowski, C.P. (1997) *Tourism and Health*. London: Cassell.

CMoT (2017) Cambodia Tourism Statistics Report March 2017. Ministry of Tourism: Statistics and Tourism Information Department. Available at: www.tourismcambodia.org/images/mot/statistic_reports/Executive%20Summary%20Report%20in%20March%202017.pdf (accessed 26 May 2017).

Coats, A. and Ferguson, S. (2013) Rubbernecking or rejuvenation: Post-earthquake perceptions and the implications for business practice in a dark tourism context. *Journal of Research for Consumers*, 23(1): 32–65.

Coccossis, H. and Mexa, A. (2004) *The Challenge of Tourism Carrying Capacity Assessment: Theory and Practice*. Abingdon: Routledge.

Cohen, E. (1972) Towards a sociology of international tourism. *Social Research*, 39(1): 64–82.

Cohen, E. (1973) Nomads from affluence: Notes on the phenomenon of drifter tourism. *International Journal of Comparative Sociology*, 14(1–2): 89–103.

Cohen, E. (1974) Who is a tourist? A conceptual clarification. *Sociological Review*, 22(4): 527–555.

Cohen, E. (1979a) Rethinking the sociology of tourism. *Annals of Tourism Research*, 6(1): 18–35.

Cohen, E. (1979b) A phenomenology of tourist experiences. *Sociology*, 13: 179–201.

Cohen, E. (1984) The sociology of tourism: Approaches, issues and findings. *Annual Review of Sociology*, 10: 373–392.

Cohen, E. (1985) The tourist guide: The origins, structure and dynamics of a role. *Annals of Tourism Research*, 12(1): 5–29.

Cohen, E. (1988a) Authenticity and commoditisation in tourism. *Annals of Tourism Research*, 15(3): 371–386.

Cohen, E. (1988b) Traditions in the qualitative sociology of tourism. *Annals of Tourism Research*, 15(1): 29–46.

Cohen, E. (2002) Authenticity, equity and sustainability in tourism. *Journal of Sustainable Tourism*, 10(4): 267–276.

Cohen, E. (2017) Mass tourism in Thailand. In D. Harrison and R. Sharpley (eds) *Mass Tourism in a Small World*. Wallingford: CABI, pp. 159–167.

Cohen, S. (2011) Lifestyle travellers: Backpacking as a way of life. *Annals of Tourism Research*, 38(4): 1535–1555.

Cohen, S. and Taylor, L. (1976) *Escape Attempts: The Theory and Practice of Resistance in Everyday Life*. Harmondsworth: Penguin.

Collins-Kreiner, N. and Gatrell, J. (2006) Tourism, heritage and pilgrimage: the case of Haifa's Bahá'í Gardens. *Journal of Heritage Tourism*, 1(1): 32–50.

Connell, J. (2012) Film tourism: Evolution, progress and prospects. *Tourism Management*, 33(5): 1007–1029.

Connolly, K. (2017) Cruise ships overwhelm Europe's ancient resorts. BBC Online. Available at: www.bbc.co.uk/news/world-europe-40592247 (accessed 7 September 2017).

Contours (2004) India promotes spiritual tourism. *Contours*, 14(1): 21.

Cooper, C. (ed.) (1991) *Progress in Tourism, Recreation and Hospitality Management Vol III*. London: Bellhaven Press.

Cooper, C., Fletcher, J., Fyall, A., Gilbert, D. and Wanhill, S. (2005) *Tourism: Principles and Practice*, 3rd Edition. Harlow: Pearson Education.

Coppock, J. (1977) *Second Homes: Curse or Blessing*. Oxford: Pergamon Press.

Cormack, B. (1998) *A History of Tourism, 1812–1998*. Volume I of P. Smith (ed.) *History of Tourism: Thomas Cook and the Origins of Travel*. London: Routledge/Thomas Cook Archives.

Corvo, P. (2011) The pursuit of happiness and the globalized tourist. *Social Indicators Research*, 102(1): 93–97.

Country Reports (n.d.) Crime information for tourists in Italy. Available at: www.countryreports.org/travel/Italy/crimes.htm (accessed 7 September 2017).

Cowe, R. and Williams, S. (2000) *Who is the Ethical Consumer?* Manchester: Co-operative Bank.

Craig-Smith, S. (1996) Economic impact of tourism in the Pacific. In C.M. Hall and S. Page (eds) *Tourism in the Pacific: Issues and Cases*. London: International Thomson Business Press, pp. 36–48.

Creighton, H. (2014) *Europe's Ageing Demography*. International Longevity Centre UK, EU Factpack. London: ILC-UK.

CREST (2016) *The Case for Responsible Travel: Trends & Statistics 2016*. Centre for Responsible Travel. Available at: www.responsibletravel.org/whatWeDo/The_Case_for_Responsible_Travel_2016_Final.pdf (accessed 30 March 2017).

Crick, M. (1989) Representations of international tourism in the social sciences. *Annual Review of Anthropology*, 18: 307–344.

Croall, J. (1995) *Preserve or Destroy: Tourism and the Environment*. London: Calouste Gulbenkian Foundation.

Crompton, J. (1979) Motivations for pleasure vacation. *Annals of Tourism Research*, 6(4): 408–424.

Cronin, L. (1990) A strategy for tourism and sustainable developments. *World Leisure and Recreation*, 32(3): 12–18.

Crouch, G. (1992) Effect of income and price on international tourism. *Annals of Tourism Research*, 19(4): 643–664.

Croy, W.G. (2010) Planning for film tourism: Active destination image management. *Tourism and Hospitality Planning & Development*, 7(1): 21–30.

Culler, J. (1981) Semiotics of tourism. *American Journal of Semiotics*. 1(1–2): 127–140.

Curry, S. (1992) Economic adjustment policies and the hotel sector in Jamaica. In P. Johnson and B. Thomas (eds) *Perspectives on Tourism Policy*. London: Mansell, pp. 193–213.

D'Amore, L. (1988) Tourism: A vital force for peace. *Annals of Tourism Research*, 15(2): 269–271.

Dalen, E. (1989) Research into values and consumer trends in Norway. *Tourism Management*, 10(3): 183–186.

Damer, S. (1990) *Glasgow: Going for a Song*. London: Lawrence and Wishart.

Dann, G. (1977) Anomie, ego-enhancement and tourism. *Annals of Tourism Research*, 4(4): 184–194.

Dann, G. (1981) Tourist motivation: An appraisal. *Annals of Tourism Research*, 8(2): 187–219.

Dann, G. (1989) The tourist as child: Some reflections. *Cahiers de Tourisme*, Série C: 135, Aix-en-Provence: CHET.

Dann, G. (1994) Tourism: The nostalgia industry of the future. In W. Theobald (ed.) *Global Tourism: The Next Decade*. Oxford: Butterworth Heinemann, pp. 55–67.

Dann, G. (1996) *The Language of Tourism: A Socio-linguistic Perspective*. Wallingford: CABI.

Dann, G. (1998) The dark side of tourism. *Etudes et Rapports*. Série L, Centre International de Recherches et d'Etudes Touristiques, Aix-en-Provence.

Dann, G. (1999) Writing out the tourist in space and time. *Annals of Tourism Research*, 26(1): 159–187.

Dann, G. (2002) *The Tourist as a Metaphor of the Social World*. Wallingford: CABI Publishing.

Dann, G. and Cohen, E. (1991) Sociology and tourism. *Annals of Tourism Research*, 18(1): 155–169.

Dann, G. and Parrinello, G. (eds) (2009a) *The Sociology of Tourism: European Origins and Developments*. Bingley: Emerald Group Publishing.

Dann, G. and Parrinello, G. (2009b) Setting the scene. In G. Dann an G. Parrinello (eds) *The Sociology of Tourism: European Origins and Developments*. Bingley: Emerald, pp. 1–63.

Dann, G. and Seaton, A. (eds) (2001) *Slavery, Contested Heritage and Thanatourism*. Binghampton, HY: Haworth Hospitality Press.

Dann, G., Nash, D. and Pearce, P. (1988) Methodology in tourism research. *Annals of Tourism Research*, 15(1): 1–28.

Darker, C., Larkin, M. and French, D. (2007) An exploration of walking behaviour: An interpretative phenomenological approach. *Social Science & Medicine*, 65(10): 2172–2183.

Dasgupta, P. and Weale, M. (1992) On measuring the quality of life. *World Development*, 20(1): 119–131.

Davidson, R. (1998) *Travel and Tourism in Europe*, 2nd Edition. Harlow: Longman.

Davidson, T. (1994) What are travel and tourism: Are they really an industry? In W. Theobald (ed.) *Global Tourism: The Next Decade*. Oxford: Butterworth Heinemann, pp. 20–26.

Davis, D., Allen, J. and Cosenza, R. (1988) Segmenting local residents by their attitudes, interests, and opinions toward tourism. *Journal of Travel Research*, 27(2): 2–8.

Davis, F. (1979) *Yearning for Yesterday: A Sociology of Nostalgia*. New York: Free Press.

de Botton, A. (2002) *The Art of Travel*. London: Penguin Books.

de Kadt, E. (1979) *Tourism: Passport to Development?* New York: Oxford University Press.

de Rivero, O. (2001) *The Myth of Development: Non-viable Economies of the 21st Century*. London: Zed Books.

Deery, M., Jago, L. and Fredline, L. (2012) Rethinking social impacts of tourism research: A new research agenda. *Tourism Management*, 33(1): 64–73.

Defoe, D. (1991) *A Tour Through the Whole Island of Great Britain*. New Haven and London: Yale University Press.

Deitch, L. (1989) The impact of tourism on the arts and crafts of the Indians of the Southwestern United States. In V. Smith (ed.) *Hosts and Guests: The Anthropology of Tourism*, 2nd Edition, Philadelphia: University of Pennsylvania Press, pp. 223–236.

del Bosque, I. and San Martin, H. (2008) Tourist satisfaction: A cognitive-affective model. *Annals of Tourism Research*, 35(2): 551–573.

del Chiappa, G., Andreu, L. and Gallarza, M. G. (2014) Emotions and visitors' satisfaction at a museum. *International Journal of Culture, Tourism and Hospitality Research*, 8(4): 420–431.

DeLeire, T. and Kalil, A. (2009) Does consumption buy happiness? Evidence from the United States. *International Review of Economics*, 57(2): 163–176.

Dernoi, L. (1981) Alternative tourism: Towards a new style in North-South relations. *International Journal of Tourism Management*, 2(4): 253–264.

Devereux, C. and Carnegie, E. (2006) Pilgrimage: Journeying beyond self. Paper presented at the *Tourism: The Spiritual Dimension* Conference, University of Lincoln, April.

DfT (2015) *Vehicle Licensing Statistics, Quarter 1 2015*. Department for Transport. Available at: www.gov.uk/government/uploads/system/uploads/attachment_data/file/433994/vls-2015-q1-release.pdf (accessed 19 March 2017).

Di John, J. (2010) The concept, causes and consequences of failed states: A critical review of the literature and agenda for research with specific reference to sub-Saharan Africa. *European Journal of Development Research*, 22(1): 10–30.

Diamantis, D. (1999) Green strategies for tourism worldwide. *Travel & Tourism Analyst*, No. 4: 89–112.

Diamond, J. (1997) Tourism's role in economic development: The case re-examined. *Economic Development and Cultural Change*, 25(3): 539–553.

Dieke, P. (1993) Tourism and development policy in The Gambia. *Annals of Tourism Research*, 20(4): 423–449.

Dieke, P. (1995) Tourism and structural adjustment policies in the African economy. *Tourism Economics*, 1(1): 71–93.

Dilley, R. (1986) Tourist brochures and tourist images. *Canadian Geographer*, 30(1): 59–65.

Dimanche, F. and Havitz, M. (1994) Consumer behaviour and tourism: Review and extension of four study areas. *Journal of Travel and Tourism Marketing*, 3(4): 37–57.

Din, K. (1982) Tourism in Malaysia: Competing needs in a plural society. *Annals of Tourism Research*, 16(4): 453–480.

Dmitrović, T., Knežević Cvelbar, L., Kolar, T., Makovec Brenčič, M., Ograjenšek, I. and Žabkar, V. (2009) Conceptualizing tourist satisfaction at the destination level. *International Journal of Culture, Tourism and Hospitality Research*, 3(2): 116–126.

Dobruszkes, F. (2006) An analysis of European low-cost airlines and their networks. *Journal of Transport Geography*, 14(4): 249–264.

Docherty, T. (2014) *Postmodernism: A Reader*. Abingdon: Routledge.

Dos Santos, T. (1970) The structure of dependency. *American Economic Review*, 60(2): 231–236.

Dowling, R. (1992) Tourism and environmental integration: The journey from idealism to realism. In C. Cooper and A. Lockwood (eds) *Progress in Tourism, Recreation and Hospitality Management Vol IV*, London: Bellhaven Press, pp. 33–46.

Doxey, G. (1975) A causation theory of visitor-resident irritants: Methodology and research inferences. *The Impact of Tourism*, Sixth Annual Conference Proceedings of the Travel Research Association, San Diego, 195–198.

Duffy, R. (2002) *A Trip Too Far; Ecotourism, Politics and Exploitation*. London: Earthscan.

Dumbrovská, V. and Fialová, D. (2014) Tourist intensity in capital cities in Central Europe: Comparative analysis of tourism in Prague, Vienna and Budapest. *Czech Journal of Tourism*, 3(1): 5–26.

Duran, H. (2017) Smartphone users will reach 3.6 billion by 2020. *A-List Daily*. Available at: www.alistdaily.com/digital/newzoo-smartphone-users-3–6-billion-by-2020/ (accessed 6 October 2017).

Durkheim, E. (2008) *The Elementary Forms of Religious Life*. Mineola, New York: Dover Publications.

Durkin, K.F. (2003) Death, dying and the dead in popular culture. In C. Bryant (ed.) *The Handbook of Death and Dying*. New York: Sage, pp. 43–49.

Dwyer, L. and Forsyth, P. (2006) *International Handbook on the Economics of Tourism*. Cheltenham: Edward Elgar Publishing.

Dwyer, L., Forsyth, P. and Dwyer, W. (2010) *Tourism Economics and Policy*. Bristol: Channel View Publications.

Eade, J. (1992) Pilgrimage and tourism at Lourdes, France. *Annals of Tourism Research*, 19(1): 18–32.

Eagles, P. (1992) The travel motivations of Canadian ecotourists. *Journal of Travel Research,* 31(2): 2–13.

Eagles, P. and Cascagnette, J. (1995) Canadian ecotourists: Who are they? *Tourism Recreation Research,* 20(1): 22–28.

Easterlin, R. (1975) Will raising the incomes of all increase the happiness of all? *Journal of Economic Behaviour and Organisation*, 27(1): 35–47.

Eco, U. (1995) Travels in Hyperreality. In *Faith in Fakes.* London: Minerva: 1–58.

Economist (2016) Chinese Society: The new class war. *The Economist*, Special Issue, 9 July.

Edensor, T. (2000) Staging tourism: Tourists as performers. *Annals of Tourism Research*, 27(2): 322–344.

Edwards, A. (1987) *Choosing Holiday Destinations: The Impact of Exchange Rates and Inflation*. Special Report No. 1109. London: Economic Intelligence Unit.

Edwards, E. (1993) The tourist icon in tourism. *In Focus*, Tourism Concern, 6: 4–5.

Egger, R. and Buhalis, D. (2008) *eTourism: Case Studies*. Oxford: Butterworth Heinemann.

Elkins, D., Hedstrom, L., Hughes, L., Leaf, J. and Saunders, C. (1988) Toward a humanistic phenomenological spirituality: Definition, description and measurement. *Journal of Humanistic Psychology*, 28(4): 5–18.

Elliott, J. (1997) *Tourism: Politics and Public Sector Management*. London: Routledge.

Elsrud, T. (2001) Risk creation in travelling: Backpacker adventure narration. *Annals of Tourism Research*, 28(3): 597–617.

Emery, F. (1981) Alternative futures in tourism. *International Journal of Tourism Management,* 2(1): 49–67.

Engel, J., Blackwell, R. and Miniard, P. (1993) *Consumer Behaviour*. Orlando: Dryden Press.

Erfurt-Cooper, P. and Cooper, M. (2009) *Heat and Wellness Tourism: Spas and Hot Springs*. Bristol: Channel View Publications.

Erisman, M. (1983) Tourism and cultural dependency in the West Indies. *Annals of Tourism Research,* 10(3): 337–361.

ETB (1991) *Tourism and the Environment: Maintaining the Balance*. London: English Tourist Board.

ETB (1993) Holiday tourism by the British. *ETB Insights, Vol IV*: F-6, London: English Tourist Board.

Faith Survey (2017) Christianity in the UK. Available at: https://faithsurvey.co.uk/uk-christianity.html (accessed 12 September 2017).

Farmaki, A. and Papatheodorou, A. (2015) Stakeholder perceptions of the role of low-cost carriers in insular tourism destinations: The case of Cyprus. *Tourism Planning & Development*, 12(4): 412–432.

Faulkner, B. and Tideswell, C. (1997) A framework for monitoring community impacts of tourism. *Journal of Sustainable Tourism*, 5(1): 3–28.

Feather, N. (1975) *Values in Education and Society*. New York: Free Press.

Featherstone, M. (1990) Perspectives on consumer culture. *Sociology*, 24(1): 5–22.

Featherstone, M. (1991) *Consumer Culture and Postmodernism*. London: Sage Publications.

Feifer, M. (1985) *Going Places*. London: Macmillan.

Fennell, D. (1999) *Ecotourism: An Introduction*. London: Routledge.

Fennell, D. (2007) *Ecotourism,* 3rd Edition. Abingdon: Routledge.

Filep, S. (2012) Positive psychology and tourism. In M. Uysal, R. Perdue and M.J. Sirgy (eds) *Handbook of Tourism and Quality-of-Life Research*. Dordrecht: Springer, pp. 31–50.

Filep, S. and Deery, M. (2010) Towards a picture of tourists' happiness. *Tourism Analysis*, 15(4): 399–410.

Filieri, R., Alguezaui, S. and McLeay, F. (2015) Why do travelers trust TripAdvisor? Antecedents of trust towards consumer-generated media and its influence on recommendation adoption and word of mouth. *Tourism Management*, 51: 174–185.

Fisher, J., Francis, L. and Johnson, P. (2000) Assessing spiritual health via four domains of spiritual wellbeing: The SH4DI. *Pastoral Psychology*, 49(2): 133–145.

Fitzgerald, F. (1983) Sociologies of development. In P. Limqueco and B. McFarlane (eds) *Neo-Marxist Theories of Development*. Beckenham: Croom Helm, pp. 12–28.

Fodness, D. (1992) The impact of family life cycle on the vacation decision-making process. *Journal of Travel Research*, 31(2): 8–13.

Foley, M. and Lennon, J. (1996a) JFK and dark tourism: A fascination with assassination. *International Journal of Heritage Studies*, 2(4): 198–211.

Foley, M. and Lennon, J. (1996b) Editorial: Heart of darkness. *International Journal of Heritage Studies*, 2(4): 195–197.

Foo, J., McGuiggan, R. and Yiannakis, A. (2004) Roles tourists play: An Australian perspective. *Annals of Tourism Research*, 31(2): 408–427.

Forster, J. (1964) The sociological consequences of tourism. *International Journal of Comparative Sociology*, 5(2): 217–227.

Fotis, J., Buhalis, D. and Rossides, N. (2012) Social media use and impact during the holiday travel planning process. In M. Fuchs, F. Ricci and L. Cantoni (eds) *Information and Communication Technologies in Tourism*. Vienna: Springer-Verlag, pp. 13–24.

Fox, C. (2017) In Pictures: Cambodia's Female Construction Workers. Available at: www.bbc.co.uk/news/in-pictures-39102989

Frank, A. (1969) The development of underdevelopment. *Monthly Review*, 18(4): 17–31.

Franklin, A. (2003) *Tourism: An Introduction*. London: Sage Publications.

Fredline, E. and Faulkner, B. (2000) Host community reactions: A cluster analysis. *Annals of Tourism Research*, 27(3): 763–784.

Fredrickson, L. and Anderson, D. (1999) A qualitative exploration of the wilderness experience as a source of spiritual inspiration. *Journal of Environmental Psychology*, 19(1): 21–29.

Freitag, T. (1994.) Enclave tourism development: For whom the benefits roll? *Annals of Tourism Research*, 21(3): 538–554.

Furnham, A. (1984) Tourism and culture shock. *Annals of Tourism Research*, 11(1): 1–57.

Galtung, J. (1986) Towards a new economics: On the theory and practice of self-reliance. In P. Ekins (ed.) *The Living Economy: A New Economy in the Making*. London: Routledge, pp. 97–109.

Gambia Experience (2017) *The Gambia*. Available at: www.gambia.co.uk (accessed 9 June 2017).

Garlick, S. (2002) Revealing the unseen: Tourism, art and photography. *Cultural Studies*, 16(2): 289–305.

Garrod, B. (2008) Understanding the relationship between tourism destination imagery and tourist photography. *Journal of Travel Research*, 47(3): 346–358.

Gee, E. (2002) Misconceptions and misapprehensions about population ageing. *International Journal of Epidemiology*, 31(4): 750–753.

Getz, D. (1991) *Festivals, Special Events and Tourism*. New York: Van Nostrand Reinhold.

Getz, D. (1992) Tourism planning and destination life cycle. *Annals of Tourism Research*, 19(4): 752–780.

Ghani, A. and Lockhart, C. (2008) *Fixing Failed States*. Oxford: Oxford University Press.

Giddens, A. (1991) *Modernity and Self Identity*. Cambridge: Polity.

Giddens, A. (2009) *Sociology*, 6th Edition. Cambridge: Polity Press.

Gilbert, D. (1990) Conceptual issues in the meaning of tourism. In C. Cooper (ed.) *Progress in Tourism, Recreation and Hospitality Management, Volume II*. London: Bellhaven Press, pp. 4–27.

Gilbert, D. (1991) An examination of the consumer behaviour process related to tourism. In C. Cooper (ed.) *Progress in Tourism, Recreation and Hospitality Management, Volume III*. London: Bellhaven Press, pp. 78–105.

Gilbert, D. and Houghton, P. (1991) An exploratory investigation of format, design, and use of U.K. tour operators' brochures. *Journal of Travel Research*, 30(2): 20–25.

Gillette, A. (1999) A (very) short history of volunteering. Available at: http://volunteering.ge/upload/pdf/b7e88087fbf77747309c21116496a0da.pdf (accessed 1 March 2017).

Gilovich, T. and Kumar, A. (2015) We'll always have Paris: The hedonic payoff from experiential and material investments. In M. Zanna and J. Olson (eds) *Advances in Experimental Social Psychology*, 51. Oxford: Elsevier, pp. 147–187.

Godfrey, K. (1996) Towards sustainability? Tourism in the Republic of Cyprus. In L. Harrison and W. Husbands (eds) *Practising Responsible Tourism: International Case Studies in Tourism Planning, Policy and Development*. Chichester: John Wiley & Sons, pp. 58–79.

Goffman, I. (1959) *The Presentation of Self in Everyday Life*. Harmondsworth: Penguin.

Goodall, B. (1991) Understanding holiday choice. In C. Cooper (ed.) *Progress in Tourism, Recreation and Hospitality Management, Volume III*. London: Bellhaven Press, pp. 58–77.

Goodland, R. (1992) The case that the world has reached its limits. In R. Goodland, H. Daly, S. el Sarafy and B. von Droste (eds) *Environmentally Sustainable Economic Development: Building on Brundtland*. Paris: UNESCO, pp. 15–27.

Goodwin, H. (2011) *Taking Responsibility for Tourism*. Oxford: Goodfellow Publishers.

Goodwin, H. and Francis, J. (2003) Ethical and responsible tourism: Consumer trends in the UK. *Journal of Vacation Marketing*, 9(3): 271–284.

Gössling, S., Hall, C.M. and Weaver, D. (2009) *Sustainable Tourism Futures: Perspectives on Systems, Restructuring and Innovations*. Abingdon: Routledge.

Gottlieb, A. (1982) Americans' vacations. *Annals of Tourism Research,* 9(2): 165–187.

Gould, K. and Lewis, Y. (2007) Viewing the wreckage: Eco-disaster tourism in the wake of Katrina. *Societies Without Borders*, 2(2): 175–197.

Goulding, C. (2000) The commodification of the past, postmodern pastiche, and the search for authentic experiences at contemporary heritage attractions. *European Journal of Marketing*, 34(7): 835–853.

Goulet, D. (1968) On the goals of development. *Cross Current*, 18: 387–405.

Goulet, D. (1992) Development: Creator and destroyer of values. *World Development*, 20(3): 467–475.

Government of Nepal (2016) *Nepal Tourism Statistics 2016*. Ministry of Culture, Tourism and Aviation, Kathmandu. Available at: www.tourism.gov.np/downloadfile/Nepal%20Tourism%20statistic_Final-2016_1498990228.pdf (accessed 7 September 2017).

Grabler, K., Maier, G., Mazanec, J. and Wöber, K. (1997) *International City Tourism: Analysis and Strategy*. London: Pinter.

Graburn, N. (1976) *Ethnic and Tourist Arts: Cultural Expressions from the Fourth World*. Berkeley: University of California Press.

Graburn, N. (1983) The anthropology of tourism. *Annals of Tourism Research,* 10(1): 9–33.

Graburn, N. (1989) Tourism: The sacred journey. In V. Smith (ed.) *Hosts and Guests: The Anthropology of Tourism,* 2nd Edition. Philadelphia: University of Pennsylvania Press, pp. 21–36.

Graburn, N. (2001) Secular ritual: A general theory of tourism. In V. Smith and M. Brent (eds) *Hosts and Guests Revisited: Tourism Issues of the 21st Century*. New York: Cognizant Communications, pp. 42–50.

Graham, C. (2009) *Happiness around the World: The Paradox of Happy Peasants and Miserable Millionaires.* Oxford: Oxford University Press.

Grahn, P. (1991) Using tourism to protect existing culture: A project in Swedish Lapland. *Leisure Studies*, 10(1): 33–47.

Grant, D. and Mason, S. (2003) *Holiday Law: The Law Relating to Travel and Tourism,* 3rd Edition. London: Sweet and Maxwell.

Gray, H. (1970) *International Travel–International Trade.* Lexington: DC Heath.

Gray, T. (1884) *Journal in the Lakes*. London: Macmillan.

Grayling, A.C. (2008) Happiness is the measure of true wealth. *Daily Telegraph*, 10 April. Available at: www.telegraph.co.uk/comment/3557112/Happiness-is-the-measure-of-true-wealth.html (accessed 16 May 2017).

Greenwood, D. (1989) Culture by the pound: An anthropological perspective on tourism as cultural commoditisation. In V. Smith (ed.) *Hosts and Guests: The Anthropology of Tourism*, 2nd Edition. Philadelphia: University of Pennsylvania Press, pp. 171–185.

Gretzel, U., Sigala, M., Xiang, Z. and Koo, C. (2015) Smart tourism: Foundations and developments. *Electronic Markets*, 25(3): 179–188.

Grihault, N. (2003) *Film Tourism*. London: Mintel International Group Limited.

Griffiths, I. and Sharpley, R. (2012) Influences of nationalism on tourist-host relationships. *Annals of Tourism Research*, 39(4): 2051–2072.

GSTC (2015) Welcome to the Global Sustainable Tourism Council. Available at: www.gstcouncil.org/about/learn-about-gstc.html (accessed 30 January 2015).

Guest, D. (2002) Perspectives on the study of work-life balance. *Social Science Information*, 41(2): 255–279.

Gursoy, D. and Rutherford, D. (2004) Host attitudes towards tourism: an improved structural model. *Annals of Tourism Research*, 31(3): 495–516.

Guttentag, D. (2009) The possible negative impacts of volunteer tourism. *International Journal of Tourism Research*, 11(6): 537–551.

Guttentag, D. (2010) Virtual reality: Applications and implications for tourism. *Tourism Management*, 31(5): 637–651.

Haldrup, M. and Larsen, J. (2003) The family gaze. *Tourist Studies*, 3(1): 23–45.

Haldrup, M. and Larsen, J. (2010) *Tourism, Performance and The Everyday: Consuming the Orient*. Abingdon: Routledge.

Hall, C., Scott, D. and Gössling, S. (2015) Tourism, climate change and development. In R. Sharpley and D. Telfer (eds) *Tourism and Development Concepts and Issues,* 2nd Edition. Bristol: Channel View Publications, pp. 332–357.

Hall, C.M. (1994) *Tourism and Politics: Policy, Power and Place*. Chichester: John Wiley & Sons.

Hall, C.M. (2005) *Tourism: Rethinking the Science of Mobility*. Harlow: Pearson Education.

Hall, C.M. (2011) Consumerism, tourism and voluntary simplicity: We all have to consume, but do we really have to travel so much to be happy? *Tourism Recreation Research*, 36(3): 298–303.

Hall, C.M. and Higham, J. (2005) *Tourism, Recreation and Climate Change*. Clevedon: Channel View Publications.

Hall, C.M. and Müller, D. (2004) *Tourism, Mobility and Second Homes: Between Elite Landscape and Common Ground*. Clevedon: Channel View Publications.

Hall, C.M. and Page, S. (2003) *Managing Urban Tourism*. Harlow: Pearson Education.

Hall, C.M. and Page, S. (2014) *The Geography of Tourism and Recreation: Environment, Space and Place,* 4th Edition. Abingdon: Routledge.

Hall, D. (1993) Tourism in Eastern Europe. In W. Pompl and P. Lavery (eds) *Tourism in Europe: Structures and Developments*. Wallingford: CAB International, pp. 341–358.

Hall, D. and Richards, G. (2003) *Tourism and Sustainable Community Development*. London: Routledge.

Hall, S., Held, D. and McGrew, G. (1992a) Introduction. In S. Hall, D. Held and T. McGrew (eds) *Modernity and its Futures*. Cambridge: Polity Press: 1–11.

Hall, S., Held, D. and McGrew, T. (eds) (1992b) *Modernity and its Futures*. Cambridge: Polity Press.

Hannam, K. and Ateljevic, I. (eds) (2007) *Backpacker Tourism: Concepts and Profiles*. Clevedon: Channel View Publications.

Hannam, K. and Diekman, A. (eds) (2011) *Beyond Backpacker Tourism: Mobilities and Experiences*. Bristol: Channel View Publications.

Haralambopoulos, N. and Pizam, A. (1996) Perceived impacts of tourism: The case of Samos. *Annals of Tourism Research*, 23(3): 503–526.

Hares, A., Dickinson, J. and Wilkes, K. (2010) Climate change and the air travel decisions of UK tourists. *Journal of Transport Geography*, 18(3): 466–473.

Harkin, M. (1995) Modernist anthropology and tourism of the authentic. *Annals of Tourism Research,* 22(3): 650–670.

Harrigan, J. and Mosley, P. (1991) Evaluating the impact of World Bank structural adjustment lending. *Journal of Development Studies*, 27(3): 63–94.

Harrill, R. (2004) Residents' attitudes toward tourism development: A literature review with implications for tourism planning. *Journal of Planning Literature*, 18(3): 251–266.

Harrison, C. (1991) *Countryside Recreation in a Changing Society*. London: TMS Partnership.

Harrison, D. (1988) *The Sociology of Modernisation and Development*. London: Routledge.

Harrison, D. (ed.) (1992a) *Tourism and the Less Developed Countries*. London: Bellhaven Press.

Harrison, D. (1992b) Tourism to less developed countries: The social consequences. In D. Harrison (ed.) *Tourism and the Less Developed Countries*. London: Bellhaven Press, pp. 19–34.

Harrison, D. (ed.) (2001) *Tourism and the Less Developed World: Issues and Case Studies*. Wallingford: CABI Publishing.

Harrison, D. and Sharpley, R. (eds) (2017a) *Mass Tourism in a Small World*. Wallingford: CABI Publishing.

Harrison, D. and Sharpley, R. (2017b) Introduction: Mass tourism in a small world. In D. Harrison and R. Sharpley (eds) *Mass Tourism in a Small World*. Wallingford: CABI Publishing, pp. 1–14.

Harrison, L. and Husbands, W. (eds) (1996) *Practising Responsible Tourism: International Case Studies in Tourism Planning, Policy and Development*. Chichester: John Wiley & Sons.

Harvey, D. (1990) *The Condition of Postmodernity*. Oxford: Blackwell.

Hay, D. and Marsh, C. (eds) (2000) *Demystifying Globalisation*. Houndmills: Macmillan Press Ltd.

Haywood, K.M. (1986) Can the tourist-area life cycle be made operational? *Tourism Management*, 7(3): 154–167.

Haywood, K.M. (1988) Responsible and responsive tourism planning in the community. *Tourism Management,* 9(2): 105–118.

Heelas, P. and Woodhead, L. (2005) *The Spiritual Revolution: Why Religion is Giving Way to Spirituality*. Oxford: Blackwell Publishing.

Heeley, J. (2011) *Inside City Tourism: A European Perspective*. Bristol: Channel View Publications.

Heintzman, P. (2007) Men's wilderness experience and spirituality: Further explorations. In *Proceedings of the 2007 Northeastern Recreation Research Symposium*. Newton Square, PA: Department of Agriculture, Forest Service.

Henderson, J. (2000) War as a tourist attraction: the case of Vietnam. *International Journal of Tourism Research*, 2(3): 269–280.

Henning, G. (2012) The habit of tourism: Experiences and their ontological meaning. In R. Sharpley and P. Stone (eds) *Contemporary Tourist Experience: Concepts and Consequences*. Abingdon: Routledge, pp. 25–37.

Herbert, D. (ed.) (1995) *Heritage, Tourism and Society*. London: Pinter.

Hewison, R. (1987) *The Heritage Industry: Britain in a Climate of Decline*. London: Methuen.

Hewison, R. (1991) Commerce and culture. In J. Corner and S. Harvey (eds) *Enterprise and Heritage: Cross-currents of National Culture*. London: Routledge, pp. 157–172.

Hewison, R. (1993) Field of Dreams. *The Sunday Times*, 3 January.

Hickman, L. (2007) *The Final Call: In Search of the True Cost of our Holidays*. London: Eden Project Books.

Hirst, P. and Thompson, C. (1999) *Globalization in Question: The International Economy and the Possibilities of Governance*. Cambridge: Polity Press.

Hoggart, K., Buller, H. and Black, R. (1995) *Rural Europe: Identity and Change*. London: Arnold.

Høivik, T. and Heiberg, T. (1980) Centre-periphery tourism and self-reliance. *International Social Science Journal*, 32(1): 69–98.

Holbrook, M. and Hirschman, E. (1982) The experiential aspects of consumption: Consumer fantasies, feelings and fun. *Journal of Consumer Research*, 9: 132–140.

Holden, P. (ed.) (1984) *Alternative Tourism with a Focus on Asia*. Bangkok: ECTWT.

Holiday, S., Lewis, M.J., Nielsen, R., Anderson, H.D. and Elinzano, M. (2016) The selfie study: Archetypes and motivations in modern self-photography. *Visual Communication Quarterly*, 23(3): 175–187.

Hollinshead, K. (1993) *The Truth About Texas: A Naturalistic Study of the Construction of Heritage*. Unpublished PhD Thesis, Austin: Texas A&M University.

Hollinshead, K. and Kuon, V. (2013) The scopic drive of tourism: Foucault and eye dialectic. In O. Moufakkir and Y. Reisinger (eds) *The Host Gaze in Global Tourism*. Wallingford: CABI, pp. 1–18.

Holloway, J.C. (1998) *The Business of Tourism*, 5th Edition. Harlow: Longman.

Holloway, J.C. (2004) *Marketing for Tourism*, 4th Edition. Harlow: Pearson Education.

Holloway, J.C. and Plant, R. (1992) *Marketing for Tourism*. London: Pitman Publishing.

Holloway, J.C. with Taylor, N. (2006) *The Business of Tourism*, 7th Edition. Harlow: Prentice Hall.

Holt, D. (1995) How consumers consume: A typology of consumption practices. *Journal of Consumer Research*, 22 (June): 1–16.

Horner, S. and Swarbrooke, J. (2016) *Consumer Behaviour in Tourism*, 3rd Edition. Abingdon: Routledge.

Hosany, S. and Gilbert, D. (2010) Measuring tourists' emotional experience toward hedonic holiday destinations. *Journal of Travel Research*, 49(4): 513–526.

Howarth, G. (2006) *Death and Dying: A Sociological Introduction*. Cambridge: Polity Press.

Høyer, K. (2000) Sustainable tourism or sustainable mobility? The Norwegian case. *Journal of Sustainable Tourism*, 8(2): 147–160.

Hughes, G. (1995) Authenticity in tourism. *Annals of Tourism Research*, 22(4): 781–803.

Hughes, K., Bond, N. and Ballantyne, R. (2013) Designing and managing interpretive experiences at religious sites: Visitors' perceptions of Canterbury Cathedral. *Tourism Management*, 36: 210–220.

Hui, T., Wan, D. and Ho, A. (2007) Tourists' satisfaction, recommendation and revisiting Singapore. *Tourism Management*, 28(4): 965–975.

Hupka, R., Lenton, A. and Hutchison, K. (1999) Universal development of emotion categories in natural language. *Journal of Personality and Social Psychology*, 77(2): 247–278.

Hunter, C. (1995) On the need to re-conceptualise sustainable tourism development. *Journal of Sustainable Tourism*, 3(3): 155–165.

Hunziker, W. and Krapf, K. (1942) *Grundriss der Allgemeinen Fremdenverkehrslehre*. Zurich: Polygraphischer Verlag.

Hvengaard, G. (1994) Ecotourism: A status report and conceptual framework. *Journal of Tourism Studies*, 5(2): 24–35.

IAATO (2017) Tourists by nationality landed. International Association of Antarctic Tour Operators. Available at: https://iaato.org/documents/10157/1444539/2015–2016+Tourists+by+Nationality+(Landed)/0b7448 86–827a-4597–82e1-eae297b7022f (accessed 27 March 2017).

IEP (2014) *Global Terrorism Index 2014.* Institute for Economics & Peace. Available at: http://economic sandpeace.org/wp-content/uploads/2015/06/Global-Terrorism-Index-Report-2014.pdf (accessed 17 April 2017).

IFTO (1994) *Planning for Sustainable Tourism: The ECOMOST Project.* Lewes: International Federation of Tour Operators.

Igbaria, M. and Chakrabarti, A. (1990) Computer anxiety and attitudes towards microcomputer use. *Behaviour & Information Technology,* 9(3): 229–241.

Inskeep, I. and Kallenberger, M. (1992) *An Integrated Approach to Resort Development, Six Case Studies.* Madrid: World Tourism Organization.

International Trade Forum (2011) *Tourism and the Least Developed Countries.* www.tradeforum.org/upload edFiles/Common/Content/TradeForum/Issues/Web%20version%20final_02.pdf (accessed 2 June 2017).

Ioannides, D. (1992) Tourism development agents: The Cypriot resort cycle. *Annals of Tourism Research,* 19(4): 711–731.

Iso-Ahola, S. (1982) Toward a social psychological theory of tourism motivation: A rejoinder. *Annals of Tourism Research,* 9(2): 256–262.

Issa, J. and Jayawardena, C. (2003) The 'all-inclusive' concept in the Caribbean. *International Journal of Contemporary Hospitality Management,* 15(3): 167–171.

IUCN (1991) *Caring for the Earth: A Strategy for Sustainable Living.* Gland, Switzerland: World Conservation Union.

Jackson, R. and Hudman, L. (1995) Pilgrimage tourism and English cathedrals: The role of religion in travel. *The Tourist Review,* 50(4): 40–48.

Jacobsen, J. and Munar, A. (2012) Tourist information search and destination choice in a digital age. *Tourism Management Perspectives,* 1(1): 39–47.

Jafari, J. (1977) Editors Page. *Annals of Tourism Research,* 5(1): 8.

Jafari, J. (1987) Tourism models: The sociocultural aspects. *Tourism Management,* 8(2): 151–159.

Jafari, J. (1989) Sociocultural dimensions of tourism: An English language literature review. In J. Bystrzanowski (ed.) *Tourism as a Factor of Change: A Sociocultural Study.* Vienna: Vienna Centre, pp. 17–60.

Jamal, T. and Dredge, D. (2015) Tourism and community development issues. In R. Sharpley and D. Telfer (eds) *Tourism and Development: Concepts and Issues,* 2nd Edition. Bristol: Channel View Publications, pp. 178–204.

Jameson, F. (1984) Postmodernism, or the cultural logic of late capitalism. *New Left Review,* 146: 53–92.

Jang, S. and Feng, R. (2007) Temporal destination revisit intention: The effects of novelty seeking and satisfaction. *Tourism Management,* 28(2): 580–590.

Jarratt, D. and Gammon, S. (2016) 'We had the most wonderful times': Seaside nostalgia at a British resort. *Tourism Recreation Research,* 41(2): 123–133.

Jarratt, D. and Sharpley, R. (2017) Tourists at the seaside: Exploring the spiritual dimension. *Tourist Studies* (online) doi: 10.1177/1468797616687560.

Jary, D. and Jary, J. (1991) *Collins Dictionary of Sociology.* London: Harper Collins.

Jebb, M. (1986) *Walkers.* London: Constable.

Jenkins, C. (1991) Tourism development strategies. In L. Likorish (ed.) *Developing Tourism Destinations,* Harlow: Longman, pp. 61–77.

Jenkins, O. (2003) Photography and travel brochures: The circle of representation. *Tourism Geographies,* 5(3): 305–328.

Jenner, P. and Smith, C. (1992) *The Tourism Industry and the Environment,* Special Report No. 2453, London: Economic Intelligence Unit.

Jepson, D. and Sharpley, R. (2015) More than sense of place? Exploring the emotional dimension of rural tourism experiences. *Journal of Sustainable Tourism,* 23(8–9): 1157–1178.

Johnson, J., Snepenger, D. and Akis, S. (1994) Residents' perceptions of tourism development. *Annals of Tourism Research,* 21(3): 629–642.

Johnson, P. and Thomas, B. (ed.) (1992) *Choice and Demand in Tourism.* London: Mansell Publishing.

Johnston, B. (2005) Naples bans motorbikes and scooters in battle against bag snatchers and the Mafia. *The Telegraph*. Available at: www.telegraph.co.uk/news/worldnews/europe/italy/1490064/Naples-bans-mo torbikes-and-scooters-in-battle-against-bag-snatchers-and-the-Mafia.html (accessed 7 September 2017).

Jones, A. (1987) Green tourism. *Tourism Management*, 8(4): 354–356.

Jorvik (2017) Jorvik Viking Centre. Available at: www.jorvikvikingcentre.co.uk/about/ (accessed 31 March 2017).

Jurowski, C. and Gursoy, D. (2004) Distance effects on residents' attitudes toward tourism. *Annals of Tourism Research*, 31(2): 296–312.

Kahle, L., Beatty, S. and Homer, P. (1986) Alternative measurement approaches to consumer values: The list of values (LOV) and values and lifestyles (VALS). *Journal of Consumer Research*, 13: 405–409.

Kalat, J. (2011) *Introduction to Psychology*, 9th Edition. Belmont, CA: Wadsworth.

Kamakura, W. and Mazzon, J. (1991) Value segmentation: A model for the measurement of values and value systems. *Journal of Consumer Research*, 18: 208–218.

Kaplan, S. (1995) The restorative benefits of nature: Towards an integrative framework. *Journal of Environmental Psychology*, 15(3): 169–182.

Kariel, H. (1989) Tourism and development: Perplexity or panacea? *Journal of Travel Research*, 28(1): 2–6.

Kelman, I. and Dodds, R. (2009) Developing a code of ethics for disaster tourism. *International Journal of Mass Emergencies and Disasters*, 27(3): 272–296.

Kemp, S. (2017) Digital in 2017: Global overview. Available at: https://wearesocial.com/special-reports/dig ital-in-2017-global-overview (accessed 6 October 2017).

Khaleeli, H. (2017) From Barcelona to Malia: how Brits on holiday have made themselves unwelcome. *The Guardian, Travel Shortcuts*. Available at www.theguardian.com/travel/shortcuts/2017/jan/17/from-barce lona-to-malia-how-brits-on-holiday-have-made-themselves-unwelcome (accessed 28 April 2017).

Kiely, T. (2013) Tapping into Mammon: Stakeholder perspectives on developing church tourism in Dublin's Liberties. *Tourism Review*, 68(2): 31–43.

Kim, H. and Richardson, S. (2003) Motion picture impacts on destination images. *Annals of Tourism Research*, 30(1): 216–237.

King, B., Pizam, A. and Milman, A. (1993) Social impacts of tourism: Host perceptions. *Annals of Tourism Research*, 20(4): 650–665.

Kinnaird, V. and Hall, D. (eds) (1994) *Tourism: A Gender Analysis*. Chichester: John Wiley & Sons.

Klemm, M. (1992) Sustainable tourism development: Languedoc-Rousillon thirty years on. *Tourism Management*, 13(2): 169–180.

Klenosky, D. (2002) The 'pull' of tourism destinations: A means-end investigation. *Journal of Travel Research*, 40(4): 385–395.

Knutsson, B. (2009) The intellectual history of development towards a widening potential repertoire. *Perspectives* No. 13, April 2009. www.gu.se/digitalAssets/1272/1272997_Perspectives_13.pdf (accessed 7 June 2017).

Koenig-Lewis, N. and Palmer, A., (2014) The effects of anticipatory emotions on service satisfaction and behavioral intention. *Journal of Services Marketing*, 28(6): 437–451.

Korpela, K. and Hartig, T. (1996) Restorative qualities of favourite places. *Journal of Environmental Psychology*, 16(3): 221–233.

Kounavis, C., Kasimati, A. and Zamani, E. (2012) Enhancing the tourism experience through mobile aug mented reality: Challenges and prospects. *International Journal of Engineering Business Management*, 4. Avail able at: http://journals.sagepub.com/doi/pdf/10.5772/51644 (accessed 12 October 2017).

Kozak, M. (2003) Measuring tourist satisfaction with multiple destination attributes. *Tourism Analysis*, 7(3–4): 229–269.

Kozak, M. and Rimmington, M. (2000) Tourist satisfaction with Mallorca, Spain, as an off-season holiday destination. *Journal of Travel Research*, 38(3): 260–269.

Krippendorf, J. (1986) Tourism in the system of industrial society. *Annals of Tourism Research,* 13(4): 517–532.

Krippendorf, J. (1987) *The Holiday Makers*. Oxford: Heinemann.

Kwon, M., Lee, J., Won, W., Park, J., Min, J., Hahn, C., Gu, X., Choi, J. and Kim, D. (2013) Development and validation of a smartphone addiction scale (SAS). *PloS ONE*, 8(2). Available at: http://journals.plos.org/ plosone/article?id=10.1371/journal.pone.0056936 (accessed 13 October 2017).

Laing, J. and Crouch, G. (2006) From the frontier: sacred journeys in far away places. Paper presented at the *Tourism: The Spiritual Dimension* Conference, University of Lincoln, UK (unpublished).

Lambert, Y. (2004) A turning point in religious evolution in Europe. *Journal of Contemporary Religion*, 19(1): 29–45.

Larsen, J. (2005) Families seen sightseeing: Performativity of tourist photography. *Space and Culture*, 8(4): 416–434.

Larsen, J. and Sandbye, M. (2014) *Digital Snaps: The New Face of Photography*. London: I.B. Taurus.

Lash, S. (1990) *Sociology of Postmodernism*. London: Routledge.

Lash, S. and Urry, J. (1987) *The End of Organised Capitalism*. Cambridge: Polity.

Lau, R. (2010) Revisiting authenticity: A social realist approach. *Annals of Tourism Research*, 37(2): 478–498.

Law, C. (2002) *Urban Tourism: The Visitor Economy and the Growth of Large Cities*, 2nd Edition. London: Continuum.

Law, R. (2006) The perceived impact of risks on travel decisions. *International Journal of Tourism Research*, 8(4): 289–300.

Lazarus, J. (2008) Participation in Poverty Reduction Strategy Papers: Reviewing the past, assessing the present and predicting the future. *Third World Quarterly*, 29(6): 1205–1221.

Lea, J. (1988) *Tourism and Development in the Third World*. London: Routledge.

Lee, D. (2017) London-Paris electric flight 'in decade'. BBC News. Available at: www.bbc.co.uk/news/technology-39350058 (accessed 24 March 2017).

Lee, G. (1987) Tourism as a factor in development co-operation. *Tourism Management*, 8(1): 2–19.

Lee, T. and Crompton, J. (1992) Measuring novelty seeking in tourism. *Annals of Tourism Research*, 19(4): 732–751.

Leigh, J. (2011) New tourism in a new society arises from 'peak oil'. *Tourismos*, 6(1): 165–191.

Lélé, S. (1991) Sustainable development: A critical review. *World Development*, 19(6): 607–621.

Lennon, J. and Foley M. (2000) *Dark Tourism: The Attraction of Death and Disaster*. London: Continuum.

Lett, J. (1983) Ludic and liminoid aspects of charter yacht tourism in the Caribbean. *Annals of Tourism Research*, 10(1): 35–56.

Lett, J. (1989) Epilogue to touristic studies in anthropological perspective. In V. Smith (ed.) *Hosts and Guests: The Anthropology of Tourism,* 2nd Edition. Philadelphia: University of Pennsylvania Press, pp, 275–279.

Levine, L. and Pizzaro, D. (2004) Emotion and memory research: A grumpy overview. *Social Cognition*, 22(5): 530–554.

Li, M., Sharpley, R. and Gammon, S. (2017) Towards an understanding of Chinese tourist photography: Evidence from the UK. *Current Issues in Tourism* (online) doi: 10.1080/13683500.2017.1377690.

Lickorish, L. (1990) Tourism facing change. In M. Quest (ed.) *The Horwath Book of Tourism*, London: Macmillan, pp. 108–127.

Liechty, M. (2005) Building the road to Kathmandu: Notes on the history of tourism in Nepal. *HIMALAYA, the Journal of the Association for Nepal and Himalayan Studies*, 25(1): 19–28.

Light, D. (2017) Progress in dark tourism and thanatourism research: An uneasy relationship with heritage tourism. *Tourism Management*, 61: 275–301.

Lillywhite, M. and Lillywhite, L. (1991) Low impact tourism. In D. Hawkins and J. Brent Ritchie (eds) *World Travel and Tourism Review: Indicators, Trends and Forecasts*, Wallingford: CAB International, pp. 162–169.

Liu, J. and Var, T. (1986) Resident attitudes toward tourism impacts in Hawaii. *Annals of Tourism Research*, 13(2): 193–214.

Liu, K. (2013) Happiness and tourism. *International Journal of Business and Social Science*, 4(15): 67–70.

Lo, I.S., McKercher, B., Lo, A., Cheung, C. and Law, R. (2011) Tourism and online photography. *Tourism Management*, 32(4): 725–731.

Lois González, R. (2013) The Camino de Santiago and its contemporary renewal: Pilgrims, tourists and territorial identities. *Culture and Religion*, 14(1): 8–22.

Loker-Murphy, L. and Pearce, P. (1995) Young budget travellers: Backpackers in Australia. *Annals of Tourism Research*, 22(4): 819–843.

Lowenthal, D. (1990) *The Past is a Foreign Country*. Cambridge: Cambridge University Press.

Lowyck, E., Van Langenhove, L. and Bollaert, L. (1992) Typologies of tourist roles. In P. Johnson and B. Thomas (eds) *Choice and Demand in Tourism*. London: Mansell Publishing, pp. 13–32.

Ludwig, D., Hilborn, R. and Walters, C. (1993) Uncertainty, resource exploitation, and conservation: Lessons from history. *Science*, 269(5104): 17 and 36.

Luk, S., de Leon, C., Leong, F. and Li, E. (1993) Value segmentation of tourists' expectations of service quality. *Journal of Travel and Tourism Marketing*, 2(4): 23–38.

Lumley, R. (ed.) (1988) *The Museum Time-Machine*. London: Routledge.

Lunden, I. (2015) 6.1B Smartphone Users Globally by 2020, Overtaking Basic Fixed Phone Subscriptions. *TecCrunch*. Available at: https://techcrunch.com/2015/06/02/6–1b-smartphone-users-globally-by-2020-overtaking-basic-fixed-phone-subscriptions/ (accessed 6 October 2017).

Lupfer, M., Brock, K. and DePaola, S. (1992) The use of secular and religious attributions to explain everyday behaviour, *Journal of the Scientific Study of Religion*, 31(4): 486–503.

Lury, C. (1996) *Consumer Culture*. Cambridge: Polity Press.

Lusher, A. (2015) A history of package holidays: Rising numbers indicate a renaissance with an updated and classier holiday experience. *The Independent*. Available at: www.independent.co.uk/travel/news-and-advice/a-history-of-package-holidays-rising-numbers-indicate-a-renaissance-with-an-updated-and-class ier-10306101.html (accessed 23 March 2017).

Lyons, K., Hanley, J., Wearing, S. and Neil, J. (2012) Gap year volunteer tourism: Myths of global citizenship? *Annals of Tourism Research*, 39(1): 361–378.

Lyotard, J. (1984) *The Postmodern Condition: A Report on Knowledge*. Manchester: Manchester University Press.

Mabogunje, A. (1980) *The Development Process: A Spatial Perspective*. London: Hutchinson.

MacCannell, D. (1973) Staged authenticity: Arrangements of social space in tourist settings. *American Journal of Sociology*, 79: 589–603.

MacCannell, D. (1976) *The Tourist: A New Theory of the Leisure Class*. New York: Schocken Books.

MacCannell, D. (1989) *The Tourist: A New Theory of the Leisure Class*, 2nd Edition. New York: Schocken Books.

MacCannell, D. (2013) *The Tourist: A New Theory of the Leisure Class*. Berkeley and Los Angeles: University of California Press.

Macnaught, T. (1982) Mass tourism and the dilemmas of modernisation in Pacific island communities. *Annals of Tourism Research*, 9(3): 359–381.

Macnaughten, P. and Urry, J. (1998) *Contested Natures*. London: Sage Publications.

Madrigal, R. and Kahle, L. (1994) Predicting vacation activity preferences on the basis of value-system segmentation. *Journal of Travel Research*, 32(3): 22–28.

Mann, M. (2000) *The Community Tourism Guide*. London: Earthscan Publications.

Mannell, R. and Iso-Ahola, S. (1987) Psychological nature of leisure and tourism experience. *Annals of Tourism Research*, 14(3): 314–331.

Mansfeld, Y. (1992) From motivation to actual travel. *Annals of Tourism Research*, 19(3): 399–419.

Mao, N., Delacy, T. and Grunfeld, H. (2013) Local livelihoods and the tourism value chain: The case of Cambodia. *Tourism Recreation Research*, 27(1): 91–102.

Marcoulides, G. (1989) Measuring computer anxiety: The computer anxiety scale. *Educational and Psychological Measurement*, 49(3): 733–739.

Markwell, K. (1997) Dimensions of photography in a nature-based tour. *Annals of Tourism Research*, 24(1): 131–155.

Martin, D., O'Neill, M., Hubbard, S. and Palmer, A. (2008) The role of emotion in explaining consumer satisfaction and future behavioural intention. *Journal of Services Marketing*, 22(3): 224–236.

Martin, W. and Mason, S. (1987) Social trends and tourism futures. *Tourism Management*, 8(2): 112–114.

Maslow, A. (1943) A theory of human motivation. *Psychological Review*, 50: 370–396.

Mason, P. (2008) *Tourism Impacts, Planning and Management*. Abingdon: Routledge.

Mason, P. and Cheyne, J. (2000) Residents' attitudes to proposed tourism development. *Annals of Tourism Research*, 27(2): 391–411.

Matthews, H. and Richter, L. (1991) Political science and tourism. *Annals of Tourism Research*, 18(1): 120–135.

Mathieson, A. and Wall, G. (1982) *Tourism: Economic, Physical and Social Impacts*. Harlow: Longman.

Mayo, E. (1975) Tourism and national parks: A psychographic and attitudinal study. *Journal of Travel Research*, 14(1): 14–17.

Mazar, N. and Zhong, C. (2010) Do green products make us better people? *Psychological Science*, 1(4): 494–498.

McAreavey, R. and McDonagh, J. (2011) Sustainable rural tourism: Lessons for rural development. *Sociologia Ruralis*, 51(2): 175–194.

McCabe, S. (2002) The tourist experience and everyday life. In G. Dann (ed.) *The Tourist as a Metaphor of the Social World*, Wallingford: CABI, pp. 61–75.

McCabe, S. (2005) 'Who is a tourist?' A critical review. *Tourist Studies*, 5(1): 85–106.

McCarthy, T. (1994) Booking trends. *Travel Weekly Plus* 2, March, p. 35.

McCracken, G. (1986) Culture and consumption: A theoretical account of the structure and movement of the cultural meaning of consumer goods. *Journal of Consumer Research*, 13: 71–84.

McGehee, N. and Andereck, K. (2004) Factors predicting rural residents' support of tourism. *Journal of Travel Research*, 43(2): 131–140.

McGillivray, M. (2008) What is development? In D. Kingsbury, J. McKay, J. Hunt, M. McGillivray and M. Clarke (eds) *International Development: Issues and Challenges*. Houndmills: Palgrave Macmillan, pp. 21–50.

McGrew, A. (1992) A global society? In S. Hall, D. Held, and T. McGrew (eds) *Modernity and its Futures,* Cambridge: Polity Press, pp. 61–116.

McIntosh, A. and Prentice, R. (1999) Affirming authenticity: consuming cultural heritage. *Annals of Tourism Research*, 26(3): 589–612.

McIntosh, R. and Goeldner, C. (1990) *Tourism: Principles, Practices and Philosophies*. New York: Wiley.

McKean, P. (1989) Towards a theoretical analysis of tourism: Economic dualism and cultural involution in Bali. In V. Smith (ed.) *Hosts and Guests: The Anthropology of Tourism,* 2nd Edition. Philadelphia: University of Pennsylvania Press, pp. 119–138.

McKelvie, J. (2005) Religious tourism. *Travel and Tourism Analyst*, (4): 1–47.

McKercher, B. (1993) Some fundamental truths about tourism. *Journal of Sustainable Tourism*, 1(1): 6–16.

McKercher, B. and du Cros, H. (2002) *Cultural Tourism: The Partnership between Tourism and Cultural Heritage Management*. Abingdon: Routledge.

McKercher, B. and du Cros, H. (2003) Testing a cultural tourism typology. *International Journal of Tourism Research*, 5(1): 45–58.

McLennan, G. (1992) The enlightenment project revisited. In S. Hall, D. Held and T. McGrew (eds) *Modernity and its Futures.* Cambridge: Polity Press, pp. 327–377.

McMinn, S. and Cater, E. (1998) Tourist typologies: Observations from Belize. *Annals of Tourism Research*, 25(3): 675–699.

McPheters, L. and Stronge, W. (1974) Crime as an environmental externality of tourism. *Land Economics*, 50: 359–381.

McQueen, M. (1983) Appropriate policies towards multinational hotel corporations in developing countries. *World Development*, 11(2): 141–152.

MDG Monitor (2017) *Millennium Development Goals: Eradicate Poverty and Hunger.* Available at: www.mdg monitor.org/mdg-1-eradicate-poverty-hunger/ (accessed 4 June 2017).

Meethan, K. (2001) *Tourism in Global Society: Place Culture, Consumption.* Basingstoke: Palgrave.

Mehmetoglu, M. (2003) *The Solitary Traveller: Why Do People Travel On Their Own?* Unpublished PhD thesis, University of Bedfordshire. Available at: http://uobrep.openrepository.com/uobrep/handle/10547/324321 (accessed 11 April 2017).

Mehmetoglu, M. and Olsen, K. (2003) Talking authenticity: What kind of experiences do solitary travellers in the Norwegian Lofoten Islands regard as authentic? *Tourism, Culture & Communication*, 4(3): 137–152.

Mehmetoglu, M., Hines, K., Graumann, C. and Greibrokk, J. (2010) The relationship between personal values and tourism behaviour: A segmentation approach. *Journal of Vacation Marketing*, 16(1): 17–27.

Mellor, P. and Shilling, C. (1993) Modernity, self-identity and the sequestration of death. *Sociology*, 27: 411–431.

Middleton, V. (1988) *Marketing in Travel and Tourism*. Oxford: Heinemann.

Middleton, V., Fyall, A., Morgan, M. and Ranchhod, A. (2009) *Marketing in Travel and Tourism,* 4th Edition. Oxford: Butterworth Heinemann.

Mihalič, T. (2015) Tourism and economic development issues. In R. Sharpley and D. Telfer (eds) *Tourism and Development: Concepts and Issues,* 2nd Edition, Bristol: Channel View Publications, pp. 77–117.

Miles, W. (2002) Auschwitz: Museum interpretation and darker tourism. *Annals of Tourism* Research, 29: 1175–1178.

Mill, R. and Morrison, A. (1985) *The Tourism System*. New Jersey: Prentice Hall International.

Miller, D. (1987) *Material Culture and Mass Consumption*. Oxford: Blackwell.

Milman, A. and Pizam, A. (1988) Social impacts of tourism on Central Florida. *Annals of Tourism Research*, 15(2): 191–204.

Milman, A., Reichal, A. and Pizam, A. (1990) The impact of tourism on ethnic attitudes: The Israeli-Egyptian case. *Journal of Travel Research*, 29(2): 45–49.

Mintel (1994) *The Green Consumer I: The Green Conscience*. London: Mintel International.

Mintel (2007) *Green and Ethical Consumers*. London: Mintel International.

Mintel (2012) *Religious and Pilgrimage Tourism*: Market Report. London: Mintel International.

Mishan, E. (1969) *The Costs of Economic Growth*. Harmondsworth: Penguin.

Momsen, J. (2004) *Gender and Development*. London: Routledge.

Moore, M. (2007) Tourists pay for being rude in Venice. *Daily Telegraph*, 9 August, p. 20.

Morris, H. (2017) Help us stem Dubrovnik tourist tide, mayor urges cruise industry. *Daily Telegraph*, Travel News, 9 September, p. 5.

Moshin, A. and Ryan, C. (2003) Backpackers in the Northern Territories of Australia: Motives, behaviours and satisfactions. *International Journal of Tourism Research*, 5(2): 113–131.

Mosley, P. and Toye, J. (1988) The design of structural adjustment programmes. *Development Policy Review*, 6(4): 395–413.

Moufakkir, O. and Kelly, I. (eds) (2010) *Tourism, Progress and Peace*. Wallingford: CABI.

Moufakkir, O. and Reisinger, Y. (2013) Introduction: Gazemaking: Le regard. Do you hear me? In O. Moufakkir and Y. Reisinger (eds) *The Host Gaze in Global Tourism*. Wallingford: CABI, pp. xi–xvi.

Moutinho, L. (1987) Consumer behaviour in tourism. *European Journal of Marketing*, 21(10): 5–44.

Mowforth, M. and Munt, I. (2009) *Tourism and Sustainability: Development, Globalisation and New Tourism in the Third World*, 3rd Edition. Abingdon: Routledge.

Müller, T. (1991) Using personal values to define segments in an international tourism market. *International Marketing Review*, 8(1): 57–70.

Munt, I. (1994) The 'other' postmodern tourism: Culture, travel and the new middle classes. *Theory, Culture and Society*, 11(3): 101–123.

Murphy, L. (2001) Exploring social interactions of backpackers. *Annals of Tourism Research*, 28(1): 50–67.

Murphy, P. (1983) Tourism as a community industry. *Tourism Management*, 4(3): 180–193.

Murphy, P. (1985) *Tourism: A Community Approach*. London: Routledge.

Murphy, P. (1988) Community driven tourism planning. *Tourism Management*, 9(2): 96–104.

Murray, R. (1989) Fordism and post-Fordism. In S. Hall and M. Jacques (eds) *New Times*: *Changing Face of Politics in the 1990s*. London: Lawrence & Wishart, pp. 38–52.

Naidoo, P. and Sharpley, R. (2016) Local perceptions of the relative contributions of enclave tourism and agritourism to community well-being: The case of Mauritius. *Journal of Destination Marketing & Management*, 5(1): 16–25.

Nash, D. (1981) Tourism as an anthropological subject. *Current Anthropology*, 22(5): 461–481.

Nash, D. (1989) Tourism as a form of imperialism. In V. Smith (ed.) *Hosts and Guests: The Anthropology of Tourism*, 2nd Edition. Philadelphia: University of Pennsylvania Press, pp. 37–52.

Nash, D. (1996) *Anthropology of Tourism*. Oxford: Pergamon Press.

Nash, D. and Smith, V. (1991) Anthropology and tourism. *Annals of Tourism Research*, 18(1): 12–25.

Nawijn, J. (2010) The holiday happiness curve: A preliminary investigation into mood during a holiday abroad. *International Journal of Tourism Research*, 12(3): 281–290.

Nawijn, J. (2011a) Happiness through vacationing: Just a temporary boost or long-term benefits? *Journal of Happiness Studies*, 12(4): 651–665.

Nawijn, J. (2011b) Determinants of daily happiness on vacation. *Journal of Travel Research*, 50(5): 559–566.

Nawijn, J. and Fricke, M. (2015) Visitor emotions and behavioral intentions: The case of concentration camp memorial Neuengamme. *International Journal of Tourism Research*, 17(3): 221–228.

Nawijn, J., Marchand, M.A., Veenhoven, R. and Vingerhoets, A. (2010) Vacationers happier, but most not happier after a holiday. *Applied Research in Quality of Life*, 5(1): 35–47.

Nepal, S. (2008) Residents' attitudes to tourism in central British Columbia, Canada. *Tourism Geographies: An International Journal of Tourism Space, Place and Environment*, 10(1): 42–65.

Neuhofer, B. (2014) The technology enhanced tourist experience. In R. Baggio, M. Sigala, A. Inversini and J. Pesonen (eds) *Information and Communication Technologies in Tourism 2014, eProceedings of the ENTER 2014*

PhD Workshop in Dublin, Ireland, pp. 90–96. Available at: www.ifitt.org/wp-content/uploads/2014/05/eProceedings_ENTER2014_PhDWS-Jan17201411.pdf#page=93 (accessed 9 October 2017).

Neumayer, E. (2004) The impact of political violence on tourism: Dynamic cross-national estimation. *Journal of Conflict Resolution,* 48(2): 259–281.

Newsome, D., Moore, S. and Dowling, R. (2013) *Natural Area Tourism: Ecology, Impacts and Management,* 2nd Edition. Bristol: Channel View Publications.

Nicolau, J. and Mas, F. (2006) The influence of distance and prices on the choice of tourist destinations: The moderating role of motivations. *Tourism Management.* 27(5): 982–996.

Nkyi, E. and Hashimoto, A. (2015) Human rights issues in tourism development. In R. Sharpley and D. Telfer (eds) *Tourism and Development: Concepts and Issues,* 2nd Edition. Bristol: Channel View Publications, pp. 378–399.

Novak, T. and MacEvoy, B. (1990) On comparing alternative segmentation schemes: The list of values (LOV) and values and lifestyles (VALS). *Journal of Consumer Research,* 17: 105–109.

Novelli, M. (ed.) (2005) *Niche Tourism: Contemporary Issues, Trends and Cases.* Oxford: Elsevier Butterworth-Heinemann.

Noy, C. (2004) The trip really changed me. *Annals of Tourism Research,* 31(1): 78–102.

Nuñez, T. (1963) Tourism, tradition and acculturation: Weekendismo in a Mexican village. *Ethnology,* 2(3): 347–352.

Nuñez, T. (1989) Touristic studies in anthropological perspective. In V. Smith (ed.) *Hosts and Guests: The Anthropology of Tourism,* 2nd Edition. Philadelphia: University of Pennsylvania Press, pp. 265–274.

Nunkoo, R., Smith, S. and Ramkissoon, M. (2013) Resident attitudes to tourism: A longitudinal study of 140 articles from 1984 to 2010. *Journal of Sustainable Tourism,* 21(1): 5–25.

O'Callahgan, L. (2016) Should we ban phones in restaurants? *The Express.* Available at: www.express.co.uk/life-style/life/665420/ban-mobile-phones-in-restaurants-say-majority-of-brits (accessed 13 October 2017).

OECD (2013) *OECD and Post 2015 Reflections: Keeping the Multiple Dimensions of Poverty at the Heart of Development.* Element 1, Paper 1. Available at: www.oecd.org/dac/POST-2015%20multidimensional%20poverty.pdf (accessed 4 June January 2017).

Okazaki, S. and Hirose, M. (2009) Does gender affect media choice in travel information search? On the use of mobile Internet. *Tourism Management,* 30(6): 794–804.

Oliver, R. (1997) *Satisfaction: A Behavioural Perspective on the Consumer.* London: McGraw-Hill.

Olsen, K. (2002) Authenticity as a concept in tourism research: The social organisation of the experience of authenticity. *Tourist Studies,* 2(2): 159–182.

Olsen, D. and Timothy, D. (2006) Tourism and religious journeys. In D. Timothy and D. Olsen (eds) *Tourism, Religion and Spiritual Journeys.* Abingdon: Routledge, pp. 1–22.

O'Neill, C. and Walton, J. (2004) Tourism and the Lake District: Social and cultural histories. In D. Hind and J. Mitchell (eds) *Sustainable Tourism in the English Lake District.* Sunderland: Business Education Publishers, pp. 19–47.

Opperman, M. (1993) Tourism space in developing countries. *Annals of Tourism Research,* 20(4): 535–556.

Opperman, M. (1998) *Sex Tourism and Prostitution: Aspects of Leisure, Recreation and Work.* New York: Cognizant.

Opperman, M. and Chon, K. (1997) *Tourism in Developing Countries.* London: International Thomson Business Press.

O'Reilly, A. (1986) Tourism carrying capacity: Concept and issues. *Tourism Management,* 7(4): 254–258.

O'Reilly, C. (2005) Tourist or traveller? Narrating backpacker identity. In A. Jaworski and A. Pritchard (eds) *Discourse, Communication and Tourism.* Bristol: Channel View Publications, pp. 150–169.

O'Reilly, C. (2006) From drifter to gap year tourist: Mainstreaming backpacker travel. *Annals of Tourism Research,* 33(4): 998–1017.

O'Reilly, K. (2003) When is a tourist? The articulation of tourism and migration in Spain's Costa del Sol. *Tourist Studies,* 3(3): 301–317.

O'Rourke, P. (1988) *Holidays in Hell.* London: Picador.

Osborne, C. (1993) Making the most out of tourism. *In Focus,* Tourism Concern, 10: 10–11.

Ousby, I. (1990) *The Englishman's England: Taste, Travel and the Rise of Tourism.* Cambridge: Cambridge University Press.

Owen, R. (1991) *A New View of Society and Other Writings*. Harmondsworth: Penguin.

Pagden, A. (2013) *The Enlightenment and Why It Still Matters*. Oxford: OUP.

Page, S. and Getz, D. (eds) (1997) *The Business of Rural Tourism: International Perspectives*. London: International Thomson Business Press.

Palacio, V. and McCool, S. (1997) Identifying ecotourists in Belize through benefit segmentation: A preliminary analysis. *Journal of Sustainable Tourism*, 5(3): 234–243.

Palacios, C. (2010) Volunteer tourism, development and education in a postcolonial world: Conceiving global connections beyond aid. *Journal of Sustainable Tourism*, 18(7): 861–878.

Palma, G. (1995) Underdevelopment and Marxism: From Marx to the theories of imperialism and dependency. In R. Ayers (ed.) *Development Studies: An Introduction through Selected Readings*. Dartford: Greenwich University Press, pp. 161–210.

Palmer, A., Koenig-Lewis, N. and Jones, L. (2013) The effects of residents' social identity and involvement on their advocacy of incoming tourism. *Tourism Management*, 38(1): 142–151.

Parker, S. (1983) *Leisure and Work*. London: Allen and Unwin.

Parrinello, G. (1993) Motivation and anticipation in post-industrial tourism. *Annals of Tourism Research*, 20(2): 233–249.

Passariello, P. (1983) Never on Sunday? Mexican tourists at the beach. *Annals of Tourism Research*, 10(1): 109–122.

Pastor, M. (1987) The effects of IMF programs in the Third World: Debate and experience from Latin America. *World Development*, 15(2): 249–262.

Pearce, B. and Pearce, D. (2000) *Setting Environmental Taxes for Aircraft: A Case Study of the UK*. Norwich: Centre for Social and Economic Research on the Global Environment.

Pearce, D. and Butler, R. (eds) (1992) *Tourism Research: Critiques and Challenges*. London: Routledge.

Pearce, D. (1989) *Tourist Development*, 2nd Edition. Harlow: Longman.

Pearce, P. (1982) *The Social Psychology of Tourist Behaviour*. Oxford: Pergamon Press.

Pearce, P. (1988) *The Ulysses Factor*. New York: Springer-Verlag.

Pearce, P. (1992) Fundamentals of tourist motivation. In D. Pearce and R. Butler (eds) *Tourism Research: Critiques and Challenges*. London: Routledge, pp. 113–134.

Pearce, P. (1994) Tourist-resident impacts: Examples, explanations and emerging solutions. In W. Theobald (ed.) *Global Tourism: The Next Decade*. Oxford: Butterworth Heinemann, pp. 103–123.

Pearce, P. (2005) *Tourist Behaviour: Themes and Conceptual Schemes*. Clevedon: Channel View Publications.

Pearce, P. (2011) *Tourist Behaviour and the Contemporary World*. Bristol: Channel View Publications.

Pearce, P. and Caltabiano, M. (1983) Inferring travel motivation from travellers' experiences. *Journal of Travel Research*, 22: 16–20.

Pearce, P. and Moscardo, G. (1986) The concept of authenticity in tourist settings. *Australian and New Zealand Journal of Sociology*, 22(1): 121–132.

Pearce, P. and Packer, J. (2013) Minds on the move: New links from psychology to tourism. *Annals of Tourism Research*, 40: 386–341.

Perdue, R., Long, P. and Allen, L. (1987) Rural resident tourism perceptions and attitudes. *Annals of Tourism Research*, 14(3): 420–429.

Perez, C. (2003) *Technological Revolutions and Financial Capital*. Cheltenham: Edward Elgar Publishing.

Pérez, E. and Nadal, J. (2005) Host community perceptions: A cluster analysis. *Annals of Tourism Research*, 32(4): 925–941.

Perlmutter, H. (1991) On the rocky road to the first global civilisation. *Human Relations*, 44(9): 897–920.

Pfaffenberger, B. (1983) Serious pilgrims and frivolous tourists, *Annals of Tourism Research*, 10(1): 57–74.

Picard, M. (1995) Cultural heritage and tourist capital: Cultural tourism in Bali. In M. Lanfant, J. Allcock and E. Bruner (eds) *International Tourism: Identity and Change*, London: Sage Publications, pp. 44–66.

Pigram, J. (1990) Sustainable tourism: Policy considerations. *Journal of Tourism Studies*, 1(2): 2–9.

Pike, S. (2002) Destination image analysis—a review of 142 papers from 1973 to 2000. *Tourism Management*, 23(5): 541–549.

Pimlott, J. (1947) *The Englishman's Holiday*. London: Faber & Faber.

Pi-Sunyer, O. (1989) Changing perceptions of tourism and tourists in a Catalan resort town. In V. Smith (ed.) *Hosts and Guests: The Anthropology of Tourism*, 2nd Edition. Philadelphia: University of Pennsylvania Press, pp. 187–199.

Pittman, M. and Reich, B. (2016) Social media and loneliness: Why an Instagram picture may be worth more than a thousand Twitter words. *Computers in Human Behavior*, 62: 155–167.

Pitts, R. and Woodside, A. (1986) Personal values and travel decisions. *Journal of Travel Research* 25(1): 20–25.

Pizam, A. (1978) Tourism's impacts: The social cost to the destination community as perceived by its residents. *Journal of Travel Research,* 16(1): 8–12.

Pizam, A. (1999) A comprehensive approach to classifying acts of crime and violence at tourist destinations. *Journal of Travel Research*, 38(1): 5–13.

Pizam, A. and Calantone, R. (1987) Beyond psychographics: values as determinants of tourist behaviour. *International Journal of Hospitality Management*, 6(3): 177–181.

Pizam, A. and Mansfeld, Y. (eds) (1996) *Tourism, Crime and International Security Issues*. Chichester: John Wiley & Sons.

Pizam, A., Milman, A. and Jafari, J. (1991) Influence of tourism on attitudes: US students visiting USSR. *Tourism Management*, 12(1): 47–54.

Pizam, A. and Sussman, S. (1995) Does nationality affect tourist behaviour? *Annals of Tourism Research*, 22(4): 901–917.

Plog, S. (1977) Why destination areas rise and fall in popularity. In E. Kelly (ed.) *Domestic and International Tourism*. Wellesley, MA: Institute of Certified Travel Agents.

Plutchik, R. (1980) *The Emotions,* 1st Edition. Lanham: University Press of America.

Plutchik, R. (1991) *The Emotions,* 2nd Edition. Lanham: University Press of America.

Plutchik, R. (2001) The nature of emotions. *American Scientist*, 89(4): 344–350.

Poira, Y., Butler, R. and Airey, D. (2003) Tourism, religion and religiosity: A holy mess. *Current Issues in Tourism*, 6(4): 340–363.

Pollock, A. (2012) Conscious travel: Signposts towards a new model for tourism. *2nd UNWTO Ethics and Tourism Congress Conscious Tourism for a New Era, September 12th, Quito*. Available at: http://3rxg9qea 18zhtl6s2u8jammft.wpengine.netdna-cdn.com/wp-content/uploads/2012/09/presentacion-anna-meira-pollock.pdf (accessed 8 June 2017).

Pompl, W. and Lavery, P. (1993) *Tourism in Europe: Structures and Developments*. Wallingford: CAB International.

Poon, A. (1993) *Tourism, Technology and Competitive Strategies*. Wallingford: CABI.

Popescu, L. (2008) *The Good Tourist: An Ethical Traveller's Guide*. London: Arcadia Books.

Porritt, J. (1984) *Seeing Green*. Oxford: Blackwell.

Postelnicu, C., Dinu, V. and Dabija, D.C. (2015. Economic deglobalization: From hypothesis to reality. *Economics and Management*, 18(2): 4–14.

Potter, D. (2000) Democratisation, 'good governance' and development. In T. Allen and A. Thomas (eds) *Poverty and Development into the 21st Century*. Oxford: OUP, pp. 365–382.

Prahalad, C. and Ramaswamy, V. (2004) Co-creation experiences: The next practice in value creation. *Journal of Interactive Marketing*, 18(3): 5–14.

Prayag, G., Hosany, S. and Odeh, K. (2013) The role of tourists' emotional experiences and satisfaction in understanding behavioural intentions. *Journal of Destination Marketing & Management*, 2: 118–127.

Prebensen, N, and Foss, L. (2011) Coping and co-creating in tourist experiences. *International Journal of Tourism Research*, 13(1): 54–67.

Pretes, M. (1995) Postmodern tourism: The Santa Claus industry. *Annals of Tourism Research*, 22(1): 1–15.

Pritchard, A. and Morgan, N. (1995) Evaluating vacation destination brochure images: The case of local authorities in Wales. *Journal of Vacation Marketing*, 2(1): 23–38.

Purvis, J. (2003) *Emmeline Pankhurst: A Biography*. Abingdon: Routledge.

Quinlan Cutler, S. and Carmichael, B. (2010) The dimensions of the tourist experience. In M. Morgan, P. Lugosi and J. Ritchie (eds) *The Leisure and Tourism Experience: Consumer and Managerial Perspectives*. Bristol: Channel View Publications, pp. 3–26.

Qurashi, J. (2017) Commodification of Islamic religious tourism: From spiritual to touristic experience. *International Journal of Religious Tourism and Pilgrimage*, 5(1): 89–104.

Raine, R. (2013) A dark tourist spectrum. *International Journal of Culture, Tourism and Hospitality Research*, 7(3): 242–256.

Raj, R. and Griffin, K.A. (eds) (2015) *Religious Tourism and Pilgrimage Management: An International Perspective*. Wallingford: CABI.

Rattachumpoth, R. (1992) Phuket: Holiday paradise where locals are banned. *Contours*, 5(8): 13–15.

Raymond, C. and Brown, G. (2007) A spatial method for assessing resident and visitor attitudes towards tourism growth and development. *Journal of Sustainable Tourism*, 15(5): 520–540.

Raymond, E. and Hall, C.M. (2008) The development of cross-cultural (mis)understanding through volunteer tourism. *Journal of Sustainable Tourism*, 16(5): 530–543.

Reader, I. (2003) Review of 'Dark Tourism; the attraction of death and disaster'. Available at: http://cult-media.com/issue2/Rreade.htm

Redclift, M. (1987) *Sustainable Development: Exploring the Contradictions*. London: Routledge.

Reid, D. (1995) *Sustainable Development: An Introductory Guide*. London: Earthscan.

Reid, D. (2003) *Tourism, Globalization and Development: Responsible Tourism Planning*. London: Pluto Press.

Reisinger, Y. and Turner, L. (2003) *Cross Cultural Behaviour in Tourism: Concepts and Analysis*. Oxford: Butterworth-Heinemann.

Reisinger, Y., Kozak, M. and Visser, E. (2013) Turkish host gaze at Russian tourists: A cultural perspective. In O. Moufakkir and Y. Reisinger (eds) *The Host Gaze in Global Tourism*. Wallingford: CABI, pp. 47–66.

Reynoso y Valle, A. and de Regt, J. (1979) Growing pains: Planned development in Ixtapa-Zihuatanejo. In E. de Kadt (ed.) *Tourism: Passport to Development?* New York: Oxford University Press, pp. 111–134.

Richards, G. (2011) Creativity and tourism: The state of the art. *Annals of Tourism Research*, 38(4): 1225–1253.

Richards, G. and Wilson, J. (2004) *The Global Nomad: Backpacker Travel in Theory and Practice*. Clevedon: Channel View Publications.

Richards, G. and Wilson, J. (2007) *Tourism, Creativity and Development*. Abingdon: Routledge.

Richter, L. (1987) The search for appropriate tourism. *Tourism Recreation Research*, 12(2): 5–7.

Richter, L. and Waugh, W. (1986) Terrorism and tourism as logical companions. *Tourism Management*, 7(4): 230–238.

Rickly, J. (2013) Existential authenticity: Place matters. *Tourism Geographies*, 15(4): 680–686.

Riley, P. (1988) Road culture of international long-term budget travellers. *Annals of Tourism Research*, 15(3): 313–328.

Riley, R., Baker, D. and Van Doren, C. (1998) Movie induced tourism. *Annals of Tourism Research*, 25(4): 919–935.

Rinschede, G. (1992) Forms of religious tourism. *Annals of Tourism Research*, 19(1): 51–67.

Ritzer, G. (2015) *The McDonaldization of Society*, 8th Edition. Thousand Oaks, California/London: Sage Publications.

Roberts, L. and Hall, D. (2001) *Rural Tourism and Recreation: Principles to Practice*. Wallingford: CABI Publishing.

Robinson, M. and Andersen, H-C. (2002) *Literature and Tourism*. London: Thomson.

Robinson, M. and Boniface, P. (1999) *Tourism and Cultural Conflicts*. Wallingford: CABI.

Roche, M. (1992) Mega-events and micro-modernisation: On the sociology of new urban tourism. *British Journal of Sociology*, 43(3): 563–600.

Rogers, E. (1995) *Diffusion of Innovations*. New York: The Free Press.

Rojek, C. (1993) *Ways of Escape*. Basingstoke: Macmillan.

Rojek, C. (1997) Indexing, dragging and the social construction of tourist sights. In C. Rojek and J. Urry (eds) *Touring Cultures: Transformations of Travel and Theory*. London: Routledge, pp. 52–74.

Rojek, C. and Urry, J. (eds) (1997) *Touring Cultures: Transformations of Travel and Theory*. London: Routledge.

Rokeach, M. (1973) *The Nature of Human Values*. New York: The Free Press.

Rosenow, J. and Pulsipher, G. (1979) *Tourism: The Good, The Bad and The Ugly*. Lincoln: Three Centuries Press.

Ross, G. (1992) Resident perception of the impact of tourism on an Australian City. *Journal of Travel Research*, 3(3): 13–17.

Ross, G. (1994) *The Psychology of Tourism*. Melbourne: Hospitality Press.

Rostow, W. (1960) *The Stages of Economic Growth: A Non-Communist Manifesto*. Cambridge: Cambridge University Press.

Rothman, R. (1978) Residents and transients: Community reaction to seasonal visitors. *Journal of Travel Research*, 16: 8–13.

Ryan, C. (1991a) *Recreational Tourism: A Social Science Perspective*. London: Routledge.

Ryan, C. (1991b) Tourism, terrorism and violence: The risks of wider world travel. *Conflict Studies 244*. London: Research Institute for the Study of Conflict and Terrorism.

Ryan, C. (1997) The chase of a dream, the end of a play. In C. Ryan (ed.) *The Tourist Experience: A New Introduction*, London: Cassell, pp. 1–24.

Ryan, C. (2002) *The Tourist Experience: A New Introduction,* 2nd Edition. London: Thomson Learning.

Ryan, C. (2005) *Researching Tourist Satisfaction: Issues, Concepts, Problems.* Wallingford: CABI.

Ryan, C. (ed.) (2007) *Battlefield Tourism: History, Place and Interpretation.* Oxford: Elsevier.

Ryan, C. and Crotts, J. (1997) Carving and tourism: A Maori perspective. *Annals of Tourism Research*, 24(4): 898–918.

Ryan, C. and Hall, C.M. (2001) *Sex Tourism: Marginal People and Liminalities.* London: Routledge.

Ryan, C. and Sterling, L. (2001) Visitors to Litchfield National Park, Australia: A typology based on behaviours. *Journal of Sustainable Tourism*, 9(1): 61–75.

Ryanair (2017) Facts and Figures. Available at: https://corporate.ryanair.com/about-us/fact-and-figures/ (accessed 23 March 2017).

Scarles, C. (2009) Becoming tourist: Renegotiating the visual in the tourist experience. *Environment and Planning D: Society and Space*, 27(3): 465–488.

Schaller, D. (2007) From the editors: Genocide tourism – Educational value or voyeurism? *Journal of Genocide Research*, 9(4): 513–515.

Schmoll, G. (1977) *Tourism Promotion.* London: Tourism International Press.

Scholte, J. (2002) What is globalization? The definitional issue – again. CSGR Working Paper No. 109/02, University of Warwick. Available at: http://wrap-test.warwick.ac.uk/2010/1/WRAP_Scholte_wp10902.pdf (accessed 31 March 2017).

Schor, J. and Holt, D. (2000) *The Consumer Society Reader.* New York: The New Press.

Schumacher, E. (1974) *Small is Beautiful: A Study of Economics as if People Mattered.* London: Abacus.

Scott, J. and Marshall, G. (2005) *A Dictionary of Sociology.* Oxford: OUP.

Seabrook, J. (1996) *Travels in the Skin Trade: Tourism and the Sex Industry.* London: Pluto Press.

Seaton, A. (1996) Guided by the dark: from thanatopsis to thanatourism. *International Journal of Heritage Studies*, 2(4): 234–244.

Seaton, A. (2002) Thanatourism's final frontiers? Visits to cemeteries, churchyards and funerary sites as sacred and secular pilgrimage. *Tourism Recreation Research*, 27(2): 73–82.

Seaton, A. and Lennon, J. (2004) Moral panics, ulterior motives and alterior desires: Thanatourism in the early 21st century. In T.V. Singh (ed.) *New Horizons in Tourism: Strange Experiences and Stranger Practices*, Wallingford: CABI Publishing, pp. 63–82.

Seers, D. (1969) The meaning of development. *International Development Review*, 11(4): 2–6.

Seers, D. (1977) The new meaning of development. *International Development Review*, 19(3): 2–7.

Selwyn, N. (2009) the digital native: Myth and reality. *Aslib Proceedings: New Information* Perspectives, 61(4): 364–379. Available at: http://ai2-s2-pdfs.s3.amazonaws.com/93c8/72a6e2729722078c2fb88b6849f85cadd151.pdf (accessed October 2017).

Selwyn, T. (1992) Tourism, society and development. *Community Development Journal*, 27(4): 353–336.

Selwyn, T. (ed.) (1996) *The Tourist Image: Myths and Myth Making in Tourism.* Chichester: John Wiley & Sons.

Sen, A. (1999) *Development as Freedom.* New York: Anchor Books.

Settis, S. (2016) *If Venice Dies*, New York: New Vessel Press.

Shackley, M. (2002) Space, sanctity and service: The English cathedral as heterotopia. *International Journal of Tourism Research*, 4: 345–352.

Shackley, M. (2006) *Atlas of Travel and Tourism Development.* Oxford: Butterworth Heinemann.

Sharpley, R. (1996) Tourism and consumer culture in postmodern society. In M. Robinson *et al.* (eds) *Tourism and Cultural Change.* Sunderland: Business Education Publishers, pp. 203–216.

Sharpley, R. (2000) Tourism and sustainable development: Exploring the theoretical divide. *Journal of Sustainable Tourism*, 8(1): 1–19.

Sharpley, R. (2001) Tourism in Cyprus: Challenges and opportunities. *Tourism Geographies,* 3(1): 64–85.

Sharpley, R. (2005a) The tsunami and tourism: A comment. *Current Issues in Tourism*, 8(4): 344–349.

Sharpley, R. (2005b) Travels to the edge of darkness: Towards a typology of dark tourism. In Ryan, C. *et al.* (eds) *Taking Tourism to the Limits: Issues, Concepts and Managerial Perspectives*, Oxford: Elsevier, pp. 217–228.

Sharpley, R. (2006) Ecotourism: A consumption perspective. *Journal of Ecotourism,* 5(1+2): 7–22.

Sharpley, R. (2007) *Tourism and Leisure in the Countryside,* 5th Edition. Huntingdon: Elm Publications.

Sharpley, R. (2009a) Tourism, religion and spirituality. In M. Robinson and T. Jamal (eds) *Handbook of Tourism Studies*. London: Sage Publications, pp. 237–253.

Sharpley, R. (2009b) *Tourism, Development and the Environment: Beyond Sustainability*. London: Earthscan Publications.

Sharpley, R. (2009c) Tourism in The Gambia: A case of planning failure? *Tourism Review International*, 12(3–4): 215–230.

Sharpley, R. (2009d) Tourism and development in the Least Developed Countries: The case of The Gambia. *Current Issues in Tourism*, 12(4): 337–358.

Sharpley, R. (2011) *The Study of Tourism: Past Trends and Future Directions*. Abingdon: Routledge.

Sharpley, R. (2012) Responsible tourism: Whose responsibility? In A. Holden and D. Fennel (eds) *Handbook of Tourism & the Environment*. Abingdon: Routledge, pp. 382–391.

Sharpley, R. (2014) Host perceptions of tourism: A review of the research. *Tourism Management,* 42(1): 37–49.

Sharpley, R. (2015) Tourism: A vehicle for development? In R. Sharpley and T. Telfer (eds) *Tourism and Development: Concepts and Issues,* 2nd Edition. Bristol: Channel View Publications, pp. 3–30.

Sharpley, R. (2017) From holiday camps to the all-inclusive: The 'Butlinization' of tourism. In D. Harrison and R. Sharpley (eds) *Mass Tourism in a Small World*, Wallingford: CABI, pp. 95–104.

Sharpley, R. and Friedrich, M. (2017) Genocide tourism in Rwanda: Contesting the concept of the 'dark tourist'. In G. Hooper and J. Lennon (eds) *Dark Tourism: Practice and Interpretation*. Abingdon: Routledge, pp. 134–146.

Sharpley, R. and Harrison, D. (2017) Conclusion: Mass tourism in the future. In D. Harrison and R. Sharpley (eds) *Mass Tourism in a Small World*, Wallingford: CABI, pp. 232–240.

Sharpley, R. and Jepson, D. (2011) Rural tourism: A spiritual experience? *Annals of Tourism Research*, 38(1): 52–71.

Sharpley, R. and McGrath, P. (2017) Tourism in Cambodia: Opportunities and challenges. In K. Brickell and S. Springer (eds) *The Handbook of Contemporary Cambodia*, Abingdon: Routledge, pp. 87–98.

Sharpley, R. and Sharpley, J. (1996) Tourism in West Africa: The Gambian experience. In A. Badger *et al.* (eds) *Trading Places: Tourism as Trade*. Wimbledon: Tourism Concern, pp. 27–33.

Sharpley, R. and Sharpley, J. (1997) *Rural Tourism: An Introduction*, London: International Thomson Business Press.

Sharpley, R. and Stone, P. (2009) *The Darker Side of Travel: The Theory and Practice of Dark Tourism*. Bristol: Channel View Publications.

Sharpley, R. and Stone, P. (2012) Introduction Experiencing tourism: Experiencing happiness? In R. Sharpley and P. Stone (eds) *Contemporary Tourist Experience: Concepts and Consequences*. Abingdon: Routledge, pp. 1–8.

Sharpley, R. and Sundaram, P. (2005) Tourism: a sacred journey? The case of ashram tourism, India. *International Journal of Tourism Research*, 7(3): 161–171.

Sharpley, R. and Telfer, D. (eds) (2002) *Tourism and Development Concepts and Issues*. Clevedon: Channel View Publications.

Sharpley, R. and Telfer, D. (eds) (2015) *Tourism and Development Concepts and Issues,* 2nd Edition. Bristol: Channel View Publications.

Sharpley, R., Sharpley, J. and Adams, J. (1996) Travel advice or trade embargo? The impacts and implications of official travel advice, *Tourism Management,* 17(1): 1–7.

Shaw, G. and Williams, A. (1994) *Critical Issues in Tourism: A Geographical Perspective*. Oxford: Blackwell.

Shaw, G. and Williams, A. (eds) (1997) *The Rise and Fall of British Coastal Resorts: Cultural and Economic Perspectives*. London: Mansell Publishing.

Shaw, G. and Williams, A. (eds) (2000) *Tourism, Leisure and Recreation Series: Tourism and Sex*. London: Pinter.

Shaw, G. and Williams, A. (2002) *Critical Issues in Tourism: A Geographical Perspective*, 2nd Edition. Oxford: Blackwell.

Sheldon, P. and Abenjona, T. (2001) Resident attitudes in a mature destination: The case of Waikiki. *Tourism Management,* 22(5): 435–443.

Sheldon, P. and Var, T. (1984) Resident attitudes towards tourism in North Wales. *Tourism Management*, 5(1): 40–48.

Shepherd, R. (2002) Commodification, culture and tourism. *Tourist Studies*, 2(2): 183–201.

Shields, R. (1991) *Places on the Margin: Alternative Geographies of Modernity*. London: Routledge.

Shih, D. (1986) VALS as a tool of tourism market research: The Pennsylvania approach. *Journal of Travel Research*, 24(4): 2–11.

Short, J. (1991) *Imagined Country: Society, Culture and Environment*. London: Routledge.

Sigaux, G. (1966) *History of Tourism*. London: Leisure Arts Ltd.

Silver, I. (1993) Marketing authenticity in Third World countries. *Annals of Tourism Research*, 20(2): 302–318.

Silverberg, K., Backman, S. and Backman, K. (1996) A preliminary investigation into the psychographics of nature-based travellers to the south-eastern United States. *Journal of Travel Research*, 35(2): 19–28.

Sim, S. (2011) *The Routledge Companion to Postmodernism*. Abingdon: Routledge.

Simon, T. (1980) *Jupiter's Travels*. Harmondsworth: Penguin.

Simon, T. (2007) *Dreaming of Jupiter*. London: Little, Brown.

Simpson, B. (1993) Tourism and tradition: From healing to heritage. *Annals of Tourism Research*, 20(2): 164–181.

Simpson, K. (2004) 'Doing development': The gap year, volunteer-tourists and a popular practice of development. *Journal of International Development*, 16(5): 681–692.

Sin, H. (2010) Who are we responsible to? Locals' tales of volunteer tourism. *Geoforum*, 41(6): 983–992.

Sinclair, M.T. (1997) *Gender, Work and Tourism*. London: Routledge.

Sion, B. (2014) *Death Tourism: Disaster Sites as Recreational Landscape*. New York: Seagull Books.

Smith, K. (2010) Work-life balance perspectives of marketing professionals in generation Y. *Services Marketing Quarterly*, 31(4): 434–447.

Smith, M. (2003) Holistic holidays: Tourism and the reconciliation of body, mind and spirit. *Tourism Recreation Research*, 8(1): 103–108.

Smith, M. (2006) *Tourism, Culture and Regeneration*. Wallingford: CABI Publishing.

Smith, R. (2007) Typhoid is brought back to Britain by Tourists. *Daily Telegraph*, 30 August. Available at: http://www.pressreader.com/uk/the-daily-telegraph/20070830/281904473791207 (Accessed 20 October 2017).

Smith, M. (2009) *Issues in Cultural Tourism Studies*, 2nd Edition. Abingdon: Routledge.

Smith, M. and Puczkó, L. (2009) *Health and Wellness Tourism*. Abingdon: Routledge.

Smith, S. (1990) A test of Plog's allocentric/psychocentric model: Evidence from seven nations. *Journal of Travel Research*, 28(4): 40–43.

Smith, V. (ed.) (1977) *Hosts and Guests: The Anthropology of Tourism*, 1st Edition. Philadelphia: University of Pennsylvania Press.

Smith, V. (ed.) (1989a) *Hosts and Guests: The Anthropology of Tourism*, 2nd Edition. Philadelphia: University of Pennsylvania Press.

Smith, V. (1989b) Eskimo tourism: Micro-models and marginal men. In V. Smith (ed.) *Hosts and Guests: The Anthropology of Tourism*, 2nd Edition. Philadelphia: University of Pennsylvania Press, pp. 55–82.

Smith, V. (1992) Introduction: The quest in guest. *Annals of Tourism Research*, 19(1): 1–17.

Smith, V. (1998) War and tourism: An American ethnography. *Annals of Tourism Research*, 25(1): 202–227.

Smith, V. and Brent, M. (eds) (2001) *Hosts and Guests Revisited: Tourism Issues of the 21st Century*. New York: Cognizant.

Smith, V. and Eadington, W. (eds) (1992) *Tourism Alternatives: Potentials and Problems in the Development of Tourism*. Philadelphia: University of Pennsylvania Press.

Snaith, T. and Haley, A. (1999) Residents' opinions of tourism development in the historical city of York. *Tourism Management*, 20(5): 595–603.

Solomon, M. (1994) *Consumer Behaviour: Buying, Having and Being*, 2nd Edition. Needham Heights, MA: Allyn and Bacon.

Sönmez, S. (1998) Tourism, terrorism and political instability. *Annals of Tourism Research*, 25(2): 416–456.

Sönmez, S. and Graefe, A. (1998) Determining future travel behavior from past travel experience and perceptions of risk and safety. *Journal of Travel Research*, 37(2): 171–177.

Sontag, S. (1977) *On Photography*. London: Penguin Books.

Southgate, C. (2006) Ecotourism in Kenya: The vulnerability of communities. *Journal of Ecotourism*, 5(1+2): 80–96.

Speake, J. (2003) *Literature of Travel and Exploration: An Encyclopedia, Volume 1*. Abingdon: Routledge.

Spirou, C. (2010) *Urban Tourism and Urban Change: Cities in a Global Economy*. Abingdon: Routledge.

Squires, N. (2016) Venetians brandish shopping trolleys and pushchairs in protest against mass tourism. *The Telegraph*, 12 September. Available at: www.telegraph.co.uk/news/2016/09/12/venetians-brandish-shopping-trolleys-and-pushchairs-in-protest-a/ (accessed 6 October 2016).

Stabler, M., Papatheodorou, A. and Sinclair, M.T. (2010) *The Economics of Tourism*, 2nd Edition. Abingdon: Routledge.

Stanton, M. (1989) The Polynesian Cultural Centre: A multi-ethnic model of seven Pacific cultures. In V. Smith (ed.) *Hosts and Guests: The Anthropology of Tourism*, 2nd Edition. Philadelphia: University of Pennsylvania Press, pp. 247–262.

Stark, R., Hamberg, E. and Miller, A. (2005) Exploring spirituality and unchurched religions in America, Sweden and Japan. *Journal of Contemporary Religion*, 20(1): 3–23.

Starmer-Smith, C. (2004) Eco-friendly tourism on the rise. *Daily Telegraph Travel*, 6 November, p. 4.

Statista (2016) International Hotel Groups by Number of Hotel Rooms Worldwide as of April 2016. *Statista*. Available at: www.statista.com/statistics/245690/number-of-hotel-rooms-of-international-hotel-groups/ (accessed 3 June 2017).

Statista (2017) Number of smartphones sold to end users worldwide from 2007 to 2016. *Statista*. Available at: www.statista.com/statistics/263437/global-smartphone-sales-to-end-users-since-2007/ (accessed 6 October 2017).

Steele, P. (1995) Ecotourism: An economic analysis. *Journal of Sustainable Tourism*, 3(1): 29–44.

Steger, M. (2003) *Globalization: A Very Short Introduction*. Oxford: OUP.

Stone, P. (2006) A dark tourism spectrum: Towards a typology of death and macabre related tourist sites, attractions and exhibitions. *Tourism: An Interdisciplinary International Journal*, 52: 145–160.

Stone, P. and Sharpley, R. (2008) Consuming dark tourism: A thanatological perspective, *Annals of Tourism Research*, 35(2): 574–595.

Strange, C. and Kempa, M. (2003) Shades of dark tourism: Alcatraz and Robben Island, *Annals of Tourism Research*, 30(2): 386–403.

Streeten, P. (1977) The basic features of a basic needs approach to development. *International Development Review*, 3: 8–16.

Stylianou-Lambert, T. (2012) Tourists with cameras: Reproducing or producing? *Annals of Tourism Research*, 39(4): 1817–1838.

Sutton, W. (1967) Travel and understanding: Notes on the social structure of touring. *International Journal of Comparative Sociology*, 8: 217–233.

Swain, M. and Momsen, J. (eds) (2002) *Gender/Tourism/Fun(?)*. New York: Cognizant Communication Corporation.

Swarbrooke, J. (1999) *Sustainable Tourism Management*. Wallingford: CABI Publishing.

Swingewood, A. (1991) *A Short History of Sociological Thought*. Basingstoke: Macmillan.

Tarlow, P. (2005) Dark tourism: The appealing 'dark' side of tourism and more. In M. Novelli (ed.) *Niche Tourism: Contemporary Issues, Trends and Cases*. Oxford: Elsevier, pp. 47–57.

Tarlow, P. (2006) Terrorism and tourism. In J. Wilks, D. Pendergast, and P. Leggatt (eds) *Tourism in Turbulent Times: Towards Safe Experiences for Visitors*. Abingdon: Routledge, pp. 79–92.

Taylor, G. (1994) Styles of travel. In W. Theobald (ed.) *Global Tourism: The Next Decade*, Oxford: Butterworth Heinemann, pp. 188–198.

Taylor, G. (1995) The community approach: Does it really work? *Tourism Management*, 16(7): 487–489.

Taylor, J. (1994) *A Dream of England: Landscape, Photography and the Tourist's Imagination*. Manchester: Manchester University Press.

Taylor, J. (2001) Authenticity and sincerity in tourism. *Annals of Tourism Research*, 28(1): 7–26.

Tearfund (2000) *Tourism – An Ethical Issue. Market Research Report*. Teddington: Tearfund.

Telfer, D. (2015) The evolution of development theory and tourism. In R. Sharpley and D. Telfer (eds) *Tourism and Development: Concepts and Issues*, 2nd Edition. Bristol: Channel View Publications, pp. 31–73.

Telfer, D. and Sharpley, R. (2016) *Tourism and Development in the Developing World*, 2nd Edition. Abingdon: Routledge.

Temperton, J. (2016) Inside Sellafield: How the UK's most dangerous nuclear site is cleaning its act. *Wired*, 17 September. Available at: www.wired.co.uk/article/inside-sellafield-nuclear-waste-decommissioning (accessed 30 May 2017).

Teymur, N. (1993) Phototourism – or the epistemology of photography in tourism. *Tourism in Focus*, 6: 6 and 16.

Theobald, W. (1994) The context, meaning and scope of tourism. In W. Theobald (ed.) *Global Tourism: The Next Decade*. Oxford: Butterworth Heinemann, pp. 3–19.

Theos (2013) *The Spirit of Things Unseen: Belief in Post-Religious Britain*. London: Theos.

Thomas, G. and Morgan-Watts, M. (1988) *Shipwreck: The Strange Fate of the Morro Castle*. Dorchester: Dorset Press.

Thompson, K. (1992) Social pluralism and post-modernity. In S. Hall, D. Held and T. McGrew (eds) *Modernity and its Futures*. Cambridge: Polity Press, pp. 221–271.

Thomsons (1994) *Winter Sun Brochure*. London: Thomson Holidays.

Thornton, P., Shaw, G. and Williams, A. (1997) Tourist group holiday decision-making and behaviour: The influence of children. *Tourism Management*, 18(5): 287–297.

Thrane, C. (1997) Values as segmentation criteria in tourism research: The Norwegian monitor approach. *Tourism Management*, 18(2): 111–113.

Thurot, J. and Thurot, G. (1983) The ideology of class and tourism: Confronting the discourse of advertising. *Annals of Tourism Research*, 10(1): 173–189.

Timothy, D. (2002) Tourism and community development issues. In R. Sharpley and D. Telfer (eds) *Tourism and Development: Concepts and Issues*. Clevedon: Channel view Publications, pp. 149–164.

Timothy, D. (2011) *Cultural Heritage and Tourism: An Introduction*. Bristol: Channel View Publications.

Timothy, D. and Boyd, S. (2003) *Heritage Tourism*. Harlow: Pearson Education.

Timothy, D. and Olsen, D. (eds) (2006) *Tourism, Religion and Spiritual Journeys*. Abingdon: Routledge.

Tisdell, C. (2013) *Handbook of Tourism Economics: Analysis, New Applications and Case Studies*. Singapore: World Scientific Publishing Co.

Todaro, M. (1994) *Economic Development in the Third World*, 5th Edition. Harlow: Longman.

Todaro, M. and Smith S. (2014) *Economic Development*, 12th Edition. Harlow: Pearson Education.

Tomasi, L. (2002) Homo viator: From pilgrimage to religious tourism. In W. Swatos and L. Tomasi (eds) *From Medieval Pilgrimage to Religious Tourism*. Praeger: London, pp. 1–25.

Tomazos, K. and Cooper, W. (2012) Volunteer tourism: At the crossroads of commercialisation and service? *Current Issues in Tourism*, 15(5): 405–423.

Tooke, N. and Baker, M. (1996) Seeing is believing: The effect of film on visitor numbers to screened locations. *Tourism Management,* 17(2): 87–94.

Torres, R. (2002) Cancun's tourism development from a Fordist spectrum of analysis. *Tourist Studies*, 2(1): 87–116.

Tosun, C. (2000) Limits to community participation in the tourism development process in developing countries. *Tourism Management,* 21(6): 613–633.

Tourism Alliance (2017) *UK Tourism Statistics 2017*. Available at: www.tourismalliance.com/downloads/TA_395_420.pdf (accessed 7 September 2017).

Tourism Council of Bhutan (2015) Bhutan Tourism Monitor, Annual Report 2015. Available at: www.tcb.img.ebizity.bt/attachments/tcb_052016_btm-2015.pdf (accessed 3 June 2017).

Towner, J. (1984) The Grand Tour: Sources and a methodology for an historical study of tourism. *Tourism Management,* 5(3): 215–222.

Towner, J. (1985) The Grand Tour: A key phase in the history of tourism. *Annals of Tourism Research*, 12(3): 297–333.

Towner, J. (1988) Approaches to tourism history. *Annals of Tourism Research*, 15(1): 47–62.

Towner, J. (1995) What is tourism's history? *Tourism Management*, 16(5): 339–343.

Towner, J. (1996) *An Historical Geography of Recreation and Tourism in the Western World 1540–1940*. Chichester: John Wiley & Sons.

Travis, A. (1982) Physical impacts: Trends affecting tourism. Managing the environmental and cultural impacts of tourism and leisure development. *Tourism Management*, 3(4): 256–262.

Tribe, J. and Mkono, M. (2017) Not such smart tourism? The concept of e-lienation. *Annals of Tourism Research*, 66: 105–115.

Tribe, J. and Snaith, T. (1998) From SERVQUAL to HOLSAT: Holiday satisfaction in Varadero, Cuba. *Tourism Management*, 19(1): 25–34.

Trilling, L. (1974) *Sincerity and Authenticity*. Oxford Paperbacks, London: Oxford University Press.

Tronvoll, B. (2011) Negative emotions and their effect on customer complaint behavior. *Journal of Service Management,* 22(1): 111–134.

Tsartas, P. (1992) Socio-economic impacts of tourism on two Greek isles. *Annals of Tourism Research*, 19(3): 516–553.

Tunbridge, J. and Ashworth, G. (1996) *Dissonant Heritage: The Management of the Past as a Resource in Conflict.* Chichester: John Wiley & Sons.

Turner, L. and Ash, J. (1975) *The Golden Hordes: International Tourism and the Pleasure Periphery*, London: Constable.

Turner, V. (1973) The centre out there: The pilgrim's goal. *History of Religions*, 10: 191–230.

Turner, V. and Turner, E. (2011) *Image and Pilgrimage in Christian Culture*. New York: Columbia University Press.

Tweedie, S. (2015) The world's first smartphone, Simon, was created 15 years before the iPhone. *Business Insider UK*. Available at: http://uk.businessinsider.com/worlds-first-smartphone-simon-launched-before-iphone-2015–6?r=US&IR=T (accessed 6 October 207).

Um, S. and Crompton, J. (1987) Measuring resident's attachment levels in a host community. *Journal of Travel Research*, 26(1): 27–29.

UN (2016) *List of Least Developed Countries (as of May 2016).* UN Committee for Development Policy. Available at: www.un.org/en/development/desa/policy/cdp/ldc/ldc_list.pdf (accessed 3 June 2017).

UN (2017) Sustainable Development Goals. Available at: https://sustainabledevelopment.un.org/?menu=1300 (accessed 4 June 2017).

UNDP (1995) *Human Development Report 1995*. New York: Oxford University Press.

UNDP (2004) *Human Development Report 2004*. New York: Oxford University Press.

UNDP (2010) *Human Development Report 2010*. New York: Oxford University Press.

UNEP/WTO (2005) *Making Tourism More Sustainable: A Guide for Policy Makers*. Paris/Madrid: United Nations Environment Programme/World Tourism Organization.

UNESCO (1976) The effects of tourism on socio-cultural values. *Annals of Tourism Research*, 4(1): 74–105.

UNFCCC (2017) *The Paris Agreement*. UN Framework Convention on Climate Change. Available at: http://unfccc.int/paris_agreement/items/9485.php (accessed 8 June 2017).

UNWTO (2005) *World Tourism Barometer 3(2)*. Madrid: UN World Tourism Organization.

UNWTO (2009) *From Davos to Copenhagen and Beyond: Advancing Tourism's Response to Climate Change*. UN World Tourism Organization. Available at: sdt.unwto.org/sites/all/files/docpdf/fromdavostocopenhagen beyondunwtopaperelectronicversion.pdf (accessed 24 March 2017).

UNWTO (2014) *Tourism Can Protect and Promote Religious Heritage*. UN World Tourism Organization Press Release, PR 14083. Available at: http://media.unwto.org/press-release/2014-12-10/tourism-can-protect-and-promote-religious-heritage (accessed 21 March 2107).

UNWTO (2016a) Exports from international tourism rise 4% in 2015. UN World Tourism Organization Press Release No. 16003. Available at: www.media.unwto.org/press-release/2016-05.../exports-international-tourism-rise-4-2015 (accessed 10 March 2017).

UNWTO (2016b) *UNWTO Tourism Highlights, 2016 Edition*. Madrid: UN World Tourism Organization.

UNWTO (2017) *UNWTO Tourism Highlights, 2017 Edition*. Madrid: UN World Tourism Organization.

UNWTO (n.d.) *The Responsible Tourist and Traveller*. UN World Tourism Organization. Available at: http://ethics.unwto.org/sites/all/files/docpdf/responsibletouristbrochureen.pdf (accessed 19 April 2017).

Uriely, N. (1997) Theories of modern and postmodern tourism. *Annals of Tourism Research*, 24(4): 982–985.

Uriely, N. (2005) The tourist experience: Conceptual developments. *Annals of Tourism Research*, 32(1): 199–216.

Uriely, N., Yonay, Y. and Simchai, D. (2002) Backpacking experiences: A type and form analysis. *Annals of Tourism Research*, 29(2): 520–538.

Urry, J. (1988) Cultural change and contemporary holiday-making. *Theory, Culture and Society*, 5: 35–55.

Urry, J. (1990a) *The Tourist Gaze*. London: Sage Publications.

Urry, J. (1990b) The consumption of tourism. *Sociology*, 24(1): 23–35.

Urry, J. (1992) The tourist gaze and the environment. *Theory, Culture and Society*, 9: 1–26.

Urry, J. (1994) Cultural change and contemporary tourism. *Leisure Studies*, 13(4): 233–238.

Urry, J. (1995) *Consuming Places*. London: Routledge.

Urry, J. (2002) *The Tourist Gaze*, 2nd Edition. London: Sage Publications.

Urry, J. (2012) *Sociology Beyond Societies: Mobilities for the Twenty-first Century*. Abingdon: Routledge.

Urry, J. and Larsen, J. (2011) *The Tourist Gaze 3.0*. London: Sage Publications.

Ussi, M. and Sharpley, R. (2014) Tourism and governance in Small Island Developing States (SIDS): The case of Zanzibar. *International Journal of Tourism Research*, 16(1): 87–96.

Uzell, D. (1984) An alternative structuralist approach to the psychology of tourism marketing. *Annals of Tourism Research*, 11(1): 79–99.

Vaillant, G. (2008) Positive emotions, spirituality and the practice of psychiatry. *Mens Sana Monographs*, 6(1): 48–62.

Van House, N. (2011) Personal photography, digital technologies and the uses of the visual. *Visual Studies*, 26(2): 125–134.

Vanhove, N. (2011) *The Economics of Tourism Destinations*. London: Elsevier.

van Raaij, W. and Francken, D. (1984) Vacation decisions, activities and satisfactions. *Annals of Tourism Research*, 11(1): 101–112.

Vargas-Sánchez, A., Plaza-Mejía, M. and Porras-Bueno, N. (2009) Understanding residents' attitudes toward the development of industrial tourism in a former mining community. *Journal of Travel Research*, 47(3): 373–387.

Vellas, F. and Bécherel, L. (1995) *International Tourism: An Economic Perspective*. Basingstoke: Macmillan.

Vijayanand, S. (2012) Socio-economic impact in pilgrimage tourism. *International Journal of Multidisciplinary Research*, 2(1): 329–343.

Visit Britain (2017) *Britain's Visitor Economy Facts*. Available at: www.visitbritain.org/visitor-economy-facts (accessed 23 March 2017).

Voase, R. (1995) *Tourism: The Human Perspective*. London: Hodder & Stoughton.

Voase, R. (2007) Visiting a cathedral: The consumer psychology of a 'rich experience'. *International Journal of Heritage Studies*, 13(1): 41–55.

Vogt, J. (1978) Wandering: Youth and travel behaviour. *Studies in Third World Societies*, 5: 19–40.

Volo, S. (2009) Conceptualizing experience: A tourist based approach. *Journal of Hospitality Marketing & Management*, 18(2–3): 111–126.

Vong, F. (2016) Application of cultural tourist typology in a gaming destination–Macao. *Current Issues in Tourism*, 19(9): 949–965.

Vukonić, B. (1996) *Tourism and Religion*. Oxford: Pergamon.

Vukonić, B. (2000) Religion. In J. Jafari (ed.) *Encyclopedia of Tourism*. London: Routledge: 497–500.

Vukonić, B. (2002) Religion, tourism and economics: A convenient symbiosis. *Tourism Recreation Research*, 27(2): 59–64.

Wahab, S. (1975) *Tourism Management*. London: Tourism International Press.

Wahab, S. and Pigram, J. (1997) *Tourism, Development and Growth: The Challenge of Sustainability*. London: Routledge.

Walby, S. (1992) Post-postmodernism: Theorising social complexity. In M. Barrett and A. Phillips (eds) *Destabilizing Theory: Contemporary Feminist Debates*. Cambridge: Polity Press, pp. 31–52.

Wall, G. (1997) Sustainable tourism: Unsustainable development. In S. Wahab and J. Pigram (eds) *Tourism, Development and Growth: The Challenge of Sustainability*. London: Routledge, pp. 33–49.

Wall, G. and Mathieson, A. (2006) *Tourism: Change, Impacts and Opportunities*. Harlow: Pearson Education.

Walsh, K. (1992) *The Representation of the Past: Museums and Heritage in the Post-Modern World*. London: Routledge.

Walter, J. (1982) Social limits to tourism. *Leisure Studies*, 1: 295–304.

Walter, T., Littlewood, J. and Pickering, M. (1995) Death in the news: The public investigation of private emotion. *Sociology*, 29: 579–596.

Walton, J. (1983) *The English Seaside Resort: A Social History, 1750–1914*. Leicester: Leicester University Press.

Walton, J. (2005) *Histories of Tourism: Representation, Identity and Conflict*. Clevedon: Channel View Publications.

Walton, J. (2009) Prospects in tourism history: Evolution, state of play and future developments. *Tourism Management*, 30(6): 783–793.

Walvin, J. (1978) *Beside the Seaside*. London: Allen Lane.

Wang, D. and Fesenmaier, D. (2013) Transforming the travel experience: The use of smartphones for travel. In L. Cantoni and Z. Xiang (eds) *Information and Communication Technologies in Tourism 2013*. Berlin/Heidelberg: Springer, pp. 58–69.

Wang, D., Park, S. and Fesenmaier, D. (2012) The role of smartphones in mediating the touristic experience. *Journal of Travel Research*, 51(4): 371–387.

Wang, N. (1999a) *Tourism and Modernity: A Sociological Analysis*. Oxford: Pergamon.

Wang, N. (1999b) Rethinking authenticity in tourism experience. *Annals of Tourism Research*, 26(2): 349–370.

Wang, Y. and Pfister, R. (2008) Residents' attitudes toward tourism and perceived personal benefits in a rural community. *Journal of Travel Research*, 47(1): 84–93.

Ward, C. and Hardy, D. (1986) *Goodnight Campers! The History of the British Holiday Camp*. London: Mansell Publishing.

Warde, A. (1992) Notes on the relationship between production and consumption. In R. Burrows and C. Marsh (eds) *Consumption and Class*, Basingstoke: Macmillan, pp. 15–31.

WCED (1987) *Our Common Future*. World Commission on Environment and Development, Oxford: Oxford University Press.

Wearing, S. (2001) *Volunteer Tourism: Experiences that Make a Difference*. Wallingford: CABI.

Wearing, S. and McGehee, N. (2013) Volunteer tourism: A review. *Tourism Management*, 38, 120–130.

Weaver, D. (1990) Grand Cayman Island and the resort cycle concept. *Journal of Travel Research*, 29(2): 9–15.

Weaver, D. (1994) Ecotourism in the Caribbean Basin. In E. Cater and G. Lowman (eds) *Ecotourism: A Sustainable Option*, Chichester: John Wiley & Sons, pp. 159–176.

Weaver, D. (2001) *The Encyclopaedia of Ecotourism*. Wallingford: CABI Publishing.

Weaver, D. (2017) Sustainability and mass tourism: A contradiction in terms? In D. Harrison and R. Sharpley (eds) *Mass Tourism in a Small World*. Wallingford: CABI, pp. 63–74.

Webber, D. (2013) Space tourism: Its history, future and importance. *Acta Astronautica*, 92(2): 138–143.

Webster, A. (1990) *Introduction to the Sociology of Development*, 2nd Edition. Basingstoke: Macmillan.

Weedon, C. (2014) *Responsible Tourist Behaviour*. Abingdon: Routledge.

Weideger, P. (1994) *Gilding the Acorn: Behind the Façade of the National Trust*. London: Simon & Schuster Ltd.

Weiler, B. and Hall, C.M. (1992) *Special Interest Tourism*. London: Belhaven Press.

Weiler, B. and Yu, X. (2007) Dimensions of cultural mediation in guiding Chinese tour groups: Implications for interpretation. *Tourism Recreation Research*, 32(3): 13–22.

Welch, R. (1984) The meaning of development: Traditional view and more recent ideas. *New Zealand Journal of Geography*, 76: 2–4.

Westerhausen, K. and Macbeth, J. (2003) Backpackers and empowered local communities: Natural allies in the struggle for sustainable and local control? *Tourism Geographies*, 5(1): 71–86.

Wheeler, M. (1992) Applying ethics to the tourism industry. *Business Ethics*, 1(4): 227–235.

Wheeller, B. (1991) Tourism's troubled times. *Tourism Management*, 12(3): 91–96.

Wheeller, B. (1992a) Eco or ego tourism: New wave tourism. *ETB Insights, Vol III*, London: English Tourist Board: D41–44.

Wheeller, B. (1992b) Alternative tourism: A deceptive ploy. In C. Cooper and A. Lockwood (eds) *Progress in Tourism, Recreation and Hospitality Management Vol IV*, London: Bellhaven Press, pp. 140–145.

Whelan, T. (ed.) (1991) *Nature Tourism: Managing for the Environment*. Washington DC: Island Press.

White, C. and Yu, Y. (2005) Satisfaction emotions and consumer behavioral intentions. *Journal of Services Marketing*, 19(6): 411–420.

Wickens, E. (2002) The sacred and the profane: A tourist typology. *Annals of Tourism Research*, 29(3): 834–851.

Wight, P. (1996) North American ecotourism markets: Motivations, preferences and destinations. *Journal of Travel Research*, 35(1): 3–10.

Wildfrontiers (2017) Wildfrontiers: Extraordinary travel experiences. Available at: www.wildfrontierstravel.com/en_GB/?gclid=CMLCmLKKjdQCFQIG0wod8iYKbw (accessed 26 May 2017).

Wilkinson, P. (1989) Strategies for tourism in island microstates. *Annals of Tourism Research*, 16(2): 153–177.

Williams, A. and Hall, C.M. (2000) Tourism and migration: New relationships between production and consumption. *Tourism Geographies*, 2(1): 5–27.

Williams, A. and Shaw, G. (1991) Tourism and development: Introduction. In A. Williams and G. Shaw (eds) *Tourism and Economic Development: Western European Experiences*. London: Bellhaven Press, pp. 1–12.

Williams, E., Francis, L., Robbins, M. and Annis, J. (2006) Visitor experiences of St. David's Cathedral: The two worlds of pilgrims and secular tourists. Paper presented at the *Tourism: The Spiritual Dimension* Conference, University of Lincoln, UK (unpublished).

Williams, S. and Lew, A. (2015) *Tourism Geography: Critical Understandings of Place, Space and Experience*, 3rd Edition. Abingdon: Routledge.

Wilson, A. (1992) *The Culture of Nature: North American Landscape from Disney to Exxon Valdez*. Cambridge, Mass: Blackwell.

Winter, T. (2008) Post-conflict heritage and tourism in Cambodia: The burden of Angkor. *International Journal of Heritage Studies*, 14(6): 524–539.

Witherspoon, S. (1994) The greening of Britain: Romance and rationality. In R. Jowell *et al.* (eds) *British Social Attitudes: the 11th Report*. Aldershot: Dartmouth, pp. 107–139.

Witt, C. and Wright, P. (1992) Tourist motivation: Life after Maslow. In P. Johnson and B. Thomas (eds) *Choice and Demand in Tourism*, London: Mansell Publishing, pp. 33–55.

Witt, S. and Moutinho, L. (eds) (1989) *Tourism Marketing and Management Handbook*. Hemel Hempstead: Prentice Hall International.

Wood, K. and House, S. (1991) *The Good Tourist: A Worldwide Guide for the Green Traveller*. London: Mandarin.

Wood, R. (1980) International tourism and cultural change in South East Asia. *Economic Development and Cultural Change*, 28: 561–581.

Woodside, A. and Pitts, R. (1976) Effects of consumer lifestyles, demographics and travel activities on foreign and domestic travel behaviour. *Journal of Travel Research*, 14(3): 15.

Woosnam, K. (2012) Using emotional solidarity to explain residents' attitudes about tourism and tourism development. *Journal of Travel Research*, 51(3): 315–327.

World Bank (2017) World Bank List of Economies 2017. Available at: www.databank.worldbank.org/data/download/site-content/CLASS.xls (accessed 2 June 2017).

Wray-Lake, L., Flanagan, C. and Osgood, D. (2010) Examining trends in adolescent environmental attitudes, beliefs, and behaviors across three decades. *Environment and Behavior*, 42(1): 61–85.

Wright, P. (1985) *On Living in an Old Country*. London: Verso.

WTO (1980) *Manila Declaration on World Tourism*. Madrid: World Tourism Organization.

WTO (1981) *The Social and Cultural Dimension of Tourism*. Madrid: World Tourism Organization.

WTO (1994) *Recommendations on Tourism Statistics*. Madrid: World Tourism Organization.

WTO (1998a) *Tourism: 2020 Vision: Influences, Directional Flows and Key Trends*. Madrid: World Tourism Organization.

WTO (2005) *A Historical Perspective of World Tourism*. World Tourism Organization, available at: www.world-tourism.org/facts/trends/historical.htm

WTO/WTTC (1996) *Agenda 21 for the Travel & Tourism Industry: Towards Environmentally Sustainable Development*. World Tourism Organization/World Travel and Tourism Council.

WTTC (2016) *Travel and Tourism World Economic Impact 2016*. World Travel & Tourism Council. Available at: www.wttc.org/-/media/files/reports/economic%20impact%20research/regions%202016/world2016.pdf (accessed 4 April 2017).

WTTC (2017) *Travel and Tourism World Economic Impact 2017*. World Travel & Tourism Council. Available at: www.wttc.org/-/media/files/reports/economic-impact-research/regions-2017/world2017.pdf (accessed 7 September 2017).

Wuthnow, R. (1998) *After Heaven: Spirituality in America since the 1950s*. Berkeley: University of California Press.

Xie, P. (2003) The bamboo-beating dance in Hainan, China: Authenticity and commodification. *Journal of Sustainable Tourism*, 11(1): 5–16.

Yafei, H. (2017) Brexit may be part of the first wave of de-globalization. *Huffington Post*. Available at: www.huffingtonpost.com/he-yafei/brexit-deglobalization_b_10755862.html (accessed 31 March 2017).

Yale, P. (1992) *Tourism in the UK*. London: Elm Publications.

Yale, P. (1995) *The Business of Tour Operations*. Harlow: Longman.

Yale, P. (2004) *From Tourist Attractions to Heritage Tourism*, 3rd Edition. Huntingdon: Elm Publications.

Yang, K. and Jolly, L. (2008) Age cohort analysis in adoption of mobile data services: gen Xers versus baby boomers. *Journal of Consumer Marketing*, 25(5): 272–280.

Yiannakis, A. and Gibson, H. (1992) Roles tourists play. *Annals of Tourism Research*, 19(2): 287–303.

Yearley, S. (1991) *The Green Case: A Sociology of Environmental Issues, Arguments and Politics*. London: Routledge.

Yeoman, I. (2011) *Tomorrow's Tourist: Scenarios and Trends*. Abingdon: Routledge.

Yeoman, I. (2012) *2050: Tomorrow's Tourism*. Bristol: Channel View Publications.

Young, G. (1973) *Tourism: Blessing or Blight?* Harmondsworth: Penguin.

Zalatan, A. (2004) Tourist typology: An ex ante approach. *Tourism Economics*, 10(3): 329–343.

Zautra, A. (2003) *Emotions, Stress and Health*. Oxford: Oxford University Press.

Zhang, J., Inbakaran, R. and Jackson, M. (2006) Understanding community attitudes towards tourism and host–guest interaction in the urban–rural border region. *Tourism Geographies: An International Journal of Tourism Space, Place and Environment*, 8(2): 182–204.

Zinnbauer, B., Pargament, K., Cole, B., Rye, M., Butter, E., Belavich, T., Hipp, K., Scott, A. and Kadar, J. (1997) Religion and spirituality: Unfuzzying the fuzzy. *Journal for the Scientific Study of Religion*, 36(4): 549–564.

Zukin, S. (1990) Socio-spatial prototypes of a new organisation of consumption: The role of real cultural capital. *Sociology*, 24(1): 37–55.

Zuzanek, J. and Mannell, R. (1983) Work leisure relationships from a sociological and social psychological perspective. *Leisure Studies*, 2: 327.

Index